D1592006

Dynamic Logic

Foundations of Computing (selected titles)

Michael Garey and Albert Meyer, editors

Algebraic Theory of Processes, Matthew Hennessy, 1988

PX: A Computational Logic, Susumu Hayashi and Hiroshi Nakano, 1989

The Stable Marriage Problem: Structure and Algorithms, Dan Gusfield and Robert Irving, 1989

Realistic Compiler Generation, Peter Lee, 1989

Basic Category Theory for Computer Scientists, Benjamin C. Pierce, 1991

Categories, Types, and Structures: An Introduction to Category Theory for the Working Computer Scientist, Andrea Asperti and Giuseppe Longo, 1991

Semantics of Programming Languages: Structures and Techniques, Carl A. Gunter, 1992

The Formal Semantics of Programming Languages: An Introduction, Glynn Winskel, 1993

Hilbert's Tenth Problem, Yuri V. Matiyasevich, 1993

Exploring Interior-Point Linear Programming: Algorithms and Software, Ami Arbel, 1993

Theoretical Aspects of Object-Oriented Programming: Types, Semantics, and Language Design, edited by Carl A. Gunter and John C. Mitchell, 1994

From Logic to Logic Programming, Kees Doets, 1994

The Structure of Typed Programming Languages, David A. Schmidt, 1994

Logic and Information Flow, edited by Jan van Eijck and Albert Visser, 1994

Circuit Complexity and Neural Networks, Ian Parberry, 1994

Control Flow Semantics, Jaco de Bakker and Erik de Vink, 1996

Algebraic Semantics of Imperative Programs, Joseph A. Goguen and Grant Malcolm, 1996

Algorithmic Number Theory, Volume I: Efficient Algorithms, Eric Bach and Jeffrey Shallit, 1996

Foundations for Programming Languages, John C. Mitchell, 1996

Computability and Complexity: From a Programming Perspective, Neil D. Jones, 1997

Proof, Language, and Interaction: Essays in Honour of Robin Milner, edited by Gordon Plotkin, Colin Stirling, and Mads Tofte, 2000

Dynamic Logic, David Harel, Dexter Kozen, and Jerzy Tiuryn, 2000

Dynamic Logic

David Harel
The Weizmann Institute

Dexter Kozen
Cornell University

Jerzy Tiuryn
University of Warsaw

The MIT Press
Cambridge, Massachusetts
London, England

This book was set in Times Roman by the author using the LaTeX document preparation system. Bound in the United States of America.

Library of Congress Cataloging-in-Publication Data

Harel, David, 1950– .
  Dynamic logic / David Harel, Dexter Kozen, Jerzy Tiuryn.
    p. cm. —(Foundations of computing)
  Includes bibliographical references and index.
  ISBN 0-262-08289-6 (alk. hc)
  1. Computer logic. 2. Formal methods (Computer science).
I. Kozen, Dexter, 1951– . II. Tiuryn, Jerzy. III. Title. IV. Series.
QA76.9.L63 H37   2000
004'.01'5113—dc21   00-030380

To Albert, Rohit, and Vaughan

If I have seen further than others,
it is by standing upon the shoulders of giants.
—Isaac Newton

Contents

Preface   xiii

I   FUNDAMENTAL CONCEPTS

1   Mathematical Preliminaries   3

1.1   Notational Conventions   3

1.2   Sets   3

1.3   Relations   5

1.4   Graphs and Dags   13

1.5   Lattices   13

1.6   Transfinite Ordinals   13

1.7   Set Operators   16

1.8   Bibliographical Notes   22

Exercises   22

2   Computability and Complexity   27

2.1   Machine Models   27

2.2   Complexity Classes   38

2.3   Reducibility and Completeness   53

2.4   Bibliographical Notes   63

Exercises   64

3   Logic   67

3.1   What is Logic?   67

3.2   Propositional Logic   71

3.3   Equational Logic   86

3.4   Predicate Logic   102

3.5   Ehrenfeucht–Fraïssé Games   119

3.6   Infinitary Logic   120

3.7   Modal Logic   127

3.8   Bibliographical Notes   134

Exercises   134

4   Reasoning About Programs   145

4.1   What are Programs?   145

4.2   States and Executions   146

4.3   Programming Constructs   147

4.4   Program Verification   152

4.5   Exogenous and Endogenous Logics   157

4.6   Bibliographical Notes   157

Exercises   158

II   PROPOSITIONAL DYNAMIC LOGIC

5   Propositional Dynamic Logic   163

5.1   Syntax   164

5.2   Semantics   167

5.3   Computation Sequences   170

5.4   Satisfiability and Validity   171

5.5   A Deductive System   173

5.6   Basic Properties   174

5.7   Encoding Hoare Logic   186

5.8   Bibliographical Notes   187

Exercises   188

6   Filtration and Decidability   191

6.1   The Fischer–Ladner Closure   191

6.2   Filtration and the Small Model Theorem   195

6.3   Filtration over Nonstandard Models   199

6.4   Bibliographical Notes   201

Exercises   202

7   Deductive Completeness   203

7.1	Deductive Completeness	203
7.2	Logical Consequences	209
7.3	Bibliographical Notes	209
	Exercises	209
8	**Complexity of** PDL	211
8.1	A Deterministic Exponential-Time Algorithm	211
8.2	A Lower Bound	216
8.3	Compactness and Logical Consequences	220
8.4	Bibliographical Notes	224
	Exercises	225
9	**Nonregular** PDL	227
9.1	Context-Free Programs	227
9.2	Basic Results	228
9.3	Undecidable Extensions	232
9.4	Decidable Extensions	237
9.5	More on One-Letter Programs	250
9.6	Bibliographical Notes	255
	Exercises	256
10	**Other Variants of** PDL	259
10.1	Deterministic PDL and **While** Programs	259
10.2	Restricted Tests	263
10.3	Representation by Automata	266
10.4	Complementation and Intersection	268
10.5	Converse	270
10.6	Well-Foundedness and Total Correctness	271
10.7	Concurrency and Communication	276
10.8	Bibliographical Notes	277

III   FIRST-ORDER DYNAMIC LOGIC

11   First-Order Dynamic Logic   283

11.1 Basic Syntax   283

11.2 Richer Programs   287

11.3 Semantics   291

11.4 Satisfiability and Validity   297

11.5 Bibliographical Notes   298

Exercises   298

12   Relationships with Static Logics   301

12.1 The Uninterpreted Level   301

12.2 The Interpreted Level   307

12.3 Bibliographical Notes   311

Exercises   311

13   Complexity   313

13.1 The Validity Problem   313

13.2 Spectral Complexity   317

13.3 Bibliographical Notes   324

Exercises   325

14   Axiomatization   327

14.1 The Uninterpreted Level   327

14.2 The Interpreted Level   333

14.3 Bibliographical Notes   341

Exercises   341

15   Expressive Power   343

15.1 The Unwind Property   344

15.2 Spectra and Expressive Power   347

15.3 Bounded Nondeterminism   355

15.4 Unbounded Memory									369

15.5 The Power of a Boolean Stack							376

15.6 Unbounded Nondeterminism							377

15.7 Bibliographical Notes								378

Exercises											380

16 Variants of DL									383

16.1 Algorithmic Logic									383

16.2 Nonstandard Dynamic Logic							384

16.3 Well-Foundedness									386

16.4 Dynamic Algebra									389

16.5 Probabilistic Programs								391

16.6 Concurrency and Communication						393

16.7 Bibliographical Notes								394

17 Other Approaches								397

17.1 Logic of Effective Definitions							397

17.2 Temporal Logic									398

17.3 Process Logic									408

17.4 The μ-Calculus									415

17.5 Kleene Algebra									418

References										425
Notation and Abbreviations								439
Index											449

Preface

Dynamic Logic is a formal system for reasoning about programs. Traditionally, this has meant formalizing correctness specifications and proving rigorously that those specifications are met by a particular program. Other activities fall into this category as well: determining the equivalence of programs, comparing the expressive power of various programming constructs, synthesizing programs from specifications, etc. Formal systems too numerous to mention have been proposed for these purposes, each with its own peculiarities.

This book presents a comprehensive introduction to one system, or rather family of systems, collectively called Dynamic Logic (DL). Among the myriad approaches to formal reasoning about programs, DL enjoys the singular advantage of strong connections with classical logic. It can be described as a blend of three complementary classical ingredients: first-order predicate logic, modal logic, and the algebra of regular events. These components merge to form a system of remarkable unity that is theoretically rich as well as practical.

The name *Dynamic Logic* emphasizes the principal feature distinguishing it from classical predicate logic. In the latter, truth is *static*: the truth value of a formula φ is determined by a valuation of its free variables over some structure. The valuation and the truth value of φ it induces are regarded as immutable; there is no formalism relating them to any other valuations or truth values. In Dynamic Logic, there are explicit syntactic constructs called *programs* whose main role is to change the values of variables, thereby changing the truth values of formulas. For example, the program $x := x + 1$ over the natural numbers changes the truth value of the formula "x is even".

Such changes occur on a metalogical level in classical predicate logic. For example, in Tarski's definition of truth of a formula, if $u : \{x, y, \ldots\} \to \mathbb{N}$ is a valuation of variables over the natural numbers $\mathbb{N}$, then the formula $\exists x \; x^2 = y$ is defined to be true under the valuation u iff there exists an $a \in \mathbb{N}$ such that the formula $x^2 = y$ is true under the valuation $u[x/a]$, where $u[x/a]$ agrees with u everywhere except x, on which it takes the value a. This definition involves a metalogical operation that produces $u[x/a]$ from u for all possible values $a \in \mathbb{N}$. This operation becomes explicit in Dynamic Logic in the form of the program $x := ?$, called a *nondeterministic* or *wildcard assignment*. This is a rather unconventional program, since it is not effective; however, it is quite useful as a descriptive tool. A more conventional way to obtain a square root of y, if it exists, would be the program

$$x := 0 \,; \textbf{while } x^2 < y \textbf{ do } x := x + 1. \tag{0.1}$$

In Dynamic Logic, such programs are first-class objects on a par with formulas,

complete with a collection of operators for forming compound programs inductively
from a basis of primitive programs. In the simplest version of DL, these program
operators are ∪ (nondeterministic choice), ; (sequential composition), * (iteration),
and ? (test). These operators are already sufficient to generate all **while** programs,
which over ℕ are sufficient to compute all partial recursive functions. To discuss the
effect of the execution of a program α on the truth of a formula φ, DL uses a modal
construct $<\alpha>\varphi$, which intuitively states, "It is possible to execute α and halt in a
state satisfying φ." For example, the first-order formula $\exists x\ x^2 = y$ is equivalent to
the DL formula

$$<x := ?>x^2 = y. \tag{0.2}$$

In order to instantiate the quantifier effectively, we might replace the nondeterministic assignment inside the < > with the **while** program (0.1); over ℕ, the resulting
formula would be equivalent to (0.2).

This book is divided into three parts. Part I reviews the fundamental concepts of
logic and computability theory that are needed in the study of Dynamic Logic. Part
II discusses Propositional Dynamic Logic and its variants, and Part III discusses
First-Order Dynamic Logic and its variants. Examples are provided throughout,
and a collection of exercises and a short historical section are included at the end
of each chapter.

Part I was included in an effort to achieve a certain level of self-containment,
although the level achieved is far from absolute, since DL draws on too many
disciplines to cover adequately. The treatment of some topics in Part I is therefore necessarily abbreviated, and a passing familiarity with the basic concepts of
mathematical logic, computability, formal languages and automata, and program
verification is a desirable prerequisite. This background material can be found in
Shoenfield (1967) (logic), Rogers (1967) (recursion theory), Kozen (1997a) (formal
languages, automata, and computability), Keisler (1971) (infinitary logic), Manna
(1974) (program verification), and Harel (1992); Lewis and Papadimitriou (1981);
Davis et al. (1994) (computability and complexity).

Apart from the obvious heavy reliance on classical logic, computability theory
and programming, the subject has its roots in the work of Thiele (1966) and
Engeler (1967) in the late 1960's, who were the first to advance the idea of
formulating and investigating formal systems dealing with properties of programs
in an abstract setting. Research in program verification flourished thereafter with
the work of many researchers, notably Floyd (1967), Hoare (1969), Manna (1974),
and Salwicki (1970). The first precise development of a Dynamic Logic-like system
was carried out by Salwicki (1970), following Engeler (1967). This system was

called Algorithmic Logic. A similar system, called Monadic Programming Logic, was developed by Constable (1977). Dynamic Logic, which emphasizes the modal nature of the program/assertion interaction, was introduced by Pratt (1976).

There are by now a number of books and survey papers treating logics of programs, program verification, and Dynamic Logic. We refer the reader to Apt and Olderog (1991); Backhouse (1986); Harel (1979, 1984); Parikh (1981); Goldblatt (1982, 1987); Knijnenburg (1988); Cousot (1990); Emerson (1990); Kozen and Tiuryn (1990).

The material of this book has been used as the basis for graduate courses at the Weizmann Institute of Science, Bar-Ilan University, Aarhus University, Warsaw University, and Cornell University.

We would like to thank the following colleagues, students, and friends for their invaluable contributions: Alex Stoulboushkin, Jan Bergstra, Peter van Emde Boas, E. Allen Emerson, Neal Glew, Joseph Halpern, Chris Jeuell, Marek Karpiński, Assaf J. Kfoury, Nils Klarlund, David McAllester, Albert Meyer, Aleksey Nogin, Rohit Parikh, Nancy Perry, Vaughan Pratt, Aleksy Schubert, Fred Smith, Geoffrey Smith, Pawel Urzyczyn, and Moshe Vardi.

We welcome comments and criticism from readers.

I FUNDAMENTAL CONCEPTS

1 Mathematical Preliminaries

1.1 Notational Conventions

The integers, the rational numbers, and the real numbers are denoted $\mathbb{Z}$, $\mathbb{Q}$, and $\mathbb{R}$, respectively. The natural numbers are denoted $\mathbb{N}$ or ω; we usually use the former when thinking of them as an algebraic structure with arithmetic operations $+$ and $\cdot$ and the latter when thinking of them as the set of finite ordinal numbers. We reserve the symbols i, j, k, m, n to denote natural numbers.

We use the symbols $\Longrightarrow$, $\rightarrow$ for implication (if-then) and $\Longleftrightarrow$, $\leftrightarrow$ for bidirectional implication (equivalence, if and only if). The single-line versions will denote logical symbols in the systems under study, whereas the double-line versions are metasymbols standing for the English "implies" and "if and only if" in verbal proofs. Some authors use $\supset$ and $\equiv$, but we will reserve these symbols for other purposes. The symbol $\rightarrow$ is also used in the specification of the type of a function, as in $f : A \rightarrow B$, indicating that f has domain A and range B.

The word "iff" is an abbreviation for "if and only if."

We use the notation $\overset{\text{def}}{=}$ and $\overset{\text{def}}{\Longleftrightarrow}$ to indicate that the object on the left is being defined in terms of the object on the right. When a term is being defined, it is written in *italics*.

We adopt the convention that for any associative binary operation $\cdot$ with left and right identity ι, the empty product is ι. For example, for the operation of addition in $\mathbb{R}$, we take the empty sum $\sum_{a \in \varnothing} a$ to be 0, and we take the empty union $\bigcup_{A \in \varnothing} A$ to be $\varnothing$.

The length of a finite sequence σ of objects is denoted $|\sigma|$. The set of all finite sequences of elements of A is denoted A^*. Elements of A^* are also called *strings*. The unique element of A^* of length 0 is called the *empty string* or *empty sequence* and is denoted ε. The set A^* is called the *asterate* of A, and the set operator * is called the *asterate operator*.

The *reverse* of a string w, denoted w^R, is w written backwards.

1.2 Sets

Sets are denoted $A, B, C, \ldots$, possibly with subscripts. The symbol $\in$ denotes set containment: $x \in A$ means x is an element of A. The symbol $\subseteq$ denotes set inclusion: $A \subseteq B$ means A is a subset of B. We write $x \notin B$ and $A \nsubseteq B$ to indicate that x is not an element of B and A is not a subset of B, respectively.

Strict inclusion is denoted $\subset$. The cardinality of a set A is denoted $\#A$.

The *powerset* of a set A is the set of all subsets of A and is denoted 2^A. The empty set is denoted $\varnothing$. The union and intersection of sets A and B are denoted $A \cup B$ and $A \cap B$, respectively. If $\mathcal{A}$ is a set of sets, then $\bigcup \mathcal{A}$ and $\bigcap \mathcal{A}$ denote the union and the intersection, respectively, of all sets in $\mathcal{A}$ (for the latter, we require $\mathcal{A} \neq \varnothing$). That is,

$$\bigcup \mathcal{A} \overset{\text{def}}{=} \{x \mid \exists B \in \mathcal{A} \ x \in B\}$$

$$\bigcap \mathcal{A} \overset{\text{def}}{=} \{x \mid \forall B \in \mathcal{A} \ x \in B\}.$$

The *complement* of A in B is the set of all elements of B that are not in A and is denoted $B - A$. If B is understood, then we sometimes write $\sim A$ for $B - A$.

We use the standard set-theoretic notation $\{x \mid \varphi(x)\}$ and $\{x \in A \mid \varphi(x)\}$ for the class of all x satisfying the property φ and the set of all $x \in A$ satisfying φ, respectively.

The *Cartesian product* of sets A and B is the set of ordered pairs

$$A \times B \overset{\text{def}}{=} \{(a, b) \mid a \in A \text{ and } b \in B\}.$$

More generally, if A_α is an indexed family of sets, $\alpha \in I$, then the *Cartesian product* of the sets A_α is the set $\prod_{\alpha \in I} A_\alpha$ consisting of all I-tuples whose α^{th} component is in A_α for all $\alpha \in I$.

In particular, if all $A_\alpha = A$, we write A^I for $\prod_{\alpha \in I} A_\alpha$; if in addition I is the finite set $\{0, 1, \ldots, n-1\}$, we write

$$
\begin{aligned}
A^n &\overset{\text{def}}{=} \prod_{i=0}^{n-1} A_i \\
&= \underbrace{A \times \cdots \times A}_{n} \\
&= \{(a_0, \ldots, a_{n-1}) \mid a_i \in A, \ 0 \le i \le n-1\}.
\end{aligned}
$$

The set A^n is called the nth *Cartesian power* of A.

Along with the Cartesian product $\prod_{\alpha \in I} A_\alpha$ come the *projection functions* $\pi_\beta : \prod_{\alpha \in I} A_\alpha \to A_\beta$. The function π_β applied to $x \in \prod_{\alpha \in I} A_\alpha$ gives the βth component of x. For example, the projection function $\pi_0 : \mathbb{N}^3 \to \mathbb{N}$ gives $\pi_0(3, 5, 7) = 3$.

A Note on Foundations

We take Zermelo–Fraenkel set theory with the axiom of choice (ZFC) as our foundational system. In pure ZFC, everything is built out of sets, and sets are the only objects that can be elements of other sets. We will not give a systematic introduction to ZFC, but just point out a few relevant features.

The axioms of ZFC allow the formation of unions, ordered pairs, powersets, and Cartesian products. Infinite sets are allowed. Representations of all common datatypes and operations on them, such as strings, natural numbers, real numbers, trees, graphs, lists, and so forth, can be defined from these basic set operations. One important feature is the construction of the ordinal numbers and the transfinite induction principle, which we discuss in more detail in Section 1.6 below.

Sets and Classes

In ZFC, there is a distinction between *sets* and *classes*. For any property φ of sets, one can form the class

$$\{X \mid \varphi(X)\} \tag{1.2.1}$$

of all sets satisfying φ, along with the corresponding deduction rule

$$A \in \{X \mid \varphi(X)\} \iff \varphi(A) \tag{1.2.2}$$

for any set A. Any set B is a class $\{X \mid X \in B\}$, but classes need not be sets. Early versions of set theory assumed that any class of the form (1.2.1) was a set; this assumption is called *comprehension*. Unfortunately, this assumption led to inconsistencies such as *Russell's paradox* involving the class of all sets that do not contain themselves:

$$\{X \mid X \notin X\}. \tag{1.2.3}$$

If this were a set, say B, then by (1.2.2), $B \in B$ if and only if $B \notin B$, a contradiction.

Russell's paradox and other similar paradoxes were resolved by weakening Cantor's original version of set theory. Comprehension was replaced by a weaker axiom that states that if A is a set, then so is $\{X \in A \mid \varphi(X)\}$, the class of all elements of A satisfying φ. Classes that are not sets, such as (1.2.3), are called *proper classes*.

1.3   Relations

A *relation* is a subset of a Cartesian product. For example, the relation "is a daughter of" is a subset of the product {female humans} × {humans}. Relations are denoted $P, Q, R, \ldots$, possibly with subscripts. If A is a set, then a *relation on A* is a subset R of A^n for some n. The number n is called the *arity* of R. The relation R

on A is called *nullary*, *unary* (or *monadic*), *binary* (or *dyadic*), *ternary*, or *n-ary* if its arity is $0, 1, 2, 3$, or n, respectively. A unary relation on A is just a subset of A. The *empty relation* $\varnothing$ is the relation containing no tuples. It can be considered as a relation of any desired arity; all other relations have a unique arity.

If R is an n-ary relation, we sometimes write $R(a_1, \ldots, a_n)$ to indicate that the tuple $(a_1, \ldots, a_n)$ is in R. For binary relations, we may write $a \; R \; b$ instead of $R(a, b)$, as dictated by custom; this is particularly common for binary relations such as $\leq$, $\subseteq$, and $=$.

Henceforth, we will assume that the use of any expression of the form $R(a_1, \ldots, a_n)$ carries with it the implicit assumption that R is of arity n. We do this to avoid having to write " ... where R is n-ary."

A relation R is said to *refine* or *be a refinement of* another relation S if $R \subseteq S$, considered as sets of tuples.

Binary Relations

A binary relation R on U is said to be

- *reflexive* if $(a, a) \in R$ for all $a \in U$;
- *irreflexive* if $(a, a) \notin R$ for all $a \in U$;
- *symmetric* if $(a, b) \in R$ whenever $(b, a) \in R$;
- *antisymmetric* if $a = b$ whenever both $(a, b) \in R$ and $(b, a) \in R$;
- *transitive* if $(a, c) \in R$ whenever both $(a, b) \in R$ and $(b, c) \in R$;
- *well-founded* if every nonempty subset $X \subseteq U$ has an R-minimal element; that is, an element $b \in X$ such that for no $a \in X$ is it the case that $a \; R \; b$.

A binary relation R on U is called

- a *preorder* or *quasiorder* if it is reflexive and transitive;
- a *partial order* if it is reflexive, antisymmetric, and transitive;
- a *strict partial order* if it is irreflexive and transitive;
- a *total order* or *linear order* if it is a partial order and for all $a, b \in U$ either $a \; R \; b$ or $b \; R \; a$;
- a *well order* if it is a well-founded total order; equivalently, if it is a partial order and every subset of U has a *unique* R-least element;
- an *equivalence relation* if it is reflexive, symmetric, and transitive.

A partial order is *dense* if there is an element strictly between any two distinct comparable elements; that is, if $a \; R \; c$ and $a \neq c$, then there exists an element b

such that $b \neq a$, $b \neq c$, $a \, R \, b$, and $b \, R \, c$.

The *identity relation* ι on a set U is the binary relation

$$\iota \stackrel{\text{def}}{=} \{(s, s) \mid s \in U\}.$$

Note that a relation is reflexive iff ι refines it.

The *universal relation* on U of arity n is U^n, the set of all n-tuples of elements of U.

An important operation on binary relations is *relational composition* ∘. If P and Q are binary relations on U, their *composition* is the binary relation

$$P \circ Q \stackrel{\text{def}}{=} \{(u, w) \mid \exists v \in U \ (u, v) \in P \text{ and } (v, w) \in Q\}.$$

The identity relation ι is a left and right identity for the operation ∘; in other words, for any R, $\iota \circ R = R \circ \iota = R$. A binary relation R is transitive iff $R \circ R \subseteq R$.

One can generalize ∘ to the case where P is an m-ary relation on U and Q is an n-ary relation on U. In this case we define $P \circ Q$ to be the $(m + n - 2)$-ary relation

$$P \circ Q \stackrel{\text{def}}{=} \{(\overline{u}, \overline{w}) \mid \exists v \in U \ (\overline{u}, v) \in P, \ (v, \overline{w}) \in Q\}.$$

In Dynamic Logic, we will find this extended notion of relational composition useful primarily in the case where the left argument is binary and the right argument is unary. In this case,

$$P \circ Q \ = \ \{s \mid \exists t \in U \ (s, t) \in P \text{ and } t \in Q\}.$$

We abbreviate the n-fold composition of a binary relation R by R^n. Formally,

$$R^0 \stackrel{\text{def}}{=} \iota,$$
$$R^{n+1} \stackrel{\text{def}}{=} R \circ R^n.$$

This notation is the same as the notation for Cartesian powers described in Section 1.2, but both notations are standard, so we will rely on context to distinguish them. One can show by induction that for all $m, n \geq 0$, $R^{m+n} = R^m \circ R^n$.

The *converse* operation $^-$ on a binary relation R reverses its direction:

$$R^- \stackrel{\text{def}}{=} \{(t, s) \mid (s, t) \in R\}.$$

Note that $R^{--} = R$. A binary relation R is symmetric iff $R^- \subseteq R$; equivalently, if $R^- = R$.

Two important operations on binary relations are

$$R^* \quad \overset{\text{def}}{=} \quad \bigcup_{n \geq 0} R^n$$

$$R^+ \quad \overset{\text{def}}{=} \quad \bigcup_{n \geq 1} R^n.$$

The relations R^+ and R^* are called the *transitive closure* and the *reflexive transitive closure* of R, respectively. The reason for this terminology is that R^+ is the smallest (in the sense of set inclusion $\subseteq$) transitive relation containing R, and R^* is the smallest reflexive and transitive relation containing R (Exercise 1.13).

We will develop some basic properties of these constructs in the exercises. Here is a useful lemma that can be used to simplify several of the arguments involving the * operation.

LEMMA 1.1:   Relational composition distributes over arbitrary unions. That is, for any binary relation P and any indexed family of binary relations Q_α,

$$P \circ (\bigcup_\alpha Q_\alpha) \;=\; \bigcup_\alpha (P \circ Q_\alpha),$$

$$(\bigcup_\alpha Q_\alpha) \circ P \;=\; \bigcup_\alpha (Q_\alpha \circ P).$$

Proof For the first equation,

$$
\begin{aligned}
(u,v) \in P \circ (\bigcup_\alpha Q_\alpha) \quad &\Longleftrightarrow \quad \exists w \; (u,w) \in P \text{ and } (w,v) \in \bigcup_\alpha Q_\alpha \\
&\Longleftrightarrow \quad \exists w \; \exists \alpha \; (u,w) \in P \text{ and } (w,v) \in Q_\alpha \\
&\Longleftrightarrow \quad \exists \alpha \; \exists w \; (u,w) \in P \text{ and } (w,v) \in Q_\alpha \\
&\Longleftrightarrow \quad \exists \alpha \; (u,v) \in P \circ Q_\alpha \\
&\Longleftrightarrow \quad (u,v) \in \bigcup_\alpha (P \circ Q_\alpha).
\end{aligned}
$$

The proof of the second equation is similar. ∎

Equivalence Relations

Recall from Section 1.3 that a binary relation on a set U is an *equivalence relation* if it is reflexive, symmetric, and transitive. Given an equivalence relation $\equiv$ on U, the $\equiv$-*equivalence class* of $a \in U$ is the set

$$\{b \in U \mid b \equiv a\},$$

typically denoted $[a]$. By reflexivity, $a \in [a]$; and if $a, b \in U$, then

$$a \equiv b \iff [a] = [b]$$

(Exercise 1.10).

A *partition* of a set U is a collection of pairwise disjoint subsets of U whose union is U. That is, it is an indexed collection $A_\alpha \subseteq U$ such that $\bigcup_\alpha A_\alpha = U$ and $A_\alpha \cap A_\beta = \varnothing$ for all $\alpha \neq \beta$.

There is a natural one-to-one correspondence between equivalence relations and partitions. The equivalence classes of an equivalence relation on U form a partition of U; conversely, any partition of U gives rise to an equivalence relation by declaring two elements to be equivalent if they are in the same set of the partition.

Recall that a binary relation $\equiv_1$ on U *refines* another binary relation $\equiv_2$ on U if for any $a, b \in U$, if $a \equiv_1 b$ then $a \equiv_2 b$. For equivalence relations, this is the same as saying that every equivalence class of $\equiv_1$ is included in an equivalence class of $\equiv_2$; equivalently, every $\equiv_2$-class is a union of $\equiv_1$-classes. Any family $\mathcal{E}$ of equivalence relations has a *coarsest common refinement*, which is the $\subseteq$-greatest relation refining all the relations in $\mathcal{E}$. This is just $\bigcap \mathcal{E}$, thinking of elements of $\mathcal{E}$ as sets of ordered pairs. Each equivalence class of the coarsest common refinement is an intersection of equivalence classes of relations in $\mathcal{E}$.

Functions

Functions are denoted $f, g, h, \ldots$, possibly with subscripts. Functions, like relations, are formally sets of ordered pairs. More precisely, a function f is a binary relation such that no two distinct elements have the same first component; that is, for all a there is at most one b such that $(a, b) \in f$. In this case we write $f(a) = b$. The a is called the *argument* and the b is called the *value*.

The *domain* of f is the set $\{a \mid \exists b \ (a, b) \in f\}$ and is denoted dom f. The function f is said to be *defined* on a if $a \in$ dom f. The *range* of f is any set containing $\{b \mid \exists a \ (a, b) \in f\} = \{f(a) \mid a \in$ dom $f\}$. We use the phrase "the range" loosely; the range is not unique. We write $f : A \rightarrow B$ to denote that f is a function with domain A and range B. The set of all functions $f : A \rightarrow B$ is denoted $A \rightarrow B$ or B^A.

A function can be specified anonymously with the symbol $\mapsto$. For example, the function $x \mapsto 2x$ on the integers is the function $\mathbb{Z} \rightarrow \mathbb{Z}$ that doubles its argument.

Formally, it is the set of ordered pairs $\{(x, 2x) \mid x \in \mathbb{Z}\}$. The symbol $\upharpoonright$ is used to restrict a function to a smaller domain. For example, if $f : \mathbb{R} \to \mathbb{R}$, then $f \upharpoonright \mathbb{Z} : \mathbb{Z} \to \mathbb{R}$ is the function that agrees with f on the integers but is otherwise undefined.

If $C \subseteq A$ and $f : A \to B$, then $f(C)$ denotes the set

$$f(C) \ \overset{\text{def}}{=} \ \{f(a) \mid a \in C\} \ \subseteq \ B.$$

This is called the *image* of C under f. The *image* of f is the set $f(A)$.

The *composition* of two functions f and g is just the relational composition $f \circ g$ as defined in Section 1.3. If $f : A \to B$ and $g : B \to C$, then $f \circ g : A \to C$, and

$$(f \circ g)(a) \ = \ g(f(a)).^1$$

A function $f : A \to B$ is *one-to-one* or *injective* if $f(a) \neq f(b)$ whenever $a, b \in A$ and $a \neq b$. A function $f : A \to B$ is *onto* or *surjective* if for all $b \in B$ there exists $a \in A$ such that $f(a) = b$. A function is *bijective* if it is both injective and surjective. A bijective function $f : A \to B$ has an *inverse* $f^{-1} : B \to A$ in the sense that $f \circ f^{-1}$ is the identity function on A and $f^{-1} \circ f$ is the identity function on B. Thinking of f as a binary relation, f^{-1} is just the converse f^- as defined in Section 1.3. Two sets are said to be in *one-to-one correspondence* if there exists a bijection between them.

We will find the following *function-patching* operator useful. If $f : A \to B$ is any function, $a \in A$, and $b \in B$, then we denote by $f[a/b] : A \to B$ the function defined by

$$f[a/b](x) \ \overset{\text{def}}{=} \ \begin{cases} b, & \text{if } x = a \\ f(x), & \text{otherwise.} \end{cases}$$

In other words, $f[a/b]$ is the function that agrees with f everywhere except possibly a, on which it takes the value b.

Partial Orders

Recall from Section 1.3 that a binary relation $\leq$ on a set A is a *preorder* (or *quasiorder*) if it is reflexive and transitive, and it is a *partial order* if in addition it is antisymmetric. Any preorder $\leq$ has a natural associated equivalence relation

$$a \equiv b \ \Longleftrightarrow \ a \leq b \text{ and } b \leq a.$$

---

1 Unfortunately, the definition $(f \circ g)(a) = f(g(a))$ is fairly standard, but this conflicts with other standard usage, namely the definition of $\circ$ for binary relations and the definition of functions as sets of (argument,value) pairs.

The order $\leq$ is well-defined on $\equiv$-equivalence classes; that is, if $a \leq b$, $a \equiv a'$, and $b \equiv b'$, then $a' \leq b'$. It therefore makes sense to define $[a] \leq [b]$ if $a \leq b$. The resulting order on $\equiv$-classes is a partial order.

A *strict partial order* is a binary relation $<$ that is irreflexive and transitive. Any strict partial order $<$ has an associated partial order $\leq$ defined by $a \leq b$ if $a < b$ or $a = b$. Any preorder $\leq$ has an associated strict partial order defined by $a < b$ if $a \leq b$ but $b \not\leq a$. For partial orders $\leq$, these two operations are inverses. For example, the strict partial order associated with the set inclusion relation $\subseteq$ is the proper inclusion relation $\subset$.

A function $f : (A, \leq) \to (A', \leq)$ between two partially ordered sets is *monotone* if it preserves order: if $a \leq b$ then $f(a) \leq f(b)$.

Let $\leq$ be a partial order on A and let $B \subseteq A$. An element $x \in A$ is an *upper bound* of B if $y \leq x$ for all $y \in B$. The element x itself need not be an element of B. If in addition $x \leq z$ for every upper bound z of B, then x is called the *least upper bound*, *supremum*, or *join* of B, and is denoted $\sup_{y \in B} y$ or $\sup B$. The supremum of a set need not exist, but if it does, then it is unique.

A function $f : (A, \leq) \to (A', \leq)$ between two partially ordered sets is *continuous* if it preserves all existing suprema: whenever $B \subseteq A$ and $\sup B$ exists, then $\sup_{x \in B} f(x)$ exists and is equal to $f(\sup B)$.

Any partial order extends to a total order. In fact, any partial order is the intersection of all its total extensions (Exercise 1.14).

Recall that a preorder $\leq$ is *well-founded* if every subset has a $\leq$-minimal element. An *antichain* is a set of pairwise $\leq$-incomparable elements.

PROPOSITION 1.2:   Let $\leq$ be a preorder on a set A. The following four conditions are equivalent:

(i) The relation $\leq$ is well-founded and has no infinite antichains.

(ii) For any infinite sequence $x_0, x_1, x_2, \ldots$, there exist i, j such that $i < j$ and $x_i \leq x_j$.

(iii) Any infinite sequence has an infinite nondecreasing subsequence; that is, for any sequence $x_0, x_1, x_2, \ldots$, there exist $i_0 < i_1 < i_2 < \cdots$ such that $x_{i_0} \leq x_{i_1} \leq x_{i_2} \leq \cdots$.

(iv) Any set $X \subseteq A$ has a finite base $X_0 \subseteq X$; that is, a finite subset X_0 such that for all $y \in X$ there exists $x \in X_0$ such that $x \leq y$.

In addition, if $\leq$ is a partial order, then the four conditions above are equivalent to the fifth condition:

(v) Any total extension of $\leq$ is a well order.

Proof Exercise 1.16. ∎

A preorder or partial order is called a *well quasiorder* or *well partial order*, respectively, if it satisfies any of the four equivalent conditions of Proposition 1.2.

Well-Foundedness and Induction

Everyone is familiar with the set $\omega = \{0, 1, 2, \ldots\}$ of *finite ordinals*, also known as the *natural numbers*. An essential mathematical tool is the *induction principle* on this set, which states that if a property is true of zero and is preserved by the successor operation, then it is true of all elements of ω.

There are more general notions of induction that we will find useful. *Transfinite induction* extends induction on ω to higher ordinals. We will discuss transfinite induction later on in Section 1.6. *Structural induction* is used to establish properties of inductively defined objects such as lists, trees, or logical formulas.

All of these types of induction are instances of a more general notion called *induction on a well-founded relation* or just *well-founded induction*. This is in a sense the most general form of induction there is (Exercise 1.15). Recall that a binary relation R on a set X is *well-founded* if every subset of X has an R-minimal element. For such relations, the following induction principle holds:

(WFI) If φ is a property that holds for x whenever it holds for all R-predecessors of x—that is, if φ is true of x whenever it is true of all y such that $y\ R\ x$—then φ is true of all x.

The "basis" of the induction is the case of R-minimal elements; that is, those with no R-predecessors. In this case, the premise "φ is true of all R-predecessors of x" is vacuously true.

LEMMA 1.3 (PRINCIPLE OF WELL-FOUNDED INDUCTION):   If R is a well-founded relation on a set X, then the well-founded induction principle (WFI) is sound.

Proof Suppose φ is a property such that, whenever φ is true of all y such that $y\ R\ x$, then φ is also true of x. Let S be the set of all elements of X satisfying property φ. Then $X - S$ is the set of all elements of X not satisfying property φ. Since R is well-founded, if $X - S$ were nonempty, it would have a minimal element x. But then φ would be true of all R-predecessors of x but not of x itself, contradicting our assumption. Therefore $X - S$ must be empty, and consequently $S = X$. ∎

In fact, the converse holds as well: if R is not well-founded, then there is a property on elements of X that violates the principle (WFI) (Exercise 1.15).

1.4   Graphs and Dags

For the purposes of this book, we define a *directed graph* to be a pair $\mathcal{D} = (D, \to_{\mathcal{D}})$, where D is a set and $\to_{\mathcal{D}}$ is a binary relation on D. Elements of D are called *vertices* and elements of $\to_{\mathcal{D}}$ are called *edges*. In graph theory, one often sees more general types of graphs allowing multiple edges or weighted edges, but we will not need them here.

A directed graph is called *acyclic* if for no $d \in D$ is it the case that $d \to^+_{\mathcal{D}} d$, where $\to^+_{\mathcal{D}}$ is the transitive closure of $\to_{\mathcal{D}}$. A directed acyclic graph is called a *dag*.

1.5   Lattices

An *upper semilattice* is a partially ordered set in which every finite subset has a supremum (join). Every semilattice has a unique smallest element, namely the join of the empty set.

A *lattice* is a partially ordered set in which every finite subset has both a supremum and an *infimum*, or *greatest lower bound*. The infimum of a set is often called its *meet*. Every lattice has a unique largest element, which is the meet of the empty set.

A *complete lattice* is a lattice in which all joins exist; equivalently, in which all meets exist. Each of these assumptions implies the other: the join of a set B is the meet of the set of upper bounds of B, and the meet of B is the join of the set of lower bounds of B. Every set B has at least one upper bound and one lower bound, namely the top and bottom elements of the lattice, respectively.

For example, the powerset 2^A of a set A is a complete lattice under set inclusion $\subseteq$. In this lattice, for any $B \subseteq 2^A$, the supremum of B is $\bigcup B$ and its infimum is $\bigcap B$.

1.6   Transfinite Ordinals

The *induction principle* on the natural numbers $\omega = \{0, 1, 2, \dots\}$ states that if a property is true of zero and is preserved by the successor operation, then it is true of all elements of ω.

In the study of logics of programs, we often run into higher ordinals, and it is useful to have a *transfinite induction principle* that applies in those situations. Cantor recognized the value of such a principle in his theory of infinite sets. Any modern account of the foundations of mathematics will include a chapter on ordinals and transfinite induction.

Unfortunately, a complete understanding of ordinals and transfinite induction is impossible outside the context of set theory, since many issues impact the very foundations of the subject. A thorough treatment would fill a large part of a basic course in set theory, and is well beyond the scope of this introduction. We provide here only a cursory account of the basic facts, tools and techniques we will need in the sequel. We encourage the student interested in foundations to consult the references at the end of the chapter for a more detailed treatment.

Set-Theoretic Definition of Ordinals

Ordinals are defined as certain sets of sets. The key facts we will need about ordinals, succinctly stated, are:

(i) There are two kinds: *successors* and *limits*.

(ii) They are well-ordered.

(iii) There are a lot of them.

(iv) We can do induction on them.

We will explain each of these statements in more detail below.

A set C of sets is said to be *transitive* if $C \subseteq 2^C$; that is, every element of C is a subset of C. In other words, if $A \in B$ and $B \in C$, then $A \in C$. Formally, an *ordinal* is defined to be a set A such that

- A is transitive

- all elements of A are transitive.

It follows that any element of an ordinal is an ordinal. We use $\alpha, \beta, \gamma, \ldots$ to refer to ordinals. The class of all ordinals is denoted **Ord**. It is not a set, but a proper class.

This rather neat but perhaps obscure definition of ordinals has some far-reaching consequences that are not at all obvious. For ordinals α, β, define $\alpha < \beta$ if $\alpha \in \beta$. Then every ordinal is equal to the set of all smaller ordinals (in the sense of $<$). The relation $<$ is a strict partial order in the sense of Section 1.3.

If α is an ordinal, then so is $\alpha \cup \{\alpha\}$. The latter is called the *successor* of α and is denoted $\alpha + 1$. Also, if A is any set of ordinals, then $\bigcup A$ is an ordinal and is the supremum of the ordinals in A under the relation $\leq$.

The smallest few ordinals are

$0 \;\overset{\text{def}}{=}\; \varnothing$

$1 \;\overset{\text{def}}{=}\; \{0\} \;=\; \{\varnothing\}$

$2 \;\overset{\text{def}}{=}\; \{0,1\} \;=\; \{\varnothing, \{\varnothing\}\}$

$3 \;\overset{\text{def}}{=}\; \{0,1,2\} \;=\; \{\varnothing, \{\varnothing\}, \{\varnothing, \{\varnothing\}\}\}$

$\vdots$

The first infinite ordinal is

$\omega \;\overset{\text{def}}{=}\; \{0,1,2,3,\ldots\}.$

An ordinal is called a *successor ordinal* if it is of the form $\alpha + 1$ for some ordinal α, otherwise it is called a *limit ordinal*. The smallest limit ordinal is 0 and the next smallest is ω. Of course, $\omega + 1 = \omega \cup \{\omega\}$ is an ordinal, so it does not stop there.

It follows from the axioms of ZFC that the relation $<$ on ordinals is a linear order. That is, if α and β are any two ordinals, then either $\alpha < \beta$, $\alpha = \beta$, or $\beta < \alpha$. This is most easily proved by induction on the well-founded relation

$$(\alpha, \beta) \leq (\alpha', \beta') \;\overset{\text{def}}{\Longleftrightarrow}\; \alpha \leq \alpha' \text{ and } \beta \leq \beta'.$$

The class of ordinals is well-founded in the sense that any nonempty set of ordinals has a least element.

Since the ordinals form a proper class, there can be no one-to-one function $\mathbf{Ord} \to A$ into a set A. This is what is meant in clause (iii) above. In practice, this fact will come up when we construct functions $f : \mathbf{Ord} \to A$ from $\mathbf{Ord}$ into a set A by induction. Such an f, regarded as a collection of ordered pairs, is necessarily a class and not a set. We will always be able to conclude that there exist distinct ordinals α, β with $f(\alpha) = f(\beta)$.

Transfinite Induction

The *transfinite induction principle* is a method of establishing that a particular property is true of all ordinals. It states that in order to prove that the property is true of all ordinals, it suffices to show that the property is true of an arbitrary ordinal α whenever it is true of all ordinals $\beta < \alpha$. Proofs by transfinite induction typically contain two cases, one for successor ordinals and one for limit ordinals. The basis of the induction is often a special case of the case for limit ordinals, since $0 = \varnothing$ is a limit ordinal; here the premise that the property holds of all ordinals

$\beta < \alpha$ is vacuously true.

The validity of this principle follows ultimately from the well-foundedness of the set containment relation $\in$. This is an axiom of ZFC called the *axiom of regularity*.

We will see many examples of definitions and proofs by transfinite induction in subsequent sections.

Zorn's Lemma and the Axiom of Choice

Related to the ordinals and transfinite induction are the *axiom of choice* and *Zorn's lemma*.

The *axiom of choice* is an axiom of ZFC. It states that for every set A of nonempty sets, there exists a function f with domain A that picks an element out of each set in A; that is, for every $B \in A$, $f(B) \in B$. Equivalently, any Cartesian product of nonempty sets is nonempty.

Zorn's lemma states that every set of sets closed under unions of chains contains a $\subseteq$-maximal element. Here a *chain* is a family of sets linearly ordered by the inclusion relation $\subseteq$, and to say that a set C of sets is closed under unions of chains means that if $B \subseteq C$ and B is a chain, then $\bigcup B \in C$. An element $B \in C$ is $\subseteq$-*maximal* if it is not properly included in any $B' \in C$.

The *well ordering principle*, also known as *Zermelo's theorem*, states that every set is in one-to-one correspondence with some ordinal. A set is *countably infinite* if it is in one-to-one correspondence with ω. A set is *countable* if it is finite or countably infinite.

The axiom of choice, Zorn's lemma, and the well ordering principle are equivalent to one another and *independent* of ZF set theory (ZFC without the axiom of choice) in the sense that if ZF is consistent, then neither they nor their negations can be proven from the axioms of ZF.

In subsequent sections, we will use the axiom of choice, Zorn's lemma, and the transfinite induction principle freely.

1.7   Set Operators

A *set operator* is a function that maps sets to sets. Set operators arise everywhere in mathematics, and we will see many applications in subsequent sections. Here we introduce some special properties of set operators such as monotonicity and closure and discuss some of their consequences. We culminate with a general theorem due to Knaster and Tarski concerning inductive definitions.

Let U be a fixed set. Recall that 2^U denotes the *powerset* of U, or the set of subsets of U:

$$2^U \quad \overset{\text{def}}{=} \quad \{A \mid A \subseteq U\}.$$

A *set operator* on U is a function $\tau : 2^U \to 2^U$.

Monotone, Continuous, and Finitary Operators

A set operator τ is said to be *monotone* if it preserves set inclusion:

$$A \subseteq B \implies \tau(A) \subseteq \tau(B).$$

A *chain of sets* in U is a family of subsets of U totally ordered by the inclusion relation $\subseteq$; that is, for every A and B in the chain, either $A \subseteq B$ or $B \subseteq A$. A set operator τ is said to be *(chain-)continuous* if for every chain of sets $\mathcal{C}$,

$$\tau(\bigcup \mathcal{C}) \;=\; \bigcup_{A \in \mathcal{C}} \tau(A).$$

A set operator τ is said to be *finitary* if its action on a set A depends only on finite subsets of A in the following sense:

$$\tau(A) \;=\; \bigcup_{\substack{B \subseteq A \\ B \text{ finite}}} \tau(B).$$

Every finitary operator is continuous and every continuous operator is monotone. However, neither inclusion holds in the opposite direction in general (Exercise 1.17). In many applications, the appropriate operators are finitary.

EXAMPLE 1.4:   For a binary relation R on a set V, let

$$\begin{aligned} \tau(R) \;&=\; \{(a,c) \mid \exists b \; (a,b), \; (b,c) \in R\} \\ &=\; R \circ R. \end{aligned}$$

The function τ is a set operator on V^2; that is,

$$\tau : 2^{V^2} \;\to\; 2^{V^2}.$$

The operator τ is finitary, because $\tau(R)$ is determined by the action of τ on two-element subsets of R.

Prefixpoints and Fixpoints

A *prefixpoint* of a set operator τ is a set A such that $\tau(A) \subseteq A$. A *fixpoint* of τ is a set A such that $\tau(A) = A$. We say that a set A is *closed* under the operator τ if A is a prefixpoint of τ. Every set operator on U has at least one prefixpoint, namely U. Monotone set operators also have fixpoints, as we shall see.

EXAMPLE 1.5: By definition, a binary relation R on a set V is *transitive* if $(a, c) \in R$ whenever $(a, b) \in R$ and $(b, c) \in R$. Equivalently, R is transitive iff it is closed under the finitary set operator τ defined in Example 1.4.

LEMMA 1.6: The intersection of any set of prefixpoints of a monotone set operator τ is a prefixpoint of τ.

Proof Let $\mathcal{C}$ be any set of prefixpoints of τ. We wish to show that $\bigcap \mathcal{C}$ is a prefixpoint of τ. For any $A \in \mathcal{C}$, $\bigcap \mathcal{C} \subseteq A$, therefore

$$\tau(\bigcap \mathcal{C}) \quad \subseteq \quad \tau(A) \quad \text{monotonicity of } \tau$$
$$\subseteq \quad A \quad \text{since } A \text{ is a prefixpoint.}$$

Since $A \in \mathcal{C}$ was arbitrary, $\tau(\bigcap \mathcal{C}) \subseteq \bigcap \mathcal{C}$. ∎

It follows from Lemma 1.6 and the characterization of complete lattices of Section 1.5 that the set of prefixpoints of a monotone operator τ forms a complete lattice under the inclusion ordering $\subseteq$. In this lattice, the meet of any set of prefixpoints $\mathcal{C}$ is the set $\bigcap \mathcal{C}$, and the join of any set of prefixpoints $\mathcal{C}$ is the set

$$\bigcap \{A \subseteq U \mid \bigcup \mathcal{C} \subseteq A, \ A \text{ is a prefixpoint of } \tau\}.$$

Note that the join of $\mathcal{C}$ is *not* $\bigcup \mathcal{C}$ in general; this is not necessarily a prefixpoint (Exercise 1.23).

By Lemma 1.6, for any set A, the meet of all prefixpoints containing A is a prefixpoint of τ containing A and is necessarily the least prefixpoint of τ containing A. That is, if we define

$$\mathcal{C}(A) \stackrel{\text{def}}{=} \{B \subseteq U \mid A \subseteq B \text{ and } \tau(B) \subseteq B\} \tag{1.7.1}$$
$$\tau^\dagger(A) \stackrel{\text{def}}{=} \bigcap \mathcal{C}(A), \tag{1.7.2}$$

then $\tau^\dagger(A)$ is the least prefixpoint of τ containing A with respect to $\subseteq$. Note that the set $\mathcal{C}(A)$ is nonempty, since it contains U at least.

LEMMA 1.7:   Any monotone set operator τ has a $\subseteq$-least fixpoint.

Proof We show that $\tau^\dagger(\varnothing)$ is the least fixpoint of τ. By Lemma 1.6, it is the least prefixpoint of τ. If it is a fixpoint, then it is the least one, since every fixpoint is a prefixpoint. But if it were not a fixpoint, then by monotonicity, $\tau(\tau^\dagger(\varnothing))$ would be a smaller prefixpoint, contradicting the fact that $\tau^\dagger(\varnothing)$ is the least. ∎

Closure Operators

A set operator σ on U is called a *closure operator* if it satisfies the following three properties:

(i) σ is monotone

(ii) $A \subseteq \sigma(A)$

(iii) $\sigma(\sigma(A)) = \sigma(A)$.

Because of clause (ii), fixpoints and prefixpoints coincide for closure operators. Thus a set is closed with respect to a closure operator σ iff it is a fixpoint of σ. As shown in Lemma 1.6, the set of closed sets of a closure operator forms a complete lattice.

LEMMA 1.8:   For any monotone set operator τ, the operator $\tau^\dagger$ defined in (1.7.2) is a closure operator.

Proof The operator $\tau^\dagger$ is monotone, since

$$A \subseteq B \implies \mathcal{C}(B) \subseteq \mathcal{C}(A) \implies \bigcap \mathcal{C}(A) \subseteq \bigcap \mathcal{C}(B),$$

where $\mathcal{C}(A)$ is the set defined in (1.7.1).

Property (ii) of closure operators follows directly from the definition of $\tau^\dagger$. Finally, to show property (iii), since $\tau^\dagger(A)$ is a prefixpoint of τ, it suffices to show that any prefixpoint of τ is a fixpoint of $\tau^\dagger$. But

$$\tau(B) \subseteq B \iff B \in \mathcal{C}(B)$$
$$\iff B = \bigcap \mathcal{C}(B) = \tau^\dagger(B).$$

∎

EXAMPLE 1.9:   The *transitive closure* of a binary relation R on a set V is the least transitive relation containing R; that is, it is the least relation containing R and closed under the finitary transitivity operator τ of Example 1.4. This is the relation $\tau^\dagger(R)$. Thus the closure operator $\tau^\dagger$ maps an arbitrary binary relation R to its transitive closure.

EXAMPLE 1.10: The *reflexive transitive closure* of a binary relation R on a set V is the least reflexive and transitive relation containing R; that is, it is the least relation that contains R, is closed under transitivity, and contains the identity relation $\iota = \{(a,a) \mid a \in V\}$. Note that "contains the identity relation" just means closed under the constant-valued monotone set operator $R \mapsto \iota$. Thus the reflexive transitive closure of R is $\sigma^\dagger(R)$, where σ denotes the finitary operator $R \mapsto \tau(R)\cup\iota$.

The Knaster–Tarski Theorem

The *Knaster–Tarski theorem* is a useful theorem that describes how least fixpoints of monotone set operators can be obtained either "from above," as in the proof of Lemma 1.7, or "from below," as a limit of a chain of sets defined by transfinite induction. In general, the Knaster–Tarski Theorem holds for monotone operators on an arbitrary complete lattice, but we will find it most useful for the lattice of subsets of a set U, so we prove it only for that case.

Let U be a set and let τ be a monotone operator on U. Let $\tau^\dagger$ be the associated closure operator defined in (1.7.2). We show how to attain $\tau^\dagger(A)$ starting from A and working up. The idea is to start with A, then apply τ repeatedly, adding new elements until achieving closure. In most applications, the operator τ is continuous, in which case this takes only countably many iterations; but for monotone operators in general, it can take more.

Formally, we construct by transfinite induction a chain of sets $\tau^\alpha(A)$ indexed by ordinals α:

$$\tau^{\alpha+1}(A) \;\overset{\text{def}}{=}\; A \cup \tau(\tau^\alpha(A))$$
$$\tau^\lambda(A) \;\overset{\text{def}}{=}\; \bigcup_{\alpha<\lambda} \tau^\alpha(A), \quad \lambda \text{ a limit ordinal}$$
$$\tau^*(A) \;\overset{\text{def}}{=}\; \bigcup_{\alpha\in\mathbf{Ord}} \tau^\alpha(A).$$

The base case is included in the case for limit ordinals:

$$\tau^0(A) \;=\; \varnothing.$$

Intuitively, $\tau^\alpha(A)$ is the set obtained by applying τ to A α times, reincluding A at successor stages.

LEMMA 1.11:   If $\alpha \leq \beta$, then $\tau^\alpha(A) \subseteq \tau^\beta(A)$.

Proof We proceed by transfinite induction. For two successor ordinals $\alpha + 1$ and $\beta + 1$ with $\alpha + 1 \leq \beta + 1$,

$$
\begin{aligned}
\tau^{\alpha+1}(A) &= A \cup \tau(\tau^\alpha(A)) \\
&\subseteq A \cup \tau(\tau^\beta(A)) \qquad \text{induction hypothesis and monotonicity} \\
&= \tau^{\beta+1}(A).
\end{aligned}
$$

If $\alpha \leq \beta$ and α is a limit ordinal,

$$
\begin{aligned}
\tau^\alpha(A) &= \bigcup_{\gamma < \alpha} \tau^\gamma(A) \\
&\subseteq \tau^\beta(A) \quad \text{induction hypothesis.}
\end{aligned}
$$

Finally, if $\alpha \leq \beta$ and β is a limit ordinal, the result is immediate from the definition of $\tau^\beta(A)$. ∎

Lemma 1.11 says that the $\tau^\alpha(A)$ form a chain of sets. The set $\tau^*(A)$ is the union of this chain over all ordinals α.

Now there must exist an ordinal κ such that $\tau^{\kappa+1}(A) = \tau^\kappa(A)$, because there is no one-to-one function from the class of ordinals to the powerset of U. The least such κ is called the *closure ordinal* of τ. If κ is the closure ordinal of τ, then $\tau^\beta(A) = \tau^\kappa(A)$ for all $\beta > \kappa$, therefore $\tau^*(A) = \tau^\kappa(A)$.

If τ is continuous, then its closure ordinal is at most ω, but not for monotone operators in general (Exercise 1.18).

THEOREM 1.12 (KNASTER–TARSKI): $\tau^\dagger(A) = \tau^*(A)$.

Proof First we show the forward inclusion. Let κ be the closure ordinal of τ. Since $\tau^\dagger(A)$ is the least prefixpoint of τ containing A, it suffices to show that $\tau^*(A) = \tau^\kappa(A)$ is a prefixpoint of τ. But

$$
\begin{aligned}
\tau(\tau^\kappa(A)) &\subseteq A \cup \tau(\tau^\kappa(A)) \\
&= \tau^{\kappa+1}(A) \\
&= \tau^\kappa(A).
\end{aligned}
$$

Conversely, we show by transfinite induction that for all ordinals α, $\tau^\alpha(A) \subseteq$

$\tau^\dagger(A)$, therefore $\tau^*(A) \subseteq \tau^\dagger(A)$. For successor ordinals $\alpha + 1$,

$$
\begin{aligned}
\tau^{\alpha+1}(A) \;=\;& A \cup \tau(\tau^\alpha(A)) \\
\subseteq\;& A \cup \tau(\tau^\dagger(A)) \quad \text{induction hypothesis and monotonicity} \\
\subseteq\;& \tau^\dagger(A) \qquad\qquad\;\; \text{definition of } \tau^\dagger.
\end{aligned}
$$

For limit ordinals λ, $\tau^\alpha(A) \subseteq \tau^\dagger(A)$ for all $\alpha < \lambda$ by the induction hypothesis; therefore

$$
\tau^\lambda(A) \;=\; \bigcup_{\alpha < \lambda} \tau^\alpha(A) \;\subseteq\; \tau^\dagger(A).
$$

∎

1.8   Bibliographical Notes

Most of the result of this chapter can be found in any basic text on discrete structures such as Gries and Schneider (1994); Rosen (1995); Graham et al. (1989). A good reference for introductory axiomatic set theory is Halmos (1960).

Exercises

1.1. Prove that relational composition is associative:

$$
P \circ (Q \circ R) \;=\; (P \circ Q) \circ R.
$$

1.2. Prove that ι is an identity and $\varnothing$ an annihilator for relational composition:

$$
\begin{aligned}
\iota \circ P \;&=\; P \circ \iota \;=\; P \\
\varnothing \circ P \;&=\; P \circ \varnothing \;=\; \varnothing.
\end{aligned}
$$

1.3. Prove that relational composition is monotone in both arguments with respect to the inclusion order $\subseteq$: if $P \subseteq P'$ and $Q \subseteq Q'$, then $P \circ Q \subseteq P' \circ Q'$.

1.4. Prove that relational composition is continuous in both arguments with respect to the inclusion order $\subseteq$: for any indexed families P_α and Q_β of binary relations on a set U,

$$
\Big(\bigcup_\alpha P_\alpha\Big) \circ \Big(\bigcup_\beta Q_\beta\Big) \;=\; \bigcup_{\alpha,\beta} (P_\alpha \circ Q_\beta).
$$

1.5. Prove that the converse operation $^-$ commutes with $\cup$ and with *:

$$\left(\bigcup_\alpha R_\alpha\right)^- = \bigcup_\alpha R_\alpha^-$$
$$(R^*)^- = (R^-)^*.$$

1.6. Prove that the converse operation commutes with relational composition, provided the order of the composition factors is reversed:

$$(P \circ Q)^- = Q^- \circ P^-.$$

1.7. Prove the following identities for binary relations:

$$P^n \circ P^m = P^{m+n}, \quad m, n \geq 0$$
$$P \circ P^* = P^* \circ P$$
$$P = P^{--}$$
$$P \subseteq P \circ P^- \circ P.$$

1.8. Give an example of a set U and a nonempty binary relation R on U such that for all m, n with $m \neq n$, $R^m \cap R^n = \varnothing$. On the other hand, show that for any binary relation R, if $m \leq n$ then $(\iota \cup R)^m \subseteq (\iota \cup R)^n$, and that

$$R^* = \bigcup_n (\iota \cup R)^n.$$

1.9. Prove that P^* is the least prefixpoint of the monotone set operator

$$X \mapsto \iota \cup (P \circ X).$$

1.10. Let $\equiv$ be an equivalence relation on a set U with equivalence classes $[a]$, $a \in U$. Show that for any $a, b \in U$,

$$a \equiv b \iff [a] = [b].$$

1.11. Let $(A, \leq)$ be a total order with associated strict order $<$. Define an order on A^* by: $a_1, \ldots, a_m \leq b_1, \ldots, b_n$ if either $a_1, \ldots, a_m$ is a prefix of $b_1, \ldots, b_n$, or there exists $i \leq m, n$ such that $a_j = b_j$ for all $j < i$ and $a_i < b_i$. Prove that this is a total order on A^n. This order is called *lexicographic order* on A^n.

1.12. Prove the following properties of binary relations R:

$$\iota \subseteq R^*$$
$$R \subseteq R^*$$
$$R^* \circ R^* = R^*$$
$$R^{**} = R^*$$
$$\iota \cup (R \circ R^*) = R^*.$$

Give purely equational proofs using Lemma 1.1 and the definition $R^* = \bigcup_n R^n$.

1.13. Prove that for any binary relation R, R^+ is the smallest (in the sense of set inclusion $\subseteq$) transitive relation containing R, and R^* is the smallest reflexive and transitive relation containing R.

1.14. Prove that any partial order is equal to the intersection of all its total extensions. That is, for any partial order R on a set X,

$$R = \bigcap \{T \subseteq X \times X \mid R \subseteq T,\ T \text{ is a total order on } X\}.$$

1.15. Let R be a binary relation on a set X. An *infinite descending R-chain* is an infinite sequence $x_0, x_1, x_2, \ldots$ of elements of X such that $x_{i+1}\ R\ x_i$ for all $i \geq 0$. Prove that the following two statements are equivalent:

(i) The relation R is well-founded.

(ii) There are no infinite descending R-chains.

1.16. Prove Proposition 1.2. *Hint.* Prove the four statements in the first part of the theorem in the order (i) $\Longrightarrow$ (ii) $\Longrightarrow$ (iii) $\Longrightarrow$ (iv) $\Longrightarrow$ (i). For (ii) $\Longrightarrow$ (iii), use *Ramsey's theorem*: if we color each element of $\{(i,j) \mid i,j \in \omega,\ i < j\}$ either red or green, then there exists an infinite set $A \subseteq \omega$ such that either all elements of $\{(i,j) \mid i,j \in A,\ i < j\}$ are red or all elements are green. In the language of graph theory, if we color the edges of the complete undirected graph on countably many vertices either red or green, then there exists either an infinite complete red subgraph or an infinite complete green subgraph. You may use Ramsey's theorem without proof.

1.17. Prove that every finitary operator is continuous and every continuous operator is monotone. Give examples showing that both inclusions are strict.

1.18. Prove that if τ is a continuous set operator, then its closure ordinal is at most ω. Give a counterexample showing that this is not true for monotone operators in general.

1.19. Show that there is a natural one-to-one correspondence between the sets of functions $A \to (B \to C)$ and $(A \times B) \to C$. *Hint.* Given $f : A \to (B \to C)$, consider the function $\mathbf{curry}(f)$ defined by

$$\mathbf{curry}(f)(x,y) \overset{\text{def}}{=} f(x)(y).$$

Applying the operator $\mathbf{curry}$ is often called "currying." These terms are named after Haskell B. Curry.

1.20. Prove that

$$(i,j) \;\mapsto\; \frac{(i+j+1)(i+j)}{2} + j$$

is a one-to-one and onto function. Conclude that $\#\omega = \#(\omega^2)$.

1.21. Prove that a countable union of countable sets is countable. That is, if each A_i is countable, then $\bigcup_{i=0}^{\infty} A_i$ is countable. (*Hint.* Use Exercise 1.20).

1.22. Show that the map $\tau \mapsto \tau^*$ is a closure operator on the set $2^U \to 2^U$ curried to $2^{2^U \times U}$, and that τ^* is the least closure operator on U containing τ. (See Exercise 1.19 for a definition of *currying*.)

1.23. Show that in the lattice of prefixpoints of a monotone set operator τ constructed in Lemma 1.6, join is not necessarily union. That is, show that if $\mathcal{C}$ is a set of prefixpoints of τ, then $\bigcup \mathcal{C}$ is not necessarily a prefixpoint of τ.

1.24. (Birkhoff (1973)) Let X and Y be two partially ordered sets. A pair of functions $f : X \to Y$ and $g : Y \to X$ is called a *Galois connection* if for all $x \in X$ and $y \in Y$,

$$x \leq g(y) \iff y \leq f(x).$$

(a) Suppose f and g form a Galois connection. Prove that f and g are *anti-*

monotone in the sense that

$$x_1 \leq x_2 \implies f(x_1) \geq f(x_2)$$
$$y_1 \leq y_2 \implies g(y_1) \geq g(y_2),$$

and that for all $x \in X$ and $y \in Y$,

$$
\begin{array}{rclcrcl}
x & \leq & g(f(x)) & \qquad & y & \leq & f(g(y)) \\
g(y) & = & g(f(g(y))) & \qquad & f(x) & = & f(g(f(x))).
\end{array}
$$

(b) Let U and V be sets, $R \subseteq U \times V$. Define $f : 2^U \to 2^V$ and $g : 2^V \to 2^U$ by:

$$f(A) \stackrel{\text{def}}{=} \{y \in V \mid \text{for all } x \in A,\ x \, R \, y\}$$

$$g(B) \stackrel{\text{def}}{=} \{x \in U \mid \text{for all } y \in B,\ x \, R \, y\}.$$

Prove that f and g form a Galois connection between 2^U and 2^V ordered by set inclusion. Conclude from (a) that $f \circ g$ and $g \circ f$ are closure operators in the sense of Section 1.7.

2 Computability and Complexity

In this chapter we review the basic definitions and results of machine models, computability theory, and complexity theory that we will need in later chapters.

2.1 Machine Models

Deterministic Turing Machines

Our basic model of computation is the *Turing machine*, named after Alan Turing, who invented it in 1936. Turing machines can compute any function normally considered computable; in fact, we normally define *computable* to mean computable by a Turing machine.

Formally, Turing machines manipulate strings over a finite alphabet. However, there is a natural one-to-one correspondence between strings in $\{0, 1\}^*$ and natural numbers $\mathbb{N} = \{0, 1, 2, \dots\}$ defined by

$$x \quad \mapsto \quad N(1x) - 1$$

where $N(y)$ is the natural number represented by the string y in binary. It is just as easy to encode other reasonable forms of data (strings over larger alphabets, trees, graphs, dags, etc.) as strings in $\{0, 1\}^*$.

We describe below the basic model. There are many apparently more powerful variations (multitape, nondeterministic, two-way infinite tape, two-dimensional tape, ...) that can be simulated by this basic model. There are also many apparently less powerful variations (two-stack machines, two counter machines) that can simulate the basic model. All these models are equivalent in the sense that they compute all the same functions, although not with equal efficiency. One can include suitably abstracted versions of modern programming languages in this list.

Informally, a Turing machine consists of a finite set Q of *states*, an *input tape* consisting of finitely many cells delimited on the left and right by endmarkers ⊢ and ⊣, a semi-infinite *worktape* delimited on the left by an endmarker ⊢ and infinite to the right, and *heads* that can move left and right over the two tapes. The input string is a finite string of symbols from a finite input alphabet Σ and is written on the input tape between the endmarkers, one symbol per cell. The input head is read-only and must stay between the endmarkers. The worktape is initially blank. The worktape head can read and write symbols from a finite worktape alphabet Γ and must stay to the right of the left endmarker, but can move arbitrarily far to the right.

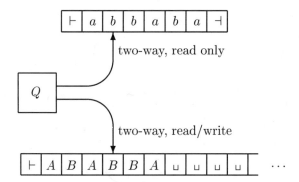

The machine starts in its start state s with its heads scanning the left end-markers ⊢ on both tapes. The worktape is initially blank. In each step it reads the symbols on the tapes under its heads, and depending on those symbols and its current state, writes a new symbol on the worktape cell, moves its heads left or right one cell or leaves them stationary, and enters a new state. The action it takes in each situation is determined by a finite transition function δ. It *accepts* its input by entering a special accept state t and *rejects* by entering a special reject state r. On some inputs it may run infinitely without ever accepting or rejecting.

Formally, a *deterministic Turing machine* is a 10-tuple

$$M \;=\; (Q,\, \Sigma,\, \Gamma,\, \sqcup,\, \vdash,\, \dashv,\, \delta,\, s,\, t,\, r)$$

where:

- Q is a finite set of *states*
- Σ is a finite *input alphabet*
- Γ is a finite *worktape alphabet*
- $\sqcup \in \Gamma$ is the *blank symbol*
- $\vdash \in \Gamma - \Sigma$ is the *left endmarker*
- $\dashv \notin \Sigma$ is the *right endmarker*
- $\delta : Q \times (\Sigma \cup \{\vdash, \dashv\}) \times \Gamma \to Q \times \Gamma \times \{-1, 0, 1\}^2$ is the *transition function*
- $s \in Q$ is the *start state*
- $t \in Q$ is the *accept state*
- $r \in Q$ is the *reject state*, $r \neq t$.

The $-1, 0, 1$ in the definition of δ stand for "move left one cell," "remain stationary," and "move right one cell," respectively. Intuitively, $\delta(p, a, b) = (q, c, d, e)$ means,

"When in state p scanning symbol a on the input tape and b on the worktape, write c on that worktape cell, move the input and work heads in direction d and e, respectively, and enter state q."

We restrict Turing machines so that the left endmarker on the worktape is never overwritten with another symbol and the machine never moves its heads outside the endmarkers. We also require that once the machine enters its accept state, it remains in that state, and similarly for its reject state. This translates into certain formal constraints on the above definition.

Configurations and Acceptance

Intuitively, at any point in time, the worktape of the machine contains a semi-infinite string of the form $\vdash y \sqcup^\omega$, where $y \in \Gamma^*$ (that is, y is a finite-length string) and $\sqcup^\omega$ denotes the semi-infinite string of blanks

$$\sqcup \; \sqcup \; \sqcup \; \sqcup \; \sqcup \; \sqcup \; \sqcup \; \sqcup \; \cdots$$

(recall that ω denotes the smallest infinite ordinal). Although the string $\vdash y\sqcup^\omega$ is infinite, it always has a finite representation, since all but finitely many of the symbols are the blank symbol $\sqcup$.

Let $x \in \Sigma^*$, $|x| = n$. We define a *configuration* of the machine on input x to be an element of $Q \times \{y\sqcup^\omega \mid y \in \Gamma^*\} \times \{0, 1, 2, \ldots, n+1\} \times \omega$. Intuitively, a configuration is a global state giving a snapshot of all relevant information about a Turing machine computation at some instant in time. The configuration (p, z, i, j) specifies a current state p of the finite control, current worktape contents z, and current positions i, j of the input and worktape heads, respectively. We denote configurations by $\alpha, \beta, \gamma, \ldots$. The *start configuration* on input $x \in \Sigma^*$ is the configuration

$$(s, \vdash\sqcup^\omega, 0, 0).$$

The last two components 0,0 mean that the machine is initially scanning the left endmarkers $\vdash$ on its two tapes.

We define a binary relation $\xrightarrow[M,x]{1}$ on configurations, called the *next configuration relation*, as follows. For a string $z \in \Gamma^\omega$, let z_j be the jth symbol of z (the leftmost symbol is z_0), and let $z[j/b]$ denote the string obtained by replacing z_j by b in z. For example,

$$\vdash b\,a\,a\,a\,c\,a\,b\,c\,a \cdots [4/b] \;=\; \vdash b\,a\,a\,b\,c\,a\,b\,c\,a \cdots$$

Let $x_0 = \vdash$ and $x_{n+1} = \dashv$. The relation $\xrightarrow[M,x]{1}$ is defined by:

$$(p, z, i, j) \xrightarrow[M,x]{1} (q, z[j/b], i + d, j + e) \quad \overset{\text{def}}{\Longleftrightarrow} \quad \delta(p, x_i, z_j) = (q, b, d, e).$$

Intuitively, if the worktape contains z and if M is in state p scanning the ith cell of the input tape and the jth cell of the worktape, and δ says that in that case M should print b on the worktape, move the input head in direction d (either -1, 0, or 1), move the worktape head in direction e, and enter state q, then immediately after that step the worktape will contain $z[j/b]$, the input head will be scanning the $i + d^{\text{th}}$ cell of the input tape, the worktape head will be scanning the $j + e^{\text{th}}$ cell of the worktape, and the new state will be q.

We define the relation $\xrightarrow[M,x]{*}$ to be the reflexive transitive closure of $\xrightarrow[M,x]{1}$. In other words,

- $\alpha \xrightarrow[M,x]{0} \alpha$
- $\alpha \xrightarrow[M,x]{n+1} \beta$ if $\alpha \xrightarrow[M,x]{n} \gamma \xrightarrow[M,x]{1} \beta$ for some γ
- $\alpha \xrightarrow[M,x]{*} \beta$ if $\alpha \xrightarrow[M,x]{n} \beta$ for some $n \geq 0$.

The machine M is said to *accept* input $x \in \Sigma^*$ if

$$(s, \vdash \sqcup^\omega, 0, 0) \quad \xrightarrow[M,x]{*} \quad (t, y, i, j)$$

for some y, i, and j, and to *reject* x if

$$(s, \vdash \sqcup^\omega, 0, 0) \quad \xrightarrow[M,x]{*} \quad (r, y, i, j)$$

for some y, i, and j. It is said to *halt* on input x if it either accepts x or rejects x. Note that it may do neither, but run infinitely on input x without ever accepting or rejecting. In that case it is said to *loop* on input x. A Turing machine M is said to be *total* if it halts on all inputs. The set $L(M)$ denotes the set of strings accepted by M.

A set of strings is called *recursively enumerable* (r.e.) if it is $L(M)$ for some Turing machine M, and *recursive* if it is $L(M)$ for some total Turing machine M.

EXAMPLE 2.1: Here is a total Turing machine that accepts the set $\{a^n b^n c^n \mid n \geq 1\}$. Informally, the machine starts in its start state s, then scans to the right over the input string, writing an A on its worktape for every a it sees on the input tape. When it sees the first symbol that is not an a on the input tape, it starts to move its worktape head to the left over the A's it has written, and continues to move its input head to the right, checking that the number of A's written on the worktape is equal to the number of b's occurring after the a's. It checks that it sees the left endmarker $\vdash$ on the worktape at the same time that it sees the first non-b on the input tape. It then continues to scan the input tape, meanwhile moving its worktape head to the right again, checking that the number of c's on the input tape is the same as the number of A's on the worktape. It accepts if it sees the right endmarker $\dashv$ on the input tape at the same time as it sees the first blank symbol $\sqcup$ on the worktape.

Formally, this machine has

$$Q = \{s, q_1, q_2, q_3, t, r\}$$
$$\Sigma = \{a, b, c\}$$
$$\Gamma = \{A, \vdash, \sqcup\}.$$

The start state, accept state, and reject state are s, t, r, respectively. The left and right endmarkers and blank symbol are $\vdash, \dashv, \sqcup$, respectively. The transition function δ is given by

$$
\begin{aligned}
\delta(s, \vdash, \vdash) &= (q_1, \vdash, 1, 1) & \delta(q_2, c, A) &= (r, -, -, -) \\
\delta(q_1, a, \sqcup) &= (q_1, A, 1, 1) & \delta(q_2, c, \vdash) &= (q_3, \vdash, 0, 1) \\
\delta(q_1, b, \sqcup) &= (q_2, \sqcup, 0, -1) & \delta(q_3, a, -) &= (r, -, -, -) \\
\delta(q_1, c, \sqcup) &= (r, -, -, -) & \delta(q_3, b, -) &= (r, -, -, -) \\
\delta(q_1, \dashv, \sqcup) &= (r, -, -, -) & \delta(q_3, c, A) &= (q_3, A, 1, 1) \\
\delta(q_2, a, -) &= (r, -, -, -) & \delta(q_3, c, \sqcup) &= (r, -, -, -) \\
\delta(q_2, b, A) &= (q_2, A, 1, -1) & \delta(q_3, \dashv, A) &= (r, -, -, -) \\
\delta(q_2, b, \vdash) &= (r, -, -, -) & \delta(q_3, \dashv, \sqcup) &= (t, -, -, -).
\end{aligned}
$$

The symbol $-$ above means "don't care." Any legal value may be substituted for $-$ without affecting the behavior of the machine. Also, transitions that can never occur (for example, $\delta(q_1, a, A)$) are omitted.

Two Stacks

A machine with a read-only input head and two stacks is as powerful as a Turing machine. Intuitively, the worktape of a Turing machine can be simulated with two stacks by storing the tape contents to the left of the head on one stack and the tape contents to the right of the head on the other stack. The motion of the head is simulated by popping a symbol off one stack and pushing it onto the other. For example,

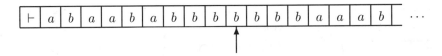

is simulated by

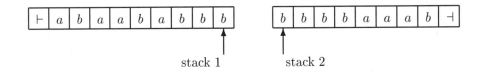

stack 1   stack 2

Counter Machines

A *k-counter machine* is a machine equipped with a two-way read-only input head and k integer counters, each of which can store an arbitrary nonnegative integer. In each step, the machine can test each counter for 0, and based on this information, the input symbol it is currently scanning, and its current state, it can increment or decrement its counters, move its input head one cell in either direction, and enter a new state.

A stack can be simulated with two counters as follows. We can assume without loss of generality that the stack alphabet of the stack to be simulated contains only two symbols, say 0 and 1. This is because we can encode each stack symbol as a binary number of some fixed length k, roughly the base 2 logarithm of the size of the stack alphabet; then pushing or popping one symbol is simulated by pushing or popping k binary digits. The contents of the stack can thus be regarded as a binary number whose least significant bit is on top of the stack. We maintain this binary number in the first of the two counters, and use the second to effect the stack operations. To simulate pushing a 0 onto the stack, we need to double the value in the first counter. This is done by entering a loop that repeatedly subtracts one from the first counter and adds two to the second until the first counter is 0. The value in the second counter is then twice the original value in the first counter. We can then transfer that value back to the first counter (or just switch the roles of the two counters). To push 1, the operation is the same, except that the value of the second counter is incremented once after doubling. To simulate popping, we need to divide the counter value by 2; this is done in a similar fashion.

Since a two-stack machine can simulate an arbitrary Turing machine, and since two counters can simulate a stack, it follows that a four-counter machine can simulate an arbitrary Turing machine.

However, we can do even better: a two-counter machine can simulate a four-counter machine. When the four-counter machine has the values i, j, k, ℓ in its counters, the two-counter machine will have the value $2^i 3^j 5^k 7^\ell$ in its first counter. It uses its second counter to effect the counter operations of the four-counter machine. For example, if the four-counter machine wanted to increment k (the value of the third counter), then the two-counter machine would have to multiply the value in its first counter by 5. This is done in the same way as above, adding 5 to the second counter for every 1 we subtract from the first counter. To simulate a test for zero, the two-counter machine has to determine whether the value in its first counter is divisible by 2, 3, 5, or 7, depending on which counter of the four-counter machine is being tested.

Combining these simulations, we see that two-counter machines are as powerful as arbitrary Turing machines (one-counter machines are strictly less powerful; see Exercise 2.10). However, as one can imagine, it takes an enormous number of steps of the two-counter machine to simulate one step of the Turing machine.

Nondeterministic Turing Machines

Nondeterministic Turing machines differ from deterministic Turing machines only in that the transition relation δ is not necessarily single-valued. Formally, the type of δ is now a relation

$$\delta \quad \subseteq \quad (Q \times (\Sigma \cup \{\vdash, \dashv\}) \times \Gamma) \times (Q \times \Gamma \times \{-1, 0, 1\}^2).$$

Intuitively, $((p, a, b), (q, c, d, e)) \in \delta$ means, "When in state p scanning symbols a and b on the input and worktapes, respectively, one possible move is to write c on that worktape cell, move the input and worktape heads in direction d and e, respectively, and enter state q." Since there may now be several pairs in δ with the same left-hand side (p, a, b), the next transition is not uniquely determined.

The next configuration relation $\xrightarrow[M,x]{1}$ on input x and its reflexive transitive closure $\xrightarrow[M,x]{*}$ are defined exactly as with deterministic machines. A nondeterministic Turing machine M is said to *accept* its input x if

$$(s, \vdash \sqcup^\omega, 0, 0) \quad \xrightarrow[M,x]{*} \quad (t, y, i, j)$$

for some y, i, and j; that is, if there exists a computation path from the start configuration to an accept configuration. The main difference here is that the next configuration is not necessarily uniquely determined.

Nondeterministic algorithms are often described in terms of a "guess and verify" paradigm. This is a good way to think of nondeterministic computation informally. The machine guesses which transition to take whenever there is a choice, then checks at the end whether its sequence of guesses was correct, rejecting if not and accepting if so.

For example, to accept the set of (encodings over Σ^* of) satisfiable propositional formulas, a nondeterministic machine might guess a truth assignment to the variables of the formula, then verify its guess by evaluating the formula on that assignment, accepting if the guessed assignment satisfies the formula and rejecting if not. Each guess is a binary choice of a truth value to assign to one of the variables. This would be represented formally as a configuration with two successor configurations.

Although next configurations are not uniquely determined, the set of *possible* next configurations is. Thus there is a uniquely determined tree of possible computation sequences on any input x. The nodes of the tree are configurations, the root is the start configuration on input x, and the edges are the next configuration relation $\xrightarrow[M,x]{1}$. This tree contains an accept configuration iff the machine accepts x. The tree might also contain a reject configuration, and might also have looping computations; that is, infinite paths that neither accept nor reject. However, as long as there is at least one path that leads to acceptance, the machine is said to accept x.

Alternating Turing Machines

Another useful way to think of a nondeterministic Turing machine is as a kind of parallel machine consisting of a potentially unbounded number of processes which can spawn new subprocesses at branch points in the computation tree. Intuitively, we associate a process with each configuration in the tree. As long as the next configuration is uniquely determined, the process computes like an ordinary deterministic machine. When a branch point is encountered, say a configuration with two possible next configurations, the process spawns two subprocesses and assigns one to each next configuration. It then suspends, waiting for reports from its subprocesses. If a process enters the accept state, it reports success to its parent process and terminates. If a process enters the reject state, it reports failure to its parent and terminates. A suspended process, after receiving a report of success from at least one of its subprocesses, reports success to its parent and terminates.

If a suspended process receives a report of failure from *all* its subprocesses, it reports failure to its parent and terminates. Of course, it is possible that neither of these things happens. The machine accepts the input if the root process receives a success report. There is no explicit formal mechanism for reporting success or failure, suspending, or terminating.

Now we extend this idea to allow machines to test whether *all* subprocesses lead to success as well as whether *some* subprocess lead to success. Intuitively, each branch point in the computation tree is either an or-branch or an and-branch, depending on the state. The or-branches are handled as described above. The and-branches are just the same, except that a process suspended at an and-branch reports success to its parent iff *all* of its subprocesses report success, and reports failure to its parent iff *at least one* of its subprocesses reports failure.

Machines with this capability are called *alternating Turing machines* in reference to the alternation of and- and or-branches. They are useful in analyzing the complexity of problems with a natural alternating and/or structure, such as games or logical theories.

Formally, an alternating Turing machine is just like a nondeterministic machine, except we include an additional function $g : Q \to \{\wedge, \vee\}$ associating either $\wedge$ (and) or $\vee$ (or) with each state. A configuration (q, y, m, n) is called an *and-configuration* if $g(q) = \wedge$ and an *or-configuration* if $g(q) = \vee$. The machine is said to *accept* input x if the computation tree on input x has a finite *accepting subtree*, which is a finite subtree T containing the root such that every node c of T is either

- an accept configuration (that is, a configuration whose state is the accept state);

- an or-configuration with at least one successor in T;

- an and-configuration with all successors in T.

In fact, we can dispense with the accept and reject states entirely by defining an *accept configuration* to be an and-configuration with no successors and a *reject configuration* to be an or-configuration with no successors. For accept configurations so defined, the condition "all successors in T" is vacuously satisfied.

Alternating machines are no more powerful than ordinary deterministic Turing machines, since an ordinary Turing machine can construct the computation tree of an alternating machine in a breadth-first fashion and check for the existence of a finite accepting subtree.

Alternating Machines with Negation

Alternating machines can also be augmented to allow *not-states* as well as and- and or-states. Perhaps contrary to expectation, these machines are no more powerful than ordinary Turing machines in terms of the sets they accept.

The formal definition of alternating machines with negation requires a bit of extra work. Here the function g is of type $Q \to \{\wedge, \vee, \neg\}$ and associates either $\wedge$ (and), $\vee$ (or), or $\neg$ (not) with each state. If $g(q) = \wedge$ (respectively, $\vee$, $\neg$), the state q is called an *and-state* (respectively, *or-state*, *not-state*) and the configuration (q, y, m, n) is called an *and-configuration* (respectively, *or-configuration*, *not-configuration*). A not-configuration is required to have exactly one successor. We also dispense with the accept and reject states, defining an *accept configuration* to be an and-configuration with no successors and a *reject configuration* to be an or-configuration with no successors.

Acceptance is defined formally in terms of a certain labeling ℓ_* of configurations with $\mathbf{1}$ (true), $\mathbf{0}$ (false), or $\bot$ (undefined). This labeling is defined as the $\sqsubseteq$-least solution ℓ of the equation

$$\ell(c) \stackrel{\text{def}}{=} \begin{cases} \bigwedge \{\ell(d) \mid c \xrightarrow[M,x]{1} d\}, & \text{if } g(c) = \wedge, \\ \bigvee \{\ell(d) \mid c \xrightarrow[M,x]{1} d\}, & \text{if } g(c) = \vee, \\ \neg \ell(d), & \text{if } g(c) = \neg \text{ and } c \xrightarrow[M,x]{1} d, \end{cases}$$

where $\sqsubseteq$ is the order defined by

i.e., $\bot \sqsubseteq \bot \sqsubseteq \mathbf{0} \sqsubseteq \mathbf{0}$ and $\bot \sqsubseteq \mathbf{1} \sqsubseteq \mathbf{1}$, and

$$\ell \sqsubseteq \ell' \stackrel{\text{def}}{\iff} \forall c\ \ell(c) \sqsubseteq \ell'(c),$$

and $\wedge$, $\vee$, and $\neg$ are computed on $\{\mathbf{0}, \bot, \mathbf{1}\}$ according to the following tables:

$\wedge$:	$\mathbf{0}$	$\bot$	$\mathbf{1}$
$\mathbf{0}$	$\mathbf{0}$	$\mathbf{0}$	$\mathbf{0}$
$\bot$	$\mathbf{0}$	$\bot$	$\bot$
$\mathbf{1}$	$\mathbf{0}$	$\bot$	$\mathbf{1}$

$\vee$:	$\mathbf{0}$	$\bot$	$\mathbf{1}$
$\mathbf{0}$	$\mathbf{0}$	$\bot$	$\mathbf{1}$
$\bot$	$\bot$	$\bot$	$\mathbf{1}$
$\mathbf{1}$	$\mathbf{1}$	$\mathbf{1}$	$\mathbf{1}$

$\neg$:	
$\mathbf{0}$	$\mathbf{1}$
$\bot$	$\bot$
$\mathbf{1}$	$\mathbf{0}$

In other words, $\wedge$ gives the greatest lower bound and $\vee$ gives the least upper bound in the order $\mathbf{0} \leq \perp \leq \mathbf{1}$, and $\neg$ inverts the order.

The labeling ℓ_* can be computed as the $\sqsubseteq$-least fixpoint of the monotone map $\tau : \{\text{labelings}\} \to \{\text{labelings}\}$, where

$$\tau(\ell)(c) \overset{\text{def}}{=} \begin{cases} \bigwedge \{\ell(d) \mid c \xrightarrow[M,x]{1} d\}, & \text{if } g(c) = \wedge, \\ \bigvee \{\ell(d) \mid c \xrightarrow[M,x]{1} d\}, & \text{if } g(c) = \vee, \\ \neg \ell(d), & \text{if } g(c) = \neg \text{ and } c \xrightarrow[M,x]{1} d, \end{cases}$$

as provided by the Knaster–Tarski theorem (Section 1.7).

Universal Turing Machines and Undecidability

An important observation about Turing machines is that they can be *uniformly simulated*. By this we mean that there exist a special Turing machine U and a coding scheme that codes a complete description of each Turing machine M as a finite string x_M in such a way that U, given any such encoding x_M and a string y, can simulate the machine M on input y, accepting iff M accepts y. The machine U is called a *universal Turing machine*. Nowadays this is perhaps not so surprising, since we can easily imagine writing a Scheme interpreter in Scheme or a C compiler in C, but it was quite an advance when it was first observed by Turing in the 1930s; it led to the notion of the *stored-program computer*, the basic architectural paradigm underlying the design of all modern general-purpose computers today.

Undecidability of the Halting Problem

Recall that a set is *recursively enumerable* (r.e.) if it is $L(M)$ for some Turing machine M and *recursive* if it is $L(M)$ for some total Turing machine M (one that halts on all inputs, i.e., either accepts or rejects). A property φ is *decidable* (or *recursive*) if the set $\{x \mid \varphi(x)\}$ is recursive, *undecidable* if not.

Two classical examples of undecidable problems are the *halting problem* and the *membership problem* for Turing machines. Define

$$\mathsf{HP} \overset{\text{def}}{=} \{(x_M, y) \mid M \text{ halts on input } y\}$$
$$\mathsf{MP} \overset{\text{def}}{=} \{(x_M, y) \mid M \text{ accepts input } y\}.$$

These sets are r.e. but not recursive; in other words, it is undecidable for a given Turing machine M and input y whether M halts on y or whether M accepts y.

PROPOSITION 2.2:   The set HP is r.e. but not recursive.

Proof   The set MP is r.e., because it is the set accepted by the universal Turing machine U. The set HP is r.e. as well, because a Turing machine can be constructed that on input (x_M, y) simulates M on input y using U, accepting if M either accepts or rejects y.

We show by contradiction that HP is not recursive. This argument is called a *diagonalization argument* and was first used by Cantor to show that the power set of a set A cannot be put in one-to-one correspondence with A. The reader will also probably notice the similarity to Russell's paradox (1.2.3).

Suppose for a contradiction that HP were recursive. Then there would be a *total* Turing machine K that decides for a given (x_M, y) whether M halts on y. Construct a Turing machine N that on input x interprets x as x_M, then determines whether M halts on input x_M by running K on (x_M, x_M). The machine K is total, so it either halts and accepts if M halts on input x_M or halts and rejects if M does not halt on input x_M. If K rejects, make N halt immediately. If K accepts, make N enter an infinite loop. Thus N halts on input x_M iff K rejects (x_M, x_M) iff M does not halt on input x_M. Now consider what happens when N is run on its own description x_N. By our construction, N halts on x_N iff N does not halt on x_N. This is a contradiction.   ∎

We will show by a different technique that the same proposition holds of MP (Example 2.14).

Most interesting questions about Turing machines turn out to be undecidable. For example, it is undecidable whether a given M accepts any string at all, whether M accepts a finite set, or whether M accepts a recursive set. In fact, *every* nontrivial property of r.e. sets is undecidable (Exercise 2.4).

2.2   Complexity Classes

By restricting the amount of time or space a Turing machine can use, we obtain various complexity classes. Most of these definitions are fairly robust in the sense that they are impervious to minor changes in the model, but extra care must be taken at lower levels of complexity.

Time and Space Complexity

Let $f : \mathbb{N} \to \mathbb{N}$ be a function. A (deterministic, nondeterministic, or alternating) Turing machine M is said to *run in time* $f(n)$ if for all sufficiently large n, all computation paths starting from the start configuration on any input of length n are of length at most $f(n)$. It is said to *run in space* $f(n)$ if for all sufficiently large

n, all configurations reachable from the start configuration on any input of length n use at most $f(n)$ worktape cells.

The machine M is said to run in time (respectively, space) $O(f(n))$ if it runs in time (respectively, space) $cf(n)$ for some constant c independent of n.

The machine M is said to run in *logarithmic space* if it runs in space $\log n$, where log denotes logarithm to the base 2. It is said to run in *polynomial time* if it runs in time $n^{O(1)}$; that is, if it runs in time n^k for some constant k independent of n. It is said to run in *exponential time* if it runs in time $2^{n^{O(1)}}$; that is, if it runs in time 2^{n^k} for some constant k independent of n. It is said to run in *double-exponential time* if it runs in time $2^{2^{n^{O(1)}}}$. It is said to run in *k-fold exponential time* if it runs in time $2 \uparrow_k n^{O(1)}$, where

$$2 \uparrow_0 n \overset{\text{def}}{=} n$$
$$2 \uparrow_{k+1} n \overset{\text{def}}{=} 2^{2\uparrow_k n}.$$

The corresponding space complexity bounds are defined analogously.

There is some disagreement in the literature as to the meaning of *exponential time*. It is often taken to mean time $2^{O(n)}$ instead of $2^{n^{O(1)}}$. We will use the latter definition, since it fits in better with results relating the complexity of deterministic and alternating Turing machines. However, in situations in which we can derive the stronger upper bound $2^{O(n)}$, we will do so and mention the bound explicitly.

The class $DTIME(f(n))$ (respectively, $NTIME(f(n))$, $ATIME(f(n))$) is the family of all sets $L(M)$ for deterministic (respectively, nondeterministic, alternating) Turing machines M running in time $f(n)$. The space complexity classes $DSPACE(f(n))$, $NSPACE(f(n))$, and $ASPACE(f(n))$ are defined similarly. We write $DTIME(n^{O(1)})$ for $\bigcup_{k\geq 0} DTIME(n^k)$, etc. A few common complexity classes have special notation:

$$LOGSPACE \overset{\text{def}}{=} DSPACE(\log n)$$
$$NLOGSPACE \overset{\text{def}}{=} NSPACE(\log n)$$
$$ALOGSPACE \overset{\text{def}}{=} ASPACE(\log n)$$
$$PTIME \overset{\text{def}}{=} DTIME(n^{O(1)})$$
$$NPTIME \overset{\text{def}}{=} NTIME(n^{O(1)})$$
$$APTIME \overset{\text{def}}{=} ATIME(n^{O(1)})$$
$$PSPACE \overset{\text{def}}{=} DSPACE(n^{O(1)})$$
$$NPSPACE \overset{\text{def}}{=} NSPACE(n^{O(1)})$$

$$APSPACE \overset{\text{def}}{=} ASPACE(n^{O(1)})$$

$$EXPTIME \overset{\text{def}}{=} DTIME(2^{n^{O(1)}})$$

$$NEXPTIME \overset{\text{def}}{=} NTIME(2^{n^{O(1)}})$$

$$AEXPTIME \overset{\text{def}}{=} ATIME(2^{n^{O(1)}})$$

$$EXPSPACE \overset{\text{def}}{=} DSPACE(2^{n^{O(1)}})$$

$$NEXPSPACE \overset{\text{def}}{=} NSPACE(2^{n^{O(1)}})$$

$$AEXPSPACE \overset{\text{def}}{=} ASPACE(2^{n^{O(1)}}).$$

These are the classes of all sets computable in, respectively: deterministic, nondeterministic, and alternating logarithmic space; deterministic, nondeterministic, and alternating polynomial time; deterministic, nondeterministic, and alternating polynomial space; deterministic, nondeterministic, and alternating exponential time; and deterministic, nondeterministic, and alternating exponential space.

The classes *PTIME* and *NPTIME* are more commonly known as P and NP, respectively.

A remarkable fact is that the following relationships hold among the deterministic and alternating complexity classes:

$$
\begin{array}{ccccccccc}
PTIME & \subseteq & PSPACE & \subseteq & EXPTIME & \subseteq & EXPSPACE & \subseteq & \cdots \\
\| & & \| & & \| & & \| & & \\
ALOGSPACE & \subseteq & APTIME & \subseteq & APSPACE & \subseteq & AEXPTIME & \subseteq & \cdots
\end{array}
$$

That is, the hierarchy of logarithmic space, polynomial time, polynomial space, exponential time, exponential space, double-exponential time, double-exponential space, etc. shifts by exactly one level when going from determinism to alternation.

One of the most important open problems in computational complexity is whether $P = NP$. Many important combinatorial optimization problems can be solved in nondeterministic polynomial time by a "guess and verify" method. Figuring out how to solve these problems efficiently without the guessing would have significant impact in real-world applications.

Oracle Machines and Relative Computability

It is sometimes useful to talk about computability *relative to a given set B*. The set B itself may not be computable, but we may be interested in what we could compute if we were given the power to test membership in B for free. One way to capture this idea formally is by *oracle Turing machines*. Another way will be discussed in Section 2.3.

An oracle Turing machine $M[\cdot]$ is like an ordinary deterministic Turing machine, except that it has three distinguished states, the *query state*, the *yes state*, and the *no state*, a finite *oracle alphabet* Δ, and a write-only tape called the *oracle query tape* on which the machine can write a string in Δ^*.

The machine can be equipped with an *oracle* $B \subseteq \Delta^*$, in which case we denote it by $M[B]$. This machine operates as follows. On input $x \in \Sigma^*$, $M[B]$ computes like an ordinary deterministic Turing machine, except that periodically it may decide to write a symbol on its oracle query tape. When it does so, the tape head is advanced one cell to the right. At some point, perhaps after writing several symbols on the oracle query tape, the machine may decide to enter its query state. When that happens, it automatically and immediately enters the yes state if $y \in B$ and the no state if $y \notin B$, where y is the string currently written on the oracle query tape. The oracle query tape is then automatically erased and the oracle query tape head returned to the left end of the tape. The contents of the worktape and the positions of the input and worktape heads are not altered. The machine then continues processing from that point. If the machine ever halts and accepts, then $x \in L(M[B])$. Note that the behavior of $M[B]$ may depend heavily on the oracle B.

An alternative formalism for oracle machines gives $M[B]$ an extra semi-infinite, two-way, read-only tape on which is written the characteristic function of B, where the elements of B are ordered in some reasonable way, perhaps lexicographically. If the machine wishes to know whether $y \in B$, it can scan out to the appropriate position on the tape containing the bit corresponding to y. The ordering on Δ^* should be sufficiently nice that this position is easily computable from y.

A set A is said to be *r.e. in B* if there is an oracle Turing machine $M[\cdot]$ such that $A = L(M[B])$; *co-r.e. in B* if $\sim A$ is r.e. in B; and *recursive in B* if there is an oracle Turing machine $M[\cdot]$ such that $A = L(M[B])$ and $M[B]$ is total (halts on all inputs). Again, whether or not $M[B]$ is total may depend heavily on the oracle B.

LEMMA 2.3:   If A is r.e. in B, then so are the sets

$$\{z_1 \# z_2 \# \cdots \# z_n \mid \bigwedge_{i=1}^{n} z_i \in A\}$$

$$\{z_1 \# z_2 \# \cdots \# z_n \mid \bigvee_{i=1}^{n} z_i \in A\}.$$

Proof Exercise 2.1. ∎

Recursive and R.E. Sets

In this section we state some basic facts about recursive and recursively enumerable (r.e.) sets that we will need in subsequent chapters. Recall that a set is *r.e.* if it is $L(M)$ for some Turing machine M and *recursive* if it is $L(M)$ for some total Turing machine M (one that halts on all inputs, i.e., either accepts or rejects). Define a set to be *co-r.e.* if its complement is r.e. A property φ is *decidable* (or *recursive*) if the set $\{x \mid \varphi(x)\}$ is recursive, *undecidable* if not.

PROPOSITION 2.4:   A set is recursive iff it is both r.e. and co-r.e.

Proof If A is recursive, then a Turing machine accepting its complement $\sim A$ can be obtained by reversing the accept and reject states of a total Turing machine for A. Conversely, if both A and $\sim A$ are r.e., then a total Turing machine for A can be obtained by simulating a machine for A and a machine for $\sim A$ in parallel in a time-sharing fashion, accepting the input if the machine for A accepts and rejecting if the machine for $\sim A$ accepts; exactly one of those two events must occur.   ∎

Here is another useful characterization of the r.e. sets:

PROPOSITION 2.5:   A set A is r.e. if and only if there exists a decidable dyadic predicate φ such that

$$A \;=\; \{x \mid \exists y \; \varphi(x,y)\}.$$

Proof If A has such a representation, then we can construct a Turing machine M for A that enumerates all y in some order, and for each one tests whether $\varphi(x,y)$, accepting if such a witness y is ever found. Conversely, if A is r.e., say $A = L(M)$, then we can take the recursive predicate $\varphi(x,y)$ to be "M accepts x in y steps." This predicate is decidable, since its truth can be determined by running M on x for y steps.   ∎

The Arithmetic Hierarchy

Propositions 2.4 and 2.5 are special cases of a more general relationship. Consider the following hierarchy of classes of sets, defined inductively as follows.

Recall from Section 2.2 that a set A is *r.e. in B* if there is an oracle Turing machine $M[\cdot]$ such that $A = L(M[B])$, *co-r.e. in B* if there is an oracle Turing machine $M[\cdot]$ such that $A = \sim L(M[B])$, and *recursive in B* if there is an oracle

Turing machine $M[\cdot]$ such that $A = L(M[B])$ and $M[B]$ halts on all inputs. Consider the following inductively defined hierarchy:

$$\Sigma_1^0 \overset{\text{def}}{=} \{A \mid A \text{ is r.e.}\}$$

$$\Pi_1^0 \overset{\text{def}}{=} \{A \mid A \text{ is co-r.e.}\}$$

$$\Delta_1^0 \overset{\text{def}}{=} \{A \mid A \text{ is recursive}\}$$

$$\Sigma_{n+1}^0 \overset{\text{def}}{=} \{A \mid A \text{ is r.e. in } B \text{ for some } B \in \Sigma_n^0\}$$

$$= \{A \mid A \text{ is r.e. in } B \text{ for some } B \in \Pi_n^0\}$$

$$\Pi_{n+1}^0 \overset{\text{def}}{=} \{A \mid A \text{ is co-r.e. in } B \text{ for some } B \in \Sigma_n^0\}$$

$$= \{A \mid A \text{ is co-r.e. in } B \text{ for some } B \in \Pi_n^0\}$$

$$\Delta_{n+1}^0 \overset{\text{def}}{=} \{A \mid A \text{ is recursive in } B \text{ for some } B \in \Sigma_n^0\}$$

$$= \{A \mid A \text{ is recursive in } B \text{ for some } B \in \Pi_n^0\}.$$

The following two theorems generalize Propositions 2.4 and 2.5, respectively.

THEOREM 2.6:   For all $n \geq 0$, $\Delta_n^0 = \Sigma_n^0 \cap \Pi_n^0$.

Proof The proof is exactly like the proof of Proposition 2.4, except that all computations are done in the presence of an oracle. ∎

THEOREM 2.7:

(i) $A \in \Sigma_n^0$ iff there exists a decidable $(n+1)$-ary predicate $\varphi(x, y_1, \ldots, y_n)$ such that

$$A = \{x \mid \exists y_1 \, \forall y_2 \, \exists y_3 \, \ldots \, Q_n y_n \, \varphi(x, y_1, \ldots, y_n)\},$$

where $Q_i = \exists$ if i is odd, $\forall$ if i is even.

(ii) $A \in \Pi_n^0$ iff there exists a decidable $(n+1)$-ary predicate $\varphi(x, y_1, \ldots, y_n)$ such that

$$A = \{x \mid \forall y_1 \, \exists y_2 \, \forall y_3 \, \ldots \, Q_n y_n \, \varphi(x, y_1, \ldots, y_n)\},$$

where $Q_i = \forall$ if i is odd, $\exists$ if i is even.

Proof We prove (i); statement (ii) follows from the fact that Π_n^0 is the class of all complements of sets in Σ_n^0.

We proceed by induction on n. The case $n = 1$ is given by Proposition 2.5. For

$n > 1$, assume first that

$$A = \{x \mid \exists y_1 \, \forall y_2 \, \exists y_3 \, \ldots \, Q_n y_n \, \varphi(x, y_1, \ldots, y_n)\}.$$

Let

$$B = \{(x, y_1) \mid \forall y_2 \, \exists y_3 \, \ldots \, Q_n y_n \, \varphi(x, y_1, \ldots, y_n)\}.$$

By the induction hypothesis, $B \in \Pi^0_{n-1}$, and

$$A = \{x \mid \exists y_1 \, (x, y_1) \in B\},$$

thus A is r.e. in B by an argument similar to that of Proposition 2.5.

Conversely, suppose $A = L(M[B])$ and $B \in \Pi^0_{n-1}$. Then $x \in A$ iff there exists a *valid computation history* y describing the computation of $M[B]$ on input x, including oracle queries and their responses, and all the responses to the oracle queries described in y are correct. Such a valid computation history might consist of a sequence of consecutive descriptions of configurations of the machine, each such configuration including a current state, tape contents, and tape head positions. Under a reasonable encoding of all this information, it is easy to check whether such a string obeys the rules of $M[\cdot]$; the only thing that is not checked easily is whether the results of the oracle queries (whether the machine enters the yes or the no state) are correct.

By Lemma 2.3, for any fixed k, the sets

$$U = \{z_1 \# z_2 \# \cdots \# z_k \mid \bigwedge_{i=1}^{k} z_i \in B\}$$

$$V = \{w_1 \# w_2 \# \cdots \# w_k \mid \bigwedge_{i=1}^{k} w_i \notin B\}$$

are in Π^0_{n-1} and Σ^0_{n-1}, respectively. By the induction hypothesis, membership in U and V can be represented by predicates with $n - 1$ alternations of quantifiers beginning with $\forall$ (respectively, $\exists$) over a recursive predicate. Then the condition $x \in A$ is equivalent to the statement:

There exists a valid computation history y of $M[B]$ on input x such that if $z_1, \ldots, z_n$ are the strings that are queried of the oracle B in the computation of $M[B]$ on input x for which the response (as represented in the string y) is positive, and if $w_1, \ldots, w_m$ are the queries for which the response is negative, then $z_1 \# z_2 \# \cdots \# z_n \in U$ and $w_1 \# w_2 \# \cdots \# w_m \in V$.

By combining the representations of U and V and the recursive predicate "y is a valid computation history of $M[B]$ on input x," we can obtain a representation of the predicate $x \in A$ with n alternations of quantifiers beginning with $\exists$ over a recursive predicate. ∎

Kleene showed that the arithmetic hierarchy is strict: for all $n \geq 0$,

$$\Sigma_n^0 \cup \Pi_n^0 \quad \subset \quad \Delta_{n+1}^0,$$

and Σ_n^0 and Π_n^0 are incomparable with respect to set inclusion.

The Analytic Hierarchy

The arithmetic hierarchy relates to first-order number theory as the *analytic hierarchy* relates to *second-order number theory*, in which quantification over sets and functions is allowed. We will be primarily interested in the first level of this hierarchy, in particular the class Π_1^1 of relations over $\mathbb{N}$ definable with one universal second-order quantifier. A remarkable theorem due to Kleene states that this is exactly the class of relations over $\mathbb{N}$ definable by first-order induction. In this section we will provide a computational characterization of the classes Π_1^1 and Δ_1^1 and sketch a proof of Kleene's theorem.

Definitions of Π_1^1 and Δ_1^1

The class Π_1^1 is the class of all relations on $\mathbb{N}$ that can be defined by a prenex universal second-order number-theoretic formula. Here *prenex* means all quantifiers appear at the front of the formula and *universal* means only universal quantification over functions is allowed. Using various transformation rules to be discussed later in Section 3.4, we can assume every such formula is of the form

$$\forall f \, \exists y \, \varphi(\overline{x}, y, f),$$

where φ is quantifier free (Exercise 3.33). This formula defines the n-ary relation

$$\{\overline{a} \in \mathbb{N}^n \mid \forall f \, \exists y \, \varphi(\overline{a}, y, f)\}.$$

The class Δ_1^1 is the class of all relations on $\mathbb{N}$ that are Π_1^1 and whose complements are Π_1^1.

The Programming Language IND

We take a rather unusual approach to the subject of first-order inductive definability: we introduce a programming language IND and use it to define the inductive and hyperarithmetic sets and the recursive ordinals. This turns out to be equivalent to more conventional approaches (see for example Moschovakis (1974)), but has a decidedly more computational flavor. Keep in mind that the relations "computed" by IND programs can be highly noncomputable.

An IND program consists of a finite sequence of labeled statements. Each statement is of one of three forms:

- assignment: $\ell :\ x := \exists$ $\ell :\ y := \forall$
- conditional jump: $\ell :\ $ **if** $R(\bar{t})$ **then go to** ℓ'
- halt statement: $\ell :\ $ **accept** $\ell :\ $ **reject**.

The semantics of programs is very much like alternating Turing machines, except that the branching is infinite. The execution of an assignment statement causes countably many subprocesses to be spawned, each assigning a different element of $\mathbb{N}$ to the variable. If the statement is $x := \exists$, the branching is existential; if it is $y := \forall$, the branching is universal. The conditional jump tests the atomic formula $R(\bar{t})$, and if true, jumps to the indicated label. The **accept** and **reject** commands halt and pass a Boolean value back up to the parent. Computation proceeds as in alternating Turing machines: the input is an initial assignment to the program variables; execution of statements causes a countably branching computation tree to be generated downward, and Boolean accept (**1**) or reject (**0**) values are passed back up the tree, a Boolean $\vee$ being computed at each existential node and a Boolean $\wedge$ being computed at each universal node. The program is said to *accept* the input if the root of the computation tree ever becomes labeled with the Boolean value **1** on that input; it is said to *reject* the input if the root ever becomes labeled with the Boolean value **0** on that input; and it is said to *halt* on an input if it either accepts or rejects that input. An IND program that halts on all inputs is said to be *total*.

These notions are completely analogous to alternating Turing machines, so we forego the formalities in favor of some revealing examples.

First, we show how to simulate a few other useful programming constructs with those listed above. An unconditional jump

goto ℓ

is simulated by the statement

if $x = x$ **then go to** ℓ

More complicated forms of conditional branching can be effected by manipulation of control flow. For example, the statement

if $R(\bar{t})$ **then reject else** ℓ

is simulated by the program segment

    if $R(\bar{t})$ **then go to** ℓ'
    goto ℓ
ℓ': **reject**

A simple assignment is effected by guessing and verifying:

$$x := y + 1$$

is simulated by

$x := \exists$
if $x \neq y + 1$ **then reject**

The process spawns infinitely many subprocesses, all but one of which immediately reject!

EXAMPLE 2.8:   Any first-order relation is definable by a loop-free program. For example, the set of natural numbers x such that

$$\exists y \ \forall z \ \exists w \ x \leq y \wedge x + z \leq w$$

is defined by the program

$y := \exists$
$z := \forall$
$w := \exists$
if $x > y$ **then reject**
if $x + z \leq w$ **then accept**
reject

The converse is true too: any loop-free program defines a first-order relation.

However, IND can also define inductively definable relations that are not first-order.

EXAMPLE 2.9:   The reflexive transitive closure of a relation R is definable by the following program, which takes its input in the variables x, z and accepts if $(x, z) \in R^*$:

ℓ: **if** $x = z$ **then accept**
    $y := \exists$

if $\neg R(x,y)$ **then reject**

$x := y$

go to ℓ

EXAMPLE 2.10:   A *two-person perfect information game* consists of a binary relation **move** on a set of *boards*. The two players alternate. If the current board is x and it is player I's turn, player I chooses y such that **move**(x,y); then player II chooses z such that **move**(y,z); and so on. A player wins by *checkmate*, i.e., by forcing the opponent into a position from which there is no legal next move. Thus a checkmate position is a board y such that $\forall z \, \neg$**move**(y,z).

We would like to know for a given board x whether the player whose turn it is has a forced win from x. Ordinarily this might be defined as the least solution **win** of the recursive equation

$$\mathbf{win}(x) \iff \exists y \, (\mathbf{move}(x,y) \wedge \forall z \, \mathbf{move}(y,z) \to \mathbf{win}(z)).$$

The base case involving an immediate win by checkmate is included: if y is a checkmate position, then the subformula $\forall z \, \mathbf{move}(y,z) \to \mathbf{win}(z)$ is vacuously true. The least solution to this recursive equation is the least fixpoint of the monotone map τ defined by

$$\tau(R) \stackrel{\text{def}}{\iff} \{x \mid \exists y \, \mathbf{move}(x,y) \wedge \forall z \, \mathbf{move}(y,z) \to R(z)\}$$

(see Section 1.7). We can express **win**(x) with an IND program as follows:

ℓ: $y := \exists$

   if $\neg$**move**(x,y) **then reject**

   $x := \forall$

   if $\neg$**move**(y,x) **then accept**

   go to ℓ

EXAMPLE 2.11:   Our last example involves well-founded relations. As observed in Section 1.3, induction and well-foundedness go hand in hand. Here is an IND program that tests whether a strict partial order $<$ is well-founded:

   $x := \forall$

ℓ: $y := \forall$

   if $\neg y < x$ **then accept**

   $x := y$

   go to ℓ

This program halts and accepts if all descending chains are finite (see Exercise 1.15).

Any property that is expressed as a least fixpoint of a monotone map defined by a positive first-order formula can be computed by an IND program. Here is what we mean by this. Let R be an n-ary relation symbol, and let $\varphi(\overline{x}, R)$ be a first-order formula with free individual variables $\overline{x} = x_1, \ldots, x_n$ and free relation variable R. Assume further that all free occurrences of R in φ are *positive*; that is, they occur in the scope of an even number of negation symbols $\neg$. For any n-ary relation B, define

$$\tau(B) \quad = \quad \{\overline{a} \mid \varphi(\overline{a}, B)\}.$$

That is, we think of φ as representing a set operator τ mapping a set of n-tuples B to another set of n-tuples $\{\overline{a} \mid \varphi(\overline{a}, B)\}$. One can show that the positivity assumption implies that the set operator τ is monotone, therefore it has a least fixpoint F_φ, which is an n-ary relation (see Section 1.7). The traditional treatment of inductive definability defines a first-order inductive relation as a projection of such a fixpoint; that is, a relation of the form

$$\{a_1, \ldots, a_m \mid F_\varphi(a_1, \ldots, a_m, b_{m+1}, \ldots, b_n)\},$$

where $b_{m+1}, \ldots, b_n$ are fixed elements of the structure. Given the formula φ and the elements $b_{m+1}, \ldots, b_n$, one can construct an IND program that assigns $b_{m+1}, \ldots, b_n$ to the variables $x_{m+1}, \ldots, x_n$, then checks whether the values of $x_1, \ldots, x_n$ satisfy F_φ by decomposing the formula top-down, executing existential assignments at existential quantifiers, executing universal assignments at universal quantifiers, using control flow for the propositional connectives, using conditional tests for the atomic formulas, and looping back to the top of the program at occurrences of the inductive variable R. The examples above involving reflexive transitive closure, games, and well-foundedness illustrate this process.

Conversely, any relation computed by an IND program is inductive in the traditional sense, essentially because the definition of acceptance for IND programs involves the least fixpoint of an inductively defined set of labelings of the computation tree.

Inductive and Hyperelementary Relations

Many of the sample IND programs of the previous section make sense when interpreted over any structure, not just $\mathbb{N}$. We define the *inductive relations* of any structure $\mathfrak{A}$ to be those relations computable by IND programs over $\mathfrak{A}$. We define the *hyperelementary relations* of $\mathfrak{A}$ to be those relations computable by *total* IND programs over $\mathfrak{A}$, i.e., programs that halt on all inputs. Note that every first-order relation is hyperelementary, since it is computed by a loop-free program.

One can show that a relation over $\mathfrak{A}$ is hyperelementary iff it is both inductive and coinductive. If there is an IND program that accepts R and another IND program that accepts $\sim R$, then one can construct a total IND program that runs the two other programs in parallel, much as in the proof of Proposition 2.4.

Now we restrict our attention to the structure of arithmetic $\mathbb{N}$. Over this structure, the hyperelementary relations are sometimes called the *hyperarithmetic relations*.

Recursive Trees, Recursive Ordinals, and ω_1^{ck}

An ordinal α is *countable* if there exists a one-to-one function $f : \alpha \to \omega$. The ordinals $\omega \cdot 2$ and ω^2, although greater than ω, are still countable. The smallest uncountable ordinal is called ω_1.

Traditionally, a *recursive ordinal* is defined as one for which there exists a *computable* one-to-one function from it to ω under some suitable encoding of ordinals and notion of computability (see Rogers (1967)). The smallest nonrecursive ordinal is called ω_1^{ck}. It is a countable ordinal, but it looks uncountable to any computable function.

We will define recursive ordinals in terms of inductive labelings of *recursive trees*. For the purposes of this chapter, a *tree* is a nonempty prefix-closed subset of ω^*. In other words, it is a set T of finite-length strings of natural numbers such that

- $\varepsilon \in T$;
- if $xy \in T$ then $x \in T$.

A *path* in T is a maximal subset of T linearly ordered by the prefix relation. The tree T is *well-founded* if it has no infinite paths; equivalently, if the converse of the prefix relation is a well-founded relation on T. A *leaf* is an element of T that is not a prefix of any other element of T.

Given a well-founded tree T, we define a labeling $\mathrm{ord} : T \to \mathbf{Ord}$ inductively as follows:

$$\mathrm{ord}(x) \stackrel{\mathrm{def}}{=} (\sup_{\substack{n \in \omega \\ xn \in T}} \mathrm{ord}(xn)) + 1.$$

Thus $\mathrm{ord}(x) = 1$ if x is a leaf; otherwise, $\mathrm{ord}(x)$ is determined by first determining $\mathrm{ord}(xn)$ for all $xn \in T$, then taking the supremum and adding 1.

For example, consider the tree consisting of ε and all sequences of the form $(n, \underbrace{0, 0, \dots, 0}_{m})$ for $n \geq 0$ and $m \leq n$. The leaves are labeled 1 by ord, the next elements above the leaves are labeled 2, and so on. The root ε is labeled $\omega + 1$.

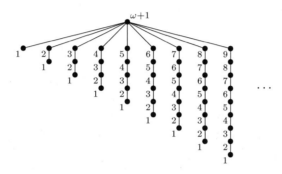

For a well-founded tree T, let $\mathrm{ord}(T)$ be the ordinal assigned to the root of T. Every $\mathrm{ord}(T)$ is a countable ordinal, and $\sup_T \mathrm{ord}(T) = \omega_1$.

Now define an ordinal to be *recursive* if it is $\mathrm{ord}(T)$ for some *recursive* tree T; that is, a tree such that the set T, suitably encoded, is a recursive set. The supremum of the recursive ordinals is ω_1^{ck}.

An alternative definition of recursive ordinals is the set of all running times of IND programs. The running time of an IND program on some input is the time it takes to label the root of the computation tree with 1 or 0. This is the closure ordinal of the inductive definition of labelings of the computation tree in the formal definition of acceptance. It is very similar to the definition of the labelings ord of recursive trees. The ordinal ω_1^{ck} is the supremum of all running times of IND programs.

Kleene's Theorem

THEOREM 2.12 (KLEENE):   Over $\mathbb{N}$, the inductive relations and the Π_1^1 relations coincide, and the hyperelementary and Δ_1^1 relations coincide.

Proof sketch.   First we show that every inductive relation is Π_1^1. This direction holds in any structure $\mathfrak{A}$, not just $\mathbb{N}$. Let $\varphi(\overline{x}, R)$ be a positive first-order formula with fixpoint $F_\varphi \subseteq A^n$, where A is the carrier of $\mathfrak{A}$. We can describe F_φ as the intersection of all relations closed under φ:

$$F_\varphi(\overline{x}) \quad \Longleftrightarrow \quad \forall R \ (\forall \overline{y} \ \varphi(\overline{y}, R) \to R(\overline{y})) \to R(\overline{x}).$$

This is a Π_1^1 formula.

Conversely, consider any Π_1^1 formula over $\mathbb{N}$. As mentioned earlier, we can assume without loss of generality that the formula is of the form

$$\forall f \ \exists y \ \varphi(x, y, f), \tag{2.2.1}$$

where f ranges over functions $\omega \to \omega$, y ranges over ω, and φ is quantifier free (Exercise 3.33).

Regarding a function $f : \omega \to \omega$ as the infinite string of its values $f(0)$, $f(1)$, $f(2), \ldots$, the functions f are in one-to-one correspondence with paths in the complete tree ω^*. Moreover, for any x and y, the truth of $\varphi(x, y, f)$ is determined by any finite prefix of this path that includes all arguments to f corresponding to terms appearing in $\varphi(x, y, f)$. Let $f \upharpoonright n$ denote the finite prefix of f of length n. We can think of $f \upharpoonright n$ either as a string of natural numbers of length n or as a partial function that agrees with f on domain $\{0, 1, \ldots, n - 1\}$. Instead of (2.2.1) we can write

$$\forall f \ \exists y \ \exists n \ \varphi'(x, y, f \upharpoonright n), \tag{2.2.2}$$

where φ' is just φ modified slightly to evaluate to $\mathbf{0}$ (false) in case n is too small to give enough information to determine whether $\varphi(x, y, f)$. Note that if $\varphi'(x, y, f \upharpoonright n)$, then $\varphi'(x, y, f \upharpoonright m)$ for all $m \geq n$. This says that (2.2.2) is essentially a well-foundedness condition: if we label the vertices $f \upharpoonright n$ of the infinite tree with the truth value of $\exists y \ \varphi'(x, y, f \upharpoonright n)$, (2.2.2) says that along every path in the tree we eventually encounter the value $\mathbf{1}$ (true). And as observed in Example 2.11, well-foundedness is inductive.

We have shown that the inductive and Π_1^1 relations over $\mathbb{N}$ coincide. Since the hyperarithmetic relations are those that are both inductive and coinductive and the Δ_1^1 relations are those that are both Π_1^1 and Σ_1^1, the hyperarithmetic and Δ_1^1 relations coincide as well. ■

Inductive is Existential over Hyperelementary

We have shown that over $\mathbb{N}$, Π_1^1 is exactly the family of sets accepted by IND programs and Δ_1^1 is the family of sets accepted by total IND programs. It is apparent from this characterization that there is a strong analogy between the inductive and the r.e. sets and between the hyperelementary and the recursive sets.

It may seem odd that that the class analogous to Σ_1^0 at the analytic level should be Π_1^1 and not Σ_1^1. This is explained by a result analogous to Proposition 2.5.

PROPOSITION 2.13: A set $A \subseteq \mathbb{N}$ is inductive iff there is a hyperelementary relation φ such that

$$
\begin{aligned}
A \quad &= \quad \{x \mid \exists \alpha < \omega_1^{ck} \; \varphi(x, \alpha)\} \\
&= \quad \{x \mid \exists y \; y \text{ encodes a recursive ordinal and } \varphi(x, y)\}.
\end{aligned}
\qquad (2.2.3)
$$

Proof sketch. If φ is hyperelementary, then we can build an IND program for (2.2.3) consisting of the statement $y := \exists$ followed by a program that in parallel checks that the Turing machine with index y accepts a well-founded recursive tree and that $\varphi(x, y)$.

Conversely, if A is inductive, say accepted by an IND program p, then we can describe A by an existential formula that says, "There exists a recursive ordinal α such that p halts and accepts x in α steps." More concretely, one would say, "There exists a recursive well-founded tree T such that on input x, p halts and accepts in $\text{ord}(T)$ steps." The quantification is then over indices of Turing machines. The predicate "p halts and accepts x in $\text{ord}(T)$ steps" is hyperelementary, since one can construct an IND program that runs p together with a program q that simply enumerates the tree T using existential branching, rejecting at the leaves. The program q rejects all inputs, but takes $\text{ord}(T)$ steps to do it. If the simulations of p and q are performed in parallel in a time-sharing fashion as in Theorem 2.4, one step at a time in each turn, then it can be shown by induction on the computation tree that the simulating machine will accept or reject depending on which of p or q takes less (ordinal) time. ∎

2.3 Reducibility and Completeness

Reducibility Relations

Reducibility is a common technique for comparing the complexity of different problems. Given decision problems $A \subseteq \Sigma^*$ and $B \subseteq \Delta^*$, a *(many-one) reduction* of A to B is a total computable function

$$
\sigma : \Sigma^* \quad \to \quad \Delta^*
$$

such that for all $x \in \Sigma^*$,

$$x \in A \iff \sigma(x) \in B. \tag{2.3.1}$$

In other words, strings in A must go to strings in B under σ, and strings not in A must go to strings not in B under σ. Intuitively, instances of the problem A are coded by σ as instances of the problem B. We may not know how to decide whether a given string x is in A or not, but we can apply σ to x to transform it into an instance $\sigma(x)$ of the problem B. Then a decision procedure for B would immediately give a decision procedure for A by composing it with σ.

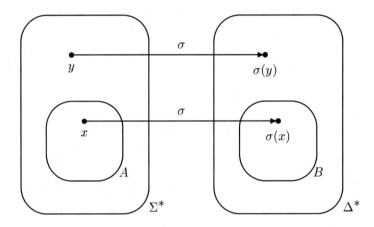

The function σ need not be one-to-one or onto. It must, however, be *total* and *effectively computable*; that is, computable by a total Turing machine that on any input x halts with $\sigma(x)$ written on its tape. When such a reduction exists, we say that A is *reducible* to B via the map σ, and we write $A \leq_m B$. The subscript m, which stands for "many-one," is used to distinguish this relation from other types of reducibility relations.

In order to obtain an *efficient* decision procedure for A from an *efficient* decision procedure for B, the reduction map σ must also be efficient. Many known reductions in the literature turn out to be very efficient, usually linear time or logspace. We write $A \leq_m^{\log} B$ if the reduction map σ is computable in logspace and $A \leq_m^P B$ if the reduction map σ is computable in polynomial time.

The reducibility relations $\leq_m$, $\leq_m^{\log}$, and $\leq_m^P$ are transitive: if $A \leq_m B$ and $B \leq_m C$, then $A \leq_m C$, and similarly for $\leq_m^{\log}$ and $\leq_m^P$. This is because if σ reduces A to B and τ reduces B to C, then their composition $\sigma \circ \tau$ reduces A to C. For the relations $\leq_m^{\log}$ and $\leq_m^P$, we must show that the composition of polynomial-time computable functions is computable in polynomial time and the composition of logspace computable functions is computable in logspace. For logspace, this is not immediate, since there is not enough space to write down an intermediate result; but with a little cleverness it can be done (Exercise 2.7).

EXAMPLE 2.14:   One can reduce HP, the halting problem for Turing machines, to the membership problem MP, the problem of determining whether a given Turing machine accepts a given string (see Section 2.1). This is done by constructing from a given description x_M of a Turing machine M and string y a description x_N of a Turing machine N that accepts ε iff M halts on y. In this example,

$$A \;=\; \mathsf{HP} \;\overset{\mathrm{def}}{=}\; \{(x_M, y) \mid M \text{ halts on input } y\},$$
$$B \;=\; \mathsf{MP} \;\overset{\mathrm{def}}{=}\; \{(x_M, y) \mid M \text{ accepts input } y\}.$$

Given x_M and y, let N be a Turing machine that on input z does the following:

(i)   erases its input z;
(ii) writes y on its tape (y is hard-coded in the finite control of N);
(iii) runs M on y (the description x_M of M is hard-coded in the finite control of N);
(iv) accepts if the computation of M on y halts.

The machine N we have constructed accepts its input z iff M halts on y. Moreover, its actions are independent of z, since it just ignores its input. Thus

$$L(N) \;=\; \begin{cases} \Sigma^*, & \text{if } M \text{ halts on } y, \\ \varnothing, & \text{if } M \text{ does not halt on } y. \end{cases}$$

In particular,

$$N \text{ accepts } \varepsilon \iff M \text{ halts on } y. \tag{2.3.2}$$

We can take our reduction σ to be the computable map $(x_M, y) \mapsto (x_N, \varepsilon)$. In this example, σ is computable in polynomial time and even in logspace. The equation (2.3.2) is just (2.3.1) in this particular case.

Here are some general results about reducibility relations that point out their usefulness in comparing the computability and complexity of decision problems.

THEOREM 2.15:

(i) If $A \leq_m B$ and B is r.e., then so is A. Equivalently, if $A \leq_m B$ and A is not r.e., then neither is B.

(ii) If $A \leq_m B$ and B is recursive, then so is A. Equivalently, if $A \leq_m B$ and A is not recursive, then neither is B.

Proof   (i) Suppose $A \leq_m B$ via the map σ and B is r.e. Let M be a Turing machine such that $B = L(M)$. Build a machine N for A as follows: on input x, first compute $\sigma(x)$, then run M on input $\sigma(x)$, accepting if M accepts. Then

$$
\begin{array}{lll}
N \text{ accepts } x & \Longleftrightarrow & M \text{ accepts } \sigma(x) \quad \text{definition of } N \\
& \Longleftrightarrow & \sigma(x) \in B \qquad\quad\ \text{definition of } M \\
& \Longleftrightarrow & x \in A \qquad\qquad\ \text{by } (2.3.1).
\end{array}
$$

(ii) Recall from Proposition 2.4 that a set is recursive iff both it and its complement are r.e. Suppose $A \leq_m B$ via the map σ and B is recursive. Note that $\sim A \leq_m \sim B$ via the same σ. If B is recursive, then both B and $\sim B$ are r.e. By (i), both A and $\sim A$ are r.e., thus A is recursive.   ∎

   We can use Theorem 2.15(i) to show that certain sets are not r.e. and Theorem 2.15(ii) to show that certain sets are not recursive. To show that a set B is not r.e., we need only give a reduction from a set A we already know is not r.e., such as the complement of the halting problem, to B. By Theorem 2.15(i), B cannot be r.e. For example, the reduction of Example 2.14, in conjunction with Proposition 2.2, shows that the membership problem MP is not decidable and that $\sim$MP is not r.e.
   A similar theorem holds in the presence of complexity bounds.

THEOREM 2.16:

(i) If $A \leq_m^p B$ and B is computable in polynomial time, then so is A. In other words, the complexity class P is closed downward under $\leq_m^p$.

(ii) If $A \leq_m^{\log} B$ and B is computable in logspace, then so is A. In other words, the complexity class $LOGSPACE$ is closed downward under $\leq_m^{\log}$.

Proof   Exercise 2.8.   ∎

Completeness

A set B is said to be *hard* for a complexity class $\mathcal{C}$ with respect to a reducibility relation $\leq$ (or just $\mathcal{C}$-hard, if $\leq$ is understood) if $A \leq B$ for all $A \in \mathcal{C}$. The set B is said to be *complete* for $\mathcal{C}$ with respect to $\leq$ (or just $\mathcal{C}$-complete) if it is hard for $\mathcal{C}$ with respect to $\leq$ and if in addition $B \in \mathcal{C}$.

Intuitively, if B is complete for $\mathcal{C}$, then B is a "hardest" problem for the class $\mathcal{C}$ in the sense that it is in $\mathcal{C}$ and encodes every other problem in $\mathcal{C}$.

For example, the Boolean satisfiability problem—to determine, given a propositional formula, whether it is satisfiable—is *NP*-complete with respect to $\leq_{\mathrm{m}}^{\mathrm{log}}$. This is known as Cook's theorem (see Hopcroft and Ullman (1979); Kozen (1991b)).

The following proposition points out the significance of these concepts.

PROPOSITION 2.17: Let $\mathcal{B}$ and $\mathcal{C}$ be complexity classes, $\mathcal{B} \subseteq \mathcal{C}$. Suppose also that $\mathcal{B}$ is closed downward under the reducibility relation $\leq$; that is, if $A \leq B$ and $B \in \mathcal{B}$, then $A \in \mathcal{B}$. If a set B is $\mathcal{C}$-complete with respect to $\leq$, then $B \in \mathcal{B}$ if and only if $\mathcal{B} = \mathcal{C}$.

In other words, the question of whether the two complexity classes are equal reduces to the question of whether the single problem B is in $\mathcal{B}$. For example, $P = NP$ if and only if the Boolean satisfiability problem is in P.

Proof If $\mathcal{B} = \mathcal{C}$, then $B \in \mathcal{B}$, since $B \in \mathcal{C}$. Conversely, suppose $B \in \mathcal{B}$. Since B is $\mathcal{C}$-hard, every element of $\mathcal{C}$ reduces to B; and since $\mathcal{B}$ is closed downward under $\leq$, all those elements are in $\mathcal{B}$. Thus $\mathcal{C} \subseteq \mathcal{B}$. ■

The complexity class *coNP* is the class of sets $A \subseteq \Sigma^*$ whose complements $\sim A = \Sigma^* - A$ are in *NP*. Usually *NP*-hardness and *coNP*-hardness are taken with respect to the reducibility relation $\leq_{\mathrm{m}}^{\mathrm{P}}$.

PROPOSITION 2.18:

(i) $A \leq_{\mathrm{m}}^{\mathrm{P}} B$ iff $\sim A \leq_{\mathrm{m}}^{\mathrm{P}} \sim B$.

(ii) A is *NP*-hard iff $\sim A$ is *coNP*-hard.

(iii) A is *NP*-complete iff $\sim A$ is *coNP*-complete.

(iv) If A is *NP*-complete then $A \in coNP$ iff $NP = coNP$.

It is unknown whether $NP = coNP$.

Tiling Problems

In this section we describe a family of *tiling problems* that are complete for various complexity classes. These problems will serve as generic problems that we can use in establishing other completeness results by reduction.

Let C be a finite set of *colors*. A *tile* is a square with colored sides. The *type* of a tile is a mapping $\{\text{north}, \text{south}, \text{east}, \text{west}\} \to C$ that gives the color of each side.

Say we are given a set of tile types and a square $n \times n$ grid consisting of n^2 cells, each of which can hold one tile. The boundary of the grid is colored with colors from C. We would like to know whether it is possible to place tiles in the cells, one tile to each cell, such that the colors on all adjacent edges match. We can use as many tiles of each of the given types as we like, but we are not allowed to rotate the tiles.

For example, the tiling problem with 2×2 grid

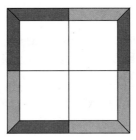

and tile types

has exactly one solution, namely

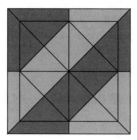

We call this problem the *first tiling problem.*

PROPOSITION 2.19:   The first tiling problem is *NP*-complete.

Proof The problem is in *NP*, since we can guess a tiling and verify quickly that the color constraints are satisfied.

To show that the problem is *NP*-hard, we show how to encode the computation of an arbitrary one-tape nondeterministic polynomial-time-bounded Turing machine on some input as an instance of a tiling problem. Let M be such a machine and let x be an input to M, $n = |x|$. Without loss of generality, the single tape is read/write and serves as both input and worktape. Say the machine M runs in time n^k for some fixed $k \geq 1$ independent of n, and let $N = n^k$. The grid will be $N \times N$. The sequence of colors along the south edges of the tiles in the jth row will represent a possible configuration of M at time j. The color of the south edge of the tile at position i, j will give the symbol occupying the ith tape cell and will indicate whether that cell is being scanned at time j, and if so, will give the current state. For example, this color might say, "M is currently in state q scanning this tape cell, and the symbol currently occupying this cell is a." The color of the north edge will represent similar information at time $j + 1$. The types of the tiles will be chosen so that only legal moves of the machine are represented. Because the tape head can move left and right, information must also move sideways, and the east/west colors are used for that. The east/west colors will say whether the head is crossing the line between this cell and an adjacent one. The possible colors on the north edge of a tile will be determined by the colors of the other three edges and the transition rules of M. The colors along the south boundary of the grid will describe the start configuration, and those along the north boundary will describe the accept configuration. The resulting tiling problem will have a solution iff M has an accepting computation on input x.

Formally, let Q be the set of states, Σ the input alphabet, Γ the work alphabet, $\sqcup$ the blank symbol, $\vdash$ the left endmarker, s the start state, t the accept state, and δ the transition relation. We assume that $\Sigma \subseteq \Gamma, \vdash, \sqcup \in \Gamma - \Sigma$, and

$$\delta \quad \subseteq \quad (Q \times \Gamma) \times (Q \times \Gamma \times \{\text{left,right}\}).$$

If $((p,a),(q,b,d)) \in \delta$, this says that when the machine is in state p scanning symbol a, it can write b on the current tape cell, move in direction d, and enter state q. The north/south colors are

$$(Q \cup \{-\}) \times \Gamma$$

and the east/west colors are

$$(Q \times \{\text{left,right}\}) \cup \{-\}.$$

The north/south color (q,a) for $q \in Q$ indicates that the tape head is currently scanning this tape cell, the machine is in state q, and the symbol currently written on this tape cell is a. The north/south color $(-,a)$ indicates that the tape head is not currently scanning this tape cell, and the symbol currently written on this tape cell is a. The east/west color (q,d) indicates that the head is crossing the line between these two tape cells in direction d and is about to enter state q. The east/west color $-$ indicates that the head is not currently crossing the line between these two tape cells.

The types of the tiles will be all types of the form

whenever $((p,a),(q,b,\text{left})) \in \delta$ and

whenever $((p,a),(q,b,\text{right})) \in \delta$, as well as all types of the form

The colors along the south boundary of the grid will represent the start configuration of M on input $x = a_1 a_2 \cdots a_n$:

$$(s, \vdash)\ (-, a_1)\ (-, a_2)\ \cdots\ (-, a_n)\ (-, \sqcup)\ \cdots\ (-, \sqcup).$$

The colors along the north boundary of the grid will represent the accept configuration of M:

$$(t, \vdash)\ (-, \sqcup)\ (-, \sqcup)\ \cdots\ (-, \sqcup)$$

(we can assume without loss of generality that M erases its tape and moves its head all the way to the left before accepting). The colors along the east and west boundaries of the grid are all $-$.

Now any accepting computation history of M on input x yields a tiling, and any tiling represents an accepting computation history, because the local consistency conditions of the tiling say that M starts in its start configuration on input x, runs according to the transition rules δ, and ends up in an accept configuration. Therefore this instance of the tiling problem has a solution iff M accepts x. ∎

Now consider a variant of the tiling problem in which we use an infinite $\omega \times \omega$ grid. The south boundary is colored with a pattern consisting of a finite string of colors followed by an infinite string of a single color, say blue. The west boundary is colored only blue. The coloring of the south and west boundaries is part of the problem specification. There is no north or east boundary. Everything else is the same as above. We call this problem the *second tiling problem*.

PROPOSITION 2.20: The second tiling problem is Π_1^0-complete (that is, co-r.e.-complete). The problem is still Π_1^0-hard even if we restrict the south boundary to be colored with a single color.

Proof sketch. The problem is in Π_1^0, since the whole grid can be tiled if and only if all southwest $n \times n$ subgrids can be tiled.[1] This is a Π_1^0 statement.

To show that the problem is Π_1^0-hard, we construct an instance of the tiling

---

1 This is not obvious! The proof uses König's lemma. See Exercise 2.6.

problem that simulates a given deterministic Turing machine on a given input as in the proof of Proposition 2.19, except that there is no bound on the size or number of configurations. All tile types with the color of the accept state on the south edge are omitted; thus the tiling can be extended indefinitely if and only if the machine does not accept the input. For any fixed Turing machine M, this construction constitutes a many-one reduction from $\sim L(M)$ to solvable instances of the tiling problem.

To show that a single color for the south boundary suffices, we could instead encode the set

$$\{x_M \mid M \text{ does not accept the empty string } \varepsilon\}$$

by constructing for a given x_M an instance of the tiling problem that simulates M on the empty input. This is a well-known Π_1^0-complete problem (Exercise 2.3).   ∎

We next consider a slightly different version of the problem. In this version, we still restrict colorings of the south boundary to consist of a finite string of colors followed by an infinite string of blue, but the coloring of the south boundary is not specified. The problem is to decide whether there exists such a coloring of the south boundary under which the tiling can be extended indefinitely. This variant is called the *third tiling problem*.

PROPOSITION 2.21:   The third tiling problem is Σ_2^0-complete.

Proof sketch.   The problem is in Σ_2^0, since the selection of the boundary coloring requires a single existential quantifier; then the statement that the grid can be tiled under that boundary coloring is Π_1^0, as in Proposition 2.20.

To show that the problem is Σ_2^0-hard, we can encode the complement of the universality problem for Turing machines. The universality problem is: given a Turing machine, does it accept all strings? In other words, is it the case that for all input strings, there exists a halting computation on that input string? This is a well-known Π_2^0-complete problem.

As in the proof of Proposition 2.20, we can construct from a given Turing machine an instance of the tiling problem that simulates the Turing machine. Here, however, the various colorings of the south boundary will represent the possible input strings. The finite multicolored part of the boundary coloring will represent the input string, and the infinite blue string to its right will represent infinitely many blank symbols on the Turing machine's tape to the right of the input. For a given boundary coloring, the tiling can be extended indefinitely iff the Turing machine on the input string corresponding to that boundary coloring does not halt.   ∎

As a final variant, consider the question of whether an $\omega \times \omega$ tiling problem has a solution in which a particular color, say red, is used infinitely often. We call this version the *fourth tiling problem*.

PROPOSITION 2.22: The fourth tiling problem is Σ_1^1-complete.

Proof sketch. The problem is in Σ_1^1 because it can be expressed with a second-order existential formula: a second-order existential quantifier can be used to select a tiling; and for a given tiling, being a solution and using red infinitely often are first-order properties.

To show that the problem is Σ_1^1-hard, we reduce to it the non-well-foundedness of recursive trees $T \subseteq \omega^*$. The construction given in the proof of Kleene's theorem (Theorem 2.12) shows that this problem is Σ_1^1-hard. Build a Turing machine that, given a recursive tree T, guesses a sequence $n_0, n_1, n_2, \ldots$ nondeterministically. After the kth guess, it checks whether the sequence $n_0, n_1, n_2, \ldots, n_{k-1}$ guessed so far is in T. If so, it enters a special red state. The tree is non-well-founded iff it has an infinite path, which happens iff there is a computation of the machine that enters the red state infinitely often. This can be coded as an instance of the fourth tiling problem as above. ∎

2.4 Bibliographical Notes

Turing machines were introduced by Turing (1936). Originally they were presented in the form of *enumeration machines*, since Turing was interested in enumerating the decimal expansions of computable real numbers and values of real-valued functions. Turing also introduced the concept of nondeterminism in his original paper, although he did not develop the idea. Alternating Turing machines were introduced in Chandra et al. (1981).

The basic properties of the r.e. sets were developed by Kleene (1943) and Post (1943, 1944). Universal Turing machines and the application of Cantor's diagonalization technique to prove the undecidability of the halting problem appeared in the original paper of Turing (1936). Reducibility relations were discussed by Post (1944). These fundamental ideas led to the development of *recursive function theory*; see Rogers, Jr. (1967); Soare (1987); Kleene (1952) for an introduction to this field.

Counter automata were studied by Fischer (1966), Fischer et al. (1968), and Minsky (1961).

Recursive function theory has been extended upward and downward. The upward extension deals with the arithmetic and analytic hierarchies, so-called *generalized* or *α-recursion theory*, descriptive set theory, and inductive definability. See Rogers, Jr. (1967); Soare (1987); Barwise (1975); Moschovakis (1974, 1980) for an introduction to these subjects. Kleene's theorem on the relation between inductive definability and Π_1^1 was proved in Kleene (1955). The programming language IND was introduced in Harel and Kozen (1984).

The downward extension is computational complexity theory. This subject got its start in the late 1960s and early 1970s; some seminal papers are Hartmanis and Stearns (1965); Karp (1972); Cook (1971). A good source on the theory of *NP*-completeness and completeness for other complexity classes is Garey and Johnson (1979). The tiling problems of Section 2.3 are from Harel (1985).

Exercises

2.1. Prove Lemma 2.3.

2.2. Prove that ω_1 is the smallest set of ordinals containing 0 and closed under successor and suprema of countable sets.

2.3. Show that the set

$$\{x_M \mid M \text{ accepts the empty string } \varepsilon\}$$

is Σ_1^0-complete. (*Hint.* Use a reduction similar to the one of Example 2.14.) Use this to argue that the tiling problem of Proposition 2.20 remains Π_1^0-hard even if the south boundary is restricted to be colored with a single color.

2.4. (Rice (1953, 1956)) A property $\varphi(x)$ of strings is called a *property of the r.e. sets* if for all Turing machines M and N, if $L(M) = L(N)$ then $\varphi(x_M) = \varphi(x_N)$, where x_M is the code of M as described in Section 2.1. It is *nontrivial* if there exist M and N such that $\varphi(x_M)$ is true and $\varphi(x_N)$ is false. Examples of nontrivial properties of r.e. sets are: "M accepts a finite set," "$L(M)$ is recursive," and "M accepts the empty string." Examples of properties that are not nontrivial properties of the r.e. sets are: "M has more than 21 states" (not a property of r.e. sets) and "there exists a Turing machine accepting twice as many strings as M" (not nontrivial). Prove that *every* nontrivial property of the r.e. sets is undecidable. (*Hint.* Encode the halting problem HP. Let Z and N be Turing machines such that $L(Z) = \varnothing$ and

$\varphi(x_N) \neq \varphi(x_Z)$. Build a Turing machine that accepts $L(N)$ if a given M halts on x_M and $\varnothing$ otherwise.)

2.5. (a) A tree $T \subseteq \omega^*$ is *finitely branching* if for every $x \in T$ there are only finitely many $n \in \omega$ such that $xn \in T$. Prove *König's lemma*: every finitely branching tree with infinitely many vertices has an infinite path.

(b) Give a counterexample showing that (a) is false without the finite-branching assumption.

2.6. In the second tiling problem (Proposition 2.20), we needed to know that the whole $\omega \times \omega$ grid can be tiled if and only if all southwest $n \times n$ subgrids can be tiled. Show that this is so. (*Hint.* Use either Exercise 2.5 or the compactness of propositional logic.)

2.7. Prove that the reducibility relation $\leq_{\mathrm{m}}^{\log}$ defined in 2.3 is transitive.

2.8. Prove Theorem 2.16.

2.9. Show that Proposition 2.22 holds even if the problem requires infinitely many occurrences of red on the westernmost column of tiles.

2.10. (a) Prove that the halting problem for one-counter Turing machines is decidable.

(b) Using (a), show that there exists an r.e. set that is accepted by no one-counter machine. Conclude that one-counter machines are strictly less powerful than arbitrary Turing machines.

2.11. Prove that the halting problem for IND programs is Π_1^1-complete.

3 Logic

3.1   What is Logic?

Logic typically consists of three ingredients:

- A *language* is a collection of well-formed expressions to which meaning can be assigned. The symbols of the language, together with the formal rules for distinguishing well-formed expressions from arbitrary aggregates of symbols, are called the *syntax* of the language.

- A *semantics* tells how to interpret well-formed expressions as statements *about* something. The "something" can be mathematical objects such as groups or graphs or the natural numbers or everyday things such as cars, employees, or the weather. The statements of the language talk about the properties of and relationships among these objects.

- A *deductive system* consists of a collection of rules that can be applied to derive, in a purely mechanical way, interesting facts about and relationships among the semantic objects. The facts and relationships are those expressible in the language.

All three of these aspects—language, semantics, and deductive system—can be adapted to particular applications and to particular levels of expressibility as desired.

  In this chapter we will introduce several classical logical systems:

- *propositional logic*, the logic of uninterpreted assertions and the basic propositional connectives: *and, or, not, if ... then ...* , and *if and only if* (Section 3.2);

- *equational logic*, the logic of equality (Section 3.3);

- *first-order predicate logic*, the logic of individual elements and their properties, especially those properties expressible using universal and existential quantification (Section 3.4);

- *infinitary logic*, a variant of predicate logic allowing certain infinite expressions (Section 3.6);

- *modal logic*, the logic of *possibility* and *necessity* (Section 3.7).

For each system, we will discuss its syntax, semantics, and deductive apparatus and derive some elementary results.

Languages

The language of a given logic typically consists of an *application-specific* part and an *application-independent* part. The application-specific part consists of those constructs that are tailored to the application at hand and may not make sense in other contexts. For example, when talking about properties of the natural numbers $\mathbb{N} = \{0, 1, 2, \dots\}$, a symbol $+$ denoting addition and a symbol $\cdot$ denoting multiplication are quite relevant, but less so if we are discussing properties of graphs. For this reason, the language of number theory and the language of graph theory look very different. In a medical expert system, the objects under discussion may be diseases, treatments, symptoms, and medications, and their relationships with one another. These differences might be called "horizontal differences" among logical systems.

There are also "vertical differences." Even within a specific application domain, there may be several possible levels of expressiveness, depending on the complexity of the properties that need to be expressed and reasoned about. A good rule of thumb when designing a logic is to make it no more detailed than necessary to handle the task at hand. This allows irrelevant information to be suppressed, so that it cannot clutter or confuse the process of deduction. If propositional letters and propositional connectives suffice to express an assertion, it is pointless to include, say, variables, constants and functions; if we are trying to establish the equality of two terms, we might as well ignore quantifiers. Classical mathematical logic—the logic of mathematical objects such as groups, graphs, or topological spaces—divides neatly into various levels of expressiveness, reflecting these differences. The same will hold true for Dynamic Logic.

Models, Satisfaction, and Validity

Nowadays, logicians generally take pains to develop formal semantics for new logics they invent. This was not always so. Up until about the 1940s, logic existed in purely syntactic form—the "sacred" form, as it is called by van Dalen (1994). Logicians did not think much about formal semantics or interpretation, but just worked mechanically with the syntax and proof apparatus, guided by intuition. But it was always clear that expressions had meaning, at least on some level. Number theory was always about the natural numbers and set theory about sets, even though we might not have been completely sure what these objects were.

A more recent approach, the *model theoretic* approach, attempts to define the meaning of expressions rigorously as true/false statements about formally defined mathematical objects. These objects are usually called *structures* or *models*.

Included in the specification of the structure is a mapping that tells how to interpret the basic symbols of the language in that structure. Certain syntactic expressions are designated as *sentences*, which are formulas that take on well-defined truth values under a given interpretation mapping. This "profane" view of logic is one of the great contributions of Alfred Tarski.

If a sentence φ is true in a structure $\mathfrak{A}$, then we say that φ is *satisfied* in the structure $\mathfrak{A}$ or that $\mathfrak{A}$ is a *model* of φ, and write $\mathfrak{A} \vDash \varphi$. If φ is satisfied in every possible structure, we say that φ is *valid* and write $\vDash \varphi$.

In some instances we wish to limit the class of structures under consideration. Often the class of structures of interest is itself specified by a set of sentences. For example, in group theory, we are interested in groups, which are mathematical objects satisfying certain properties that can be expressed in the language of groups. If Φ is a set of sentences (finite or infinite), we say that $\mathfrak{A}$ is a model of Φ and write $\mathfrak{A} \vDash \Phi$ if $\mathfrak{A}$ is a model of every element of Φ. For example, Φ might be the set of sentences defining groups; by definition, a structure is a group iff it is a model of this set. We write $\Phi \vDash \varphi$ if φ is satisfied in every model of Φ, and say that φ is a *logical consequence* of Φ. The set of logical consequences of Φ is called the *theory of* Φ and is denoted **Th** Φ. For example, group theory is the set of logical consequences of the set of sentences defining groups; that is, the set of all sentences that are true in all groups.

There are modern logical systems for which the semantics is not fully defined, either because set theory does not provide adequate support or there is not complete agreement on how expressions should be interpreted. Indeed, there exist systems for which it is still not understood how to give any complete and rigorous formal interpretation at all.

Deduction

Many different types of deductive systems have been proposed for the various logics we will consider in this book: sequent systems, natural deduction, tableau systems, and resolution, to name a few. Each of these systems has its advantages and disadvantages.

For uniformity and consistency, we will concentrate on one style of deductive system called a *Hilbert system* after the mathematician David Hilbert, who advocated its use in mechanizing mathematics. A Hilbert system consists of a set of *axioms*, or sentences in the language that are postulated to be true, and *rules of inference* of the form

$$\frac{\varphi_1, \quad \varphi_2, \quad \cdots, \quad \varphi_n}{\psi}$$

from which new theorems can be derived. The statements $\varphi_1, \dots, \varphi_n$ above the line are called the *premises* of the rule and the statement ψ below the line is called the *conclusion*. In Hilbert systems, usually the axioms are emphasized and the rules of inference are few and very basic.

A *proof* in a Hilbert system is a sequence $\varphi_1, \dots, \varphi_m$ of statements such that each φ_i is either an axiom or the conclusion of a rule all of whose premises occur earlier in the sequence. The sequence $\varphi_1, \dots, \varphi_m$ is said to be a *proof of* φ_m, and φ_m is called a *theorem* of the system. We write $\vdash \varphi$ if φ is a theorem.

More generally, we may wish to reason in the presence of extra assumptions. If Φ is a set of sentences (finite or infinite), we write $\Phi \vdash \varphi$ if there is a proof of φ using the elements of Φ as if they were extra axioms. In other words, $\Phi \vdash \varphi$ if there is a sequence $\varphi_1, \dots, \varphi_m$ of statements such that each φ_i is either an axiom, an element of Φ, or the conclusion of a rule all of whose premises occur earlier in the sequence, and $\varphi = \varphi_m$. If $\Phi \vdash \varphi$, we say that φ is a *deductive consequence* of Φ. A theorem is just a deductive consequence of the empty set of assumptions.

Soundness and Completeness

A deductive system $\vdash$ is said to be *sound* with respect to a semantics $\vDash$ if for all sentences φ,

$$\vdash \varphi \;\Longrightarrow\; \vDash \varphi;$$

that is, every theorem is valid. A deductive system $\vdash$ is said to be *complete* with respect to $\vDash$ if for all φ,

$$\vDash \varphi \;\Longrightarrow\; \vdash \varphi;$$

that is, every valid sentence is a theorem.

Consistency and Refutability

Many logics have a negation operator $\neg$. For such logics, we say that a formula φ is *refutable* if $\neg \varphi$ is a theorem; that is, if $\vdash \neg \varphi$. If the logic contains a conjunction operator $\wedge$ as well, then we say that a set Φ of sentences is *refutable* if some finite conjunction of elements of Φ is refutable. We say that φ or Φ is *consistent* if it is not refutable.

Axiom Schemes

In many cases, axioms and rules are given as *schemes*, which are rules standing for infinitely many *instances*. For example, the rule

$$\frac{\varphi, \quad \psi}{\varphi \wedge \psi}$$

says that from the truth of φ and ψ we can infer that the single statement $\varphi \wedge \psi$ is true. This really stands for infinitely many rules, one for each possible choice of φ and ψ. The rules themselves are the instances of this scheme obtained by substituting a particular φ and ψ. For example,

$$\frac{p \to q, \quad q \to p}{(p \to q) \wedge (q \to p)}$$

might be one such instance.

3.2 Propositional Logic

We often need to make basic deductions such as:

If p implies q, and if q is false, then p must also be false.

This deduction is valid independent of the truth or falsity of p and q. Propositional logic formalizes this type of reasoning.

Syntax

The basic symbols of propositional logic are the *propositional letters* $p, q, r, \ldots$ representing atomic assertions, which can be either true or false. We assume that there are countably many such symbols available.

In addition to these symbols, there are *propositional operators* or *connectives*

- $\wedge$ *conjunction, "and"*;
- $\vee$ *disjunction, "or"*;
- $\neg$ *negation, "not"*;
- **1**   *truth*;
- **0**   *falsity*;
- $\to$ *implication, "if ... then ... "*;
- $\leftrightarrow$ *equivalence, "if and only if", "iff"*;

and parentheses. We will actually take only $\rightarrow$ and $\mathbf{0}$ as primitive symbols and define all the others in terms of them.

Propositions or *propositional formulas*, denoted $\varphi, \psi, \rho, \ldots$, are built up inductively according to the following rules:

- all atomic propositions $p, q, r, \ldots$ and $\mathbf{0}$ are propositions;
- if φ and ψ are propositions, then so is $\varphi \rightarrow \psi$.

We define the other propositional operators as follows:

$$\neg\varphi \overset{\text{def}}{=} \varphi \rightarrow \mathbf{0}$$
$$\mathbf{1} \overset{\text{def}}{=} \neg\mathbf{0}$$
$$\varphi \vee \psi \overset{\text{def}}{=} (\neg\varphi) \rightarrow \psi$$
$$\varphi \wedge \psi \overset{\text{def}}{=} \neg((\neg\varphi) \vee (\neg\psi))$$
$$\varphi \leftrightarrow \psi \overset{\text{def}}{=} (\varphi \rightarrow \psi) \wedge (\psi \rightarrow \varphi).$$

Note that by replacing left-hand sides with right-hand sides, we can systematically remove the operators $\leftrightarrow, \wedge, \vee, \mathbf{1}$, and $\neg$ and reduce every formula to a formula over $\rightarrow$ and $\mathbf{0}$ only.

Parentheses and Precedence

We parenthesize using the symbols ( ) where necessary to ensure unique readability. For example, if we just write

$$p \vee q \wedge r \tag{3.2.1}$$

it is not clear whether we intend

$$(p \vee q) \wedge r \qquad \text{or} \qquad p \vee (q \wedge r); \tag{3.2.2}$$

and these two expressions have very different meaning.

However, if we used parentheses everywhere, they would quickly get out of hand. We can avoid the proliferation of parentheses by assigning a *precedence* to the connectives, which tells which ones bind more tightly than others. The precedence is:

- the negation symbol $\neg$ has highest precedence (binds most tightly);
- the conjunction and disjunction symbols $\wedge$ and $\vee$ have next highest and equal precedence;

- the implication symbol $\rightarrow$ has next highest precedence; and
- the equivalence symbol $\leftrightarrow$ has lowest precedence.

For example, the expression

$$\neg\varphi \rightarrow \psi \quad \leftrightarrow \quad \neg\psi \rightarrow \varphi \qquad (3.2.3)$$

should be read

$$((\neg\varphi) \rightarrow \psi) \quad \leftrightarrow \quad ((\neg\psi) \rightarrow \varphi).$$

If we want (3.2.3) to be read another way, say

$$(\neg((\varphi \rightarrow \psi) \leftrightarrow \neg\psi)) \quad \rightarrow \quad \varphi,$$

then we have to use parentheses.

We associate symbols of equal precedence from left to right. Thus the expression (3.2.1) should be read as the left-hand expression in (3.2.2).

In the text, we often also use spacing to help with readability, as we have done in (3.2.3); but formally, spacing has no significance.

Metasymbols, or symbols that we use as abbreviations for English phrases in our discourse, always have lower precedence than symbols in the language under study. For example, the meta-expression

$$\vDash \psi \implies \vDash \varphi \rightarrow \psi$$

says, "if ψ is valid, then so is $\varphi \rightarrow \psi$," as if written

$$(\vDash \psi) \implies (\vDash (\varphi \rightarrow \psi))$$

with parentheses. The symbol $\rightarrow$, which is a propositional connective, has higher precedence than the metasymbols $\vDash$ and $\implies$. It is important to distinguished the propositional implication symbol $\rightarrow$ from the meta-implication symbol $\implies$. The distinction is necessary because we are *using* propositional logic even as we define it.

Semantics

The truth or falsity of a proposition depends on the truth or falsity of the atomic propositions appearing in it. For example, the proposition $p \wedge q$ (read: "p and q") is true iff both of the propositions p and q are true; and the proposition $\neg p$ (read: "not p") is true iff p is false.

There are two possible *truth values*, which we denote by **0** (false) and **1** (true).

We can think of the atomic propositions $p, q, r, \ldots$ as variables ranging over the set $\{\mathbf{0}, \mathbf{1}\}$. Any assignment of truth values to the atomic propositions appearing in a proposition φ automatically determines a truth value for φ inductively, as described formally below.

We define a *truth assignment* to be a map

$$u : \{p, q, r, \ldots\} \quad \rightarrow \quad \{\mathbf{0}, \mathbf{1}\}.$$

The value $u(p)$ is the *truth value* of the atomic proposition p under the truth assignment u. Any such map extends inductively to all propositions as follows:

$$u(\mathbf{0}) \quad \overset{\text{def}}{=} \quad \mathbf{0}$$

$$u(\varphi \rightarrow \psi) \quad \overset{\text{def}}{=} \quad \begin{cases} \mathbf{1}, & \text{if } u(\varphi) = \mathbf{0} \text{ or } u(\psi) = \mathbf{1} \\ \mathbf{0}, & \text{otherwise.} \end{cases}$$

It follows that

$$u(\varphi \wedge \psi) \quad = \quad \begin{cases} \mathbf{1}, & \text{if } u(\varphi) = u(\psi) = \mathbf{1} \\ \mathbf{0}, & \text{otherwise} \end{cases}$$

$$u(\varphi \vee \psi) \quad = \quad \begin{cases} \mathbf{1}, & \text{if } u(\varphi) = \mathbf{1} \text{ or } u(\psi) = \mathbf{1} \\ \mathbf{0}, & \text{otherwise} \end{cases}$$

$$u(\neg\varphi) \quad = \quad \begin{cases} \mathbf{0}, & \text{if } u(\varphi) = \mathbf{1} \\ \mathbf{1}, & \text{otherwise} \end{cases}$$

$$u(\mathbf{1}) \quad = \quad \mathbf{1}$$

$$u(\varphi \leftrightarrow \psi) \quad = \quad \begin{cases} \mathbf{1}, & \text{if } u(\varphi) = u(\psi) \\ \mathbf{0}, & \text{otherwise.} \end{cases}$$

We say that the truth assignment u *satisfies* φ if $u(\varphi) = \mathbf{1}$, and write $u \vDash \varphi$ and $u(\varphi) = \mathbf{1}$ interchangeably. If Φ is any set of propositions, finite or infinite, we say that u *satisfies* Φ and write $u \vDash \Phi$ if u satisfies all the propositions in Φ. A proposition or set of propositions is *satisfiable* if there is a truth assignment that satisfies it.

The formula φ is said to be *valid* if $u \vDash \varphi$ for all u. A valid formula is also called a *(propositional) tautology*. We write $\vDash \varphi$ to indicate that φ is a tautology. A tautology is a formula that is always true, no matter what the truth values of its atomic propositions are.

Observe that $\vDash \varphi$ iff $\neg\varphi$ is not satisfiable.

EXAMPLE 3.1:   The following are some examples of basic tautologies:

(i) $\varphi \lor \neg\varphi$

(ii) $\neg\neg\varphi \leftrightarrow \varphi$

(iii) $\psi \rightarrow (\varphi \rightarrow \psi)$

(iv) $\varphi \rightarrow \psi \leftrightarrow \neg\varphi \lor \psi$

(v) $\varphi \leftrightarrow \psi \leftrightarrow (\varphi \rightarrow \psi) \land (\psi \rightarrow \varphi)$

(vi) $\neg\varphi \land \neg\psi \leftrightarrow \neg(\varphi \lor \psi)$

(vii) $\varphi \land (\psi \lor \rho) \leftrightarrow (\varphi \land \psi) \lor (\varphi \land \rho)$

(viii) $\varphi \lor (\psi \land \rho) \leftrightarrow (\varphi \lor \psi) \land (\varphi \lor \rho)$

(ix) $\varphi \land \varphi \leftrightarrow \varphi$

(x) $\varphi \lor \varphi \leftrightarrow \varphi$

(xi) $\varphi \rightarrow \psi \leftrightarrow \neg\psi \rightarrow \neg\varphi$

(xii) $\neg\varphi \leftrightarrow \varphi \rightarrow \mathbf{0}$

(xiii) $\varphi \lor \psi \leftrightarrow \neg(\neg\varphi \land \neg\psi)$

(xiv) $\varphi \land \psi \leftrightarrow \neg(\neg\varphi \lor \neg\psi)$

(xv) $(\varphi \land \psi) \lor (\neg\varphi \land \rho) \leftrightarrow (\varphi \rightarrow \psi) \land (\neg\varphi \rightarrow \rho)$.

If φ and ψ take the same truth values on all truth assignments, we say that φ and ψ are *equivalent* and write $\varphi \equiv \psi$. Note that φ and ψ are equivalent iff $\varphi \leftrightarrow \psi$ is a tautology.

We have defined all the propositional connectives in terms of $\rightarrow$ and $\mathbf{0}$. This was by no means the only possible choice of a primitive set of connectives. For example, because of (iv), we could have defined $\rightarrow$ in terms of $\neg$ and $\lor$. A set of connectives is called *complete* if every formula is equivalent to a formula containing only those connectives. For example, the sets $\{\rightarrow, \mathbf{0}\}$, $\{\lor, \neg\}$, and $\{\land, \neg\}$ are all complete. We study some of these properties in the exercises (Exercises 3.2 and 3.3).

Although there are infinitely many propositional letters, it follows from the definition that $u(\varphi)$ depends only on $u(p)$ for p appearing in φ. This observation gives a decision procedure for satisfiability and validity:

THEOREM 3.2:   Given any φ, it is decidable whether φ is satisfiable.

Proof   Suppose φ contains propositional letters $p_1, \ldots, p_n$. For each possible truth assignment $u : \{p_1, \ldots, p_n\} \rightarrow \{\mathbf{0}, \mathbf{1}\}$, compute $u(\varphi)$ inductively according to the rules given above. Then φ is satisfiable iff $u(\varphi) = \mathbf{1}$ for at least one such u.   ∎

COROLLARY 3.3:   It is decidable whether φ is valid.

Proof Check whether $\neg\varphi$ is satisfiable. ■

The decision problem of Theorem 3.2 is the Boolean satisfiability problem discussed in Section 2.3. The decision procedure given in the proof of that theorem, naively implemented, takes exponential time in the size of φ, since there are 2^n possible truth assignments $u : \{p_1, \ldots, p_n\} \to \{\mathbf{0}, \mathbf{1}\}$. The question of whether there exists a polynomial-time algorithm is equivalent to the $P = NP$ problem (see Section 2.3).

Set-Theoretic Representation

Let S be a set. The propositional operators $\vee$, $\wedge$, $\neg$, $\mathbf{0}$, and $\mathbf{1}$ behave very much like certain set-theoretic operators on subsets of S, namely $\cup$ (union), $\cap$ (intersection), $\sim$ (complementation in S), $\varnothing$ (emptyset), and S, respectively. This correspondence is more than just coincidental. If we take S to be set of truth assignments $u : \{p, q, r, \ldots\} \to \{\mathbf{0}, \mathbf{1}\}$ and define

$$\varphi' \;=\; \{u \in S \mid u \vDash \varphi\}$$

then the map $'$, which takes propositions to subsets of S, is a *homomorphism* with respect to these operators:

THEOREM 3.4:

$$\begin{aligned}
(\varphi \wedge \psi)' &= \varphi' \cap \psi' \\
(\varphi \vee \psi)' &= \varphi' \cup \psi' \\
(\neg\varphi)' &= S - \varphi' \\
\mathbf{1}' &= S \\
\mathbf{0}' &= \varnothing.
\end{aligned}$$

Moreover,

$$\begin{aligned}
\vDash \varphi &\iff \varphi' = S \\
\varphi \text{ is satisfiable} &\iff \varphi' \neq \varnothing \\
\vDash \varphi \to \psi &\iff \varphi' \subseteq \psi' \\
\vDash \varphi \leftrightarrow \psi &\iff \varphi \equiv \psi \iff \varphi' = \psi'.
\end{aligned}$$

Proof Exercise 3.1. ■

A Deductive System

We will discuss two Hilbert-style deductive systems for propositional logic and prove their soundness and completeness. For the sake of simplicity, our first system will be rather meager. Later we will consider a richer system that includes all the propositional operators and that is much easier to work with in practice; but for the sake of proving completeness, we restrict our attention to formulas over $\to$ and $\mathbf{0}$ only. This assumption is without loss of generality, since the other operators are defined from these.

Our system consists of three axioms and a rule of inference.

AXIOM SYSTEM 3.5:

(S) $\qquad (\varphi \to (\psi \to \sigma)) \ \to \ ((\varphi \to \psi) \to (\varphi \to \sigma))$

(K) $\qquad \varphi \ \to \ (\psi \to \varphi)$

(DN) $\qquad ((\varphi \to \mathbf{0}) \to \mathbf{0}) \to \varphi$

(MP) $\qquad \dfrac{\varphi, \quad \varphi \to \psi}{\psi}.$

The axiom (DN) is called the *law of double negation*. Considering $\neg\varphi$ as an abbreviation for $\varphi \to \mathbf{0}$, this law takes the form $\neg\neg\varphi \to \varphi$. The rule of inference (MP) is called *modus ponens*.

The following are some sample derivations in this system.

EXAMPLE 3.6: Let us start off with something very simple: $\varphi \to \varphi$. Here is a proof. Let $Q \stackrel{\text{def}}{=} \varphi \to \varphi$.

(i) $\varphi \to (Q \to \varphi)$

(ii) $\varphi \to Q$

(iii) $(\varphi \to (Q \to \varphi)) \ \to \ ((\varphi \to Q) \to (\varphi \to \varphi))$

(iv) $(\varphi \to Q) \to (\varphi \to \varphi)$

(v) $\varphi \to \varphi$.

Statements (i) and (ii) are both instances of (K); (iii) is an instance of (S); (iv) follows from (i) and (iii) by modus ponens; and (v) follows from (ii) and (iv) by modus ponens.

EXAMPLE 3.7:   We prove the transitivity of implication:

$$(\psi \to \sigma) \quad \to \quad ((\varphi \to \psi) \to (\varphi \to \sigma)).$$ (3.2.4)

Let

$$P \stackrel{\text{def}}{=} \psi \to \sigma$$

$$Q \stackrel{\text{def}}{=} \varphi \to (\psi \to \sigma)$$

$$R \stackrel{\text{def}}{=} (\varphi \to \psi) \to (\varphi \to \sigma).$$

The theorem (3.2.4) we would like to prove is $P \to R$. Here is a proof.

(i) $P \to Q$

(ii) $Q \to R$

(iii) $(Q \to R) \to (P \to (Q \to R))$

(iv) $P \to (Q \to R)$

(v) $(P \to (Q \to R)) \to ((P \to Q) \to (P \to R))$

(vi) $(P \to Q) \to (P \to R)$

(vii) $P \to R$.

Statement (i) is an instance of (K); (ii) is an instance of (S); (iii) is an instance of (K); (iv) follows from (ii) and (iii) by modus ponens; (v) is an instance of (S); (vi) follows from (iv) and (v) by modus ponens; and (vii) follows from (i) and (vi) by modus ponens.

EXAMPLE 3.8:   We show that the statement

(EFQ) $\mathbf{0} \to \varphi$

is a theorem. The name EFQ stands for *e falso quodlibet* ("from falsity, anything you like"). Let us abbreviate $\varphi \to \mathbf{0}$ by $\neg\varphi$. Here is a proof of (EFQ):

(i) $\mathbf{0} \to \neg\neg\varphi$

(ii) $\neg\neg\varphi \to \varphi$

(iii) $(\neg\neg\varphi \to \varphi) \to ((\mathbf{0} \to \neg\neg\varphi) \to (\mathbf{0} \to \varphi))$

(iv) $(\mathbf{0} \to \neg\neg\varphi) \to (\mathbf{0} \to \varphi)$

(v) $\mathbf{0} \to \varphi$.

Statement (i) is an instance of (K), since it is really $\mathbf{0} \to (\neg\varphi \to \mathbf{0})$; (ii) is just (DN); (iii) is an instance of the theorem proved in Example 3.7; (iv) follows from

(ii) and (iii) by modus ponens; and (v) follows from (i) and (iv) by modus ponens.

If we omit the axiom (DN) and take (K), (S), and (EFQ) as axioms along with the rule (MP), we get a weaker system called *intuitionistic propositional logic*. The propositional tautology (DN) is not provable in this system; see Exercise 3.5.

The Deduction Theorem

Here is a useful theorem about this system that has to do with reasoning in the presence of assumptions. It says that if the proposition ψ can be derived in the presence of an extra assumption φ, then the proposition $\varphi \to \psi$ can be derived without any assumptions; that is, the assumption φ can be coded into the theorem itself.

THEOREM 3.9 (DEDUCTION THEOREM):   Let Φ be a finite or infinite set of propositions. Then

$$\Phi \cup \{\varphi\} \vdash \psi \quad \Longleftrightarrow \quad \Phi \vdash \varphi \to \psi.$$

Proof First suppose $\Phi \vdash \varphi \to \psi$. Certainly $\Phi \cup \{\varphi\} \vdash \varphi \to \psi$. Also $\Phi \cup \{\varphi\} \vdash \varphi$ by a one-line proof. Therefore $\Phi \cup \{\varphi\} \vdash \psi$ by modus ponens. This was the easy direction.

Conversely, suppose $\Phi \cup \{\varphi\} \vdash \psi$. We proceed by induction on the length of proofs to show that $\Phi \vdash \varphi \to \psi$. Consider the last step in a proof of ψ under the assumptions $\Phi \cup \{\varphi\}$. If $\psi \in \Phi$, then $\Phi \vdash \psi$, and $\Phi \vdash \psi \to (\varphi \to \psi)$ by (K), therefore $\Phi \vdash \varphi \to \psi$ by modus ponens. If $\psi = \varphi$, then $\Phi \vdash \varphi \to \varphi$ by the theorem proved in Example 3.6. Finally, if ψ is the conclusion of an application of modus ponens, then there is a σ such that $\Phi \cup \{\varphi\} \vdash \sigma \to \psi$ and $\Phi \cup \{\varphi\} \vdash \sigma$ by shorter proofs. By the induction hypothesis, $\Phi \vdash \varphi \to (\sigma \to \psi)$ and $\Phi \vdash \varphi \to \sigma$. By (S),

$$\Phi \vdash (\varphi \to (\sigma \to \psi)) \quad \to \quad ((\varphi \to \sigma) \to (\varphi \to \psi));$$

then by two applications of modus ponens, $\Phi \vdash \varphi \to \psi$. ∎

Completeness

In this section we prove the completeness of Axiom System 3.5. First, we observe that the system is sound, since the axioms (K), (S), and (DN) are tautologies and the rule (MP) preserves validity; therefore by induction, every formula φ such that $\vdash \varphi$ is a tautology. The more interesting part is the converse: every tautology has a proof in this system.

First we prove a preliminary lemma whose proof contains most of the work. We will also find this lemma useful later on when we study compactness. Recall from Section 3.1 that a finite or infinite set Φ of formulas is *refutable* if $\neg\varphi$ is a theorem, where φ is some finite conjunction of elements of Φ. In light of Theorem 3.9, this is equivalent to saying that $\Phi \vdash \mathbf{0}$. The set Φ is *consistent* if it is not refutable.

LEMMA 3.10:   If Φ is consistent, then it is satisfiable.

Proof   Suppose Φ is consistent. Then Φ is contained in a setwise maximal consistent set $\widehat{\Phi}$; that is, a consistent set such that $\Phi \subseteq \widehat{\Phi}$ and any proper superset of $\widehat{\Phi}$ is refutable. Such a set $\widehat{\Phi}$ can be obtained as follows. Line up all the propositions $\varphi_0, \varphi_1, \varphi_2, \ldots$ in some order. Set $\Phi_0 \stackrel{\text{def}}{=} \Phi$. For each φ_i, set

$$\Phi_{i+1} \stackrel{\text{def}}{=} \begin{cases} \Phi_i \cup \{\varphi_i\}, & \text{if } \Phi_i \cup \{\varphi_i\} \text{ is consistent,} \\ \Phi_i, & \text{otherwise.} \end{cases}$$

Let $\widehat{\Phi} \stackrel{\text{def}}{=} \bigcup_i \Phi_i$. The set $\widehat{\Phi}$ is consistent, since each Φ_i is consistent and only finitely many formulas can be used in a refutation; and it is maximal, since each φ_i was included unless it was inconsistent with formulas already taken.

We now claim that for each φ, exactly one of the following holds: $\varphi \in \widehat{\Phi}$ or $\varphi \to \mathbf{0} \in \widehat{\Phi}$. Certainly not both are true, because then we would have $\widehat{\Phi} \vdash \mathbf{0}$ by (MP), contradicting the fact that $\widehat{\Phi}$ is consistent. But if neither is true, then $\widehat{\Phi} \cup \{\varphi\}$ and $\widehat{\Phi} \cup \{\varphi \to \mathbf{0}\}$ must both be inconsistent; thus $\widehat{\Phi} \cup \{\varphi\} \vdash \mathbf{0}$ and $\widehat{\Phi} \cup \{\varphi \to \mathbf{0}\} \vdash \mathbf{0}$. By the deduction theorem (Theorem 3.9), $\widehat{\Phi} \vdash \varphi \to \mathbf{0}$ and $\widehat{\Phi} \vdash (\varphi \to \mathbf{0}) \to \mathbf{0}$; therefore by (MP), $\widehat{\Phi} \vdash \mathbf{0}$, a contradiction. It follows that $\widehat{\Phi}$ is *deductively closed* in the sense that if $\widehat{\Phi} \vdash \varphi$, then $\varphi \in \widehat{\Phi}$.

Now we construct a truth assignment satisfying $\widehat{\Phi}$. Set

$$u(\varphi) \stackrel{\text{def}}{=} \begin{cases} \mathbf{1}, & \text{if } \varphi \in \widehat{\Phi}, \\ \mathbf{0}, & \text{if } \varphi \notin \widehat{\Phi}. \end{cases}$$

This certainly satisfies $\widehat{\Phi}$; we only have to show that it is a legal truth assignment. According to the definition, we need to show

$$u(\varphi \to \psi) = \mathbf{1} \iff u(\varphi) = \mathbf{0} \text{ or } u(\psi) = \mathbf{1},$$

or in other words,

$$\varphi \to \psi \in \widehat{\Phi} \iff \varphi \notin \widehat{\Phi} \text{ or } \psi \in \widehat{\Phi}.$$

Suppose first that $\varphi \to \psi \in \widehat{\Phi}$. If $\varphi \notin \widehat{\Phi}$, we are done. Otherwise $\varphi \in \widehat{\Phi}$, in which case $\psi \in \widehat{\Phi}$ by modus ponens.

Conversely, if $\psi \in \widehat{\Phi}$, then $\varphi \to \psi \in \widehat{\Phi}$ by (K) and modus ponens. If $\varphi \notin \widehat{\Phi}$, then $\varphi \to \mathbf{0} \in \widehat{\Phi}$. Then by (EFQ) and transitivity of implication (Examples 3.8 and 3.7 respectively), $\varphi \to \psi \in \widehat{\Phi}$.

Also, $u(\mathbf{0}) = \mathbf{0}$ because $\mathbf{0} \notin \widehat{\Phi}$; otherwise $\widehat{\Phi}$ would be trivially inconsistent.   ■

THEOREM 3.11 (COMPLETENESS):   If $\Phi \vDash \varphi$ then $\Phi \vdash \varphi$.

Proof

$$\Phi \vDash \varphi \quad \Longrightarrow \quad \Phi \cup \{\varphi \to \mathbf{0}\} \text{ is unsatisfiable}$$
$$\Longrightarrow \quad \Phi \cup \{\varphi \to \mathbf{0}\} \text{ is refutable} \qquad \text{by Lemma 3.10}$$
$$\Longrightarrow \quad \Phi \vdash (\varphi \to \mathbf{0}) \to \mathbf{0} \qquad \text{by the Deduction Theorem}$$
$$\Longrightarrow \quad \Phi \vdash \varphi \qquad\qquad\qquad \text{by (DN).}$$

■

Compactness

Let Φ be a set of propositions, finite or infinite. Recall that a set Φ is *satisfiable* if there is a truth assignment u such that $u \vDash \varphi$ for every $\varphi \in \Phi$. Let us say that Φ is *finitely satisfiable* if every finite subset of Φ is satisfiable.

THEOREM 3.12 (COMPACTNESS OF PROPOSITIONAL LOGIC):   Let Φ be any set of propositions. Then Φ is finitely satisfiable iff it is satisfiable.

Proof   Trivially, any satisfiable set is finitely satisfiable. The interesting direction is that finite satisfiability implies satisfiability.

Suppose Φ is finitely satisfiable. By the soundness of the system 3.5, every finite subset of Φ is consistent. Since refutations can only use finitely many formulas, the set Φ itself is consistent. By Lemma 3.10, Φ is satisfiable.   ■

Compactness has many applications. For example, one can show using compactness that an infinite graph is k-colorable iff every finite subgraph is k-colorable.

The term *compactness* is from topology. Let S be the topological space whose points are the truth assignments $u : \{p, q, r, \dots\} \to \{\mathbf{1}, \mathbf{0}\}$ and whose basic open sets are the sets $\{\varphi' \mid \varphi \text{ is a proposition}\}$. A family of sets has the *finite intersection property* if every finite subfamily has a nonempty intersection. A topological space is *compact* if every family Δ of closed sets with the finite intersection property has a nonempty intersection $\bigcap \Delta$. Theorem 3.12 asserts exactly that the topological space S is compact.

An Equational System

Here is another complete deductive system for propositional logic. Whereas Axiom System 3.5 is as austere as possible, this system errs in the opposite direction. No attempt has been made to reduce it to the minimum possible number of costructs. It is thus much richer and more suitable for reasoning.

The system is an equational-style system for deriving theorems of the form $\varphi \leftrightarrow \psi$. Recall that $\varphi \equiv \psi$ iff $\vDash \varphi \leftrightarrow \psi$. The relation $\equiv$ is an equivalence relation on formulas. Later on in Section 3.3 we will give a general introduction to equational logic. In that section, the system we are about to present would be called *Boolean algebra* (see Exercise 3.8).

Let φ be a proposition containing only the propositional letters $p_1, \ldots, p_n$. Let S be the set of all 2^n truth assignments to $p_1, \ldots, p_n$. As observed in Section 3.2, $\vDash \varphi$ iff $\varphi' = S$, where

$$\varphi' = \{u \in S \mid u \vDash \varphi\}.$$

Define a *literal* of $\{p_1, \ldots, p_n\}$ to be a propositional letter p_i or its negation $\neg p_i$. There is a one-to-one correspondence between truth assignments u and conjunctions of literals

$$q_1 \wedge q_2 \wedge \cdots \wedge q_n,$$

where each q_i is either p_i or $\neg p_i$. Such a formula is called an *atom* of $\{p_1, \ldots, p_n\}$. For each truth assignment u there is exactly one atom satisfied by u, and each atom is satisfied by exactly one truth assignment. For example, the atom

$$p_1 \wedge p_2 \wedge \neg p_3$$

of $\{p_1, p_2, p_3\}$ corresponds to the truth assignment $u(p_1) = u(p_2) = \mathbf{1}$, $u(p_3) = \mathbf{0}$.

If $\alpha_1, \ldots, \alpha_k$ are atoms, then the disjunction

$$\alpha_1 \vee \alpha_2 \vee \cdots \vee \alpha_k$$

is satisfied by exactly those truth assignments corresponding to the atoms $\alpha_1, \ldots, \alpha_k$. It follows that every subset of S is φ' for some φ. If $\vDash \varphi$, then $\varphi' = S$, in which case φ is equivalent to the disjunction of all 2^n possible atoms.

Our deductive system is a Hilbert-style system of equational axioms and rules.

It can be used to show that any formula φ is equivalent to another formula of a special form, called complete disjunctive normal form. A formula is in *complete disjunctive normal form* if it is a disjunction of atoms of $\{p_1, \ldots, p_n\}$ in which each atom occurs at most once. The complete disjunctive normal form consisting of no atoms is **0**.

AXIOM SYSTEM 3.13:

(i) **1**

(ii) De Morgan laws:

$$\neg(\varphi \wedge \psi) \quad \leftrightarrow \quad \neg\varphi \vee \neg\psi$$
$$\neg(\varphi \vee \psi) \quad \leftrightarrow \quad \neg\varphi \wedge \neg\psi$$

(iii) Law of double negation:

$$\neg\neg\varphi \quad \leftrightarrow \quad \varphi$$

(iv) Associative laws:

$$(\varphi \wedge \psi) \wedge \rho \quad \leftrightarrow \quad \varphi \wedge (\psi \wedge \rho)$$
$$(\varphi \vee \psi) \vee \rho \quad \leftrightarrow \quad \varphi \vee (\psi \vee \rho)$$

(v) Commutative laws:

$$\varphi \vee \psi \quad \leftrightarrow \quad \psi \vee \varphi$$
$$\varphi \wedge \psi \quad \leftrightarrow \quad \psi \wedge \varphi$$

(vi) Distributive laws:

$$\varphi \vee (\psi \wedge \rho) \quad \leftrightarrow \quad (\varphi \vee \psi) \wedge (\varphi \vee \rho)$$
$$\varphi \wedge (\psi \vee \rho) \quad \leftrightarrow \quad (\varphi \wedge \psi) \vee (\varphi \wedge \rho)$$

(vii) Idempotency laws:

$$\varphi \vee \varphi \quad \leftrightarrow \quad \varphi$$
$$\varphi \wedge \varphi \quad \leftrightarrow \quad \varphi$$

(viii) Zero-one laws:

$$\varphi \wedge \mathbf{0} \;\leftrightarrow\; \mathbf{0}$$
$$\varphi \vee \mathbf{0} \;\leftrightarrow\; \varphi$$
$$\varphi \vee \neg\varphi \;\leftrightarrow\; \mathbf{1}$$
$$\varphi \wedge \mathbf{1} \;\leftrightarrow\; \varphi$$
$$\varphi \vee \mathbf{1} \;\leftrightarrow\; \mathbf{1}$$
$$\varphi \wedge \neg\varphi \;\leftrightarrow\; \mathbf{0}$$

(ix) Elimination of implications:

$$(\varphi \rightarrow \psi) \;\leftrightarrow\; \neg\varphi \vee \psi$$
$$(\varphi \leftrightarrow \psi) \;\leftrightarrow\; (\varphi \wedge \psi) \vee (\neg\varphi \wedge \neg\psi)$$

(x) Substitution of equals for equals:

$$\frac{\varphi \leftrightarrow \psi, \quad \sigma[p/\varphi]}{\sigma[p/\psi]}$$

where $\sigma[p/\varphi]$ denotes a formula σ with the proposition φ substituted for all occurrences of the atomic proposition p.

The substitution rule (x) says that if we have established the equivalence of two expressions φ and ψ, and we have proved a theorem containing φ as a subexpression, then we may substitute ψ for φ in that theorem and the resulting formula will be a theorem.

THEOREM 3.14:   Axiom System 3.13 is sound.

Proof We need to show that every theorem derivable in the system is valid. Using induction on the lengths of proofs, it suffices to show that all the axioms are valid and the rule of inference preserves validity.

The validity of the axioms can be established by reasoning set theoretically with φ'. For example, for (v), we need to show

$$\models \varphi \vee \psi \;\leftrightarrow\; \psi \vee \varphi.$$

But this is true since

$$(\varphi \vee \psi)' \;=\; (\psi \vee \varphi)' \;=\; \varphi' \cup \psi'$$

and $\cup$ is commutative. Axiom (i) is valid since $\mathbf{1}' = S$. We leave the verification of the remaining axioms as exercises (Exercise 3.6).

In order to establish the soundness of the substitution rule (x), we observe first that if $\varphi \leftrightarrow \psi$ is a tautology then so is $\sigma[p/\varphi] \leftrightarrow \sigma[p/\psi]$. In other words, if $\varphi \equiv \psi$, then $\sigma[p/\varphi] \equiv \sigma[p/\psi]$. This can be proved by induction on the depth of σ. If $\sigma = p$, then the substitution gives $\varphi \equiv \psi$, which is true by assumption. If $\sigma = q \neq p$, then the substitution gives $q \equiv q$.

For the induction step, we need only observe that if $\sigma_1 \equiv \sigma_2$ and $\tau_1 \equiv \tau_2$, then $\sigma_1 \rightarrow \tau_1 \equiv \sigma_2 \rightarrow \tau_2$, and similarly for the other operators.

Now if $\vDash \varphi \leftrightarrow \psi$, then $\vDash \sigma[p/\varphi] \leftrightarrow \sigma[p/\psi]$, as we have just shown. If in addition $\vDash \sigma[p/\varphi]$, then $\vDash \sigma[p/\psi]$. Thus if both premises of the inference rule (x) are valid, then so is the conclusion. Since every axiom is valid and the rule of inference preserves validity, any theorem derivable in this system is valid. ■

THEOREM 3.15:   Axiom System 3.13 is complete.

Proof sketch.   Intuitively, our axioms and inference rule allow us to transform any proposition φ into an equivalent join of atoms of $p_1, \dots, p_n$, the propositional letters occurring in φ. If φ is valid, then this join of atoms must contain all 2^n possible atoms, in which case the formula can be further transformed to $\mathbf{1}$.

In the following, we use axioms (iv) and (v) implicitly to rearrange parentheses and formulas in conjunctions and disjunctions. Thus we may write $\varphi_1 \vee \varphi_2 \vee \cdots \vee \varphi_k$ without parentheses and without regard to the order of the φ_i.

Starting with φ, first apply the axioms (ix) in the left-to-right direction to replace any subexpression of the form $\varphi \rightarrow \psi$ with $\neg\varphi \vee \psi$ and any subexpression of the form $\varphi \leftrightarrow \psi$ with $(\varphi \wedge \psi) \vee (\neg\varphi \wedge \neg\psi)$ until the resulting term has no occurrence of $\rightarrow$ or $\leftrightarrow$. Now apply the De Morgan laws (ii) in the left-to-right direction to move all occurrences of $\neg$ inward. Whenever a subexpression of the form $\neg\neg\varphi$ occurs, replace it by φ using (iii). Keep doing this until all occurrences of $\neg$ are applied only to atomic p. Use the second distributive law (vi) in the left-to-right direction to move occurrences of $\vee$ outward and occurrences of $\wedge$ inward until obtaining *disjunctive normal form*: a disjunction of conjunctions of literals p or $\neg p$.

If some p occurs twice in one of the conjunctions, use (vii) to get rid of the double occurrence. If p and $\neg p$ both occur, use (viii) in the left-to-right direction. If neither p nor $\neg p$ occurs in a conjunction ψ, use (viii) and then (vi) to replace ψ with $(\psi \wedge p) \vee (\psi \wedge \neg p)$. The result is a disjunction of atoms of $p_1, \dots, p_n$. Since φ was valid and the transformations preserve validity (Theorem 3.14), the resulting formula is valid; thus all 2^n atoms must appear in the disjunction, since otherwise the truth assignment corresponding to an omitted atom would falsify the formula.

Now we use the rules in the opposite direction to reduce the formula to **1**. Note that each atom of $p_1, \ldots, p_n$ is of the form $\psi \wedge p_n$ or $\psi \wedge \neg p_n$, where ψ is an atom of $p_1, \ldots, p_{n-1}$. Moreover, since all 2^n atoms of $p_1, \ldots, p_n$ occur in the disjunction, both $\psi \wedge p_n$ and $\psi \wedge \neg p_n$ occur for each of the 2^{n-1} atoms ψ of $p_1, \ldots, p_{n-1}$. For each such ψ, apply the second distributive law (vi) in the right-to-left direction to $(\psi \wedge p_n) \vee (\psi \wedge \neg p_n)$ to obtain $\psi \wedge (p \vee \neg p)$, then (viii) to obtain $\psi \wedge \mathbf{1}$, then (viii) again to obtain ψ. We are left with the disjunction of all 2^{n-1} atoms of $p_1, \ldots, p_{n-1}$. Continue in this fashion until we are left with **1**.   ∎

3.3   Equational Logic

Equational logic is a formalization of equational reasoning. The properties of pure equality are captured in the axioms for equivalence relations: *reflexivity, symmetry,* and *transitivity* (see Section 1.3). In the presence of function symbols, a fourth rule of *congruence* is added.

The language of equational logic is a sublanguage of first order logic, so it makes sense to treat this special case before moving on to full first-order logic in Section 3.4.

Syntax

A *signature* or *vocabulary* consists of a set Σ of *function symbols*, each with an associated *arity* (number of input places). There is only one relation symbol, the *equality symbol* =, and it is of arity 2.[1] Function symbols of arity 0, 1, 2, 3, and n are called *nullary, unary, binary, ternary,* and *n-ary*, respectively. Nullary symbols are often called *constants*.

EXAMPLE 3.16:   The signature for groups consists of function symbols $\cdot$, $^{-1}$, and 1, where $\cdot$ is a binary symbol for multiplication, $^{-1}$ is a unary symbol for multiplicative inverse, and 1 is a nullary (constant) symbol for the multiplicative identity.

EXAMPLE 3.17:   The signature of Boolean algebra consists of the function symbols $\wedge, \vee, \neg, \mathbf{0}, \mathbf{1}$ with arities $2, 2, 1, 0, 0$ respectively.

---

1 When we discuss first-order logic in Section 3.4, the signature may also include other relation symbols of various arities.

We will work with an arbitrary but fixed signature Σ of function symbols. We use the symbols $f, g, h, \ldots$ to denote typical elements of Σ and $a, b, c, \ldots$ to denote typical constants in Σ. So that we do not have to keep writing " $\ldots$ where f is n-ary," we will adopt the convention that any use of the expression $f(t_1, \ldots, t_n)$ carries with it the implicit proviso that the symbol f is of arity n.

The language of equational logic is built from the symbols of Σ, the binary equality symbol $=$, a countable set X of *individual variables* $x, y, \ldots$, and parentheses.

A *term* is a well formed expression built from the function symbols and variables. By "well formed," we mean that it respects the arities of all the symbols, where variables are considered to have arity 0. Terms are denoted $s, t, \ldots$. Formally, terms are defined inductively:

- any variable x is a term;
- if $t_1, \ldots, t_n$ are terms and f is n-ary, then $f(t_1, \ldots, t_n)$ is a term.

Note that every constant symbol c is a term: this is the case $n = 0$ in the second clause above. The following is a typical term, where f is binary, g is unary, c is a constant, and x, y are variables:

$$f(f(x, g(c)), g(f(y, c))).$$

The set of all terms over Σ and X is denoted $T_\Sigma(X)$. A term is called a *ground term* if it contains no variables. The set of ground terms over Σ is denoted T_Σ. We sometimes write $t(x_1, \ldots, x_n)$ to indicate that all variables occurring in t are among $x_1, \ldots, x_n$. (It is not necessary that all of $x_1, \ldots, x_n$ appear in t.)

EXAMPLE 3.18: Terms over the signature of Boolean algebra described in Example 3.17 are exactly the propositional formulas over $\wedge$, $\vee$, $\neg$, $\mathbf{0}$, and $\mathbf{1}$ as described in Section 3.2. The propositional letters are the variables.

Over an abstract signature Σ, we always write terms in *prefix notation*, which means function symbol first: $f(t_1, \ldots, t_n)$. In various applications, however, we often use infix or postfix notation for certain operators as dictated by custom. For example, the binary Boolean operators $\vee$ and $\wedge$ are written in infix: $s \vee t$, $s \wedge t$. The unary Boolean operator $\neg$ is customarily written in prefix as $\neg t$, whereas the unary group inverse operator $^{-1}$ is customarily written in postfix as t^{-1}.

An *equation* is a formal expression $s = t$ consisting of two terms separated by the equality symbol $=$. A *Horn formula* is a formal expression of the form

$$s_1 = t_1 \wedge \cdots \wedge s_k = t_k \quad \rightarrow \quad s = t, \tag{3.3.1}$$

where the $s_i = t_i$ and $s = t$ are equations. When $k = 0$, the Horn formula (3.3.1) is equivalent to the equation $s = t$.

Semantics

Σ-algebras

Terms and equations over an alphabet Σ take on meaning when interpreted over an algebraic structure called a Σ-*algebra* (or just an *algebra* when Σ is understood). This is a structure

$$\mathfrak{A} \;=\; (A, \, \mathfrak{m}_{\mathfrak{A}})$$

consisting of

- a nonempty set A called the *carrier* or *domain* of $\mathfrak{A}$, the elements of which are called *individuals*;
- a *meaning function* $\mathfrak{m}_{\mathfrak{A}}$ that assigns an n-ary function $\mathfrak{m}_{\mathfrak{A}}(f) : A^n \rightarrow A$ to each n-ary function symbol $f \in \Sigma$. We abbreviate $\mathfrak{m}_{\mathfrak{A}}(f)$ by $f^{\mathfrak{A}}$.

We regard 0-ary functions $A^0 \rightarrow A$ as just elements of A. Thus the constant symbol $c \in \Sigma$ is interpreted as an element $c^{\mathfrak{A}} \in A$. The carrier of $\mathfrak{A}$ is sometimes denoted $|\mathfrak{A}|$.

When we discuss the syntax of first-order logic in Section 3.4, the signature will include relation symbols p of various arities, and the meaning function $\mathfrak{m}_{\mathfrak{A}}$ will assign relations $\mathfrak{m}_{\mathfrak{A}}(p) = p^{\mathfrak{A}}$ on A to those symbols as well. In equational logic, however, there is only one (binary) relation symbol $=$, and unless we say otherwise, its interpretation $=^{\mathfrak{A}}$ in $\mathfrak{A}$ is always assumed to be the binary *identity relation*

$$\{(a,a) \mid a \in A\}.$$

As is customary, we omit the superscript $\mathfrak{A}$ from $=^{\mathfrak{A}}$ and denote by $=$ both the equality symbol itself and its meaning as the identity relation on A. To complicate matters further, we also use $=$ as our metasymbol for equality. The proper interpretation should be clear from context.

EXAMPLE 3.19:   The signature of Boolean algebra was described in Example 3.17. Let K be a set, and let 2^K denote the powerset of K. We define an algebra $\mathfrak{B}$ for this signature consisting of carrier 2^K, $\vee^{\mathfrak{B}}$ the operation of set union, $\wedge^{\mathfrak{B}}$ the operation of set intersection, $\neg^{\mathfrak{B}}$ the operation of set complementation in K, $\mathbf{0}^{\mathfrak{B}}$ the empty set, and $\mathbf{1}^{\mathfrak{B}}$ the set K. The algebra of sets of truth assignments described in Section 3.2 is an example of such a Boolean algebra.

EXAMPLE 3.20:   For any signature Σ, the set of terms $T_\Sigma(X)$ forms a Σ-algebra, where each $f \in \Sigma$ is given the *syntactic interpretation*

$$f^{T_\Sigma(X)}(t_1, \ldots, t_n) \;\; = \;\; f(t_1, \ldots, t_n).$$

There is no meaning associated with the f appearing on the right-hand side; it is merely a symbol, and the expression $f(t_1, \ldots, t_n)$ is merely a term—a syntactic object. The $f^{T_\Sigma(X)}$ on the left-hand side, however, is a semantic object; it is the function $f^{T_\Sigma(X)} : T_\Sigma(X)^n \to T_\Sigma(X)$ which on input $t_1, \ldots, t_n$ gives the term $f(t_1, \ldots, t_n)$ as result.

The algebra $T_\Sigma(X)$ is called a *term algebra*.

Subalgebras and Generating Sets

Let $\mathfrak{A}$ and $\mathfrak{B}$ be two Σ-algebras with carriers A and B, respectively. The algebra $\mathfrak{A}$ is a *subalgebra* of $\mathfrak{B}$ if $A \subseteq B$ and $f^{\mathfrak{A}} = f^{\mathfrak{B}} \restriction A^n$ for all n-ary $f \in \Sigma$.

If $C \subseteq B$, the *subalgebra of $\mathfrak{B}$ generated by C* is the smallest subalgebra of $\mathfrak{B}$ containing C. Its domain is the smallest subset of B containing C and the constants $c^{\mathfrak{B}}$ and closed under the action of the functions $f^{\mathfrak{B}}$, as described in Section 1.7.

The set C is called a *generating set* of $\mathfrak{B}$, and is said to *generate* $\mathfrak{B}$, if the subalgebra of $\mathfrak{B}$ generated by C is $\mathfrak{B}$ itself. For example, X generates the term algebra $T_\Sigma(X)$.

Homomorphisms

Homomorphisms are structure-preserving functions between Σ-algebras. Formally, if $\mathfrak{A} = (A, \mathfrak{m}_{\mathfrak{A}})$ and $\mathfrak{B} = (B, \mathfrak{m}_{\mathfrak{B}})$ are Σ-algebras, a *homomorphism* $h : \mathfrak{A} \to \mathfrak{B}$ is a function $h : A \to B$ that commutes with the distinguished functions in the sense that for any $a_1, \ldots, a_n \in A$ and $f \in \Sigma$,

$$h(f^{\mathfrak{A}}(a_1, \ldots, a_n)) \;\; = \;\; f^{\mathfrak{B}}(h(a_1), \ldots, h(a_n)). \tag{3.3.2}$$

This includes the case $n = 0$ (constants), for which (3.3.2) reduces to

$$h(c^{\mathfrak{A}}) \;\; = \;\; c^{\mathfrak{B}}.$$

A homomorphism is called a *monomorphism* if it is one-to-one, an *epimorphism* if it is onto, and an *isomorphism* if it is both. An algebra $\mathfrak{B}$ is a *homomorphic image* of $\mathfrak{A}$ if there is an epimorphism $h : \mathfrak{A} \to \mathfrak{B}$.

The identity map $\mathfrak{A} \to \mathfrak{A}$ is an isomorphism, and if $g : \mathfrak{A} \to \mathfrak{B}$ and $h : \mathfrak{B} \to \mathfrak{C}$ are homomorphisms, then so is $g \circ h : \mathfrak{A} \to \mathfrak{C}$. Because of (3.3.2), any homomorphism is uniquely determined by its action on a generating set.

The *kernel* of a homomorphism $h : \mathfrak{A} \to \mathfrak{B}$ is the relation

$$\ker h \;\stackrel{\text{def}}{=}\; \{(a, b) \mid h(a) = h(b)\} \tag{3.3.3}$$

on $\mathfrak{A}$.

Valuations and Substitutions

A homomorphism $u : T_\Sigma(X) \to \mathfrak{A}$ defined on a term algebra over variables X is called a *valuation*. A valuation is uniquely determined by its values on X, since X generates $T_\Sigma(X)$. Moreover, any map $u : X \to \mathfrak{A}$ extends uniquely to a valuation $u : T_\Sigma(X) \to \mathfrak{A}$ by induction using (3.3.2).

Note that in the case $n = 0$, we have $u(c) = c^{\mathfrak{A}}$. Note also that the value of $u(t)$ depends only on the values $u(x)$ for those x appearing in t. In particular, a ground term t always has a fixed value in $\mathfrak{A}$, independent of the valuation u. Thus in the case of ground terms t, we can write $t^{\mathfrak{A}}$ for $u(t)$.

A homomorphism $u : T_\Sigma(X) \to T_\Sigma(Y)$ from one term algebra to another is called a *substitution*. We can think of these maps as substitutions in the usual sense: the value of the substitution u applied to a term $t \in T_\Sigma(X)$ is the term in $T_\Sigma(Y)$ obtained by substituting the term $u(x)$ for all occurrences of x in t simultaneously for all $x \in X$:

$$u(t) \;=\; t[x/u(x) \mid x \in X].$$

If $u : T_\Sigma(X) \to T_\Sigma(Y)$ is a substitution and $s, t \in T_\Sigma(X)$, then the term $u(s)$ and the equation $u(s) = u(t)$ are called *substitution instances* over $T_\Sigma(Y)$ of s and $s = t$, respectively.

Satisfaction

We say that the Σ-algebra $\mathfrak{A}$ *satisfies* the equation $s = t$ under valuation $u : T_\Sigma(X) \to \mathfrak{A}$, and write $\mathfrak{A}, u \vDash s = t$, if $u(s) = u(t)$; that is, if $u(s)$ and $u(t)$ are the same element of A. More generally, we say that the Σ-algebra $\mathfrak{A}$ *satisfies* the Horn formula

$$s_1 = t_1 \wedge \cdots \wedge s_k = t_k \quad \rightarrow \quad s = t$$

under valuation $u : T_\Sigma(X) \rightarrow \mathfrak{A}$, and write

$$\mathfrak{A}, u \ \vDash \ s_1 = t_1 \wedge \cdots \wedge s_k = t_k \rightarrow s = t,$$

if either

- $u(s_i) \neq u(t_i)$ for some i, $1 \leq i \leq k$; or
- $u(s) = u(t)$.

If φ is an equation or a Horn formula, we write $\mathfrak{A} \vDash \varphi$ if $\mathfrak{A}, u \vDash \varphi$ for all valuations u and say that φ is *valid* in $\mathfrak{A}$, or that $\mathfrak{A}$ *satisfies* φ, or that $\mathfrak{A}$ is a *model* of φ.[2] If Φ is a set of equations or Horn formulas, we write $\mathfrak{A} \vDash \Phi$ if $\mathfrak{A}$ satisfies all elements of Φ and say that $\mathfrak{A}$ *satisfies* Φ, or that $\mathfrak{A}$ is a *model* of Φ. We denote by **Mod** Φ the class of all models of Φ.

Let **Th** $\mathfrak{A}$ denote the set of equations over X that are valid in $\mathfrak{A}$:

$$\mathbf{Th}\,\mathfrak{A} \ \overset{\text{def}}{=} \ \{s = t \mid \mathfrak{A} \vDash s = t\}.$$

If $\mathcal{D}$ is a class of Σ-algebras, let **Th** $\mathcal{D}$ denote the set of equations valid in all elements of $\mathcal{D}$:

$$\mathbf{Th}\,\mathcal{D} \ \overset{\text{def}}{=} \ \bigcap_{\mathfrak{A} \in \mathcal{D}} \mathbf{Th}\,\mathfrak{A}.$$

The set **Th** $\mathcal{D}$ is called the *equational theory* of $\mathcal{D}$. An equation $s = t$ is called a *logical consequence* of Φ if $s = t$ is satisfied by all models of Φ; that is, if $s = t \in \mathbf{Th}\,\mathbf{Mod}\,\Phi$.

EXAMPLE 3.21: Any group satisfies the following equations:

$$
\begin{aligned}
x \cdot (y \cdot z) &= (x \cdot y) \cdot z \\
x^{-1} \cdot x &= 1 \\
x \cdot x^{-1} &= 1 \\
x \cdot 1 &= x \\
1 \cdot x &= x.
\end{aligned}
\tag{3.3.4}
$$

---

2 Thus we think of the variables in φ as *universally quantified*. This terminology will make sense after we have introduced the universal quantifier $\forall$ in Section 3.4.

In fact, a group is *defined* to be any algebra over the signature of groups that satisfies these five equations. A group is *Abelian* or *commutative* if it satisfies the extra equation $x \cdot y = y \cdot x$.

The equational theory of groups is the set of equations that are true in all groups. This is the set of logical consequences of the axioms (3.3.4).

Varieties

As noted in Example 3.21, the class of groups and the class of Abelian groups are defined by sets of equations. Such classes are called *equationally defined classes* or *varieties*.

Formally, a class $\mathcal{C}$ of Σ-algebras is an *equationally defined class* or *variety* if there is a set of equations Φ over $T_\Sigma(X)$ such that $\mathcal{C} = \mathbf{Mod}\,\Phi$.

The following are examples of varieties:

EXAMPLE 3.22: A semigroup is any structure with an associative binary operation $\cdot$; i.e., it is an algebraic structure over an alphabet consisting of a single binary operator $\cdot$ and satisfying the equation $x \cdot (y \cdot z) = (x \cdot y) \cdot z$.

EXAMPLE 3.23: Monoids are semigroups with a left and right identity element 1. In other words, the nullary symbol 1 is added to the signature along with equations $1 \cdot x = x$ and $x \cdot 1 = x$.

EXAMPLE 3.24:   Rings are algebraic structures over the alphabet $+, \cdot, -, 0, 1$ of arity $2, 2, 1, 0, 0$, respectively, defined by equations that say that the structure under the operations $+, -, 0$ forms an Abelian group, that the structure under the operations $\cdot, 1$ forms a monoid, and that the following *distributive laws* describing the interaction of the additive and multiplicative structure hold:

$$
\begin{aligned}
x \cdot (y + z) &= (x \cdot y) + (x \cdot z) \\
(x + y) \cdot z &= (x \cdot z) + (y \cdot z).
\end{aligned}
$$

A ring is *commutative* if it satisfies the extra equation $x \cdot y = y \cdot x$.

EXAMPLE 3.25:   *Semilattices* and *lattices* as described in Section 1.5 are varieties. Complete lattices are not (Exercise 3.34). The signature for lattices is $\vee, \wedge, \bot, \top$ (join, meet, bottom, top) of arity $2, 2, 0, 0$, respectively. The signature for semilattices is $\vee, \bot$ only. No special symbol for $\leq$ is necessary, because $x \leq y$ can be considered an abbreviation for $x \vee y = y$. This is true for semilattices, but not for partial orders in general (Exercise 3.24).

EXAMPLE 3.26:   A *Boolean algebra* is an algebra over the signature described in Example 3.17 satisfying (ii)–(viii) of Axiom System 3.13, regarding $\leftrightarrow$ as equality (see Exercise 3.8). Boolean algebra is the algebraic analog of propositional logic.

EXAMPLE 3.27:   A *vector space* over the real numbers $\mathbb{R}$ is an Abelian group with a unary operator for each real number a denoting the operation of scalar multiplication by a, and satisfying the following infinite set of equations:

$$
\begin{aligned}
a(x + y) &= ax + ay \\
(a + b)x &= ax + bx \\
(ab)x &= a(bx)
\end{aligned}
$$

for all $a, b \in \mathbb{R}$. We can regard this as a Σ-algebra over an infinite Σ containing the signature $+, -, 0$ of Abelian groups as well as infinitely many unary symbols, one for each $a \in \mathbb{R}$.

THEOREM 3.28:   Any variety $\mathcal{C}$ is closed under homomorphic images. In other words, if $h : \mathfrak{A} \to \mathfrak{B}$ is an epimorphism and $\mathfrak{A} \in \mathcal{C}$, then $\mathfrak{B} \in \mathcal{C}$.

Proof   It suffices to show that if $h : \mathfrak{A} \to \mathfrak{B}$ is an epimorphism and $\mathfrak{A} \vDash s = t$, then $\mathfrak{B} \vDash s = t$.

   Let X be a set of variables containing all the variables occurring in s and t. Let $v : T_\Sigma(X) \to \mathfrak{B}$ be an arbitrary valuation. Define the function $u : X \to \mathfrak{A}$ such that $h(u(x)) = v(x)$. This is always possible, since h is onto. The function u extends uniquely to a homomorphism $u : T_\Sigma(X) \to \mathfrak{A}$. Since homomorphisms are determined by their values on a generating set, and since the valuations $u \circ h$ and v agree on the generating set X, they are equal.

   Now since $\mathfrak{A} \vDash s = t$, we have that $u(s) = u(t)$. Then

$$
v(s) = h(u(s)) = h(u(t)) = v(t).
$$

Since v was arbitrary, $\mathfrak{B} \vDash s = t$.   ∎

LEMMA 3.29:   Let $h_1 : \mathfrak{A} \to \mathfrak{B}_1$ and $h_2 : \mathfrak{A} \to \mathfrak{B}_2$ be homomorphisms defined on $\mathfrak{A}$ such that h_1 is an epimorphism and $\ker h_1$ refines $\ker h_2$; that is, $\ker h_1 \subseteq \ker h_2$. Then there exists a unique homomorphism $g : \mathfrak{B}_1 \to \mathfrak{B}_2$ such that $h_2 = h_1 \circ g$.

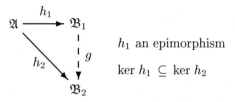

h_1 an epimorphism

$\ker h_1 \subseteq \ker h_2$

Proof Since h_1 is an epimorphism, any element of $\mathfrak{B}_1$ is of the form $h_1(a)$ for some $a \in \mathfrak{A}$. To satisfy the lemma, we had better define $g(h_1(a)) = h_2(a)$. This determines the function g uniquely, provided it is well defined. But it is well defined, for if a' is any other element of $\mathfrak{A}$ such that $h_1(a') = h_1(a)$, then $h_2(a') = h_2(a)$. Moreover, g is a homomorphism: if $b_i = h_1(a_i)$, $1 \leq i \leq n$, then

$$
\begin{aligned}
g(f^{\mathfrak{B}_1}(b_1, \ldots, b_n)) &= g(f^{\mathfrak{B}_1}(h_1(a_1), \ldots, h_1(a_n))) \\
&= g(h_1(f^{\mathfrak{A}}(a_1, \ldots, a_n))) \\
&= h_2(f^{\mathfrak{A}}(a_1, \ldots, a_n)) \\
&= f^{\mathfrak{B}_2}(h_2(a_1), \ldots, h_2(a_n)) \\
&= f^{\mathfrak{B}_2}(g(h_1(a_1)), \ldots, g(h_1(a_n))) \\
&= f^{\mathfrak{B}_2}(g(b_1), \ldots, g(b_n)).
\end{aligned}
$$

∎

Congruences

A *congruence* $\equiv$ on a Σ-algebra $\mathfrak{A}$ with carrier A is an equivalence relation on A that respects the functions $f^{\mathfrak{A}}$, $f \in \Sigma$, in the sense that

$$a_i \equiv b_i, \ 1 \leq i \leq n \ \implies \ f^{\mathfrak{A}}(a_1, \ldots, a_n) \equiv f^{\mathfrak{A}}(b_1, \ldots, b_n). \tag{3.3.5}$$

The $\equiv$-*congruence class* of an element a is the set

$$[a] \ \stackrel{\text{def}}{=} \ \{b \mid b \equiv a\}.$$

Since any congruence is an equivalence relation, the congruences classes partition A in the sense that they are pairwise disjoint and their union is A (Section 1.3).

EXAMPLE 3.30:   The identity relation and the universal relation are always congruences. They are the finest and coarsest congruences, respectively, on any algebra. The congruence classes of the identity relation are all singleton sets, and the universal relation has one congruence class consisting of all elements.

EXAMPLE 3.31:   On the ring of integers $\mathbb{Z}$, any positive integer n defines a congruence

$$a \equiv_n b \iff b - a \text{ is divisible by } n.$$

In the number theory literature, this relation is commonly written $a \equiv b \ (n)$ or $a \equiv b \pmod{n}$. There are n congruence classes, namely $[0], [1], \dots, [n-1]$. The congruence class $[0]$ is the set of all multiples of n.

EXAMPLE 3.32:   An *ideal* of a commutative ring $\mathfrak{R}$ is a nonempty subset I such that if $a, b \in I$ then $a + b \in I$, and if $a \in I$ and $b \in \mathfrak{R}$, then $ab \in I$. If $\mathfrak{R}$ is any commutative ring and I is an ideal in $\mathfrak{R}$, then the relation

$$a \equiv_I b \iff b - a \in I$$

is a congruence. This relation is often written $a \equiv b \ (I)$. Conversely, given any congruence $\equiv$, the congruence class $[0]$ is an ideal. Example 3.31 is a special case.

EXAMPLE 3.33:   A subgroup $\mathfrak{H}$ of a group $\mathfrak{G}$ is a *normal* (or *self-conjugate*) subgroup of $\mathfrak{G}$, in symbols $\mathfrak{H} \triangleleft \mathfrak{G}$, if for all $x \in \mathfrak{H}$ and $a \in \mathfrak{G}$, $a^{-1}xa \in \mathfrak{H}$. If $\mathfrak{G}$ is any group and $\mathfrak{H} \triangleleft \mathfrak{G}$, then the relation

$$a \equiv_{\mathfrak{H}} b \iff b^{-1}a \in \mathfrak{H}$$

is a congruence. Conversely, given any congruence on $\mathfrak{G}$, the congruence class of the identity element is a normal subgroup.

Let $\mathfrak{A}$ be a Σ-algebra with carrier A and let S be any binary relation on A. By considerations of Section 1.7, there is a unique minimal congruence on $\mathfrak{A}$ containing S, called the *congruence closure* of S. It is the least relation that contains S and is closed under the monotone set operators

$$R \mapsto \iota \tag{3.3.6}$$
$$R \mapsto R^- \tag{3.3.7}$$
$$R \mapsto R \circ R \tag{3.3.8}$$
$$R \mapsto \{(f^{\mathfrak{A}}(a_1, \dots, a_n), f^{\mathfrak{A}}(b_1, \dots, b_n)) \mid f \in \Sigma \text{ and } (a_i, b_i) \in R, 1 \leq i \leq n\} \tag{3.3.9}$$

corresponding to reflexivity, symmetry, transitivity, and congruence, respectively.

It follows from the results of Section 1.7 that the set of congruences on $\mathfrak{A}$ under the partial order of refinement forms a complete lattice. The meet of a set of congruences $\equiv_i$ is their intersection $\bigcap_i \equiv_i$, and the join of the $\equiv_i$ is the congruence generated by $\bigcup_i \equiv_i$; that is, the smallest congruence containing all the $\equiv_i$.

The Quotient Construction

The following theorem shows that there is a strong relationship between homomorphisms and congruences. Its proof illustrates an important construction called the *quotient construction.*

THEOREM 3.34:

(i) The kernel of any homomorphism is a congruence.

(ii) Any congruence is the kernel of a homomorphism.

Proof Statement (i) follows in a straightforward way from the definition of homomorphism and congruence and is left as an exercise (Exercise 3.17).

To show (ii), we need to construct, given a congruence $\equiv$ on $\mathfrak{A}$, a Σ-algebra $\mathfrak{B}$ and a homomorphism $h : \mathfrak{A} \to \mathfrak{B}$ with kernel $\equiv$. It will turn out that the homomorphism h we construct is an epimorphism; thus $\mathfrak{B}$ is a homomorphic image of $\mathfrak{A}$. Moreover, up to isomorphism, $\mathfrak{B}$ is the unique homomorphic image of $\mathfrak{A}$ under a homomorphism with kernel $\equiv$. This construction is known as the *quotient construction.*

Let A be the carrier of $\mathfrak{A}$. For $a \in A$, let $[a]$ denote the $\equiv$-congruence class of a, and define

$$A/\equiv \ \overset{\text{def}}{=} \ \{[a] \mid a \in A\}.$$

Define the Σ-algebra

$$\mathfrak{A}/\equiv \ \overset{\text{def}}{=} \ (A/\equiv, \ \mathfrak{m}_{\mathfrak{A}/\equiv})$$

where

$$f^{\mathfrak{A}/\equiv}([a_1], \dots, [a_n]) \ \overset{\text{def}}{=} \ [f^{\mathfrak{A}}(a_1, \dots, a_n)]. \qquad (3.3.10)$$

We must argue that the function $f^{\mathfrak{A}/\equiv}$ is well defined; that is, if $[a_i] = [b_i]$ for $1 \le i \le n$, then $[f^{\mathfrak{A}}(a_1, \dots, a_n)] = [f^{\mathfrak{A}}(b_1, \dots, b_n)]$. But this is precisely (3.3.5).

The Σ-algebra $\mathfrak{A}/\equiv$ is called the *quotient of $\mathfrak{A}$ by $\equiv$* or *$\mathfrak{A}$ modulo $\equiv$.* Moreover, by (3.3.10), the map $a \mapsto [a]$ is a homomorphism $\mathfrak{A} \to \mathfrak{A}/\equiv$, which we call the *canonical homomorphism.* Since $[a] = [b]$ iff $a \equiv b$, the kernel of the canonical homomorphism is $\equiv$. ∎

In Example 3.31, the quotient $\mathbb{Z}/\equiv_n$ is the ring of integers modulo n. In Example 3.32, we defined a congruence $\equiv_I$ on a commutative ring in terms of an ideal I. Similarly, in Example 3.33, we defined a congruence $\equiv_{\mathfrak{H}}$ on a group $\mathfrak{G}$ in terms of a normal subgroup $\mathfrak{H}$. By Theorem 3.34, these congruences are kernels of homomorphisms. In ring theory and group theory, the *kernel* is normally defined to be the ideal or normal subgroup itself, not the congruence it generates. However, there is a one-to-one correspondence between congruences and ideals of a commutative ring and between congruences and normal subgroups of a group, so the definition of kernel as given in (3.3.3) subsumes these as special cases.

The relationship between congruences and homomorphisms is even stronger than Theorem 3.34 would suggest. As mentioned in Section 3.3, the set of congruences on $\mathfrak{A}$ under the partial order of refinement forms a complete lattice. Similarly, consider the class of all epimorphisms with domain $\mathfrak{A}$. For two such epimorphisms $h_1 : \mathfrak{A} \to \mathfrak{B}_1$ and $h_2 : \mathfrak{A} \to \mathfrak{B}_2$, let us write $h_1 \leq h_2$ if there exists an epimorphism $g : \mathfrak{B}_1 \to \mathfrak{B}_2$ such that $h_2 = h_1 \circ g$ and $h_1 \approx h_2$ if both $h_1 \leq h_2$ and $h_2 \leq h_1$. Using Lemma 3.29, one can show that $h_1 \approx h_2$ iff there is an isomorphism $\iota : \mathfrak{B}_1 \to \mathfrak{B}_2$ such that $h_2 = h_1 \circ \iota$ (Exercise 3.19). The set of $\approx$-classes of epimorphisms on $\mathfrak{A}$ forms a complete lattice under the partial order $\leq$.

THEOREM 3.35:   Up to $\approx$, the congruences on $\mathfrak{A}$ and the epimorphisms on $\mathfrak{A}$ are in one-to-one correspondence under the map that associates an epimorphism with its kernel. This correspondence is an isomorphism of lattices.

Proof Exercise 3.20. ∎

Free Algebras

One recurring phenomenon in algebra that turns out to be very useful is the notion of a *free algebra*. The essential idea is that for any set Φ of equations and for any set Y, there is an algebra generated by Y that satisfies Φ and all of its logical consequences, but no more. Thus it is as "free" of extra equations as possible, satisfying only those equations it is forced to satisfy by Φ. The free algebra is unique up to isomorphism.

The free algebra on generators Y satisfying Φ can be constructed as the quotient of $T_\Sigma(Y)$ modulo the smallest congruence containing all substitution instances over $T_\Sigma(Y)$ of equations in Φ. We denote this quotient by $T_\Sigma(Y)/\Phi$.

In more detail, assume that Φ is a set of equations over $T_\Sigma(X)$. (No relationship between X and Y is assumed.) Let $\equiv$ be the smallest congruence on $T_\Sigma(Y)$

containing all pairs $u(s) \equiv u(t)$ for any substitution $u : T_\Sigma(X) \to T_\Sigma(Y)$ and $s = t \in \Phi$. For example, if $f, g, a \in \Sigma$ are of arity $2, 1, 0$ respectively, $x, y \in X$, $z, w \in Y$, and $f(x, y) = f(y, x)$ is in Φ, then $f(g(z), f(a, w)) \equiv f(f(a, w), g(z))$. The algebra $T_\Sigma(Y)/\Phi$ is defined to be the quotient $T_\Sigma(Y)/\equiv$.

The following theorem asserts formally the key property of "freeness" that we described intuitively above.

THEOREM 3.36:

(i) $T_\Sigma(Y)/\Phi$ is a model of Φ;

(ii) for any model $\mathfrak{A}$ of Φ and for any valuation $u : T_\Sigma(Y) \to \mathfrak{A}$, there exists a unique homomorphism $v : T_\Sigma(Y)/\Phi \to \mathfrak{A}$ such that $u = [\,]\circ v$, where $[\,] : T_\Sigma(Y) \to T_\Sigma(Y)/\Phi$ is the canonical homomorphism.

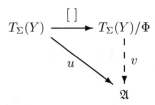

Proof (i) Let $u : T_\Sigma(X) \to T_\Sigma(Y)/\Phi$ be any valuation and let $s = t$ be any equation in Φ. We wish to show that $T_\Sigma(Y)/\Phi, u \vDash s = t$; that is, $u(s) = u(t)$. For $x \in X$, let $v(x) \in T_\Sigma(Y)$ be any element of the congruence class $u(x)$. Then for any $x \in X$, $u(x) = [v(x)]$. Extend v to a substitution $v : T_\Sigma(X) \to T_\Sigma(Y)$. Since the two valuations u and $v \circ [\,]$ agree on the generating set X, they are equal. But $v(s) \equiv v(t)$ by definition of $\equiv$, therefore $u(s) = u(t)$ and $T_\Sigma(Y)/\Phi, u \vDash s = t$. Since u was arbitrary, $T_\Sigma(Y)/\Phi \vDash s = t$.

(ii) The kernel of u is a congruence, and since $\mathfrak{A} \vDash \Phi$, it contains all substitution instances of equations in Φ. Since $\equiv$, the kernel of the canonical homomorphism $[\,]$, is the minimal such congruence, $\equiv$ refines $\ker u$. The result then follows from Lemma 3.29. ∎

EXAMPLE 3.37: The free monoid on generators A is the asterate A^*, the set of finite length strings over A with the operation of concatenation and identity element ε, the empty string.

EXAMPLE 3.38: The free commutative ring on generators X is the ring of polynomials $\mathbb{Z}[X]$. In particular, the free commutative ring on no generators is $\mathbb{Z}$.

EXAMPLE 3.39:   The free vector space over $\mathbb{R}$ on n generators is just the Euclidean space $\mathbb{R}^n$.

A Deductive System

A sound and complete deductive system for equational logic can be obtained from the definition of congruence.

AXIOM SYSTEM 3.40:

(REF) $s = s$

(SYM) $\dfrac{s = t}{t = s}$

(TRANS) $\dfrac{s = t, \quad t = u}{s = u}$

(CONG) $\dfrac{s_i = t_i, \ 1 \leq i \leq n}{f(s_1, \ldots, s_n) = f(t_1, \ldots, t_n)}.$

These are the laws of *reflexivity, symmetry, transitivity,* and *congruence,* respectively. Let X be a set of variables and let Φ be a set of equations over $T_\Sigma(X)$. A *proof* of an equation $s = t$ from assumptions Φ in this system consists of a sequence of equations containing $s = t$ in which each equation is either

• a substitution instance of an equation in Φ, or

• a consequence of an axiom or rule whose premises occur earlier in the sequence.

We write $\Phi \vdash s = t$ if there is a proof of $s = t$ from assumptions Φ.

Starting from a set of equations A on a term algebra, the four rules of Axiom System 3.40 generate exactly the congruence closure of A. This is because the rules implement exactly the monotone operators (3.3.6)–(3.3.9) defining congruence closure. If A is the set of all substitution instances over $T_\Sigma(Y)$ of equations in Φ, the rules will therefore generate exactly those pairs $s = t$ such that $T_\Sigma(Y)/\Phi, [\,] \vDash s = t$.

THEOREM 3.41 (SOUNDNESS AND COMPLETENESS OF EQUATIONAL LOGIC):
Let Φ be a set of equations over $T_\Sigma(X)$ and let $s = t$ be an equation over $T_\Sigma(Y)$. Let $[\,] : T_\Sigma(Y) \to T_\Sigma(Y)/\Phi$ be the canonical homomorphism. The following three statements are equivalent:

(i) $\Phi \vdash s = t$;

(ii) $[s] = [t]$;

(iii) $s = t \in \mathbf{Th\,Mod}\,\Phi$.

Proof (i) $\Longleftrightarrow$ (ii) The four rules of Axiom System 3.40 implement exactly the four monotone set operators (3.3.6)–(3.3.9) on $T_\Sigma(Y)$ defining congruence closure. Let T be this set of operators and let $T^\dagger$ be the associated closure operator as described in Section 1.7. Let R be the set of substitution instances over $T_\Sigma(Y)$ of equations in Φ. By Theorem 1.12, $T^\dagger(R)$ is the congruence closure of R, and this is ker $[\,]$ by definition. But by the definition of proof,

$$\{s = t \mid \Phi \vdash s = t\} \;=\; T^\omega(R),$$

and $T^\omega(R) = T^\dagger(R)$ since the operators T are finitary (Exercises 1.17 and 1.18).

(iii) $\Longrightarrow$ (ii) Since $[s] = [t]$ iff $T_\Sigma(Y)/\Phi, [\,] \vDash s = t$, this follows immediately from Theorem 3.36(i).

(ii) $\Longrightarrow$ (iii) Let $\mathfrak{A}$ be any model of Φ. By Theorem 3.36(ii), for any valuation $u : T_\Sigma(Y) \to \mathfrak{A}$ there exists a valuation $v : T_\Sigma(Y)/\Phi \to \mathfrak{A}$ such that $u = [\,] \circ v$. Since $[s] = [t]$ by assumption, we have $u(s) = v([s]) = v([t]) = u(t)$. Since u was arbitrary, $\mathfrak{A} \vDash s = t$. Since $\mathfrak{A}$ was arbitrary, $s = t$ is a logical consequence of Φ. ∎

The HSP Theorem

We conclude this section with a remarkable theorem of Birkhoff that characterizes varieties in terms of closure properties. It states that a class of algebras is a variety—that is, it is defined by equations—if and only if it is closed under the formation of subalgebras, products, and homomorphic images.

Homomorphic images and subalgebras were defined in Section 3.3. Products are defined as follows. Recall from Section 1.2 that if $\{A_i \mid i \in I\}$ is an indexed family of sets, the *Cartesian product* of the A_i is the set $\prod_{i \in I} A_i$ of all functions $a : I \to \bigcup_{i \in I} A_i$ such that $a(i) \in A_i$. We write a_i for $a(i)$ and think of an element $a \in \prod_{i \in I} A_i$ as a tuple $(a_i \mid i \in I)$ whose components are indexed by I. If $\{\mathfrak{A}_i \mid i \in I\}$ is an indexed family of algebras, where the carrier of $\mathfrak{A}_i$ is A_i, the *product* $\mathfrak{A} = \prod_{i \in I} \mathfrak{A}_i$ is the algebra whose carrier is $A = \prod_{i \in I} A_i$ and whose distinguished functions $f^{\mathfrak{A}} : A^n \to A$ are defined componentwise: $f^{\mathfrak{A}}(a)_i = f^{\mathfrak{A}_i}(a_i)$.

Let Φ be a set of equations over variables X. Recall from Section 3.3 that $\mathbf{Mod}\,\Phi$ denotes the class of models of Φ, that is, $\mathbf{Mod}\,\Phi = \{\mathfrak{A} \mid \mathfrak{A} \vDash \Phi\}$; if $\mathfrak{A}$ is a Σ-algebra, then $\mathbf{Th}\,\mathfrak{A}$ denotes the set of equations valid in $\mathfrak{A}$; and if $\mathcal{D}$ is a class of Σ-algebras, then $\mathbf{Th}\,\mathcal{D}$ denotes the set of equations valid in all elements of $\mathcal{D}$. Recall that a *variety* is a class of algebras of the form $\mathbf{Mod}\,\Phi$ for some set of equations Φ.

We define the operators **H**, **S**, and **P** that when applied to a class $\mathcal{D}$ of algebras give the class of (isomorphic copies of) homomorphic images, subalgebras, and products of algebras in $\mathcal{D}$, respectively. Thus we write $\mathbf{H\,S\,P}\,\mathcal{D}$ for the class of all homomorphic images of subalgebras of products of algebras in $\mathcal{D}$. We write $\{\mathbf{H},\mathbf{S},\mathbf{P}\}^*\,\mathcal{D}$ for the smallest class of algebras containing $\mathcal{D}$ and closed under the formation of homomorphic images, subalgebras, and products.

THEOREM 3.42:   Let $\mathcal{D}$ be a class of algebras. Then

$$\mathbf{Mod\,Th}\,\mathcal{D}\ =\ \mathbf{H\,S\,P}\,\mathcal{D}\ =\ \{\mathbf{H},\mathbf{S},\mathbf{P}\}^*\,\mathcal{D}.$$

Proof We show first that $\{\mathbf{H},\mathbf{S},\mathbf{P}\}^*\,\mathcal{D}\subseteq\mathbf{Mod\,Th}\,\mathcal{D}$. Surely $\mathcal{D}\subseteq\mathbf{Mod\,Th}\,\mathcal{D}$. Any product of algebras satisfying $\mathbf{Th}\,\mathcal{D}$ also satisfies $\mathbf{Th}\,\mathcal{D}$, because an equation holds in the product iff it holds in all the factor algebras. Any subalgebra of an algebra $\mathfrak{A}$ satisfying $\mathbf{Th}\,\mathcal{D}$ also satisfies $\mathbf{Th}\,\mathcal{D}$, because any valuation over the subalgebra is a valuation over $\mathfrak{A}$, therefore must verify any equation in $\mathbf{Th}\,\mathcal{D}$. Finally, any homomorphic image of an algebra satisfying $\mathbf{Th}\,\mathcal{D}$ also satisfies $\mathbf{Th}\,\mathcal{D}$ by Theorem 3.28.

The inclusion $\mathbf{H\,S\,P}\,\mathcal{D}\subseteq\{\mathbf{H},\mathbf{S},\mathbf{P}\}^*\,\mathcal{D}$ is obvious.

Finally, we show that $\mathbf{Mod\,Th}\,\mathcal{D}\subseteq\mathbf{H\,S\,P}\,\mathcal{D}$. Suppose $\mathfrak{A}\in\mathbf{Mod\,Th}\,\mathcal{D}$. We wish to show that $\mathfrak{A}\in\mathbf{H\,S\,P}\,\mathcal{D}$. Let B be any set of generators of $\mathfrak{A}$. Considering B as just a set, form the free algebra $T_\Sigma(B)/\mathbf{Th}\,\mathcal{D}$. By Theorem 3.36(ii), the valuation $\iota:T_\Sigma(B)\to\mathfrak{A}$ such that $\iota\restriction B$ is the identity factors through $T_\Sigma(B)/\mathbf{Th}\,\mathcal{D}$, giving a homomorphism $\iota':T_\Sigma(B)/\mathbf{Th}\,\mathcal{D}\to\mathfrak{A}$.

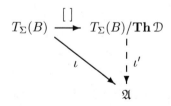

Moreover, since B generates $\mathfrak{A}$, ι' is an epimorphism, thus $\mathfrak{A}$ is a homomorphic image of $T_\Sigma(B)/\mathbf{Th}\,\mathcal{D}$. It thus suffices to show that $T_\Sigma(B)/\mathbf{Th}\,\mathcal{D}\in\mathbf{S\,P}\,\mathcal{D}$.

For each pair s,t in $T_\Sigma(B)$ such that $[s]\neq[t]$, the equation $s=t$ cannot be in $\mathbf{Th}\,\mathcal{D}$. Thus there must exist an algebra $\mathfrak{B}_{s,t}\in\mathcal{D}$ and valuation $u_{s,t}:T_\Sigma(B)\to\mathfrak{B}_{s,t}$ such that $u_{s,t}(s)\neq u_{s,t}(t)$. Set

$$\mathfrak{B}\ =\ \prod_{[s]\neq[t]}\mathfrak{B}_{s,t}$$

and let $u : T_\Sigma(B) \to \mathfrak{B}$ be the valuation

$$u(r) \quad = \quad \prod_{[s] \neq [t]} u_{s,t}(r).$$

Since all components $\mathfrak{B}_{s,t}$ are models of $\mathbf{Th}\,\mathcal{D}$, so is their product $\mathfrak{B}$. By Theorem 3.36(ii), u factors through $T_\Sigma(B)/\mathbf{Th}\,\mathcal{D}$ as $[\ ] \circ v$, where $v : T_\Sigma(B)/\mathbf{Th}\,\mathcal{D} \to \mathfrak{B}$. Moreover, v is injective, since if $[s] \neq [t]$, then $v(s) \neq v(t)$ in at least one component, namely $\mathfrak{B}_{s,t}$. Thus $T_\Sigma(B)/\mathbf{Th}\,\mathcal{D}$ is isomorphic under v to a subalgebra of the product $\mathfrak{B}$. ∎

COROLLARY 3.43 (BIRKHOFF):   Let $\mathcal{D}$ be a class of Σ-algebras. The following are equivalent:

(i) $\mathcal{D}$ is a variety;

(ii) $\mathcal{D} = \mathbf{H\,S\,P}\,\mathcal{D}$;

(iii) $\mathcal{D} = \{\mathbf{H}, \mathbf{S}, \mathbf{P}\}^*\,\mathcal{D}$.

Proof   That (ii) and (iii) are equivalent and imply (i) are immediate from Theorem 3.42. That (i) implies (ii) follows from Theorem 3.42 and the fact that for any set of formulas Φ, $\mathbf{Mod}\,\Phi = \mathbf{Mod}\,\mathbf{Th}\,\mathbf{Mod}\,\Phi$ (Exercise 3.21). ∎

3.4   Predicate Logic

First-order predicate logic is the logic of predicates and quantification ($\forall, \exists$) over elements of a structure.

Syntax

Syntactically, we start with a countable signature as with equational logic, except that we include some *relation* or *predicate symbols* $p, q, r, \ldots$ in addition to the function symbols $f, g, \ldots$. A *signature* or *vocabulary* then consists of a set Σ of function and relation symbols, each with an associated *arity* (number of inputs). Function and relation symbols of arity 0, 1, 2, 3, and n are called *nullary, unary, binary, ternary*, and *n-ary*, respectively. Nullary elements are often called *constants*. One of the relation symbols may be the binary *equality symbol* $=$. In most applications, Σ is finite.

The language consists of:

- the function and relation symbols in Σ
- a countable set X of *individual variables* $x, y, \ldots$
- the propositional connectives $\rightarrow$ and $\mathbf{0}$
- the universal quantifier symbol $\forall$ ("for all")
- parentheses.

As in Section 3.2, the other propositional connectives $\vee$, $\wedge$, $\mathbf{1}$, $\neg$, and $\leftrightarrow$ can all be defined in terms of $\rightarrow$ and $\mathbf{0}$. Similarly, we will define below the existential quantifier $\exists$ ("there exists") in terms of $\forall$.

Terms $s, t, \ldots$ are exactly as in equational logic (see Section 3.3). A term is a *ground term* if it contains no variables.

Formulas $\varphi, \psi, \ldots$ are defined inductively. A formula is either

- an *atomic formula* $p(t_1, \ldots, t_n)$, where p is an n-ary relation symbol and $t_1, \ldots, t_n$ are terms; or
- $\varphi \rightarrow \psi$, $\mathbf{0}$, or $\forall x\ \varphi$, where φ and ψ are formulas and x is a variable.

Intuitively, in the formula $\forall x\ \varphi$, we think of φ as a property of an object x; then the formula $\forall x\ \varphi$ says that that property φ holds for all objects x.

The other propositional operators are defined from $\rightarrow$ and $\mathbf{0}$ as described in Section 3.2. The quantifier $\exists$ is defined as follows:

$$\exists x\ \varphi \quad \overset{\text{def}}{\Longleftrightarrow} \quad \neg \forall x\ \neg\varphi. \tag{3.4.1}$$

Intuitively, in the formula $\exists x\ \varphi$, we again think of φ as a property of an object x; then the formula $\exists x\ \varphi$ says that that there exists an object x for which the property φ holds. The formal definition (3.4.1) asserts the idea that there exists an x for which φ is true if and only if it is not the case that for all x, φ is false.

As with propositional logic, we will assume a natural precedence of the operators and use parentheses where necessary to ensure that a formula can be read in one and only one way. The precedence of the propositional operators is the same as in Section 3.2. The quantifier $\forall$ binds more tightly than the propositional operators; thus $\forall x\ \varphi \rightarrow \psi$ should be parsed as $(\forall x\ \varphi) \rightarrow \psi$.

The family of languages we have just defined will be denoted collectively by $L_{\omega\omega}$. The two subscripts ω refer to the fact that we allow only finite (that is, $< \omega$) conjunctions and disjunctions and finitely many variables.

EXAMPLE 3.44:   The first-order language of number theory is suitable for expressing properties of the natural numbers $\mathbb{N}$. The signature consists of binary function symbols $+$ and $\cdot$ (written in infix), constants 0 and 1, and binary relation symbol $=$ (also written in infix). A typical term is $(x+1) \cdot y$ and a typical atomic formula is $x + y = z$. The formula

$$\forall x \; \exists y \; (x \leq y \wedge \forall z \; (z \mid y \rightarrow (z = 1 \vee z = y)))$$

expresses the statement that there are infinitely many primes. Here $s \leq t$ is an abbreviation for $\exists w \; s + w = t$ and $s \mid t$ (read "s divides t") is an abbreviation for $\exists w \; s \cdot w = t$.

Scope, Bound and Free Variables

Let $\mathbf{Q}$ be either $\forall$ or $\exists$. If $\mathbf{Q}x \; \varphi$ occurs as a subformula of some formula ψ, then that occurrence of φ in ψ is called the *scope* of that occurrence of $\mathbf{Q}x$ in ψ. An occurrence of a variable y in ψ that occurs in a term is a *free occurrence of y in ψ* if it is not in the scope of any quantifier $\mathbf{Q}y$ with the same variable y. If $\mathbf{Q}y \; \varphi$ occurs as a subformula of ψ and y occurs free in φ, then that occurrence of y is said to be *bound to* that occurrence of $\mathbf{Q}y$. Thus an occurrence of y in ψ is bound to the $\mathbf{Q}y$ with smallest scope containing that occurrence of y, if such a $\mathbf{Q}y$ exists; otherwise it is free.

We say that a term t is *free for y in φ* if no free occurrence of y in φ occurs in the scope of a quantifier $\mathbf{Q}x$, where x occurs in t. This condition says that it is safe to substitute t for free occurrences of y in φ without fear of some variable x of t being inadvertently captured by a quantifier.

EXAMPLE 3.45:   In the formula

$$\exists x \; ((\forall y \; \exists x \; q(x,y)) \wedge p(x,y,z)),$$

the scope of the first $\exists x$ is $(\forall y \; \exists x \; q(x,y)) \wedge p(x,y,z)$, the scope of the $\forall y$ is $\exists x \; q(x,y)$, and the scope of the second $\exists x$ is $q(x,y)$. The occurrence of x in $q(x,y)$ is bound to the second $\exists x$. The x in $p(x,y,z)$ occurs free in the subformula $(\forall y \; \exists x \; q(x,y)) \wedge p(x,y,z)$ but is bound to the first $\exists x$. The occurrence of y in $q(x,y)$ is bound to the $\forall y$, but the occurrence of y in $p(x,y,z)$ is free. The only occurrence of z in the formula is a free occurrence. The term $f(x)$ is not free for either y or z in the formula, because substitution of $f(x)$ for y or z would result in the capture of x by the first $\exists x$.

Note that the adjectives "free" and "bound" apply not to variables but to *occurrences* of variables in a formula. A formula may have free and bound occurrences of the same variable. For example, the variable y in the formula of Example 3.45 has one free and one bound occurrence. Note also that occurrences of variables in quantifiers—occurrences of the form $\forall y$ and $\exists y$—do not figure in the definition of free and bound.

A variable is called a *free variable* of a formula φ if it has a free occurrence in φ. The notation $\varphi[x_1/t_1, \ldots, x_n/t_n]$ or $\varphi[x_i/t_i \mid 1 \leq i \leq n]$ denotes the formula φ with all free occurrences of x_i replaced with t_i, $1 \leq i \leq n$. The substitution is done for all variables simultaneously. Note that $\varphi[x/s, y/t]$ can differ from $\varphi[x/s][y/t]$ if s has an occurrence of y. Although notationally similar, the substitution operator $[x/t]$ should not be confused with the function-patching operator defined in Section 1.3.

We occasionally write $\varphi(x_1, \ldots, x_n)$ to indicate that all free variables of φ are among $x_1, \ldots, x_n$. The variables $x_1, \ldots, x_n$ need not all appear in $\varphi(x_1, \ldots, x_n)$, however. When $\varphi = \varphi(x_1, \ldots, x_n)$, we sometimes write $\varphi(t_1, \ldots, t_n)$ instead of $\varphi[x_1/t_1, \ldots, x_n/t_n]$.

A formula is a *closed formula* or *sentence* if it contains no free variables. The *universal closure* of a formula φ is the sentence obtained by preceding φ with enough universal quantifiers $\forall x$ to bind all the free variables of φ.

Semantics

A *relational structure* over signature Σ is a structure $\mathfrak{A} = (A, \mathfrak{m}_{\mathfrak{A}})$ where A is a nonempty set, called the *carrier* or *domain* of $\mathfrak{A}$, and $\mathfrak{m}_{\mathfrak{A}}$ is a function assigning an n-ary function $f^{\mathfrak{A}} : A^n \to A$ to each n-ary function symbol $f \in \Sigma$ and an n-ary relation $p^{\mathfrak{A}} \subseteq A^n$ to each n-ary relation symbol $p \in \Sigma$. As with equational logic, nullary functions are considered elements of A; thus constant symbols $c \in \Sigma$ are interpreted as elements $c^{\mathfrak{A}} \in A$.

As in equational logic, we define a *valuation* to be a Σ-homomorphism $u : T_{\Sigma}(X) \to \mathfrak{A}$. A valuation u is uniquely determined by its values on the variables X.

Given a valuation u, we define $u[x/a]$ to be the new valuation obtained from u by changing the value of x to a and leaving the values of the other variables intact; thus

$$u[x/a](y) \overset{\text{def}}{=} u(y), \quad y \neq x,$$
$$u[x/a](x) \overset{\text{def}}{=} a.$$

This is the same as in equational logic.

The *satisfaction relation* $\vDash$ is defined inductively as follows:

$$\mathfrak{A}, u \vDash p(t_1, \ldots, t_n) \quad \overset{\text{def}}{\Longleftrightarrow} \quad p^{\mathfrak{A}}(u(t_1), \ldots, u(t_n))$$

$$\mathfrak{A}, u \vDash \varphi \to \psi \quad \overset{\text{def}}{\Longleftrightarrow} \quad (\mathfrak{A}, u \vDash \varphi \Longrightarrow \mathfrak{A}, u \vDash \psi)$$

$$\mathfrak{A}, u \vDash \forall x \; \varphi \quad \overset{\text{def}}{\Longleftrightarrow} \quad \text{for all } a \in A, \; \mathfrak{A}, u[x/a] \vDash \varphi.$$

It follows that

$$\mathfrak{A}, u \vDash \varphi \lor \psi \quad \Longleftrightarrow \quad \mathfrak{A}, u \vDash \varphi \text{ or } \mathfrak{A}, u \vDash \psi$$

$$\mathfrak{A}, u \vDash \varphi \land \psi \quad \Longleftrightarrow \quad \mathfrak{A}, u \vDash \varphi \text{ and } \mathfrak{A}, u \vDash \psi$$

$$\mathfrak{A}, u \vDash \neg\varphi \quad \Longleftrightarrow \quad \mathfrak{A}, u \nvDash \varphi; \text{ that is, if it is } not \text{ the case that } \mathfrak{A}, u \vDash \varphi$$

$$\mathfrak{A}, u \vDash \exists x \; \varphi \quad \Longleftrightarrow \quad \text{there exists an } a \in A \text{ such that } \mathfrak{A}, u[x/a] \vDash \varphi.$$

Also, $\mathfrak{A}, u \nvDash \mathbf{0}$ and $\mathfrak{A}, u \vDash \mathbf{1}$.

If $\mathfrak{A}, u \vDash \varphi$, we say that φ is *true in $\mathfrak{A}$ under valuation u*, or that $\mathfrak{A}, u$ is a *model* of φ, or that $\mathfrak{A}, u$ *satisfies* φ. If Φ is a set of formulas, we write $\mathfrak{A}, u \vDash \Phi$ if $\mathfrak{A}, u \vDash \varphi$ for all $\varphi \in \Phi$ and say that $\mathfrak{A}, u$ *satisfies* Φ. If φ is true in all models of Φ, we write $\Phi \vDash \varphi$ and say that φ is a *logical consequence*[3] of Φ. If $\varnothing \vDash \varphi$, we write $\vDash \varphi$ and say that φ is *valid*.

It can be shown that if φ is a sentence, then $\vDash$ does not depend on the valuation u; that is, if $\mathfrak{A}, u \vDash \varphi$ for some u, then $\mathfrak{A}, u \vDash \varphi$ for all u (Exercise 3.29). In this case, we omit the u and just write $\mathfrak{A} \vDash \varphi$. If Φ is a set of sentences, then $\mathfrak{A} \vDash \Phi$ means that $\mathfrak{A} \vDash \varphi$ for all $\varphi \in \Phi$.

Two formulas φ, ψ are said to be *logically equivalent* if $\vDash \varphi \leftrightarrow \psi$.

The following lemma establishes a relationship between the function-patching operator $[x/a]$ on valuations and the substitution operator $[x/t]$ on terms and formulas.

LEMMA 3.46:

(i) For any valuation u and terms $s, t \in T_\Sigma(X)$,

$$u[x/u(t)](s) \quad = \quad u(s[x/t]).$$

(ii) If t is free for x in φ, then

$$\mathfrak{A}, u[x/u(t)] \vDash \varphi \quad \Longleftrightarrow \quad \mathfrak{A}, u \vDash \varphi[x/t].$$

---

3 This notion of logical consequence is slightly different from the one used in equational logic (Section 3.3). There, the free variables of formulas were assumed to be implicitly universally quantified. We abandon that assumption here because we have explicit quantification.

Proof (i)   Proceeding by induction on the structure of s, if s is the variable x, then

$$u[x/u(t)](x) \;=\; u(t) \;=\; u(x[x/t]).$$

If s is a variable y different from x, then

$$u[x/u(t)](y) \;=\; u(y) \;=\; u(y[x/t]).$$

Finally, if $s = f(t_1, \dots, t_n)$, then

$$
\begin{aligned}
u[x/u(t)](f(t_1, \dots, t_n)) &= f^{\mathfrak{A}}(u[x/u(t)](t_1), \dots, u[x/u(t)](t_n)) \\
&= f^{\mathfrak{A}}(u(t_1[x/t]), \dots, u(t_n[x/t])) \\
&= u(f(t_1[x/t], \dots, t_n[x/t])) \\
&= u(f(t_1, \dots, t_n)[x/t]).
\end{aligned}
$$

(ii)   We proceed by induction on the structure of φ. For atomic formulas, using (i) we have that

$$
\begin{aligned}
\mathfrak{A}, u[x/u(t)] \vDash p(t_1, \dots, t_n) &\iff p^{\mathfrak{A}}(u[x/u(t)](t_1), \dots, u[x/u(t)](t_n)) \\
&\iff p^{\mathfrak{A}}(u(t_1[x/t]), \dots, u(t_n[x/t])) \\
&\iff \mathfrak{A}, u \vDash p(t_1[x/t], \dots, t_n[x/t]) \\
&\iff \mathfrak{A}, u \vDash p(t_1, \dots, t_n)[x/t].
\end{aligned}
$$

For formulas of the form $\varphi \to \psi$, if t is free for x in $\varphi \to \psi$, then t is free for x in both φ and ψ. Then

$$
\begin{aligned}
\mathfrak{A}, u[x/u(t)] \vDash \varphi \to \psi &\iff (\mathfrak{A}, u[x/u(t)] \vDash \varphi \implies \mathfrak{A}, u[x/u(t)] \vDash \psi) \\
&\iff (\mathfrak{A}, u \vDash \varphi[x/t] \implies \mathfrak{A}, u \vDash \psi[x/t]) \\
&\iff \mathfrak{A}, u \vDash \varphi[x/t] \to \psi[x/t] \\
&\iff \mathfrak{A}, u \vDash (\varphi \to \psi)[x/t].
\end{aligned}
$$

Finally, for formulas of the form $\forall y\ \varphi$, if x has no free occurrence in $\forall y\ \varphi$, then the result is a straightforward consequence of Exercise 3.29. This includes the case $y = x$. Otherwise, y is different from x and t is free for x in φ. Since φ contains a free occurrence of x, t must not contain an occurrence of y, therefore $u(t) = u[y/a](t)$.

Then

$$\mathfrak{A}, u[x/u(t)] \vDash \forall y \; \varphi \;\; \Longleftrightarrow \;\; \text{for all } a \in \mathfrak{A}, \;\;\; \mathfrak{A}, u[x/u(t)][y/a] \vDash \varphi$$
$$\Longleftrightarrow \;\; \text{for all } a \in \mathfrak{A}, \;\;\; \mathfrak{A}, u[y/a][x/u(t)] \vDash \varphi$$
$$\Longleftrightarrow \;\; \text{for all } a \in \mathfrak{A}, \;\;\; \mathfrak{A}, u[y/a][x/u[y/a](t)] \vDash \varphi$$
$$\Longleftrightarrow \;\; \text{for all } a \in \mathfrak{A}, \;\;\; \mathfrak{A}, u[y/a] \vDash \varphi[x/t]$$
$$\Longleftrightarrow \;\; \mathfrak{A}, u \vDash \forall y \; (\varphi[x/t])$$
$$\Longleftrightarrow \;\; \mathfrak{A}, u \vDash (\forall y \; \varphi)[x/t].$$

∎

LEMMA 3.47:   The following formulas are valid under the provisos indicated:

(i) $\forall x \; (\varphi \to \psi) \; \to \; (\forall x \; \varphi \to \forall x \; \psi)$;

(ii) $\forall x \; \varphi \; \to \; \varphi[x/t]$, provided t is free for x in φ;

(iii) $\varphi \to \forall x \; \varphi$, provided x does not occur free in φ.

Proof (i)   Suppose that $\mathfrak{A}, u \vDash \forall x \; (\varphi \to \psi)$ and $\mathfrak{A}, u \vDash \forall x \; \varphi$. Then for any $a \in \mathfrak{A}$, $\mathfrak{A}, u[x/a] \vDash \varphi \to \psi$ and $\mathfrak{A}, u[x/a] \vDash \varphi$. By the semantics of $\to$,

$$\mathfrak{A}, u[x/a] \vDash \varphi \;\; \Longrightarrow \;\; \mathfrak{A}, u[x/a] \vDash \psi,$$

therefore $\mathfrak{A}, u[x/a] \vDash \psi$. Since a was arbitrary, $\mathfrak{A}, u \vDash \forall x \; \psi$. We have shown that

$$\mathfrak{A}, u \vDash \forall x \; (\varphi \to \psi) \;\; \Longrightarrow \;\; (\mathfrak{A}, u \vDash \forall x \; \varphi \;\; \Longrightarrow \;\; \mathfrak{A}, u \vDash \forall x \; \psi),$$

which by the semantics of $\to$ implies that

$$\mathfrak{A}, u \;\; \vDash \;\; \forall x \; (\varphi \to \psi) \; \to \; (\forall x \; \varphi \to \forall x \; \psi).$$

Since $\mathfrak{A}$ and u were arbitrary, (i) is valid.

(ii)   If $\mathfrak{A}, u \vDash \forall x \; \varphi$, then $\mathfrak{A}, u[x/u(t)] \vDash \varphi$. Since t is free for x in φ, by Lemma 3.46(ii), $\mathfrak{A}, u \vDash \varphi[x/t]$. Thus $\mathfrak{A}, u \vDash \forall x \; \varphi \; \to \; \varphi[x/t]$. Since $\mathfrak{A}, u$ was arbitrary, $\forall x \; \varphi \to \varphi[x/t]$ is valid.

(iii)   Since the truth value of $\mathfrak{A}, u \vDash \varphi$ is independent of $u(x)$ if x does not occur free in φ (Exercise 3.29), we have

$$\mathfrak{A}, u \vDash \varphi \;\; \Longrightarrow \;\; \text{for any } a \in \mathfrak{A}, \mathfrak{A}, u[x/a] \vDash \varphi$$
$$\Longrightarrow \;\; \mathfrak{A}, u \vDash \forall x \; \varphi.$$

Combining these implications, we have

$$\mathfrak{A}, u \quad \vDash \quad \varphi \to \forall x \ \varphi.$$

∎

Prenex Form

A formula is in *prenex form* if it is of the form

$$Q_1 x_1 \ Q_2 x_2 \ \ldots \ Q_k x_k \ \varphi,$$

where each Q_i is either $\forall$ or $\exists$ and φ is quantifier-free. The following lemmas will allow us to transform any formula to an equivalent formula in prenex form.

LEMMA 3.48 (CHANGE OF BOUND VARIABLE):   If y is free for x in φ and if y does not occur free in φ, then the formula

$$\forall x \ \varphi \quad \leftrightarrow \quad \forall y \ \varphi[x/y]$$

is valid.

Proof   ($\to$) By Lemma 3.47(ii), the formula

$$\forall x \ \varphi \quad \to \quad \varphi[x/y]$$

is valid, therefore so is

$$\forall y \ (\forall x \ \varphi \quad \to \quad \varphi[x/y]).$$

But then

$$\forall y \ \forall x \ \varphi \quad \to \quad \forall y \ \varphi[x/y]$$
$$\forall x \ \varphi \quad \to \quad \forall y \ \forall x \ \varphi$$

are valid by Lemma 3.47(i) and (iii) respectively, therefore

$$\forall x \ \varphi \quad \to \quad \forall y \ \varphi[x/y]$$

is valid.

($\leftarrow$) Since y is free for x in φ, every free occurrence of x in φ turns into a free occurrence of y in $\varphi[x/y]$. Since y does not occur free in φ, every free occurrence of y in $\varphi[x/y]$ must have come from a free occurrence of x in φ. Also, x does not occur free in $\varphi[x/y]$, since y was substituted for all free occurrences of x; and x is free for y in $\varphi[x/y]$, since y could not have replaced a bound occurrence of x. It follows that $\varphi[x/y][y/x] = \varphi$, thus the situation is completely symmetric to the previous case, and the reverse implication follows from the argument above. ∎

Neither of the two provisos in the statement of Lemma 3.48 can be omitted. We must have y free for x in φ, as can be seen by taking φ to be the formula $\exists y\ y = x + 1$ interpreted over $\mathbb{N}$; and we must not have y occurring free in φ, as can be seen by taking φ to be the formula $y \neq x + 1$ interpreted over $\mathbb{N}$.

The practical significance of Lemma 3.48 is that it can be used to change bound variable names to avoid capture during substitution. Say we wish to substitute into a formula φ a term t with an occurrence of x that would be captured by a quantifier $\forall x$. We can avoid the capture by replacing the x in the quantifier $\forall x$ and all free occurrences of x in the scope of the $\forall x$ with y, where y is a new variable (one with no occurrences in φ). The lemma says that the resulting formula is equivalent.

LEMMA 3.49:   If x does not occur free in ψ, then the following formulas are valid:

$$(\forall x\ \varphi) \to \psi \quad\leftrightarrow\quad \exists x\ (\varphi \to \psi)$$
$$(\exists x\ \varphi) \to \psi \quad\leftrightarrow\quad \forall x\ (\varphi \to \psi)$$
$$\psi \to (\forall x\ \varphi) \quad\leftrightarrow\quad \forall x\ (\psi \to \varphi)$$
$$\psi \to (\exists x\ \varphi) \quad\leftrightarrow\quad \exists x\ (\psi \to \varphi).$$

Proof Exercise 3.31. ∎

A special case of the first two formulas of Lemma 3.49 are the formulas

$$\neg\forall x\ \varphi \quad\leftrightarrow\quad \exists x\ \neg\varphi$$
$$\neg\exists x\ \varphi \quad\leftrightarrow\quad \forall x\ \neg\varphi,$$

which are essentially the definition of $\exists$.

LEMMA 3.50 (PRENEX FORM):   Every formula is equivalent to a formula in prenex form.

Proof Quantifiers can be moved outward outside all occurrences of the propositional operator $\to$ by applying the rules of Lemma 3.49 from left to right. If we wish to apply one of these rules at some point and cannot because of the proviso regarding free variables, then Lemma 3.48 can be used to rename the bound variables. ∎

A Deductive System

In this section we give a complete Hilbert-style deductive system for first-order logic.

AXIOM SYSTEM 3.51:   The axioms of our deductive system consist of the laws of propositional logic and the universal closures of the valid formulas of Lemma 3.47:

(i) $\forall x\ (\varphi \to \psi)\ \to\ (\forall x\ \varphi \to \forall x\ \psi)$;

(ii) $\forall x\ \varphi\ \to\ \varphi[x/t]$, provided t is free for x in φ;

(iii) $\varphi \to \forall x\ \varphi$, provided x does not occur free in φ.

There are two rules of inference:

(MP) $$\frac{\varphi,\quad \varphi \to \psi}{\psi}$$

(GEN) $$\frac{\varphi}{\forall x\ \varphi}.$$

When reasoning in the presence of assumptions, the rule (GEN) may only be applied with the proviso that x does not occur free in any assumption.

The rule (MP) is the rule *modus ponens* of propositional logic (Section 3.2). The rule (GEN) is known as the *generalization rule*.

    This system is easily shown to be sound (Exercise 3.32). Intuitively, the generalization rule is sound because if one could prove $\varphi(x)$ without any assumptions about x, then $\varphi(x)$ is true for arbitrary x.

The Deduction Theorem

THEOREM 3.52 (DEDUCTION THEOREM):   For any set of formulas Φ and formulas φ, ψ,

$$\Phi \cup \{\varphi\} \vdash \psi \quad \Longleftrightarrow \quad \Phi \vdash \varphi \to \psi.$$

Proof The proof is identical to the corresponding proof for propositional logic (Theorem 3.9), except that in the direction ($\Longrightarrow$) there is an extra case for the rule (GEN). Suppose $\Phi \cup \{\varphi\} \vdash \forall x\ \psi$ by an application of the rule (GEN). Then $\Phi \cup \{\varphi\} \vdash \psi$ by a shorter proof, and x is not free in φ or any formula of Φ. By the induction hypothesis, $\Phi \vdash \varphi \to \psi$. By (GEN), $\Phi \vdash \forall x\ (\varphi \to \psi)$. By Axiom 3.51(i) and an application of modus ponens,

$$\Phi \;\vdash\; \forall x\, \varphi \to \forall x\, \psi.$$

But since x does not occur free in φ, by Axiom 3.51(iii) and the transitivity of implication we have

$$\Phi \;\vdash\; \varphi \to \forall x\, \psi.$$

∎

Completeness

As with propositional logic, we will prove completeness of the system 3.51 by proving that every consistent set of formulas Φ, finite or infinite, has a model. However, the situation is complicated somewhat by the presence of quantifiers. We must ensure that the model we construct contains a witness a for every existential formula $\exists x\, \psi$ in Φ. We use a technique of Henkin (1949) in which we include extra variables to provide these witnesses.

We augment the language with the new variables as follows. Let X_0 be the original set of variables, and let L_0 be the original set of formulas over these variables. Now suppose X_n and L_n have been constructed. For each formula $\varphi \in L_n$, let x_φ be a new variable. Let

$$X_{n+1} \;\stackrel{\text{def}}{=}\; X_n \cup \{x_\varphi \mid \varphi \in L_n\},$$

and let L_{n+1} be the language augmented with these new variables. Let

$$X_\omega \;\stackrel{\text{def}}{=}\; \bigcup_n X_n$$
$$L_\omega \;\stackrel{\text{def}}{=}\; \bigcup_n L_n.$$

The sets X_ω and L_ω are still countable, because they are countable unions of countable sets (Exercise 1.21).

Now let $\Psi \subseteq L_\omega$ be the set of all formulas of the form

$$\exists x\, \psi \;\;\to\;\; \psi[x/x_{\exists x\psi}]. \tag{3.4.2}$$

Intuitively, this formula says that if there exists an element x satisfying ψ at all, then the value of $x_{\exists x\psi}$ gives such an element.

LEMMA 3.53:   Let $\Phi \subseteq L_0$. If Φ is consistent, then so is $\Phi \cup \Psi$.

Proof Suppose $\Phi \cup \Psi$ is refutable. Then there is a minimal finite subset Ψ' of Ψ such that $\Phi \cup \Psi'$ is refutable. Also, there must be an existential formula $\varphi = \exists x\, \psi$ and $\varphi \to \psi[x/x_\varphi] \in \Psi'$ such that x_φ does not appear in any other formula in $\Phi \cup \Psi'$: surely x_φ does not occur in any formula of Φ, since $\Phi \subseteq L_0$; and if x_φ occurs in $\exists y \rho \to \rho[y/x_{\exists y \rho}] \in \Psi'$, then x_φ occurs in $\exists y \rho$, therefore $x_{\exists y \rho}$ was introduced strictly later in the inductive definition of X_ω. This can be avoided by choosing x_φ to be the latest such variable introduced among those appearing in Ψ'.

Let $\Psi'' \stackrel{\text{def}}{=} \Psi' - \{\varphi \to \psi[x/x_\varphi]\}$. Then

$$\Phi \cup \Psi'' \cup \{\varphi \to \psi[x/x_\varphi]\} \;\vdash\; \mathbf{0},$$

therefore by the deduction theorem (Theorem 3.52),

$$\Phi \cup \Psi'' \;\vdash\; \neg(\varphi \to \psi[x/x_\varphi]).$$

By propositional logic, we have

$$\Phi \cup \Psi'' \;\vdash\; \varphi$$
$$\Phi \cup \Psi'' \;\vdash\; \neg\psi[x/x_\varphi].$$

By (GEN),

$$\Phi \cup \Psi'' \;\vdash\; \forall x_\varphi \, \neg\psi[x/x_\varphi];$$

changing the bound variable (Exercise 3.30) then gives

$$\Phi \cup \Psi'' \;\vdash\; \forall x \, \neg\psi.$$

Since $\varphi = \exists x\, \psi$, this leads immediately to a refutation of $\Phi \cup \Psi''$, contradicting the minimality of Ψ'. ∎

THEOREM 3.54 (COMPLETENESS):   The deductive system (3.51) is complete; that is, any consistent set of formulas has a model.

Proof Suppose Φ is consistent. By Lemma 3.53, so is $\Phi \cup \Psi$. Extend $\Phi \cup \Psi$ to a maximal consistent set $\widehat{\Phi}$ as in the proof of Lemma 3.10. As argued there, for all $\varphi \in L_\omega$, either $\varphi \in \widehat{\Phi}$ or $\neg\varphi \in \widehat{\Phi}$, and $\widehat{\Phi}$ is deductively closed in the sense that if $\widehat{\Phi} \vdash \psi$ then $\psi \in \widehat{\Phi}$.

Now we construct a model $\mathfrak{A}$ from $\widehat{\Phi}$. The domain of $\mathfrak{A}$ will be the set of terms

$T_\Sigma(X_\omega)$. The function symbols f are interpreted in $\mathfrak{A}$ syntactically:

$$f^{\mathfrak{A}}(t_1, \ldots, t_n) \overset{\text{def}}{=} f(t_1, \ldots, t_n).$$

The truth value of atomic formulas is defined as follows:

$$p^{\mathfrak{A}}(t_1, \ldots, t_n) = \mathbf{1} \overset{\text{def}}{\iff} p(t_1, \ldots, t_n) \in \widehat{\Phi}.$$

Let $u : X_\omega \to T_\Sigma(X_\omega)$ be the valuation $x \mapsto x$. The unique homomorphic extension $u : T_\Sigma(X_\omega) \to T_\Sigma(X_\omega)$ is the identity map. (Here all terms, including variables x, are both syntactic and semantic objects.) We prove by induction on the structure of formulas that for all $\varphi \in L_\omega$,

$$\mathfrak{A}, u \vDash \varphi \iff \varphi \in \widehat{\Phi}.$$

The basis of the induction,

$$\mathfrak{A}, u \vDash p(t_1, \ldots, t_n) \iff p(t_1, \ldots, t_n) \in \widehat{\Phi},$$

is by the definition of $p^{\mathfrak{A}}$. The inductive argument for $\to$ is the same as in the propositional case (Lemma 3.10). Finally, for the case of the existential quantifier, we show that

$$\mathfrak{A}, u \vDash \exists y\, \varphi \iff \exists y\, \varphi \in \widehat{\Phi}.$$

By the definition of the meaning of $\exists$,

$$\mathfrak{A}, u \vDash \exists y\, \varphi \iff \exists t \in T_\Sigma(X_\omega)\ \mathfrak{A}, u[y/t] \vDash \varphi.$$

Assume without loss of generality that all quantified variables in φ have been renamed so as to be different from variables appearing in t; thus t is free for y in φ. Then

$$\exists t \in T_\Sigma(X_\omega)\ \mathfrak{A}, u[y/t] \vDash \varphi$$
$$\iff\ \exists t \in T_\Sigma(X_\omega)\ \mathfrak{A}, u \vDash \varphi[y/t] \qquad \text{by Lemma 3.46(ii)}$$
$$\iff\ \exists t \in T_\Sigma(X_\omega)\ \varphi[y/t] \in \widehat{\Phi} \qquad \text{by the induction hypothesis}$$
$$\iff\ \exists y\, \varphi \in \widehat{\Phi}.$$

In the last step, the direction ($\Longrightarrow$) is from Axiom 3.51(ii) and the direction ($\Longleftarrow$) is from the fact that the formulas (3.4.2) are included in $\widehat{\Phi}$. ∎

Completeness with Equality

First-order logic with equality typically means that the binary equality symbol $=$ is included in the signature Σ and that we restrict the semantics to include only models in which $=$ is interpreted as the identity relation. As it turns out, this is actually not much of a restriction: a structure $\mathfrak{A}$ for which $=^{\mathfrak{A}}$ is not equality but obeys all the laws of equality (Axioms 3.55(ii) and (iii) below) can be collapsed by a quotient construction to give an equivalent model in which $=$ is interpreted as the identity relation.

AXIOM SYSTEM 3.55:   The axioms and rules of inference for first order logic with equality are:

(i) Axiom System 3.51 for first-order logic;

(ii) Axiom System 3.40 for equational logic;

(iii) the rule

$$\frac{s_i = t_i, \quad 1 \le i \le n}{p(s_1, \ldots, s_n) \leftrightarrow p(t_1, \ldots, t_n)}.$$

We regard (iii) as part of the rule (CONG) of Axiom System 3.40.

THEOREM 3.56 (COMPLETENESS WITH EQUALITY):   Axiom System 3.55 is complete for first order logic with equality; that is, any consistent set of formulas has a model.

Proof sketch.   The proof is the same as without equality (Theorem 3.54), except that instead of the term model $T_\Sigma(X_\omega)$, we take its quotient by the congruence

$$s \equiv t \quad \overset{\text{def}}{\Longleftrightarrow} \quad s = t \in \widehat{\Phi}.$$

The new rule (iii) ensures that $p^{\mathfrak{A}}$ is well-defined on $\equiv$-congruence classes. ∎

Compactness

We proved in Section 3.4 that any consistent set of first-order formulas has a model. The *compactness theorem* is an immediate consequence of this. Recall that a set of formulas Φ is *finitely satisfiable* if all finite subsets of Φ have a model.

THEOREM 3.57 (COMPACTNESS):   A set Φ of first-order formulas is satisfiable if and only if it is finitely satisfiable.

Proof The proof is the same as for propositional logic (Theorem 3.12), using Theorem 3.54. ∎

The Löwenheim–Skolem Theorem

Our proof of the completeness theorem constructed models from terms, or in the presence of equality, from congruence classes of terms. Since the language has only countably many terms, the models constructed were countable (either finite or countably infinite). We thus have

COROLLARY 3.58:   Let Φ be a countable set of formulas. If Φ has a model, then it has a countable model.

The first part of Theorem 3.59 below is a slight strengthening of this.

THEOREM 3.59 (LÖWENHEIM–SKOLEM):   Let Φ be a countable set of formulas.

(i) If Φ has an infinite model, then it has a countably infinite model.

(ii) If Φ has a countably infinite model, then it has a model of every infinite cardinality.

Parts (i) and (ii) of Theorem 3.59 are known as the *downward* and *upward Löwenheim–Skolem theorem*, respectively.

Proof sketch.   (i)   Suppose $\mathfrak{A}, u \vDash \Phi$, $\mathfrak{A}$ infinite. Let

$$\Phi^+ \overset{\text{def}}{=} \Phi \cup \{\theta_n \mid n \geq 0\},$$

where

$$\theta_n \overset{\text{def}}{=} \exists x_1 \, \exists x_2 \, \ldots \, \exists x_n \bigwedge_{1 \leq i < j \leq n} x_i \neq x_j.$$

The sentence θ_n says, "There are at least n elements." Then Φ^+ is consistent, since it has a model $\mathfrak{A}$. By Corollary 3.58, Φ^+ has a countable model, say $\mathfrak{B}$. But $\mathfrak{B}$ cannot be finite, since $\mathfrak{B} \vDash \theta_n$ for all n.

(ii)   Let κ be any infinite cardinality, and let

$$X \overset{\text{def}}{=} \{x_\alpha \mid \alpha < \kappa\}$$

be a set of new variables. Then $\#X = \kappa$. Suppose Φ has an infinite model $\mathfrak{A}$. Let

$$\Phi^+ \;\overset{\text{def}}{=}\; \Phi \cup \{x_\alpha \neq x_\beta \mid \alpha < \beta < \kappa\}.$$

Note that $\#\Phi^+ = \kappa$, so we are no longer necessarily working in a countable language. Nevertheless, the technique of the completeness theorem (Theorem 3.54) still applies. The set Φ^+ is consistent, because any refutation would involve only a finite subset of Φ^+, and every such subset has a model, namely $\mathfrak{A}$. We then construct a maximal consistent extension of Φ^+ as in the proof of Theorem 3.54, the only difference here being that we need transfinite induction. We form a term algebra $\mathfrak{A}$ and valuation u such that $\mathfrak{A}, u \vDash \Phi^+$. Now $\#\mathfrak{A} \leq \kappa$, since the number of terms is at most κ; and $\#\mathfrak{A} \geq \kappa$, since $\mathfrak{A}, u \vDash x_\alpha \neq x_\beta$ for all $\alpha < \beta < \kappa$. $\blacksquare$

Undecidability

It is undecidable for given a sentence φ of first-order logic whether $\vDash \varphi$. In fact, the problem is Σ_1^0-complete.

THEOREM 3.60:   The validity problem for first-order logic is Σ_1^0-complete.

Proof   That the problem is in Σ_1^0 follows from the completeness theorem. Since a formula is valid iff it has a proof, the set of valid formulas can be recursively enumerated in a uniform way simply by enumerating all proofs and checking their validity.

For Σ_1^0-hardness, we work with the complement of the validity problem, namely the *satisfiability problem*: given a first-order formula φ, is it satisfied in some model? We show that this problem is Π_1^0-hard by a reduction from the Π_1^0-complete tiling problem of Proposition 2.20: given a finite set of tile types, is there a tiling of the infinite $\omega \times \omega$ grid in which the south and west boundaries are colored blue?

We will work in a fixed first-order language consisting of one constant symbol a, one unary function symbol f, and four ternary relation symbols $\text{NORTH}(x, y, z)$, $\text{SOUTH}(x, y, z)$, $\text{EAST}(x, y, z)$, and $\text{WEST}(x, y, z)$. Intuitively, the arguments x, y will denote a grid position and z a color. The grid position $(i, j) \in \omega^2$ will be encoded by the pair $(f^i(a), f^j(a))$, where $f^0(a) \overset{\text{def}}{=} a$ and $f^{n+1}(a) \overset{\text{def}}{=} f(f^n(a))$. A color $c \in \mathbb{N}$ will be encoded by the term $f^c(a)$. Intuitively, the predicate $\text{EAST}(f^i(a), f^j(a), f^c(a))$ says, "The east edge of the tile at position i, j is colored c." Although we are thinking intuitively of an $\omega \times \omega$ grid, keep in mind that we are interpreting formulas over arbitrary structures, not just ω.

Let T be a given finite set of tile types. Each tile type is determined by the colors of the four edges. Let C be the finite set of colors appearing in T. For each tile type $A \in T$, we can define a predicate that says that the tile at position x, y is of type A. For instance, if A is the type

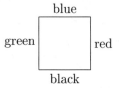

we can define

$$\text{TILE}_A(x,y) \overset{\text{def}}{\iff} \text{NORTH}(x,y,f^{\text{blue}}(a)) \wedge \bigwedge_{\substack{c \in C \\ c \neq \text{blue}}} \neg\text{NORTH}(x,y,f^c(a))$$

$$\wedge \text{SOUTH}(x,y,f^{\text{black}}(a)) \wedge \bigwedge_{\substack{c \in C \\ c \neq \text{black}}} \neg\text{SOUTH}(x,y,f^c(a))$$

$$\wedge \text{EAST}(x,y,f^{\text{red}}(a)) \wedge \bigwedge_{\substack{c \in C \\ c \neq \text{red}}} \neg\text{EAST}(x,y,f^c(a))$$

$$\wedge \text{WEST}(x,y,f^{\text{green}}(a)) \wedge \bigwedge_{\substack{c \in C \\ c \neq \text{green}}} \neg\text{WEST}(x,y,f^c(a))$$

This says that each of the four edges of the tile at position x, y is colored with exactly one color, and the colors correspond to the tile type A.

Let φ_T be the conjunction of the following five sentences:

$$\forall x \, \forall y \, \bigvee_{A \in T} \text{TILE}_A(x,y) \tag{3.4.3}$$

$$\forall x \, \text{SOUTH}(x,a,f^{\text{blue}}(a)) \tag{3.4.4}$$

$$\forall y \, \text{WEST}(a,y,f^{\text{blue}}(a)) \tag{3.4.5}$$

$$\forall x \, \forall y \, \bigwedge_{c \in C}(\text{EAST}(x,y,f^c(a)) \rightarrow \text{WEST}(f(x),y,f^c(a))) \tag{3.4.6}$$

$$\forall x \, \forall y \, \bigwedge_{c \in C}(\text{NORTH}(x,y,f^c(a)) \rightarrow \text{SOUTH}(x,f(y),f^c(a))) \tag{3.4.7}$$

The predicate (3.4.3) says that every grid position is tiled with exactly one tile. The predicates (3.4.4) and (3.4.5) say that the south and west boundaries of the grid are colored blue. The predicates (3.4.6) and (3.4.7) say that the edges of adjacent tiles match.

We now argue that φ_T is satisfiable iff there exists a tiling of the grid with the given set of tile types.

First assume that $\mathfrak{A} \vDash \varphi_T$. Tile the grid as follows. Place a tile of type A at position (i, j), where A is the unique tile type such that $\mathfrak{A} \vDash \text{TILE}_A(f^i(a), f^j(a))$. At least one such tile type must exist, because $\mathfrak{A}$ satisfies (3.4.3); and no more than one such tile type can exist, because the definition of $\text{TILE}_A(f^i(a), f^j(a))$ rules out all other colorings. The remaining four clauses of φ_T assert that the local coloring conditions are satisfied by this tiling.

Conversely, suppose that the grid can be tiled with tile types from T. We can satisfy φ_T in a structure $\mathfrak{A}$ with carrier ω in which a is interpreted as 0 and f is interpreted as the successor function $x \mapsto x + 1$. The interpretation of the ternary relation symbols depends on the tiling. For example, we take $\text{EAST}(i, j, k)$ to be true if the east edge of the tile at position (i, j) has color k, and similarly for the other relation symbols. It is easy to see that φ_T holds in $\mathfrak{A}$. ∎

3.5   Ehrenfeucht–Fraïssé Games

Ehrenfeucht–Fraïssé games are a technique for proving results about the expressiveness of logical languages involving quantification. There are different variations, depending on the application. Here is one:

Consider the following game between two players called the *duplicator* and the *spoiler*. The game board consists of two first-order structures $\mathfrak{A}$ and $\mathfrak{B}$. Each player is given n pebbles, one of each of n different colors.

The play alternates between the players with the spoiler going first. In each round, the spoiler places one of his pebbles on an element of either structure. The duplicator then places her pebble of the same color on an element of the other structure. The play alternates until all the pebbles have been played. If the final configuration of pebbles is a *local isomorphism*, then the duplicator wins; otherwise the spoiler wins. A configuration is a *local isomorphism* if for any atomic formula $\varphi(x_1, \ldots, x_n)$,

$$\mathfrak{A}, u \vDash \varphi(x_1, \ldots, x_n) \iff \mathfrak{B}, v \vDash \varphi(x_1, \ldots, x_n),$$

where u, v are valuations assigning to each variable x_i, $1 \leq i \leq n$, the element occupied by the pebble of color i in $\mathfrak{A}$ and $\mathfrak{B}$, respectively.

The interesting fact about this game is that the duplicator has a forced win—that is, can always assure a win for herself by playing optimally—if and only if $\mathfrak{A}$ and $\mathfrak{B}$ are indistinguishable by any first-order sentence of quantifier depth n or less. (The *quantifier depth* of a sentence is the maximum number of quantifiers in whose scope any symbol occurs.)

For example, consider the two-pebble game played on the total orders $(\mathbb{Z}, \leq)$ and $(\mathbb{Q}, \leq)$ (we ignore the algebraic structure of $\mathbb{Z}$ and $\mathbb{Q}$ and only consider their order structure). Think of the elements of these structures laid out on a line in increasing order from left to right. The duplicator can always achieve a win by the following strategy. In the first round, the spoiler plays his red pebble somewhere, then the duplicator plays her red pebble on an arbitrary element of the other structure. In the second round, if the spoiler plays his blue pebble to the left, on top, or to the right of the red pebble on either structure, then the duplicator plays her blue pebble to the left, on top, or to the right of the red pebble on the other structure, respectively. This always gives a local isomorphism, so the duplicator wins. This says that these two structures agree on any first-order sentence of quantifier depth two or less.

On the other hand, the spoiler can always win the three-pebble game on these structures by the following strategy. In the first round, he plays his red pebble on $0 \in \mathbb{Z}$. The duplicator must respond by playing her red pebble on some element $x \in \mathbb{Q}$. In the second round, the spoiler plays his blue pebble on $1 \in \mathbb{Z}$. The duplicator must respond by playing her blue pebble on some element $y \in \mathbb{Q}$, and she had better play it on some $y > x$, otherwise she loses immediately. In the third round, the spoiler plays his green pebble on some element of $\mathbb{Q}$ strictly between x and y, and the duplicator has nowhere to play on $\mathbb{Z}$ to maintain the local isomorphism. The spoiler wins.

These arguments reflect the fact that the ordered structure $(\mathbb{Q}, \leq)$ is dense, whereas $(\mathbb{Z}, \leq)$ is not. The two structures are distinguished by the sentence

$$\forall x \ \forall z \ (x < z \rightarrow \exists y \ (x < y \wedge y < z))$$

of quantifier depth three, and this is the minimum quantifier depth needed to express density.

3.6 Infinitary Logic

In some cases, we will find it convenient to allow infinite conjunctions and disjunctions of formulas; that is, formulas of form $\bigwedge_{\alpha \in A} \varphi_\alpha$ and $\bigvee_{\alpha \in A} \varphi_\alpha$, where $\{\varphi_\alpha \mid \alpha \in A\}$ is an indexed family of formulas, possibly infinite. The meaning of these formulas is just what one would expect: $\mathfrak{A}, u \vDash \bigwedge_{\alpha \in A} \varphi_\alpha$ iff for all $\alpha \in A$, $\mathfrak{A}, u \vDash \varphi_\alpha$, and $\mathfrak{A}, u \vDash \bigvee_{\alpha \in A} \varphi_\alpha$ iff for at least one $\alpha \in A$, $\mathfrak{A}, u \vDash \varphi_\alpha$.

Two particular infinitary systems that will arise in Chapter 12 and thereafter are $L_{\omega_1 \omega}$ and $L_{\omega_1^{ck} \omega}$. The language $L_{\omega_1 \omega}$ is obtained by extending first-order logic to allow formulas with countable conjunctions and disjunctions but only finitely many variables.

Unlike first-order logic, formulas are now possibly infinite objects. However, each formula may contain only finitely many variables. The ω_1 in $L_{\omega_1\omega}$ signifies that countable conjunctions and disjunctions are allowed, and the ω signifies the restriction to finitely many variables.

Syntax

Formally, we amend the inductive definition of formulas as follows. Let C be a fixed *finite* set of variables. The set L_C of *formulas over* C is the smallest set of formulas containing all atomic formulas all of whose variables are in C and closed under the usual closure rules for first-order logic as given Section 3.4, allowing quantification only over elements of C. In addition, we include in the inductive definition the extra clause

If $\{\varphi_\alpha \mid \alpha \in A\}$ is an indexed family of formulas of L_C and A is countable, then $\bigwedge_{\alpha \in A} \varphi_\alpha$ and $\bigvee_{\alpha \in A} \varphi_\alpha$ are formulas of L_C.

The set $L_{\omega_1\omega}$ is the union of all L_C for all finite subsets C of some fixed countable set of variables.

The language $L_{\omega_1^{ck}\omega}$ is the sublanguage of $L_{\omega_1\omega}$ in which the countable conjunctions and disjunctions are further restricted to be over *recursively enumerable* sets of formulas. Thus we can form a countable conjunction $\bigwedge_{\varphi \in A} \varphi$ or disjunction $\bigvee_{\varphi \in A} \varphi$ provided the set A is r.e.

It is convenient to think of a formula of $L_{\omega_1\omega}$ as a well-founded infinitary labeled tree. Each vertex of the tree is labeled with $\forall x$, $\exists x$, $\neg$, $\bigvee$, $\bigwedge$, or an atomic formula. Vertices labeled $\forall x$, $\exists x$, or $\neg$ have one child; vertices labeled $\bigvee$ or $\bigwedge$ have countably many children; and atomic formulas label the leaves. The tree is well-founded (no infinite paths) because the definition of formulas is inductive.

Under a suitable encoding, the tree corresponding to a formula of $L_{\omega_1^{ck}\omega}$ is recursively enumerable. Such trees were encountered in Section 2.2. This gives us a computational handle on infinitary formulas. For example, our encoding might represent the formula $\bigwedge_{\varphi \in A} \varphi$ as the pair of numbers $(5, i)$, where 5 indicates that the formula is a conjunction and the i is a description of a Turing machine enumerating the codes of the formulas in the r.e. set A. A universal Turing machine can then be used to enumerate the entire tree.

Another advantage of $L_{\omega_1^{ck}\omega}$ over $L_{\omega_1\omega}$ is that over a countable signature, there are only countably many formulas of $L_{\omega_1^{ck}\omega}$. This is not true for $L_{\omega_1\omega}$.

The language $L_{\omega_1^{ck}\omega}$ is not compact, nor does it satisfy the upward Löwenheim–Skolem theorem: the countable set

$$\{ \bigvee_{n<\omega} p(f^n(a))\} \;\cup\; \{\neg p(f^n(a)) \mid n < \omega\}$$

is finitely satisfiable but not satisfiable (Exercise 3.35), and the sentence

$$\forall x \bigvee_{n<\omega} x = f^n(a) \tag{3.6.1}$$

has a countable model but no model of higher cardinality (Exercise 3.36). The same holds *a fortiori* for the language $L_{\omega_1\omega}$. However, the downward Löwenheim–Skolem holds, and one can give a complete infinitary deductive system for both $L_{\omega_1\omega}$ and $L_{\omega_1^{ck}\omega}$. These are the topics of the next section.

An Infinitary Deductive System

To obtain a deductive system for $L_{\omega_1\omega}$ and $L_{\omega_1^{ck}\omega}$, we augment the deductive system for first-order predicate logic given in Section 3.4 with the axioms

$$\varphi_\beta \;\rightarrow\; \bigvee_{\alpha \in A} \varphi_\alpha, \qquad \beta \in A, \tag{3.6.2}$$

$$\bigwedge_{\alpha \in A} \varphi_\alpha \;\rightarrow\; \varphi_\beta, \qquad \beta \in A, \tag{3.6.3}$$

as well as the infinitary rules of inference

$$\frac{\varphi_\alpha \rightarrow \psi, \; \alpha \in A}{(\bigvee_{\alpha \in A} \varphi_\alpha) \rightarrow \psi} \tag{3.6.4}$$

$$\frac{\varphi \rightarrow \psi_\alpha, \; \alpha \in A}{\varphi \rightarrow \bigwedge_{\alpha \in A} \psi_\alpha}. \tag{3.6.5}$$

The new rules of inference may have infinitely many premises. Thus proofs, like formulas, are no longer finite objects. However, like formulas, proofs can be represented as well-founded infinitary labeled trees, with the axioms labeling the leaves and the theorem labeling the root. Moreover, in $L_{\omega_1^{ck}\omega}$, because infinite conjunctions and disjunctions must be r.e., proof trees are r.e. as well.

Like formulas, we artificially restrict proofs to contain only finitely many variables. By definition, a proof is not a proof unless there is a finite set of variables C such that all formulas labeling the vertices of the proof tree are in L_C.

EXAMPLE 3.61:   The deductive system can be used to prove infinitary versions of the basic propositional tautologies. For example, consider the infinitary De Morgan law

$$\neg \bigvee_\alpha \varphi_\alpha \; \leftrightarrow \; \bigwedge_\alpha \neg\varphi_\alpha. \tag{3.6.6}$$

We prove the implication in both directions using the deductive system.

($\rightarrow$)   By (3.6.5), it suffices to show

$$\neg \bigvee_\alpha \varphi_\alpha \; \rightarrow \; \neg\varphi_\beta$$

for each β. By (finitary) propositional logic, this is equivalent to

$$\varphi_\beta \; \rightarrow \; \bigvee_\alpha \varphi_\alpha.$$

But this is just (3.6.2).

($\leftarrow$)   By propositional logic, the implication is equivalent to

$$\bigvee_\alpha \varphi_\alpha \; \rightarrow \; \neg \bigwedge_\alpha \neg\varphi_\alpha.$$

By (3.6.4), it suffices to show

$$\varphi_\beta \; \rightarrow \; \neg \bigwedge_\alpha \neg\varphi_\alpha$$

for each β, which by propositional logic is equivalent to

$$\bigwedge_\alpha \neg\varphi_\alpha \; \rightarrow \; \neg\varphi_\beta.$$

But this is just an instance of (3.6.3).

EXAMPLE 3.62:   For another example, consider the infinitary distributive law

$$\varphi \vee \bigwedge_\alpha \psi_\alpha \; \leftrightarrow \; \bigwedge_\alpha (\varphi \vee \psi_\alpha). \tag{3.6.7}$$

We prove the implication in both directions.

($\rightarrow$)   By (3.6.5), it suffices to show

$$\varphi \vee \bigwedge_\alpha \psi_\alpha \; \rightarrow \; \varphi \vee \psi_\beta$$

for each β. This follows immediately from (3.6.3) and propositional logic.

($\leftarrow$)   By propositional logic, the implication is equivalent to

$$\neg\varphi \wedge \bigwedge_{\alpha}(\varphi \vee \psi_\alpha) \;\; \rightarrow \;\; \bigwedge_{\alpha} \psi_\alpha. \tag{3.6.8}$$

For all β, we have

$$\neg\varphi \wedge \bigwedge_{\alpha}(\varphi \vee \psi_\alpha) \;\; \rightarrow \;\; \neg\varphi \wedge (\varphi \vee \psi_\beta) \quad \text{by (3.6.3)}$$

$$\rightarrow \;\; \psi_\beta;$$

then (3.6.8) follows from (3.6.5).

Infinitary versions of other basic properties are given in Exercise 3.37.

THEOREM 3.63 (INFINITARY DEDUCTION THEOREM):   For any set of formulas Φ and formulas φ, ψ of $L_{\omega_1\omega}$,

$$\Phi \cup \{\varphi\} \vdash \psi \;\; \Longleftrightarrow \;\; \Phi \vdash \varphi \rightarrow \psi.$$

Proof   The proof is the same as for first-order logic (Theorem 3.52), except that in the direction ($\Longrightarrow$) there are extra cases for the rules (3.6.4) and (3.6.5). We argue the case (3.6.5) explicitly and leave the case (3.6.4) as an exercise (Exercise 3.38).

Suppose $\Phi \cup \{\varphi\} \vdash \psi \rightarrow \bigwedge_{\alpha} \psi_\alpha$ by an application of the rule (3.6.5). Then for each β, $\Phi \cup \{\varphi\} \vdash \psi \rightarrow \psi_\beta$ by a shorter proof; here "shorter" means the well-founded proof tree is shallower.[4] By the induction hypothesis, $\Phi \vdash \varphi \rightarrow (\psi \rightarrow \psi_\beta)$, and by propositional logic, $\Phi \vdash (\varphi \wedge \psi) \rightarrow \psi_\beta$. By (3.6.5), $\Phi \vdash (\varphi \wedge \psi) \rightarrow \bigwedge_{\alpha} \psi_\alpha$, and again by propositional logic, $\Phi \vdash \varphi \rightarrow (\psi \rightarrow \bigwedge_{\alpha} \psi_\alpha)$.   ∎

Now we show that the deductive system is complete. The proof mirrors closely that for first-order logic given in Theorem 3.52 with appropriate modifications to handle infinitary conjunctions and disjunctions.

First we note that for any formula φ of $L_{\omega_1\omega}$, the number of subformulas of φ is countable. This can be proved by induction using the fact that a countable union of countable sets is countable (Exercise 1.21). It follows that if Φ is a countable set of formulas, then the set of all subformulas of formulas in Φ and their negations is countable.

We form the sets X_n, L_n, X_ω, and L_ω as in the proof of Theorem 3.52, except that we must amend the definition slightly to ensure that the resulting set of

---

4 Formally, the ordinal $\text{ord}(T)$ labeling the root of the proof tree T under the labeling scheme described in Section 2.2 is smaller.

formulas is countable whenever Φ is. Starting with a set of formulas L_0 over a set of variables X_0, we form L_n and X_n inductively as follows. For each φ in L_n, create a new variable $x_\varphi \in X_{n+1}$ and let

$$X_{n+1} \stackrel{\text{def}}{=} X_n \cup \{x_\varphi \mid \varphi \in L_n\}.$$

Now let L_{n+1} be the set of formulas obtained from L_n by changing any bound variable to one of the new variables in X_{n+1} (Lemma 3.48) and by substituting any term over X_{n+1} for any free variable. Thus in this construction we do not consider the set of all $L_{\omega_1\omega}$ formulas, which is uncountable, but only those that are similar to a formula of L_0 except for change of bound variable or substitution of a term for a free variable. By Exercise 1.21, if the original sets L_0 and X_0 are countable, then the resulting sets L_ω and X_ω will be countable as well. In our application, we will take L_0 to be the set of subformulas of formulas in Φ and their negations.

As in the proof of Theorem 3.52, we take Ψ to be the set of all formulas of L_ω of the form

$$\exists x \, \psi \;\; \rightarrow \;\; \psi[x/x_{\exists x\psi}]. \tag{3.6.9}$$

LEMMA 3.64:   Let $\Phi \subseteq L_0$. If Φ is consistent, then so is $\Phi \cup \Psi$.

Proof   In the proof of the corresponding theorem for first-order logic (Theorem 3.52), the first step was to observe that if $\Phi \cup \Psi$ is refutable, then there exists a finite subset $\Psi' \subseteq \Psi$ such that $\Phi \cup \Psi'$ is refutable. This was obvious there, since proofs were finite objects, therefore could refer to at most finitely many members of Ψ. Here formulas and proofs are no longer finite objects; nevertheless, the observation still holds, since proofs may contain only finitely many variables, and each formula (3.6.9) contains a distinct variable $x_{\exists x\psi}$, therefore at most finitely many of them can appear in the refutation. The remainder of the proof is the same as the proof for first-order logic (Theorem 3.52). ∎

THEOREM 3.65 (COMPLETENESS):   The infinitary deductive system is complete; that is, any consistent set of formulas has a model.

Proof   Everything is the same as in the first-order case (Theorem 3.54), except that in the inductive argument that

$$\mathfrak{A}, u \vDash \varphi \;\; \Longleftrightarrow \;\; \varphi \in \widehat{\Phi},$$

we have two extra cases for infinitary join and meet. For infinitary meet, we have

$$\mathfrak{A}, u \vDash \bigwedge_\alpha \varphi_\alpha \iff \text{for all } \beta, \quad \mathfrak{A}, u \vDash \varphi_\beta \quad \text{definition of } \vDash$$

$$\iff \text{for all } \beta, \quad \varphi_\beta \in \widehat{\Phi} \quad \text{induction hypothesis}$$

$$\iff \textstyle\bigwedge_\alpha \varphi_\alpha \in \widehat{\Phi} \quad \text{consistency and maximality of } \widehat{\Phi}.$$

The case of infinitary join is similar. ∎

The Downward Löwenheim–Skolem Theorem

THEOREM 3.66 (DOWNWARD LÖWENHEIM–SKOLEM):   Let Φ be a countable set of formulas of $L_{\omega_1 \omega}$. If Φ has a model, then it has a countable model.

Proof If Φ has a model, then it is consistent, since the deductive system is sound. In the construction of the term model of the completeness theorem, if we restrict our attention to subformulas of formulas in Φ and their negations, the resulting model is countable. ∎

Complexity

THEOREM 3.67:   Deciding the validity of $L_{\omega_1^{ck}\omega}$ formulas is Π_1^1-complete.

Proof The problem is in Π_1^1, because by the completeness theorem (Theorem 3.65), a formula is valid iff it has a recursively enumerable well-founded proof tree, and this is a statement of the form (2.2.3). Alternatively, one can give an explicit IND program (see Section 2.2) accepting the code of a formula of $L_{\omega_1^{ck}\omega}$ iff it is provable (Exercise 3.39).

To show that the problem is Π_1^1-hard, we encode (the complement of) the tiling problem of Proposition 2.22. The construction is very similar to that of Theorem 3.60, except that we include the formula (3.6.1) to restrict to models consisting essentially of the natural numbers, as well as a formula ψ_{red} that says that red occurs only finitely often in the tiling:

$$\mathrm{RED}(x,y) \stackrel{\text{def}}{\iff} \mathrm{NORTH}(x,y,f^{\mathrm{red}}(a)) \vee \mathrm{SOUTH}(x,y,f^{\mathrm{red}}(a))$$
$$\vee \mathrm{EAST}(x,y,f^{\mathrm{red}}(a)) \vee \mathrm{WEST}(x,y,f^{\mathrm{red}}(a))$$
$$\psi_{\mathrm{red}} \stackrel{\text{def}}{\iff} \exists x \, \forall y \, \forall z \; z \geq x \to (\neg \mathrm{RED}(y,z) \wedge \neg \mathrm{RED}(z,y)).$$

If φ is the formula constructed in the proof of Theorem 3.60, which says that we have a valid tiling, and if ψ is the sentence (3.6.1), then the desired formula is

$$\varphi \wedge \psi \;\; \rightarrow \;\; \psi_{\mathrm{red}},$$

which says that if the model represents a valid tiling of the $\omega \times \omega$ grid, then red is used only finitely often. Unlike the case of Theorem 3.60, we must include ψ here to ensure that the existential quantifiers in ψ_{red} refer to grid elements. ∎

3.7 Modal Logic

Modal logic is the logic of *possibility* and *necessity*. There is not a single system of modal logic, but many different systems depending on the application. Modal logic is good for reasoning in situations involving incomplete information or dependence on time. It is also useful in applications involving knowledge, belief, and provability.

Propositional Modal Logic

Propositional logic (Section 3.2) can be extended to propositional modal logic by adding a new unary operator $\Box$, the *necessity* operator. Thus if φ is a formula, then so is $\Box\varphi$. This clause is added as part of the inductive definition of the language. There is a dual operator $\Diamond\varphi$, the *possibility* operator, defined by

$$\Diamond\varphi \;\; \overset{\text{def}}{\Longleftrightarrow} \;\; \neg\Box\neg\varphi. \tag{3.7.1}$$

The formula $\Box\varphi$ is read, "it is *necessary* that φ," or "φ holds in all possible worlds," or just "box φ." The formula $\Diamond\varphi$ is read, "it is *possible* that φ," or "there is a possible world that realizes φ," or just "diamond φ." The property (3.7.1) expresses a duality between $\Box$ and $\Diamond$; intuitively, φ is necessarily true iff it is impossible that φ is false.

Semantically, we interpret modal formulas in structures called *Kripke frames*. A *Kripke frame* is a structure $\mathfrak{K} = (K, R_\mathfrak{K}, \mathfrak{m}_\mathfrak{K})$, where K is a nonempty set, $R_\mathfrak{K}$ is a binary relation on K called the *accessibility relation*, and $\mathfrak{m}_\mathfrak{K}$ is a function assigning a subset of K to each atomic proposition. The class K is called the *universe* of $\mathfrak{K}$ and the elements of K are called *states* or *worlds*. Intuitively, $R_\mathfrak{K}$ specifies which worlds are *accessible* (or possible) from the point of view of a given world; that is, $(u, v) \in R_\mathfrak{K}$ says that v is a possible world from the point of view of u.

The function $\mathfrak{m}_\mathfrak{K}$ determines a truth assignment to the primitive propositions in each state; we write $u \vDash p$ if $u \in \mathfrak{m}_\mathfrak{K}(p)$. We extend $\mathfrak{m}_\mathfrak{K}$ inductively to all modal formulas according to the following rules:

$$\mathsf{m}_{\mathfrak{K}}(\varphi \to \psi) \stackrel{\text{def}}{=} (K - \mathsf{m}_{\mathfrak{K}}(\varphi)) \cup \mathsf{m}_{\mathfrak{K}}(\psi), \tag{3.7.2}$$

$$\mathsf{m}_{\mathfrak{K}}(\mathbf{0}) \stackrel{\text{def}}{=} \varnothing, \tag{3.7.3}$$

$$\mathsf{m}_{\mathfrak{K}}(\Box\varphi) \stackrel{\text{def}}{=} K - (R_{\mathfrak{K}} \circ (K - \mathsf{m}_{\mathfrak{K}}(\varphi))), \tag{3.7.4}$$

where $\circ$ denotes relational composition (see Section 1.3). It follows that

$$\mathsf{m}_{\mathfrak{K}}(\Diamond\varphi) = R_{\mathfrak{K}} \circ \mathsf{m}_{\mathfrak{K}}(\varphi). \tag{3.7.5}$$

Writing $s \vDash \varphi$ for $s \in \mathsf{m}_{\mathfrak{K}}(\varphi)$, we see that (3.7.2)–(3.7.5) are equivalent to

$$u \vDash \varphi \to \psi \iff (u \vDash \varphi \implies u \vDash \psi),$$
$$u \nvDash \mathbf{0},$$
$$u \vDash \Box\varphi \iff \text{for all } v, \text{ if } (u,v) \in R_{\mathfrak{K}} \text{ then } v \vDash \varphi,$$
$$u \vDash \Diamond\varphi \iff \text{there exists } v \text{ such that } (u,v) \in R_{\mathfrak{K}} \text{ and } v \vDash \varphi,$$

respectively. The rules (3.7.2) and (3.7.3) are the same as in propositional logic, and (3.7.4) and (3.7.5) interpret the modalities.

We write $\mathfrak{K}, u \vDash \varphi$ if $u \vDash \varphi$ in the Kripke frame $\mathfrak{K}$, or just $u \vDash \varphi$ if $\mathfrak{K}$ is understood. We write $\mathfrak{K} \vDash \varphi$ iff $\mathfrak{K}, u \vDash \varphi$ for all states u of $\mathfrak{K}$. We write $\vDash \varphi$ if $\mathfrak{K} \vDash \varphi$ for all frames $\mathfrak{K}$ and say that φ is *valid*.

If Φ is a set of modal formulas, we write $\mathfrak{K}, u \vDash \Phi$ if $\mathfrak{K}, u \vDash \varphi$ for all $\varphi \in \Phi$, and we write $\mathfrak{K} \vDash \Phi$ if $\mathfrak{K}, u \vDash \Phi$ for all $u \in K$. If there exists a Kripke frame $\mathfrak{K}$ and state u of $\mathfrak{K}$ such that $\mathfrak{K}, u \vDash \Phi$, then we say that Φ is *satisfiable*. As in propositional and predicate logic, a formula φ is valid iff its negation is not satisfiable.

If $\varphi_1, \ldots, \varphi_n$ and φ are modal formulas, the rule of inference

$$\frac{\varphi_1, \ldots, \varphi_n}{\varphi}$$

is *sound* if $\mathfrak{K} \vDash \varphi$ whenever $\mathfrak{K} \vDash \varphi_i$, $1 \le i \le n$. Note that this is *not* the same as saying that $\mathfrak{K}, u \vDash \varphi$ whenever $\mathfrak{K}, u \vDash \varphi_i$, $1 \le i \le n$.

The modalities $\Box$ and $\Diamond$ capture various properties of our metalogic that we have been using in previous sections. The following are some examples.

EXAMPLE 3.68: Let P be a set of atomic propositions, and let $\mathfrak{K} = (K, R_{\mathfrak{K}}, \mathsf{m}_{\mathfrak{K}})$

be the Kripke frame with

$$
\begin{aligned}
K &= \{\text{truth assignments to } P\}, \\
R_{\mathfrak{K}} &= K \times K, \\
\mathfrak{m}_{\mathfrak{K}}(p) &= \{u \mid u(p) = \mathbf{1}\}.
\end{aligned}
$$

Then a propositional formula φ is a tautology iff $\mathfrak{K} \vDash \Box \varphi$, and φ is satisfiable iff $\mathfrak{K} \vDash \Diamond \varphi$.

EXAMPLE 3.69: Let $(P, <)$ be a strict partial order with bottom element 0. In a Kripke frame $\mathfrak{K}$ with states P and accessibility relation $<$,

- $\mathfrak{K}, a \vDash \Box \mathbf{0}$ if a is a maximal element of P;

- $\mathfrak{K}, 0 \vDash \Diamond \Box \mathbf{0}$ iff P contains a maximal element;

- $\mathfrak{K}, 0 \vDash \Box \Diamond \Box \mathbf{0}$ iff every element is below a maximal element.

THEOREM 3.70: The following are valid formulas of propositional modal logic:

(i) $\Diamond(\varphi \vee \psi) \;\leftrightarrow\; \Diamond \varphi \vee \Diamond \psi$

(ii) $\Box(\varphi \wedge \psi) \;\leftrightarrow\; \Box \varphi \wedge \Box \psi$

(iii) $\Diamond \varphi \wedge \Box \psi \;\rightarrow\; \Diamond(\varphi \wedge \psi)$

(iv) $\Box(\varphi \rightarrow \psi) \;\rightarrow\; (\Box \varphi \rightarrow \Box \psi)$

(v) $\Diamond(\varphi \wedge \psi) \;\rightarrow\; \Diamond \varphi \wedge \Diamond \psi$

(vi) $\Box \varphi \vee \Box \psi \;\rightarrow\; \Box(\varphi \vee \psi)$

(vii) $\Diamond \mathbf{0} \;\leftrightarrow\; \mathbf{0}$

(viii) $\Box \varphi \;\leftrightarrow\; \neg \Diamond \neg \varphi.$

Proof These results are straightforward exercises in relational algebra. We prove (i) explicitly and leave the rest as exercises (Exercise 3.40).

To prove (i), we must show that for any Kripke frame $\mathfrak{K} = (K, R_{\mathfrak{K}}, \mathfrak{m}_{\mathfrak{K}})$,

$$
\mathfrak{m}_{\mathfrak{K}}(\Diamond(\varphi \vee \psi)) \;=\; \mathfrak{m}_{\mathfrak{K}}(\Diamond \varphi \vee \Diamond \psi).
$$

But

$\mathfrak{m}_\mathfrak{K}(\Diamond(\varphi \lor \psi))$

$$
\begin{array}{lll}
= & R \circ \mathfrak{m}_\mathfrak{K}(\varphi \lor \psi) & \text{semantics of } \Diamond \\
= & R \circ (\mathfrak{m}_\mathfrak{K}(\varphi) \cup \mathfrak{m}_\mathfrak{K}(\psi)) & \text{semantics of proposition logic} \\
= & (R \circ \mathfrak{m}_\mathfrak{K}(\varphi)) \cup (R \circ \mathfrak{m}_\mathfrak{K}(\psi)) & \text{Lemma 1.1} \\
= & \mathfrak{m}_\mathfrak{K}(\Diamond\varphi) \cup \mathfrak{m}_\mathfrak{K}(\Diamond\psi) & \text{semantics of } \Diamond \\
= & \mathfrak{m}_\mathfrak{K}(\Diamond\varphi \lor \Diamond\psi) & \text{semantics of proposition logic.}
\end{array}
$$

∎

THEOREM 3.71:   The following rules are sound:

(i) Modal generalization (GEN):

$$\frac{\varphi}{\Box\varphi}$$

(ii) Monotonicity of $\Diamond$:

$$\frac{\varphi \to \psi}{\Diamond\varphi \to \Diamond\psi}$$

(iii) Monotonicity of $\Box$:

$$\frac{\varphi \to \psi}{\Box\varphi \to \Box\psi}.$$

Proof   Let $\mathfrak{K} = (K, R_\mathfrak{K}, \mathfrak{m}_\mathfrak{K})$ be a Kripke frame.

(i)   If $\mathfrak{m}_\mathfrak{K}(\varphi) = K$, then $R_\mathfrak{K} \circ (K - \mathfrak{m}_\mathfrak{K}(\varphi)) = \varnothing$, therefore $K - (R_\mathfrak{K} \circ (K - \mathfrak{m}_\mathfrak{K}(\varphi))) = K$.

(ii)   By monotonicity of $\circ$ (Exercise 1.3), if $\mathfrak{m}_\mathfrak{K}(\varphi) \subseteq \mathfrak{m}_\mathfrak{K}(\psi)$, then $R_\mathfrak{K} \circ \mathfrak{m}_\mathfrak{K}(\varphi) \subseteq R_\mathfrak{K} \circ \mathfrak{m}_\mathfrak{K}(\psi)$.

(iii)   If $\mathfrak{m}_\mathfrak{K}(\varphi) \subseteq \mathfrak{m}_\mathfrak{K}(\psi)$, then $(K - \mathfrak{m}_\mathfrak{K}(\psi)) \subseteq (K - \mathfrak{m}_\mathfrak{K}(\varphi))$. By (ii), we have $R_\mathfrak{K} \circ (K - \mathfrak{m}_\mathfrak{K}(\psi)) \subseteq R_\mathfrak{K} \circ (K - \mathfrak{m}_\mathfrak{K}(\varphi))$, therefore $K - (R_\mathfrak{K} \circ (K - \mathfrak{m}_\mathfrak{K}(\varphi))) \subseteq K - (R_\mathfrak{K} \circ (K - \mathfrak{m}_\mathfrak{K}(\psi)))$.   ∎

Multimodal Logic

More generally, let $A = \{a, \dots\}$ be a set of *modalities*. Instead of augmenting propositional logic with one modality as in Section 3.7, we can augment it with a separate modality for each $a \in A$. We add to the inductive definition of formulas the clause:

- If φ is a formula and $a \in A$, then $[a]\varphi$ is a formula.

We also define

$$<a>\varphi \quad \overset{\text{def}}{=} \quad \neg[a]\neg\varphi.$$

A *Kripke frame* is now a structure $\mathfrak{K} = (K, \mathfrak{m}_{\mathfrak{K}})$, where the map $\mathfrak{m}_{\mathfrak{K}}$, in addition to interpreting the atomic propositions as described in Section 3.7, associates a binary relation $\mathfrak{m}_{\mathfrak{K}}(a) \subseteq K \times K$ to each modality $a \in A$. The semantics of $[a]\varphi$ and $<a>\varphi$ is defined as for $\Box\varphi$ and $\Diamond\varphi$, respectively, with $\mathfrak{m}_{\mathfrak{K}}(a)$ taking the place of $R_{\mathfrak{K}}$.

EXAMPLE 3.72:   Consider a propositional logic whose atomic propositions are the atomic formulas $p(t_1, \dots, t_n)$ of predicate logic over a signature Σ and a countable set X of first-order variables. Let $\mathfrak{A}$ be a first-order structure of signature Σ. The structure $\mathfrak{A}$ gives rise to a multimodal Kripke frame $(K, \mathfrak{m}_{\mathfrak{A}})$ with modalities X defined as follows:

$$K \quad \overset{\text{def}}{=} \quad \{\text{valuations } u : T_{\Sigma}(X) \to |\mathfrak{A}|\},$$
$$\mathfrak{m}_{\mathfrak{A}}(p(t_1, \dots, t_n)) \quad \overset{\text{def}}{=} \quad \{u \mid \mathfrak{A}, u \vDash p(t_1, \dots, t_n)\},$$
$$\mathfrak{m}_{\mathfrak{A}}(x) \quad \overset{\text{def}}{=} \quad \{(u, v) \mid u(y) = v(y), \ y \neq x\}.$$

That is, $\mathfrak{m}_{\mathfrak{A}}(x)$ is a symmetric relation connecting any pair of valuations over $\mathfrak{A}$ that agree on all variables except possibly x. For any quantifier-free formula φ and $u \in K$, $\mathfrak{A}, u \vDash [x]\varphi$ iff $\mathfrak{A}, u \vDash \forall x \ \varphi$ in the usual sense of predicate logic as defined in Section 3.4, and $\mathfrak{A}, u \vDash <x>\varphi$ iff $\mathfrak{A}, u \vDash \exists x \ \varphi$ in the usual sense of predicate logic. More generally, if φ is a first-order formula and φ' is obtained from φ by changing all $\forall x$ to $[x]$ and all $\exists x$ to $<x>$, then $\mathfrak{A}, u \vDash \varphi'$ in the modal sense iff $\mathfrak{A}, u \vDash \varphi$ in the usual sense of predicate logic.

EXAMPLE 3.73:   Consider a finite-state automaton with states Q, start state $s \in Q$, accept states $F \subseteq Q$, and input alphabet Σ. Let the set of modalities be Σ^*. Let there be a single atomic formula f satisfied by all and only the states in F. Let $\mathfrak{M} = (Q, \mathfrak{m}_{\mathfrak{M}})$, where

$$\mathfrak{m}_{\mathfrak{M}}(w) \quad \overset{\text{def}}{=} \quad \{(p, q) \mid p, q \in Q, \ q \text{ is reachable from } p \text{ under input string } w\}.$$

Then $\mathfrak{M}$ accepts w iff $\mathfrak{M}, s \vDash <w>f$.

Unwinding

For a multimodal logic with modalities A, one can without loss of generality restrict attention to models that resemble trees. Any Kripke frame can be "unwound" into an equivalent treelike structure. By *equivalent* we mean that the two structures cannot be distinguished by any modal formula.

Given a Kripke frame $\mathfrak{K} = (K, \mathfrak{m}_\mathfrak{K})$ and $s \in K$, we construct an equivalent treelike model $\mathfrak{K}'$ whose states are the paths in $\mathfrak{K}$ out of s. Formally, a *path* in $\mathfrak{K}$ is a finite sequence $\sigma = s_0 a_0 s_1 a_1 s_2 a_2 \cdots a_{n-1} s_n$ of alternating states of $\mathfrak{K}$ and modalities, beginning and ending with a state, such that $(s_i, s_{i+1}) \in \mathfrak{m}_\mathfrak{K}(a_i)$, $0 \leq i < n$. For a path σ, let $\mathrm{first}(\sigma)$ and $\mathrm{last}(\sigma)$ denote the first and last states of σ, respectively. We take the states K' of $\mathfrak{K}'$ to be the set of all paths σ in $\mathfrak{K}$ with $\mathrm{first}(\sigma) = s$. The modalities are interpreted in $\mathfrak{K}'$ as

$$\mathfrak{m}_{\mathfrak{K}'}(a) \ \overset{\mathrm{def}}{=} \ \{(\sigma, \sigma a t) \mid (\mathrm{last}(\sigma), t) \in \mathfrak{m}_\mathfrak{K}(a)\}.$$

For the atomic propositions, we define

$$\mathfrak{m}_{\mathfrak{K}'}(p) \ \overset{\mathrm{def}}{=} \ \{\sigma \mid \mathrm{last}(\sigma) \in \mathfrak{m}_\mathfrak{K}(p)\}.$$

Then $\mathfrak{K}'$ is a tree with root s. Moreover, the states s in the two models are indistinguishable by any modal formula:

THEOREM 3.74:   For any propositional modal formula φ and any path σ in $\mathfrak{K}$,

$$\mathfrak{K}', \sigma \vDash \varphi \quad \Longleftrightarrow \quad \mathfrak{K}, \mathrm{last}(\sigma) \vDash \varphi.$$

In particular,

$$\mathfrak{K}', s \vDash \varphi \quad \Longleftrightarrow \quad \mathfrak{K}, s \vDash \varphi.$$

Proof The second statement is the special case of the first with $\sigma = s$. The first statement is proved by induction on the structure of φ and is left as an exercise (Exercise 3.41). ∎

A useful corollary of this result is that every satisfiable formula is satisfied in a countable frame; that is, one with only countably many states. In fact, one can show that every satisfiable formula is satisfied in a tree model in which each state has only finitely many successors (Exercise 3.42). For propositional modal logic, one can show an even stronger result: every satisfiable formula is satisfied in a finite frame. We will prove a generalization of this result in Chapter 6 in the context of Propositional Dynamic Logic.

Modal Logic and Programs

Modal logic is particularly well suited for reasoning in *dynamic* situations—situations in which the truth values of statements are not fixed, but may vary over time. Classical first-order logic is *static*, in the sense that the truth values of its statements are immutable.

Sentences of classical first-order logic are interpreted over a single structure, or *world*. In modal logic, an interpretation consists of a collection K of many possible worlds or states. If states can change somehow, then so can truth values.

One successful dynamic interpretation of modal logic is *temporal logic*. In this approach, a state t is accessible from s if t lies in the future of s. The accessibility relation is sometimes taken to be a linear ordering of K (linear-time temporal logic) or a tree (branching-time temporal logic). We will have more to say about temporal logic in Section 17.2.

These ideas also fit nicely into the framework of program execution. We can take the set of states K to be the universe of all possible execution states of a program. With any program α, one can associate a binary accessibility relation over K such that (s, t) is in this relation iff t is a possible final state of the program α with initial state s; that is, iff there is a computation of α starting in s and terminating in t. We say "possible" here since we might wish to consider *nondeterministic programs*, which can have more than a single final state associated with a given initial one.

Syntactically, each program gives rise to a modality of a multimodal logic. We place the program α inside the modality symbol: $[\alpha]$, $\langle\alpha\rangle$. Thus programs become an explicit part of the language. The expression $\langle\alpha\rangle\varphi$ says that it is possible to execute α and halt in a state satisfying φ; the expression $[\alpha]\varphi$ says that whenever α halts, it does so in a state satisfying φ. The resulting system is called Dynamic Logic (DL). Since the inductive definition of formulas allows arbitrary prefixes of modal operators, the syntax is more flexible and expressive than the partial correctness assertions of Hoare Logic. For example, if $\langle\alpha\rangle\varphi$ and $\langle\beta\rangle\varphi$ are logically equivalent, then for every initial state s the program α can terminate in a state satisfying φ iff β can.

Dynamic Logic is not limited merely to augmenting classical logic with a fixed modality for each program; this would be little more than multimodal logic. Rather, it uses various calculi of programs, which in conjunction with the rules of classical propositional and predicate logic give a rich family of systems for analyzing the interaction of programs and formulas. By analogy with the construction of composite formulas from atomic ones, the calculi of programs allow the construction of complex programs from atomic ones. Typical atomic programs are assignment statements and basic tests; the operators used to construct composite programs may be familiar programming constructs such as **if-then-else** and **while-do**. There are rules for analyzing the behavior of programs in terms of the behavior of their subprograms, as well as for analyzing the interaction of programs and formulas. The resulting framework gives a powerful set of tools for understanding the relative power and complexity of programming constructs. It constitutes the subject matter of the remainder of this book.

3.8 Bibliographical Notes

Most of the topics discussed in this chapter are classical. Good introductory sources are Kleene (1952); Bell and Slomson (1971); Chang and Keisler (1973); van Dalen (1994) (propositional and predicate logic), Grätzer (1978) (equational logic and universal algebra), Keisler (1971) (infinitary logic), and Emerson (1990); Chellas (1980); Hughes and Cresswell (1968) (modal logic).

Logic has been with us since the time of Aristotle. Perhaps the first person to view logic as mathematics was Boole (1847). Logic came to the fore as a foundation of mathematics around the beginning of the twentieth century as part of a trend toward increased rigor in mathematical arguments. This movement was championed by Whitehead and Russell (1913) and by Hilbert. The model-theoretic approach to logic owes much to the work of Tarski (1935). The relationship between propositional logic and set theory was observed by Stone (1936).

There are many proofs of the completeness of first-order predicate logic. The first such proof was given by Gödel (1930). The approach here is due to Henkin (1949).

The HSP Theorem (Theorem 3.42 and Corollary 3.43) is due to Birkhoff (1935). Ehrenfeucht–Fraïssé games were introduced in Ehrenfeucht (1961). Kripke (1963) developed the semantics of modal logic.

Exercises

3.1. Prove Theorem 3.4.

3.2. Let S_n be the set of all truth assignments to atomic propositional symbols $p_1, \ldots, p_n$. Elements of S_n are maps $u : \{p_1, \ldots, p_n\} \to \{0, 1\}$ and $\#S_n = 2^n$. A *truth table* over $p_1, \ldots, p_n$ is a function $T : S_n \to \{0, 1\}$. There are 2^{2^n} truth tables over $p_1, \ldots, p_n$.

Every propositional formula φ determines a truth table T_φ:

$$T_\varphi(u) \quad \overset{\text{def}}{=} \quad u(\varphi),$$

where the u on the right-hand side is the inductive extension of the truth assignment u to all formulas over $p_1, \ldots, p_n$ as defined in Section 3.2. An interesting question is the converse: is it true that for every truth table T there is a corresponding propositional formula φ such that $T = T_\varphi$? Show that this is so.

3.3. Truth tables and the notation T_φ were defined in Exercise 3.2. A set F of propositional operators is *complete* if for every n and every truth table T over $p_1, \ldots, p_n$ there is a propositional formula φ over $p_1, \ldots, p_n$ and F only such that $T = T_\varphi$. As shown in Exercise 3.2, the set $\{\mathbf{0}, \rightarrow\}$ is complete.

(a) Show that the sets $\{\wedge, \neg\}$ and $\{\vee, \neg\}$ are also complete.

(b) Show that none of the operators $\wedge, \vee, \neg, \mathbf{0}, \mathbf{1}, \rightarrow, \leftrightarrow$ by themselves are complete.

(c) Show that $\{\leftrightarrow, \neg, \mathbf{0}, \mathbf{1}\}$ is not complete. (*Hint.* Show by induction that for any truth assignment to a formula φ built from these connectives alone, if the truth value of p is changed, then the truth value of φ changes iff p has an odd number of occurrences in φ.)

(d) Show that $\{\vee, \wedge\}$ is not complete. Formulas built from the connectives $\vee, \wedge$ only are called *monotone*.

(e) Show that $\{\vee, \wedge, \rightarrow\}$ is not complete. (*Hint.* Consider the truth assignment that assigns $\mathbf{0}$ to every atomic proposition.)

(f) Define a single propositional operator that is complete. Specify the operator by giving its truth table (see Exercise 3.2). Prove that it is complete.

3.4. In this exercise we develop a useful duality principle for formulas expressed over the propositional connectives $\wedge$, $\vee$, and $\neg$. For any such propositional formula φ, define its *dual* φ' inductively as follows:

- $p' = p$ for atomic propositions p,
- $(\varphi \wedge \psi)' = \varphi' \vee \psi'$,
- $(\varphi \vee \psi)' = \varphi' \wedge \psi'$,
- $(\neg\varphi)' = \neg\varphi'$.

In other words, we just change all occurrences of $\vee$ to $\wedge$ and vice versa. Note that $\varphi'' = \varphi$.

(a) Considering $\varphi \to \psi$ as an abbreviation for $\neg\varphi \vee \psi$, $\mathbf{0}$ as an abbreviation for $p \wedge \neg p$ (where p is an arbitrary atomic proposition), $\mathbf{1}$ as an abbreviation for $p \vee \neg p$, $\varphi \leftrightarrow \psi$ as an abbreviation for $(\varphi \to \psi) \wedge (\psi \to \varphi)$, and $\varphi \oplus \psi$ as an abbreviation for $(\neg\varphi \wedge \psi) \vee (\neg\psi \wedge \varphi)$, show that

- $\mathbf{0}' = \mathbf{1}$ and $\mathbf{1}' = \mathbf{0}$,
- $(\varphi \leftrightarrow \psi)' = \varphi' \oplus \psi'$ and $(\varphi \oplus \psi)' = \varphi' \leftrightarrow \psi'$.

(b) Let φ be a propositional formula. Let $\overline{\varphi}$ denote the formula obtained by replacing all atomic propositions by their negations; that is, if all of the atomic propositions of φ are among $p_1, \dots, p_n$, then $\overline{\varphi} = \varphi[p_1/\neg p_1, \dots, p_n/\neg p_n]$. Prove that φ' and $\neg\overline{\varphi}$ are propositionally equivalent. (*Hint.* Prove this by induction on the structure of φ using Axioms 3.13(ii) and (iii)).

(c) Show that φ is satisfiable iff φ' is valid.

(d) Show that $\varphi \equiv \psi$ iff $\varphi' \equiv \psi'$.

(e) Formulate and prove a generalization of these duality results for predicate logic using (3.4.1).

(f) Formulate and prove a generalization of these duality results for modal logic using (3.7.1).

3.5. Intuitionistic propositional logic was defined in Section 3.2. Show that the following propositions are intuitionistically equivalent:

(i) law of double negation: $\neg\neg\varphi \to \varphi$;

(ii) reductio ad absurdum: $(\neg\varphi \to \mathbf{0}) \to \varphi$;

(iii) law of the excluded middle: $\neg\varphi \vee \varphi$;

(iv) law of contraposition: $(\neg\psi \to \neg\varphi) \to (\varphi \to \psi)$;

(v) Peirce's law: $((\varphi \to \psi) \to \varphi) \to \varphi$.

3.6. Prove the validity of axioms (ii)–(iv) and (vi)–(ix) of Axiom System 3.13.

3.7. Prove that the free Σ-algebra generated by a set of a given cardinality is unique up to isomorphism.

3.8. A *Boolean algebra* is a structure

$$\mathfrak{B} = (B, \wedge, \vee, \neg, 0, 1)$$

satisfying the following equations:

$$
\begin{aligned}
(x \vee y) \vee z &= x \vee (y \vee z) & (x \wedge y) \wedge z &= x \wedge (y \wedge z) \\
x \vee y &= y \vee x & x \wedge y &= y \wedge x \\
x \vee (y \wedge z) &= (x \vee y) \wedge (x \vee z) & x \wedge (y \vee z) &= (x \wedge y) \vee (x \wedge z) \\
x \vee 0 &= x & x \wedge 1 &= x \\
x \vee 1 &= 1 & x \wedge 0 &= 0 \\
x \vee \neg x &= 1 & x \wedge \neg x &= 0 \\
x \vee x &= x & x \wedge x &= x.
\end{aligned}
$$

For example, a *Boolean algebra of sets* is a structure

$$
\mathfrak{B} = (B, \cap, \cup, \sim, \varnothing, S)
$$

where S is a set, B is a collection of subsets of S, $\cap$ is set intersection, $\cup$ is set union, $\sim$ is set complementation in S, and $\varnothing$ is the empty set.

(a) Show that in any Boolean algebra $\mathfrak{B}$, for any $a, b \in \mathfrak{B}$, $a \vee b = b$ iff $a \wedge b = a$. (*Hint.* Prove first the equations $x \vee (x \wedge y) = x$ and $x \wedge (x \vee y) = x$.)

(b) Prove the *De Morgan laws*

$$
\begin{aligned}
\neg(x \vee y) &= \neg x \wedge \neg y \\
\neg(x \wedge y) &= \neg x \vee \neg y
\end{aligned}
$$

and the double-negation law

$$
\neg\neg x = x.
$$

(*Hint.* Use (a) to show that for all $a, b \in \mathfrak{B}$, if $a \wedge b = 0$ and $a \vee b = 1$, then $a = \neg b$.)

3.9. Let A be a set of propositional letters and let T denote the set of propositions over A and $\wedge, \vee, \neg$. For $x, y \in T$, define $\varphi \equiv \psi$ if $\varphi \leftrightarrow \psi$ is a propositional tautology. Prove that $T/\equiv$ is the free Boolean algebra on $\#A$ generators. (*Hint.* Consider the set of Boolean functions on n inputs $f : \{0, 1\}^n \to \{0, 1\}$.)

3.10. For finite n, how many elements does the free Boolean algebra on n generators have?

3.11. Define $a \leq b$ in a Boolean algebra if $a \wedge b = a$ (equivalently, by Exercise 3.8(a), if $a \vee b = b$). Prove that $\leq$ is a partial order with bottom 0 and top 1.

3.12. A *filter* F on a Boolean algebra $\mathfrak{B}$ is a nonempty subset of $\mathfrak{B}$ such that

$$a \in F, \ b \in F \quad \Longrightarrow \quad a \wedge b \in F$$
$$a \in F, \ a \leq b \quad \Longrightarrow \quad b \in F.$$

Find a natural one-to-one correspondence between filters on $\mathfrak{B}$ and congruences on $\mathfrak{B}$. (*Hint.* If $h : \mathfrak{A} \to \mathfrak{B}$ is a homomorphism, consider the set $h^{-1}(1) = \{a \in \mathfrak{A} \mid h(a) = 1^{\mathfrak{B}}\}$.)

3.13. An *ideal* I on a Boolean algebra $\mathfrak{B}$ is a nonempty subset of $\mathfrak{B}$ such that

$$a \in I, \ b \in I \quad \Longrightarrow \quad a \vee b \in I$$
$$b \in I, \ a \leq b \quad \Longrightarrow \quad a \in I.$$

Find a natural one-to-one correspondence between filters and ideals on $\mathfrak{B}$ (see Exercise 3.12). State the relationship between ideals and congruences analogous to the hint for Exercise 3.12.

3.14. A filter is *consistent* if $0 \notin F$. An *ultrafilter* is a maximal consistent filter; that is, one that is not properly included in any consistent filter. Show that every consistent filter is contained in an ultrafilter. (*Hint.* Show first that if F is a consistent filter and $a \in \mathfrak{B}$, then either $F(a)$ of $F(\neg a)$ is a consistent filter, where $F(x) = \{y \in \mathfrak{B} \mid \exists z \in F \ x \wedge z \leq y\}$ is the smallest filter containing F and x. Then use Zorn's lemma (see Section 1.6)).

3.15. Show that every Boolean algebra is isomorphic to a Boolean algebra of sets. (*Hint.* Given $\mathfrak{B} = (B, \wedge, \vee, \neg, 0, 1)$, take

$$S \ \stackrel{\text{def}}{=} \ \{\text{ultrafilters of } \mathfrak{B}\},$$
$$a' \ \stackrel{\text{def}}{=} \ \{F \in S \mid a \in F\},$$
$$B' \ \stackrel{\text{def}}{=} \ \{a' \mid a \in B\},$$
$$\mathfrak{B}' \ \stackrel{\text{def}}{=} \ (B', \cap, \cup, \sim, \varnothing, S),$$

where $\sim$ denotes complementation in S.)

3.16. The rule of congruence is a special case of the following *substitution rule*:

$$\frac{s_i = t_i, \ 1 \leq i \leq n}{t(s_1, \ldots, s_n) = t(t_1, \ldots, t_n)}$$

where $t(x_1, \ldots, x_n)$ is a term and $t(t_1, \ldots, t_n)$ denotes the result of simultaneously replacing all occurrences of x_i in t with t_i, $1 \le i \le n$. Show how to derive this rule from the other rules of equality.

3.17. Prove Theorem 3.34(i).

3.18. Prove Theorem 3.35. (*Hint.* First establish that the map $h \mapsto \ker h$ is invertible up to $\approx$. The inverse operation takes a congruence $\equiv$ on $\mathfrak{A}$ to the canonical epimorphism $[\,] : \mathfrak{A} \to \mathfrak{A}/\equiv$. To verify that the correspondence preserves the lattice structure, argue that for epimorphisms $h_1 : \mathfrak{A} \to \mathfrak{B}_1$ and $h_2 : \mathfrak{A} \to \mathfrak{B}_2$, there exists an epimorphism $g : \mathfrak{B}_1 \to \mathfrak{B}_2$ such that $h_2 = h_1 \circ g$ iff $\ker h_1$ refines $\ker h_2$.)

3.19. Consider the class of all epimorphisms with domain $\mathfrak{A}$. For two such epimorphisms $h_1 : \mathfrak{A} \to \mathfrak{B}_1$ and $h_2 : \mathfrak{A} \to \mathfrak{B}_2$, write $h_1 \le h_2$ if there exists an epimorphism $g : \mathfrak{B}_1 \to \mathfrak{B}_2$ such that $h_2 = h_1 \circ g$, and $h_1 \approx h_2$ if both $h_1 \le h_2$ and $h_2 \le h_1$. Show that $h_1 \approx h_2$ iff there is an isomorphism $\iota : \mathfrak{B}_1 \to \mathfrak{B}_2$ such that $h_2 = h_1 \circ \iota$.

3.20. Prove Theorem 3.35.

3.21. (a) Prove that the maps **Mod** and **Th** defined in Section 3.3 form a Galois connection (see Exercise 1.24). Conclude that for any set of equational formulas Φ, **Mod** $\Phi = $ **Mod Th Mod** Φ, as required in the proof of Corollary 3.43.

(b) By Exercise 1.24, the maps **Mod** $\circ$ **Th** and **Th** $\circ$ **Mod** are closure operators. What are their closed sets?

3.22. Prove that every homomorphism factors into a composition of a monomorphism and an epimorphism. In other words, for every homomorphism $f : \mathfrak{A} \to \mathfrak{C}$, there exist an intermediate algebra $\mathfrak{B}$, an epimorphism $g : \mathfrak{A} \to \mathfrak{B}$, and a monomorphism $h : \mathfrak{B} \to \mathfrak{C}$ such that $f = g \circ h$.

3.23. Prove that $0x = 0$ and $x0 = 0$ are logical consequences of the axioms for rings (see Example 3.24).

3.24. In Section 1.5, semilattices were defined as partial orders in which every finite set of elements has a join (lease upper bound). Show that semilattices form a variety over the signature $\vee$ (join) and $\perp$ (least element of the semilattice). (*Hint.* Consider $x \le y$ an abbreviation for $x \vee y = y$. Your axiomatization must ensure that $\le$ is a partial order, that $\perp$ is the $\leq$-least element of the structure, and that $\vee$ gives the least upper bound of two elements.)

3.25. Extend Axiom System 3.40 to handle Horn formulas. Prove that your deductive system is sound and complete.

3.26. Define a *quasivariety* to be a class of models defined by infinitary Horn formulas of the form

$$\Phi \quad \rightarrow \quad s = t,$$

where Φ is a possibly infinite set of equations. Prove the following variant of Birkhoff's theorem (Corollary 3.43). Let $\mathcal{D}$ be a class of Σ-algebras. The following are equivalent:

(i) $\mathcal{D}$ is a quasivariety

(ii) $\mathcal{D} = \mathbf{S}\,\mathbf{P}\,\mathcal{D}$

(iii) $\mathcal{D} = \{\mathbf{S}, \mathbf{P}\}^* \mathcal{D}$.

(*Hint.* Define the infinitary Horn theory of a class of algebras $\mathcal{D}$. Formulate and prove a theorem similar to Theorem 3.42 for infinitary Horn theories. In the last part of the proof, modify the definition of $\mathfrak{B}_{s,t}$ as follows. Let B be a set of generators of $\mathfrak{A}$ and let Δ be the kernel of the unique homomorphism $T_\Sigma(B) \to \mathfrak{A}$ extending the identity on B. Define $\mathfrak{B}_{s,t}$ and $u_{s,t}$ such that

$$\mathfrak{B}_{s,t}, u_{s,t} \quad \not\models \quad \Delta \to s = t$$

whenever $\Delta \to s = t$ is not in the Horn theory of $\mathcal{D}$.)

3.27. Let x, y, z be first-order variables ranging over $\mathbb{N}$. Show how to express the following predicate in the language of first-order number theory (see Example 3.44): "At least one of y and z is nonzero, and x is their greatest common divisor."

3.28. Prove that the following first-order formulas are valid:

$$\exists x\, \varphi \vee \exists x\, \psi \quad \leftrightarrow \quad \exists x\, (\varphi \vee \psi)$$
$$\varphi \quad \leftrightarrow \quad \exists x\, \varphi, \quad x \text{ not free in } \varphi$$

Show by example that the proviso "x not free in φ" is necessary in the second formula.

3.29. Show that if valuations u and v agree on all variables occurring free in φ, then

$$\mathfrak{A}, u \vDash \varphi \iff \mathfrak{A}, v \vDash \varphi.$$

Conclude that if φ is a sentence, that is, if φ has no free variables, then $\vDash$ does not depend on the valuation u; that is, if $\mathfrak{A}, u \vDash \varphi$ for some u, then $\mathfrak{A}, u \vDash \varphi$ for all u.

3.30. Lemma 3.48 gives conditions under which bound variables can be renamed, but the proof in the text establishes the equivalence of the two formulas by a semantic argument. Show that if the conditions of Lemma 3.48 hold, then the same equivalence can be derived using Axiom System 3.51.

3.31. Prove Lemma 3.49.

3.32. Prove the soundness of Axiom System 3.51.

3.33. A second-order number-theoretic formula in prenex form is *universal* if all second-order quantifiers are universal quantifiers; that is, if it is of the form

$$\forall f_1 \ \overline{\mathsf{Q}}_1 \overline{y}_1 \ \ldots \ \forall f_n \ \overline{\mathsf{Q}}_n \overline{y}_n \ \varphi, \tag{3.8.1}$$

where each f_i ranges over functions $\mathbb{N}^{k_i} \to \mathbb{N}$ for some k_i, the $\overline{\mathsf{Q}}_i \overline{y}_i$ are blocks of arbitrary first order quantifiers over individual variables y_{ij} ranging over $\mathbb{N}$, and φ is quantifier-free. In the proof of Theorem 2.12, we needed to know that every universal second-order number-theoretic formula can be transformed to an equivalent formula of the form

$$\forall f \ \exists y \ \varphi, \tag{3.8.2}$$

where f is a single function variable ranging over functions $\mathbb{N} \to \mathbb{N}$, y is a single individual variable ranging over $\mathbb{N}$, and φ is quantifier-free. In this exercise we establish this normal form.

(a) Give rules for second-order quantifiers analogous to the rules of Lemma 3.49 for first-order quantifiers. State a theorem analogous to Lemma 3.50 for second-order formulas.

(b) Show that the formula $\forall y \ \psi$, where y is an individual variable, is equivalent to the formula $\forall g \ \psi[y/g(0)]$, where g is a function variable of type $\mathbb{N} \to \mathbb{N}$. Conclude that (3.8.1) can be transformed into an equivalent second-order universal formula containing no universally quantified individual variables.

(c) By (a), we can assume without loss of generality that the first-order quantifier blocks $\overline{Q}_i \overline{y}_i$ in (3.8.1) contain only existential quantifiers. Argue that the formula

$$\forall y \; \exists f \; \psi,$$

where y is an individual variable and f is a function variable of type $\mathbb{N}^k \to \mathbb{N}$, is equivalent to the formula

$$\exists g \; \forall y \; \psi[f/g(y)],$$

where g is a function variable of type $\mathbb{N} \to (\mathbb{N}^k \to \mathbb{N})$. This transformation is called *Skolemization*, and the function g is called a *Skolem function*.

(d) Using the transformation of (b) and currying the resulting Skolem functions (see Exercise 1.19), argue that (3.8.1) can be transformed to an equivalent formula of the form

$$\forall f_1 \; \ldots \; \forall f_m \; \exists y_1 \; \ldots \; \exists y_n \; \varphi, \tag{3.8.3}$$

where each f_i is a function variable of type $\mathbb{N}^{k_i} \to \mathbb{N}$ for some k_i and the y_j are individual variables.

(e) Using the pairing function of Exercise 1.20, show how to transform the formula (3.8.3) into an equivalent formula of the desired form (3.8.2).

3.34. Show that complete lattices are not a variety. (*Hint.* Use Theorem 3.42.)

3.35. Show that the languages $L_{\omega_1^{ck}\omega}$ and $L_{\omega_1\omega}$ are not compact. (*Hint.* Consider the countable set

$$\{ \bigvee_{n<\omega} p(f^n(a)) \} \; \cup \; \{ \neg p(f^n(a)) \mid n < \omega \}$$

of infinitary formulas.)

3.36. Show that the languages $L_{\omega_1^{ck}\omega}$ and $L_{\omega_1\omega}$ do not satisfy the upward Löwenheim–Skolem theorem. (*Hint.* Consider the sentence

$$\forall x \; \bigvee_{n<\omega} x = f^n(a)$$

of $L_{\omega_1^{ck}\omega}$.)

3.37. Prove the following infinitary tautologies using the deductive system of Section 3.6.

(a) $\bigvee_\alpha \varphi \leftrightarrow \varphi$ (infinitary idempotence)

(b) $\neg \bigwedge_\alpha \varphi_\alpha \leftrightarrow \bigvee_\alpha \neg \varphi_\alpha$ (infinitary De Morgan law)

(c) $\varphi \wedge \bigvee_\alpha \psi_\alpha \leftrightarrow \bigvee_\alpha (\varphi \wedge \psi_\alpha)$ (infinitary distributive law)

3.38. Complete the proof of Theorem 3.63.

3.39. Give an IND program (see Section 2.2) that accepts a given code of a formula of $L_{\omega_1^{ck}\omega}$ iff the formula is provable. Conclude from Exercise 2.11 that deciding validity of $L_{\omega_1^{ck}\omega}$ formulas is in Π_1^1.

3.40. Prove clauses (ii)–(viii) of Theorem 3.70.

3.41. Prove Theorem 3.74.

3.42. Prove that every propositional modal formula is satisfied in a tree model in which each state has only finitely many successors. (*Hint.* Start with the tree model of Theorem 3.74 satisfying the given formula φ at the root. Describe an inductive procedure to move down the tree, labeling certain states with subformulas of φ that need to be satisfied at that state in order to make φ true at the root. Make sure only finitely many successors of each state are labeled. Delete unlabeled states. Prove by induction that each state of the resulting tree model satisfies its label.)

4 Reasoning About Programs

In subsequent chapters, we will study in depth a family of program logics collectively called Dynamic Logic (DL). Before embarking on this task, we take the opportunity here to discuss program verification in general and introduce some key concepts on an informal level. Many of the ideas discussed in this chapter will be developed in more detail later on.

4.1 What are Programs?

For us, a *program* is a recipe written in a formal language for computing desired output data from given input data.

EXAMPLE 4.1: The following program implements the Euclidean algorithm for calculating the greatest common divisor (gcd) of two integers. It takes as input a pair of integers in variables x and y and outputs their gcd in variable x:

while $y \neq 0$ **do**
  begin
    $z := x \bmod y$;
    $x := y$;
    $y := z$
  end

The value of the expression $x \bmod y$ is the (nonnegative) remainder obtained when dividing x by y using ordinary integer division.

Programs normally use *variables* to hold input and output values and intermediate results. Each variable can assume values from a specific *domain of computation*, which is a structure consisting of a set of data values along with certain distinguished constants, basic operations, and tests that can be performed on those values, as described in Section 3.4. In the program above, the domain of x, y, and z might be the integers $\mathbb{Z}$ along with basic operations including integer division with remainder and tests including $\neq$. In contrast with the usual use of variables in mathematics, a variable in a program normally assumes different values during the course of the computation. The value of a variable x may change whenever an assignment $x := t$ is performed with x on the left-hand side.

In order to make these notions precise, we will have to specify the programming language and its semantics in a mathematically rigorous way. In this text we will consider several programming languages with various properties, and each will be defined formally. In this chapter we give a brief introduction to some of these languages and the role they play in program verification.

4.2   States and Executions

As mentioned above, a program can change the values of variables as it runs. However, if we could freeze time at some instant during the execution of the program, we could presumably read the values of the variables at that instant, and that would give us an instantaneous snapshot of all information that we would need to determine how the computation would proceed from that point. This leads to the concept of a *state*—intuitively, an instantaneous description of reality.

Formally, we will define a *state* to be a function that assigns a value to each program variable. The value for variable x must belong to the domain associated with x. In logic, such a function is called a *valuation* (see Sections 3.3 and 3.4). At any given instant in time during its execution, the program is thought to be "in" some state, determined by the instantaneous values of all its variables. If an assignment statement is executed, say $x := 2$, then the state changes to a new state in which the new value of x is 2 and the values of all other variables are the same as they were before. We assume that this change takes place instantaneously; note that this is a mathematical abstraction, since in reality basic operations take some time to execute.

A typical state for the gcd program above is $(15, 27, 0, \ldots)$, where (say) the first, second, and third components of the sequence denote the values assigned to x, y, and z respectively. The ellipsis "$\ldots$" refers to the values of the other variables, which we do not care about, since they do not occur in the program.

A program can be viewed as a transformation on states. Given an initial (input) state, the program will go through a series of intermediate states, perhaps eventually halting in a final (output) state. A sequence of states that can occur from the execution of a program α starting from a particular input state is called a *trace*. As a typical example of a trace for the program above, consider the initial state $(15, 27, 0)$ (we suppress the ellipsis). The program goes through the following sequence of states:

$(15, 27, 0)$, $(15, 27, 15)$, $(27, 27, 15)$, $(27, 15, 15)$, $(27, 15, 12)$, $(15, 15, 12)$,

$(15, 12, 12)$, $(15, 12, 3)$, $(12, 12, 3)$, $(12, 3, 3)$, $(12, 3, 0)$, $(3, 3, 0)$, $(3, 0, 0)$.

The value of x in the last (output) state is 3, the gcd of 15 and 27.

The binary relation consisting of the set of all pairs of the form (input state, output state) that can occur from the execution of a program α, or in other words, the set of all first and last states of traces of α, is called the *input/output relation* of α. For example, the pair $((15, 27, 0), (3, 0, 0))$ is a member of the input/output relation of the gcd program above, as is the pair $((-6, -4, 303), (2, 0, 0))$. The values of other variables besides x, y, and z are not changed by the program. These values are therefore the same in the output state as in the input state. In this example, we may think of the variables x and y as the *input variables*, x as the *output variable*, and z as a *work variable*, although formally there is no distinction between any of the variables, including the ones not occurring in the program.

4.3   Programming Constructs

In subsequent sections we will consider a number of programming constructs. In this section we introduce some of these constructs and define a few general classes of languages built on them.

In general, programs are built inductively from *atomic programs* and *tests* using various *program operators*.

While Programs

A popular choice of programming language in the literature on DL is the family of deterministic **while** programs. This language is a natural abstraction of familiar imperative programming languages such as Pascal or C. Different versions can be defined depending on the choice of tests allowed and whether or not nondeterminism is permitted.

The language of **while** programs is defined inductively. There are atomic programs and atomic tests, as well as program constructs for forming compound programs from simpler ones.

In the propositional version of Dynamic Logic (PDL), atomic programs are simply letters $a, b, \ldots$ from some alphabet. Thus PDL abstracts away from the nature of the domain of computation and studies the pure interaction between programs and propositions. For the first-order versions of DL, atomic programs are *simple assignments* $x := t$, where x is a variable and t is a term. In addition, a *nondeterministic* or *wildcard assignment* $x :=?$ or *nondeterministic choice* construct may be allowed.

Tests can be *atomic tests*, which for propositional versions are simply propositional letters p, and for first-order versions are atomic formulas $p(t_1, \ldots, t_n)$, where $t_1, \ldots, t_n$ are terms and p is an n-ary relation symbol in the signature of the domain of computation. In addition, we include the *constant tests* **1** and **0**. Boolean combinations of atomic tests are often allowed, although this adds no expressive power. These versions of DL are called *poor test*.

More complicated tests can also be included. These versions of DL are sometimes called *rich test*. In rich test versions, the families of programs and tests are defined by mutual induction.

Compound programs are formed from the atomic programs and tests by induction, using the *composition*, *conditional*, and *while* operators. Formally, if φ is a test and α and β are programs, then the following are programs:

- $\alpha \, ; \, \beta$
- **if** φ **then** α **else** β
- **while** φ **do** α.

We can also parenthesize with **begin** ... **end** where necessary. The gcd program of Example 4.1 above is an example of a **while** program.

The semantics of these constructs is defined to correspond to the ordinary operational semantics familiar from common programming languages. We will give more detail about these programs in Sections 5.1 and 5.2.

Regular Programs

Regular programs are more general than **while** programs, but not by much. The advantage of regular programs is that they reduce the relatively more complicated **while** program operators to much simpler constructs. The deductive system becomes comparatively simpler too. They also incorporate a simple form of nondeterminism.

For a given set of atomic programs and tests, the set of *regular programs* is defined as follows:

(i) any atomic program is a program

(ii) if φ is a test, then $\varphi?$ is a program

(iii) if α and β are programs, then $\alpha \, ; \, \beta$ is a program;

(iv) if α and β are programs, then $\alpha \cup \beta$ is a program;

(v) if α is a program, then α^* is a program.

These constructs have the following intuitive meaning:

(i) Atomic programs are basic and indivisible; they execute in a single step. They are called *atomic* because they cannot be decomposed further.

(ii) The program φ? tests whether the property φ holds in the current state. If so, it continues without changing state. If not, it blocks without halting.

(iii) The operator ; is the *sequential composition* operator. The program α ; β means, "Do α, then do β."

(iv) The operator $\cup$ is the *nondeterministic choice* operator. The program $\alpha \cup \beta$ means, "Nondeterministically choose one of α or β and execute it."

(v) The operator * is the *iteration* operator. The program α means, "Execute α some nondeterministically chosen finite number of times."

Keep in mind that these descriptions are meant only as intuitive aids. A formal semantics will be given in Section 5.2, in which programs will be interpreted as binary input/output relations and the programming constructs above as operators on binary relations.

The operators $\cup$, ; , * may be familiar from automata and formal language theory (see Kozen (1997a)), where they are interpreted as operators on sets of strings over a finite alphabet. The language-theoretic and relation-theoretic semantics share much in common; in fact, they have the same equational theory, as shown in Kozen (1994a).

The operators of deterministic **while** programs can be defined in terms of the regular operators:

$$\textbf{if } \varphi \textbf{ then } \alpha \textbf{ else } \beta \ \stackrel{\text{def}}{=} \ \varphi? \, ; \, \alpha \cup \neg\varphi? \, ; \, \beta \tag{4.3.1}$$

$$\textbf{while } \varphi \textbf{ do } \alpha \ \stackrel{\text{def}}{=} \ (\varphi? \, ; \, \alpha)^* \, ; \, \neg\varphi? \tag{4.3.2}$$

The class of **while** programs is equivalent to the subclass of the regular programs in which the program operators $\cup$, ?, and * are constrained to appear only in these forms.

The definitions (4.3.1) and (4.3.2) may seem a bit mysterious at first, but we will be able to justify them after we have discussed binary relation semantics in Section 5.2.

Recursion

Recursion can appear in programming languages in several forms. We will study two such manifestations: *recursive calls* and *stacks*. We will show that under certain very general conditions, the two constructs can simulate each other. We will also show that recursive programs and **while** programs are equally expressive over the natural numbers, whereas over arbitrary domains, **while** programs are strictly weaker. **While** programs correspond to what is often called *tail recursion* or *iteration*.

R.E. Programs

A *finite computation sequence* of a program α, or *seq* for short, is a finite-length string of atomic programs and tests representing a possible sequence of atomic steps that can occur in a halting execution of α. Seqs are denoted $\sigma, \tau, \ldots$. The set of all seqs of a program α is denoted $CS(\alpha)$. We use the word "possible" loosely—$CS(\alpha)$ is determined by the syntax of α alone. Because of tests that evaluate to false, $CS(\alpha)$ may contain seqs that are never executed under any interpretation.

The set $CS(\alpha)$ is a subset of A^*, where A is the set of atomic programs and tests occurring in α. For **while** programs, regular programs, or recursive programs, we can define the set $CS(\alpha)$ formally by induction on syntax. For example, for regular programs,

$$
\begin{aligned}
CS(a) &\stackrel{\text{def}}{=} \{a\}, \quad a \text{ an atomic program or test}\\
CS(\textbf{skip}) &\stackrel{\text{def}}{=} \{\varepsilon\}\\
CS(\textbf{fail}) &\stackrel{\text{def}}{=} \varnothing\\
CS(\alpha\,;\,\beta) &\stackrel{\text{def}}{=} \{\sigma\,;\,\tau \mid \sigma \in CS(\alpha),\ \tau \in CS(\beta)\}\\
CS(\alpha \cup \beta) &\stackrel{\text{def}}{=} CS(\alpha) \cup CS(\beta)\\
CS(\alpha^*) &\stackrel{\text{def}}{=} CS(\alpha)^*\\
&= \bigcup_{n \geq 0} CS(\alpha^n),
\end{aligned}
$$

where

$$
\begin{aligned}
\alpha^0 &\stackrel{\text{def}}{=} \textbf{skip}\\
\alpha^{n+1} &\stackrel{\text{def}}{=} \alpha^n\,;\,\alpha.
\end{aligned}
$$

For example, if a is an atomic program and p an atomic formula, then the program

$$\textbf{while } p \textbf{ do } a \;=\; (p?\,;\,a)^*\,;\,\neg p?$$

has as seqs all strings of the form

$$(p?\,;\,a)^n\,;\,\neg p? \;=\; \underbrace{p?; a; p?; a; \cdots; p?; a; \neg p?}_{n}$$

for all $n \geq 0$. Note that each seq σ of a program α is itself a program, and

$$CS(\sigma) = \{\sigma\}.$$

While programs and regular programs give rise to regular sets of seqs, and recursive programs give rise to context-free sets of seqs. Taking this a step further, we can define an *r.e. program* to be simply a recursively enumerable set of seqs. This is the most general programming language we will consider in the context of DL; it subsumes all the others in expressive power.

Nondeterminism

We should say a few words about the concept of *nondeterminism* and its role in the study of logics and languages, since this concept often presents difficulty the first time it is encountered.

In some programming languages we will consider, the traces of a program need not be uniquely determined by their start states. When this is possible, we say that the program is *nondeterministic*. A nondeterministic program can have both divergent and convergent traces starting from the same input state, and for such programs it does not make sense to say that the program halts on a certain input state or that it loops on a certain input state; there may be different computations starting from the same input state that do each.

There are several concrete ways nondeterminism can enter into programs. One construct is the *nondeterministic* or *wildcard assignment* $x := ?$. Intuitively, this operation assigns an arbitrary element of the domain to the variable x, but it is not determined which one.[1] Another source of nondeterminism is the unconstrained use of the choice operator $\cup$ in regular programs. A third source is the iteration operator * in regular programs. A fourth source is r.e. programs, which are just r.e. sets of seqs; initially, the seq to execute is chosen nondeterministically. For example, over $\mathbb{N}$, the r.e. program

$$\{x := n \mid n \geq 0\}$$

is equivalent to the regular program

$$x := 0 \,;\, (x := x + 1)^*.$$

Nondeterministic programs provide no explicit mechanism for resolving the nondeterminism. That is, there is no way to determine which of many possible

---

1 This construct is often called *random assignment* in the literature. This terminology is misleading, because it has nothing at all to do with probability.

next steps will be taken from a given state. This is hardly realistic. So why study nondeterminism at all if it does not correspond to anything operational? One good answer is that nondeterminism is a valuable tool that helps us understand the expressiveness of programming language constructs. It is useful in situations in which we cannot necessarily predict the outcome of a particular choice, but we may know the range of possibilities. In reality, computations may depend on information that is out of the programmer's control, such as input from the user or actions of other processes in the system. Nondeterminism is useful in modeling such situations.

The importance of nondeterminism is not limited to logics of programs. Indeed, the most important open problem in the field of computational complexity theory, the $P{=}NP$ problem, is formulated in terms of nondeterminism.

4.4 Program Verification

Dynamic Logic and other program logics are meant to be useful tools for facilitating the process of producing correct programs. One need only look at the miasma of buggy software to understand the dire need for such tools. But before we can produce correct software, we need to know what it means for it to be correct. It is not good enough to have some vague idea of what is supposed to happen when a program is run or to observe it running on some collection of inputs. In order to apply formal verification tools, we must have a formal specification of correctness for the verification tools to work with.

In general, a *correctness specification* is a formal description of how the program is supposed to behave. A given program is *correct* with respect to a correctness specification if its behavior fulfills that specification. For the gcd program of Example 4.1, the correctness might be specified informally by the assertion

If the input values of x and y are positive integers c and d, respectively, then

    (i) the output value of x is the gcd of c and d, and

    (ii) the program halts.

Of course, in order to work with a formal verification system, these properties must be expressed formally in a language such as first-order logic.

The assertion (ii) is part of the correctness specification because programs do not necessarily halt, but may produce infinite traces for certain inputs. A finite trace, as for example the one produced by the gcd program above on input state (15,27,0), is called *halting*, *terminating*, or *convergent*. Infinite traces are called *looping* or *divergent*. For example, the program

while $x > 7$ **do** $x := x + 3$

loops on input state $(8, \ldots)$, producing the infinite trace

$(8, \ldots)$, $(11, \ldots)$, $(14, \ldots)$, $\ldots$

For the purposes of this book, we will limit our attention to the behavior of a program that is manifested in its input/output relation. Dynamic Logic is not tailored to reasoning about program behavior manifested in intermediate states of a computation (although there are close relatives, such as Process Logic and Temporal Logic, that are). This is not to say that all interesting program behavior is captured by the input/output relation, and that other types of behavior are irrelevant or uninteresting. Indeed, the restriction to input/output relations is reasonable only when programs are supposed to halt after a finite time and yield output results. This approach will not be adequate for dealing with programs that normally are not supposed to halt, such as operating systems.

For programs that are supposed to halt, correctness criteria are traditionally given in the form of an *input/output specification* consisting of a formal relation between the input and output states that the program is supposed to maintain, along with a description of the set of input states on which the program is supposed to halt. The input/output relation of a program carries all the information necessary to determine whether the program is correct relative to such a specification. Dynamic Logic is well suited to this type of verification.

It is not always obvious what the correctness specification ought to be. Sometimes, producing a formal specification of correctness is as difficult as producing the program itself, since both must be written in a formal language. Moreover, specifications are as prone to bugs as programs. Why bother then? Why not just implement the program with some vague specification in mind?

There are several good reasons for taking the effort to produce formal specifications:

1. Often when implementing a large program from scratch, the programmer may have been given only a vague idea of what the finished product is supposed to do. This is especially true when producing software for a less technically inclined employer. There may be a rough informal description available, but the minor details are often left to the programmer. It is very often the case that a large part of the programming process consists of taking a vaguely specified problem and making it precise. The process of formulating the problem precisely can be considered a *definition* of what the program is supposed to do. And it is just good programming practice to have a very clear idea of what we want to do before we start doing it.

2. In the process of formulating the specification, several unforeseen cases may become apparent, for which it is not clear what the appropriate action of the program should be. This is especially true with error handling and other exceptional situations. Formulating a specification can define the action of the program in such situations and thereby tie up loose ends.

3. The process of formulating a rigorous specification can sometimes suggest ideas for implementation, because it forces us to isolate the issues that drive design decisions. When we know all the ways our data are going to be accessed, we are in a better position to choose the right data structures that optimize the tradeoffs between efficiency and generality.

4. The specification is often expressed in a language quite different from the programming language. The specification is *functional*—it tells *what* the program is supposed to do—as opposed to *imperative*—*how* to do it. It is often easier to specify the desired functionality independent of the details of how it will be implemented. For example, we can quite easily express what it means for a number x to be the gcd of y and z in first-order logic without even knowing how to compute it.

5. Verifying that a program meets its specification is a kind of sanity check. It allows us to give two solutions to the problem—once as a functional specification, and once as an algorithmic implementation—and lets us verify that the two are compatible. Any incompatibilities between the program and the specification are either bugs in the program, bugs in the specification, or both. The cycle of refining the specification, modifying the program to meet the specification, and reverifying until the process converges can lead to software in which we have much more confidence.

Partial and Total Correctness

Typically, a program is designed to implement some functionality. As mentioned above, that functionality can often be expressed formally in the form of an input/output specification. Concretely, such a specification consists of an *input condition* or *precondition* φ and an *output condition* or *postcondition* ψ. These are properties of the input state and the output state, respectively, expressed in some formal language such as the first-order language of the domain of computation. The program is supposed to halt in a state satisfying the output condition whenever the input state satisfies the input condition. We say that a program is *partially correct* with respect to a given input/output specification φ, ψ if, whenever the program is started in a state satisfying the input condition φ, then if and when it ever halts, it does so in a state satisfying the output condition ψ. The definition of partial correctness does not stipulate that the program halts; this is what we mean by *partial*.

A program is *totally correct* with respect to an input/output specification φ, ψ if

- it is partially correct with respect to that specification; and
- it halts whenever it is started in a state satisfying the input condition φ.

The input/output specification imposes no requirements when the input state does not satisfy the input condition φ—the program might as well loop infinitely or erase memory. This is the "garbage in, garbage out" philosophy. If we really do care what the program does on some of those input states, then we had better rewrite the input condition to include them and say formally what we want to happen in those cases.

For example, in the gcd program of Example 4.1, the output condition ψ might be the condition (i) stating that the output value of x is the gcd of the input values of x and y. We can express this completely formally in the language of first-order number theory (we show how to do this later on). We may try to start off with the input specification $\varphi_0 = \mathbf{1}$ (*true*); that is, no restrictions on the input state at all. Unfortunately, if the initial value of y is 0 and x is negative, the final value of x will be the same as the initial value, thus negative. If we expect all gcds to be positive, this would be wrong. Another problematic situation arises when the initial values of x and y are both 0; in this case the gcd is not defined. Therefore, the program as written is not partially correct with respect to the specification φ_0, ψ.

We can remedy the situation by providing an input specification that rules out these troublesome input values. We can limit the input states to those in which x and y are both nonnegative and not both zero by taking the input specification

$$\varphi_1 \quad = \quad (x \geq 0 \wedge y > 0) \ \vee \ (x > 0 \wedge y \geq 0).$$

The gcd program of Example 4.1 above would be partially correct with respect to the specification φ_1, ψ. It is also totally correct, since the program halts on all inputs satisfying φ_1.

Perhaps we want to allow any input in which not both x and y are zero. In that case, we should use the input specification $\varphi_2 = \neg(x = 0 \wedge y = 0)$. But then the program of Example 4.1 is not partially correct with respect to φ_2, ψ; we must amend the program to produce the correct (positive) gcd on negative inputs.

Hoare Logic

A precursor to Dynamic Logic, and one of the first formal verification systems, was *Hoare Logic*, introduced by Hoare (1969). This is a system for proving partial correctness of deterministic **while** programs related to the invariant assertion method of Floyd (1967). Hoare Logic allows statements of the form

$$\{\varphi\}\, \alpha \,\{\psi\}, \tag{4.4.1}$$

which says that the program α is partially correct with respect to the input/output specification φ, ψ; that is, if α is started in an input state satisfying φ, then if and when it halts, it does so in a state satisfying ψ.

The deductive system for Hoare Logic consists of a small set of rules for deriving partial correctness assertions of the form (4.4.1) for compound programs inductively from similar assertions about their subprograms. There is one rule for each programming construct:

Assignment rule:

$$\{\varphi[x/e]\}\, x := e \,\{\varphi\},$$

where e is free for x in φ (see Section 3.4);

Composition rule:

$$\frac{\{\varphi\}\, \alpha \,\{\sigma\}, \quad \{\sigma\}\, \beta \,\{\psi\}}{\{\varphi\}\, \alpha \,;\, \beta \,\{\psi\}}$$

Conditional rule:

$$\frac{\{\varphi \wedge \sigma\}\, \alpha \,\{\psi\}, \quad \{\varphi \wedge \neg\sigma\}\, \beta \,\{\psi\}}{\{\varphi\}\, \textbf{if } \sigma \textbf{ then } \alpha \textbf{ else } \beta \,\{\psi\}}$$

While rule:

$$\frac{\{\varphi \wedge \sigma\}\, \alpha \,\{\varphi\}}{\{\varphi\}\, \textbf{while } \sigma \textbf{ do } \alpha \,\{\varphi \wedge \neg\sigma\}}.$$

In addition, we include a rule

Weakening rule:

$$\frac{\varphi' \to \varphi, \quad \{\varphi\}\, \alpha \,\{\psi\}, \quad \psi \to \psi'}{\{\varphi'\}\, \alpha \,\{\psi'\}}$$

that will allow us to incorporate the deductive apparatus of the underlying logic in which the pre- and postconditions are written.

We will see later on in Section 5.7 how these rules are subsumed by Dynamic Logic.

4.5   Exogenous and Endogenous Logics

There are two main approaches to modal logics of programs: the *exogenous* approach, exemplified by Dynamic Logic and its precursor Hoare Logic (Hoare (1969)), and the *endogenous* approach, exemplified by Temporal Logic and its precursor, the invariant assertions method of Floyd (1967). A logic is *exogenous* if its programs are explicit in the language. Syntactically, a Dynamic Logic program is a well-formed expression built inductively from primitive programs using a small set of program operators. Semantically, a program is interpreted as its input/output relation. The relation denoted by a compound program is determined by the relations denoted by its parts. This aspect of *compositionality* allows analysis by structural induction.

The importance of compositionality is discussed in van Emde Boas (1978). In Temporal Logic, the program is fixed and is considered part of the structure over which the logic is interpreted. The current location in the program during execution is stored in a special variable for that purpose, called the *program counter*, and is part of the state along with the values of the program variables. Instead of program operators, there are temporal operators that describe how the program variables, including the program counter, change with time. Thus Temporal Logic sacrifices compositionality for a less restricted formalism. We discuss Temporal Logic further in Section 17.2.

4.6   Bibliographical Notes

Systematic program verification originated with the work of Floyd (1967) and Hoare (1969). Hoare Logic was introduced in Hoare (1969); see Cousot (1990); Apt (1981); Apt and Olderog (1991) for surveys.

The *digital abstraction*, the view of computers as state transformers that operate by performing a sequence of discrete and instantaneous primitive steps, can be attributed to Turing (1936). Finite-state transition systems were defined formally by McCulloch and Pitts (1943). State-transition semantics is based on this idea and is quite prevalent in early work on program semantics and verification; see Hennessy and Plotkin (1979). The relational-algebraic approach taken here, in which programs are interpreted as binary input/output relations, was introduced in the context of DL by Pratt (1976).

The notions of partial and total correctness were present in the early work of Hoare (1969). Regular programs were introduced by Fischer and Ladner (1979) in the context of **PDL**. The concept of nondeterminism was introduced in the original paper of Turing (1936), although he did not develop the idea. Nondeterminism was further developed by Rabin and Scott (1959) in the context of finite automata.

Exercises

4.1. In this exercise we will illustrate the use of Hoare Logic by proving the correctness of the gcd program of Example 4.1 on p. 145. The program is of the form **while** σ **do** α, where σ is the test $y \neq 0$ and α is the program

$z := x \bmod y \,;\, x := y \,;\, y := z.$

We will use the precondition

$$\neg(x = 0 \wedge y = 0) \wedge x = x_0 \wedge y = y_0, \tag{4.6.1}$$

where x_0 and y_0 are new variables not appearing in the program. The purpose of x_0 and y_0 is to remember the initial values of x and y. The condition $\neg(x = 0 \wedge y = 0)$ ensures that the gcd exists.

The postcondition is

$$x \;\; = \;\; \gcd(x_0, y_0), \tag{4.6.2}$$

which says that the final value of the program variable x is the gcd of the values of x_0 and y_0. This can be expressed in the language of first order number theory if desired (see Exercise 3.27), although you do not need to do so for this exercise.

We assume that the variables range over $\mathbb{N}$, the natural numbers, thus we do not have to worry about fractional or negative values. The practical significance of this is that we may omit conditions such as $x \geq 0$ in our pre- and postconditions, since these are satisfied automatically by all elements of our domain of computation.

The partial correctness assertion that asserts the correctness of the gcd program is

$\{\neg(x = 0 \wedge y = 0) \wedge x = x_0 \wedge y = y_0\}$ **while** σ **do** α $\{x = \gcd(x_0, y_0)\}.$

(a) Let φ be the formula

$\neg(x = 0 \wedge y = 0) \wedge \gcd(x, y) = \gcd(x_0, y_0).$

This will be the invariant of our loop. Using informal number-theoretic arguments, prove that the precondition (4.6.1) implies φ and that $\varphi \wedge \neg\sigma$ implies the postcondition (4.6.2). Conclude using the weakening rule of Hoare Logic that it suffices to establish the partial correctness assertion

$\{\varphi\}$ **while** σ **do** α $\{\varphi \wedge \neg\sigma\}$.

(b) By (a) and the **while** rule of Hoare Logic, it suffices to prove the partial correctness assertion

$\{\varphi \wedge \sigma\}\, \alpha\, \{\varphi\}$.

Prove this using a sequence of applications of the composition and weakening rules of Hoare Logic. You may use common number-theoretic facts such as

$$y \neq 0 \quad \rightarrow \quad \gcd(x,y) = \gcd(x \bmod y, y)$$

without proof.

4.2. When the domain of computation is the natural numbers $\mathbb{N}$, we can define a **for** loop construct. The syntax of the construct is **for** y **do** α, where y is a variable and α is a program. The intuitive operation of the **for** loop is as follows: upon entering the loop **for** y **do** α, the current (nonnegative integral) value of variable y is determined, and the program α is executed that many times. Assignment to the variable y within α does not change the number of times the loop is executed, nor does execution of α alone decrement y or change its value in any way except by explicit assignment.

(a) Show how to encode a **for** loop as a **while** loop. You may introduce new variables if necessary.

(b) Argue that **while** programs with **for** loops only but no **while** loops must always halt. (*Hint.* Use induction on the depth of nesting of **for** loops in the program.)

4.3. The **repeat-until** construct **repeat** α **until** φ is like the **while** loop, except that the body of the loop α is executed *before* the test φ (therefore is always executed at least once), and control exits the loop if the test is true. Show that in the presence of the other program operators, **repeat-until** and **while-do** are equivalent.

II PROPOSITIONAL DYNAMIC LOGIC

5 Propositional Dynamic Logic

Propositional Dynamic Logic (PDL) plays the same role in Dynamic Logic that classical propositional logic plays in classical predicate logic. It describes the properties of the interaction between programs and propositions that are independent of the domain of computation. Just as propositional logic is the appropriate place to begin the study of classical predicate logic, so too is PDL the appropriate place to begin our investigation of Dynamic Logic. Since PDL is a subsystem of first-order DL, we can be sure that all properties of PDL that we establish in Part II of the book will also be valid in first-order DL, which we will deal with in Part III.

Since there is no domain of computation in PDL, there can be no notion of assignment to a variable. Instead, primitive programs are interpreted as arbitrary binary relations on an abstract set of states K. Likewise, primitive assertions are just atomic propositions and are interpreted as arbitrary subsets of K. Other than this, no special structure is imposed.

This level of abstraction may at first appear too general to say anything of interest. On the contrary, it is a very natural level of abstraction at which many fundamental relationships between programs and propositions can be observed.

For example, consider the PDL formula

$$[\alpha](\varphi \wedge \psi) \quad \leftrightarrow \quad [\alpha]\varphi \wedge [\alpha]\psi. \tag{5.0.1}$$

The left-hand side asserts that the formula $\varphi \wedge \psi$ must hold after the execution of program α, and the right-hand side asserts that φ must hold after execution of α and so must ψ. The formula (5.0.1) asserts that these two statements are equivalent. This implies that to verify a conjunction of two postconditions, it suffices to verify each of them separately. The assertion (5.0.1) holds universally, regardless of the domain of computation and the nature of the particular α, φ, and ψ.

As another example, consider

$$[\alpha \,;\, \beta]\varphi \quad \leftrightarrow \quad [\alpha][\beta]\varphi. \tag{5.0.2}$$

The left-hand side asserts that after execution of the composite program $\alpha \,;\, \beta$, φ must hold. The right-hand side asserts that after execution of the program α, $[\beta]\varphi$ must hold, which in turn says that after execution of β, φ must hold. The formula (5.0.2) asserts the logical equivalence of these two statements. It holds regardless of the nature of α, β, and φ. Like (5.0.1), (5.0.2) can be used to simplify the verification of complicated programs.

As a final example, consider the assertion

$$[\alpha]p \quad \leftrightarrow \quad [\beta]p \tag{5.0.3}$$

where p is a primitive proposition symbol and α and β are programs. If this formula is true under all interpretations, then α and β are *equivalent* in the sense that they behave identically with respect to any property expressible in PDL or any formal system containing PDL as a subsystem. This is because the assertion will hold for any substitution instance of (5.0.3). For example, the two programs

$$\alpha \quad = \quad \textbf{if } \varphi \textbf{ then } \gamma \textbf{ else } \delta$$
$$\beta \quad = \quad \textbf{if } \neg\varphi \textbf{ then } \delta \textbf{ else } \gamma$$

are equivalent in the sense of (5.0.3).

5.1   Syntax

Syntactically, PDL is a blend of three classical ingredients: propositional logic, modal logic, and the algebra of regular expressions. There are several versions of PDL, depending on the choice of program operators allowed. In this chapter we will introduce the basic version, called *regular* PDL. Variations of this basic version will be considered in later chapters.

The language of regular PDL has expressions of two sorts: *propositions* or *formulas* $\varphi, \psi, \ldots$ and *programs* $\alpha, \beta, \gamma, \ldots$. There are countably many *atomic symbols* of each sort. Atomic programs are denoted $a, b, c, \ldots$ and the set of all atomic programs is denoted Π_0. Atomic propositions are denoted $p, q, r, \ldots$ and the set of all atomic propositions is denoted Φ_0. The set of all programs is denoted Π and the set of all propositions is denoted Φ. Programs and propositions are built inductively from the atomic ones using the following operators:

Propositional operators:

    $\rightarrow$ implication
    0   falsity

Program operators:

    ;   composition
    $\cup$ choice
    *   iteration

Mixed operators:

[ ]   necessity
?   test

The definition of programs and propositions is by mutual induction. All atomic programs are programs and all atomic propositions are propositions. If φ, ψ are propositions and α, β are programs, then

$\varphi \to \psi$ propositional implication
$\mathbf{0}$ propositional falsity
$[\alpha]\varphi$ program necessity

are propositions and

$\alpha \, ; \, \beta$ sequential composition
$\alpha \cup \beta$ nondeterministic choice
α^* iteration
$\varphi?$ test

are programs. In more formal terms, we define the set Π of all programs and the set Φ of all propositions to be the smallest sets such that

- $\Phi_0 \subseteq \Phi$

- $\Pi_0 \subseteq \Pi$

- if $\varphi, \psi \in \Phi$, then $\varphi \to \psi \in \Phi$ and $\mathbf{0} \in \Phi$

- if $\alpha, \beta \in \Pi$, then $\alpha; \beta$, $\alpha \cup \beta$, and $\alpha^* \in \Pi$

- if $\alpha \in \Pi$ and $\varphi \in \Phi$, then $[\alpha]\varphi \in \Phi$

- if $\varphi \in \Phi$ then $\varphi? \in \Pi$.

Note that the inductive definitions of programs Π and propositions Φ are intertwined and cannot be separated. The definition of propositions depends on the definition of programs because of the construct $[\alpha]\varphi$, and the definition of programs depends on the definition of propositions because of the construct $\varphi?$. Note also that we have allowed all formulas as tests. This is the *rich test* version of PDL.

Compound programs and propositions have the following intuitive meanings:

$[\alpha]\varphi$ "It is necessary that after executing α, φ is true."

$\alpha; \beta$ "Execute α, then execute β."

$\alpha \cup \beta$ "Choose either α or β nondeterministically and execute it."

α^* "Execute α a nondeterministically chosen finite number of times (zero or more)."

$\varphi?$ "Test φ; proceed if true, fail if false."

We avoid parentheses by assigning precedence to the operators: unary operators, including $[\alpha]$, bind tighter than binary ones, and ; binds tighter than $\cup$. Thus the expression

$$[\alpha; \beta^* \cup \gamma^*]\varphi \vee \psi$$

should be read

$$([(\alpha; (\beta^*)) \cup (\gamma^*)]\varphi) \vee \psi.$$

Of course, parentheses can always be used to enforce a particular parse of an expression or to enhance readability. Also, under the semantics to be given in the next section, the operators ; and $\cup$ will turn out to be associative, so we may write $\alpha ; \beta ; \gamma$ and $\alpha \cup \beta \cup \gamma$ without ambiguity. We often omit the symbol ; and write the composition $\alpha ; \beta$ as $\alpha\beta$.

The primitive operators may at first seem rather unconventional. They are chosen for their mathematical simplicity. A number of more conventional constructs can be defined from them. The propositional operators $\wedge, \vee, \neg, \leftrightarrow$, and $\mathbf{1}$ are defined from $\rightarrow$ and $\mathbf{0}$ as in propositional logic (see Section 3.2).

The possibility operator $< >$ is the modal dual of the necessity operator $[\ ]$ as described in Section 3.7. It is defined by

$$<\alpha>\varphi \ \overset{\text{def}}{=} \ \neg[\alpha]\neg\varphi.$$

The propositions $[\alpha]\varphi$ and $<\alpha>\varphi$ are read "box α φ" and "diamond α φ," respectively. The latter has the intuitive meaning, "There is a computation of α that terminates in a state satisfying φ."

One important difference between $< >$ and $[\ ]$ is that $<\alpha>\varphi$ implies that α terminates, whereas $[\alpha]\varphi$ does not. Indeed, the formula $[\alpha]\mathbf{0}$ asserts that no computation of α terminates, and the formula $[\alpha]\mathbf{1}$ is always true, regardless of α.

In addition, we define

$$
\begin{aligned}
\mathbf{skip} &\stackrel{\text{def}}{=} \mathbf{1}? \\[4pt]
\mathbf{fail} &\stackrel{\text{def}}{=} \mathbf{0}? \\[4pt]
\mathbf{if}\ \varphi_1 \to \alpha_1\ |\cdots|\ \varphi_n \to \alpha_n\ \mathbf{fi} &\stackrel{\text{def}}{=} \varphi_1?; \alpha_1 \cup \cdots \cup \varphi_n?; \alpha_n \\[4pt]
\mathbf{do}\ \varphi_1 \to \alpha_1\ |\cdots|\ \varphi_n \to \alpha_n\ \mathbf{od} &\stackrel{\text{def}}{=} (\varphi_1?; \alpha_1 \cup \cdots \cup \varphi_n?; \alpha_n)^*; (\neg\varphi_1 \wedge \cdots \wedge \neg\varphi_n)? \\[4pt]
\mathbf{if}\ \varphi\ \mathbf{then}\ \alpha\ \mathbf{else}\ \beta &\stackrel{\text{def}}{=} \mathbf{if}\ \varphi \to \alpha\ |\ \neg\varphi \to \beta\ \mathbf{fi} \\[4pt]
&= \varphi?; \alpha \cup \neg\varphi?; \beta \\[4pt]
\mathbf{while}\ \varphi\ \mathbf{do}\ \alpha &\stackrel{\text{def}}{=} \mathbf{do}\ \varphi \to \alpha\ \mathbf{od} \\[4pt]
&= (\varphi?; \alpha)^*; \neg\varphi? \\[4pt]
\mathbf{repeat}\ \alpha\ \mathbf{until}\ \varphi &\stackrel{\text{def}}{=} \alpha; \mathbf{while}\ \neg\varphi\ \mathbf{do}\ \alpha \\[4pt]
&= \alpha; (\neg\varphi?; \alpha)^*; \varphi? \\[4pt]
\{\varphi\}\, \alpha\, \{\psi\} &\stackrel{\text{def}}{=} \varphi \to [\alpha]\psi.
\end{aligned}
$$

The programs **skip** and **fail** are the program that does nothing (no-op) and the failing program, respectively. The ternary **if-then-else** operator and the binary **while-do** operator are the usual *conditional* and *while loop* constructs found in conventional programming languages. The constructs **if-|-fi** and **do-|-od** are the *alternative guarded command* and *iterative guarded command* constructs, respectively. The construct $\{\varphi\}\, \alpha\, \{\psi\}$ is the Hoare partial correctness assertion described in Section 4.4. We will argue later that the formal definitions of these operators given above correctly model their intuitive behavior.

5.2 Semantics

The semantics of PDL comes from the semantics for modal logic (see Section 3.7). The structures over which programs and propositions of PDL are interpreted are called *Kripke frames* in honor of Saul Kripke, the inventor of the formal semantics of modal logic. A *Kripke frame* is a pair

$$\mathfrak{K} = (K, \mathfrak{m}_{\mathfrak{K}}),$$

where K is a set of elements $u, v, w, \ldots$ called *states* and $\mathfrak{m}_{\mathfrak{K}}$ is a *meaning function* assigning a subset of K to each atomic proposition and a binary relation on K to each atomic program. That is,

$$m_{\mathfrak{K}}(p) \quad \subseteq \quad K, \qquad p \in \Phi_0$$
$$m_{\mathfrak{K}}(a) \quad \subseteq \quad K \times K, \quad a \in \Pi_0.$$

We will extend the definition of the function $m_{\mathfrak{K}}$ by induction below to give a meaning to all elements of Π and Φ such that

$$m_{\mathfrak{K}}(\varphi) \quad \subseteq \quad K, \qquad \varphi \in \Phi$$
$$m_{\mathfrak{K}}(\alpha) \quad \subseteq \quad K \times K, \quad \alpha \in \Pi.$$

Intuitively, we can think of the set $m_{\mathfrak{K}}(\varphi)$ as the set of states *satisfying* the proposition φ in the model $\mathfrak{K}$, and we can think of the binary relation $m_{\mathfrak{K}}(\alpha)$ as the set of input/output pairs of states of the program α.

Formally, the meanings $m_{\mathfrak{K}}(\varphi)$ of $\varphi \in \Phi$ and $m_{\mathfrak{K}}(\alpha)$ of $\alpha \in \Pi$ are defined by mutual induction on the structure of φ and α. The basis of the induction, which specifies the meanings of the atomic symbols $p \in \Phi_0$ and $a \in \Pi_0$, is already given in the specification of $\mathfrak{K}$. The meanings of compound propositions and programs are defined as follows.

$$m_{\mathfrak{K}}(\varphi \to \psi) \stackrel{\text{def}}{=} (K - m_{\mathfrak{K}}(\varphi)) \cup m_{\mathfrak{K}}(\psi)$$

$$m_{\mathfrak{K}}(\mathbf{0}) \stackrel{\text{def}}{=} \varnothing$$

$$m_{\mathfrak{K}}([\alpha]\varphi) \stackrel{\text{def}}{=} K - (m_{\mathfrak{K}}(\alpha) \circ (K - m_{\mathfrak{K}}(\varphi)))$$
$$= \{u \mid \forall v \in K \text{ if } (u,v) \in m_{\mathfrak{K}}(\alpha) \text{ then } v \in m_{\mathfrak{K}}(\varphi)\}$$

$$m_{\mathfrak{K}}(\alpha;\beta) \stackrel{\text{def}}{=} m_{\mathfrak{K}}(\alpha) \circ m_{\mathfrak{K}}(\beta) \tag{5.2.1}$$
$$= \{(u,v) \mid \exists w \in K \ (u,w) \in m_{\mathfrak{K}}(\alpha) \text{ and } (w,v) \in m_{\mathfrak{K}}(\beta)\}$$

$$m_{\mathfrak{K}}(\alpha \cup \beta) \stackrel{\text{def}}{=} m_{\mathfrak{K}}(\alpha) \cup m_{\mathfrak{K}}(\beta)$$

$$m_{\mathfrak{K}}(\alpha^*) \stackrel{\text{def}}{=} m_{\mathfrak{K}}(\alpha)^* = \bigcup_{n \geq 0} m_{\mathfrak{K}}(\alpha)^n \tag{5.2.2}$$

$$m_{\mathfrak{K}}(\varphi?) \stackrel{\text{def}}{=} \{(u,u) \mid u \in m_{\mathfrak{K}}(\varphi)\}.$$

The operator $\circ$ in (5.2.1) is relational composition (Section 1.3). In (5.2.2), the first occurrence of * is the iteration symbol of PDL, and the second is the reflexive transitive closure operator on binary relations (Section 1.3). Thus (5.2.2) says that the program α^* is interpreted as the reflexive transitive closure of $m_{\mathfrak{K}}(\alpha)$.

We write $\mathfrak{K}, u \vDash \varphi$ and $u \in m_{\mathfrak{K}}(\varphi)$ interchangeably, and say that u *satisfies* φ in $\mathfrak{K}$, or that φ is *true* at state u in $\mathfrak{K}$. We may omit the $\mathfrak{K}$ and write $u \vDash \varphi$ when $\mathfrak{K}$ is understood. The notation $u \nvDash \varphi$ means that u does not satisfy φ, or in other words that $u \notin \mathfrak{m}_{\mathfrak{K}}(\varphi)$. In this notation, we can restate the definition above equivalently as follows:

$$u \vDash \varphi \to \psi \quad \overset{\text{def}}{\Longleftrightarrow} \quad u \vDash \varphi \text{ implies } u \vDash \psi$$

$$u \nvDash \mathbf{0}$$

$$u \vDash [\alpha]\varphi \quad \overset{\text{def}}{\Longleftrightarrow} \quad \forall v \text{ if } (u,v) \in \mathfrak{m}_{\mathfrak{K}}(\alpha) \text{ then } v \vDash \varphi$$

$$(u,v) \in \mathfrak{m}_{\mathfrak{K}}(\alpha\beta) \quad \overset{\text{def}}{\Longleftrightarrow} \quad \exists w \; (u,w) \in \mathfrak{m}_{\mathfrak{K}}(\alpha) \text{ and } (w,v) \in \mathfrak{m}_{\mathfrak{K}}(\beta)$$

$$(u,v) \in \mathfrak{m}_{\mathfrak{K}}(\alpha \cup \beta) \quad \overset{\text{def}}{\Longleftrightarrow} \quad (u,v) \in \mathfrak{m}_{\mathfrak{K}}(\alpha) \text{ or } (u,v) \in \mathfrak{m}_{\mathfrak{K}}(\beta)$$

$$(u,v) \in \mathfrak{m}_{\mathfrak{K}}(\alpha^*) \quad \overset{\text{def}}{\Longleftrightarrow} \quad \exists n \geq 0 \; \exists u_0, \dots, u_n \; u = u_0, \; v = u_n,$$

$$\text{and } (u_i, u_{i+1}) \in \mathfrak{m}_{\mathfrak{K}}(\alpha), \; 0 \leq i \leq n-1$$

$$(u,v) \in \mathfrak{m}_{\mathfrak{K}}(\varphi?) \quad \overset{\text{def}}{\Longleftrightarrow} \quad u = v \text{ and } u \vDash \varphi.$$

The defined operators inherit their meanings from these definitions:

$$\mathfrak{m}_{\mathfrak{K}}(\varphi \vee \psi) \quad \overset{\text{def}}{=} \quad \mathfrak{m}_{\mathfrak{K}}(\varphi) \cup \mathfrak{m}_{\mathfrak{K}}(\psi)$$

$$\mathfrak{m}_{\mathfrak{K}}(\varphi \wedge \psi) \quad \overset{\text{def}}{=} \quad \mathfrak{m}_{\mathfrak{K}}(\varphi) \cap \mathfrak{m}_{\mathfrak{K}}(\psi)$$

$$\mathfrak{m}_{\mathfrak{K}}(\neg\varphi) \quad \overset{\text{def}}{=} \quad K - \mathfrak{m}_{\mathfrak{K}}(\varphi)$$

$$\mathfrak{m}_{\mathfrak{K}}(\mathord{<}\alpha\mathord{>}\varphi) \quad \overset{\text{def}}{=} \quad \{u \mid \exists v \in K \; (u,v) \in \mathfrak{m}_{\mathfrak{K}}(\alpha) \text{ and } v \in \mathfrak{m}_{\mathfrak{K}}(\varphi)\}$$

$$= \quad \mathfrak{m}_{\mathfrak{K}}(\alpha) \circ \mathfrak{m}_{\mathfrak{K}}(\varphi)$$

$$\mathfrak{m}_{\mathfrak{K}}(\mathbf{1}) \quad \overset{\text{def}}{=} \quad K$$

$$\mathfrak{m}_{\mathfrak{K}}(\mathbf{skip}) \quad \overset{\text{def}}{=} \quad \mathfrak{m}_{\mathfrak{K}}(\mathbf{1}?) \;=\; \iota, \text{ the identity relation}$$

$$\mathfrak{m}_{\mathfrak{K}}(\mathbf{fail}) \quad \overset{\text{def}}{=} \quad \mathfrak{m}_{\mathfrak{K}}(\mathbf{0}?) \;=\; \varnothing.$$

In addition, the **if-then-else**, **while-do**, and guarded commands inherit their semantics from the above definitions, and the input/output relations given by the formal semantics capture their intuitive operational meanings. For example, the relation associated with the program **while** φ **do** α is the set of pairs (u, v) for which there exist states $u_0, u_1, \dots, u_n$, $n \geq 0$, such that $u = u_0$, $v = u_n$, $u_i \in \mathfrak{m}_{\mathfrak{K}}(\varphi)$ and $(u_i, u_{i+1}) \in \mathfrak{m}_{\mathfrak{K}}(\alpha)$ for $0 \leq i < n$, and $u_n \notin \mathfrak{m}_{\mathfrak{K}}(\varphi)$. A thorough analysis will require more careful attention, so we defer further discussion until later.

This version of **PDL** is usually called *regular* **PDL** and the elements of Π are called *regular programs* because of the primitive operators $\cup$, ;, and *, which are familiar from regular expressions. Programs can be viewed as regular expressions over the atomic programs and tests. In fact, it can be shown that if p is an atomic proposition symbol, then any two test-free programs α, β are equivalent as regular

170 Chapter 5

expressions—that is, they represent the same regular set—if and only if the formula
$\langle\alpha\rangle p \leftrightarrow \langle\beta\rangle p$ is valid (Exercise 5.13).

EXAMPLE 5.1:   Let p be an atomic proposition, let a be an atomic program, and
let $\mathfrak{K} = (K,\ \mathfrak{m}_{\mathfrak{K}})$ be a Kripke frame with

$$K = \{u,v,w\}$$
$$\mathfrak{m}_{\mathfrak{K}}(p) = \{u,v\}$$
$$\mathfrak{m}_{\mathfrak{K}}(a) = \{(u,v),(u,w),(v,w),(w,v)\}.$$

The following diagram illustrates $\mathfrak{K}$.

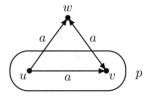

In this structure, $u \vDash \langle a\rangle\neg p \wedge \langle a\rangle p$, but $v \vDash [a]\neg p$ and $w \vDash [a]p$. Moreover, every
state of $\mathfrak{K}$ satisfies the formula

$$\langle a^*\rangle[(aa)^*]p \wedge \langle a^*\rangle[(aa)^*]\neg p.$$

5.3   Computation Sequences

Let α be a program. Recall from Section 4.3 that a *finite computation sequence*
of α is a finite-length string of atomic programs and tests representing a possible
sequence of atomic steps that can occur in a halting execution of α. These strings are
called *seqs* and are denoted $\sigma, \tau, \dots$. The set of all such sequences is denoted $CS(\alpha)$.
We use the word "possible" here loosely—$CS(\alpha)$ is determined by the syntax of α
alone, and may contain strings that are never executed in any interpretation.

Formally, the set $CS(\alpha)$ is defined by induction on the structure of α:

$$CS(a) \stackrel{\text{def}}{=} \{a\}, \ a \text{ an atomic program}$$

$$CS(\varphi?) \stackrel{\text{def}}{=} \{\varphi?\}$$

$$CS(\alpha; \beta) \stackrel{\text{def}}{=} \{\gamma\delta \mid \gamma \in CS(\alpha), \ \delta \in CS(\beta)\}$$

$$CS(\alpha \cup \beta) \stackrel{\text{def}}{=} CS(\alpha) \cup CS(\beta)$$

$$CS(\alpha^*) \stackrel{\text{def}}{=} \bigcup_{n \geq 0} CS(\alpha^n)$$

where $\alpha^0 = \mathbf{skip}$ and $\alpha^{n+1} = \alpha\alpha^n$. For example, if a is an atomic program and p is an atomic formula, then the program

$$\mathbf{while} \ p \ \mathbf{do} \ a \ = \ (p?; a)^*; \neg p?$$

has as computation sequences all strings of the form

$$p? \, a \, p? \, a \, \cdots \, p? \, a \, \mathbf{skip} \, \neg p?.$$

Note that each finite computation sequence β of a program α is itself a program, and $CS(\beta) = \{\beta\}$. Moreover, the following proposition is not difficult to prove by induction on the structure of α:

PROPOSITION 5.2:

$$\mathfrak{m}_{\mathfrak{K}}(\alpha) \ = \ \bigcup_{\sigma \in CS(\alpha)} \mathfrak{m}_{\mathfrak{K}}(\sigma).$$

Proof Exercise 5.1. ∎

5.4   Satisfiability and Validity

The definitions of satisfiability and validity of propositions are identical to those of modal logic (see Section 3.7). Let $\mathfrak{K} = (K, \mathfrak{m}_{\mathfrak{K}})$ be a Kripke frame and let φ be a proposition. We have defined in Section 5.2 what it means for $\mathfrak{K}, u \vDash \varphi$. If $\mathfrak{K}, u \vDash \varphi$ for some $u \in K$, we say that φ is *satisfiable* in $\mathfrak{K}$. If φ is satisfiable in some $\mathfrak{K}$, we say that φ is *satisfiable*.

If $\mathfrak{K}, u \vDash \varphi$ for all $u \in K$, we write $\mathfrak{K} \vDash \varphi$ and say that φ is *valid* in $\mathfrak{K}$. If $\mathfrak{K} \vDash \varphi$ for all Kripke frames $\mathfrak{K}$, we write $\vDash \varphi$ and say that φ is *valid*.

If Σ is a set of propositions, we write $\mathfrak{K} \vDash \Sigma$ if $\mathfrak{K} \vDash \varphi$ for all $\varphi \in \Sigma$. A proposition

ψ is said to be a *logical consequence* of Σ if $\mathfrak{K} \vDash \psi$ whenever $\mathfrak{K} \vDash \Sigma$, in which case we write $\Sigma \vDash \psi$. (Note that this is *not* the same as saying that $\mathfrak{K}, u \vDash \psi$ whenever $\mathfrak{K}, u \vDash \Sigma$.) We say that an inference rule

$$\frac{\varphi_1, \ldots, \varphi_n}{\varphi}$$

is *sound* if φ is a logical consequence of $\{\varphi_1, \ldots, \varphi_n\}$.

Satisfiability and validity are dual in the same sense that $\exists$ and $\forall$ are dual and $<\,>$ and $[\,]$ are dual: a proposition is valid (in $\mathfrak{K}$) if and only if its negation is not satisfiable (in $\mathfrak{K}$).

EXAMPLE 5.3:   Let p, q be atomic propositions, let a, b be atomic programs, and let $\mathfrak{K} = (K, \mathfrak{m}_\mathfrak{K})$ be a Kripke frame with

$$
\begin{aligned}
K &= \{s, t, u, v\} \\
\mathfrak{m}_\mathfrak{K}(p) &= \{u, v\} \\
\mathfrak{m}_\mathfrak{K}(q) &= \{t, v\} \\
\mathfrak{m}_\mathfrak{K}(a) &= \{(t, v), (v, t), (s, u), (u, s)\} \\
\mathfrak{m}_\mathfrak{K}(b) &= \{(u, v), (v, u), (s, t), (t, s)\}.
\end{aligned}
$$

The following figure illustrates $\mathfrak{K}$.

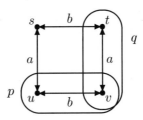

The following formulas are valid in $\mathfrak{K}$.

$$p \leftrightarrow [(ab^*a)^*]p$$
$$q \leftrightarrow [(ba^*b)^*]q.$$

Also, let α be the program

$$\alpha = (aa \cup bb \cup (ab \cup ba)(aa \cup bb)^*(ab \cup ba))^*. \tag{5.4.1}$$

Thinking of α as a regular expression, α generates all words over the alphabet $\{a, b\}$ with an even number of occurrences of each of a and b. It can be shown that for any proposition φ, the proposition $\varphi \leftrightarrow [\alpha]\varphi$ is valid in $\mathfrak{K}$ (Exercise 5.5).

EXAMPLE 5.4:   The formula

$$p \wedge [a^*]((p \to [a]\neg p) \wedge (\neg p \to [a]p)) \quad \leftrightarrow \quad [(aa)^*]p \wedge [a(aa)^*]\neg p \qquad (5.4.2)$$

is valid. Both sides assert in different ways that p is alternately true and false along
paths of execution of the atomic program a. See Exercise 5.6.

5.5   A Deductive System

The following list of axioms and rules constitutes a sound and complete Hilbert-style
deductive system for PDL.

AXIOM SYSTEM 5.5:

(i) Axioms for propositional logic
(ii) $[\alpha](\varphi \to \psi) \quad \to \quad ([\alpha]\varphi \to [\alpha]\psi)$
(iii) $[\alpha](\varphi \wedge \psi) \quad \leftrightarrow \quad [\alpha]\varphi \wedge [\alpha]\psi$
(iv) $[\alpha \cup \beta]\varphi \quad \leftrightarrow \quad [\alpha]\varphi \wedge [\beta]\varphi$
(v) $[\alpha \,;\, \beta]\varphi \quad \leftrightarrow \quad [\alpha][\beta]\varphi$
(vi) $[\psi?]\varphi \quad \leftrightarrow \quad (\psi \to \varphi)$
(vii) $\varphi \wedge [\alpha][\alpha^*]\varphi \quad \leftrightarrow \quad [\alpha^*]\varphi$
(viii) $\varphi \wedge [\alpha^*](\varphi \to [\alpha]\varphi) \quad \to \quad [\alpha^*]\varphi \qquad$ (induction axiom)

(MP) $\dfrac{\varphi, \quad \varphi \to \psi}{\psi}$

(GEN) $\dfrac{\varphi}{[\alpha]\varphi}$

The axioms (ii) and (iii) and the two rules of inference are not particular to PDL,
but come from modal logic (see Section 3.7). The rules (MP) and (GEN) are called
modus ponens and *(modal) generalization*, respectively.

Axiom (viii) is called the PDL *induction axiom*. Intuitively, (viii) says: "Suppose
φ is true in the current state, and suppose that after any number of iterations of
α, if φ is still true, then it will be true after one more iteration of α. Then φ will
be true after any number of iterations of α." In other words, if φ is true initially,
and if the truth of φ is preserved by the program α, then φ will be true after any
number of iterations of α.

Notice the similarity of the formula (viii) to the usual induction axiom of Peano arithmetic:

$$\varphi(0) \wedge \forall n \, (\varphi(n) \rightarrow \varphi(n+1)) \quad \rightarrow \quad \forall n \, \varphi(n).$$

Here $\varphi(0)$ is the basis of the induction and $\forall n \, (\varphi(n) \rightarrow \varphi(n+1))$ is the induction step, from which the conclusion $\forall n \, \varphi(n)$ can be drawn. In the **PDL** axiom (viii), the basis is φ and the induction step is $[\alpha^*](\varphi \rightarrow [\alpha]\varphi)$, from which the conclusion $[\alpha^*]\varphi$ can be drawn.

We write $\vdash \varphi$ if the proposition φ is a theorem of this system, and say that φ is *consistent* if $\nvdash \neg\varphi$; that is, if it is not the case that $\vdash \neg\varphi$. A set Σ of propositions is *consistent* if all finite conjunctions of elements of Σ are consistent.

The soundness of these axioms and rules over Kripke frames can be established by elementary arguments in relational algebra using the semantics of Section 5.2. We will do this in Section 5.6. We will prove the completeness of this system in Chapter 7.

5.6   Basic Properties

We establish some basic facts that follow from the definitions of Sections 5.1–5.5. Most of these results are in the form of valid formulas and rules of inference of **PDL**. In the course of proving these results, we will establish the soundness of the deductive system for **PDL** given in Section 5.5.

Properties Inherited from Modal Logic

We start with some properties that are not particular to **PDL**, but are valid in all modal systems. They are valid in **PDL** by virtue of the fact that **PDL** includes propositional modal logic. Theorems 5.6 and 5.7 were essentially proved in Section 3.7 (Theorems 3.70 and 3.71, respectively); these in turn were proved using the basic properties of relational composition given in Section 1.3. We restate them here in the framework of **PDL**.

THEOREM 5.6:   The following are valid formulas of **PDL**:

(i) $\langle\alpha\rangle(\varphi \vee \psi) \leftrightarrow \langle\alpha\rangle\varphi \vee \langle\alpha\rangle\psi$

(ii) $[\alpha](\varphi \wedge \psi) \leftrightarrow [\alpha]\varphi \wedge [\alpha]\psi$

(iii) $\langle\alpha\rangle\varphi \wedge [\alpha]\psi \rightarrow \langle\alpha\rangle(\varphi \wedge \psi)$

(iv) $[\alpha](\varphi \rightarrow \psi) \rightarrow ([\alpha]\varphi \rightarrow [\alpha]\psi)$

(v) $\langle\alpha\rangle(\varphi \wedge \psi) \;\;\rightarrow\;\; \langle\alpha\rangle\varphi \wedge \langle\alpha\rangle\psi$

(vi) $[\alpha]\varphi \vee [\alpha]\psi \;\;\rightarrow\;\; [\alpha](\varphi \vee \psi)$

(vii) $\langle\alpha\rangle 0 \;\;\leftrightarrow\;\; \mathbf{0}$

(viii) $[\alpha]\varphi \;\;\leftrightarrow\;\; \neg\langle\alpha\rangle\neg\varphi.$

Proof See Theorem 3.70. ∎

The converses of Theorem 5.6(iii)–(vi) are not valid. For example, (iii) is violated in state u of the following Kripke frame:

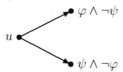

One can construct similar counterexamples for the others (Exercise 5.10).

THEOREM 5.7:   The following are sound rules of inference of PDL:

(i) Modal generalization (GEN):

$$\frac{\varphi}{[\alpha]\varphi}$$

(ii) Monotonicity of $\langle\alpha\rangle$:

$$\frac{\varphi \rightarrow \psi}{\langle\alpha\rangle\varphi \rightarrow \langle\alpha\rangle\psi}$$

(iii) Monotonicity of $[\alpha]$:

$$\frac{\varphi \rightarrow \psi}{[\alpha]\varphi \rightarrow [\alpha]\psi}$$

Proof See Theorem 3.71. ∎

The properties expressed in Theorem 5.7(ii) and (iii) are quite useful. They say that the constructs < > and [ ] are *monotone* in their second argument with respect to the ordering of logical implication. Corollary 5.9 below asserts that these constructs are also monotone and antitone, respectively, in their first argument.

Properties of ∪, ;, and ?

In this section we develop the basic properties of the choice operator ∪, the composition operator ;, and the test operator ?.

THEOREM 5.8: The following are valid formulas of PDL:

(i) $<\alpha \cup \beta>\varphi \quad \leftrightarrow \quad <\alpha>\varphi \vee <\beta>\varphi$

(ii) $[\alpha \cup \beta]\varphi \quad \leftrightarrow \quad [\alpha]\varphi \wedge [\beta]\varphi.$

Proof For (i), we need to show that for any Kripke frame $\mathfrak{K}$,

$$\mathfrak{m}_{\mathfrak{K}}(<\alpha \cup \beta>\varphi) \quad = \quad \mathfrak{m}_{\mathfrak{K}}(<\alpha>\varphi \vee <\beta>\varphi).$$

By the semantics of PDL (Section 5.2), the left-hand side is equivalent to

$$(\mathfrak{m}_{\mathfrak{K}}(\alpha) \cup \mathfrak{m}_{\mathfrak{K}}(\beta)) \circ \mathfrak{m}_{\mathfrak{K}}(\varphi)$$

and the right-hand side is equivalent to

$$(\mathfrak{m}_{\mathfrak{K}}(\alpha) \circ \mathfrak{m}_{\mathfrak{K}}(\varphi)) \cup (\mathfrak{m}_{\mathfrak{K}}(\beta) \circ \mathfrak{m}_{\mathfrak{K}}(\varphi)).$$

The equivalence of these two expressions follows from the fact that relational composition $\circ$ distributes over union $\cup$ (Lemma 1.1).

Statement (ii) follows from (i) by duality (Exercise 3.4). ∎

Intuitively, Theorem 5.8(i) says that the program $\alpha \cup \beta$ can halt in a state satisfying φ iff either α or β can. Theorem 5.8(ii) says that any halting state of the program $\alpha \cup \beta$ must satisfy φ iff this is true for both α and β.

It follows that the box and diamond operators are monotone and antitone, respectively, in their first argument α:

COROLLARY 5.9: If $\mathfrak{m}_{\mathfrak{K}}(\alpha) \subseteq \mathfrak{m}_{\mathfrak{K}}(\beta)$, then for all φ,

(i) $\mathfrak{K} \models <\alpha>\varphi \quad \rightarrow \quad <\beta>\varphi$

(ii) $\mathfrak{K} \models [\beta]\varphi \quad \rightarrow \quad [\alpha]\varphi.$

Proof Equivalently, if $\mathfrak{m}_{\mathfrak{K}}(\alpha) \subseteq \mathfrak{m}_{\mathfrak{K}}(\beta)$, then for all φ,

(i) $\mathfrak{m}_{\mathfrak{K}}(<\alpha>\varphi) \subseteq \mathfrak{m}_{\mathfrak{K}}(<\beta>\varphi)$

(ii) $\mathfrak{m}_{\mathfrak{K}}([\beta]\varphi) \subseteq \mathfrak{m}_{\mathfrak{K}}([\alpha]\varphi).$

These statements follow from Theorem 5.8 by virtue of the fact that $\mathfrak{m}_{\mathfrak{K}}(\alpha) \subseteq \mathfrak{m}_{\mathfrak{K}}(\beta)$ iff $\mathfrak{m}_{\mathfrak{K}}(\alpha) \cup \mathfrak{m}_{\mathfrak{M}}(\beta) = \mathfrak{m}_{\mathfrak{K}}(\beta)$. We leave the details as an exercise (Exercise 5.11). ∎

THEOREM 5.10: The following are valid formulas of PDL:

(i) $<\alpha\,;\,\beta>\varphi \;\leftrightarrow\; <\alpha><\beta>\varphi$

(ii) $[\alpha\,;\,\beta]\varphi \;\leftrightarrow\; [\alpha]\,[\beta]\varphi.$

Proof We need to show that in all models $\mathfrak{K}$,

(i) $\mathrm{m}_{\mathfrak{K}}(<\alpha\,;\,\beta>\varphi) \;=\; \mathrm{m}_{\mathfrak{K}}(<\alpha><\beta>\varphi)$

(ii) $\mathrm{m}_{\mathfrak{K}}([\alpha\,;\,\beta]\varphi) \;=\; \mathrm{m}_{\mathfrak{K}}([\alpha]\,[\beta]\,\varphi).$

According to the semantics of PDL, statement (i) says

$$(\mathrm{m}_{\mathfrak{K}}(\alpha) \circ \mathrm{m}_{\mathfrak{K}}(\beta)) \circ \mathrm{m}_{\mathfrak{K}}(\varphi) \;=\; \mathrm{m}_{\mathfrak{K}}(\alpha) \circ (\mathrm{m}_{\mathfrak{K}}(\beta) \circ \mathrm{m}_{\mathfrak{K}}(\varphi)).$$

This follows from the associativity of relational composition (Exercise 1.1). Statement (ii) follows from (i) by duality (Exercise 3.4). ∎

THEOREM 5.11: The following are valid formulas of PDL:

(i) $<\varphi?>\psi \;\leftrightarrow\; (\varphi \wedge \psi)$

(ii) $[\varphi?]\psi \;\leftrightarrow\; (\varphi \to \psi).$

Proof We need to show that in all models $\mathfrak{K}$,

(i) $\mathrm{m}_{\mathfrak{K}}(<\varphi?>\psi) \;=\; \mathrm{m}_{\mathfrak{K}}(\varphi \wedge \psi)$

(ii) $\mathrm{m}_{\mathfrak{K}}([\varphi?]\psi) \;=\; \mathrm{m}_{\mathfrak{K}}(\varphi \to \psi).$

To show (i),

$$\begin{aligned}
\mathrm{m}_{\mathfrak{K}}(<\varphi?>\psi) &= \{(u,u) \mid u \in \mathrm{m}_{\mathfrak{K}}(\varphi)\} \circ \mathrm{m}_{\mathfrak{K}}(\psi) \\
&= \{u \mid u \in \mathrm{m}_{\mathfrak{K}}(\varphi)\} \cap \mathrm{m}_{\mathfrak{K}}(\psi) \\
&= \mathrm{m}_{\mathfrak{K}}(\varphi) \cap \mathrm{m}_{\mathfrak{K}}(\psi) \\
&= \mathrm{m}_{\mathfrak{K}}(\varphi \wedge \psi).
\end{aligned}$$

Then (ii) follows from (i) by duality (Exercise 3.4). ∎

The Converse Operator $^-$

The following properties deal with the converse operator $^-$ with semantics

$$\mathrm{m}_{\mathfrak{K}}(\alpha^-) \;=\; \mathrm{m}_{\mathfrak{K}}(\alpha)^- \;=\; \{(v,u) \mid (u,v) \in \mathrm{m}_{\mathfrak{K}}(\alpha)\}.$$

Intuitively, the converse operator allows us to "run a program backwards;" semantically, the input/output relation of the program α^- is the output/input relation of α. Although this is not always possible to realize in practice, it is nevertheless a useful expressive tool. For example, it gives us a convenient way to talk about *backtracking*, or rolling back a computation to a previous state.

THEOREM 5.12:   For any programs α and β,

(i) $\mathfrak{m}_{\mathfrak{K}}((\alpha \cup \beta)^-) = \mathfrak{m}_{\mathfrak{K}}(\alpha^- \cup \beta^-)$

(ii) $\mathfrak{m}_{\mathfrak{K}}((\alpha \,;\, \beta)^-) = \mathfrak{m}_{\mathfrak{K}}(\beta^- \,;\, \alpha^-)$

(iii) $\mathfrak{m}_{\mathfrak{K}}(\varphi?^-) = \mathfrak{m}_{\mathfrak{K}}(\varphi?)$

(iv) $\mathfrak{m}_{\mathfrak{K}}(\alpha^{*-}) = \mathfrak{m}_{\mathfrak{K}}(\alpha^{-*})$

(v) $\mathfrak{m}_{\mathfrak{K}}(\alpha^{--}) = \mathfrak{m}_{\mathfrak{K}}(\alpha)$.

Proof   All of these follow directly from the properties of binary relations (Section 1.3). For example, (i) follows from the fact that the converse operation $^-$ on binary relations commutes with set union $\cup$ (Exercise 1.5):

$$
\begin{aligned}
\mathfrak{m}_{\mathfrak{K}}((\alpha \cup \beta)^-) &= \mathfrak{m}_{\mathfrak{K}}(\alpha \cup \beta)^- \\
&= (\mathfrak{m}_{\mathfrak{K}}(\alpha) \cup \mathfrak{m}_{\mathfrak{K}}(\beta))^- \\
&= \mathfrak{m}_{\mathfrak{K}}(\alpha)^- \cup \mathfrak{m}_{\mathfrak{K}}(\beta)^- \\
&= \mathfrak{m}_{\mathfrak{K}}(\alpha^-) \cup \mathfrak{m}_{\mathfrak{K}}(\beta^-) \\
&= \mathfrak{m}_{\mathfrak{K}}(\alpha^- \cup \beta^-).
\end{aligned}
$$

Similarly, (ii) uses Exercise 1.6, (iii) follows from the fact that $\mathfrak{m}_{\mathfrak{K}}(\varphi?)$ is a subset of the identity relation ι and is therefore symmetric, (iv) uses Exercise 1.5, and (v) uses Exercise 1.7.   ■

Theorem 5.12 can be used to transform any program containing occurrences of the operator $^-$ into an equivalent program in which all occurrences of $^-$ are applied to atomic programs only. The equivalent program is obtained by replacing any subprogram which looks like the left-hand side of one of Theorem 5.12(i)–(v) with the corresponding right-hand side. These rules are applied, moving occurrences of $^-$ inward, until they cannot be applied any more; that is, until all $^-$ are applied to primitive programs only. The resulting program is equivalent to the original.

Theorem 5.12 discusses the interaction of $^-$ with the other program operators. The interaction of $^-$ with the modal operations $<\alpha>$ and $[\alpha]$ is described in the following theorem.

THEOREM 5.13:   The following are valid formulas of PDL:

(i) $\varphi \;\rightarrow\; [\alpha]{<}\alpha^-{>}\varphi$

(ii) $\varphi \;\rightarrow\; [\alpha^-]{<}\alpha{>}\varphi$

(iii) ${<}\alpha{>}[\alpha^-]\varphi \;\rightarrow\; \varphi$

(iv) ${<}\alpha^-{>}[\alpha]\varphi \;\rightarrow\; \varphi.$

Proof   We need to show that in any model $\mathfrak{K}$,

(i) $\mathfrak{m}_{\mathfrak{K}}(\varphi) \;\subseteq\; \mathfrak{m}_{\mathfrak{K}}([\alpha]{<}\alpha^-{>}\varphi)$

(ii) $\mathfrak{m}_{\mathfrak{K}}(\varphi) \;\subseteq\; \mathfrak{m}_{\mathfrak{K}}([\alpha^-]{<}\alpha{>}\varphi)$

(iii) $\mathfrak{m}_{\mathfrak{K}}({<}\alpha{>}[\alpha^-]\varphi) \;\subseteq\; \mathfrak{m}_{\mathfrak{K}}(\varphi)$

(iv) $\mathfrak{m}_{\mathfrak{K}}({<}\alpha^-{>}[\alpha]\varphi) \;\subseteq\; \mathfrak{m}_{\mathfrak{K}}(\varphi).$

To show (i), suppose $u \in \mathfrak{m}_{\mathfrak{K}}(\varphi)$. For any state v such that $(u,v) \in \mathfrak{m}_{\mathfrak{K}}(\alpha)$, $v \in \mathfrak{m}_{\mathfrak{K}}({<}\alpha^-{>}\varphi)$, thus $u \in \mathfrak{m}_{\mathfrak{M}}([\alpha]{<}\alpha^-{>}\varphi)$. Statement (ii) follows immediately from (i) using Exercise 1.7, and (iii) and (iv) are dual to (i) and (ii). ∎

Theorem 5.13 has a rather powerful consequence: in the presence of the converse operator $^-$, the operator ${<}\alpha{>}$ is *continuous* on any Kripke frame $\mathfrak{K}$ (see Section 1.7) with respect to the partial order of implication. In **PDL** without $^-$, a Kripke frame can be constructed such that ${<}\alpha{>}$ is not continuous (Exercise 5.12).

Let $\mathfrak{K}$ be any Kripke frame for **PDL**. Let $\mathfrak{m}_{\mathfrak{K}}(\Phi)$ be the set of interpretations of **PDL** propositions:

$$\mathfrak{m}_{\mathfrak{K}}(\Phi) \;\overset{\text{def}}{=}\; \{\mathfrak{m}_{\mathfrak{K}}(\varphi) \mid \varphi \in \Phi\}.$$

The set $\mathfrak{m}_{\mathfrak{K}}(\Phi)$ is partially ordered by inclusion $\subseteq$. Under this order, the supremum of any finite set $\{\mathfrak{m}_{\mathfrak{K}}(\varphi_1), \dots, \mathfrak{m}_{\mathfrak{K}}(\varphi_n)\}$ always exists and is in $\mathfrak{m}_{\mathfrak{K}}(\Phi)$; it is

$$\mathfrak{m}_{\mathfrak{K}}(\varphi_1) \cup \cdots \cup \mathfrak{m}_{\mathfrak{K}}(\varphi_n) \;=\; \mathfrak{m}_{\mathfrak{K}}(\varphi_1 \vee \cdots \vee \varphi_n).$$

Moreover, ${<}\alpha{>}$ always preserves suprema of finite sets:

$$\sup_{i=1}^{n} \mathfrak{m}_{\mathfrak{K}}({<}\alpha{>}\varphi_i) \;=\; \mathfrak{m}_{\mathfrak{K}}\left(\bigvee_{i=1}^{n} {<}\alpha{>}\varphi_i\right)$$

$$=\; \mathfrak{m}_{\mathfrak{K}}\left({<}\alpha{>}\bigvee_{i=1}^{n} \varphi_i\right).$$

This follows from $n-1$ applications of Theorem 5.6(i). However, if $A \subseteq \Phi$ is infinite, then $\sup_{\varphi \in A} \mathfrak{m}_{\mathfrak{K}}(\varphi)$ may not exist. Note that in general $\bigcup_{\varphi \in A} \mathfrak{m}_{\mathfrak{K}}(\varphi)$ is not the supremum, since it may not even be in $\mathfrak{m}_{\mathfrak{K}}(\Phi)$. Even if $\sup_{\varphi \in A} \mathfrak{m}_{\mathfrak{K}}(\varphi)$ does exist (that is, if it is $m_{\mathfrak{K}}(\psi)$ for some $\psi \in \Phi$), it is not necessarily equal to $\bigcup_{\varphi \in A} m_{\mathfrak{K}}(\varphi)$.

The following theorem says that in the presence of $^-$, all existing suprema are preserved by the operator $<\alpha>$.

THEOREM 5.14:   In PDL with $^-$, the map $\varphi \mapsto <\alpha>\varphi$ is continuous with respect to the order of logical implication. That is, if $\mathfrak{K}$ is a Kripke frame, A a (finite or infinite) set of formulas, and φ a formula such that

$$m_{\mathfrak{K}}(\varphi) \;=\; \sup_{\psi \in A} m_{\mathfrak{K}}(\psi),$$

then $\sup_{\psi \in A} m_{\mathfrak{K}}(<\alpha>\psi)$ exists and is equal to $m_{\mathfrak{K}}(<\alpha>\varphi)$.

Proof   Since $m_{\mathfrak{K}}(\varphi)$ is an upper bound for $\{m_{\mathfrak{K}}(\psi) \mid \psi \in A\}$, we have that

$$m_{\mathfrak{K}}(<\alpha>\psi) \;\subseteq\; m_{\mathfrak{K}}(<\alpha>\varphi)$$

for each $\psi \in A$ by the monotonicity of $<\alpha>$ (Theorem 5.7(ii)), thus $m_{\mathfrak{K}}(<\alpha>\varphi)$ is an upper bound for $\{m_{\mathfrak{K}}(<\alpha>\psi) \mid \psi \in A\}$. To show it is the least upper bound, suppose ρ is any other upper bound; that is,

$$m_{\mathfrak{K}}(<\alpha>\psi) \;\subseteq\; m_{\mathfrak{K}}(\rho)$$

for all $\psi \in A$. By the monotonicity of $[\alpha^-]$ (Theorem 5.7(iii)),

$$m_{\mathfrak{K}}([\alpha^-]<\alpha>\psi) \;\subseteq\; m_{\mathfrak{K}}([\alpha^-]\rho)$$

for all $\psi \in A$, and by Theorem 5.13(ii),

$$m_{\mathfrak{K}}(\psi) \;\subseteq\; m_{\mathfrak{K}}([\alpha^-]<\alpha>\psi)$$

for all $\psi \in A$, thus $m_{\mathfrak{K}}([\alpha^-]\rho)$ is an upper bound for $\{m_{\mathfrak{K}}(\psi) \mid \psi \in A\}$. Since $m_{\mathfrak{K}}(\varphi)$ is the least upper bound,

$$m_{\mathfrak{K}}(\varphi) \;\subseteq\; m_{\mathfrak{K}}([\alpha^-]\rho).$$

By the monotonicity of $<\alpha>$ again,

$$m_{\mathfrak{K}}(<\alpha>\varphi) \;\subseteq\; m_{\mathfrak{K}}(<\alpha>[\alpha^-]\rho),$$

and by Theorem 5.13(iii),

$$m_{\mathfrak{K}}(<\alpha>[\alpha^-]\rho) \;\subseteq\; m_{\mathfrak{K}}(\rho),$$

therefore

$$m_{\mathfrak{K}}(\text{<}\alpha\text{>}\varphi) \;\subseteq\; m_{\mathfrak{K}}(\rho).$$

Since $m_{\mathfrak{K}}(\rho)$ was an arbitrary upper bound for $\{m_{\mathfrak{K}}(\text{<}p\text{>}\psi) \mid \psi \in A\}$, $m_{\mathfrak{K}}(\text{<}\alpha\text{>}\varphi)$ must be the least upper bound. ∎

The Iteration Operator *

The iteration operator * is interpreted as the reflexive transitive closure operator on binary relations. It is the means by which iteration is coded in PDL. This operator differs from the other operators in that it is infinitary in nature, as reflected by its semantics:

$$m_{\mathfrak{K}}(\alpha^*) \;=\; m_{\mathfrak{K}}(\alpha)^* \;=\; \bigcup_{n<\omega} m_{\mathfrak{K}}(\alpha)^n$$

(see Section 5.2). This introduces a level of complexity to PDL beyond the other operators. Because of it, PDL is not compact: the set

$$\{\text{<}\alpha^*\text{>}\varphi\} \;\cup\; \{\neg\varphi,\ \neg\text{<}\alpha\text{>}\varphi,\ \neg\text{<}\alpha^2\text{>}\varphi,\ \dots\} \tag{5.6.1}$$

is finitely satisfiable but not satisfiable. Because of this infinitary behavior, it is rather surprising that PDL should be decidable and that there should be a finitary complete axiomatization.

   The properties of the * operator of PDL come directly from the properties of the reflexive transitive closure operator * on binary relations, as described in Section 1.3 and Exercises 1.12 and 1.13. In a nutshell, for any binary relation R, R^* is the $\subseteq$-least reflexive and transitive relation containing R.

THEOREM 5.15:   The following are valid formulas of PDL:

(i) $[\alpha^*]\varphi \;\rightarrow\; \varphi$

(ii) $\varphi \;\rightarrow\; \text{<}\alpha^*\text{>}\varphi$

(iii) $[\alpha^*]\varphi \;\rightarrow\; [\alpha]\varphi$

(iv) $\text{<}\alpha\text{>}\varphi \;\rightarrow\; \text{<}\alpha^*\text{>}\varphi$

(v) $[\alpha^*]\varphi \;\leftrightarrow\; [\alpha^*\alpha^*]\varphi$

(vi) $\text{<}\alpha^*\text{>}\varphi \;\leftrightarrow\; \text{<}\alpha^*\alpha^*\text{>}\varphi$

(vii) $[\alpha^*]\varphi \;\leftrightarrow\; [\alpha^{**}]\varphi$

(viii) $\text{<}\alpha^*\text{>}\varphi \;\leftrightarrow\; \text{<}\alpha^{**}\text{>}\varphi$

(ix) $[\alpha^*]\varphi \;\leftrightarrow\; \varphi \wedge [\alpha][\alpha^*]\varphi.$

(x) $<\alpha^*>\varphi \ \leftrightarrow \ \varphi \lor <\alpha><\alpha^*>\varphi$.

(xi) $[\alpha^*]\varphi \ \leftrightarrow \ \varphi \land [\alpha^*](\varphi \to [\alpha]\varphi)$.

(xii) $<\alpha^*>\varphi \ \leftrightarrow \ \varphi \lor <\alpha^*>(\neg\varphi \land <\alpha>\varphi)$.

Proof   These properties follow immediately from the semantics of PDL (Section 5.2) and the properties of reflexive transitive closure (Exercises 1.7, 1.12, and 1.13).   ∎

Semantically, α^* is a reflexive and transitive relation containing α, and Theorem 5.15 captures this. That α^* is reflexive is captured in (ii); that it is transitive is captured in (vi); and that it contains α is captured in (iv). These three properties are captured by the single property (x).

Reflexive Transitive Closure and Induction

To prove properties of iteration, it is not enough to know that α^* is a reflexive and transitive relation containing α. So is the universal relation $K \times K$, and that is not very interesting. We also need some way of capturing the idea that α^* is the *least* reflexive and transitive relation containing α. There are several equivalent ways this can be done:

(RTC)   The *reflexive transitive closure rule*:

$$\frac{(\varphi \lor <\alpha>\psi) \to \psi}{<\alpha^*>\varphi \to \psi}$$

(LI)   The *loop invariance rule*:

$$\frac{\psi \to [\alpha]\psi}{\psi \to [\alpha^*]\psi}$$

(IND)   The *induction axiom* (box form):

$$\varphi \land [\alpha^*](\varphi \to [\alpha]\varphi) \ \to \ [\alpha^*]\varphi$$

(IND)   The *induction axiom* (diamond form):

$$<\alpha^*>\varphi \ \to \ \varphi \lor <\alpha^*>(\neg\varphi \land <\alpha>\varphi)$$

The rule (RTC) is called the *reflexive transitive closure rule*. Its importance is best described in terms of its relationship to the valid **PDL** formula of Theorem 5.15(x). Observe that the right-to-left implication of this formula is obtained by substituting $\langle\alpha^*\rangle\varphi$ for R in the expression

$$\varphi \vee \langle\alpha\rangle R \quad \rightarrow \quad R. \tag{5.6.2}$$

Theorem 5.15(x) implies that $\langle\alpha^*\rangle\varphi$ is a solution of (5.6.2); that is, (5.6.2) is valid when $\langle\alpha^*\rangle\varphi$ is substituted for R. The rule (RTC) says that $\langle\alpha^*\rangle\varphi$ is the *least* such solution with respect to logical implication. That is, it is the least **PDL**-definable set of states that when substituted for R in (5.6.2) results in a valid formula.

The dual propositions labeled (IND) are jointly called the **PDL** *induction axiom*. Intuitively, the box form of (IND) says, "If φ is true initially, and if, after any number of iterations of the program α, the truth of φ is preserved by one more iteration of α, then φ will be true after any number of iterations of α." The diamond form of (IND) says, "If it is possible to reach a state satisfying φ in some number of iterations of α, then either φ is true now, or it is possible to reach a state in which φ is false but becomes true after one more iteration of α."

As mentioned in Section 5.5, the box form of (IND) bears a strong resemblance to the induction axiom of Peano arithmetic:

$$\varphi(0) \wedge \forall n \; (\varphi(n) \rightarrow \varphi(n+1)) \quad \rightarrow \quad \forall n \; \varphi(n).$$

In Theorem 5.18 below, we argue that in the presence of the other axioms and rules of **PDL**, the rules (RTC), (LI), and (IND) are interderivable. First, however, we argue that the rule (RTC) is sound. The soundness of (LI) and (IND) will follow from Theorem 5.18.

THEOREM 5.16:   The reflexive transitive closure rule (RTC) is sound.

Proof We need to show that in any model $\mathfrak{K}$, if $\mathfrak{m}_\mathfrak{K}(\varphi) \subseteq \mathfrak{m}_\mathfrak{K}(\psi)$ and $\mathfrak{m}_\mathfrak{K}(\langle\alpha\rangle\psi) \subseteq \mathfrak{m}_\mathfrak{K}(\psi)$, then $\mathfrak{m}_\mathfrak{K}(\langle\alpha^*\rangle\varphi) \subseteq \mathfrak{m}_\mathfrak{K}(\psi)$. We show by induction on n that $\mathfrak{m}_\mathfrak{K}(\langle\alpha^n\rangle\varphi) \subseteq \mathfrak{m}_\mathfrak{K}(\psi)$. Certainly $\mathfrak{m}_\mathfrak{K}(\varphi) = \mathfrak{m}_\mathfrak{K}(\langle\mathbf{skip}\rangle\varphi)$, since $\mathfrak{m}_\mathfrak{K}(\mathbf{skip}) = \iota$, and ι is an identity for relational composition (Exercise 1.2). By definition, $\alpha^0 = \mathbf{skip}$, so $\mathfrak{m}_\mathfrak{K}(\langle\alpha^0\rangle\varphi) \subseteq \mathfrak{m}_\mathfrak{K}(\psi)$.

Now suppose $\mathfrak{m}_{\mathfrak{K}}(\langle\alpha^n\rangle\varphi) \subseteq \mathfrak{m}_{\mathfrak{K}}(\psi)$. Then

$$
\begin{aligned}
\mathfrak{m}_{\mathfrak{K}}(\langle\alpha^{n+1}\rangle\varphi) \;&=\; \mathfrak{m}_{\mathfrak{K}}(\langle\alpha\rangle\langle\alpha^n\rangle\varphi) \\
&\subseteq\; \mathfrak{m}_{\mathfrak{K}}(\langle\alpha\rangle\psi) \qquad \text{by the monotonicity of } \langle\alpha\rangle \\
&\subseteq\; \mathfrak{m}_{\mathfrak{K}}(\psi) \qquad\quad\; \text{by assumption.}
\end{aligned}
$$

Thus for all n, $\mathfrak{m}_{\mathfrak{K}}(\langle\alpha^n\rangle\varphi) \subseteq \mathfrak{m}_{\mathfrak{K}}(\psi)$. Since $\mathfrak{m}_{\mathfrak{K}}(\langle\alpha^*\rangle\varphi) = \bigcup_{n<\omega} \mathfrak{m}_{\mathfrak{K}}(\langle\alpha^n\rangle\varphi)$, we have that $\mathfrak{m}_{\mathfrak{K}}(\langle\alpha^*\rangle\varphi) \subseteq \mathfrak{m}_{\mathfrak{K}}(\psi)$. ∎

The deductive relationship between the induction axiom (IND), the reflexive transitive closure rule (RTC), and the rule of loop invariance (LI) is summed up in the following lemma and theorem. We emphasize that these results are purely proof-theoretic and independent of the semantics of Section 5.2.

LEMMA 5.17:   The monotonicity rules of Theorem 5.7(ii) and (iii) are derivable in PDL without the induction axiom.

Proof This is really a theorem of modal logic. First we show that the rule of Theorem 5.7(iii) is derivable in PDL without induction. Assuming the premise $\varphi \to \psi$ and applying modal generalization, we obtain $[\alpha](\varphi \to \psi)$. The conclusion $[\alpha]\varphi \to [\alpha]\psi$ then follows from Axiom 5.5(ii) and modus ponens. The dual monotonicity rule, Theorem 5.7(ii), can be derived from (iii) by pure propositional reasoning. ∎

THEOREM 5.18:   In PDL without the induction axiom, the following axioms and rules are interderivable:

- the induction axiom (IND);
- the loop invariance rule (LI);
- the reflexive transitive closure rule (RTC).

Proof (IND) $\to$ (LI)   Assume the premise of (LI):

$$\varphi \;\to\; [\alpha]\varphi.$$

By modal generalization,

$$[\alpha^*](\varphi \to [\alpha]\varphi),$$

thus

$$\varphi \;\; \rightarrow \;\; \varphi \wedge [\alpha^*](\varphi \rightarrow [\alpha]\varphi)$$
$$\rightarrow \;\; [\alpha^*]\varphi.$$

The first implication is by propositional reasoning and the second is by (IND). By transitivity of implication (Example 3.7), we obtain

$$\varphi \;\; \rightarrow \;\; [\alpha^*]\varphi,$$

which is the conclusion of (LI).

(LI) → (RTC)   Dualizing (RTC) by purely propositional reasoning, we obtain a rule

$$\frac{\psi \;\rightarrow\; \varphi \wedge [\alpha]\psi}{\psi \;\rightarrow\; [\alpha^*]\varphi} \tag{5.6.3}$$

equivalent to (RTC). It thus suffices to derive (5.6.3) from (LI). From the premise of (5.6.3), we obtain by propositional reasoning the two formulas

$$\psi \;\; \rightarrow \;\; \varphi \tag{5.6.4}$$
$$\psi \;\; \rightarrow \;\; [\alpha]\psi. \tag{5.6.5}$$

Applying (LI) to (5.6.5), we obtain

$$\psi \;\; \rightarrow \;\; [\alpha^*]\psi,$$

which by (5.6.4) and monotonicity (Lemma 5.17) gives

$$\psi \;\; \rightarrow \;\; [\alpha^*]\varphi.$$

This is the conclusion of (5.6.3).

(RTC) → (IND)   By Axiom 5.5(iii) and (vii) and propositional reasoning, we have

$$\varphi \wedge [\alpha^*](\varphi \rightarrow [\alpha]\varphi)$$
$$\rightarrow \;\; \varphi \wedge (\varphi \rightarrow [\alpha]\varphi) \wedge [\alpha][\alpha^*](\varphi \rightarrow [\alpha]\varphi)$$
$$\rightarrow \;\; \varphi \wedge [\alpha]\varphi \wedge [\alpha][\alpha^*](\varphi \rightarrow [\alpha]\varphi)$$
$$\rightarrow \;\; \varphi \wedge [\alpha](\varphi \wedge [\alpha^*](\varphi \rightarrow [\alpha]\varphi)).$$

By transitivity of implication (Example 3.7),

$$\varphi \wedge [\alpha^*](\varphi \rightarrow [\alpha]\varphi) \;\; \rightarrow \;\; \varphi \wedge [\alpha](\varphi \wedge [\alpha^*](\varphi \rightarrow [\alpha]\varphi)).$$

Applying (5.6.3), which we have argued is equivalent to (RTC), we obtain (IND):

$$\varphi \wedge [\alpha^*](\varphi \rightarrow [\alpha]\varphi) \;\;\rightarrow\;\; [\alpha^*]\varphi.$$

∎

5.7   Encoding Hoare Logic

Recall that the Hoare partial correctness assertion $\{\varphi\}\,\alpha\,\{\psi\}$ is encoded as $\varphi \rightarrow [\alpha]\psi$ in **PDL**. The following theorem says that under this encoding, Dynamic Logic subsumes Hoare Logic.

THEOREM 5.19:   The following rules of Hoare Logic are derivable in **PDL**:

(i) Composition rule:

$$\frac{\{\varphi\}\,\alpha\,\{\sigma\}, \quad \{\sigma\}\,\beta\,\{\psi\}}{\{\varphi\}\,\alpha\,;\,\beta\,\{\psi\}}$$

(ii) Conditional rule:

$$\frac{\{\varphi \wedge \sigma\}\,\alpha\,\{\psi\}, \quad \{\neg\varphi \wedge \sigma\}\,\beta\,\{\psi\}}{\{\sigma\}\,\text{if }\varphi\text{ then }\alpha\text{ else }\beta\,\{\psi\}}$$

(iii) **While** rule:

$$\frac{\{\varphi \wedge \psi\}\,\alpha\,\{\psi\}}{\{\psi\}\,\text{while }\varphi\text{ do }\alpha\,\{\neg\varphi \wedge \psi\}}$$

(iv) Weakening rule:

$$\frac{\varphi' \rightarrow \varphi, \quad \{\varphi\}\,\alpha\,\{\psi\}, \quad \psi \rightarrow \psi'}{\{\varphi'\}\,\alpha\,\{\psi'\}}$$

Proof We derive the **while** rule (iii) in **PDL**. The other Hoare rules are also derivable, and we leave them as exercises (Exercise 5.14).
    Assuming the premise

$$\{\varphi \wedge \psi\}\,\alpha\,\{\psi\} \;\; = \;\; (\varphi \wedge \psi) \rightarrow [\alpha]\psi, \tag{5.7.1}$$

we wish to derive the conclusion

$$\{\psi\}\,\text{while }\varphi\text{ do }\alpha\,\{\neg\varphi \wedge \psi\} \;\; = \;\; \psi \rightarrow [(\varphi?;\alpha)^*;\neg\varphi?](\neg\varphi \wedge \psi). \tag{5.7.2}$$

Using propositional reasoning, (5.7.1) is equivalent to

$$\psi \;\rightarrow\; (\varphi \rightarrow [\alpha]\psi),$$

which by Axioms 5.5(v) and (vi) is equivalent to

$$\psi \;\rightarrow\; [\varphi?;\alpha]\psi.$$

Applying the loop invariance rule (LI), we obtain

$$\psi \;\rightarrow\; [(\varphi?;\alpha)^*]\psi.$$

By the monotonicity of $[(\varphi?;\alpha)^*]$ (Lemma 5.17) and propositional reasoning,

$$\psi \;\rightarrow\; [(\varphi?;\alpha)^*](\neg\varphi \rightarrow (\neg\varphi \wedge \psi)),$$

and by Axiom 5.5(vi), we obtain

$$\psi \;\rightarrow\; [(\varphi?;\alpha)^*][\neg\varphi?](\neg\varphi \wedge \psi).$$

By Axiom 5.5(v), this is equivalent to the desired conclusion (5.7.2). ∎

5.8   Bibliographical Notes

Burstall (1974) suggested using modal logic for reasoning about programs, but it
was not until the work of Pratt (1976), prompted by a suggestion of R. Moore, that
it was actually shown how to extend modal logic in a useful way by considering a
separate modality for every program. The first research devoted to propositional
reasoning about programs seems to be that of Fischer and Ladner (1977, 1979) on
PDL. As mentioned in the Preface, the general use of logical systems for reasoning
about programs was suggested by Engeler (1967).

Other semantics besides Kripke semantics have been studied; see Berman
(1979); Nishimura (1979); Kozen (1979b); Trnkova and Reiterman (1980); Kozen
(1980b); Pratt (1979b). Modal logic has many applications and a vast literature;
good introductions can be found in Hughes and Cresswell (1968); Chellas (1980).
Alternative and iterative guarded commands were studied in Gries (1981). Partial
correctness assertions and the Hoare rules given in Section 5.7 were first formulated
by Hoare (1969). Regular expressions, on which the regular program operators
are based, were introduced by Kleene (1956). Their algebraic theory was further
investigated by Conway (1971). They were first applied in the context of DL by
Fischer and Ladner (1977, 1979). The axiomatization of PDL given in Axioms 5.5
was formulated by Segerberg (1977). Tests and converse were investigated by various

authors; see Peterson (1978); Berman (1978); Berman and Paterson (1981); Streett (1981, 1982); Vardi (1985b). Theorem 5.14 is due to Trnkova and Reiterman (1980).

Exercises

5.1. Prove Proposition 5.2.

5.2. A program α is said to be *semantically deterministic* in a Kripke frame $\mathfrak{K}$ if its traces are uniquely determined by their first states. Show that if α and β are semantically deterministic in a structure $\mathfrak{K}$, then so are **if** φ **then** α **else** β and **while** φ **do** α.

5.3. We say that two programs α and β are *equivalent* if they represent the same binary relation in all Kripke frames; that is, if $\mathfrak{m}_{\mathfrak{K}}(\alpha) = \mathfrak{m}_{\mathfrak{K}}(\beta)$ for all $\mathfrak{K}$. Let p be an atomic proposition not occurring in α or β. Prove that α and β are equivalent iff the PDL formula $\langle\alpha\rangle p \leftrightarrow \langle\beta\rangle p$ is valid.

5.4. Prove in PDL that the following pairs of programs are equivalent in the sense of Exercise 5.3. For (c), use the encodings (4.3.1) and (4.3.2) of Section 4.3 and reason in terms of the regular operators.

(a) $a(ba)^*$ $(ab)^*a$

(b) $(a \cup b)^*$ $(a^*b)^*a^*$

(c) **while** b **do begin**

               p;

                  while c **do** q

      end

    if b **then begin**

               p;

            while $b \vee c$ **do**

                  if c **then** q **else** p

      end

5.5. Let α be the program (5.4.1) of Example 5.3. Show that for any proposition φ, the proposition $\varphi \leftrightarrow [\alpha]\varphi$ is valid in the model $\mathfrak{K}$ of that example.

5.6. Prove that the formula (5.4.2) of Example 5.4 is valid. Give a semantic argument using the semantics of **PDL** given in Section 5.2, not the deductive system of Section 5.5.

5.7. Prove that the box and diamond forms of the **PDL** induction axiom are equivalent. See Section 5.6.

5.8. Prove that the following statements are valid:

$$<\alpha>\varphi \quad \rightarrow \quad <\alpha\alpha^-\alpha>\varphi$$
$$<\alpha^*\alpha>\varphi \quad \leftrightarrow \quad <\alpha\alpha^*>\varphi$$
$$<\alpha^*>\varphi \quad \leftrightarrow \quad \varphi \vee <\alpha>\varphi \vee <\alpha\alpha>\varphi \vee \cdots \vee <\alpha^{n-1}>\varphi \vee <\alpha^n\alpha^*>\varphi.$$

5.9. Prove that the following are theorems of **PDL**. Use Axiom System 5.5, do not reason semantically.

(i) $<\alpha>\varphi \wedge [\alpha]\psi \quad \rightarrow \quad <\alpha>(\varphi \wedge \psi)$

(ii) $<\alpha>(\varphi \vee \psi) \leftrightarrow <\alpha>\varphi \vee <\alpha>\psi$

(iii) $<\alpha \cup \beta>\varphi \leftrightarrow <\alpha>\varphi \vee <\beta>\varphi$

(iv) $<\alpha\beta>\varphi \leftrightarrow <\alpha><\beta>\varphi$

(v) $<\psi?>\varphi \quad \leftrightarrow \quad \psi \wedge \varphi$

(vi) $<\alpha^*>\varphi \quad \leftrightarrow \quad \varphi \vee <\alpha\alpha^*>\varphi$

(vii) $<\alpha^*>\varphi \quad \rightarrow \quad \varphi \vee <\alpha^*>(\neg\varphi \wedge <\alpha>\varphi)$.

(viii) $<\alpha^*>\varphi \quad \leftrightarrow \quad \varphi \vee <\alpha^*>(\neg\varphi \wedge <\alpha>\varphi)$.

In the presence of the converse operator $^-$,

(ix) $<\alpha>[\alpha^-]\varphi \quad \rightarrow \quad \varphi$

(x) $<\alpha^->[\alpha]\varphi \quad \rightarrow \quad \varphi$.

5.10. Give counterexamples showing that the converses of Theorem 5.6(iv)–(vi) are not valid.

5.11. Supply the missing details in the proof of Corollary 5.9.

5.12. Show that Theorem 5.14 fails in **PDL** without the converse operator $^-$. Construct a Kripke model such that the operator $<a>$ is not continuous.

5.13. Let Σ be a set of atomic programs and let Σ^* be the set of finite-length strings over Σ. A *regular expression* over Σ is a PDL program over Σ with only operators $\cup$, *, and ;. A regular expression α denotes a set $L(\alpha)$ of strings in Σ^* as follows:

$$L(a) \overset{\text{def}}{=} \{a\}, \quad a \in \Sigma$$

$$L(\alpha\beta) \overset{\text{def}}{=} L(\alpha) \cdot L(\beta)$$

$$= \{xy \mid x \in L(\alpha),\ y \in L(\beta)\}$$

$$L(\alpha \cup \beta) \overset{\text{def}}{=} L(\alpha) \cup L(\beta)$$

$$L(\alpha^*) \overset{\text{def}}{=} \bigcup_{n<\omega} L(\alpha)^n,$$

where $L(\alpha)^0 = \{\varepsilon\}$, $L(\alpha^{n+1}) = L(\alpha^n) \cdot L(\alpha)$, and ε is the empty string. Let p be an atomic proposition. Prove that for any two regular expressions α, β, $L(\alpha) = L(\beta)$ iff $<\alpha>p \leftrightarrow <\beta>p$ is a theorem of PDL.

5.14. Prove that the composition, conditional, and weakening rules of Hoare Logic (Theorem 5.19(i), (ii), and (iv), respectively) are derivable in PDL.

6 Filtration and Decidability

In this chapter we will establish a *small model property* for PDL. This result and the technique used to prove it, called *filtration*, come directly from modal logic.

The small model property says that if φ is satisfiable, then it is satisfied at a state in a Kripke frame with no more than $2^{|\varphi|}$ states, where $|\varphi|$ is the number of symbols of φ. This immediately gives a naive decision procedure for the satisfiability problem for PDL: to determine whether φ is satisfiable, construct all Kripke frames with at most $2^{|\varphi|}$ states and check whether φ is satisfied at some state in one of them. Considering only interpretations of the primitive formulas and primitive programs appearing in φ, there are roughly $2^{2^{|\varphi|}}$ such models, so this algorithm is too inefficient to be practical. A more efficient algorithm will be given in Chapter 8.

6.1   The Fischer–Ladner Closure

Many proofs in simpler modal systems use induction on the well-founded subformula relation. In PDL, the situation is complicated by the simultaneous inductive definitions of programs and propositions and by the behavior of the * operator, which make the induction proofs somewhat tricky. Nevertheless, we can still use the well-founded subexpression relation in inductive proofs. Here an *expression* can be either a program or a proposition. Either one can be a subexpression of the other because of the mixed operators [ ] and ?.

We start by defining two functions

$$FL \ : \ \Phi \ \to \ 2^{\Phi}$$
$$FL^{\square} \ : \ \{[\alpha]\varphi \mid \alpha \in \Psi, \ \varphi \in \Phi\} \ \to \ 2^{\Phi}$$

by simultaneous induction. The set $FL(\varphi)$ is called the *Fischer–Ladner closure* of φ. The filtration construction of Lemma 6.3 uses the Fischer–Ladner closure of a given formula where the corresponding proof for propositional modal logic would use the set of subformulas.

The functions FL and $FL^{\square}$ are defined inductively as follows:

(a) $FL(p) \overset{\text{def}}{=} \{p\}, \quad p$ an atomic proposition

(b) $FL(\varphi \to \psi) \overset{\text{def}}{=} \{\varphi \to \psi\} \cup FL(\varphi) \cup FL(\psi)$

(c) $FL(\mathbf{0}) \overset{\text{def}}{=} \{\mathbf{0}\}$

(d) $FL([\alpha]\varphi) \overset{\text{def}}{=} FL^{\square}([\alpha]\varphi) \cup FL(\varphi)$

(e) $FL^{\square}([a]\varphi) \overset{\text{def}}{=} \{[a]\varphi\}, \quad a$ an atomic program

(f) $FL^{\square}([\alpha \cup \beta]\varphi) \overset{\text{def}}{=} \{[\alpha \cup \beta]\varphi\} \cup FL^{\square}([\alpha]\varphi) \cup FL^{\square}([\beta]\varphi)$

(g) $FL^{\square}([\alpha\,;\,\beta]\varphi) \overset{\text{def}}{=} \{[\alpha\,;\,\beta]\varphi\} \cup FL^{\square}([\alpha][\beta]\varphi) \cup FL^{\square}([\beta]\varphi)$

(h) $FL^{\square}([\alpha^*]\varphi) \overset{\text{def}}{=} \{[\alpha^*]\varphi\} \cup FL^{\square}([\alpha][\alpha^*]\varphi)$

(i) $FL^{\square}([\psi?]\varphi) \overset{\text{def}}{=} \{[\psi?]\varphi\} \cup FL(\psi)$.

This definition is apparently quite a bit more involved than for mere subexpressions. In fact, at first glance it may appear circular because of the rule (h). The auxiliary function $FL^{\square}$ is introduced for the express purpose of avoiding any such circularity. It is defined only for formulas of the form $[\alpha]\varphi$ and intuitively produces those elements of $FL([\alpha]\varphi)$ obtained by breaking down α and ignoring φ.

Even after convincing ourselves that the definition is noncircular, it may not be clear how the size of $FL(\varphi)$ depends on the length of φ. Indeed, the right-hand side of rule (h) involves a formula that is larger than the formula on the left-hand side. We will be able to establish a linear relationship by induction on the well-founded subexpression relation (Lemma 6.3).

First we show a kind of transitivity property of FL and $FL^{\square}$ that will be useful in later arguments.

LEMMA 6.1:

(i) If $\sigma \in FL(\varphi)$, then $FL(\sigma) \subseteq FL(\varphi)$.

(ii) If $\sigma \in FL^{\square}([\alpha]\varphi)$, then $FL(\sigma) \subseteq FL^{\square}([\alpha]\varphi) \cup FL(\varphi)$.

Proof We prove (i) and (ii) by simultaneous induction on the well-founded subexpression relation.

First we show (i), assuming by the induction hypothesis that (i) and (ii) hold for proper subexpressions of φ. There are four cases, depending on the form of φ: an atomic proposition p, $\varphi \to \psi$, $\mathbf{0}$, or $[\alpha]\varphi$. We argue the second and fourth cases explicitly and leave the first and third as exercises (Exercise 6.1).

If $\sigma \in FL(\varphi \to \psi)$, then by clause (b) in the definition of FL, either $\sigma = \varphi \to \psi$, $\sigma \in FL(\varphi)$, or $\sigma \in FL(\psi)$. In the first case, $FL(\sigma) = FL(\varphi \to \psi)$, and we are done. In the second and third cases, we have $FL(\sigma) \subseteq FL(\varphi)$ and $FL(\sigma) \subseteq FL(\psi)$, respectively, by the induction hypothesis (i). In either case, $FL(\sigma) \subseteq FL(\varphi \to \psi)$ by clause (b) in the definition of FL.

If $\sigma \in FL([\alpha]\varphi)$, then by clause (d) in the definition of FL, either $\sigma \in$

$FL^{\Box}([\alpha]\varphi)$ or $\sigma \in FL(\varphi)$. In the former case, $FL(\sigma) \subseteq FL^{\Box}([\alpha]\varphi) \cup FL(\varphi)$ by the induction hypothesis (ii). (The induction hypothesis holds here because α is a proper subexpression of $[\alpha]\varphi$.) In the latter case, $FL(\sigma) \subseteq FL(\varphi)$ by the induction hypothesis (i). Thus in either case, $FL(\sigma) \subseteq FL([\alpha]\varphi)$ by clause (d) in the definition of FL.

Now we show (ii), again assuming that (i) and (ii) hold for proper subexpressions. There are five cases, depending on the form of the program: an atomic program a, $\alpha \cup \beta$, $\alpha \, ; \, \beta$, α^*, or $\psi?$. We argue the third and fourth cases explicitly, leaving the remaining three as exercises (Exercise 6.1).

If $\sigma \in FL^{\Box}([\alpha \, ; \, \beta]\varphi)$, then by clause (g) in the definition of $FL^{\Box}$, either

(A) $\sigma = [\alpha \, ; \, \beta]\varphi$,

(B) $\sigma \in FL^{\Box}([\alpha][\beta]\varphi)$, or

(C) $\sigma \in FL^{\Box}([\beta]\varphi)$.

In case (A), $FL(\sigma) = FL^{\Box}([\alpha \, ; \, \beta]\varphi) \cup FL(\varphi)$ by clause (d) in the definition of FL, and we are done. In case (B), we have

$$
\begin{aligned}
FL(\sigma) \ &\subseteq\ FL^{\Box}([\alpha][\beta]\varphi) \cup FL([\beta]\varphi) \quad \text{by the induction hypothesis (ii)} \\
&=\ FL^{\Box}([\alpha][\beta]\varphi) \cup FL^{\Box}([\beta]\varphi) \cup FL(\varphi) \\
&\qquad\qquad\qquad\qquad\qquad \text{by clause (d) in the definition of } FL \\
&\subseteq\ FL^{\Box}([\alpha \, ; \, \beta]\varphi) \cup FL(\varphi) \quad\ \text{by clause (g) in the definition of } FL^{\Box}.
\end{aligned}
$$

In case (C),

$$
\begin{aligned}
FL(\sigma) \ &\subseteq\ FL^{\Box}([\beta]\varphi) \cup FL(\varphi) \qquad\ \text{by the induction hypothesis (ii)} \\
&\subseteq\ FL^{\Box}([\alpha \, ; \, \beta]\varphi) \cup FL(\varphi) \quad \text{by clause (g) in the definition of } FL^{\Box}.
\end{aligned}
$$

If $\sigma \in FL^{\Box}([\alpha^*]\varphi)$, then by clause (h) in the definition of $FL^{\Box}$, either $\sigma = [\alpha^*]\varphi$ or $\sigma \in FL^{\Box}([\alpha][\alpha^*]\varphi)$. In the former case, $FL(\sigma) = FL^{\Box}([\alpha^*]\varphi) \cup FL(\varphi)$ by clause (d) in the definition of FL. In the latter case, we have

$$
\begin{aligned}
FL(\sigma) \ &\subseteq\ FL^{\Box}([\alpha][\alpha^*]\varphi) \cup FL([\alpha^*]\varphi) \\
&=\ FL^{\Box}([\alpha][\alpha^*]\varphi) \cup FL^{\Box}([\alpha^*]\varphi) \cup FL(\varphi) \\
&\subseteq\ FL^{\Box}([\alpha^*]\varphi) \cup FL(\varphi)
\end{aligned}
$$

by the induction hypothesis (ii) and clauses (d) and (h) in the definition of FL and $FL^{\Box}$. ∎

The following closure properties of FL are straightforward consequences of

Lemma 6.1.

Lemma 6.2:

(i) If $[\alpha]\psi \in FL(\varphi)$, then $\psi \in FL(\varphi)$.
(ii) If $[\rho?]\psi \in FL(\varphi)$, then $\rho \in FL(\varphi)$.
(iii) If $[\alpha \cup \beta]\psi \in FL(\varphi)$, then $[\alpha]\psi \in FL(\varphi)$ and $[\beta]\psi \in FL(\varphi)$.
(iv) If $[\alpha \,;\, \beta]\psi \in FL(\varphi)$, then $[\alpha][\beta]\psi \in FL(\varphi)$ and $[\beta]\psi \in FL(\varphi)$.
(v) If $[\alpha^*]\psi \in FL(\varphi)$, then $[\alpha][\alpha^*]\psi \in FL(\varphi)$.

Proof   Exercise 6.2.   ∎

The following lemma bounds the cardinality of $FL(\varphi)$ as a function of the length of φ. Recall that $\#A$ denotes the cardinality of a set A. Let $|\varphi|$ and $|\alpha|$ denote the length (number of symbols) of φ and α, respectively, excluding parentheses.

Lemma 6.3:

(i) For any formula φ, $\#FL(\varphi) \le |\varphi|$.
(ii) For any formula $[\alpha]\varphi$, $\#FL^{\square}([\alpha]\varphi) \le |\alpha|$.

Proof   The proof is by simultaneous induction on the well-founded subexpression relation. First we show (i). If φ is an atomic formula p, then

$$\#FL(p) \;=\; 1 \;=\; |p|.$$

If φ is of the form $\psi \to \rho$, then

$$
\begin{aligned}
\#FL(\psi \to \rho) \;&\le\; 1 + \#FL(\psi) + \#FL(\rho) \\
&\le\; 1 + |\psi| + |\rho| \quad \text{by the induction hypothesis (i)} \\
&=\; |\psi \to \rho|.
\end{aligned}
$$

The argument for φ of the form $\mathbf{0}$ is easy. Finally, if φ is of the form $[\alpha]\psi$, then

$$
\begin{aligned}
\#FL([\alpha]\psi) \;&\le\; \#FL^{\square}([\alpha]\psi) + \#FL(\psi) \\
&\le\; |\alpha| + |\psi| \quad \text{by the induction hypothesis (i) and (ii)} \\
&\le\; |[\alpha]\psi|.
\end{aligned}
$$

Now we show (ii). If α is an atomic program a, then

$$\#FL^{\square}([a]\varphi) \;=\; 1 \;=\; |a|.$$

If α is of the form $\beta \cup \gamma$, then

$$
\begin{aligned}
\#FL^{\square}([\beta \cup \gamma]\varphi) \;&\leq\; 1 + \#FL^{\square}([\beta]\varphi) + \#FL^{\square}([\gamma]\varphi) \\
&\leq\; 1 + |\beta| + |\gamma| \\
&=\; |\beta \cup \gamma|.
\end{aligned}
$$

If α is of the form $\beta \,;\, \gamma$, then

$$
\begin{aligned}
\#FL^{\square}([\beta \,;\, \gamma]\varphi) \;&\leq\; 1 + \#FL^{\square}([\beta][\gamma]\varphi) + \#FL^{\square}([\gamma]\varphi) \\
&\leq\; 1 + |\beta| + |\gamma| \\
&=\; |\beta \,;\, \gamma|.
\end{aligned}
$$

If α is of the form β^*, then

$$
\begin{aligned}
\#FL^{\square}([\beta^*]\varphi) \;&\leq\; 1 + \#FL^{\square}([\beta][\beta^*]\varphi) \\
&\leq\; 1 + |\beta| \\
&=\; |\beta^*|.
\end{aligned}
$$

Finally, if α is of the form $\psi?$, then

$$
\begin{aligned}
\#FL^{\square}([\psi?]\varphi) \;&\leq\; 1 + \#FL(\psi) \\
&\leq\; 1 + |\psi| \quad \text{by the induction hypothesis (i)} \\
&=\; |\psi?|.
\end{aligned}
$$

∎

6.2 Filtration and the Small Model Theorem

Given a PDL proposition φ and a Kripke frame $\mathfrak{K} = (K, \mathfrak{m}_{\mathfrak{K}})$, we define a new frame $\mathfrak{K}/FL(\varphi) = (K/FL(\varphi), \mathfrak{m}_{\mathfrak{K}/FL(\varphi)})$, called the *filtration of* $\mathfrak{K}$ *by* $FL(\varphi)$, as follows. Define a binary relation $\equiv$ on states of $\mathfrak{K}$ by:

$$
u \equiv v \;\overset{\text{def}}{\Longleftrightarrow}\; \forall \psi \in FL(\varphi)\ (u \in \mathfrak{m}_{\mathfrak{K}}(\psi) \Longleftrightarrow v \in \mathfrak{m}_{\mathfrak{K}}(\psi)).
$$

In other words, we collapse states u and v if they are not distinguishable by any formula of $FL(\varphi)$. Let

$$[u] \stackrel{\text{def}}{=} \{v \mid v \equiv u\}$$

$$K/FL(\varphi) \stackrel{\text{def}}{=} \{[u] \mid u \in K\}$$

$$\mathfrak{m}_{\mathfrak{K}/FL(\varphi)}(p) \stackrel{\text{def}}{=} \{[u] \mid u \in \mathfrak{m}_{\mathfrak{K}}(p)\}, \quad p \text{ an atomic proposition}$$

$$\mathfrak{m}_{\mathfrak{K}/FL(\varphi)}(a) \stackrel{\text{def}}{=} \{([u],[v]) \mid (u,v) \in \mathfrak{m}_{\mathfrak{K}}(a)\}, \quad a \text{ an atomic program.}$$

The map $\mathfrak{m}_{\mathfrak{K}/FL(\varphi)}$ is extended inductively to compound propositions and programs as described in Section 5.2.

The following key lemma relates $\mathfrak{K}$ and $\mathfrak{K}/FL(\varphi)$. Most of the difficulty in the following lemma is in the correct formulation of the induction hypotheses in the statement of the lemma. Once this is done, the proof is a fairly straightforward induction on the well-founded subexpression relation.

LEMMA 6.4 (FILTRATION LEMMA):   Let $\mathfrak{K}$ be a Kripke frame and let u, v be states of $\mathfrak{K}$.

(i) For all $\psi \in FL(\varphi)$, $u \in \mathfrak{m}_{\mathfrak{K}}(\psi)$ iff $[u] \in \mathfrak{m}_{\mathfrak{K}/FL(\varphi)}(\psi)$.

(ii) For all $[\alpha]\psi \in FL(\varphi)$,

(a) if $(u,v) \in \mathfrak{m}_{\mathfrak{K}}(\alpha)$ then $([u],[v]) \in \mathfrak{m}_{\mathfrak{K}/FL(\varphi)}(\alpha)$;

(b) if $([u],[v]) \in \mathfrak{m}_{\mathfrak{K}/FL(\varphi)}(\alpha)$ and $u \in \mathfrak{m}_{\mathfrak{K}}([\alpha]\psi)$, then $v \in \mathfrak{m}_{\mathfrak{K}}(\psi)$.

Proof The proof is by simultaneous induction on the well-founded subexpression relation. We start with (i). There are four cases, depending on the form of ψ.

Case 1   For atomic propositions $p \in FL(\varphi)$, if $u \in \mathfrak{m}_{\mathfrak{K}}(p)$, then by definition of $\mathfrak{K}/FL(\varphi)$, $[u] \in \mathfrak{m}_{\mathfrak{K}/FL(\varphi)}(p)$. Conversely, if $[u] \in \mathfrak{m}_{\mathfrak{K}/FL(\varphi)}(p)$, then there exists a u' such that $u' \equiv u$ and $u' \in \mathfrak{m}_{\mathfrak{K}}(p)$. But then $u \in \mathfrak{m}_{\mathfrak{K}}(p)$ as well.

Case 2   If $\psi \to \rho \in FL(\varphi)$, then by Lemma 6.1, both $\psi \in FL(\varphi)$ and $\rho \in FL(\varphi)$. By the induction hypothesis, (i) holds for ψ and ρ, therefore

$$s \in \mathfrak{m}_{\mathfrak{K}}(\psi \to \rho) \iff s \in \mathfrak{m}_{\mathfrak{K}}(\psi) \Longrightarrow s \in \mathfrak{m}_{\mathfrak{K}}(\rho)$$

$$\iff [s] \in \mathfrak{m}_{\mathfrak{K}/FL(\varphi)}(\psi) \Longrightarrow [s] \in \mathfrak{m}_{\mathfrak{K}/FL(\varphi)}(\rho)$$

$$\iff [s] \in \mathfrak{m}_{\mathfrak{K}/FL(\varphi)}(\psi \to \rho).$$

Case 3   The case of $\mathbf{0}$ is easy. We leave the details as an exercise (Exercise 6.3).

Case 4   If $[\alpha]\psi \in FL(\varphi)$, we use the induction hypothesis for α and ψ. By Lemma 6.2(i), $\psi \in FL(\varphi)$. By the induction hypothesis, (i) holds for ψ and (ii) holds for $[\alpha]\psi$. Using the latter fact, we have

$$s \in \mathfrak{m}_{\mathfrak{K}}([\alpha]\psi) \implies \forall t\,(([s],[t]) \in \mathfrak{m}_{\mathfrak{K}/FL(\varphi)}(\alpha) \implies t \in \mathfrak{m}_{\mathfrak{K}}(\psi)) \qquad (6.2.1)$$

by clause (b) of (ii). Conversely,

$$\begin{aligned}
&\forall t\,(([s],[t]) \in \mathfrak{m}_{\mathfrak{K}/FL(\varphi)}(\alpha) \implies t \in \mathfrak{m}_{\mathfrak{K}}(\psi))\\
&\implies \forall t\,((s,t) \in \mathfrak{m}_{\mathfrak{K}}(\alpha) \implies t \in \mathfrak{m}_{\mathfrak{K}}(\psi)) \qquad\qquad\qquad (6.2.2)\\
&\implies s \in \mathfrak{m}_{\mathfrak{K}}([\alpha]\psi)
\end{aligned}$$

by clause (a) of (ii). Then

$$\begin{aligned}
&s \in \mathfrak{m}_{\mathfrak{K}}([\alpha]\psi)\\
&\iff \forall t\,(([s],[t]) \in \mathfrak{m}_{\mathfrak{K}/FL(\varphi)}(\alpha) \implies t \in \mathfrak{m}_{\mathfrak{K}}(\psi)) \qquad \text{by (6.2.1) and (6.2.2)}\\
&\iff \forall t\,(([s],[t]) \in \mathfrak{m}_{\mathfrak{K}/FL(\varphi)}(\alpha) \implies [t] \in \mathfrak{m}_{\mathfrak{K}/FL(\varphi)}(\psi)) \qquad \text{by (i) for } \psi\\
&\iff [s] \in \mathfrak{m}_{\mathfrak{K}/FL(\varphi)}([\alpha]\psi).
\end{aligned}$$

This completes the proof of (i).

For (ii), there are five cases, depending on the form of α.

Case 1   For an atomic program a, part (a) of (ii) is immediate from the definition of $\mathfrak{m}_{\mathfrak{K}/FL(\varphi)}(a)$. For part (b), if $([s],[t]) \in \mathfrak{m}_{\mathfrak{K}/FL(\varphi)}(a)$, then by the definition of $\mathfrak{m}_{\mathfrak{K}/FL(\varphi)}(a)$, there exist $s' \equiv s$ and $t' \equiv t$ such that $(s',t') \in \mathfrak{m}_{\mathfrak{K}}(a)$. If $s \in \mathfrak{m}_{\mathfrak{K}}([a]\psi)$, then since $s' \equiv s$ and $[a]\psi \in FL(\varphi)$, we have $s' \in \mathfrak{m}_{\mathfrak{K}}([a]\psi)$ as well, thus $t' \in \mathfrak{m}_{\mathfrak{K}}(\psi)$ by the semantics of $[a]$. But $\psi \in FL(\varphi)$ by Lemma 6.2(i), and since $t \equiv t'$, we have $t \in \mathfrak{m}_{\mathfrak{K}}(\psi)$.

Case 2   For a test $\rho?$, by Lemma 6.2(ii) we have $\rho \in FL(\varphi)$, thus (i) holds for ρ by the induction hypothesis. Part (a) of (ii) is immediate from this. For (b),

$$\begin{aligned}
&([s],[s]) \in \mathfrak{m}_{\mathfrak{K}/FL(\varphi)}(\rho?) \text{ and } s \in \mathfrak{m}_{\mathfrak{K}}([\rho?]\psi)\\
&\implies [s] \in \mathfrak{m}_{\mathfrak{K}/FL(\varphi)}(\rho) \text{ and } s \in \mathfrak{m}_{\mathfrak{K}}(\rho \to \psi)\\
&\implies s \in \mathfrak{m}_{\mathfrak{K}}(\rho) \text{ and } s \in \mathfrak{m}_{\mathfrak{K}}(\rho \to \psi)\\
&\implies s \in \mathfrak{m}_{\mathfrak{K}}(\psi).
\end{aligned}$$

Case 3 The case $\alpha = \beta \cup \gamma$ is left as an exercise (Exercise 6.3).

Case 4 For the case $\alpha = \beta \,;\, \gamma$, to show (a), we have by Lemma 6.2(iv) that $[\beta][\gamma]\psi \in FL(\varphi)$ and $[\gamma]\psi \in FL(\varphi)$, so (a) holds for β and γ; then

$(s,t) \in \mathfrak{m}_{\mathfrak{K}}(\beta \,;\, \gamma)$

$\implies \exists u \ (s,u) \in \mathfrak{m}_{\mathfrak{K}}(\beta)$ and $(u,t) \in \mathfrak{m}_{\mathfrak{K}}(\gamma)$

$\implies \exists u \ ([s],[u]) \in \mathfrak{m}_{\mathfrak{K}/FL(\varphi)}(\beta)$ and $([u],[t]) \in \mathfrak{m}_{\mathfrak{K}/FL(\varphi)}(\gamma)$

$\implies ([s],[t]) \in \mathfrak{m}_{\mathfrak{K}/FL(\varphi)}(\beta \,;\, \gamma).$

To show (b), we have by the induction hypothesis that (b) holds for $[\beta][\gamma]\psi$ and $[\gamma]\psi$. Then

$([s],[t]) \in \mathfrak{m}_{\mathfrak{K}/FL(\varphi)}(\beta \,;\, \gamma)$ and $s \in \mathfrak{m}_{\mathfrak{K}}([\beta \,;\, \gamma]\psi)$

$\implies \exists u \ ([s],[u]) \in \mathfrak{m}_{\mathfrak{K}/FL(\varphi)}(\beta), \ ([u],[t]) \in \mathfrak{m}_{\mathfrak{K}/FL(\varphi)}(\gamma),$ and $s \in \mathfrak{m}_{\mathfrak{K}}([\beta][\gamma]\psi)$

$\implies \exists u \ ([u],[t]) \in \mathfrak{m}_{\mathfrak{K}/FL(\varphi)}(\gamma)$ and $u \in \mathfrak{m}_{\mathfrak{K}}([\gamma]\psi)$ by (b) for $[\beta][\gamma]\psi$

$\implies t \in \mathfrak{m}_{\mathfrak{K}}(\psi)$ by (b) for $[\gamma]\psi.$

Case 5 Finally, consider the case $\alpha = \beta^*$. By Lemma 6.2(v), $[\beta][\beta^*]\psi \in FL(\varphi)$, so we can assume that (ii) holds for $[\beta][\beta^*]\psi$. (The induction hypothesis holds because β is a proper subexpression of β^*.) By part (a) of (ii), if $(u,v) \in \mathfrak{m}_{\mathfrak{K}}(\beta)$, then $([u],[v]) \in \mathfrak{m}_{\mathfrak{K}/FL(\varphi)}(\beta)$. Therefore if $(s,t) \in \mathfrak{m}_{\mathfrak{K}}(\beta^*)$, then there exist $n \geq 0$ and $t_0,\ldots,t_n$ such that $s = t_0$, $(t_i,t_{i+1}) \in \mathfrak{m}_{\mathfrak{K}}(\beta)$ for $0 \leq i < n$, and $t_n = t$. This implies that $([t_i],[t_{i+1}]) \in \mathfrak{m}_{\mathfrak{K}/FL(\varphi)}(\beta)$ for $0 \leq i < n$, therefore $([s],[t]) = ([t_0],[t_n]) \in \mathfrak{m}_{\mathfrak{K}/FL(\varphi)}(\beta^*)$. This establishes (a).

To show (b), suppose $([s],[t]) \in \mathfrak{m}_{\mathfrak{K}/FL(\varphi)}(\beta^*)$ and $s \in \mathfrak{m}_{\mathfrak{K}}([\beta^*]\psi)$. Then there exist $t_0,\ldots,t_n$ such that $s = t_0$, $t = t_n$, and $([t_i],[t_{i+1}]) \in \mathfrak{m}_{\mathfrak{K}/FL(\varphi)}(\beta)$ for $0 \leq i < n$. We have that $t_0 = s \in \mathfrak{m}_{\mathfrak{K}}([\beta^*]\psi)$ by assumption. Now suppose $t_i \in \mathfrak{m}_{\mathfrak{K}}([\beta^*]\psi)$, $i < n$. Then $t_i \in \mathfrak{m}_{\mathfrak{K}}([\beta][\beta^*]\psi)$. By the induction hypothesis for $[\beta][\beta^*]\psi \in FL(\varphi)$, $t_{i+1} \in \mathfrak{m}_{\mathfrak{K}}([\beta^*]\psi)$. Continuing for n steps, we get $t = t_n \in \mathfrak{m}_{\mathfrak{K}}([\beta^*]\psi)$, therefore $t \in \mathfrak{m}_{\mathfrak{K}}(\psi)$, as desired. ∎

Using the filtration lemma, we can prove the small model theorem easily.

THEOREM 6.5 (SMALL MODEL THEOREM): Let φ be a satisfiable formula of PDL. Then φ is satisfied in a Kripke frame with no more than $2^{|\varphi|}$ states.

Proof If φ is satisfiable, then there is a Kripke frame $\mathfrak{K}$ and state $u \in \mathfrak{K}$ with

$u \in \mathfrak{m}_{\mathfrak{K}}(\varphi)$. Let $FL(\varphi)$ be the Fischer-Ladner closure of φ. By the filtration lemma (Lemma 6.4), $[u] \in \mathfrak{m}_{\mathfrak{K}/FL(\varphi)}(\varphi)$. Moreover, $\mathfrak{K}/FL(\varphi)$ has no more states than the number of truth assignments to formulas in $FL(\varphi)$, which by Lemma 6.3(i) is at most $2^{|\varphi|}$. ∎

It follows immediately that the satisfiability problem for PDL is decidable, since there are only finitely many possible Kripke frames of size at most $2^{|\varphi|}$ to check, and there is a polynomial-time algorithm to check whether a given formula is satisfied at a given state in a given Kripke frame (Exercise 6.4). We will give a more efficient algorithm in Section 8.1.

6.3 Filtration over Nonstandard Models

In Chapter 7 we will prove the completeness of a deductive system for PDL. The proof will also make use of the filtration lemma (Lemma 6.4), but in a somewhat stronger form. We will show that it also holds for *nonstandard Kripke frames* (to be defined directly) as well as the standard Kripke frames defined in Section 5.2. The completeness theorem will be obtained by constructing a nonstandard Kripke frame from terms, as we did for propositional and first-order logic in Sections 3.2 and 3.4, and then applying the filtration technique to get a finite standard Kripke frame.

A *nonstandard Kripke frame* is any structure $\mathfrak{N} = (N, \mathfrak{m}_{\mathfrak{N}})$ that is a Kripke frame in the sense of Section 5.2 in every respect, except that $\mathfrak{m}_{\mathfrak{N}}(\alpha^*)$ need not be the reflexive transitive closure of $\mathfrak{m}_{\mathfrak{N}}(\alpha)$, but only a reflexive, transitive binary relation containing $\mathfrak{m}_{\mathfrak{N}}(\alpha)$ satisfying the PDL axioms for * (Axioms 5.5(vii) and (viii)). In other words, we rescind the definition

$$\mathfrak{m}_{\mathfrak{N}}(\alpha^*) \overset{\text{def}}{=} \bigcup_{n \geq 0} \mathfrak{m}_{\mathfrak{N}}(\alpha)^n, \tag{6.3.1}$$

and replace it with the weaker requirement that $\mathfrak{m}_{\mathfrak{N}}(\alpha^*)$ be a reflexive, transitive binary relation containing $\mathfrak{m}_{\mathfrak{N}}(\alpha)$ such that

$$\mathfrak{m}_{\mathfrak{N}}([\alpha^*]\varphi) = \mathfrak{m}_{\mathfrak{N}}(\varphi \wedge [\alpha\,;\,\alpha^*]\varphi) \tag{6.3.2}$$

$$\mathfrak{m}_{\mathfrak{N}}([\alpha^*]\varphi) = \mathfrak{m}_{\mathfrak{N}}(\varphi \wedge [\alpha^*](\varphi \to [\alpha]\varphi)). \tag{6.3.3}$$

Otherwise, $\mathfrak{N}$ must satisfy all other requirements as given in Section 5.2. For example, it must still satisfy the properties

$$\mathfrak{m}_{\mathfrak{N}}(\alpha \, ; \, \beta) \;\; = \;\; \mathfrak{m}_{\mathfrak{N}}(\alpha) \circ \mathfrak{m}_{\mathfrak{N}}(\beta)$$

$$\mathfrak{m}_{\mathfrak{N}}(\alpha^*) \;\; \supseteq \;\; \bigcup_{n \geq 0} \mathfrak{m}_{\mathfrak{N}}(\alpha)^n.$$

A nonstandard Kripke frame *standard* if it satisfies (6.3.1). According to our definition, all standard Kripke frames are nonstandard Kripke frames, since standard Kripke frames satisfy (6.3.2) and (6.3.3), but not necessarily vice-versa (Exercise 7.3).

It is easily checked that all the axioms and rules of **PDL** (Axiom System 5.5) are still sound over nonstandard Kripke frames. One consequence of this is that all theorems and rules derived in this system are valid for nonstandard frames as well as standard ones. In particular, we will use the results of Theorem 5.18 in the proof of Lemma 6.6 below.

Let $\mathfrak{N}$ be a nonstandard Kripke frame and let φ be a proposition. We can construct the finite standard Kripke frame $\mathfrak{N}/FL(\varphi)$ exactly as before, and $\mathfrak{N}/FL(\varphi)$ will have at most $2^{|\varphi|}$ states. Note that in $\mathfrak{N}/FL(\varphi)$, the semantics of α^* is defined in the standard way using (6.3.1).

The filtration lemma (Lemma 6.4) holds for nonstandard Kripke frames as well as standard ones:

LEMMA 6.6 (FILTRATION FOR NONSTANDARD MODELS):   Let $\mathfrak{N}$ be a nonstandard Kripke frame and let u, v be states of $\mathfrak{N}$.

(i) For all $\psi \in FL(\varphi)$, $u \in \mathfrak{m}_{\mathfrak{N}}(\psi)$ iff $[u] \in \mathfrak{m}_{\mathfrak{N}/FL(\varphi)}(\psi)$.

(ii) For all $[\alpha]\psi \in FL(\varphi)$,

   (a)if $(u, v) \in \mathfrak{m}_{\mathfrak{N}}(\alpha)$ then $([u],[v]) \in \mathfrak{m}_{\mathfrak{N}/FL(\varphi)}(\alpha)$;

   (b)if $([u],[v]) \in \mathfrak{m}_{\mathfrak{N}/FL(\varphi)}(\alpha)$ and $u \in \mathfrak{m}_{\mathfrak{N}}([\alpha]\psi)$, then $v \in \mathfrak{m}_{\mathfrak{N}}(\psi)$.

Proof The argument is exactly the same as in the previous version for standard frames (Lemma 6.4) except for the cases involving $*$. Also, part (b) of (ii) for the case $\alpha = \beta^*$ uses only the fact that $\mathfrak{N}/FL(\varphi)$ is standard, not that $\mathfrak{N}$ is standard, so this argument will hold for the nonstandard case as well. Thus the only extra work we need to do for the nonstandard version is part (a) of (ii) for the case $\alpha = \beta^*$.

The proof for standard Kripke frames $\mathfrak{K}$ given in Lemma 6.4 depended on the fact that $\mathfrak{m}_{\mathfrak{K}}(\alpha^*)$ was the reflexive transitive closure of $\mathfrak{m}_{\mathfrak{K}}(\alpha)$. This does not hold in nonstandard Kripke frames in general, so we must depend on the weaker induction axiom.

For the nonstandard Kripke frame $\mathfrak{N}$, suppose $(u, v) \in \mathfrak{m}_{\mathfrak{N}}(\alpha^*)$. We wish to show that $([u], [v]) \in \mathfrak{m}_{\mathfrak{N}/FL(\varphi)}(\alpha^*)$, or equivalently that $v \in E$, where

$$E \stackrel{\text{def}}{=} \{t \in \mathfrak{N} \mid ([u], [t]) \in \mathfrak{m}_{\mathfrak{N}/FL(\varphi)}(\alpha^*)\}.$$

There is a **PDL** formula ψ_E defining E in $\mathfrak{N}$; that is, $E = \mathfrak{m}_{\mathfrak{N}}(\psi_E)$. This is because E is a union of equivalence classes defined by truth assignments to the elements of $FL(\varphi)$. The formula ψ_E is a disjunction of conjunctive formulas $\psi_{[t]}$, one for each equivalence class $[t]$ contained in E. The conjunction $\psi_{[t]}$ includes either ρ or $\neg\rho$ for all $\rho \in FL(\varphi)$, depending on whether the truth assignment defining $[t]$ takes value $\mathbf{1}$ or $\mathbf{0}$ on ρ, respectively.

Now $u \in E$ since $([u], [u]) \in \mathfrak{m}_{\mathfrak{N}/FL(\varphi)}(\alpha^*)$. Also, E is closed under the action of $\mathfrak{m}_{\mathfrak{N}}(\alpha)$; that is,

$$s \in E \text{ and } (s, t) \in \mathfrak{m}_{\mathfrak{N}}(\alpha) \implies t \in E. \qquad (6.3.4)$$

To see this, observe that if $s \in E$ and $(s, t) \in \mathfrak{m}_{\mathfrak{N}}(\alpha)$, then $([s], [t]) \in \mathfrak{m}_{\mathfrak{N}/FL(\varphi)}(\alpha)$ by the induction hypothesis (ii), and $([u], [s]) \in \mathfrak{m}_{\mathfrak{N}/FL(\varphi)}(\alpha^*)$ by the definition of E, therefore $([u], [t]) \in \mathfrak{m}_{\mathfrak{N}/FL(\varphi)}(\alpha^*)$. By the definition of E, $t \in E$.

These facts do not immediately imply that $v \in E$, since $\mathfrak{m}_{\mathfrak{N}}(\alpha^*)$ is not necessarily the reflexive transitive closure of $\mathfrak{m}_{\mathfrak{N}}(\alpha)$. However, since $E = \mathfrak{m}_{\mathfrak{N}}(\psi_E)$, (6.3.4) is equivalent to

$$\mathfrak{N} \vDash \psi_E \;\rightarrow\; [\alpha]\psi_E.$$

Using the loop invariance rule (LI) of Section 5.6, we get

$$\mathfrak{N} \vDash \psi_E \;\rightarrow\; [\alpha^*]\psi_E.$$

By Theorem 5.18, (LI) is equivalent to the induction axiom (IND). (The proof of equivalence was obtained deductively, not semantically, therefore is valid for nonstandard models.) Now $(u, v) \in \mathfrak{m}_{\mathfrak{N}}(\alpha^*)$ by assumption, and $u \in E$, therefore $v \in E$. By definition of E, $([u], [v]) \in \mathfrak{m}_{\mathfrak{N}/FL(\varphi)}(\alpha^*)$. ∎

6.4   Bibliographical Notes

The filtration argument and the small model property for **PDL** are due to Fischer and Ladner (1977, 1979). Nonstandard Kripke frames for **PDL** were studied by Berman (1979, 1982), Parikh (1978a), Pratt (1979a, 1980a), and Kozen (1979c,b, 1980a,b, 1981b).

Exercises

6.1. Complete the proof of Lemma 6.1. For part (i), fill in the argument for the cases of an atomic proposition p and the constant proposition $\mathbf{0}$. For (ii), fill in the argument for the cases of an atomic program a and compound programs of the form $\beta \cup \gamma$ and $\varphi?$.

6.2. Prove Lemma 6.2.

6.3. Complete the proof of Lemma 6.4 by filling in the arguments for part (i), case 3 and part (ii), case 3.

6.4. Give a polynomial time algorithm to check whether a given **PDL** formula is satisfied at a given state in a given Kripke frame. Describe briefly the data structures you would use to represent the formula and the Kripke frame. Specify your algorithm at a high level and give a brief complexity analysis.

6.5. Prove that all finite nonstandard Kripke frames are standard.

7 Deductive Completeness

In Section 5.5 we gave a formal deductive system (Axiom System 5.5) for deducing properties of Kripke frames expressible in the language of PDL. For convenience, we collect the axioms and rules of inference here. To the right of each axiom or rule appears a reference to the proof of its soundness.

Axioms of PDL

(i) Axioms for propositional logic $\qquad$ Section 3.2

(ii) $[\alpha](\varphi \to \psi) \;\to\; ([\alpha]\varphi \to [\alpha]\psi)$ $\qquad$ Theorem 5.6(iv)

(iii) $[\alpha](\varphi \land \psi) \;\leftrightarrow\; [\alpha]\varphi \land [\alpha]\psi$ $\qquad$ Theorem 5.6(ii)

(iv) $[\alpha \cup \beta]\varphi \;\leftrightarrow\; [\alpha]\varphi \land [\beta]\varphi$ $\qquad$ Theorem 5.8(ii)

(v) $[\alpha\,;\,\beta]\varphi \;\leftrightarrow\; [\alpha][\beta]\varphi$ $\qquad$ Theorem 5.10(ii)

(vi) $[\psi?]\varphi \;\leftrightarrow\; (\psi \to \varphi)$ $\qquad$ Theorem 5.11(ii)

(vii) $\varphi \land [\alpha][\alpha^*]\varphi \;\leftrightarrow\; [\alpha^*]\varphi$ $\qquad$ Theorem 5.15(ix)

(viii) $\varphi \land [\alpha^*](\varphi \to [\alpha]\varphi) \;\to\; [\alpha^*]\varphi$ $\qquad$ Theorem 5.15(xi)

In PDL with converse $^-$, we also include

(ix) $\varphi \;\to\; [\alpha]{<}\alpha^-{>}\varphi$ $\qquad$ Theorem 5.13(i)

(x) $\varphi \;\to\; [\alpha^-]{<}\alpha{>}\varphi$ $\qquad$ Theorem 5.13(ii)

Rules of Inference

(MP) $\dfrac{\varphi,\;\; \varphi \to \psi}{\psi}$ $\qquad$ Section 3.2

(GEN) $\dfrac{\varphi}{[\alpha]\varphi}$ $\qquad$ Theorem 5.7(i).

We write $\vdash \varphi$ if the formula φ is provable in this deductive system. Recall from Section 3.1 that a formula φ is *consistent* if $\nvdash \neg\varphi$, that is, if it is not the case that $\vdash \neg\varphi$; that a finite set Σ of formulas is *consistent* if its conjunction $\bigwedge \Sigma$ is consistent; and that an infinite set of formulas is *consistent* if every finite subset is consistent.

7.1 Deductive Completeness

This deductive system is complete: all valid formulas are theorems. To prove this fact, we will use techniques from Section 3.2 to construct a nonstandard Kripke frame from maximal consistent sets of formulas. Then we will use the filtration lemma for nonstandard models (Lemma 6.6) to collapse this nonstandard model to a finite standard model.

Since our deductive system contains propositional logic as a subsystem, the following lemma holds. The proof is similar to the proof of Lemma 3.10 for propositional logic.

LEMMA 7.1:   Let Σ be a set of formulas of PDL. Then

(i) Σ is consistent iff either $\Sigma \cup \{\varphi\}$ is consistent or $\Sigma \cup \{\neg\varphi\}$ is consistent;
(ii) if Σ is consistent, then Σ is contained in a maximal consistent set.

In addition, if Σ is a maximal consistent set of formulas, then

(iii) Σ contains all theorems of PDL;
(iv) if $\varphi \in \Sigma$ and $\varphi \to \psi \in \Sigma$, then $\psi \in \Sigma$;
(v) $\varphi \vee \psi \in \Sigma$ iff $\varphi \in \Sigma$ or $\psi \in \Sigma$;
(vi) $\varphi \wedge \psi \in \Sigma$ iff $\varphi \in \Sigma$ and $\psi \in \Sigma$;
(vii) $\varphi \in \Sigma$ iff $\neg\varphi \notin \Sigma$;
(viii) $\mathbf{0} \notin \Sigma$.

Proof   Exercise 7.1.   ∎

We also have an interesting lemma peculiar to PDL.

LEMMA 7.2:   Let Σ and Γ be maximal consistent sets of formulas and let α be a program. The following two statements are equivalent:

(a) For all formulas ψ, if $\psi \in \Gamma$, then $\langle\alpha\rangle\psi \in \Sigma$.
(b) For all formulas ψ, if $[\alpha]\psi \in \Sigma$, then $\psi \in \Gamma$.

Proof   (a) $\implies$ (b):

$$[\alpha]\psi \in \Sigma \implies \langle\alpha\rangle\neg\psi \notin \Sigma \quad \text{by Lemma 7.1(vii)}$$
$$\implies \neg\psi \notin \Gamma \quad \text{by (a)}$$
$$\implies \psi \in \Gamma \quad \text{by Lemma 7.1(vii).}$$

(b) $\Longrightarrow$ (a):

$$\begin{aligned}
\psi \in \Gamma \quad &\Longrightarrow \quad \neg\psi \notin \Gamma && \text{by Lemma 7.1(vii)} \\
&\Longrightarrow \quad [\alpha]\neg\psi \notin \Sigma && \text{by (b)} \\
&\Longrightarrow \quad \langle\alpha\rangle\psi \in \Sigma && \text{by Lemma 7.1(vii).}
\end{aligned}$$

■

Now we construct a nonstandard Kripke frame $\mathfrak{N} = (N, \mathfrak{m}_\mathfrak{N})$ as defined in Section 6.3. The states N will be the maximal consistent sets of formulas. We will write $s, t, u, \ldots$ for elements of N and call them *states*, but bear in mind that every $s \in N$ is a maximal consistent set of formulas, therefore it makes sense to write $\varphi \in s$.

Formally, let $\mathfrak{N} = (N, \mathfrak{m}_\mathfrak{N})$ be defined by:

$$\begin{aligned}
N \quad &\overset{\text{def}}{=} \quad \{\text{maximal consistent sets of formulas of PDL}\} \\
\mathfrak{m}_\mathfrak{N}(\varphi) \quad &\overset{\text{def}}{=} \quad \{s \mid \varphi \in s\} \\
\mathfrak{m}_\mathfrak{N}(\alpha) \quad &\overset{\text{def}}{=} \quad \{(s,t) \mid \text{for all } \varphi, \text{ if } \varphi \in t, \text{ then } \langle\alpha\rangle\varphi \in s\} \\
&= \quad \{(s,t) \mid \text{for all } \varphi, \text{ if } [\alpha]\varphi \in s, \text{ then } \varphi \in t\}.
\end{aligned}$$

The two definitions of $\mathfrak{m}_\mathfrak{N}(\alpha)$ are equivalent by Lemma 7.2. Note that the definitions of $\mathfrak{m}_\mathfrak{N}(\varphi)$ and $\mathfrak{m}_\mathfrak{N}(\alpha)$ apply to *all* propositions φ and programs α, not just the atomic ones; thus the meaning of compound propositions and programs is not defined inductively from the meaning of the atomic ones as usual. However, $\mathfrak{m}_\mathfrak{N}(\alpha^*)$ will satisfy the axioms of *, and all the other operators will behave in $\mathfrak{N}$ as they do in standard models; that is, as if they were defined inductively. We will have to prove this in order to establish that $\mathfrak{N}$ is a nonstandard Kripke frame according to the definition of Section 6.3. We undertake that task now.

LEMMA 7.3:

(i) $\mathfrak{m}_\mathfrak{N}(\varphi \to \psi) \;=\; (N - \mathfrak{m}_\mathfrak{N}(\varphi)) \cup \mathfrak{m}_\mathfrak{N}(\psi)$

(ii) $\mathfrak{m}_\mathfrak{N}(\mathbf{0}) \;=\; \varnothing$

(iii) $\mathfrak{m}_\mathfrak{N}([\alpha]\varphi) \;=\; N - \mathfrak{m}_\mathfrak{N}(\alpha) \circ (N - \mathfrak{m}_\mathfrak{N}(\varphi))$.

Proof The equations (i) and (ii) follow from Lemma 7.1(iv) and (viii), respectively. It follows that $\mathfrak{m}_\mathfrak{N}(\neg\varphi) = N - \mathfrak{m}_\mathfrak{N}(\varphi)$; this is also a consequence of Lemma 7.1(vii).

For (iii), it suffices to show that

$$\mathfrak{m}_{\mathfrak{N}}(\langle\alpha\rangle\varphi) \;=\; \mathfrak{m}_{\mathfrak{N}}(\alpha) \circ \mathfrak{m}_{\mathfrak{N}}(\varphi).$$

We prove both inclusions separately.

$$
\begin{aligned}
s \in \mathfrak{m}_{\mathfrak{N}}(\alpha) \circ \mathfrak{m}_{\mathfrak{N}}(\varphi) \;&\Longleftrightarrow\; \exists t \;(s,t) \in \mathfrak{m}_{\mathfrak{N}}(\alpha) \text{ and } t \in \mathfrak{m}_{\mathfrak{N}}(\varphi) \\
&\Longleftrightarrow\; \exists t \;(\forall \psi \in t \;\langle\alpha\rangle\psi \in s) \text{ and } \varphi \in t \\
&\Longrightarrow\; \langle\alpha\rangle\varphi \in s \\
&\Longleftrightarrow\; s \in \mathfrak{m}_{\mathfrak{N}}(\langle\alpha\rangle\varphi).
\end{aligned}
$$

Conversely, suppose $s \in \mathfrak{m}_{\mathfrak{N}}(\langle\alpha\rangle\varphi)$; that is, $\langle\alpha\rangle\varphi \in s$. We would like to construct t such that $(s,t) \in \mathfrak{m}_{\mathfrak{N}}(\alpha)$ and $t \in \mathfrak{m}_{\mathfrak{N}}(\varphi)$. We first show that the set

$$\{\varphi\} \;\cup\; \{\psi \mid [\alpha]\psi \in s\} \tag{7.1.1}$$

is consistent. Let $\{\psi_1, \dots, \psi_k\}$ be an arbitrary finite subset of $\{\psi \mid [\alpha]\psi \in s\}$. Then

$$\langle\alpha\rangle\varphi \wedge [\alpha]\psi_1 \wedge \cdots \wedge [\alpha]\psi_k \;\in\; s$$

by Lemma 7.1(vi), therefore

$$\langle\alpha\rangle(\varphi \wedge \psi_1 \wedge \cdots \wedge \psi_k) \;\in\; s$$

by Exercise 5.9(i) and Lemma 7.1(iii) and (iv). Since s is consistent, the formula

$$\langle\alpha\rangle(\varphi \wedge \psi_1 \wedge \cdots \wedge \psi_k)$$

is consistent, therefore so is the formula

$$\varphi \wedge \psi_1 \wedge \cdots \wedge \psi_k$$

by the rule (GEN). This says that the finite set $\{\varphi, \psi_1, \dots, \psi_k\}$ is consistent. Since these elements were chosen arbitrarily from the set (7.1.1), that set is consistent.

As in the proof of Lemma 3.10, (7.1.1) extends to a maximal consistent set t, which is a state of $\mathfrak{N}$. Then $(s,t) \in \mathfrak{m}_{\mathfrak{N}}(\alpha)$ and $t \in \mathfrak{m}_{\mathfrak{N}}(\varphi)$ by the definition of $\mathfrak{m}_{\mathfrak{N}}(\alpha)$ and $\mathfrak{m}_{\mathfrak{N}}(\varphi)$, therefore $s \in \mathfrak{m}_{\mathfrak{N}}(\alpha) \circ \mathfrak{m}_{\mathfrak{N}}(\varphi)$. ∎

LEMMA 7.4:

(i) $\mathfrak{m}_{\mathfrak{N}}(\alpha \cup \beta) \;=\; \mathfrak{m}_{\mathfrak{N}}(\alpha) \cup \mathfrak{m}_{\mathfrak{N}}(\beta)$

(ii) $\mathfrak{m}_{\mathfrak{N}}(\alpha\,;\,\beta) \;=\; \mathfrak{m}_{\mathfrak{N}}(\alpha) \circ \mathfrak{m}_{\mathfrak{N}}(\beta)$

(iii) $\mathfrak{m}_{\mathfrak{N}}(\psi?) \;=\; \{(s,s) \mid s \in \mathfrak{m}_{\mathfrak{N}}(\psi)\}$.

In PDL with converse $^-$,

(iv) $\mathfrak{m}_{\mathfrak{N}}(\alpha^-) \;=\; \mathfrak{m}_{\mathfrak{N}}(\alpha)^-.$

Proof We argue (ii) and (iii) explicitly and leave the others as exercises (Exercise 7.2).

For the reverse inclusion $\supseteq$ of (ii),

$$
\begin{aligned}
(u,v) \in \mathfrak{m}_{\mathfrak{N}}(\alpha) \circ \mathfrak{m}_{\mathfrak{N}}(\beta) \;&\Longleftrightarrow\; \exists w \; (u,w) \in \mathfrak{m}_{\mathfrak{N}}(\alpha) \text{ and } (w,v) \in \mathfrak{m}_{\mathfrak{N}}(\beta) \\
&\Longleftrightarrow\; \exists w \; \forall \varphi \in v \; {<}\beta{>}\varphi \in w \text{ and } \forall \psi \in w \; {<}\alpha{>}\psi \in u \\
&\Longrightarrow\; \forall \varphi \in v \; {<}\alpha{>}{<}\beta{>}\varphi \in u \\
&\Longleftrightarrow\; \forall \varphi \in v \; {<}\alpha \,;\, \beta{>}\varphi \in u \\
&\Longleftrightarrow\; (u,v) \in \mathfrak{m}_{\mathfrak{N}}(\alpha \,;\, \beta).
\end{aligned}
$$

For the forward inclusion, suppose $(u,v) \in \mathfrak{m}_{\mathfrak{N}}(\alpha \,;\, \beta)$. We claim that the set

$$\{\varphi \mid [\alpha]\varphi \in u\} \;\cup\; \{{<}\beta{>}\psi \mid \psi \in v\} \tag{7.1.2}$$

is consistent. Let

$$
\begin{aligned}
\{\varphi_1, \dots, \varphi_k\} \;&\subseteq\; \{\varphi \mid [\alpha]\varphi \in u\} \\
\{{<}\beta{>}\psi_1, \dots, {<}\beta{>}\psi_m\} \;&\subseteq\; \{{<}\beta{>}\psi \mid \psi \in v\}
\end{aligned}
$$

be arbitrarily chosen finite subsets, and let

$$
\begin{aligned}
\varphi \;&=\; \varphi_1 \wedge \cdots \wedge \varphi_k, \\
\psi \;&=\; \psi_1 \wedge \cdots \wedge \psi_m.
\end{aligned}
$$

Then $\psi \in v$ by Lemma 7.1(vi), and since $(u,v) \in \mathfrak{m}_{\mathfrak{N}}(\alpha \,;\, \beta)$, we have by the definition of $\mathfrak{m}_{\mathfrak{N}}(\alpha \,;\, \beta)$ that ${<}\alpha \,;\, \beta{>}\psi \in u$. Also $[\alpha]\varphi \in u$, since

$$[\alpha]\varphi \;\leftrightarrow\; [\alpha]\varphi_1 \wedge \cdots \wedge [\alpha]\varphi_k$$

is a theorem of PDL, and the right-hand side is in u by Lemma 7.1(vi). It follows that $[\alpha]\varphi \wedge {<}\alpha{>}{<}\beta{>}\psi \in u$. By Exercise 5.9(i), ${<}\alpha{>}(\varphi \wedge {<}\beta{>}\psi) \in u$, thus by (GEN), $\varphi \wedge {<}\beta{>}\psi$ is consistent. But

$$\vdash \; \varphi \wedge {<}\beta{>}\psi \;\rightarrow\; \varphi_1 \wedge \cdots \wedge \varphi_k \wedge {<}\beta{>}\psi_1 \wedge \cdots \wedge {<}\beta{>}\psi_m,$$

so the right-hand side of the implication is consistent. As this was the conjunction of an arbitrary finite subset of (7.1.2), (7.1.2) is consistent, thus extends to a maximal consistent set w. By the definition of $\mathfrak{m}_{\mathfrak{N}}(\alpha)$ and $\mathfrak{m}_{\mathfrak{N}}(\beta)$, $(u,w) \in \mathfrak{m}_{\mathfrak{N}}(\alpha)$ and

$(w, v) \in \mathfrak{m}_{\mathfrak{N}}(\beta)$, therefore $(u, v) \in \mathfrak{m}_{\mathfrak{N}}(\alpha) \circ \mathfrak{m}_{\mathfrak{N}}(\beta)$.

For (iii),

$$
\begin{aligned}
(s, t) \in \mathfrak{m}_{\mathfrak{N}}(\psi?) &\iff \forall \varphi \in t \ <\psi?>\varphi \in s &&\text{definition of } \mathfrak{m}_{\mathfrak{N}}(\psi?) \\
&\iff \forall \varphi \in t \ \psi \wedge \varphi \in s &&\text{Exercise 5.9(v)} \\
&\iff \forall \varphi \in t \ \psi \in s \text{ and } \varphi \in s &&\text{Lemma 7.1(vi)} \\
&\iff t \subseteq s \text{ and } \psi \in s \\
&\iff t = s \text{ and } \psi \in s &&\text{since } t \text{ is maximal} \\
&\iff t = s \text{ and } s \in \mathfrak{m}_{\mathfrak{N}}(\psi).
\end{aligned}
$$

∎

THEOREM 7.5:   The structure $\mathfrak{N}$ is a nonstandard Kripke frame according to the definition of Section 6.3.

Proof   By Lemmas 7.3 and 7.4, the operators $\rightarrow$, $\mathbf{0}$, $[\ ]$, $;$, $\cup$, $^-$, and $?$ behave in $\mathfrak{N}$ as in standard models. It remains to argue that the properties

$$
\begin{aligned}
[\alpha^*]\varphi &\leftrightarrow \varphi \wedge [\alpha ; \alpha^*]\varphi \\
[\alpha^*]\varphi &\leftrightarrow \varphi \wedge [\alpha^*](\varphi \rightarrow [\alpha]\varphi)
\end{aligned}
$$

of the * operator hold at all states. But this is immediate, since both these properties are theorems of PDL (Exercise 5.9), thus by Lemma 7.1(iii) they must be in every maximal consistent set. This guarantees that $\mathfrak{N}$ satisfies conditions (6.3.2) and (6.3.3) in the definition of nonstandard Kripke frames.   ∎

The definition of the nonstandard Kripke frame $\mathfrak{N}$ is independent of any particular φ. It is a *universal model* in the sense that every consistent formula is satisfied at some state of $\mathfrak{N}$.

THEOREM 7.6 (COMPLETENESS OF PDL):   If $\vDash \varphi$ then $\vdash \varphi$.

Proof   Equivalently, we need to show that if φ is consistent, then it is satisfied in a standard Kripke frame. If φ is consistent, then by Lemma 7.1(ii), it is contained in a maximal consistent set u, which is a state of the nonstandard Kripke frame $\mathfrak{N}$ constructed above. By the filtration lemma for nonstandard models (Lemma 6.6), φ is satisfied at the state $[u]$ in the finite Kripke frame $\mathfrak{N}/FL(\varphi)$, which is a standard Kripke frame by definition.   ∎

7.2   Logical Consequences

In classical logics, a completeness theorem of the form of Theorem 7.6 can be adapted to handle the relation of logical consequence $\varphi \models \psi$ between formulas because of the deduction theorem, which says

$$\varphi \vdash \psi \quad \Longleftrightarrow \quad \vdash \varphi \rightarrow \psi.$$

Unfortunately, the deduction theorem fails in PDL, as can be seen by taking $\psi = [a]p$ and $\varphi = p$. However, the following result allows Theorem 7.6, as well as Algorithm 8.2 of the next section, to be extended to handle the logical consequence relation:

THEOREM 7.7:   Let φ and ψ be any PDL formulas. Then

$$\varphi \models \psi \quad \Longleftrightarrow \quad \models [(a_1 \cup \cdots \cup a_n)^*]\varphi \rightarrow \psi,$$

where $a_1, \ldots, a_n$ are all atomic programs appearing in φ or ψ. Allowing infinitary conjunctions, if Σ is a set of formulas in which only finitely many atomic programs appear, then

$$\Sigma \models \psi \quad \Longleftrightarrow \quad \models \bigwedge \{[(a_1 \cup \cdots \cup a_n)^*]\varphi \mid \varphi \in \Sigma\} \rightarrow \psi,$$

where $a_1, \ldots, a_n$ are all atomic programs appearing in Σ or ψ.

We leave the proof of Theorem 7.7 as an exercise (Exercise 7.4).

7.3   Bibliographical Notes

The axiomatization of PDL used here (Axiom System 5.5) was introduced by Segerberg (1977). Completeness was shown independently by Gabbay (1977) and Parikh (1978a). A short and easy-to-follow proof is given in Kozen and Parikh (1981). Completeness is also treated in Pratt (1978, 1980a); Berman (1979); Nishimura (1979). The completeness proof given here is from Kozen (1981a) and is based on the approach of Berman (1979); Pratt (1980a).

Exercises

7.1. Prove Lemma 7.1. (*Hint*. Study the proof of Lemma 3.10.)

7.2. Supply the missing proofs of parts (i) and (iv) of Lemma 7.4.

7.3. Prove that PDL is compact over nonstandard models; that is, every finitely satisfiable set of propositions is satisfiable in a nonstandard Kripke frame. Conclude that there exists a nonstandard Kripke frame that is not standard.

7.4. Prove Theorem 7.7.

8 Complexity of PDL

In this chapter we ask the question: how difficult is it to determine whether a given formula φ of PDL is satisfiable? This is known as the *satisfiability problem* for PDL.

8.1 A Deterministic Exponential-Time Algorithm

The small model theorem (Theorem 6.5) gives a naive deterministic algorithm for the satisfiability problem: construct all Kripke frames of at most $2^{|\varphi|}$ states and check whether φ is satisfied at any state in any of them. Although checking whether a given formula is satisfied in a given state of a given Kripke frame can be done quite efficiently (Exercise 6.4), the naive satisfiability algorithm is highly inefficient. For one thing, the models constructed are of exponential size in the length of the given formula; for another, there are $2^{2^{O(|\varphi|)}}$ of them. Thus the naive satisfiability algorithm takes double exponential time in the worst case.

Here we develop an algorithm that runs in deterministic single-exponential time. One cannot expect to get a much more efficient algorithm than this due to a corresponding lower bound (Corollary 8.6). In fact, the problem is deterministic exponential-time complete (Theorem 8.5).

The algorithm attempts to construct the small model

$$\mathfrak{M} \;=\; (M, \mathfrak{m}_{\mathfrak{M}}) \;=\; \mathfrak{N}/FL(\varphi)$$

described in the proof of Theorem 7.6 explicitly. Here $\mathfrak{N}$ is the universal nonstandard Kripke frame constructed in Section 7.1 and $\mathfrak{M}$ is the small model obtained by filtration with respect to φ. If φ is satisfiable, then it is consistent, by the soundness of Axiom System 5.5; then φ will be satisfied at some state u of $\mathfrak{N}$, hence also at the state $[u]$ of $\mathfrak{M}$. If φ is not satisfiable, then the attempt to construct a model will fail; in this case the algorithm will halt and report failure.

Our approach will be to start with a superset of the set of states of $\mathfrak{M}$, then repeatedly delete states when we discover some inconsistency. This will give a sequence of approximations

$$\mathfrak{M}_0 \;\supseteq\; \mathfrak{M}_1 \;\supseteq\; \mathfrak{M}_2 \;\supseteq\; \cdots$$

converging to $\mathfrak{M}$.

We start with the set M_0 of all subsets

$$u \;\subseteq\; FL(\varphi) \cup \{\neg\psi \mid \psi \in FL(\varphi)\}$$

such that for each $\psi \in FL(\varphi)$, exactly one of ψ or $\neg\psi$ is in u. (Alternatively, we could take M_0 to be the set of truth assignments to $FL(\varphi)$.) By Lemma 7.1(vii), each state s of $\mathfrak{N}$ determines a unique element of M_0, namely

$$u_s \ \overset{\text{def}}{=} \ s \ \cap \ (FL(\varphi) \cup \{\neg\psi \mid \psi \in FL(\varphi)\}).$$

Moreover, by the definition of the equivalence relation $\equiv$ of Section 6.2,

$$[s] = [t] \ \Longleftrightarrow \ s \equiv t \ \Longleftrightarrow \ u_s = u_t,$$

thus the map $s \mapsto u_s$ is well-defined on $\equiv$-equivalence classes and gives a one-to-one embedding $[s] \mapsto u_s : M \to M_0$. We henceforth identify the state $[s]$ of $\mathfrak{M}$ with its image u_s in M_0 under this embedding. This allows us to regard M as a subset of M_0. However, there are some elements of M_0 that do not correspond to any state of $\mathfrak{M}$, and these are the ones to be deleted.

Now we are left with the question: how do we distinguish the sets u_s from those not corresponding to any state of $\mathfrak{M}$? This question is answered in the following lemma.

LEMMA 8.1:   Let $u \in M_0$. Then $u \in M$ if and only if u is consistent.

Proof By Lemma 6.6(i), every u_s is consistent, because it has a model: it is satisfied at the state $[s]$ of $\mathfrak{M}$.

Conversely, if $u \in M_0$ is consistent, then by Lemma 7.1(ii) it extends to a maximal consistent set $\hat{u}$, which is a state of the nonstandard Kripke frame $\mathfrak{N}$; and by Lemma 6.6(i), $[\hat{u}]$ is a state of $\mathfrak{M}$ satisfying u. ∎

We now construct a sequence of structures $\mathfrak{M}_i = (M_i, \mathfrak{m}_{\mathfrak{M}_i})$, $i \geq 0$, approximating $\mathfrak{M}$. The domains M_i of these structures will be defined below and will satisfy

$$M_0 \ \supseteq \ M_1 \ \supseteq \ M_2 \ \supseteq \ \cdots$$

The interpretations of the atomic formulas and programs in $\mathfrak{M}_i$ will be defined in the same way for all i:

$$\mathfrak{m}_{\mathfrak{M}_i}(p) \ \overset{\text{def}}{=} \ \{u \in M_i \mid p \in u\} \tag{8.1.1}$$

$$\mathfrak{m}_{\mathfrak{M}_i}(a) \ \overset{\text{def}}{=} \ \{(u,v) \in M_i^2 \mid \text{for all } [a]\psi \in FL(\varphi), \text{ if } [a]\psi \in u, \text{ then } \psi \in v\} \tag{8.1.2}$$

The map $\mathfrak{m}_{\mathfrak{M}_i}$ extends inductively in the usual way to compound programs and propositions to determine the frame $\mathfrak{M}_i$.

Here is the algorithm for constructing the domains M_i of the frames $\mathfrak{M}_i$.

ALGORITHM 8.2:

Step 1   Construct M_0.

Step 2   For each $u \in M_0$, check whether u respects Axioms 5.5(i) and (iv)–(vii), all of which can be checked locally. For example, to check Axiom 5.5(iv), which says

$$[\alpha \cup \beta]\psi \quad \leftrightarrow \quad [\alpha]\psi \wedge [\beta]\psi,$$

check for any formula of the form $[\alpha \cup \beta]\psi \in FL(\varphi)$ that $[\alpha \cup \beta]\psi \in u$ if and only if both $[\alpha]\psi \in u$ and $[\beta]\psi \in u$. Let M_1 be the set of all $u \in M_0$ passing this test. The model $\mathfrak{M}_1$ is defined by (8.1.1) and (8.1.2) above.

Step 3   Repeat the following for $i = 1, 2, \ldots$ until no more states are deleted. Find a formula $[\alpha]\psi \in FL(\varphi)$ and a state $u \in M_i$ violating the property

$$(\forall v \, ((u, v) \in \mathfrak{m}_{\mathfrak{M}_i}(\alpha) \Longrightarrow \psi \in v)) \quad \Longrightarrow \quad [\alpha]\psi \in u; \tag{8.1.3}$$

that is, such that $\neg[\alpha]\psi \in u$, but for no v such that $(u, v) \in \mathfrak{m}_{\mathfrak{M}_i}(\alpha)$ is it the case that $\neg\psi \in v$. Pick such an $[\alpha]\psi$ and u for which $|\alpha|$ is minimum. Delete u from M_i to get M_{i+1}. ∎

Step 3 can be justified intuitively as follows. To say that u violates the condition (8.1.3) says that u would like to go under α to some state satisfying $\neg\psi$, since u contains the formula $\neg[\alpha]\psi$, which is equivalent to $\langle\alpha\rangle\neg\psi$; but the left-hand side of (8.1.3) says that none of the states it currently goes to under α want to satisfy $\neg\psi$. This is evidence that u might not be in $\mathfrak{M}$, since in $\mathfrak{M}$ every state w satisfies every $\psi \in w$ by Lemma 6.6(i). But u may violate (8.1.3) not because $u \notin \mathfrak{M}$, but because there is some other state $v \notin \mathfrak{M}$ whose presence affects the truth of some subformula of $[\alpha]\psi$. This situation can be avoided by choosing $|\alpha|$ minimum.

The algorithm must terminate, since there are only finitely many states initially, and at least one state must be deleted in each iteration of step 3 in order to continue.

The correctness of this algorithm will follow from the following lemma. Note the similarity of this lemma to Lemmas 6.4 and 6.6.

LEMMA 8.3:   Let $i \geq 0$, and assume that $M \subseteq M_i$. Let $\rho \in FL(\varphi)$ be such that every $[\alpha]\psi \in FL(\rho)$ and $u \in M_i$ satisfy (8.1.3).

(i) For all $\psi \in FL(\rho)$ and $u \in M_i$, $\psi \in u$ iff $u \in \mathfrak{m}_{\mathfrak{M}_i}(\psi)$.

(ii) For all $[\alpha]\psi \in FL(\rho)$ and $u, v \in M_i$, (a)if $(u,v) \in \mathfrak{m}_\mathfrak{M}(\alpha)$, then $(u,v) \in \mathfrak{m}_{\mathfrak{M}_i}(\alpha)$;

(b)if $(u,v) \in \mathfrak{m}_{\mathfrak{M}_i}(\alpha)$ and $[\alpha]\psi \in u$, then $\psi \in v$.

Proof The proof is by simultaneous induction on the subterm relation.

(i)   The basis for atomic p is by definition as given in (8.1.1). The induction steps for $\rightarrow$ and $\mathbf{0}$ are easy and are left as exercises (Exercise 8.1). For the case $[\alpha]\psi$,

$[\alpha]\psi \in u$

$\Longrightarrow \quad \forall v\ (u,v) \in \mathfrak{m}_{\mathfrak{M}_i}(\alpha) \Longrightarrow \psi \in v$ induction hypothesis (ii)(b)

$\Longrightarrow \quad \forall v\ (u,v) \in \mathfrak{m}_{\mathfrak{M}_i}(\alpha) \Longrightarrow v \in \mathfrak{m}_{\mathfrak{M}_i}(\psi)$ induction hypothesis (i)

$\Longrightarrow \quad u \in \mathfrak{m}_{\mathfrak{M}_i}([\alpha]\psi)$.

Conversely,

$u \in \mathfrak{m}_{\mathfrak{M}_i}([\alpha]\psi)$

$\Longrightarrow \quad \forall v\ (u,v) \in \mathfrak{m}_{\mathfrak{M}_i}(\alpha) \Longrightarrow v \in \mathfrak{m}_{\mathfrak{M}_i}(\psi)$

$\Longrightarrow \quad \forall v\ (u,v) \in \mathfrak{m}_{\mathfrak{M}_i}(\alpha) \Longrightarrow \psi \in v$ induction hypothesis (i)

$\Longrightarrow \quad [\alpha]\psi \in u$ by (8.1.3).

(ii)(a)   For the basis, let a be an atomic program.

$(u,v) \in \mathfrak{m}_\mathfrak{M}(a) \quad \Longrightarrow \quad \forall \psi\ ([a]\psi \in FL(\varphi)$ and $[a]\psi \in u) \Longrightarrow \psi \in v$

$\Longrightarrow \quad (u,v) \in \mathfrak{m}_{\mathfrak{M}_i}(a)$ by (8.1.2).

The case $\alpha \cup \beta$ is left as an exercise (Exercise 8.1).
For the case $\alpha\,;\,\beta$,

$(u,v) \in \mathfrak{m}_\mathfrak{M}(\alpha\,;\,\beta) \quad \Longleftrightarrow \quad \exists w \in M\ (u,w) \in \mathfrak{m}_\mathfrak{M}(\alpha)$ and $(w,v) \in \mathfrak{m}_\mathfrak{M}(\beta)$

$\Longrightarrow \quad \exists w \in M_i\ (u,w) \in \mathfrak{m}_{\mathfrak{M}_i}(\alpha)$ and $(w,v) \in \mathfrak{m}_{\mathfrak{M}_i}(\beta)$

$\Longleftrightarrow \quad (u,v) \in \mathfrak{m}_{\mathfrak{M}_i}(\alpha\,;\,\beta)$.

The second step uses the induction hypothesis and the fact that $M \subseteq M_i$. The induction hypothesis holds for α and β because $[\alpha][\beta]\psi \in FL(\rho)$ and $[\beta]\psi \in FL(\rho)$ by Lemma 6.2(iv).

The case α^* follows from this case by iteration, and is left as an exercise (Exercise 8.1).

For the case $\psi?$,

$$
\begin{aligned}
(u,v) \in \mathfrak{m}_{\mathfrak{M}}(\psi?) &\iff u = v \text{ and } u \in \mathfrak{m}_{\mathfrak{M}}(\psi) \\
&\implies u = v \text{ and } \psi \in u \qquad &\text{Lemma 6.6(i)} \\
&\iff u = v \text{ and } u \in \mathfrak{m}_{\mathfrak{M}_i}(\psi) \qquad &\text{induction hypothesis (i)} \\
&\iff (u,v) \in \mathfrak{m}_{\mathfrak{M}_i}(\psi?).
\end{aligned}
$$

(ii)(b)   For the basis, let a be an atomic program. Then

$$
(u,v) \in \mathfrak{m}_{\mathfrak{M}_i}(a) \text{ and } [a]\psi \in u \implies \psi \in v \qquad \text{by (8.1.2)}.
$$

The cases $\alpha \cup \beta$ and $\alpha\,;\,\beta$ are left as exercises (Exercise 8.1).

For the case α^*, suppose $(u,v) \in \mathfrak{m}_{\mathfrak{M}_i}(\alpha^*)$ and $[\alpha^*]\psi \in u$. Then there exist $u_0,\dots,u_n$, $n \geq 0$, such that $u = u_0$, $v = u_n$, and $(u_i, u_{i+1}) \in \mathfrak{m}_{\mathfrak{M}_i}(\alpha)$, $0 \leq i \leq n-1$. Also $[\alpha][\alpha^*]\psi \in u_0$, otherwise u_0 would have been deleted in step 2. By the induction hypothesis (ii)(b), $[\alpha^*]\psi \in u_1$. Continuing in this fashion, we can conclude after n steps of this argument that $[\alpha^*]\psi \in u_n = v$. Then $\psi \in v$, otherwise v would have been deleted in step 2.

Finally, for the case $\psi?$, if $(u,v) \in \mathfrak{m}_{\mathfrak{M}_i}(\psi?)$ and $[\psi?]\sigma \in u$, then $u = v$ and $u \in \mathfrak{m}_{\mathfrak{M}_i}(\psi)$. By the induction hypothesis (i), $\psi \in u$. Thus $\sigma \in u$, otherwise u would have been deleted in step 2. ∎

Note that Lemma 8.3(ii)(a) actually holds of $[\alpha]\psi \in FL(\varphi)$ even if there exists $u \in M_i$ violating (8.1.3), provided $|\alpha|$ is minimum. This is because the condition regarding (8.1.3) in the statement of the lemma holds on strict subformulas of α, and that is all that is needed in the inductive proof of (ii)(a) for α. This says that no $u \in M$ is ever deleted in step 3, since for $u \in M$,

$$
\begin{aligned}
\forall v \in M_i \,((u,v) \in \mathfrak{m}_{\mathfrak{M}_i}(\alpha) \implies \psi \in v) & \\
\implies \forall v \in M \,((u,v) \in \mathfrak{m}_{\mathfrak{M}}(\alpha) \implies \psi \in v) \qquad &\text{Lemma 8.3(ii)(a)} \\
\iff \forall v \in M \,((u,v) \in \mathfrak{m}_{\mathfrak{M}}(\alpha) \implies v \in \mathfrak{m}_{\mathfrak{M}}(\psi)) \qquad &\text{Lemma 6.6(i)} \\
\iff u \in \mathfrak{m}_{\mathfrak{M}}([\alpha]\psi) \qquad &\text{definition of } \mathfrak{m}_{\mathfrak{M}} \\
\implies [\alpha]\psi \in u \qquad &\text{Lemma 6.6(i)}.
\end{aligned}
$$

Since every $u \in M$ passes the test of step 2 of the algorithm, and since no $u \in M$ is ever deleted in step 3, we have $M \subseteq M_i$ for all $i \geq 0$. Moreover, when the algorithm terminates with some model $\mathfrak{M}_n$, by Lemma 8.3(i), every $u \in M_n$ is satisfiable, since it is satisfied by the state u in the model $\mathfrak{M}_n$; thus $\mathfrak{M}_n = \mathfrak{M}$. We can now test the satisfiability of φ by checking whether $\varphi \in u$ for some $u \in M_n$.

Algorithm 8.2 can be programmed to run in exponential time without much difficulty. The efficiency can be further improved by observing that the minimal α in the $[\alpha]\psi$ violating (8.1.3) in step 3 must be either atomic or of the form β^* because of the preprocessing in step 2. This follows easily from Lemma 8.3. We have shown:

THEOREM 8.4:   There is an exponential-time algorithm for deciding whether a given formula of PDL is satisfiable.

As previously noted, Theorem 7.7 allows this algorithm to be adapted to test whether one formula is a logical consequence of another.

8.2   A Lower Bound

In the previous section we gave an exponential-time algorithm for deciding satisfiability in PDL. Here we establish the corresponding lower bound.

THEOREM 8.5:   The satisfiability problem for PDL is *EXPTIME*-complete.

Proof   In light of Theorem 8.4, we need only show that PDL is *EXPTIME*-hard (see Section 2.3). We do this by constructing a formula of PDL whose models encode the computation of a given linear-space-bounded one-tape alternating Turing machine M on a given input x of length n over M's input alphabet. We show how to define a formula $\text{ACCEPTS}_{M,x}$ involving the single atomic program NEXT, atomic propositions SYMBOL_i^a and STATE_i^q for each symbol a in M's tape alphabet, q a state of M's finite control, and $0 \le i \le n$, and an atomic proposition ACCEPT. The formula $\text{ACCEPTS}_{M,x}$ will have the property that any satisfying Kripke frame encodes an accepting computation of M on x. In any such Kripke frame, states u will represent configurations of M occurring in the computation tree of M on input x; the truth values of SYMBOL_i^a and STATE_i^q at state u will give the tape contents, current state, and tape head position in the configuration corresponding to u. The truth value of the atomic proposition ACCEPT will be $\mathbf{1}$ at u iff the computation beginning in state u is an accepting computation according to the rules of alternating Turing machine acceptance (Section 2.1).

Let Γ be M's tape alphabet and Q the set of states. We assume without loss of generality that the machine is $2^{O(n)}$-time bounded. This can be enforced by requiring M to count each step it takes on a separate track and to shut off after

c^n steps, where c^n bounds the number of possible configurations of M on inputs of length n. There are at most $\Gamma^{n+2} \cdot Q \cdot (n+2)$ such configurations, and c can be chosen large enough that c^n bounds this number.

We also assume without loss of generality that the input is enclosed in left and right endmarkers $\vdash$ and $\dashv$, respectively, that these symbols are never overwritten, and that M is constrained never to move to the left of $\vdash$ nor to the right of $\dashv$.

Now we encode configurations as follows. The atomic proposition SYMBOL_i^a says, "Tape cell i currently has symbol a written on it." The atomic proposition STATE_i^q says, "The tape head is currently scanning tape cell i in state q." We also allow STATE_i^ℓ and STATE_i^r, where $\ell, r \notin Q$ are special annotations used to indicate that the tape head is currently scanning a cell somewhere to the left or right, respectively, of cell i.

- "Exactly one symbol occupies every tape cell."

$$\bigwedge_{0 \le i \le n+1} \bigvee_{a \in \Gamma} \left(\text{SYMBOL}_i^a \wedge \bigwedge_{\substack{b \in \Gamma \\ b \ne a}} \neg \text{SYMBOL}_i^b \right)$$

- "The symbols occupying the first and last tape cells are the endmarkers $\vdash$ and $\dashv$, respectively."

$$\text{SYMBOL}_0^\vdash \wedge \text{SYMBOL}_{n+1}^\dashv$$

- "The machine is in exactly one state scanning exactly one tape cell."

$$\bigvee_{0 \le i \le n+1} \bigvee_{q \in Q} \text{STATE}_i^q$$

$$\wedge \bigwedge_{0 \le i \le n+1} \bigvee_{q \in Q \cup \{\ell, r\}} \left(\text{STATE}_i^q \wedge \bigwedge_{\substack{p \in Q \cup \{\ell, r\} \\ p \ne q}} \neg \text{STATE}_i^p \right)$$

$$\wedge \bigwedge_{0 \le i \le n} \bigwedge_{q \in Q \cup \{\ell\}} \left(\text{STATE}_i^q \to \text{STATE}_{i+1}^\ell \right)$$

$$\wedge \bigwedge_{1 \le i \le n+1} \bigwedge_{q \in Q \cup \{r\}} \left(\text{STATE}_i^q \to \text{STATE}_{i-1}^r \right).$$

Let CONFIG be the conjunction of these three formulas. Then $u \vDash \text{CONFIG}$ iff u represents a configuration of M on an input of length n.

Now we can write down formulas that say that M moves correctly. Here we use the atomic program NEXT to represent the binary next-configuration relation. For each (state, tape symbol) pair (q, a), let $\Delta(q, a)$ be the set of all (state, tape symbol, direction) triples describing a possible action M can take when scanning symbol

a in state q. For example, if $(p, b, -1) \in \Delta(q, a)$, this means that when scanning a tape cell containing a in state q, M can print b on that tape cell, move its head one cell to the left, and enter state p.

- "If the tape head is not currently scanning cell i, then the symbol written on cell i does not change."

$$\bigwedge_{0 \leq i \leq n+1} ((\text{STATE}_i^\ell \vee \text{STATE}_i^r) \to \bigwedge_{a \in \Gamma} (\text{SYMBOL}_i^a \to [\text{NEXT}]\text{SYMBOL}_i^a))$$

- "The machine moves according to its transition relation."

$$\bigwedge_{\substack{0 \leq i \leq n+1}} \bigwedge_{\substack{a \in \Gamma \\ q \in Q}} ((\text{SYMBOL}_i^a \wedge \text{STATE}_i^q) \to$$

$$(\bigwedge_{(p,b,d) \in \Delta(q,a)} \langle\text{NEXT}\rangle(\text{SYMBOL}_i^b \wedge \text{STATE}_{i+d}^p)) \tag{8.2.1}$$

$$\wedge \quad [\text{NEXT}](\bigvee_{(p,b,d) \in \Delta(q,a)} (\text{SYMBOL}_i^b \wedge \text{STATE}_{i+d}^p))) \tag{8.2.2}$$

Note that when $\Delta(q, a) = \varnothing$, clause (8.2.1) reduces to $\mathbf{1}$ and clause (8.2.2) reduces to $[\text{NEXT}]\mathbf{0}$. This figures into the definition of acceptance below.

Let MOVE be the conjunction of these two formulas. Then $u \vDash$ MOVE if the configurations represented by states v such that (u, v) is in the relation denoted by NEXT are exactly the configurations that follow from the configuration represented by u in one step according to the transition relation of M.

We can describe the start configuration of the machine M on input x:

- "The machine is in its start state s with its tape head scanning the left endmarker, and $x = x_1 \cdots x_n$ is written on the tape."

$$\text{STATE}_0^s \wedge \bigwedge_{1 \leq i \leq n} \text{SYMBOL}_i^{x_i}$$

Let this formula be called START.

Finally, we can describe the condition of acceptance for alternating Turing machines. Let $U \subseteq Q$ be the set of universal states of M and let $E \subseteq Q$ be the set of existential states of M. Then $Q = U \cup E$ and $U \cap E = \varnothing$.

- "If q is an existential state, then q leads to acceptance if at least one of its successor configurations leads to acceptance."

$$\bigwedge_{0 \leq i \leq n+1} \bigwedge_{q \in E} (\text{STATE}_i^q \to (\text{ACCEPT} \leftrightarrow \text{<NEXT>ACCEPT})) \qquad (8.2.3)$$

- "If q is a universal state, then q leads to acceptance if all its successor configurations lead to acceptance."

$$\bigwedge_{0 \leq i \leq n+1} \bigwedge_{q \in U} (\text{STATE}_i^q \to (\text{ACCEPT} \leftrightarrow [\text{NEXT}]\text{ACCEPT})) \qquad (8.2.4)$$

Let ACCEPTANCE denote the conjunction of these two formulas.

Recall from Section 2.1 that an *accept configuration* of M is a universal configuration with no next configuration and a *reject configuration* is an existential configuration with no next configuration. As observed above, when this occurs, clauses (8.2.1) and (8.2.2) reduce to **1** and [NEXT]**0**, respectively. In conjunction with ACCEPTANCE, this implies that ACCEPT is always true at accept configurations and always false at reject configurations.

Now let $\text{ACCEPTS}_{M,x}$ be the formula

$$\text{START} \wedge [\text{NEXT}^*](\text{CONFIG} \wedge \text{MOVE} \wedge \text{ACCEPTANCE}) \wedge \text{ACCEPT}.$$

Then M accepts x if and only if $\text{ACCEPTS}_{M,x}$ is satisfiable.

We have given an efficient reduction from the membership problem for linear-space alternating Turing machines to the problem of PDL satisfiability. For *EXPTIME*-hardness, we need to give a reduction from the membership problem for polynomial-space alternating Turing machines, but essentially the same construction works. The only differences are that instead of the bound n we use the bound n^k for some fixed constant k in the definition of the formulas, and the formula START is modified to pad the input out to length n^k with blanks:

$$\text{STATE}_0^s \wedge \bigwedge_{1 \leq i \leq n} \text{SYMBOL}_i^{x_i} \wedge \bigwedge_{n+1 \leq i \leq n^k} \text{SYMBOL}_i^{\sqcup}.$$

Since the membership problem for alternating polynomial-space machines is *EXPTIME*-hard (Chandra et al. (1981)), so is the satisfiability problem for PDL. ∎

COROLLARY 8.6: There is a constant $c > 1$ such that the satisfiability problem for PDL is not solvable in deterministic time $c^{n/\log n}$, where n is the size of the input formula.

Proof An analysis of the construction of $\text{ACCEPTS}_{M,x}$ in the proof of Theorem

8.5 reveals that its length is bounded above by $an \log n$ for some constant a, where $n = |x|$, and the time to construct $\text{ACCEPTS}_{M,x}$ from x is at most polynomial in n. The number of symbols in Γ and states in Q are constants and contribute at most a constant factor to the length of the formula.

Now we can use the fact that the complexity class $DTIME(2^n)$ contains a set A not contained in any complexity class $DTIME(d^n)$ for any $d < 2$ (see Hopcroft and Ullman (1979)). Since $A \in DTIME(2^n)$, it is accepted by an alternating linear-space Turing machine M (Chandra et al. (1981); see Section 2.1). We can decide membership in A by converting a given input x to the formula $\text{ACCEPTS}_{M,x}$ using the reduction of Theorem 8.5, then deciding whether $\text{ACCEPTS}_{M,x}$ is satisfiable. Since $|\text{ACCEPTS}_{M,x}| \leq an \log n$, if the satisfiability problem is in $DTIME(c^{n/\log n})$ for some constant c, then we can decide membership in A in time

$$n^k + c^{an \log n / \log(an \log n)};$$

the term n^k is the time required to convert x to $\text{ACCEPTS}_{M,x}$, and the remaining term is the time required to decide the satisfiability of $\text{ACCEPTS}_{M,x}$. But, assuming $a \geq 1$,

$$n^k + c^{an \log n / \log(an \log n)} \leq n^k + c^{an \log n / \log n}$$
$$\leq n^k + c^{an},$$

which for $c < 2^{1/a}$ is asymptotically less than 2^n. This contradicts the choice of A. ∎

It is interesting to compare the complexity of satisfiability in PDL with the complexity of satisfiability in propositional logic. In the latter, satisfiability is *NP*-complete; but at present it is not known whether the two complexity classes *EXPTIME* and *NP* differ. Thus, as far as current knowledge goes, the satisfiability problem is no easier in the worst case for propositional logic than for its far richer superset PDL.

8.3   Compactness and Logical Consequences

As we have seen, current knowledge does not permit a significant difference to be observed between the complexity of satisfiability in propositional logic and in PDL. However, there is one easily verified and important behavioral difference: propositional logic is *compact*, whereas PDL is not.

Compactness has significant implications regarding the relation of logical consequence. If a propositional formula φ is a consequence of a set Γ of propositional formulas, then it is already a consequence of some finite subset of Γ; but this is not true in PDL.

Recall that we write $\Gamma \vDash \varphi$ and say that φ is a *logical consequence* of Γ if φ satisfied in any state of any Kripke frame $\mathfrak{K}$ all of whose states satisfy all the formulas of Γ. That is, if $\mathfrak{K} \vDash \Gamma$, then $\mathfrak{K} \vDash \varphi$.

An alternative intepretation of logical consequence, not equivalent to the above, is that in any Kripke frame, the formula φ holds in any state satisfying all formulas in Γ. Allowing infinite conjunctions, we might write this as $\vDash \bigwedge \Gamma \to \varphi$. This is not the same as $\Gamma \vDash \varphi$, since $\vDash \bigwedge \Gamma \to \varphi$ implies $\Gamma \vDash \varphi$, but not necessarily vice versa. A counterexample is provided by $\Gamma = \{p\}$ and $\varphi = [a]p$. However, if Γ contains only finitely many atomic programs, we can reduce the problem $\Gamma \vDash \varphi$ to the problem $\vDash \bigwedge \Gamma' \to \varphi$ for a related Γ', as shown in Theorem 7.7.

Under either interpretation, compactness fails:

THEOREM 8.7:   There is an infinite set of formulas Γ and a formula φ such that $\vDash \bigwedge \Gamma \to \varphi$ (hence $\Gamma \vDash \varphi$), but for no proper subset $\Gamma' \subseteq \Gamma$ is it the case that $\Gamma' \vDash \varphi$ (hence neither is it the case that $\vDash \bigwedge \Gamma' \to \varphi$).

Proof   Take

$$\varphi \overset{\text{def}}{=} p \to [a^*]q$$
$$\Gamma \overset{\text{def}}{=} \{p \to q, \ p \to [a]q, \ p \to [aa]q, \ \ldots, \ p \to [a^i]q, \ \ldots\}.$$

Then $\vDash \bigwedge \Gamma \to \varphi$. But for $\Gamma' \subsetneq \Gamma$, say with $p \to [a^i]q \in \Gamma - \Gamma'$, consider a structure with states ω, atomic program a interpreted as the successor relation, p true only at 0, and q false only at i.

Then all formulas of Γ' are true in all states of this model, but φ is false in state 0. ∎

As shown in Theorem 7.7, logical consequences $\Gamma \vDash \varphi$ for finite Γ are no more difficult to decide than validity of single formulas. But what if Γ is infinite? Here compactness is the key factor. If Γ is an r.e. set and the logic is compact, then the consequence problem is r.e.: to check whether $\Gamma \vDash \varphi$, the finite subsets of Γ can be effectively enumerated, and checking $\Gamma \vDash \varphi$ for finite Γ is a decidable problem.

Since compactness fails in **PDL**, this observation does us no good, even when Γ is known to be recursively enumerable. However, the following result shows that the situation is much worse than we might expect: even if Γ is taken to be the set of substitution instances of a single formula of **PDL**, the consequence problem becomes very highly undecidable. This is a rather striking manifestation of **PDL**'s lack of compactness.

Let φ be a given formula. The set S_φ of *substitution instances* of φ is the set of all formulas obtained by substituting a formula for each atomic proposition appearing in φ.

THEOREM 8.8:   The problem of deciding whether $S_\varphi \vDash \psi$ is Π_1^1-complete. The problem is Π_1^1-hard even for a particular fixed φ.

Proof For the upper bound, it suffices to consider only countable models. The problem is to decide whether for all countable Kripke frames $\mathfrak{M}$, if $\mathfrak{M} \vDash S_\varphi$, then $\mathfrak{M} \vDash \psi$. The Kripke frame $\mathfrak{M}$ is first selected with universal second-order quantification, which determines the interpretation of the atomic program and proposition symbols. Once $\mathfrak{M}$ is selected, the check that $\mathfrak{M} \vDash S_\varphi \implies \mathfrak{M} \vDash \psi$ is first-order: either $\mathfrak{M}, u \vDash \psi$ at all states u of $\mathfrak{M}$, or there exists a substitution instance φ' of φ and a state u of $\mathfrak{M}$ such that $\mathfrak{M}, u \vDash \neg\varphi'$.

For the lower bound, we encode (the complement of) the tiling problem of Proposition 2.22. The fixed scheme φ is used to ensure that any model consists essentially of an $\omega \times \omega$ grid. Let NORTH and EAST be atomic programs and p an atomic proposition. Take φ to be the scheme

$$[(\text{NORTH} \cup \text{EAST})^*](<\text{NORTH}>\mathbf{1} \wedge <\text{EAST}>\mathbf{1}$$
$$\wedge (<\text{NORTH}>p \rightarrow [\text{NORTH}]p) \wedge (<\text{EAST}>p \rightarrow [\text{EAST}]p) \tag{8.3.1}$$
$$\wedge (<\text{NORTH}; \text{EAST}>p \rightarrow [\text{EAST}; \text{NORTH}]p)).$$

The first line of (8.3.1) says that from any reachable point, one can always continue the grid in either direction. The second line says that any two states reachable from any state under NORTH are indistinguishable by any **PDL** formula (note that any formula can be substituted for p), and similarly for EAST. The third line is a commutativity condition; it says that any state reachable by going NORTH and then EAST is indistinguishable from any state reachable by going EAST and then NORTH. It follows by induction that if σ and τ are any seqs over atomic programs NORTH, EAST such that σ and τ contain the same number of occurrences of each atomic program—that is, if σ and τ are permutations of each other—then any model of all substitution instances of (8.3.1) must also satisfy all substitution instances of the formula

$$[(\text{NORTH} \cup \text{EAST})^*](<\sigma>p \to <\tau>p)$$

(Exercise 8.3).

Now we will construct the formula ψ, which will be used in two ways:

(i) to describe the legal tilings of the grid with some given set T of tile types, and

(ii) to say that red occurs only finitely often.

For (i), we mimic the construction of Theorem 3.60. We use atomic propositions $\text{NORTH}_c, \text{SOUTH}_c, \text{EAST}_c, \text{WEST}_c$ for each color c. For example, the proposition $\text{NORTH}_{\text{blue}}$ says that the north edge of the tile is colored blue, and similarly for the other colors and directions. As in Theorem 3.60, for each tile type $A \in T$, one can construct a formula TILE_A from these propositions that is true at a state iff the truth values of $\text{NORTH}_c, \text{SOUTH}_c, \text{EAST}_c, \text{WEST}_c$ at that state describe a tile of type A. For example, the formula corresponding to the example given in Theorem 3.60 would be

$$\text{TILE}_A \stackrel{\text{def}}{\Longleftrightarrow} \text{NORTH}_{\text{blue}} \wedge \bigwedge_{\substack{c \in C \\ c \neq \text{blue}}} \neg \text{NORTH}_c$$

$$\wedge\ \text{SOUTH}_{\text{black}} \wedge \bigwedge_{\substack{c \in C \\ c \neq \text{black}}} \neg \text{SOUTH}_c$$

$$\wedge\ \text{EAST}_{\text{red}} \wedge \bigwedge_{\substack{c \in C \\ c \neq \text{red}}} \neg \text{EAST}_c$$

$$\wedge\ \text{WEST}_{\text{green}} \wedge \bigwedge_{\substack{c \in C \\ c \neq \text{green}}} \neg \text{WEST}_c.$$

Let ψ_T be the conjunction

$$[(\text{NORTH} \cup \text{EAST})^*] \bigvee_{A \in T} \text{TILE}_A$$

$$\wedge \ [\text{EAST}^*]\text{SOUTH}_{\text{blue}}$$

$$\wedge \ [\text{NORTH}^*]\text{WEST}_{\text{blue}}$$

$$\wedge \ [(\text{NORTH} \cup \text{EAST})^*] \bigwedge_{c \in C} (\text{EAST}_c \rightarrow <\text{EAST}>\text{WEST}_c)$$

$$\wedge \ [(\text{NORTH} \cup \text{EAST})^*] \bigwedge_{c \in C} (\text{NORTH}_c \rightarrow <\text{NORTH}>\text{SOUTH}_c).$$

These correspond to the sentences (3.4.3)–(3.4.7) of Theorem 3.60. As in that theorem, any model of ψ_T must be a legal tiling.

Finally, we give a formula that says that red occurs only finitely often in the tiling:

$$\text{RED} \ \overset{\text{def}}{\Longleftrightarrow} \ \text{NORTH}_{\text{red}} \vee \text{SOUTH}_{\text{red}} \vee \text{EAST}_{\text{red}} \vee \text{WEST}_{\text{red}}$$

$$\psi_{\text{red}} \ \overset{\text{def}}{\Longleftrightarrow} \ <\text{NORTH}^*>[(\text{NORTH} \cup \text{EAST})^*]\neg\text{RED}$$

$$\wedge \ <\text{EAST}^*>[(\text{NORTH} \cup \text{EAST})^*]\neg\text{RED}.$$

Then all valid tilings use only finitely many tiles with a red edge iff

$$S_\varphi \ \vDash \ \psi_T \rightarrow \psi_{\text{red}}.$$

■

The proof of Theorem 8.8 can be refined so as to yield similar results for more restricted versions of **PDL** discussed in Chapter 10. Specifically, the result holds for **SDPDL** of Section 10.1 and $\text{PDL}^{(0)}$ of Section 10.2. Of course, since the result is negative in nature, it holds for any extensions of these logics.

8.4 Bibliographical Notes

The exponential-time lower bound for **PDL** was established by Fischer and Ladner (1977, 1979) by showing how **PDL** formulas can encode computations of linear-space-bounded alternating Turing machines.

Deterministic exponential-time algorithms were first given in Pratt (1978, 1979b, 1980b). The algorithm given here is essentially from Pratt (1979b). The algorithm has been implemented by Pratt and reportedly works well on small formulas.

Theorem 8.8 showing that the problem of deciding whether $\Gamma \models \psi$, where Γ is a fixed r.e. set of PDL formulas, is Π_1^1-complete is due to Meyer et al. (1981).

Exercises

8.1. Supply the missing arguments in the proof of Lemma 8.3: part (i) for the cases $\rightarrow$ and $\mathbf{0}$, part (ii)(a) for the cases $\cup$ and *, and part (ii)(b) for the cases $\cup$ and ;.

8.2. Show how to encode the acceptance problem for linear-space alternating Turing machines in the validity problem for PDL. In other words, given such a machine M and an input x, show how to construct a PDL formula that is valid (true at all states in all Kripke frames) iff M accepts x. (*Hint.* Use the machinery constructed in Section 8.2.)

8.3. In the proof of Theorem 8.8, argue that if σ and τ are any seqs over atomic programs NORTH, EAST such that σ and τ contain the same number of occurrences of each atomic program—that is, if σ and τ are permutations of each other—then any model of all substitution instances of (8.3.1) must also satisfy all substitution instances of the formula

$[(\text{NORTH} \cup \text{EAST})^*](\langle\sigma\rangle p \rightarrow \langle\tau\rangle p).$

9 Nonregular PDL

In this chapter we enrich the class of regular programs in **PDL** by introducing programs whose control structure requires more than a finite automaton. For example, the class of *context-free programs* requires a pushdown automaton (PDA), and moving up from regular to context-free programs is really going from iterative programs to ones with parameterless recursive procedures. Several questions arise when enriching the class of programs of **PDL**, such as whether the expressive power of the logic grows, and if so whether the resulting logics are still decidable. We first show that any nonregular program increases **PDL**'s expressive power and that the validity problem for **PDL** with context-free programs is undecidable. The bulk of the chapter is then devoted to the difficult problem of trying to characterize the borderline between decidable and undecidable extensions. On the one hand, validity for **PDL** with the addition of even a single extremely simple nonregular program is shown to be already Π_1^1-complete; but on the other hand, when we add another equally simple program, the problem remains decidable. Besides these results, which pertain to very specific extensions, we discuss some broad decidability results that cover many languages, including some that are not even context-free. Since no similarly general undecidability results are known, we also address the weaker issue of whether nonregular extensions admit the finite model property and present a negative result that covers many cases.

9.1 Context-Free Programs

Consider the following self-explanatory program:

while p do a ; now do b the same number of times $\qquad\qquad$ (9.1.1)

This program is meant to represent the following set of computation sequences:

$$\{(p? \, ; \, a)^i \, ; \, \neg p? \, ; \, b^i \mid i \geq 0\}.$$

Viewed as a language over the alphabet $\{a, b, p, \neg p\}$, this set is not regular, thus cannot be programmed in **PDL**. However, it can be represented by the following parameterless recursive procedure:

proc V {
  if p **then** { a ; **call** V ; b }
    else return
  }

The set of computation sequences of this program is captured by the context-free grammar

$$V \quad \to \quad \neg p? \mid p?aVb.$$

We are thus led to the idea of allowing context-free programs inside the boxes and diamonds of PDL. From a pragmatic point of view, this amounts to extending the logic with the ability to reason about parameterless recursive procedures. The particular representation of the context-free programs is unimportant; we can use pushdown automata, context-free grammars, recursive procedures, or any other formalism that can be effectively translated into these.

In the rest of the chapter, a number of specific programs will be of interest, and we employ special abbreviations for them. For example, we define:

$$a^\Delta b a^\Delta \quad \overset{\text{def}}{=} \quad \{a^i b a^i \mid i \geq 0\}$$
$$a^\Delta b^\Delta \quad \overset{\text{def}}{=} \quad \{a^i b^i \mid i \geq 0\}$$
$$b^\Delta a^\Delta \quad \overset{\text{def}}{=} \quad \{b^i a^i \mid i \geq 0\}.$$

Note that $a^\Delta b^\Delta$ is really just a nondeterministic version of the program (9.1.1) in which there is simply no p to control the iteration. In fact, (9.1.1) could have been written in this notation as $(p?a)^\Delta \neg p?b^\Delta$.[1] In programming terms, we can compare the regular program $(ab)^*$ with the nonregular one $a^\Delta b^\Delta$ by observing that if a is "purchase a loaf of bread" and b is "pay \$1.00," then the former program captures the process of paying for each loaf when purchased, while the latter one captures the process of paying for them all at the end of the month.

9.2   Basic Results

We first show that enriching PDL with even a single arbitrary nonregular program increases expressive power.

---

1 It is noteworthy that the results of this chapter do not depend on nondeterminism. For example, the negative Theorem 9.6 holds for the deterministic version (9.1.1) too. Also, most of the results in the chapter involve nonregular programs over atomic programs only, but can be generalized to allow tests as well.

DEFINITION 9.1:   If L is any language over atomic programs and tests, then
PDL $+ L$ is defined exactly as PDL, but with the additional syntax rule stating
that for any formula φ, the expression $<L>\varphi$ is a new formula. The semantics of
PDL $+ L$ is like that of PDL with the addition of the clause

$$\mathfrak{m}_{\mathfrak{K}}(L) \quad \stackrel{\text{def}}{=} \quad \bigcup_{\beta \in L} \mathfrak{m}_{\mathfrak{K}}(\beta).$$

Note that PDL $+ L$ does not allow L to be used as a formation rule for new
programs or to be combined with other programs. It is added to the programming
language as a single new stand-alone program only.

DEFINITION 9.2:   If PDL$_1$ and PDL$_2$ are two extensions of PDL, we say that PDL$_1$
is *as expressive as* PDL$_2$ if for each formula φ of PDL$_2$ there is a formula ψ of PDL$_1$
such that $\vDash \varphi \leftrightarrow \psi$. If PDL$_1$ is as expressive as PDL$_2$ but PDL$_2$ is not as expressive
as PDL$_1$, we say that PDL$_1$ is *strictly more expressive than* PDL$_2$.

Thus, one version of PDL is strictly more expressive than another if anything
the latter can express the former can too, but there is something the former can
express that the latter cannot.
    A language is *test-free* if it is a subset of Π_0^*; that is, if its seqs contain no tests.

THEOREM 9.3:   If L is any nonregular test-free language, then PDL $+ L$ is strictly
more expressive than PDL.

Proof   The result can be proved by embedding PDL into SkS, the monadic second-
order theory of k successors (Rabin (1969)). It is possible to show that any set of
nodes definable in SkS is regular, so that the addition of a nonregular predicate
increases its expressive power.
    A more direct proof can be obtained as follows. Fix a subset $\{a_0, \dots, a_{k-1}\} \subseteq$
Π_0. Define the Kripke frame $\mathfrak{K} = (K, \mathfrak{m}_{\mathfrak{K}})$ in which

$$K \quad \stackrel{\text{def}}{=} \quad \{a_0, \dots, a_{k-1}\}^*$$
$$\mathfrak{m}_{\mathfrak{K}}(a_i) \quad \stackrel{\text{def}}{=} \quad \{(a_i x, x) \mid x \in \{a_0, \dots, a_{k-1}\}^*\}$$
$$\mathfrak{m}_{\mathfrak{K}}(p) \quad \stackrel{\text{def}}{=} \quad \{\varepsilon\}.$$

The frame $\mathfrak{K}$ can be viewed as a complete k-ary tree in which p holds at the root
only and each node has k offspring, one for each atomic program a_i, but with all

edges pointing upward. Thus, the only seq from the node $x \in \{a_0, \ldots, a_{k-1}\}^*$ that leads to a state satisfying p is x itself.

Now for any formula φ of PDL, the set $\mathfrak{m}_{\mathfrak{K}}(\varphi)$ is the set of words over $\{a_0, \ldots, a_{k-1}\}$ describing paths in $\mathfrak{K}$ leading from states that satisfy φ to the root. It is easy to show by induction on the structure of φ that $\mathfrak{m}_{\mathfrak{K}}(\varphi)$ is a regular set over the alphabet $\{a_0, \ldots, a_{k-1}\}$ (Exercise 9.1). Since $\mathfrak{m}_{\mathfrak{K}}(\texttt{<}L\texttt{>}p) = L$ is nonregular, $\texttt{<}L\texttt{>}p$ cannot be equivalent to any PDL formula. ∎

We can view the decidability of regular PDL as showing that propositional-level reasoning about iterative programs is computable. We now wish to know if the same is true for recursive procedures. We define *context-free* PDL to be PDL extended with context-free programs, where a *context-free program* is one whose seqs form a context-free language. The precise syntax is unimportant, but for definiteness we might take as programs the set of context-free grammars G over atomic programs and tests and define

$$\mathfrak{m}_{\mathfrak{K}}(G) \overset{\text{def}}{=} \bigcup_{\beta \in CS(G)} \mathfrak{m}_{\mathfrak{K}}(\beta),$$

where $CS(G)$ is the set of computation sequences generated by G as described in Section 4.3.

THEOREM 9.4:   The validity problem for context-free PDL is undecidable.

Proof Consider the formula $\texttt{<}G\texttt{>}p \leftrightarrow \texttt{<}G'\texttt{>}p$ for context-free grammars G and G' and atomic p. It can be shown that if $CS(G)$ and $CS(G')$ are test-free, then this formula is valid iff $CS(G) = CS(G')$ (Exercise 9.2). This reduces the equivalence problem for context-free languages to the validity problem for context-free PDL. The equivalence problem for context-free languages is well known to be undecidable; see Hopcroft and Ullman (1979) or Kozen (1997a). ∎

Theorem 9.4 leaves several interesting questions unanswered. What is the level of undecidability of context-free PDL? What happens if we want to add only a small number of specific nonregular programs? The first of these questions arises from the fact that the equivalence problem for context-free languages is co-r.e., or in the notation of the arithmetic hierarchy (Section 2.2), it is complete for Π_1^0. Hence, all Theorem 9.4 shows is that the validity problem for context-free PDL is Π_1^0-hard, while it might in fact be worse. The second question is far more general. We might be interested in reasoning only about deterministic or linear context-free programs,[2] or we might be interested only in a few special context-free programs such as $a^\triangle ba^\triangle$ or $a^\triangle b^\triangle$. Perhaps PDL remains decidable when these programs are added. The general question is to determine the borderline between the decidable and the undecidable when it comes to enriching the class of programs allowed in PDL.

Interestingly, if we wish to consider such simple nonregular extensions as PDL $+ a^\triangle ba^\triangle$ or PDL $+ a^\triangle b^\triangle$, we will not be able to prove undecidability by the technique used for context-free PDL in Theorem 9.4, since standard problems that are undecidable for context-free languages, such as equivalence and inclusion, are decidable for classes containing the regular languages and the likes of $a^\triangle ba^\triangle$ and $a^\triangle b^\triangle$. Moreover, we cannot prove decidability by the technique used for PDL in Section 6.2, since logics like PDL $+ a^\triangle ba^\triangle$ and PDL $+ a^\triangle b^\triangle$ do not enjoy the finite model property, as we now show. Thus, if we want to determine the decidability status of such extensions, we will have to work harder.

THEOREM 9.5:   There is a satisfiable formula in PDL $+ a^\triangle b^\triangle$ that is not satisfied in any finite structure.

Proof   Let φ be the formula

$$p \;\wedge\; [a^*]\langle ab^*\rangle p \;\wedge\; [(a \cup b)^* ba]\mathbf{0} \;\wedge\; [a^* a][a^\triangle b^\triangle]\neg p \;\wedge\; [a^\triangle b^\triangle][b]\mathbf{0}.$$

Let $\mathfrak{K}_0$ be the infinite structure illustrated in Fig. 9.1 in which the only states satisfying p are the dark ones. It is easy to see that $\mathfrak{K}_0, u \vDash \varphi$. Now let $\mathfrak{K}$ be a finite structure with a state u such that $\mathfrak{K}, u \vDash \varphi$. Viewing $\mathfrak{K}$ as a finite graph, we associate paths with the sequences of atomic programs along them. Consider the set U of paths in $\mathfrak{K}$ leading from u to states satisfying p. The fact that $\mathfrak{K}$ is finite implies that U is a regular set of words. However, the third conjunct of φ eliminates from U paths that contain b followed by a, forcing U to be contained in $a^* b^*$; the fourth and fifth conjuncts force U to be a subset of $\{a^i b^i \mid i \geq 0\}$; and the first two conjuncts force U to contain a word in $a^i b^*$ for each $i \geq 0$. Consequently, U must be exactly $\{a^i b^i \mid i \geq 0\}$, contradicting regularity. ∎

---

2 A *linear program* is one whose seqs are generated by a context-free grammar in which there is at most one nonterminal symbol on the right-hand side of each rule. This corresponds to a family of recursive procedures in which there is at most one recursive call in each procedure.

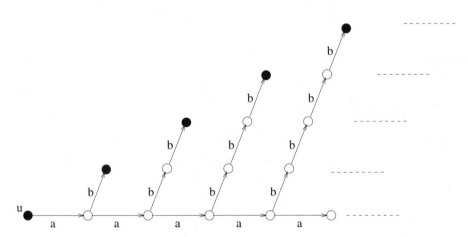

Figure 9.1

9.3 Undecidable Extensions

Two-Letter Programs

The proof of Theorem 9.5 can be modified easily to work for $\mathsf{PDL} + a^\Delta b a^\Delta$ (Exercise 9.3). However, for this extension the news is worse than mere undecidability:

THEOREM 9.6:   The validity problem for $\mathsf{PDL} + a^\Delta b a^\Delta$ is Π_1^1-complete.

Proof   To show that the problem is in Π_1^1, we use the Löwenheim–Skolem Theorem (Section 3.4) to write the notion of validity in the general form "For every countable structure ... ," then observe that the question of whether a given formula is satisfied in a given countable structure is arithmetical.

To show that the problem is Π_1^1-hard, we reduce the tiling problem of Proposition 2.22 to it. Recall that in this tiling problem, we are given a set T of tile types, and we wish to know whether the $\omega \times \omega$ grid can be tiled so that the color red appears infinitely often.

We proceed as in the proof of the lower bound of Theorem 8.8. We use the same atomic propositions $\mathrm{NORTH}_c, \mathrm{SOUTH}_c, \mathrm{EAST}_c, \mathrm{WEST}_c$ for each color c. For example, NORTH_c says that the north edge of the current tile is colored c. As in Theorem 8.8, for each tile type $A \in T$, we construct a formula TILE_A from these propositions

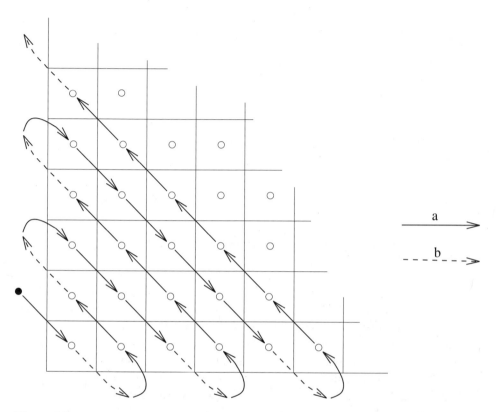

Figure 9.2

that is true at a state if the truth values of $\text{NORTH}_c, \text{SOUTH}_c, \text{EAST}_c, \text{WEST}_c$ at that
state describe a tile of type A.

The construction of the grid must be different here, since the extension of **PDL**
with the new program $a^\triangle b a^\triangle$ does not offer a direct way of setting up two atomic
programs, such as NORTH and EAST, to correspond to the two directions on a grid,
as was done in Theorems 3.60 and 8.8. The imaginary grid that we want to tile
must be set up in a subtler manner.

Denoting $a^\triangle b a^\triangle$ by α and a^*ab by β, let φ_{snake} be the formula

$$\langle ab \rangle 1 \quad \wedge \quad [\beta^*](\langle \beta \rangle 1 \wedge [a^*a][\alpha][ab]0 \wedge [\alpha][aa]0).$$

This formula forces the existence of an infinite path of the form $\sigma = aba^2ba^3ba^4b\cdots$.
Fig. 9.2 shows how this path is to be imagined as snaking through $\omega \times \omega$, and the
details of the proof are based on this correspondence.

We now have to state that the grid implicit in the path σ is tiled legally with tiles from T and that red occurs infinitely often. For this we use the formula RED from Theorem 8.8:

$$\text{RED} \quad \overset{\text{def}}{\Longleftrightarrow} \quad \text{NORTH}_{\text{red}} \vee \text{SOUTH}_{\text{red}} \vee \text{EAST}_{\text{red}} \vee \text{WEST}_{\text{red}}.$$

We then construct the general formula φ_T as the conjunction of φ_{snake} and the following formulas:

$$[(a \cup b)^* a] \bigvee_{A \in T} \text{TILE}_A \tag{9.3.1}$$

$$[(\beta\beta)^* a^* a] \bigwedge_{c \in C} ((\text{EAST}_c \to [\alpha a] \text{WEST}_c) \wedge (\text{NORTH}_c \to [\alpha a a] \text{SOUTH}_c)) \tag{9.3.2}$$

$$[(\beta\beta)^* \beta a^* a] \bigwedge_{c \in C} ((\text{EAST}_c \to [\alpha a a] \text{WEST}_c) \wedge (\text{NORTH}_c \to [\alpha a] \text{SOUTH}_c)) \tag{9.3.3}$$

$$[\beta^*] < \beta^* a^* a > \text{RED}. \tag{9.3.4}$$

Clause (9.3.1) associates tiles from T with those points of σ that follow a's, which are exactly the points of $\omega \times \omega$. Clauses (9.3.2) and (9.3.3) force the matching of colors by using $a^\Delta b a^\Delta$ to reach the correct neighbor, coming from above or below depending on the parity of β's. Finally, clause (9.3.4) can be shown to force the recurrence of red. This is not straightforward. In the case of the consequence problem of Theorem 8.8, the ability to substitute arbitrary formulas for the atomic proposition p made it easy to enforce the uniformity of properties in the grid. In contrast, here the $<\beta^*>$ portion of the formula could be satisfied along different paths that branch off the main path σ. Nevertheless, a König-like argument can be used to show that indeed there is an infinite recurrence of red in the tiling along the chosen path σ (Exercise 9.4).

It follows that φ_T is satisfiable if and only if T can tile $\omega \times \omega$ with red recurring infinitely often. ∎

The Π_1^1 result holds also for PDL extended with the two programs $a^\Delta b^\Delta$ and $b^\Delta a^\Delta$ (Exercise 9.5).

It is easy to show that the validity problem for context-free PDL in its entirety remains in Π_1^1. Together with the fact that $a^\Delta b a^\Delta$ is a context-free language, this yields an answer to the first question mentioned earlier: context-free PDL is Π_1^1-complete. As to the second question, Theorem 9.6 shows that the high undecidability phenomenon starts occurring even with the addition of one very simple nonregular program.

One-Letter Programs

We now turn to nonregular programs over a single letter. Consider the language of powers of 2:

$$a^{2^*} \stackrel{\text{def}}{=} \{a^{2^i} \mid i \geq 0\}.$$

Here we have:

THEOREM 9.7:   The validity problem for $\mathsf{PDL} + a^{2^*}$ is undecidable.

Proof sketch.   This proof is also carried out by a reduction from a tiling problem, but this time on a subset of the $\omega \times \omega$ grid. It makes essential use of simple properties of powers of 2.

The idea is to arrange the elements of the set $S = \{2^i + 2^j \mid i, j \geq 0\}$ in a grid as shown in Fig. 9.3. Elements of this set are reached by executing the new program a^{2^*} twice from the start state. The key observation in the proof has to do with the points that are reached when a^{2^*} is executed once more from a point u already in S. If u is not a power of two (that is, if $u = 2^i + 2^j$ for $i \neq j$), then the only points in S that can be reached by adding a third power of 2 to u are u's upper and right-hand neighbors in Fig. 9.3. If u is a power of 2 (that is, if $u = 2^i + 2^i$), then the points in S reached in this manner form an infinite set consisting of one row (finite) and one column (infinite) in the figure. A particularly delicate part of the proof involves setting things up so that the upper neighbor can be distinguished from the right-hand one. This is done by forcing a periodic marking of the grid with three diagonal stripes encoded by three new atomic programs. In this way, the two neighbors will always be associated with different detectable stripes. Exercise 9.6 asks for the details. ∎

It is actually possible to prove this result for powers of any fixed $k \geq 2$. Thus PDL with the addition of any language of the form $\{a^{k^i} \mid i \geq 0\}$ for fixed $k \geq 2$ is undecidable. Another class of one-letter extensions that has been proven to be undecidable consists of Fibonacci-like sequences:

THEOREM 9.8:   Let f_0, f_1 be arbitrary elements of $\mathbb{N}$ with $f_0 < f_1$, and let F be the sequence $f_0, f_1, f_2, \ldots$ generated by the recurrence $f_i = f_{i-1} + f_{i-2}$ for $i \geq 2$. Let $a^F \stackrel{\text{def}}{=} \{a^{f_i} \mid i \geq 0\}$. Then the validity problem for $\mathsf{PDL} + a^F$ is undecidable.

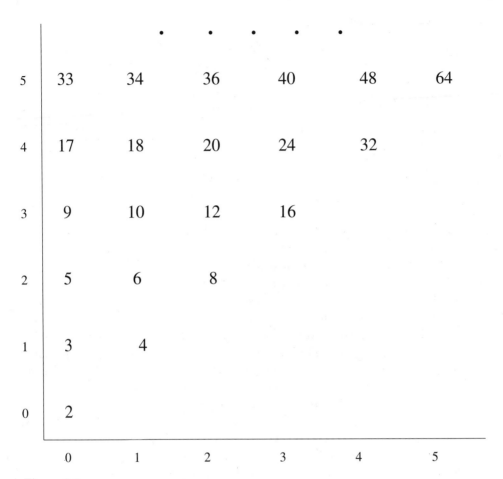

Figure 9.3

The proof of this result follows the general lines of the proof of Theorem 9.7, but is more complicated. It is based on a careful analysis of the properties of sums of elements of F.

In both these theorems, the fact that the sequences of a's in the programs grow exponentially is crucial to the proofs. Indeed, we know of no undecidability results for any one-letter extension in which the lengths of the sequences of a's grow subexponentially. Particularly intriguing are the cases of squares and cubes:

$$a^{*^2} \quad \stackrel{\text{def}}{=} \quad \{a^{i^2} \mid i \geq 0\},$$
$$a^{*^3} \quad \stackrel{\text{def}}{=} \quad \{a^{i^3} \mid i \geq 0\}.$$

Are $\mathsf{PDL} + a^{*^2}$ and $\mathsf{PDL} + a^{*^3}$ undecidable?

In Section 9.5 we shall describe a decidability result for a slightly restricted version of the squares extension, which seems to indicate that the full unrestricted version $\mathsf{PDL} + a^{*^2}$ is decidable too. However, we conjecture that for cubes the problem is undecidable. Interestingly, several classical open problems in number theory reduce to instances of the validity problem for $\mathsf{PDL} + a^{*^3}$. For example, while no one knows whether every integer greater than 10000 is the sum of five cubes, the following formula is valid if and only if the answer is yes:

$$[(a^{*^3})^5]p \quad \rightarrow \quad [a^{10001}a^*]p.$$

(The 5-fold and 10001-fold iterations have to be written out in full, of course.) If $\mathsf{PDL} + a^{*^3}$ were decidable, then we could compute the answer in a simple manner, at least in principle.

9.4 Decidable Extensions

We now turn to positive results. In Theorem 9.5 we showed that $\mathsf{PDL} + a^\Delta b^\Delta$ does not have the finite model property. Nevertheless, we have the following:

THEOREM 9.9:   The validity problem for $\mathsf{PDL} + a^\Delta b^\Delta$ is decidable.

When contrasted with Theorem 9.6, the decidability of $\mathsf{PDL} + a^\Delta b^\Delta$ is very surprising. We have two of the simplest nonregular languages—$a^\Delta b a^\Delta$ and $a^\Delta b^\Delta$— which are extremely similar, yet the addition of one to PDL yields high undecidability while the other leaves the logic decidable.

Theorem 9.9 was proved originally by showing that, although $\mathsf{PDL} + a^\Delta b^\Delta$ does not always admit finite models, it does admit finite *pushdown models*, in which transitions are labeled not only with atomic programs but also with push and pop instructions for a particular kind of stack. A close study of the proof (which relies heavily on the idiosyncrasies of the language $a^\Delta b^\Delta$) suggests that the decidability or undecidability has to do with the manner in which an automaton accepts the languages involved. For example, in the usual way of accepting $a^\Delta b a^\Delta$, a pushdown automaton (PDA) reading an a will carry out a push or a pop, depending upon its location in the input word. However, in the standard way of accepting $a^\Delta b^\Delta$, the a's are always pushed and the b's are always popped, regardless of the location; the input symbol alone determines what the automaton does. More recent work, which we now set out to describe, has yielded a general decidability result that confirms this intuition. It is of special interest due to its generality, since it does not depend on specific programs.

DEFINITION 9.10:   Let $M = (Q, \Sigma, \Gamma, q_0, z_0, \delta)$ be a PDA that accepts by empty stack. We say that M is *simple-minded* if, whenever $\delta(q, \sigma, \gamma) = (p, b)$, then for each q' and γ', either $\delta(q', \sigma, \gamma') = (p, b)$ or $\delta(q', \sigma, \gamma')$ is undefined. A context-free language is said to be *simple-minded* (a simple-minded CFL) if there exists a simple-minded PDA that accepts it.

In other words, the action of a simple-minded automaton is determined uniquely by the input symbol; the state and stack symbol are only used to help determine whether the machine halts (rejecting the input) or continues. Note that such an automaton is necessarily deterministic.

It is noteworthy that simple-minded PDAs accept a large fragment of the context-free languages, including $a^\Delta b^\Delta$ and $b^\Delta a^\Delta$, as well as all balanced parenthesis languages (Dyck sets) and many of their intersections with regular languages.

EXAMPLE 9.11:   Let $M = (\{q_0, q\}, \Sigma, \Gamma, q_0, z_0, \delta)$ be a PDA, where $\Sigma = \{a, b\}$, $\Gamma = \{z, z_0\}$, and the transition function δ is given by:

$$\begin{aligned}
\delta(q_0, a, z_0) &= (q_0, \mathbf{pop}; \mathbf{push}(z)) \\
\delta(q_0, a, z) &= (q_0, \mathbf{push}(z)) \\
\delta(q_0, b, z) &= (q, \mathbf{pop}) \\
\delta(q, b, z) &= (q, \mathbf{pop}).
\end{aligned}$$

The function δ is undefined for all other possibilities. Since M accepts by empty stack, the language accepted is precisely $\{a^i b^i \mid i \geq 1\}$. The automaton M is simple-minded, since it always performs $\mathbf{push}(z)$ when the input is a and $\mathbf{pop}$ when the input is b.

EXAMPLE 9.12:   Let $M = (\{q\}, \Sigma \cup \Sigma', \Gamma, q, z_0, \delta)$ be a PDA, where $\Sigma = \{[,]\}$, Σ' is some finite alphabet of interest disjoint from Σ, $\Gamma = \{[, z_0\}$, and the transition function δ is given by:

$$\begin{aligned}
\delta(q, [, z_0) &= (q, \mathbf{pop}; \mathbf{push}([)) \\
\delta(q, a, [) &= (q, \mathbf{sp}) \quad \text{for } a \in \Sigma' \\
\delta(q,], [) &= (q, \mathbf{pop}).
\end{aligned}$$

Here $\mathbf{sp}$ stands for "stay put," and can be considered an abbreviation for $\mathbf{push}(\varepsilon)$. The function δ is undefined for all other possibilities. Since the automaton only accepts by empty stack, the language accepted by M is precisely the set of expressions over $\Sigma \cup \Sigma'$ beginning with [and ending with] in which the parentheses are balances. The automaton M is simple-minded, since it always performs $\mathbf{push}([)$ when the input is [, $\mathbf{pop}$ when the input is], and $\mathbf{sp}$ when the input is a letter from Σ'.

The main purpose of this entire section is to prove the following:

THEOREM 9.13:   If L is accepted by a simple-minded PDA, then PDL + L is decidable.

First, however, we must discuss a certain class of models of PDL.

Tree Models

We first prove that PDL + L has the *tree model property*. Let ψ be a formula of PDL + L containing n distinct atomic programs, including those used in L. A *tree structure* for ψ in PDL + L is a Kripke frame $\mathfrak{K} = (K, \mathfrak{m}_{\mathfrak{K}})$ such that

- K is a nonempty prefix-closed subset of $[k]^*$, where $[k] = \{0, \ldots, k-1\}$ for some $k \geq 0$ a multiple of n;
- for all atomic programs a, $\mathfrak{m}_{\mathfrak{K}}(a) \subseteq \{(x, xi) \mid x \in [k]^*, \ i \in [k]\}$;
- if a, b are atomic programs and $a \neq b$, then $\mathfrak{m}_{\mathfrak{K}}(a) \cap \mathfrak{m}_{\mathfrak{K}}(b) = \varnothing$.

A tree structure $\mathfrak{K} = (K, \mathfrak{m}_{\mathfrak{K}})$ is a *tree model* for ψ if $\mathfrak{K}, \varepsilon \vDash \psi$, where ε is the null string, the root of the tree.

We now show that for any L, if a PDL + L formula ψ is satisfiable, then it has a tree model. To do this we first unwind any model of ψ into a tree as in Theorem 3.74, then use a construction similar to Exercise 3.42 to create a substructure in which every state has a finite number of successors. In order to proceed, we want to be able to refer to the Fischer–Ladner closure $FL(\psi)$ of a formula ψ in PDL+L. The definition of Section 6.1 can be adopted as is, except that we take $FL^{\square}([L]\sigma) = \varnothing$

(we will not need it). Note however that if $[L]\sigma \in FL(\psi)$, then $\sigma \in FL(\psi)$ as well.

Now for the tree result:

PROPOSITION 9.14:   A formula ψ in $\mathsf{PDL} + L$ is satisfiable iff it has a tree model.

Proof Suppose that $\mathfrak{K}, u \vDash \psi$ for some Kripke frame $\mathfrak{K} = (K, \mathfrak{m}_{\mathfrak{K}})$ and $u \in K$. Let C_i for $0 \le i < 2^{|FL(\psi)|}$ be an enumeration of the subsets of $FL(\psi)$, let $k = n2^{|FL(\psi)|}$, and let

$$\mathbf{Th}_\psi(t) \;\overset{\text{def}}{=}\; \{\xi \in FL(\psi) \mid \mathfrak{K}, t \vDash \xi\}.$$

To show that ψ has a tree model, we first define a partial mapping $\rho : [k]^* \to 2^K$ by induction on the length of words in $[k]^*$:

$$\rho(\varepsilon) \;\overset{\text{def}}{=}\; \{u\}$$
$$\rho(x(i+nj)) \;\overset{\text{def}}{=}\; \{t \in K \mid \exists s \in \rho(x)\ (s,t) \in \mathfrak{m}_{\mathfrak{K}}(a_i) \text{ and } C_j = \mathbf{Th}_\psi(t)\}$$

for all $0 \le i < n$ and $0 \le j < 2^{|FL(\psi)|}$. Note that if $\rho(x)$ is the empty set, then so is $\rho(xi)$.

We now define a Kripke frame $\mathfrak{K}' = (K', \mathfrak{m}_{\mathfrak{K}'})$ as follows:

$$K' \;\overset{\text{def}}{=}\; \{x \mid \rho(x) \ne \varnothing\},$$
$$\mathfrak{m}_{\mathfrak{K}'}(a_i) \;\overset{\text{def}}{=}\; \{(x, x(i+nj)) \mid 0 \le j < 2^{|FL(\psi)|},\ x(i+nj) \in K'\},$$
$$\mathfrak{m}_{\mathfrak{K}'}(p) \;\overset{\text{def}}{=}\; \{x \mid \exists t \in \rho(x)\ t \in \mathfrak{m}_{\mathfrak{K}}(p)\}.$$

Note that $\mathfrak{m}_{\mathfrak{K}'}$ is well defined by the definitions of ρ and $\mathfrak{m}_{\mathfrak{K}}$. It is not difficult to show that $\mathfrak{K}'$ is a tree structure and that if $x \in K'$ and $\xi \in FL(\psi)$, then $\mathfrak{K}', x \vDash \xi$ iff $\mathfrak{K}, t \vDash \xi$ for some $t \in \rho(x)$. In particular, $\mathfrak{K}', \varepsilon \vDash \psi$.

The converse is immediate. ∎

Let $CL(\psi)$ be the set of all formulas in $FL(\psi)$ and their negations. Applying the De Morgan laws and the PDL identities

$$\neg[\alpha]\varphi \;\leftrightarrow\; {<}\alpha{>}\neg\varphi$$
$$\neg{<}\alpha{>}\varphi \;\leftrightarrow\; [\alpha]\neg\varphi$$
$$\neg\neg\varphi \;\leftrightarrow\; \varphi$$

from left to right, we can assume without loss of generality that negations in formulas of $CL(\psi)$ are applied to atomic formulas only.

Let

$$CL^{\perp}(\psi) \quad \overset{\text{def}}{=} \quad CL(\psi) \cup \{\perp\}.$$

We would now like to embed the tree model $\mathfrak{K}' = (K', \mathfrak{m}_{\mathfrak{K}'})$ constructed above into a certain labeled complete k-ary tree. Every node in K' will be labeled by the formulas in $CL(\psi)$ that it satisfies, and all the nodes not in K' are labeled by the special symbol $\perp$. These trees satisfy some special properties, as we shall now see.

DEFINITION 9.15:   A *unique diamond path Hintikka tree* (or UDH tree for short) for a $\mathsf{PDL} + L$ formula ψ with atomic programs $a_0, \dots, a_{n-1}$ consists of a k-ary tree $[k]^*$ for some k a multiple of n and two labeling functions

$$T : [k]^* \quad \rightarrow \quad 2^{CL^{\perp}(\psi)}$$
$$\Phi : [k]^* \quad \rightarrow \quad CL^{\perp}(\psi)$$

such that $\psi \in T(\varepsilon)$; for all $x \in [k]^*$, $\Phi(x)$ is either a single diamond formula or the special symbol $\perp$; and

1. either $T(x) = \{\perp\}$ or $\perp \notin T(x)$, and in the latter case, $\xi \in T(x)$ iff $\neg\xi \notin T(x)$ for all $\xi \in FL(\psi)$;

2. if $\xi \rightarrow \sigma \in T(x)$ and $\xi \in T(x)$, then $\sigma \in T(x)$, and $\xi \wedge \sigma \in T(x)$ iff both $\xi \in T(x)$ and $\sigma \in T(x)$;

3. if $<\gamma>\xi \in T(x)$, and

   (a) if γ is an atomic program a_i, then there exists j such that $i + nj < k$ and $\xi \in T(x(i + nj))$;

   (b) if $\gamma = \alpha \,;\, \beta$, then $<\alpha><\beta>\xi \in T(x)$;

   (c) if $\gamma = \alpha \cup \beta$, then either $<\alpha>\xi \in T(x)$ or $<\beta>\xi \in T(x)$;

   (d) if $\gamma = \varphi?$, then both $\varphi \in T(x)$ and $\xi \in T(x)$;

   (e) if $\gamma = \alpha^*$, then there exists a word $w = w_1 \cdots w_m \in CS(\alpha^*)$ and $u_0, \dots, u_m \in [k]^*$ such that $u_0 = x$, $\xi \in T(u_m)$, and for all $1 \leq i \leq m$, $\Phi(u_i) = <\alpha^*>\xi$; moreover, if w_i is $\varphi?$, then $\varphi \in T(u_{i-1})$ and $u_i = u_{i-1}$, and if w_i is $a_j \in \Pi_0$, then $u_i = u_{i-1}r$, where $r = j + n\ell < k$ for some ℓ;

   (f) if $\gamma = L$, then there exists a word $w = w_1 \cdots w_m \in L$ and $u_0, \dots, u_m \in [k]^*$ such that $u_0 = x$, $\xi \in T(u_m)$, and for all $1 \leq i \leq m$, $\Phi(u_i) = <L>\xi$; moreover, if $w_i = a_j \in \Pi_0$, then $u_i = u_{i-1}r$, where $r = j + n\ell < k$ for some ℓ;

4. if $[\gamma]\xi \in T(x)$, and

(a)if γ is an atomic program a_j, then for all $r = j + n\ell < k$, if $T(xr) \neq \{\bot\}$ then $\xi \in T(xr)$;

(b)if $\gamma = \alpha\,;\,\beta$, then $[\alpha]\,[\beta]\xi \in T(x)$;

(c)if $\gamma = \alpha \cup \beta$, then both $[\alpha]\xi \in T(x)$ and $[\beta]\xi \in T(x)$;

(d)if $\gamma = \varphi?$ and if $\varphi \in T(x)$, then $\xi \in T(x)$;

(e)if $\gamma = \alpha^*$, then $\xi \in T(x)$ and $[\alpha]\,[\alpha^*]\xi \in T(x)$;

(f)if $\gamma = L$, then for all words $w = w_1 \cdots w_m \in L$ and $u_0, \ldots, u_m \in [k]^*$ such that $u_0 = x$ and for all $1 \leq i \leq m$, if $w_i = a_j \in \Pi_0$, then $u_i = u_{i-1}r$, where $r = j + n\ell < k$ for some ℓ, we have that either $T(u_m) = \{\bot\}$ or $\xi \in T(u_m)$.

PROPOSITION 9.16:   A formula ψ in PDL $+ L$ has a UDH if and only if it has a model.

Proof   Exercise 9.9.   ∎

Pushdown Automata on Infinite Trees

We now discuss pushdown automata on infinite trees. We show later that such an automaton accepts precisely the UDH's of some formula.

A *pushdown k-ary ω-tree automaton* (PTA) is a machine

$$M = (Q, \Sigma, \Gamma, q_0, z_0, \delta, F),$$

where Q is a finite set of states, Σ is a finite input alphabet, Γ is a finite stack alphabet, $q_0 \in Q$ is the initial state, $z_0 \in \Gamma$ is the initial stack symbol, and $F \subseteq Q$ is the set of accepting states.

The transition function δ is of type

$$\delta : Q \times \Sigma \times \Gamma \;\rightarrow\; (2^{(Q \times B)^k} \cup 2^{Q \times B}),$$

where $B = \{\mathbf{pop}\} \cup \{\mathbf{push}(w) \mid w \in \Gamma^*\}$. The transition function reflects the fact that M works on trees with outdegree k that are labeled by Σ. The number of rules in δ is denoted by $|\delta|$.

A good informal way of viewing PTA's is as a pushdown machine that operates on an infinite tree of outdegree k. At each node u of the tree, the machine can read the input symbol $T(u)$ there. It can either stay at that node, performing some action on the stack and entering a new state as determined by an element of $Q \times B$; or it can split into k copies, each copy moving down to one of the k children of u, as determined by an element of $(Q \times B)^k$.

The set of *stack configurations* is $S = \{\gamma z_0 \mid \gamma \in \Gamma^*\}$. The top of the stack is to the left. The *initial stack configuration* is z_0. A *configuration* is a pair $(q, \gamma) \in Q \times S$. The *initial configuration* is (q_0, z_0). Let head $: S \rightarrow \Gamma$ be a function given by $\mathrm{head}(z\gamma) = z$. This describes the letter on top of the stack. If the stack is empty, then head is undefined.

In order to capture the effect of δ on stack configurations, we define the partial function apply $: B \times S \rightarrow S$ that provides the new contents of the stack:

$$\mathrm{apply}(\mathbf{pop}, z\gamma) \stackrel{\text{def}}{=} \gamma;$$
$$\mathrm{apply}(\mathbf{push}(w), \gamma) \stackrel{\text{def}}{=} w\gamma.$$

The latter includes the case $w = \varepsilon$, in which case the stack is unchanged; we abbreviate $\mathbf{push}(\varepsilon)$ by $\mathbf{sp}$.

The automaton M runs on complete labeled k-ary trees over Σ. That is, the input consists of the complete k-ary tree $[k]^*$ with labeling function

$$T : [k]^* \rightarrow \Sigma.$$

We denote the labeled tree by T. A *computation* of M on input T is a labeling

$$C : [k]^* \rightarrow (Q \times S)^+$$

of the nodes of T with sequences of configurations satisfying the following conditions. If $u \in [k]^*$, $T(u) = a \in \Sigma$, and $C(u) = ((p_0, \gamma_0), \ldots, (p_m, \gamma_m))$, then

- $(p_{i+1}, b_{i+1}) \in \delta(p_i, a, \mathrm{head}(\gamma_i))$ and $\mathrm{apply}(b_{i+1}, \gamma_i) = \gamma_{i+1}$ for $0 \le i < m$; and
- there exists $((r_0, b_0), \ldots, (r_{k-1}, b_{k-1})) \in \delta(p_m, a, \mathrm{head}(\gamma_m))$ such that for all $0 \le j < k$, the first element of $C(uj)$ is $(r_j, \mathrm{apply}(b_j, \gamma_m))$.

Intuitively, a computation is an inductive labeling of the nodes of the tree $[k]^*$ with configurations of the machine. The label of a node is the sequence of configurations that the machine goes through while visiting that node.

A computation C is said to be *Büchi accepting*, or just *accepting* for short, if the first configuration of $C(\varepsilon)$ is the start configuration (q_0, z_0) and every path in the tree contains infinitely many nodes u such that $q \in F$ for some $(q, \gamma) \in C(u)$. A tree T is *accepted* by M if there exists an accepting computation of M on T.

The *emptiness problem* is the problem of determining whether a given automaton M accepts some tree.

A PTA that uses only the symbol $\mathbf{sp}$ from B (that is, never $\mathbf{push}$es nor $\mathbf{pop}$s) is simply a Büchi k-ary ω-tree automaton as defined in Vardi and Wolper (1986a). Our definition is a simplified version of the more general definition of stack tree automata from Harel and Raz (1994) and is similar to that appearing in Saudi (1989). If $k = 1$, the infinite trees become infinite sequences.

Our main result is the following.

THEOREM 9.17:   The emptiness problem for PTA's is decidable.

The proof in Harel and Raz (1994) establishes decidability in 4-fold exponential time for STA's and in triple-exponential time for PTA's. A single-exponential-time algorithm for PTA's is given by Peng and Iyer (1995).

Decidability for Simple-Minded Languages

Given a simple-minded CFL L, we now describe the construction of a PTA A_ψ for each ψ in PDL + L. This PTA will be shown to accept precisely the UDH trees of the formula ψ. The PTA A_ψ is a parallel composition of three machines. The first, called A_ℓ, is a tree automaton with no stack that tests the input tree for local consistency properties. The second component of A_ψ, called $A_\square$, is a tree PDA that deals with box formulas that contain L. The third component, called $A_\diamond$, is a tree PDA that deals with the diamond formulas of $CL(\psi)$.

Let $M_L = (Q, \Sigma, \Gamma, q_0, z_0, \rho)$ be a simple-minded PDA that accepts the language L, and let ψ be a formula in PDL + L. Define the function $\Omega : \Sigma \times \Gamma \to \Gamma^*$ by: $\Omega(a, z) = w$ if there exist $p, q \in Q$ such that $\delta(p, a, z) = (q, w)$. Note that for a simple-minded PDA, Ω is a partial function.

The *local automaton* for ψ is

$$A_\ell \stackrel{\text{def}}{=} (2^{CL^\perp(\psi)}, 2^{CL^\perp(\psi)}, N_\psi, \delta, 2^{CL^\perp(\psi)}),$$

where:

- $CL^\perp(\psi) = CL(\psi) \cup \{\perp\}$;
- the starting set N_ψ consists of all sets s such that $\psi \in s$;
- $(s_0, \ldots, s_{k-1}) \in \delta(s, a)$ iff $s = a$, and

    —either $s = \{\perp\}$ or $\perp \notin s$, and in the latter case, $\xi \in s$ iff $\neg\xi \notin s$;

    —if $\xi \to \sigma \in s$ and $\xi \in s$, then $\sigma \in s$, and $\xi \wedge \sigma \in s$ iff both $\xi \in s$ and $\sigma \in s$;

    —if $<\gamma>\xi \in s$, then:

       *if γ is an atomic program a_j, then there exists $r = j + n\ell < k$ for some ℓ such that $\xi \in s_r$;

       *if $\gamma = \alpha \,;\, \beta$, then $<\alpha><\beta>\xi \in s$;

       *if $\gamma = \alpha \cup \beta$, then either $<\alpha>\xi \in s$ or $<\beta>\xi \in s$;

*if $\gamma = \varphi$? then both $\varphi \in s$ and $\xi \in s$;

−if $[\gamma]\xi \in s$, then:

*if γ is an atomic program a_j, then for all $r = j + n\ell < k$, if $s_r \neq \{\bot\}$ then $\xi \in s$;

*if $\gamma = \alpha\,;\,\beta$, then $[\alpha]\,[\beta]\xi \in s$;

*if $\gamma = \alpha \cup \beta$, then both $[\alpha]\xi \in s$ and $[\beta]\xi \in s$;

*if $\gamma = \varphi$? and $\varphi \in s$, then $\xi \in s$;

*if $\gamma = \alpha^*$, then both $\xi \in s$ and $[\alpha]\,[\alpha^*]\xi \in s$.

PROPOSITION 9.18:   The automaton A_ℓ accepts precisely the trees that satisfy conditions 1, 2, 3(a)–(d), and 4(a)–(e) of Definition 9.15.

Proof A computation of an automaton M on an infinite tree $T : [k]^* \to \Sigma$ is an infinite tree $C : [k]^* \to Q'$, where Q' is the set of states of M. Clearly, if T satisfies conditions 1, 2, 3(a)–(d) and 4(a)–(e) of Definition 9.15, then T is also an accepting computation of A_ℓ on T.

Conversely, if C is an accepting computation of A_ℓ on some tree T, then C is itself an infinite tree over $2^{CL^\perp(\psi)}$ that satisfies the desired conditions. By the first rule of A_ℓ, for every node a we have $a = s$, hence $T = C$, and T satisfies conditions 1, 2, 3(a)–(d), and 4(a)–(e) of Definition 9.15. ∎

The aim of the the next component of A_ψ is to check satisfaction of condition 4(f) of Definition 9.15, the condition that deals with box formulas containing the symbol L.

The *box automaton* for ψ is

$$A_\square \overset{\text{def}}{=} (Q_\square,\, 2^{CL^\perp(\psi)},\, \Gamma \times 2^{CL^\perp(\psi)},\, q_0,\, (z_0, \varnothing),\, \delta,\, Q_\square),$$

where $Q_\square = Q$ and δ is given by: $((p_0, w_0), \ldots, (p_{k-1}, w_{k-1})) \in \delta(q, \mathbf{a}, (z, \mathbf{s}))$ iff

1. either $a = \bot$ or $\mathbf{s} \subseteq \mathbf{a}$, and

2. for all $0 \leq j < n$ and for all $i = j + n\ell < k$ we have:

   (a) if $\rho(q, a_j, z) = (q', \varepsilon)$, then $p_i = q'$ and $w_i = \varepsilon$,

   (b) if $\rho(q, a_j, z) = (q', z)$, then $p_i = q'$ and $w_i = (z, \mathbf{s} \cup \mathbf{s}')$,

   (c) if $\rho(q, a_j, z) = (q', zz')$, then $p_i = q'$ and $w_i = (z, \mathbf{s} \cup \mathbf{s}'), (z', \varnothing)$, and

   (d) if $\rho(q, a_j, z)$ is undefined, then

       i. if $\rho(q_0, a_j, z_0)$ is undefined, then $p_i = q_0$ and $w_i = (z_0, \varnothing)$;

ii.if $\rho(q_0, a_j, z_0) = (q', z_0)$, then $p_i = q'$ and $w_i = (z_0, \mathbf{s}')$; and

iii.if $\rho(q_0, a_j, z_0) = (q', z_0 z)$, then $p_i = q'$ and $w_i = (z_0, \mathbf{s}'), (z', \varnothing)$.

Here, if $\rho(q_0, a_j, z_0)$ is defined and $[L]\xi \in \mathbf{a}$, then $\xi \in \mathbf{s}'$, otherwise $\mathbf{s}' = \varnothing$.

In clause 1 we check whether old box promises that involve the language L are kept, while in clause 2 we put new such box promises on the stack to be checked later on. Note that the stack behavior of $A_\square$ depends only on the path in the tree and not on the values of the tree nodes.

LEMMA 9.19:   Let $x \in [k]^*$ and $T : [k]^* \to 2^{CL^\perp(\psi)}$, and let

$$C_\square(x) \quad \stackrel{\text{def}}{=} \quad (q, (z_0, \mathbf{s}_0), \dots, (z_m, \mathbf{s}_m)),$$

where $C_\square$ is a computation of $A_\square$ over T. Then for each $w = a_{j_1} \cdots a_{j_\ell} \in L$ and $r_m = j_m + n\ell_m < k$, the following two conditions hold:

- $C_\square(xr_1 \cdots r_\ell) = (q', (z_0, \mathbf{s}_0), \dots, (z_{m-1}, \mathbf{s}_{m-1}), (z_m, \mathbf{s}'_m))$;
- $\mathbf{s}'_m$ contains all formulas ξ for which $[L]\xi \in T(x)$.

Proof Define $\psi_m : Q \times (\Gamma \times 2^{CL^\perp(\psi)})^+ \to Q_\square \times \Gamma^+$ by

$$\psi(q, (z_0, \mathbf{s}_0) \cdots (z_m, \mathbf{s}_m) \cdots (z_r, \mathbf{s}_r)) \quad \stackrel{\text{def}}{=} \quad (q, z_m, \dots, z_r).$$

Let $(q_0, \gamma_0) \cdots (q_\ell, \gamma_\ell)$ be a computation of M that accepts w. Since w is in L, for all $r_1 = j_1 + n\ell_1 < k$ we have that $\delta(q_0, a_j, z_0)$ is defined; hence by the definition of $\mathbf{s}'$ in $A_\square$ we have that

$$C_\square(xr_1) \quad = \quad (q', (z_0, \mathbf{s}_0), \dots, (z_m, \mathbf{s}'_m), \gamma'),$$

where γ' may be empty and $\mathbf{s}'_m$ contains all formulas ξ such that $[L]\xi \in T(x)$.

We proceed by induction on i to prove that $\psi_m(C_\square(xr_1 \cdots r_i)) = (q_i, \gamma_i)$ for all $1 \le i \le \ell$. The base case has just been established, and the general case follows immediately from the definition of $A_\square$. For $i = \ell$, this proves the lemma. ∎

PROPOSITION 9.20:   The box automaton $A_\square$ accepts precisely the trees that satisfy condition 4(f) of Definition 9.15.

Proof We must show that $A_\square$ has an accepting computation over some tree T iff for all $x \in [k]^*$ the following holds: if $[L]\xi \in T(x)$, then for all $r_m = j_m + n\ell_m < k$, we have $\xi \in T(xr_1 \cdots r_\ell)$ or $T(xr_1 \cdots r_\ell) = \{\perp\}$.

($\Longrightarrow$) Suppose for a contradiction that there exist $x_0 \in [k]^*$, $[L]\xi \in T(x_0)$, and $w = a_{j_1}, \ldots, a_{j_\ell} \in L$ such that $T(xr_1 \cdots r_\ell) \neq \{\bot\}$ and $\xi \notin T(xr_1 \cdots r_\ell)$ for some $r_m = j_m + n\ell m < k$. Let C be any computation of $A_\square$. By Lemma 9.19, we know that $C(xr_1 \cdots r_\ell) = (q', (z_0, s_0') \cdots (z_m, s_m'))$, and $\xi \in s_m'$. This yields a contradiction to our assumption, since clause 1 in the definition of $A_\square$ requires that $\mathbf{s} \subseteq \mathbf{a}$, which implies $\xi \in T(xr_1 \cdots r_\ell)$.

($\Longleftarrow$) If T satisfies the above condition and at each stage of the computation we add to $\mathbf{s}'$ exactly all ξ for which $[L]\xi \in T(x)$ when $\delta(q_0, a_j, z_0)$ is defined and add $\varnothing$ otherwise, we obtain an infinite computation of $A_\square$ over T. This computation is accepting because $F_\square = Q_\square$. ■

The third component of A_ψ deals with diamond formulas. Note that unlike the box case, some diamond formulas are non-local in nature, thus cannot be handled by the local automaton. The special nature of UDH's is the key for the following construction, since it ensures that each diamond formula is satisfied along a unique path. All $A_\diamond$ must do is guess nondeterministically which successor lies on the appropriate path and check that there is indeed a finite path through that successor satisfying the diamond formula.

For technical reasons, we must define a finite automaton for each α such that $\langle \alpha^* \rangle \xi \in CL(\psi)$ for some ξ. Define $\Sigma_\psi = \Pi \cup \{\varphi? \mid \varphi? \in CL(\psi)\}$, and let $M_\alpha = (Q_\alpha, \Sigma_\psi, q_{0_\alpha}, \delta_\alpha, F_\alpha)$ be an automaton for $CS(\alpha)$.

The *diamond automaton* for ψ is

$$A_\diamond \overset{\text{def}}{=} (Q_\diamond, 2^{CL^\perp(\psi)}, \Gamma \times \{0,1\}, (1, \bot, \bot), (z_0, 0), \delta, F_\diamond),$$

where

- $Q_\diamond \overset{\text{def}}{=} \{0,1\} \times CL^\perp(\psi) \times (Q \cup \bigcup\{Q_\alpha \mid \langle \alpha^* \rangle \xi \in CL(\psi) \text{ for some } \xi\})$. The first component is used to indicate acceptance, the second points to the diamond formula that is being verified or to $\bot$ if no such formula exists, and the third is used to simulate the computation of either M_L or M_α.

- $F_\diamond$ is the set of all triples in $Q_\diamond$ containing 1 in the first component or $\bot$ in the second.

- Define

$$\psi_M(a_j, z) \overset{\text{def}}{=} \begin{cases} \varepsilon & \text{if } \Omega(a_j, z) = \varepsilon \\ (z, 0) & \text{if } \Omega(a_j, z) = z \\ (z, 0)(z', 1) & \text{if } \Omega(a_j, z) = zz' \end{cases}$$

and

$$\psi_N(a_j, z) \;\overset{\text{def}}{=}\; \begin{cases} \varepsilon & \text{if} \quad \Omega(a_j, z) = \varepsilon \\ (z, 1) & \text{if} \quad \Omega(a_j, z) = z \\ (z, 1)(z', 1) & \text{if} \quad \Omega(a_j, z) = zz'. \end{cases}$$

Then $((p_0, w_0), \dots, (p_{k-1}, w_{k-1})) \in \delta((c, g, q), \mathbf{a}, (z, b))$ iff the following three conditions hold:

1. (a) for each $<\alpha>^*\chi \in \mathbf{a}$, either $\chi \in \mathbf{a}$ or there exists $i = j + n\ell < k$ and a word $v = \varphi_1? \cdots \varphi_m?$ such that $\{\varphi_1, \dots, \varphi_m\} \subseteq \mathbf{a}$ and $p_i = (c_i, <\alpha>\chi, p)$, $p \in \delta_\alpha(q_{0\alpha}, va_j)$, and $w_i = \psi_M(a_j, z)$;

   (b) if $<L>\chi \in \mathbf{a}$, then there exists $i = j + n\ell < k$ such that $p_i = (c_i, <L>\chi, p)$, $p = \rho(q_{0\alpha}, a_j, z_0)$, and $w_i = \psi_N(a_j, z)$;

2. (a) if $\xi = <L>\chi$, then either we are in an accepting state (that is, $c = 1$, $b = 0$, and $\chi \in \mathbf{a}$) or $c = 0$ and there exists $i = j + n\ell < k$ such that $p_i = (c_i, <L>\chi, p)$, $p = \rho(q, a_j, z)$, $w_i = \psi_N(a_j, z)$, and if $w_i = \varepsilon$ then $b = 1$;

   (b) if $\xi = <\alpha>\chi$, then there exists a word $v = \varphi_1? \cdots \varphi_m?$ such that $\{\varphi_1, \dots, \varphi_m\} \subseteq \mathbf{a}$ and either we are in an accepting state (that is, $c = 1$, $\delta_\alpha(q, v) \in F_\alpha$, and $\chi \in \mathbf{a}$) or $c = 0$ and there exists $i = j + n\ell < k$ such that $p_i = (c_i, <\alpha>\chi, p)$, $p \in \delta_\alpha(q_{0\alpha}, va_j)$, and $w_i = \psi_N(a_j, z)$;

3. for all $0 \le j < n$ and $i = j + n\ell < k$, we have $w_i = \psi_N(a_j, z)$ or $w_i = \psi_M(a_j, z)$.

The idea here is much simpler than it might appear from the detailed construction. Condition 1 takes care of new diamond formulas. Each such formula is either satisfied in $\mathbf{a}$ or is written in the machine to be satisfied later. Condition 2 takes care of old promises which are either fulfilled or remain as promises in the machine. Condition 3 deals with the stack. We make sure that all stack operations coincide with those of M_L and use the extra bit on the stack to indicate the beginning of new simulations of M_L.

PROPOSITION 9.21:   The automaton $A_\diamond$ accepts precisely the trees that satisfy both conditions 3(e) and 3(f) of Definition 9.15.

Proof Exercise 9.10.   ∎

LEMMA 9.22:   There is a pushdown k-ary tree automaton A_ψ such that $L(A_\psi) = L(A_\ell) \cap L(A_\diamond) \cap L(A_\square)$ and the size of A_ψ is at most $|A_\ell| \cdot |A_\diamond| \cdot |A_\square|$.

Proof Define

$$A_\psi \overset{\text{def}}{=} (Q_\psi, 2^{CL^\perp(\psi)}, \Gamma_\psi, q_{0\psi}, z_{0\psi}, \delta_\psi, F_\psi)$$

as follows:

$$Q_\psi \overset{\text{def}}{=} Q_\ell \times Q_\square \times Q_\diamond$$

$$q_{0\psi} \overset{\text{def}}{=} N_\psi \times q_{0\square} \times q_{0\diamond}$$

$$F_\psi \overset{\text{def}}{=} Q_\ell \times Q_\square \times F_\diamond$$

$$\Gamma_\psi \overset{\text{def}}{=} \Gamma_\square \times \Gamma_\diamond$$

$$z_{0\psi} \overset{\text{def}}{=} z_{0\square} \times z_{0\diamond}$$

and the transition function δ_ψ is the Cartesian product of the appropriate δ functions of the component automata.

Since all the states of both the local automaton and the box automaton are accepting states, and since we have taken the third component of A_ψ to be $F_\diamond$, the accepted language is as required. Also, the size bound is immediate. We have only to show that this definition indeed describes a tree PDA; in other words, we have to show that the transition function δ_ψ is well defined. This is due to the simple-mindedness of the language L. More formally, for each $x \in [k]^*$ and each $i_m = j_m + n\ell_m < k$, the stack operations of $A_\diamond$ are the same as the stack operations of $A_\square$, since they both depend only on the letter a_{j_m}. ∎

Lemma 9.22, together with the preceding results, yields:

PROPOSITION 9.23: Given a formula ψ in PDL $+ L$, where L is a simple-minded CFL, one can construct a PTA A_ψ such that ψ has a model iff there is some tree T accepted by A_ψ.

Theorem 9.13 now follows.

Other Decidable Classes

Using techniques very similar to those of the previous proof, we can obtain another general decidability result involving languages accepted by deterministic stack automata. A stack automaton is a one-way PDA whose head can travel up and down the stack reading its contents, but can make changes only at the top of the stack. Stack automata can accept non-context-free languages such as $a^\Delta b^\Delta c^\Delta$ and its generalizations $a_1^\Delta a_2^\Delta \ldots a_n^\Delta$ for any n, as well as many variants thereof. It would be nice to be able to prove decidability of PDL when augmented by any language accepted by such a machine, but this is not known. What has been proven, however, is that if each word in such a language is preceded by a new symbol to mark its beginning, then the enriched PDL is decidable:

THEOREM 9.24:   Let $e \notin \Pi_0$, and let L be a language over Π_0 that is accepted by a deterministic stack automaton. If we let eL denote the language $\{eu \mid u \in L\}$, then PDL $+ eL$ is decidable.

While Theorems 9.13 and 9.24 are general and cover many languages, they do not prove decidability of PDL $+ a^{\Delta}b^{\Delta}c^{\Delta}$, which may be considered the simplest non-context-free extension of PDL. Nevertheless, the constructions used in the proofs of the two general results have been combined to yield:

THEOREM 9.25:   PDL $+ a^{\Delta}b^{\Delta}c^{\Delta}$ is decidable.

9.5   More on One-Letter Programs

A Decidable Case

The results of the previous section provide sufficient conditions for an extension of PDL with a nonregular language to remain decidable.[3] If we consider one-letter languages, none of these results apply. Theorem 9.13 involves context-free languages, and by Parikh's theorem (see Kozen (1997a)) nonregular one-letter languages cannot be context-free; Theorem 9.24 involves adding a new letter to each word, and therefore does not apply to one-letter languages; and Theorem 9.25 talks about a specific three-letter language. The only negative results on one-letter extensions are those of Theorems 9.7 and Theorem 9.8, in which the words grow exponentially. We have no negative results for languages with subexponential growth. However, we do have a recent positive result, which we now describe.

The aim was to prove that the squares extension, PDL $+ a^{*^2}$, is decidable. The basic idea is to take advantage of the fact that the *difference sequence* of the squares language is linear and is in fact very simple: $(n+1)^2 - n^2 = 2n + 1$. We exploit this in a construction similar in ways to that of Section 9.4, but using stack automata instead of pushdown automata. For technical reasons, the proof as it stands at the time of writing falls short of being applicable to the full PDL $+ a^{*^2}$. Accordingly, we

---

3 There are other decidable extensions that do not satisfy these conditions, so we do not have a tight characterization.

have had to restrict somewhat the context in which the squares language appears in formulas. Here is a definition of a restricted version of $\mathsf{PDL} + a^{*^2}$, which we call Restricted-$\mathsf{PDL} + a^{*^2}$.

Denote by L the squares language a^{*^2}. It is easy to see that $L^* = a^*$. Also, for any infinite regular language α over the alphabet $\{a\}$, the concatenation $L\alpha$ is regular (Exercise 9.14).

Now, given a formula φ, we say that φ is *clean* if L does not appear in φ. We say that L *appears simply* in φ (or in a program α) if all its appearances are either alone (that is, as the sole program within a box or diamond) or concatenated with a finite language over $\{a\}$ and then combined as a union with some regular language over $\{a\}$, as for example $Laa \cup (aa)^*$. A *nice box formula* is a formula of the form $[\alpha]\varphi$, where φ is clean and L appears simply in α. A regular expression α is said to be *unrestricted* if $\alpha \subseteq \{a, L\}^*$.

We now define inductively the set of formulas Φ in our PDL extension Restricted-$\mathsf{PDL} + a^{*^2}$:

- $p, \neg p \in \Phi$ for all atomic propositions p;
- $[\alpha]\varphi \in \Phi$ whenever $\varphi \in \Phi$ and at least one of the following holds:

  −both α and φ are clean,

  −$[\alpha]\varphi$ is a nice box-formula,

  −α is clean and φ is a nice box-formula;

- $<\alpha>\varphi \in \Phi$ whenever $\varphi \in \Phi$ and α is unrestricted;
- $\varphi \vee \psi \in \Phi$ whenever $\varphi, \psi \in \Phi$;
- $\varphi \wedge \psi \in \Phi$ whenever $\varphi, \psi \in \Phi$ and at least one of the following holds:

  −either φ or ψ is clean,

  −φ and ψ are nice box-formulas.

We now have:

THEOREM 9.26:   Restricted-$\mathsf{PDL} + a^{*^2}$ is decidable.

Cases with no Finite Model Property

As explained, we know of no undecidabile extension of PDL with a polynomially growing language, although we conjecture that the cubes extension is undecidable. Since the decidability status of such extensions seems hard to determine, we now address a weaker notion: the presence or absence of a finite model property. The technique used in Theorem 9.5 to show that $\mathsf{PDL} + a^{\Delta}b^{\Delta}$ violates the finite model property uses the two-letter comb-like model of Fig. 9.1, thus does not work for one-letter alphabets. Nevertheless, we now prove a general result leading to many one-letter extensions that violate the finite model property. In particular, the theorem will yield the following:

PROPOSITION 9.27 (SQUARES AND CUBES): The logics $\mathsf{PDL}+a^{*^2}$ and $\mathsf{PDL}+a^{*^3}$ do not have the finite model property.

Let us now prepare for the theorem.

DEFINITION 9.28: For a program β over Π_0 with $a \in \Pi_0$, we let $\mathrm{n}(\beta)$ denote the set $\{i \mid a^i \in CS(\beta)\}$. For $S \subseteq \mathbb{N}$, we let a^S denote the set $\{a^i \mid i \in S\}$; hence $\mathrm{n}(a^S) = S$.

THEOREM 9.29: Let $S \subseteq \mathbb{N}$. Suppose that for some program β in $\mathsf{PDL}+a^S$ with $CS(\beta) \subseteq a^*$, the following conditions are satisfied:

(i) there exists n_0 such that for all $x \geq n_0$ and $i \in \mathrm{n}(\beta)$,

$$x \in S \implies x+i \notin S;$$

(ii) for every $\ell, m > 0$, there exists $x, y \in S$ with $x > y \geq \ell$ and $d \in \mathrm{n}(\beta)$ such that $(x - y) \equiv d \pmod{m}$.

Then $\mathsf{PDL} + a^S$ does not have the finite model property.

Proof Every infinite path in a finite model must "close up" in a circular fashion. Thus, formulas satisfied along such a path must exhibit some kind of periodicity. Let S and β satisfy the conditions of the theorem. We use the nonperiodic nature of the set S given in property (i) in the statement of the theorem to construct a satisfiable formula φ in $\mathsf{PDL} + a^S$ that has no finite model.

Let φ be the conjunction of the following three formulas:

$\varphi_1 \overset{\text{def}}{=} [a^*]\langle a\rangle\mathbf{1}$

$\varphi_2 \overset{\text{def}}{=} [a^S]p$

$\varphi_3 \overset{\text{def}}{=} [a^{n_0}][a^*](p \to [\beta]\neg p)$.

Here n_0 is the constant from (i) and a^{n_0} is written out in full.

To show that φ is satisfiable, take the infinite model consisting of a sequence of

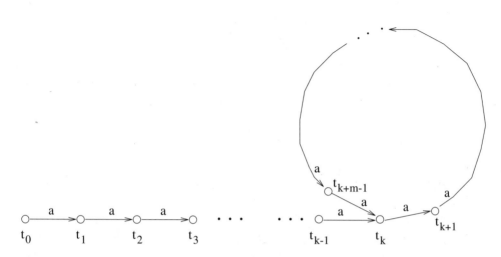

Figure 9.4

states $t_0, t_1, \ldots$ connected in order by the atomic program a. Assign p true in t_i iff $i \in S$. Then $t_0 \vDash \varphi$, since (i) guarantees that φ_3 holds in t_0.

We now show that φ does not have a finite model. Suppose $\mathfrak{K}, u_0 \vDash \varphi$ for some finite model $\mathfrak{K}$. By φ_1 and the finiteness of $\mathfrak{K}$, there must be a path in $\mathfrak{K}$ of the form shown in Fig. 9.4, where m denotes the size of the cycle. For every $z \in \mathbb{N}$, let z' be the remainder of $(z - k)$ when divided by m. Note that for $z \geq k$, the state $t_{k+z'}$ can be reached from t_0 by executing the program a^z.

By property (ii) in the statement of the theorem, we can find $x, y \in S$ and $d \in n(\beta)$ such that

$$x > y > \max(n_0, k) \quad \text{and} \quad (x - y) \equiv d \pmod{m}.$$

That φ_2 holds at t_0 implies that $t_{k+y'} \vDash p$ and $t_{k+x'} \vDash p$. Since $y > n_0$, it follows from φ_3 that $t_{k+(y+d)'} \vDash \neg p$. However, $(x - y) \equiv d \pmod{m}$ implies that $(y + d)' = x'$, so that $t_{k+x'} \vDash \neg p$, which is a contradiction. ■

It is sometimes useful to replace condition (ii) of Theorem 9.29 with a weaker condition, call it (ii'), in which the consequent does not have to hold for every modulus m, but only for every $m >= m_0$ for some fixed m_0 (Exercise 9.12).

Now to some corollaries of the theorem. First, we prove the "squares" part of Proposition 9.27.

Proof Let $S_{\mathrm{sqr}} = \{i^2 \mid i \in \mathbb{N}\}$. To satisfy Theorem 9.29(i), take $n_0 = 1$ and $\beta = a$;

thus $n(\beta) = \{1\}$. As for property (ii) of that theorem, given $\ell, m > 0$, let $d = 1$ and choose $y = (qm)^2 > \ell$ and $x = (qm + 1)^2$. Then $x, y \in S_{\text{sqr}}$, $x > y \geq \ell$, and $x - y = (qm + 1)^2 - (qm)^2 \equiv d \pmod{m}$. ∎

In fact, all polynomials of degree 2 or more exhibit the same property:

PROPOSITION 9.30 (POLYNOMIALS):   For every polynomial of the form

$$p(n) = c_i n^i + c_{i-1} n^{i-1} + \cdots + c_0 \in \mathbb{Z}[n]$$

with $i \geq 2$ and positive leading coefficient $c_i > 0$, let $S_p = \{p(m) \mid m \in \mathbb{N}\} \cap \mathbb{N}$. Then $\mathsf{PDL} + a^{S_p}$ does not have the finite model property.

Proof   To satisfy the conditions of Theorem 9.29, choose j_0 such that $p(j_0) - c_0 > 0$. Take β such that $n(\beta) = \{p(j_0) - c_0\}$. Find some n_0 such that each $x \geq n_0$ will satisfy $p(x + 1) - p(x) > p(j_0) - c_0$. This takes care of property (i) of the theorem.

Now, given $\ell, m > 0$, for $d = p(j_0) - c_0, y = p(qm) > \ell$, and $x = p(q'm + j_0) > y$, we have $x - y = p(q'm + j_0) - p(qm) \equiv p(j_0) - c_0 \pmod{m}$. ∎

PROPOSITION 9.31 (SUMS OF PRIMES):   Let p_i be the ith prime (with $p_1 = 2$), and define

$$S_{\text{sop}} \stackrel{\text{def}}{=} \{\sum_{i=1}^{n} p_i \mid n \geq 1\}.$$

Then $\mathsf{PDL} + a^{S_{\text{sop}}}$ does not have the finite model property.

Proof   Clearly, property (i) of Theorem 9.29 holds with $n_0 = 3$ and $\beta = a$. To see that (ii) holds, we use a well known theorem of Dirichlet to the effect that there are infinitely many primes in the arithmetic progression $s + jt$, $j \geq 0$, if and only if $\gcd(s, t) = 1$. Given $\ell, m > 0$, find some i_0 such that $p_{i_0 - 1} > \ell$ and $p_{i_0} \equiv 1 \pmod{m}$. The existence of such a p_{i_0} follows from Dirichlet's theorem applied to the arithmetic progression $1 + jm$, $j \geq 0$.

Now let $d = 1$, $y = \sum_{i=1}^{i_0-1} p_i$, and $x = \sum_{i=1}^{i_0} p_i$. Then $x, y \in S_{\text{sop}}$, $x > y \geq \ell$, and $x - y = p_{i_0} \equiv d \pmod{m}$. ∎

PROPOSITION 9.32 (FACTORIALS):   Let $S_{\text{fac}} \stackrel{\text{def}}{=} \{n! \mid n \in \mathbb{N}\}$. Then $\mathsf{PDL} + a^{S_{\text{fac}}}$ does not have the finite model property.

Proof   Exercise 9.11. ∎

Since undecidable extensions of PDL cannot satisfy the finite model property, there is no need to prove that the powers of a fixed k or the Fibonacci numbers violate the finite model property.

The finite model property fails for any sufficiently fast-growing integer linear recurrence, not just the Fibonacci sequence, although we do not know whether these extensions also render PDL undecidable. A kth-*order integer linear recurrence* is an inductively defined sequence

$$\ell_n \stackrel{\text{def}}{=} c_1\ell_{n-1} + \cdots + c_k\ell_{n-k} + c_0, \quad n \geq k, \tag{9.5.1}$$

where $k \geq 1$, $c_0, \ldots, c_k \in \mathbb{N}$, $c_k \neq 0$, and $\ell_0, \ldots, \ell_{k-1} \in \mathbb{N}$ are given.

PROPOSITION 9.33 (LINEAR RECURRENCES):   Let $S_{\text{lr}} = \{\ell_n \mid n \geq 0\}$ be the set defined inductively by (9.5.1). The following conditions are equivalent:

(i) $a^{S_{\text{lr}}}$ is nonregular;

(ii) PDL + $a^{S_{\text{lr}}}$ does not have the finite model property;

(iii) not all $\ell_0, \ldots, \ell_{k-1}$ are zero and $\sum_{i=1}^{k} c_i > 1$.

Proof Exercise 9.13. ∎

9.6   Bibliographical Notes

The main issues discussed in this chapter—the computational difficulty of the validity problem for nonregular PDL and the borderline between the decidable and undecidable—were raised in Harel et al. (1983). The fact that any nonregular program adds expressive power to PDL, Theorem 9.3, first appeared explicitly in Harel and Singerman (1996). Theorem 9.4 on the undecidability of context-free PDL was observed by Ladner (1977).

Theorems 9.5 and 9.6 are from Harel et al. (1983), but the proof of Theorem 9.6 using tiling is taken from Harel (1985). The existence of a primitive recursive one-letter extension of PDL that is undecidable was shown already in Harel et al. (1983), but undecidability for the particular case of a^{2^*}, Theorem 9.7, is from Harel and Paterson (1984). Theorem 9.8 is from Harel and Singerman (1996).

As to decidable extensions, Theorem 9.9 was proved in Koren and Pnueli (1983). The more general results of Section 9.4, namely Theorems 9.13, 9.24, and 9.25, are from Harel and Raz (1993), as is the notion of a simple-minded PDA. The decidability of emptiness for pushdown and stack automata on trees that is needed for the proofs of these (Section 9.4) is from Harel and Raz (1994). A better bound on the complexity of the emptiness results can be found in Peng and Iyer (1995).

Theorem 9.29 is from Harel and Singerman (1996) and Theorem 9.26 is from Ferman and Harel (2000).

Exercises

9.1. Complete the proof of Theorem 9.3.

9.2. Consider the formula $<G>p \leftrightarrow <G'>p$ for context-free grammars G and G' over atomic programs $\{a_0, \dots, a_{k-1}\}$. Show that this formula is valid iff $CS(G) = CS(G')$, where $CS(G)$ is the language over $\{a_0, \dots, a_{k-1}\}$ generated by G.

9.3. Modify the proof of Theorem 9.5 to show that $\mathsf{PDL} + a^\Delta b a^\Delta$ does not have the finite model property.

9.4. Complete the proof of Theorem 9.6 by showing why (9.3.4) forces the recurrence of red.

9.5. Prove that PDL with the addition of both $a^\Delta b^\Delta$ and $b^\Delta a^\Delta$ is Π_1^1-complete.

9.6. Complete the proof of Theorem 9.7.

9.7. Show that $a^i b^{2i}$ is a simple-minded CFL.

9.8. Extend Example 9.12 to show that the language of balanced strings of parentheses over an alphabet with $k > 1$ pairs of different parentheses is simple-minded.

9.9. Prove Proposition 9.16.

9.10. Prove Proposition 9.21.

9.11. Prove Proposition 9.32.

9.12. Show that Theorem 9.29 still holds when condition (ii) is replaced by the weaker condition

(ii') there exists an m_0 such that for every $m > m_0$ and $\ell > 0$, there exists $x, y \in S$

with $x > y \geq \ell$ and $d \in n(\beta)$ such that $(x - y) \equiv d \pmod{m}$.

9.13. Show that the terms ℓ_n of a kth-order integer linear recurrence of the form (9.5.1) grow either linearly or exponentially, and that condition (iii) of Proposition 9.33 is necessary and sufficient for exponential growth. Use this fact to prove the proposition. (*Hint.* Use Exercise 9.12.)

9.14. Prove that for any language L over the alphabet $\{a\}$ and any infinite regular language α over $\{a\}$, the concatenation language $L\alpha$ is regular.

10 Other Variants of PDL

A number of interesting variants are obtained by extending or restricting the standard version of PDL in various ways. In this section we describe some of these variants and review some of the known results concerning relative expressive power, complexity, and proof theory. These investigations are aimed at revealing the power of such programming features as recursion, testing, concurrency, and nondeterminism when reasoning on a propositional level.

The extensions and restrictions we consider are varied. One can require that programs be deterministic (Section 10.1), that tests not appear or be simple (Section 10.2), or that programs be expressed by finite automata (Section 10.3). We studied nonregular programs in Chapter 9; one can also augment the language of regular programs by adding operators for converse, intersection, or complementation (Sections 10.4 and 10.5), or the ability to assert that a program cannot execute forever (Section 10.6), or a form of concurrency and communication (Section 10.7).

Wherever appropriate, questions of expressiveness, complexity, and axiomatic completeness are addressed anew.

10.1 Deterministic PDL and While Programs

Nondeterminism arises in PDL in two ways:

- atomic programs can be interpreted in a structure as (not necessarily single-valued) binary relations on states; and
- the programming constructs $\alpha \cup \beta$ and α^* involve nondeterministic choice.

Many modern programming languages have facilities for concurrency and distributed computation, certain aspects of which can be modeled by nondeterminism. Nevertheless, the majority of programs written in practice are still deterministic. In this section we investigate the effect of eliminating either one or both of these sources of nondeterminism from PDL.

A program α is said to be (*semantically*) *deterministic* in a Kripke frame $\mathfrak{K}$ if its traces are uniquely determined by their first states. If α is an atomic program a, this is equivalent to the requirement that $\mathfrak{m}_{\mathfrak{K}}(a)$ be a partial function; that is, if both (s,t) and $(s,t') \in \mathfrak{m}_{\mathfrak{K}}(a)$, then $t = t'$. A *deterministic Kripke frame* $\mathfrak{K} = (K, \mathfrak{m}_{\mathfrak{K}})$ is one in which all atomic a are semantically deterministic.

The class of *deterministic* **while** *programs*, denoted DWP, is the class of programs in which

- the operators $\cup$, ?, and * may appear only in the context of the conditional test, **while** loop, **skip**, or **fail**;

- tests in the conditional test and **while** loop are purely propositional; that is, there is no occurrence of the $<\ >$ or $[\ ]$ operators.

The class of *nondeterministic* **while** *programs*, denoted WP, is the same, except unconstrained use of the nondeterministic choice construct $\cup$ is allowed. It is easily shown that if α and β are semantically deterministic in $\mathfrak{K}$, then so are **if** φ **then** α **else** β and **while** φ **do** α (Exercise 5.2).

By restricting either the syntax or the semantics or both, we obtain the following logics:

- DPDL (deterministic PDL), which is syntactically identical to PDL, but interpreted over deterministic structures only;

- SPDL (strict PDL), in which only deterministic **while** programs are allowed; and

- SDPDL (strict deterministic PDL), in which both restrictions are in force.

Validity and satisfiability in DPDL and SDPDL are defined just as in PDL, but with respect to deterministic structures only. If φ is valid in PDL, then φ is also valid in DPDL, but not conversely: the formula

$$<a>\varphi \quad \rightarrow \quad [a]\varphi \tag{10.1.1}$$

is valid in DPDL but not in PDL. Also, SPDL and SDPDL are strictly less expressive than PDL or DPDL, since the formula

$$<(a \cup b)^*>\varphi \tag{10.1.2}$$

is not expressible in SPDL, as shown in Halpern and Reif (1983).

THEOREM 10.1:   If the axiom scheme

$$<a>\varphi \quad \rightarrow \quad [a]\varphi, \quad a \in \Pi_0 \tag{10.1.3}$$

is added to Axiom System 5.5, then the resulting system is sound and complete for DPDL.

Proof sketch.   The extended system is certainly sound, since (10.1.3) is a straightforward consequence of semantic determinacy.

Completeness can be shown by modifying the construction of Section 7.1 with some special provisions for determinacy. For example, in the construction leading up to Lemma 7.3, we defined a nonstandard Kripke frame $\mathfrak{N}$ whose states were maximal consistent sets of formulas such that

$$
\begin{aligned}
\mathfrak{m}_{\mathfrak{N}}(a) \;&\stackrel{\text{def}}{=}\; \{(s,t) \mid \forall\varphi\ \varphi \in t \rightarrow \text{<}a\text{>}\varphi \in s\} \\
&=\; \{(s,t) \mid \forall\varphi\ [a]\varphi \in s \rightarrow \varphi \in t\}.
\end{aligned}
$$

The structure $\mathfrak{N}$ produced in this way need not be deterministic, but it can be "unwound" into a treelike deterministic structure which satisfies the given satisfiable formula. ∎

The proof sketched above also yields:

THEOREM 10.2:   Validity in DPDL is deterministic exponential-time complete.

Proof sketch.   The upper bound is shown in Ben-Ari et al. (1982). For the lower bound, a formula φ is valid in PDL iff φ' is valid in DPDL, where φ' is obtained from φ by replacing all atomic programs a by ab^* for some new atomic program b. The possibility of reaching many new states via a from some state s in PDL is modeled in DPDL by the possibility of executing b many times from the single state reached via a from s. The result follows from the linearity of this transformation. ∎

Now we turn to SPDL, in which atomic programs can be nondeterministic but can be composed into larger programs only with deterministic constructs.

THEOREM 10.3:   Validity in SPDL is deterministic exponential-time complete.

Proof sketch.   Since we have restricted the syntax only, the upper bound carries over directly from PDL. For the lower bound, a formula φ of PDL is valid iff φ' is valid in SPDL, where φ' involves new nondeterministic atomic programs acting as "switches" for deciding when the tests that control the determinism of **if-then-else** and **while-do** statements are true. For example, the nondeterministic program α^* can be simulated in SPDL by the program $b;$ **while** p **do** $(\alpha; b)$. ∎

The final version of interest is SDPDL, in which both the syntactic restrictions of SPDL and the semantic ones of DPDL are adopted. Note that the crucial $[\text{NEXT}^*]$ that appears in the simulation of the alternating Turing machine in Section 8.2 can no longer be written as it is, because we do not have the use of the * construct, and it apparently cannot be simulated with nondeterministic atomic programs as above either. Indeed, the exponential-time lower bound fails here, and we have:

THEOREM 10.4:   The validity problem for SDPDL is complete in polynomial space.

Proof sketch.   For the upper bound, the following two nontrivial properties of formulas of SDPDL are instrumental:

(i) if φ is satisfiable, then it is satisfiable in a treelike structure with only polynomially many nodes at each level. (In Theorem 10.5 a counterexample for DPDL and PDL is given.)

(ii) if φ is satisfied in a treelike structure $\mathfrak{A}$, then $\mathfrak{A}$ can be collapsed into a finite structure by "bending" certain edges back to ancestors, resulting in a treelike structure with back edges of depth at most exponential in $|\varphi|$ that has no nested or crossing backedges.

   The polynomial-space procedure attempts to construct a treelike model for a given formula by carrying out a depth-first search of potential structures, deciding nondeterministically whether or not to split nodes and whether or not to bend edges backwards. The size of the stack for such a procedure can be made to be polynomial in the size of the formula, since we have a treelike object of exponential depth but only polynomial width, hence exponential size. Savitch's theorem is then invoked to eliminate the nondeterminism while remaining in polynomial space.

   For the lower bound, we proceed as in the proof of the lower bound for PDL in Theorem 8.5. Given a polynomial space-bounded one-tape deterministic Turing machine M accepting a set $L(M)$, a formula φ_x of SDPDL is constructed for each word x that simulates the computation of M on x. The formula φ_x will be polynomial-time computable and satisfiable iff $x \in K$. Since we do not have the program NEXT*, the entire formula constructed in the proof of Theorem 8.5 must be restructured, and will now take on the form

<while $\neg\sigma$ do (NEXT; ψ?)**>1**,

where σ describes an accepting configuration of M and ψ verifies that configurations and transitions behave correctly. These parts of the formula can be constructed similarly to those used in the proof of Theorem 8.5.   ∎

   The question of relative power of expression is of interest here. Is DPDL < PDL? Is SDPDL < DPDL? The first of these questions is inappropriate, since the syntax of both languages is the same but they are interpreted over different classes of structures. Considering the second, we have:

THEOREM 10.5:   SDPDL < DPDL and SPDL < PDL.

Proof The DPDL formula

$$[(a \cup b)^*](<a>1 \wedge <b>1) \tag{10.1.4}$$

is satisfied in the full infinite binary tree (with a modeled, say, by left transitions and b by right ones), but in no tree structure with polynomially many nodes at each level. This contradicts property (i) of SDPDL in the proof of Theorem 10.4. The argument goes through even if (10.1.4) is thought of as a PDL formula and is compared with SPDL. ∎

In summary, we have the following diagram describing the relations of expressiveness between these logics. The solid arrows indicate added expressive power and broken ones a difference in semantics. The validity problem is exponential-time complete for all but SDPDL, for which it is *PSPACE*-complete. Straightforward variants of Axiom System 5.5 are complete for all versions.

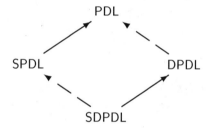

10.2 Restricted Tests

Tests φ? in PDL are defined for arbitrary propositions φ. This is sometimes called *rich test* PDL. Rich tests give substantially more power than one would normally find in a conventional programming language. For example, if φ is the formula $[\alpha]\psi$, the test φ? in effect allows a program to pause during the computation and ask the question: "Had we run program α now, would ψ have been true upon termination?" without actually running α. For example, the formula $[([\alpha]p)?;\alpha]p$ is valid. In general, however, this kind of question would be undecidable.

A more realistic model would allow tests with Boolean combinations of atomic formulas only. This is called *poor-test* PDL.

To refine this distinction somewhat, we introduce a hierarchy of subsets of Φ determined by the depth of nesting of tests. We then establish that each level of the hierarchy is strictly more expressive than all lower levels.

Let $\Phi^{(0)}$ be the subset of Φ in which programs contain no tests. This actually means that programs are regular expressions over the set Π_0 of atomic programs. Now let $\Phi^{(i+1)}$ be the subset of Φ in which programs can contain tests $\varphi?$ only for $\varphi \in \Phi^{(i)}$. The logic restricted to formulas $\Phi^{(i)}$ is called $\mathsf{PDL}^{(i)}$. Clearly, $\Phi = \bigcup_i \Phi^{(i)}$, and we can also write $\mathsf{PDL} = \bigcup_i \mathsf{PDL}^{(i)}$. The logic $\mathsf{PDL}^{(0)}$ is sometimes called *test-free* PDL.

The language fragment $\mathsf{PDL}^{(1)}$ can test test-free formulas of PDL and these themselves can contain test-free programs. Poor-test PDL, which can test only Boolean combinations of atomic formulas, fits in between $\mathsf{PDL}^{(0)}$ and $\mathsf{PDL}^{(1)}$ (we might call it $\mathsf{PDL}^{(0.5)}$).

Since the lower bound proof of Theorem 8.5 does not make use of tests at all, the exponential time lower bound carries over even to $\mathsf{PDL}^{(0)}$, the weakest version considered here, and of course the upper bound of Section 8.1 holds too. Also, omitting axiom (vi) from Axiom System 5.5 yields a complete axiom system for $\mathsf{PDL}^{(0)}$.

The question we now ask is whether even atomic tests add to the expressive power of PDL. The answer is affirmative.

THEOREM 10.6: $\mathsf{PDL}^{(0)}$ < poor-test PDL.

Proof sketch.   Axioms 5.5(iv), (v), and (vi) enable one to eliminate from formulas all tests that do not appear under a * operator. Consequently, a proof of the theorem will have to make use of iterating a test. Let φ be the the poor-test PDL formula

$$\varphi \overset{\text{def}}{=} \ <(p?a)^*(\neg p)?a>p$$

for atomic a and p. Consider the structure $\mathfrak{A}_m$ illustrated in the following figure, where arrows indicate a-transitions.

For $0 \le k < m$, $\mathfrak{A}_m, u_k \vDash \varphi$, but $\mathfrak{A}_m, u_{k+m} \nvDash \varphi$.

The rest of the proof is devoted to formalizing the following intuition. Without the ability to test p inside a loop, it is impossible to tell in general whether the current state belongs to the left- or right-hand portion of the structure, since it is always possible to proceed and find oneself eventually in the other portion.

To that end, it becomes necessary to see to it that a test-free a^* or $(a^i)^*$ program cannot distinguish between these possibilities. The constants m and k are therefore chosen carefully, taking into account the eventual periodicity of one-letter regular sets. Specifically, it can be shown that for any test-free formula ψ there are m and k such that $\mathfrak{A}_m, u_k \vDash \psi$ iff $\mathfrak{A}_m, u_{k+m} \vDash \psi$, hence φ cannot be equivalent to any formula of $\mathsf{PDL}^{(0)}$. ∎

Theorem 10.6 can be generalized to

THEOREM 10.7:   For every $i \geq 0$, $\mathsf{PDL}^{(i)} < \mathsf{PDL}^{(i+1)}$.

Proof sketch.   The proof is very similar in nature to the previous one. In particular, let φ_0 be the φ of the previous proof with a_0 replacing a, and let φ_{j+1} be φ with a_{j+1} replacing a and φ_j replacing the atomic formula p. Clearly, $\varphi_i \in \Phi^{(i+1)} - \Phi^{(i)}$.

The idea is to build an elaborate multi-layered version of the structure $\mathfrak{A}_m$ described above, in which states satisfying p or $\neg p$ in $\mathfrak{A}_m$ now have transitions leading down to appropriate distinct points in lower levels of the structure. The lowest level is identical to $\mathfrak{A}_m$. The intuition is that descending a level in the structure corresponds to nesting a test in the formula. The argument that depth of nesting $i+1$ is required to distinguish between appropriately chosen states u_k and u_{k+m} is more involved but similar. ∎

The proofs of these results make no essential use of nondeterminism and can be easily seen to hold for the deterministic versions of PDL from Section 10.1 (similarly refined according to test depth).

COROLLARY 10.8:   For every $i \geq 0$, we have

$$\mathsf{DPDL}^{(i)} < \mathsf{DPDL}^{(i+1)},$$
$$\mathsf{SPDL}^{(i)} < \mathsf{SPDL}^{(i+1)},$$
$$\mathsf{SDPDL}^{(i)} < \mathsf{SDPDL}^{(i+1)}.$$

In fact, it seems that the ability to test is in a sense independent of the ability to branch nondeterministically. The proof of Theorem 10.5 uses no tests and therefore actually yields a stronger result:

THEOREM 10.9:   There is a formula of $\mathsf{DPDL}^{(0)}$ (respectively, $\mathsf{PDL}^{(0)}$) that is not expressible in SDPDL (respectively SPDL).

We thus have the following situation: for nondeterministic structures,

$$\mathsf{SPDL}^{(0)} \quad < \quad \mathsf{SPDL}^{(1)} \quad < \quad \cdots \quad < \quad \mathsf{SPDL},$$
$$\mathsf{PDL}^{(0)} \quad < \quad \mathsf{PDL}^{(1)} \quad < \quad \cdots \quad < \quad \mathsf{PDL},$$

and for deterministic structures,

$$\mathsf{SDPDL}^{(0)} \quad < \quad \mathsf{SDPDL}^{(1)} \quad < \quad \cdots \quad < \quad \mathsf{SDPDL}$$
$$\mathsf{DPDL}^{(0)} \quad < \quad \mathsf{DPDL}^{(1)} \quad < \quad \cdots \quad < \quad \mathsf{DPDL}.$$

10.3   Representation by Automata

A **PDL** program represents a regular set of computation sequences. This same regular set could possibly be represented exponentially more succinctly by a finite automaton. The difference between these two representations corresponds roughly to the difference between **while** programs and flowcharts.

Since finite automata are exponentially more succinct in general, the upper bound of Section 8.1 could conceivably fail if finite automata were allowed as programs. Moreover, we must also rework the deductive system of Section 5.5.

However, it turns out that the completeness and exponential-time decidability results of **PDL** are not sensitive to the representation and still go through in the presence of finite automata as programs, provided the deductive system of Section 5.5 and the techniques of Chapter 7 and Section 8.1 are suitably modified, as shown in Pratt (1979b, 1981b) and Harel and Sherman (1985).

In recent years, the automata-theoretic approach to logics of programs has yielded significant insight into propositional logics more powerful than **PDL**, as well as substantial reductions in the complexity of their decision procedures. Especially enlightening are the connections with automata on infinite strings and infinite trees. By viewing a formula as an automaton and a treelike model as an input to that automaton, the satisfiability problem for a given formula becomes the emptiness problem for a given automaton. Logical questions are thereby transformed into purely automata-theoretic questions.

This connection has prompted renewed inquiry into the complexity of automata on infinite objects, with considerable success. See Courcoubetis and Yannakakis (1988); Emerson (1985); Emerson and Jutla (1988); Emerson and Sistla (1984); Manna and Pnueli (1987); Muller et al. (1988); Pecuchet (1986); Safra (1988); Sistla et al. (1987); Streett (1982); Vardi (1985a,b, 1987); Vardi and Stockmeyer (1985); Vardi and Wolper (1986c,b); Arnold (1997a,b); and Thomas (1997). Especially noteworthy in this area is the result of Safra (1988) involving the complexity of converting a nondeterministic automaton on infinite strings into an equivalent deterministic one. This result has already had a significant impact on the complexity of decision procedures for several logics of programs; see Courcoubetis and Yannakakis (1988); Emerson and Jutla (1988, 1989); and Safra (1988).

We assume that nondeterministic finite automata are given in the form

$$M \;=\; (n,\,i,\,j,\,\delta), \tag{10.3.1}$$

where $\bar{n} = \{0, \dots, n-1\}$ is the set of states, $i, j \in \bar{n}$ are the start and final states respectively, and δ assigns a subset of $\Pi_0 \cup \{\varphi? \mid \varphi \in \Phi\}$ to each pair of states. Intuitively, when visiting state ℓ and seeing symbol a, the automaton may move to state k if $a \in \delta(\ell, k)$.

The fact that the automata (10.3.1) have only one accept state is without loss of generality. If M is an arbitrary nondeterministic finite automaton with accept states F, then the set accepted by M is the union of the sets accepted by M_k for $k \in F$, where M_k is identical to M except that it has unique accept state k. A desired formula $[M]\varphi$ can be written as a conjunction

$$\bigwedge_{k \in F} [M_k]\varphi$$

with at most quadratic growth.

We now obtain a new logic APDL (*automata* PDL) by defining Φ and Π inductively using the clauses for Φ from Section 5.1 and letting $\Pi = \Pi_0 \cup \{\varphi? \mid \varphi \in \Phi\} \cup F$, where F is the set of automata of the form (10.3.1).

Exponential time decidability and completeness can be proved by adapting and generalizing the techniques used in Chapter 7 and Section 8.1 for PDL. We shall not supply full details here, except to make a couple of comments that will help give the reader the flavor of the adaptations needed.

There is an analogue $AFL(\varphi)$ of the Fischer–Ladner closure $FL(\varphi)$ of a formula φ defined in Section 6.1. The inductive clauses for $\alpha\,;\,\beta$, $\alpha \cup \beta$, and α^* are replaced by:

- if $[n, i, j, \delta]\psi \in AFL(\varphi)$, then for every $k \in \bar{n}$ and $\alpha \in \delta(i, k)$,

$[\alpha]\,[n, k, j, \delta]\psi \in AFL(\varphi)$;

- in addition, if $i = j$, then $\psi \in AFL(\varphi)$.

Axioms 5.5(iv), (v), and (vii) are replaced by:

$$[n, i, j, \delta]\varphi \;\leftrightarrow\; \bigwedge_{\substack{k \in \overline{n} \\ \alpha \in \delta(i,k)}} [\alpha] [n, k, j, \delta]\varphi, \quad i \neq j \tag{10.3.2}$$

$$[n, i, i, \delta]\varphi \;\leftrightarrow\; \varphi \wedge \bigwedge_{\substack{k \in \overline{n} \\ \alpha \in \delta(i,k)}} [\alpha] [n, k, i, \delta]\varphi. \tag{10.3.3}$$

The induction axiom 5.5(viii) becomes

$$(\bigwedge_{k \in \overline{n}} [n, i, k, \delta](\varphi_k \;\rightarrow\; \bigwedge_{\substack{m \in \overline{n} \\ \alpha \in \delta(k,m)}} [\alpha]\varphi_m)) \;\rightarrow\; (\varphi_i \;\rightarrow\; [n, i, j, \delta]\varphi_j). \tag{10.3.4}$$

These and other similar changes can be used to prove:

THEOREM 10.10:   Validity in APDL is decidable in exponential time.

THEOREM 10.11:   The axiom system described above is complete for APDL.

10.4   Complementation and Intersection

In previous sections we exploited the fact that programs in PDL are regular expressions, hence denote sets of computations recognizable by finite automata. Consequently, those operations on programs that do not lead outside the class of regular sets, such as the shuffle operator $\alpha \parallel \beta$ (of importance in reasoning about concurrent programs) need not be added explicitly to PDL. Thus the intersection of programs and the complement of a program are expressible in PDL by virtue of these operations being regular operations.

However, this is so only when the operations are regarded as being applied to the languages denoted by the programs, so that for example the intersection of α and β contains all execution sequences of atomic programs and tests contained in both. In this section we are interested in a more refined notion of such operations. Specifically, we consider the complementation and intersection of the binary relations on states denoted by programs. Let $-\alpha$ and $\alpha \cap \beta$ stand for new programs with semantics

$$\mathfrak{m}_{\mathfrak{K}}(-\alpha) \;\overset{\text{def}}{=}\; (K \times K) - \mathfrak{m}_{\mathfrak{K}}(\alpha)$$

$$\mathfrak{m}_{\mathfrak{K}}(\alpha \cap \beta) \;\overset{\text{def}}{=}\; \mathfrak{m}_{\mathfrak{K}}(\alpha) \cap \mathfrak{m}_{\mathfrak{K}}(\beta).$$

It is clear that $\alpha \cap \beta$ can be defined as $-(-\alpha \cup -\beta)$, so we might have considered adding complementation only. However, for this case we have the following immediate result.

THEOREM 10.12: The validity problem for PDL with the complementation operator is undecidable.

Proof The result follows from the known undecidability of the equivalence problem for the algebra of binary relations with complementation. ∎

However, it is of interest to consider the logic IPDL, defined as PDL with $\alpha \cap \beta$ in Π for each $\alpha, \beta \in \Pi$. The corresponding equivalence problem for binary relations is not known to be undecidable and can be shown to be no higher than Π_1^0 in the arithmetic hierarchy. This should be contrasted with Theorem 10.14 below. First, we establish the following.

THEOREM 10.13: There is a satisfiable formula of IPDL that has no finite model.

Proof sketch. Take α to be

$[a^*](\langle a\rangle 1 \wedge [a^*a \cap 1?]0)$.

Satisfiability is seen to hold in an infinite a-path. The second conjunct, however, states that non-empty portions of a-paths do not bend backwards; therefore no two states on such an infinite path can be identical. ∎

The following result is the strongest available. It concerns the version IDPDL of IPDL in which structures are deterministic.

THEOREM 10.14: The validity problem for IDPDL (hence also for DPDL with complementation of programs) is Π_1^1-complete.

Proof sketch. We reduce the recurring tiling problem of Proposition 2.22 to the satisfiability of formulas in IDPDL. First we construct a formula that forces its models to contain a (possibly cyclic) two-dimensional grid. This is done using atomic programs NORTH and EAST as follows:

$[(\text{NORTH} \cup \text{EAST})^*](\langle(\text{NORTH}; \text{EAST}) \cap (\text{EAST}; \text{NORTH})\rangle 1$.

The proof then continues along the lines of the proof of Theorem 9.6. ∎

It is interesting to observe that the techniques used in proving Theorem 10.14 do not seem to apply to the nondeterministic cases. It is not known at present whether IPDL is decidable, although it would be very surprising if were.

10.5   Converse

The *converse operator* $^-$ is a program operator that allows a program to be "run backwards":

$$m_{\mathfrak{K}}(\alpha^-) \ \stackrel{\text{def}}{=} \ \{(s,t) \mid (t,s) \in m_{\mathfrak{K}}(\alpha)\}.$$

PDL with converse is called CPDL.

The following identities, proved valid in Theorem 5.12, allow us to assume without loss of generality that the converse operator is applied to atomic programs only.

$$\begin{aligned}
(\alpha \,;\, \beta)^- &\ \leftrightarrow\ \beta^- \,;\, \alpha^- \\
(\alpha \cup \beta)^- &\ \leftrightarrow\ \alpha^- \cup \beta^- \\
\alpha^{*-} &\ \leftrightarrow\ \alpha^{-*}.
\end{aligned}$$

The converse operator strictly increases the expressive power of PDL, since the formula $<\alpha^->\mathbf{1}$ is not expressible without it.

THEOREM 10.15:   PDL $<$ CPDL.

Proof   Consider the structure described in the following figure:

In this structure, $s \vDash <a^->\mathbf{1}$ but $u \nvDash <a^->\mathbf{1}$. On the other hand, it can be shown by induction on the structure of formulas that if s and u agree on all atomic formulas, then no formula of PDL can distinguish between the two.   ∎

More interestingly, the presence of the converse operator implies that the operator $<\alpha>$ is *continuous* in the sense that if A is any (possibly infinite) family of formulas possessing a join $\bigvee A$, then $\bigvee <\alpha>A$ exists and is logically equivalent to $<\alpha> \bigvee A$ (Theorem 5.14). In the absence of the converse operator, one can construct nonstandard models for which this fails (Exercise 5.12).

The completeness and exponential time decidability results of Chapter 7 and Section 8.1 can be extended to **CPDL** provided the following two axioms are added:

$$\varphi \;\; \rightarrow \;\; [\alpha] <\alpha^{-}> \varphi$$
$$\varphi \;\; \rightarrow \;\; [\alpha^{-}] <\alpha> \varphi.$$

The filtration lemma (Lemma 6.4) still holds in the presence of $^{-}$, as does the finite model property.

10.6   Well-Foundedness and Total Correctness

If α is a deterministic program, the formula $\varphi \rightarrow <\alpha> \psi$ asserts the total correctness of α with respect to pre- and postconditions φ and ψ, respectively. For *nondeterministic* programs, however, this formula does not express the right notion of total correctness. It asserts that φ implies that *there exists* a halting computation sequence of α yielding ψ, whereas we would really like to assert that φ implies that *all* computation sequences of α terminate and yield ψ. Let us denote the latter property by

$$TC(\varphi, \alpha, \psi).$$

Unfortunately, this is not expressible in **PDL**.

The problem is intimately connected with the notion of *well-foundedness*. A program α is said to be *well-founded* at a state u_0 if there exists no infinite sequence of states $u_0, u_1, u_2, \ldots$ with $(u_i, u_{i+1}) \in \mathfrak{m}_{\mathfrak{K}}(\alpha)$ for all $i \geq 0$. This property is not expressible in **PDL** either, as we will see.

Several very powerful logics have been proposed to deal with this situation. The most powerful is perhaps the propositional μ-calculus, which is essentially propositional modal logic augmented with a least fixpoint operator μ. Using this operator, one can express any property that can be formulated as the least fixpoint of a monotone transformation on sets of states defined by the **PDL** operators. For example, the well-foundedness of a program α is expressed

$$\mu X. [\alpha] X \tag{10.6.1}$$

in this logic. We will discuss the propositional μ-calculus in more detail in Section 17.4.

Two somewhat weaker ways of capturing well-foundedness without resorting to the full μ-calculus have been studied. One is to add to **PDL** an explicit predicate

---

wf for well-foundedness:

$$\mathfrak{m}_{\mathfrak{K}}(\mathbf{wf}\,\alpha) \overset{\text{def}}{=} \{s_0 \mid \neg\exists s_1, s_2, \dots \;\forall i \geq 0\; (s_i, s_{i+1}) \in \mathfrak{m}_{\mathfrak{K}}(\alpha)\}.$$

Another is to add an explicit predicate **halt**, which asserts that all computations of its argument α terminate. The predicate **halt** can be defined inductively from **wf** as follows:

$$\mathbf{halt}\,a \overset{\text{def}}{\Longleftrightarrow} \mathbf{1}, \quad a \text{ an atomic program or test,} \tag{10.6.2}$$

$$\mathbf{halt}\,\alpha;\beta \overset{\text{def}}{\Longleftrightarrow} \mathbf{halt}\,\alpha \wedge [\alpha]\mathbf{halt}\,\beta, \tag{10.6.3}$$

$$\mathbf{halt}\,\alpha \cup \beta \overset{\text{def}}{\Longleftrightarrow} \mathbf{halt}\,\alpha \wedge \mathbf{halt}\,\beta, \tag{10.6.4}$$

$$\mathbf{halt}\,\alpha^* \overset{\text{def}}{\Longleftrightarrow} \mathbf{wf}\,\alpha \wedge [\alpha^*]\mathbf{halt}\,\alpha. \tag{10.6.5}$$

These constructs have been investigated in Harel and Pratt (1978), Harel and Sherman (1982), Niwinski (1984), and Streett (1981, 1982, 1985b) under the various names **loop**, **repeat**, and Δ. The predicates **loop** and **repeat** are just the complements of **halt** and **wf**, respectively:

$$\mathbf{loop}\,\alpha \overset{\text{def}}{\Longleftrightarrow} \neg\mathbf{halt}\,\alpha$$

$$\mathbf{repeat}\,\alpha \overset{\text{def}}{\Longleftrightarrow} \neg\mathbf{wf}\,\alpha.$$

Clause (10.6.5) is equivalent to the assertion

$$\mathbf{loop}\,\alpha^* \overset{\text{def}}{\Longleftrightarrow} \mathbf{repeat}\,\alpha \vee \langle\alpha^*\rangle\mathbf{loop}\,\alpha.$$

It asserts that a nonhalting computation of α^* consists of either an infinite sequence of halting computations of α or a finite sequence of halting computations of α followed by a nonhalting computation of α.

Let RPDL and LPDL denote the logics obtained by augmenting PDL with the **wf** and **halt** predicates, respectively.[1] It follows from the preceding discussion that

$$\mathsf{PDL} \;\leq\; \mathsf{LPDL} \;\leq\; \mathsf{RPDL} \;\leq\; \text{the propositional } \mu\text{-calculus.}$$

Moreover, all these inclusions are known to be strict.

The logic LPDL is powerful enough to express the total correctness of nondeterministic programs. The total correctness of α with respect to precondition φ and postcondition ψ is expressed

$$TC(\varphi, \alpha, \psi) \overset{\text{def}}{\Longleftrightarrow} \varphi \to \mathbf{halt}\,\alpha \wedge [\alpha]\psi.$$

---

1 The L in LPDL stands for "loop" and the R in RPDL stands for "repeat." We retain these names for historical reasons.

Conversely, **halt** can be expressed in terms of TC:

$$\textbf{halt}\,\alpha \quad \Longleftrightarrow \quad TC(\mathbf{1}, \alpha, \mathbf{1}).$$

The filtration lemma fails for RPDL, LPDL, and the propositional μ-calculus (except under certain strong syntactic restrictions which render formulas like (10.6.1) ineffable; see Pratt (1981a)). This can be seen by considering the model $\mathfrak{K} = (K, \mathfrak{m}_{\mathfrak{K}})$ with

$$K \;\overset{\text{def}}{=}\; \{(i, j) \in \mathbb{N}^2 \mid 0 \le j \le i\} \cup \{u\}$$

and atomic program a with

$$\mathfrak{m}_{\mathfrak{K}}(a) \;\overset{\text{def}}{=}\; \{((i, j), (i, j - 1)) \mid 1 \le j \le i\} \cup \{(u, (i, i)) \mid i \in \mathbb{N}\}.$$

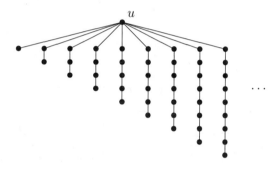

The state u satisfies **halt** a^* and **wf** a, but its equivalence class in any finite filtrate does not satisfy either of these formulas. It follows that

THEOREM 10.16:   PDL < LPDL.

Proof By the preceding argument and Lemma 6.4, neither **halt** a^* nor **wf** a is equivalent to any PDL formula. ∎

THEOREM 10.17:   LPDL < RPDL.

Proof sketch.   For any i, let $\mathfrak{A}_n$ and $\mathfrak{B}_n$ be the structures of Figures 10.1 and 10.2, respectively. The state t_i of $\mathfrak{B}_n$ is identified with the state s_0 in its own copy of $\mathfrak{A}_n$. For any n and $i \le n$, $\mathfrak{A}_n, s_i \vDash \textbf{wf}\,a^*b$, but $\mathfrak{B}_n, t_i \vDash \neg\textbf{wf}\,a^*b$. However, for each formula φ of LPDL, it is possible to find a large enough n such that for all $i \le n$, $\mathfrak{B}_n, t_i \vDash \varphi$ iff $\mathfrak{A}_n, s_0 \vDash \varphi$. This is proved by induction on the structure of φ. For the

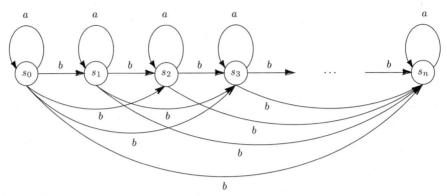

Figure 10.1
The structure $\mathfrak{A}_n$

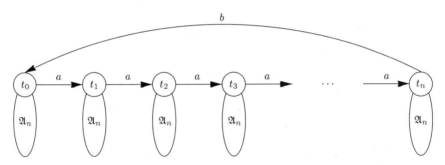

Figure 10.2
The structure $\mathfrak{B}_n$

case of **halt** α, one uses the fact that in order to capture the infinite path of a's and b's in $\mathfrak{B}_n$ with a $\neg$**halt** α clause, say $\neg$**halt** $(a^*b)^*$ for example, there must exist an infinite computation of α that after some finite bounded length consists solely of a's. Hence, this particular $\neg$**halt** α clause is already satisfied in $\mathfrak{A}_n$ for sufficient large n. The argument is similar to the proof of the pumping lemma for regular languages; see Hopcroft and Ullman (1979) or Kozen (1997a). ■

It is possible to extend Theorem 10.17 to versions **CRPDL** and **CLPDL** in which converse is allowed in addition to **wf** or **halt**. Also, the proof of Theorem 10.15 goes through for **LPDL** and **RPDL**, so that $<a^->1$ is not expressible in either. Theorem 10.16 goes through for the converse versions too. We obtain the situation illustrated in the following figure, in which the arrows indicate $<$ and the absence of a path between two logics means that each can express properties that the other cannot.

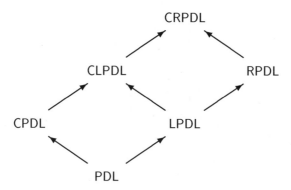

The filtration lemma fails for all **halt** and **wf** versions as in the proof of Theorem 10.16. However, satisfiable formulas of the μ-calculus (hence of RPDL and LPDL) do have finite models. This finite model property is not shared by CLPDL or CRPDL.

THEOREM 10.18:   The CLPDL formula

$$\neg\mathbf{halt}\,a^* \wedge [a^*]\mathbf{halt}\,a^{*-}$$

is satisfiable but has no finite model.

Proof Let φ be the formula in the statement of the theorem. This formula is satisfied in the infinite model

To show it is satisfied in no finite model, suppose $\mathfrak{K}, s \vDash \varphi$. By (10.6.2) and (10.6.5),

$$\mathbf{halt}\,a^* \iff \mathbf{wf}\,a \wedge [a^*]\mathbf{halt}\,a$$
$$\iff \mathbf{wf}\,a \wedge [a^*]\mathbf{1}$$
$$\iff \mathbf{wf}\,a,$$

thus $\mathfrak{K}, s \vDash \neg\mathbf{wf}\,a$. This says that there must be an infinite a-path starting at s. However, no two states along that path can be identical without violating the clause $[a^*]\mathbf{halt}\,a^{*-}$ of φ, thus $\mathfrak{K}$ is infinite. ∎

As it turns out, Theorem 10.18 does not prevent CRPDL from being decidable.

THEOREM 10.19:   The validity problems for CRPDL, CLPDL, RPDL, LPDL, and the propositional μ-calculus are all decidable in deterministic exponential time.

Obviously, the simpler the logic, the simpler the arguments needed to show exponential time decidability. Over the years all these logics have been gradually shown to be decidable in exponential time by various authors using various techniques. Here we point to the exponential time decidability of the propositional μ-calculus with forward and backward modalities, proved in Vardi (1998b), from which all these can be seen easily to follow. The proof in Vardi (1998b) is carried out by exhibiting an exponential time decision procedure for two-way alternating automata on infinite trees.

As mentioned above, RPDL possesses the finite (but not necessarily the small and not the collapsed) model property.

THEOREM 10.20:   Every satisfiable formula of RPDL, LPDL, and the propositional μ-calculus has a finite model.

Proof sketch.   The proof uses the fact that every automaton on infinite trees that accepts some tree accepts a tree obtained by unwinding a finite graph. For a satisfiable formula φ in these logics, it is possible to transform the finite graph obtained in this way from the automaton for φ into a finite model of φ. ∎

CRPDL and CLPDL are extensions of PDL that, like $PDL + a^\Delta b^\Delta$ (Theorems 9.5 and 9.9), are decidable despite lacking a finite model property.

Complete axiomatizations for RPDL and LPDL can be obtained by embedding them into the μ-calculus (see Section 17.4).

10.7   Concurrency and Communication

Another interesting extension of PDL concerns concurrent programs. Recall the intersection operator ∩ introduced in Section 10.4. The binary relation on states corresponding to the program $\alpha \cap \beta$ is the intersection of the binary relations corresponding to α and β. This can be viewed as a kind of concurrency operator that admits transitions to those states that both α and β would have admitted.

In this section, we consider a different and perhaps more natural notion of concurrency. The interpretation of a program will not be a binary relation on states, which relates initial states to possible final states, but rather a relation between states and *sets* of states. Thus $\mathfrak{m}_{\mathfrak{K}}(\alpha)$ will relate a start state u to a collection of sets of states U. The intuition is that starting in state u, the (concurrent) program α can be run with its concurrent execution threads ending in the set of final states U. The basic concurrency operator will be denoted here by $\wedge$, although in the original work on concurrent Dynamic Logic (Peleg (1987b,c,a)) the notation $\cap$ is used.

The syntax of *concurrent* PDL is the same as PDL, with the addition of the clause:

- if $\alpha, \beta \in \Pi$, then $\alpha \wedge \beta \in \Pi$.

The program $\alpha \wedge \beta$ means intuitively, "Execute α and β in parallel."

The semantics of concurrent PDL is defined on Kripke frames $\mathfrak{K} = (K, \mathfrak{m}_\mathfrak{K})$ as with PDL, except that for programs α,

$$\mathfrak{m}_\mathfrak{K}(\alpha) \quad \subseteq \quad K \times 2^K.$$

Thus the meaning of α is a collection of *reachability pairs* of the form (u, U), where $u \in K$ and $U \subseteq K$. In this brief description of concurrent PDL, we require that structures assign to atomic programs *sequential*, non-parallel, meaning; that is, for each $a \in \Pi_0$, we require that if $(u, U) \in \mathfrak{m}_\mathfrak{K}(a)$, then $\#U = 1$. The true parallelism will stem from applying the concurrency operator to build larger sets U in the reachability pairs of compound programs. We shall not provide the details here; the reader is referred to Peleg (1987b,c).

The relevant results for this logic are the following:

THEOREM 10.21:   PDL $<$ concurrent PDL.

THEOREM 10.22:   The validity problem for concurrent PDL is decidable in deterministic exponential time.

Axiom System 5.5, augmented with the following axiom, can be be shown to be complete for concurrent PDL:

$<\alpha \wedge \beta>\varphi \quad \leftrightarrow \quad <\alpha>\varphi \wedge <\beta>\varphi.$

10.8   Bibliographical Notes

Completeness and exponential time decidability for DPDL, Theorem 10.1 and the upper bound of Theorem 10.2, are proved in Ben-Ari et al. (1982) and Valiev (1980).

The lower bound of Theorem 10.2 is from Parikh (1981). Theorems 10.4 and 10.5 on SDPDL are from Halpern and Reif (1981, 1983).

That tests add to the power of PDL (Theorem 10.6) is proved in Berman and Paterson (1981), and Theorem 10.7 appears in Berman (1978) and Peterson (1978). It can be shown (Peterson (1978); Berman (1978); Berman and Paterson (1981)) that rich-test PDL is strictly more expressive than poor-test PDL. These results also hold for SDPDL (see Section 10.1).

The results on programs as automata (Theorems 10.10 and 10.11) appear in Pratt (1981b) but the proofs sketched are from Harel and Sherman (1985). The material of Section 10.4 on the intersection of programs is from Harel et al. (1982). That the axioms in Section 10.5 yield completeness for CPDL is proved in Parikh (1978a).

The complexity of PDL with converse and various forms of well-foundedness constructs is studied in Vardi (1985b). Many authors have studied logics with a least-fixpoint operator, both on the propositional and first-order levels (Scott and de Bakker (1969); Hitchcock and Park (1972); Park (1976); Pratt (1981a); Kozen (1982, 1983, 1988); Kozen and Parikh (1983); Niwinski (1984); Streett (1985b); Vardi and Stockmeyer (1985)). The version of the propositional μ-calculus presented here was introduced in Kozen (1982, 1983).

That the propositional μ-calculus is strictly more expressive than PDL with **wf** was show in Niwinski (1984) and Streett (1985b). That this logic is strictly more expressive than PDL with **halt** was shown in Harel and Sherman (1982). That this logic is strictly more expressive than PDL was shown in Streett (1981).

The **wf** construct (actually its complement, **repeat**) is investigated in Streett (1981, 1982), in which Theorems 10.16 (which is actually due to Pratt) and 10.18–10.20 are proved. The **halt** construct (actually its complement, **loop**) was introduced in Harel and Pratt (1978) and Theorem 10.17 is from Harel and Sherman (1982). Finite model properties for the logics LPDL, RPDL, CLPDL, CRPDL, and the propositional μ-calculus were established in Streett (1981, 1982) and Kozen (1988). Decidability results were obtained in Streett (1981, 1982); Kozen and Parikh (1983); Vardi and Stockmeyer (1985); and Vardi (1985b). Deterministic exponential-time completeness was established in Emerson and Jutla (1988) and Safra (1988). For the strongest variant, CRPDL, exponential-time decidability follows from Vardi (1998b).

Concurrent PDL is defined in Peleg (1987b), in which the results of Section 10.7 are proved. Additional versions of this logic, which employ various mechanisms for communication among the concurrent parts of a program, are considered in Peleg (1987c,a). These papers contain many results concerning expressive power, decidability and undecidability for concurrent PDL with communication.

Other work on **PDL** not described here includes work on nonstandard models, studied in Berman (1979, 1982) and Parikh (1981); **PDL** with Boolean assignments, studied in Abrahamson (1980); and restricted forms of the consequence problem, studied in Parikh (1981).

III FIRST-ORDER DYNAMIC LOGIC

11 First-Order Dynamic Logic

In this chapter we begin the study of first-order Dynamic Logic. The main difference between first-order DL and the propositional version PDL discussed in Part II of the book is the presence of a first-order structure $\mathfrak{A}$, called the *domain of computation*, over which first-order quantification is allowed. States are no longer abstract points, but *valuations* of a set of variables over A, the *carrier* of $\mathfrak{A}$. Atomic programs in DL are no longer abstract binary relations, but *assignment statements* of various forms, all based on assigning values to variables during the computation. The most basic example of such an assignment is the *simple assignment* $x := t$, where x is a variable and t is a term. The atomic formulas of DL are generally taken to be atomic first-order formulas.

In addition to the constructs introduced in Part II, the basic DL syntax contains individual variables ranging over A, function and predicate symbols for distinguished functions and predicates of $\mathfrak{A}$, and quantifiers ranging over A, exactly as in classical first-order logic. More powerful versions of the logic contain array and stack variables and other constructs, as well as primitive operations for manipulating them, and assignments for changing their values. Sometimes the introduction of a new construct increases expressive power and sometimes not; sometimes it has an effect on the complexity of deciding satisfiability and sometimes not. Indeed, one of the central goals of Part III of the book is to classify these constructs in terms of their relative expressive power and complexity.

In this chapter we lay the groundwork for this by defining the various logical and programming constructs we shall be needing.

11.1 Basic Syntax

The language of first-order Dynamic Logic is built upon classical first-order logic as described in Section 3.4. There is always an underlying first-order vocabulary Σ, which involves a vocabulary of function symbols and predicate (or relation) symbols. On top of this vocabulary, we define a set of *programs* and a set of *formulas*. These two sets interact by means of the modal construct [ ] exactly as in the propositional case. Programs and formulas are usually defined by mutual induction.

Let $\Sigma = \{f, g, \ldots, p, r, \ldots\}$ be a finite first-order vocabulary. Here f and g denote typical function symbols of Σ, and p and r denote typical relation symbols. Associated with each function and relation symbol of Σ is a fixed *arity* (number of arguments), although we do not represent the arity explicitly. We assume that Σ always contains the equality symbol $=$, whose arity is 2. Functions and relations of arity $0, 1, 2, 3$ and n are called *nullary, unary, binary, ternary,* and *n-ary,* respectively. Nullary functions are also called *constants.* We shall be using a countable set of *individual variables* $V = \{x_0, x_1, \dots\}$.

The definitions of DL programs and formulas below depend on the vocabulary Σ, but in general we shall not make this dependence explicit unless we have some specific reason for doing so.

Atomic Formulas and Programs

In all versions of DL that we will consider, atomic formulas are atomic formulas of the first-order vocabulary Σ; that is, formulas of the form

$r(t_1, \dots, t_n)$,

where r is an n-ary relation symbol of Σ and $t_1, \dots, t_n$ are terms of Σ.

As in PDL, programs are defined inductively from atomic programs using various programming constructs. The meaning of a compound program is given inductively in terms of the meanings of its constituent parts. Different classes of programs are obtained by choosing different classes of atomic programs and programming constructs.

In the basic version of DL, an atomic program is a *simple assignment*

$$x := t, \tag{11.1.1}$$

where $x \in V$ and t is a term of Σ. Intuitively, this program assigns the value of t to the variable x. This is the same form of assignment found in most conventional programming languages.

More powerful forms of assignment such as stack and array assignments and nondeterministic "wildcard" assignments will be discussed later. The precise choice of atomic programs will be made explicit when needed, but for now, we use the term *atomic program* to cover all of these possibilities.

Tests

As in PDL, DL contains a test operator ?, which turns a formula into a program. In most versions of DL that we shall discuss, we allow only quantifier-free first-order formulas as tests. We sometimes call these versions *poor test.* Alternatively, we might allow any first-order formula as a test. Most generally, we might place no restrictions on the form of tests, allowing any DL formula whatsoever, including those that contain other programs, perhaps containing other tests, etc. These versions of DL are labeled *rich test* as in Section 10.2. Whereas programs can be defined independently from formulas in poor test versions, rich test versions require a mutually inductive definition of programs and formulas.

As with atomic programs, the precise logic we consider at any given time depends on the choice of tests we allow. We will make this explicit when needed, but for now, we use the term *test* to cover all possibilities.

Regular Programs

For a given set of atomic programs and tests, the set of *regular programs* is defined as in PDL (see Section 5.1):

- any atomic program or test is a program;
- if α and β are programs, then $\alpha \,;\, \beta$ is a program;
- if α and β are programs, then $\alpha \cup \beta$ is a program;
- if α is a program then α^* is a program.

While Programs

Some of the literature on DL is concerned with the class of **while** *programs*. This class was defined formally in Section 10.1 for PDL (see also Section 5.1); the definition is the same here.

Formally, *deterministic* **while** *programs* form the subclass of the regular programs in which the program operators $\cup$, ?, and * are constrained to appear only in the forms

$$\mathbf{skip} \overset{\mathrm{def}}{=} \mathbf{1}?$$

$$\mathbf{fail} \overset{\mathrm{def}}{=} \mathbf{0}?$$

$$\textbf{if } \varphi \textbf{ then } \alpha \textbf{ else } \beta \overset{\mathrm{def}}{=} (\varphi?; \alpha) \cup (\neg\varphi?; \beta) \tag{11.1.2}$$

$$\textbf{while } \varphi \textbf{ do } \alpha \overset{\mathrm{def}}{=} (\varphi?; \alpha)^*; \neg\varphi? \tag{11.1.3}$$

The class of *nondeterministic* **while** *programs* is the same, except that we allow unrestricted use of the nondeterministic choice construct $\cup$. Of course, unrestricted use of the sequential composition operator is allowed in both languages.

Restrictions on the form of atomic programs and tests apply as with regular programs. For example, if we are allowing only poor tests, then the φ occurring in the programs (11.1.2) and (11.1.3) must be a quantifier-free first-order formula.

The class of deterministic **while** programs is important because it captures the basic programming constructs common to many real-life imperative programming languages. Over the standard structure of the natural numbers $\mathbb{N}$, deterministic **while** programs are powerful enough to define all partial recursive functions, and thus over $\mathbb{N}$ they are as as expressive as regular programs. A similar result holds for a wide class of models similar to $\mathbb{N}$, for a suitable definition of "partial recursive functions" in these models. However, it is not true in general that **while** programs, even nondeterministic ones, are universally expressive. We discuss these results in Chapter 15.

Formulas

A *formula* of DL is defined in way similar to that of PDL, with the addition of a rule for quantification. Equivalently, we might say that a formula of DL is defined in a way similar to that of first-order logic, with the addition of a rule for modality. The basic version of DL is defined with regular programs:

- the false formula **0** is a formula;
- any atomic formula is a formula;
- if φ and ψ are formulas, then $\varphi \to \psi$ is a formula;
- if φ is a formula and $x \in V$, then $\forall x \; \varphi$ is a formula;
- if φ is a formula and α is a program, then $[\alpha]\varphi$ is a formula.

The only missing rule in the definition of the syntax of DL are the tests. In our basic version we would have:

- if φ is a quatifier-free first-order formula, then φ? is a test.

For the rich test version, the definitions of programs and formulas are mutually dependent, and the rule defining tests is simply:

- if φ is a formula, then φ? is a test.

We will use the same notation as in propositional logic that $\neg\varphi$ stands for $\varphi \to \mathbf{0}$. As in first-order logic, the first-order existential quantifier $\exists$ is considered a defined construct: $\exists x \; \varphi$ abbreviates $\neg\forall x \; \neg\varphi$. Similarly, the modal construct < > is considered a defined construct as in Section 5.1, since it is the modal dual of [ ]. The other propositional constructs $\land$, $\lor$, $\leftrightarrow$ are defined as in Section 3.2. Of course, we use parentheses where necessary to ensure unique readability.

Note that the individual variables in V serve a dual purpose: they are both program variables and logical variables.

11.2 Richer Programs

Seqs and R.E. Programs

Some classes of programs are most conveniently defined as certain sets of seqs. Recall from Section 5.3 that a *seq* is a program of the form $\sigma_1; \cdots ; \sigma_k$, where each σ_i is an assignment statement or a quantifier-free first-order test. Each regular program α is associated with a unique set of seqs $CS(\alpha)$ (Section 5.3). These definitions were made in the propositional context, but they apply equally well to the first-order case; the only difference is in the form of atomic programs and tests.

Construing the word in the broadest possible sense, we can consider a *program* to be an arbitrary set of seqs. Although this makes sense semantically—we can assign an input/output relation to such a set in a meaningful way—such programs can hardly be called executable. At the very least we should require that the set of seqs be recursively enumerable, so that there will be some effective procedure that can list all possible executions of a given program. However, there is a subtle issue that arises with this notion. Consider the set of seqs

$$\{x_i := f^i(c) \mid i \in \mathbb{N}\}.$$

This set satisfies the above restriction, yet it can hardly be called a program. It uses infinitely many variables, and as a consequence it might change a valuation at infinitely many places. Another pathological example is the set of seqs

$$\{x_{i+1} := f(x_i) \mid i \in \mathbb{N}\},$$

which not only could change a valuation at infinitely many locations, but also depends on infinitely many locations of the input valuation.

In order to avoid such pathologies, we will require that each program use only finitely many variables. This gives rise to the following definition of *r.e. programs*, which is the most general family of programs we will consider. Specifically, an r.e. program α is a Turing machine that enumerates a set of seqs over a finite set of variables. The set of seqs enumerated will be called $CS(\alpha)$. By $FV(\alpha)$ we will denote the finite set of variables that occur in seqs of $CS(\alpha)$.

An important issue connected with r.e. programs is that of *bounded memory*. The assignment statements or tests in an r.e. program may have infinitely many terms with increasingly deep nesting of function symbols (although, as discussed, these terms only use finitely many variables), and these could require an unbounded amount of memory to compute. We define a set of seqs to be *bounded memory* if the depth of terms appearing in it is bounded. In fact, without sacrificing computational power, we could require that all terms be of the form $f(x_1, \ldots, x_n)$ in a bounded-memory set of seqs (Exercise 15.4).

Arrays and Stacks

Interesting variants of the programming language we use in DL arise from allowing auxiliary data structures. We shall define versions with *arrays* and *stacks*, as well as a version with a nondeterministic assignment statement called *wildcard assignment*.

Besides these, one can imagine augmenting **while** programs with many other kinds of constructs such as blocks with declarations, recursive procedures with various parameter passing mechanisms, higher-order procedures, concurrent processes, etc. It is easy to arrive at a family consisting of thousands of programming languages, giving rise to thousands of logics. Obviously, we have had to restrict ourselves. It is worth mentioning, however, that certain kinds of recursive procedures are captured by our stack operations, as explained below.

Arrays

To handle arrays, we include a countable set of *array variables*

$$V_{\text{array}} = \{F_0, F_1, \ldots\}.$$

Each array variable has an associated *arity*, or number of arguments, which we do not represent explicitly. We assume that there are countably many variables of each arity $n \geq 0$. In the presence of array variables, we equate the set V of individual variables with the set of nullary array variables; thus $V \subseteq V_{\text{array}}$.

The variables in V_{array} of arity n will range over n-ary functions with arguments and values in the domain of computation. In our exposition, elements of the domain of computation play two roles: they are used both as *indices* into an array and as *values* that can be stored in an array. One might equally well introduce a separate sort for array indices; although conceptually simple, this would complicate the notation and would give no new insight.

We extend the set of first-order terms to allow the unrestricted occurrence of array variables, provided arities are respected.

The classes of *regular programs with arrays* and *deterministic* and *nondeterministic* **while** *programs with arrays* are defined similarly to the classes without, except that we allow *array assignments* in addition to simple assignments. Array assignments are similar to simple assignments, but on the left-hand side we allow a term in which the outermost symbol is an array variable:

$$F(t_1, \ldots, t_n) := t.$$

Here F is an n-ary array variable and $t_1, \ldots, t_n, t$ are terms, possibly involving other array variables. Note that when $n = 0$, this reduces to the ordinary simple assignment.

Recursion via an Algebraic Stack

We now consider DL in which the programs can manipulate a stack. The literature in automata theory and formal languages often distinguishes a stack from a pushdown store. In the former, the automaton is allowed to inspect the contents of the stack but to make changes only at the top. We shall use the term stack to denote the more common pushdown store, where the only inspection allowed is at the top of the stack.

The motivation for this extension is to be able to capture recursion. It is well known that recursive procedures can be modeled using a stack, and for various technical reasons we prefer to extend the data-manipulation capabilities of our programs than to introduce new control constructs. When it encounters a recursive call, the stack simulation of recursion will push the return location and values of local variables and parameters on the stack. It will pop them upon completion of the call. The LIFO (last-in-first-out) nature of stack storage fits the order in which control executes recursive calls.

To handle the stack in our stack version of DL, we add two new atomic programs

push(t) and   **pop**(y),

where t is a term and $y \in V$. Intuitively, **push**(t) pushes the current value of t onto the top of the stack, and **pop**(y) pops the top value off the top of the stack and assigns that value to the variable y. If the stack is empty, the pop operation does not change anything. We could have added a test for stack emptiness, but it can be shown to be redundant (Exercise 11.3). Formally, the stack is simply a finite string of elements of the domain of computation.

The classes of *regular programs with stack* and *deterministic* and *nondeterministic* **while** *programs with stack* are obtained by augmenting the respective classes of programs with the **push** and **pop** operations as atomic programs in addition to simple assignments.

In contrast to the case of arrays, here there is only a single stack. In fact, expressiveness changes dramatically when two or more stacks are allowed (Exercise 15.7). Also, in order to be able to simulate recursion, the domain must have at least two distinct elements so that return addresses can be properly encoded in the stack. One way of doing this is to store the return address itself in unary using one element of the domain, then store one occurrence of the second element as a delimiter symbol, followed by domain elements constituting the current values of parameters and local variables.

The kind of stack described here is often termed *algebraic*, since it contains elements from the domain of computation. It should be contrasted with the Boolean stack described next.

Parameterless Recursion via a Boolean Stack

An interesting special case is when the stack can contain only two distinct elements. This version of our programming language can be shown to capture recursive procedures without parameters or local variables. This is because we only need to store return addresses, but no actual data items from the domain of computation. This can be achieved using two values, as described above. We thus arrive at the idea of a Boolean stack.

To handle such a stack in this version of DL, we add three new kinds of atomic programs and one new test. The atomic programs are

  push-1   **push-0**   **pop**,

and the test is simply

top?.

Intuitively, **push-1** and **push-0** push the corresponding distinct Boolean values on the stack, **pop** removes the top element, and the test **top**? evaluates to true iff the top element of the stack is **1**, but with no side effect.

With the test **top**? only, there is no explicit operator that distinguishes a stack with top element **0** from the empty stack. We might have defined such an operator, and in a more realistic language we would certainly do so. However, it is mathematically redundant, since it can be simulated with the operators we already have (Exercise 11.1).

Wildcard Assignment

The nondeterministic assignment

$x := ?$

is a device that arises in the study of fairness; see Apt and Plotkin (1986). It has often been called *random assignment* in the literature, although it has nothing to do with randomness or probability. We shall call it *wildcard assignment*. Intuitively, it operates by assigning a nondeterministically chosen element of the domain of computation to the variable x. This construct together with the [ ] modality is similar to the first-order universal quantifier, since it will follow from the semantics that the two formulas

$$[x := ?]\varphi \qquad \text{and} \qquad \forall x\ \varphi$$

are equivalent. However, wildcard assignment may appear in programs and can therefore be iterated.

11.3   Semantics

In this section we assign meanings to the syntactic constructs described in the previous sections. We interpret programs and formulas over a first-order structure $\mathfrak{A}$. Variables range over the carrier of this structure. We take an *operational* view of program semantics: programs change the values of variables by sequences of simple assignments $x := t$ or other assignments, and flow of control is determined by the truth values of tests performed at various times during the computation.

States as Valuations

An instantaneous snapshot of all relevant information at any moment during the computation is determined by the values of the program variables. Thus our *states* will be *valuations* $u, v, \ldots$ of the variables V over the carrier of the structure $\mathfrak{A}$. Our formal definition will associate the pair (u, v) of such valuations with the program α if it is possible to start in valuation u, execute the program α, and halt in valuation v. In this case, we will call (u, v) an *input/output pair* of α and write $(u, v) \in \mathfrak{m}_{\mathfrak{A}}(\alpha)$. This will result in a Kripke frame exactly as in Chapter 5.

Let

$$\mathfrak{A} \;=\; (A,\ \mathfrak{m}_{\mathfrak{A}})$$

be a first-order structure for the vocabulary Σ as defined in Section 3.4. We call $\mathfrak{A}$ the *domain of computation*. Here A is a set, called the *carrier* of $\mathfrak{A}$, and $\mathfrak{m}_{\mathfrak{A}}$ is a *meaning function* such that $\mathfrak{m}_{\mathfrak{A}}(f)$ is an n-ary function $\mathfrak{m}_{\mathfrak{A}}(f) : A^n \to A$ interpreting the n-ary function symbol f of Σ, and $\mathfrak{m}_{\mathfrak{A}}(r)$ is an n-ary relation $\mathfrak{m}_{\mathfrak{A}}(r) \subseteq A^n$ interpreting the n-ary relation symbol r of Σ. The equality symbol $=$ is always interpreted as the identity relation.

For $n \geq 0$, let $A^n \to A$ denote the set of all n-ary functions in A. By convention, we take $A^0 \to A = A$. Let A^* denote the set of all finite-length strings over A.

The structure $\mathfrak{A}$ determines a Kripke frame, which we will also denote by $\mathfrak{A}$, as follows. A *valuation* over $\mathfrak{A}$ is a function u assigning an n-ary function over A to each n-ary array variable. It also assigns meanings to the stacks as follows. We shall use the two unique variable names STK and $BSTK$ to denote the algebraic stack and the Boolean stack, respectively. The valuation u assigns a finite-length string of elements of A to STK and a finite-length string of Boolean values $\mathbf{1}$ and $\mathbf{0}$ to $BSTK$. Formally:

$$\begin{aligned}
u(F) &\in A^n \to A, \quad \text{if } F \text{ is an } n\text{-ary array variable,} \\
u(STK) &\in A^*, \\
u(BSTK) &\in \{\mathbf{1}, \mathbf{0}\}^*.
\end{aligned}$$

By our convention $A^0 \to A = A$, and assuming that $V \subseteq V_{\text{array}}$, the individual variables (that is, the nullary array variables) are assigned elements of A under this definition:

$u(x) \in A$ if $x \in V$.

The valuation u extends uniquely to terms t by induction. For an n-ary function symbol f and an n-ary array variable F,

$$\begin{aligned}
u(f(t_1, \ldots, t_n)) &\overset{\text{def}}{=} \mathfrak{m}_{\mathfrak{A}}(f)(u(t_1), \ldots, u(t_n)) \\
u(F(t_1, \ldots, t_n)) &\overset{\text{def}}{=} u(F)(u(t_1), \ldots, u(t_n)).
\end{aligned}$$

Recall the *function-patching* operator defined in Section 1.3: if X and D are sets, $f : X \to D$ is any function, $x \in X$, and $d \in D$, then $f[x/d] : X \to D$ is the function defined by

$$f[x/d](y) \overset{\text{def}}{=} \begin{cases} d, & \text{if } x = y \\ f(y), & \text{otherwise.} \end{cases}$$

We will be using this notation in several ways, both at the logical and metalogical levels. For example:

- If u is a valuation, x is an individual variable, and $a \in A$, then $u[x/a]$ is the new valuation obtained from u by changing the value of x to a and leaving the values of all other variables intact.

- If F is an n-ary array variable and $f : A^n \to A$, then $u[F/f]$ is the new valuation that assigns the same value as u to the stack variables and to all array variables other than F, and

$$u[F/f](F) = f.$$

- If $f : A^n \to A$ is an n-ary function and $a_1, \dots, a_n, a \in A$, then the expression $f[a_1, \dots, a_n/a]$ denotes the n-ary function that agrees with f everywhere except for input $a_1, \dots, a_n$, on which it takes the value a. More precisely,

$$f[a_1, \dots, a_n/a](b_1, \dots, b_n) \quad = \quad \begin{cases} a, & \text{if } b_i = a_i, \ 1 \leq i \leq n \\ f(b_1, \dots, b_n), & \text{otherwise.} \end{cases}$$

We call valuations u and v *finite variants* of each other if

$$u(F)(a_1, \dots, a_n) \quad = \quad v(F)(a_1, \dots, a_n)$$

for all but finitely many array variables F and n-tuples $a_1, \dots, a_n \in A^n$. In other words, u and v differ on at most finitely many array variables, and for those F on which they do differ, the functions $u(F)$ and $v(F)$ differ on at most finitely many values.

The relation "is a finite variant of" is an equivalence relation on valuations. Since a halting computation can run for only a finite amount of time, it can execute only finitely many assignments. It will therefore not be able to cross equivalence class boundaries; that is, in the binary relation semantics given below, if the pair (u, v) is an input/output pair of the program α, then v is a finite variant of u.

We are now ready to define the *states* of our Kripke frame. For $a \in A$, let w_a be the valuation in which the stacks are empty and all array and individual variables are interpreted as constant functions taking the value a everywhere. A *state* of $\mathfrak{A}$ is any finite variant of a valuation w_a. The set of states of $\mathfrak{A}$ is denoted $S^{\mathfrak{A}}$.

Call a state *initial* if it differs from some w_a only at the values of individual variables.

It is meaningful, and indeed useful in some contexts, to take as states the set of *all* valuations. Our purpose in restricting our attention to states as defined above is to prevent arrays from being initialized with highly complex oracles that would compromise the value of the relative expressiveness results of Chapter 15.

Assignment Statements

As in Section 5.2, with every program α we associate a binary relation

$$\mathfrak{m}_{\mathfrak{A}}(\alpha) \quad \subseteq \quad S^{\mathfrak{A}} \times S^{\mathfrak{A}}$$

(called the *input/output relation* of p), and with every formula φ we associate a set

$$\mathfrak{m}_{\mathfrak{A}}(\varphi) \quad \subseteq \quad S^{\mathfrak{A}}.$$

The sets $\mathfrak{m}_\mathfrak{A}(\alpha)$ and $\mathfrak{m}_\mathfrak{A}(\varphi)$ are defined by mutual induction on the structure of α and φ.

For the basis of this inductive definition, we first give the semantics of all the assignment statements discussed earlier.

- The array assignment $F(t_1, \ldots, t_n) := t$ is interpreted as the binary relation

$$\mathfrak{m}_\mathfrak{A}(F(t_1, \ldots, t_n) := t) \overset{\text{def}}{=} \{(u, u[F/u(F)[u(t_1), \ldots, u(t_n)/u(t)]]) \mid u \in S^\mathfrak{A}\}.$$

In other words, starting in state u, the array assignment has the effect of changing the value of F on input $u(t_1), \ldots, u(t_n)$ to $u(t)$, and leaving the value of F on all other inputs and the values of all other variables intact. For $n = 0$, this definition reduces to the following definition of simple assignment:

$$\mathfrak{m}_\mathfrak{A}(x := t) \overset{\text{def}}{=} \{(u, u[x/u(t)]) \mid u \in S^\mathfrak{A}\}.$$

- The push operations, **push**(t) for the algebraic stack and **push-1** and **push-0** for the Boolean stack, are interpreted as the binary relations

$$\mathfrak{m}_\mathfrak{A}(\mathbf{push}(t)) \overset{\text{def}}{=} \{(u, u[STK/(u(t) \cdot u(STK))]) \mid u \in S^\mathfrak{A}\}$$

$$\mathfrak{m}_\mathfrak{A}(\mathbf{push\text{-}1}) \overset{\text{def}}{=} \{(u, u[BSTK/(\mathbf{1} \cdot u(BSTK))]) \mid u \in S^\mathfrak{A}\}$$

$$\mathfrak{m}_\mathfrak{A}(\mathbf{push\text{-}0}) \overset{\text{def}}{=} \{(u, u[BSTK/(\mathbf{0} \cdot u(BSTK))]) \mid u \in S^\mathfrak{A}\},$$

respectively. In other words, **push**(t) changes the value of the algebraic stack variable STK from $u(STK)$ to the string $u(t) \cdot u(STK)$, the concatenation of the value $u(t)$ with the string $u(STK)$, and everything else is left intact. The effects of **push-1** and **push-0** are similar, except that the special constants $\mathbf{1}$ and $\mathbf{0}$ are concatenated with $u(BSTK)$ instead of $u(t)$.

- The pop operations, **pop**(y) for the algebraic stack and **pop** for the Boolean stack, are interpreted as the binary relations

$$\mathfrak{m}_\mathfrak{A}(\mathbf{pop}(y)) \overset{\text{def}}{=} \{(u, u[STK/\mathbf{tail}(u(STK))][y/\mathbf{head}(u(STK), u(y))]) \mid u \in S^\mathfrak{A}\}$$

$$\mathfrak{m}_\mathfrak{A}(\mathbf{pop}) \overset{\text{def}}{=} \{(u, u[BSTK/\mathbf{tail}(u(BSTK))]) \mid u \in S^\mathfrak{A}\},$$

respectively, where

$$\mathbf{tail}(a \cdot \sigma) \overset{\text{def}}{=} \sigma$$
$$\mathbf{tail}(\varepsilon) \overset{\text{def}}{=} \varepsilon$$
$$\mathbf{head}(a \cdot \sigma, b) \overset{\text{def}}{=} a$$
$$\mathbf{head}(\varepsilon, b) \overset{\text{def}}{=} b$$

and ε is the empty string. In other words, if $u(STK) \neq \varepsilon$, this operation changes the value of STK from $u(STK)$ to the string obtained by deleting the first element of $u(STK)$ and assigns that element to the variable y. If $u(STK) = \varepsilon$, then nothing is changed. Everything else is left intact. The Boolean stack operation **pop** changes the value of $BSTK$ only, with no additional changes. We do not include explicit constructs to test whether the stacks are empty, since these can be simulated (Exercise 11.3). However, we do need to be able to refer to the value of the top element of the Boolean stack, hence we include the **top**? test.

- The Boolean test program **top**? is interpreted as the binary relation

$$\mathrm{m}_{\mathfrak{A}}(\mathbf{top}?) \overset{\text{def}}{=} \{(u, u) \mid u \in S^{\mathfrak{A}}, \ \mathbf{head}(u(BSTK)) = \mathbf{1}\}.$$

In other words, this test changes nothing at all, but allows control to proceed iff the top of the Boolean stack contains $\mathbf{1}$.

- The wildcard assignment $x := ?$ for $x \in V$ is interpreted as the relation

$$\mathrm{m}_{\mathfrak{A}}(x := ?) \overset{\text{def}}{=} \{(u, u[x/a]) \mid u \in S^{\mathfrak{A}}, \ a \in A\}.$$

As a result of executing this statement, x will be assigned some arbitrary value of the carrier set A, and the values of all other variables will remain unchanged.

Programs and Formulas

The meanings of compound programs and formulas are defined by mutual induction on the structure of α and φ essentially as in the propositional case (see Section 5.2). We include these definitions below for completeness.

Regular Programs and While Programs

Here are the semantic definitions for the four constructs of regular programs.

$$m_{\mathfrak{A}}(\alpha\,;\,\beta) \overset{\text{def}}{=} m_{\mathfrak{A}}(\alpha) \circ m_{\mathfrak{A}}(\beta)$$

$$= \{(u,v) \mid \exists w \ (u,w) \in m_{\mathfrak{A}}(\alpha) \text{ and } (w,v) \in m_{\mathfrak{A}}(\beta)\} \tag{11.3.1}$$

$$m_{\mathfrak{A}}(\alpha \cup \beta) \overset{\text{def}}{=} m_{\mathfrak{A}}(\alpha) \cup m_{\mathfrak{A}}(\beta) \tag{11.3.2}$$

$$m_{\mathfrak{A}}(\alpha^*) \overset{\text{def}}{=} m_{\mathfrak{A}}(\alpha)^* = \bigcup_{n \geq 0} m_{\mathfrak{A}}(\alpha)^n$$

$$m_{\mathfrak{A}}(\varphi?) \overset{\text{def}}{=} \{(u,u) \mid u \in m_{\mathfrak{A}}(\varphi)\}. \tag{11.3.3}$$

The semantics of defined constructs such as **if-then-else** and **while-do** are obtained using their definitions exactly as in **PDL**.

Seqs and R.E. Programs

Recall that an r.e. program is a Turing machine enumerating a set $CS(\alpha)$ of seqs. If α is an r.e. program, we define

$$m_{\mathfrak{A}}(\alpha) \overset{\text{def}}{=} \bigcup_{\sigma \in CS(\alpha)} m_{\mathfrak{A}}(\sigma).$$

Thus, the meaning of α is defined to be the union of the meanings of the seqs in $CS(\alpha)$. The meaning $m_{\mathfrak{A}}(\sigma)$ of a seq σ is determined by the meanings of atomic programs and tests and the sequential composition operator.

There is an interesting point here regarding the translation of programs using other programming constructs into r.e. programs. This can be done for arrays and stacks (for Booleans stacks, even into r.e. programs with bounded memory), but not for wildcard assignment. Since later in the book we shall be referring to the r.e. set of seqs associated with such programs, it is important to be able to carry out this translation. To see how this is done for the case of arrays, for example, consider an algorithm for simulating the execution of a program by generating only ordinary assignments and tests. It does not generate an array assignment of the form $F(t_1,\ldots,t_n) := t$, but rather "remembers" it and when it reaches an assignment of the form $x := F(t_1,\ldots,t_n)$ it will aim at generating $x := t$ instead. This requires care, since we must keep track of changes in the variables inside t and $t_1,\ldots,t_n$ and incorporate them into the generated assignments. We leave the details to the reader (Exercises 11.5–11.7).

Formulas

Here are the semantic definitions for the constructs of formulas of DL. The reader is referred to Section 3.4 for the semantic definitions of atomic first-order formulas.

$$\mathfrak{m}_{\mathfrak{A}}(\mathbf{0}) \overset{\text{def}}{=} \varnothing \tag{11.3.4}$$

$$\mathfrak{m}_{\mathfrak{A}}(\varphi \to \psi) \overset{\text{def}}{=} \{u \mid \text{if } u \in \mathfrak{m}_{\mathfrak{A}}(\varphi) \text{ then } u \in \mathfrak{m}_{\mathfrak{A}}(\psi)\} \tag{11.3.5}$$

$$\mathfrak{m}_{\mathfrak{A}}(\forall x\ \varphi) \overset{\text{def}}{=} \{u \mid \forall a \in A\ u[x/a] \in \mathfrak{m}_{\mathfrak{A}}(\varphi)\} \tag{11.3.6}$$

$$\mathfrak{m}_{\mathfrak{A}}([\alpha]\varphi) \overset{\text{def}}{=} \{u \mid \forall v \text{ if } (u,v) \in \mathfrak{m}_{\mathfrak{A}}(\alpha) \text{ then } v \in \mathfrak{m}_{\mathfrak{A}}(\varphi)\}. \tag{11.3.7}$$

Equivalently, we could define the first-order quantifiers $\forall$ and $\exists$ in terms of the wildcard assignment:

$$\forall x\ \varphi \ \leftrightarrow \ [x := ?]\varphi \tag{11.3.8}$$

$$\exists x\ \varphi \ \leftrightarrow \ \langle x := ?\rangle\varphi. \tag{11.3.9}$$

Note that for *deterministic* programs α (for example, those obtained by using the **while** programming language instead of regular programs and disallowing wildcard assignments), $\mathfrak{m}_{\mathfrak{A}}(\alpha)$ is a partial function from states to states; that is, for every state u, there is at most one v such that $(u, v) \in \mathfrak{m}_{\mathfrak{A}}(\alpha)$. The partiality of the function arises from the possibility that α may not halt when started in certain states. For example, $\mathfrak{m}_{\mathfrak{A}}(\textbf{while 1 do skip})$ is the empty relation. In general, the relation $\mathfrak{m}_{\mathfrak{A}}(\alpha)$ need not be single-valued.

If K is a given set of syntactic constructs, we refer to the version of Dynamic Logic with programs built from these constructs as *Dynamic Logic with K* or simply as $\mathsf{DL}(K)$. Thus, we have $\mathsf{DL}(\text{r.e.})$, $\mathsf{DL}(\text{array})$, $\mathsf{DL}(\text{stk})$, $\mathsf{DL}(\text{bstk})$, $\mathsf{DL}(\text{wild})$, and so on. As a default, these logics are the poor-test versions, in which only quantifier-free first-order formulas may appear as tests. The unadorned DL is used to abbreviate $\mathsf{DL}(\text{reg})$, and we use $\mathsf{DL}(\text{dreg})$ to denote DL with **while** programs, which are really deterministic regular programs. Again, **while** programs use only poor tests. Combinations such as $\mathsf{DL}(\text{dreg+wild})$ are also allowed.

11.4   Satisfiability and Validity

The concepts of satisfiability, validity, etc. are defined as for PDL in Chapter 5 or as for first-order logic in Section 3.4.

Let $\mathfrak{A} = (A, \mathfrak{m}_{\mathfrak{A}})$ be a structure, and let u be a state in $S^{\mathfrak{A}}$. For a formula φ, we write $\mathfrak{A}, u \vDash \varphi$ if $u \in \mathfrak{m}_{\mathfrak{A}}(\varphi)$ and say that u *satisfies* φ *in* $\mathfrak{A}$. We sometimes write $u \vDash \varphi$ when $\mathfrak{A}$ is understood. We say that φ is $\mathfrak{A}$-*valid* and write $\mathfrak{A} \vDash \varphi$ if $\mathfrak{A}, u \vDash \varphi$

for all u in $\mathfrak{A}$. We say that φ is *valid* and write $\vDash \varphi$ if $\mathfrak{A} \vDash \varphi$ for all $\mathfrak{A}$. We say that φ is *satisfiable* if $\mathfrak{A}, u \vDash \varphi$ for some $\mathfrak{A}, u$.

For a set of formulas Δ, we write $\mathfrak{A} \vDash \Delta$ if $\mathfrak{A} \vDash \varphi$ for all $\varphi \in \Delta$.

Informally, $\mathfrak{A}, u \vDash [\alpha]\varphi$ iff every terminating computation of α starting in state u terminates in a state satisfying φ, and $\mathfrak{A}, u \vDash <\alpha>\varphi$ iff there exists a computation of α starting in state u and terminating in a state satisfying φ. For a pure first-order formula φ, the metastatement $\mathfrak{A}, u \vDash \varphi$ has the same meaning as in first-order logic (Section 3.4).

11.5   Bibliographical Notes

First-order DL was defined in Harel et al. (1977), where it was also first named Dynamic Logic. That paper was carried out as a direct continuation of the original work of Pratt (1976).

Many variants of DL were defined in Harel (1979). In particular, DL(stk) is very close to the context-free Dynamic Logic investigated there.

Exercises

11.1. Show that in the presence of the Boolean stack operations **push-1**, **push-0**, **pop**, and **top?**, there is no need for a Boolean stack operation that tests whether the top element is **0**.

11.2. Show how to write the recursive procedure appearing in Section 9.1 using a Boolean stack.

11.3. Show that a test for stack emptiness is redundant in DL with an algebraic stack.

11.4. Prove that the meaning of a regular program is the same as the meaning of the corresponding (regular) r.e. program.

11.5. Show how to translate any regular program with array assignments into an r.e. set of seqs with simple assignments only.

11.6. Show how to translate any regular program with an algebraic stack into an r.e. set of seqs with simple assignments only.

11.7. Show how to translate any regular program with a Boolean stack into a bounded-memory r.e. set of seqs with simple assignments only.

11.8. Define DL with integer counters. Show how to translate this logic into bounded-memory DL(r.e.).

11.9. Prove the equivalences (11.3.8) and (11.3.9) for relating wildcard assignment to quantification.

12 Relationships with Static Logics

Reasoning in first-order Dynamic Logic can take two forms: *uninterpreted* and *interpreted*. The former involves properties expressible in the logic that are independent of the domain of interpretation. The latter involves the use of the logic to reason about computation over a particular domain or a limited class of domains. In this chapter we discuss these two levels of reasoning and the relationships they engender between DL and classical static logics.

12.1   The Uninterpreted Level

Uninterpreted Reasoning: Schematology

In contrast to the propositional version PDL discussed in Part II, DL formulas involve variables, functions, predicates, and quantifiers, a state is a mapping from variables to values in some domain, and atomic programs are assignment statements. To give semantic meaning to these constructs requires a first-order structure $\mathfrak{A}$ over which to interpret the function and predicate symbols. Nevertheless, we are not obliged to assume anything special about $\mathfrak{A}$ or the nature of the interpretations of the function and predicate symbols, except as dictated by first-order semantics. Any conclusions we draw from this level of reasoning will be valid under all possible interpretations. *Uninterpreted reasoning* refers to this style of reasoning.

For example, the formula

$$p(f(x), g(y, f(x))) \quad \rightarrow \quad \texttt{<}z := f(x)\texttt{>}p(z, g(y, z))$$

is true over any domain, irrespective of the interpretations of p, f, and g.

Another example of a valid formula is

$$z = y \ \wedge \ \forall x \ f(g(x)) = x$$
$$\rightarrow \quad \texttt{[while } p(y) \textbf{ do } y := g(y)]\texttt{<while } y \neq z \textbf{ do } y := f(y)\texttt{>}1.$$

Note the use of [ ] applied to < >. This formula asserts that under the assumption that f "undoes" g, any computation consisting of applying g some number of times to z can be backtracked to the original z by applying f some number of times to the result.

This level of reasoning is the most appropriate for comparing features of programming languages, since we wish such comparisons not to be influenced by the coding capabilities of a particular domain of interpretation. For example, if we abandon the uninterpreted level and assume the fixed domain $\mathbb{N}$ of the natural numbers with zero, addition and multiplication, all reasonable programming languages are equivalent in computation power—they all compute exactly the partial recursive functions. In contrast, on the uninterpreted level, it can be shown that recursion is a strictly more powerful programming construct than iteration. Research comparing the expressive power of programming languages on the uninterpreted level is sometimes called *schematology*, and uninterpreted programs are often called *program schemes*.

As an example, let us consider regular programs and nondeterministic **while** programs. The former are as powerful as the latter, since every **while** program is obviously regular, as can be seen by recalling the definitions from Section 11.1:

$$\textbf{if } \varphi \textbf{ then } \alpha \textbf{ else } \beta \;\overset{\text{def}}{=}\; (\varphi?;\alpha) \cup (\neg\varphi?;\beta)$$
$$\textbf{while } \varphi \textbf{ do } \alpha \;\overset{\text{def}}{=}\; (\varphi?;\alpha)^*;\neg\varphi?.$$

Conversely, over any structure, nondeterministic **while** programs are as powerful as regular programs (Exercise 12.2). We define our logics using the regular operators since they are simpler to manipulate in mathematical arguments, but the **while** program operators are more natural for expressing algorithms.

If we do not allow nondeterminism in **while** programs, the situation is different. We show in Chapter 15 that DL with deterministic **while** programs is strictly less expressive than DL with regular programs when considered over all structures. However, over $\mathbb{N}$ they are equivalent (Theorem 12.6).

Failure of Classical Theorems

We now show that three basic properties of classical (uninterpreted) first-order logic, the *Löwenheim–Skolem theorem*, *completeness*, and *compactness*, fail for even fairly weak versions of DL.

The Löwenheim–Skolem theorem (Theorem 3.59) states that if a formula φ has an infinite model then it has models of all infinite cardinalities. Because of this theorem, classical first-order logic cannot define the structure of elementary arithmetic

$$\mathbb{N} \;=\; (\omega, +, \cdot, 0, 1, =)$$

up to isomorphism. That is, there is no first-order sentence that is true in a structure $\mathfrak{A}$ if and only if $\mathfrak{A}$ is isomorphic to $\mathbb{N}$. However, this can be done in DL.

PROPOSITION 12.1:   There exists a formula $\Theta_{\mathbb{N}}$ of DL(dreg) that defines $\mathbb{N}$ up to isomorphism.

Proof   Take as $\Theta_\mathbb{N}$ the conjunction of the following six first-order formulas:

- $\forall x\ x + 1 \neq 0$
- $\forall x\ \forall y\ x + 1 = y + 1 \rightarrow x = y$
- $\forall x\ x + 0 = x$
- $\forall x\ \forall y\ x + (y + 1) = (x + y) + 1$
- $\forall x\ x \cdot 0 = 0$
- $\forall x\ \forall y\ x \cdot (y + 1) = (x \cdot y) + x,$

plus the DL(dreg) formula

$$\forall x\ \texttt{<}y := 0\,;\ \textbf{while}\ y \neq x\ \textbf{do}\ y := y + 1\texttt{>}\mathbf{1}. \tag{12.1.1}$$

The sentence (12.1.1) says that the program inside the diamond halts for all x; in other words, every element of the structure is obtained from 0 by adding 1 a finite number of times. This is inexpressible in first-order logic. A side effect of (12.1.1) is that we may use the induction principle in all models of $\Theta_\mathbb{N}$.

The first two of the above first-order formulas imply that every model of $\Theta_\mathbb{N}$ is infinite. The remaining first-order formulas are the inductive definitions of addition and multiplication. It follows that every model of $\Theta_\mathbb{N}$ is isomorphic to $\mathbb{N}$.   ∎

The Löwenheim–Skolem theorem does not hold for DL, because $\Theta_\mathbb{N}$ has an infinite model (namely $\mathbb{N}$), but all models are isomorphic to $\mathbb{N}$ and are therefore countable.

Besides the Löwenheim–Skolem Theorem, compactness fails in DL as well. Consider the following countable set Γ of formulas:

$$\{\texttt{<while}\ p(x)\ \textbf{do}\ x := f(x)\texttt{>}\mathbf{1}\}\ \cup\ \{p(f^n(x)) \mid n \geq 0\}.$$

It is easy to see that Γ is not satisfiable, but it is finitely satisfiable, i.e. each finite subset of it is satisfiable.

Worst of all, completeness cannot hold for any deductive system as we normally think of it (a finite effective system of axioms schemes and finitary inference rules). The set of theorems of such a system would be r.e., since they could be enumerated by writing down the axioms and systematically applying the rules of inference in all possible ways. However, the set of valid statements of DL is not r.e. (Exercise 12.1). In fact, we will show in Chapter 13 exactly how bad the situation is.

This is not to say that we cannot say anything meaningful about proofs and deduction in DL. On the contrary, there is a wealth of interesting and practical results on axiom systems for DL that we will cover in Chapter 14.

Expressive Power

In this section we investigate the power of DL relative to classical static logics on the uninterpreted level. In particular, we will introduce *rich test* DL *of r.e. programs* and show that it is equivalent to the infinitary language $L_{\omega_1^{ck}\omega}$. Some consequences of this fact are drawn in later sections.

First we introduce a definition that allows to compare different variants of DL. Let us recall from Section 11.3 that a state is *initial* if it differs from a constant state w_a only at the values of individual variables. If DL_1 and DL_2 are two variants of DL over the same vocabulary, we say that DL_2 is *as expressive as* DL_1 and write $DL_1 \leq DL_2$ if for each formula φ in DL_1 there is a formula ψ in DL_2 such that $\mathfrak{A}, u \vDash \varphi \leftrightarrow \psi$ for all structures $\mathfrak{A}$ and initial states u. If DL_2 is as expressive as DL_1 but DL_1 is not as expressive as DL_2, we say that DL_2 is *strictly more expressive than* DL_1, and write $DL_1 < DL_2$. If DL_2 is as expressive as DL_1 and DL_1 is as expressive as DL_2, we say that DL_1 and DL_2 are of *equal expressive power*, or are simply *equivalent*, and write $DL_1 \equiv DL_2$. We will also use these notions for comparing versions of DL with static logics such as $L_{\omega\omega}$.

There is a technical reason for the restriction to initial states in the above definition. If DL_1 and DL_2 have access to different sets of data types, then they may be trivially incomparable for uninteresting reasons, unless we are careful to limit the states on which they are compared. We shall see examples of this in Chapter 15.

Also, in the definition of $DL(K)$ given in Section 11.4, the programming language K is an explicit parameter. Actually, the particular first-order vocabulary Σ over which $DL(K)$ and K are considered should be treated as a parameter too. It turns out that the relative expressiveness of versions of DL is sensitive not only to K, but also to Σ. This second parameter is often ignored in the literature, creating a source of potential misinterpretation of the results. For now, we assume a fixed first-order vocabulary Σ.

Rich Test Dynamic Logic of R.E. Programs

We are about to introduce the most general version of DL we will ever consider. This logic is called *rich test Dynamic Logic of r.e. programs*, and it will be denoted DL(rich-test r.e.). Programs of DL(rich-test r.e.) are r.e. sets of seqs as defined in Section 11.2, except that the seqs may contain tests φ? for any previously constructed formula φ.

The formal definition is inductive. All atomic programs are programs and all atomic formulas are formulas. If φ, ψ are formulas, α, β are programs, $\{\alpha_n \mid n \in \omega\}$

is an r.e. set of programs over a finite set of variables (free or bound), and x is a variable, then

- **0**
- $\varphi \rightarrow \psi$
- $[\alpha]\varphi$
- $\forall x \; \varphi$

are formulas and

- $\alpha \, ; \, \beta$
- $\{\alpha_n \mid n \in \omega\}$
- $\varphi?$

are programs. The set $CS(\alpha)$ of computation sequences of a rich test r.e. program α is defined as usual.

Recall from Section 3.6 that $L_{\omega_1\omega}$ is the language with the formation rules of the first-order language $L_{\omega\omega}$, but in which countably infinite conjunctions and disjunctions $\bigwedge_{i \in I} \varphi_i$ and $\bigvee_{i \in I} \varphi_i$ are also allowed. In addition, if $\{\varphi_i \mid i \in I\}$ is recursively enumerable, then the resulting language is denoted $L_{\omega_1^{ck}\omega}$ and is sometimes called *constructive* $L_{\omega_1\omega}$.

PROPOSITION 12.2:   DL(rich-test r.e.) $\equiv L_{\omega_1^{ck}\omega}$.

Proof In the translations below, φ ranges over $L_{\omega_1^{ck}\omega}$ formulas, ψ ranges over DL(rich-test r.e.) formulas, and α ranges over rich test r.e. programs. The translation from $L_{\omega_1^{ck}\omega}$ to DL(rich-test r.e.) is obtained via the mapping μ. The main clause of its definition is given below. Recall that $\neg\varphi$ stands for $\varphi \rightarrow \mathbf{0}$ and $<\alpha>\varphi$ stands for $\neg[\alpha]\neg\varphi$.

$$\mu(\bigvee_{i \in I} \varphi_i) \;\stackrel{\text{def}}{=}\; <\{\mu(\varphi_i)? \mid i \in I\}>\mathbf{1}.$$

The reverse translation is obtained via a mapping ν with the help of a mapping $(\;)_\alpha$ that tranforms $L_{\omega_1^{ck}\omega}$ formulas into $L_{\omega_1^{ck}\omega}$ formulas. Here α is an arbitrary rich test r.e. program. The main clause of the definition of ν is

$$\nu(<\alpha>\psi) \;\stackrel{\text{def}}{=}\; \nu(\psi)_\alpha,$$

and the main defining clauses for $(\ )_\alpha$ are as follows:

$$\varphi_{x:=t} \;\stackrel{\text{def}}{=}\; \varphi[x/t]$$

$$\varphi_{\alpha\,;\,\beta} \;\stackrel{\text{def}}{=}\; (\varphi_\alpha)_\beta$$

$$\varphi_{\{\alpha_n\mid n\in\omega\}} \;\stackrel{\text{def}}{=}\; \bigvee_{n\in\omega} \varphi_{\alpha_n}$$

$$\varphi_{\psi?} \;\stackrel{\text{def}}{=}\; \varphi \wedge \nu(\psi).$$

∎

Since r.e. programs as defined in Section 11.2 are clearly a special case of general rich-test r.e. programs, it follows that $\mathsf{DL}(\text{rich-test r.e.})$ is as expressive as $\mathsf{DL}(\text{r.e.})$. In fact they are not of the same expressive power.

THEOREM 12.3: $\mathsf{DL}(\text{r.e.}) \;<\; \mathsf{DL}(\text{rich-test r.e.})$.

Proof sketch.   One can use an Ehrenfeucht–Fraïssé argument to show that $\mathsf{DL}(\text{r.e.})$ cannot distinguish between the recursive ordinals ω^ω and $\omega^\omega \cdot 2$, whereas any recursive ordinal can be defined by a formula of $\mathsf{DL}(\text{rich-test r.e.})$ up to isomorphism. Details can be found in Meyer and Parikh (1981). ∎

Henceforth, we shall assume that the first-order vocabulary Σ contains at least one function symbol of positive arity. Under this assumption, DL can easily be shown to be strictly more expressive than $L_{\omega\omega}$:

THEOREM 12.4: $L_{\omega\omega} \;<\; \mathsf{DL}$.

Proof In Section 12.1 we saw how to construct an infinite model for Σ that is uniquely definable in DL up to isomorphism. By the upward Löwenheim–Skolem theorem, this is impossible in $L_{\omega\omega}$. ∎

COROLLARY 12.5:

$$L_{\omega\omega} \;<\; \mathsf{DL} \;\leq\; \mathsf{DL}(\text{r.e.}) \;<\; \mathsf{DL}(\text{rich-test r.e.}) \;\equiv\; L_{\omega_1^{ck}\omega}.$$

The situation with the intermediate versions of DL, e.g. $\mathsf{DL}(\text{stk})$, $\mathsf{DL}(\text{bstk})$, $\mathsf{DL}(\text{wild})$, etc., is of interest. We deal with the relative expressive power of these in Chapter 15, where we also show that the second inequality in Corollary 12.5 is strict.

12.2   The Interpreted Level

Interpreted Reasoning: Arithmetical Structures

This is the most detailed level we will consider. It is the closest to the actual process of reasoning about concrete, fully specified programs. Syntactically, the programs and formulas are as on the uninterpreted level, but here we assume a fixed structure or class of structures.

In this framework, we can study programs whose computational behavior depends on (sometimes deep) properties of the particular structures over which they are interpreted. In fact, almost any task of verifying the correctness of an actual program falls under the heading of interpreted reasoning.

One specific structure we will look at carefully is the natural numbers with the usual arithemetic operations:

$$\mathbb{N} \;=\; (\omega,\, 0,\, 1,\, +,\, \cdot,\, =).$$

Let $-$ denote the (first-order-definable) operation of subtraction and let $\gcd(x, y)$ denote the first-order-definable operation giving the greatest common divisor of x and y. The following formula of $\mathbf{DL}$ is $\mathbb{N}$-valid, i.e., true in all states of $\mathbb{N}$:

$$x = x' \wedge y = y' \wedge xy \geq 1 \quad \rightarrow \quad <\alpha>(x = \gcd(x', y')) \tag{12.2.1}$$

where α is the **while** program of Example 4.1 or the regular program

$$(x \neq y?;((x > y?; x := x - y) \cup (x < y?; y := y - x)))^{*}x = y?.$$

Formula (12.2.1) states the correctness and termination of an actual program over $\mathbb{N}$ computing the greatest common divisor.

As another example, consider the following formula over $\mathbb{N}$:

$$\forall x \geq 1 \; <(\textbf{if even}(x) \textbf{ then } x := x/2 \textbf{ else } x := 3x + 1)^{*}>(x = 1).$$

Here / denotes integer division, and **even**( ) is the relation that tests if its argument is even. Both of these are first-order definable. This innocent-looking formula asserts that starting with an arbitrary positive integer and repeating the following two operations, we will eventually reach 1:

- if the number is even, divide it by 2;
- if the number is odd, triple it and add 1.

The truth of this formula is as yet unknown, and it constitutes a problem in number theory (dubbed "the $3x + 1$ problem") that has been open for over 60 years. The formula $\forall x \geq 1\ <\alpha>\mathbf{1}$, where α is

while $x \neq 1$ **do if even**(x) **then** $x := x/2$ **else** $x := 3x + 1$,

says this in a slightly different way.

The specific structure $\mathbb{N}$ can be generalized, resulting in the class of *arithmetical structures*. We shall not give a full definition here. Briefly, a structure $\mathfrak{A}$ is *arithmetical* if it contains a first-order-definable copy of $\mathbb{N}$ and has first-order definable functions for coding finite sequences of elements of $\mathfrak{A}$ into single elements and for the corresponding decoding.

Arithmetical structures are important because (i) most structures arising naturally in computer science (e.g., discrete structures with recursively defined data types) are arithmetical, and (ii) any structure can be extended to an arithmetical one by adding appropriate encoding and decoding capabilities. While most of the results we present for the interpreted level are given in terms of $\mathbb{N}$ alone, many of them hold for any arithmetical structure, so their significance is greater.

Expressive Power over $\mathbb{N}$

The results of Section 12.1 establishing that

$$ L_{\omega\omega}\quad <\quad \mathsf{DL}\quad \leq\quad \mathsf{DL}(\text{r.e.})\quad <\quad \mathsf{DL}(\text{rich-test r.e.}) $$

were on the uninterpreted level, where all structures are taken into account.[1] Thus first-order logic, regular DL, and $\mathsf{DL}(\text{rich-test r.e.})$ form a sequence of increasingly more powerful logics when interpreted uniformly over all structures.

What happens if one fixes a structure, say $\mathbb{N}$? Do these differences in expressive power still hold? We now address these questions.

First, we introduce notation for comparing expressive power over $\mathbb{N}$. If DL_1 and DL_2 are variants of DL (or static logics, such as $L_{\omega\omega}$) and are defined over the vocabulary of $\mathbb{N}$, we write $\mathsf{DL}_1 \leq_{\mathbb{N}} \mathsf{DL}_2$ if for each $\varphi \in \mathsf{DL}_1$ there is $\psi \in \mathsf{DL}_2$ such that $\mathbb{N} \vDash \varphi \leftrightarrow \psi$. We define $<_{\mathbb{N}}$ and $\equiv_{\mathbb{N}}$ from $\leq_{\mathbb{N}}$ the same way $<$ and $\equiv$ were defined from $\leq$ in Section 12.1.

We now show that over $\mathbb{N}$, DL is no more expressive than first-order logic $L_{\omega\omega}$. This is true even for finite-test DL. The result is stated for $\mathbb{N}$, but is actually true for any arithmetical structure.

THEOREM 12.6: $L_{\omega\omega} \equiv_{\mathbb{N}} \mathsf{DL} \equiv_{\mathbb{N}} \mathsf{DL}(\text{r.e.})$.

---

1 As mentioned, the second inequality is also strict.

Proof   The direction $\leq$ of both equivalences is trivial. For the other direction, we sketch the construction of a first-order formula φ_L for each $\varphi \in \mathsf{DL}(\text{r.e.})$ such that $\mathbb{N} \vDash \varphi \leftrightarrow \varphi_L$.

The construction of φ_L is carried out by induction on the structure of φ. The only nontrivial case is for φ of the form $[\alpha]\psi$. For a formula of this form, suppose ψ_L has been constructed. Let $FV(\alpha) \subseteq \{x_1, \ldots, x_k\}$ for some $k \geq 0$. Consider the set of seqs σ over the vocabulary of arithmetic such that $FV(\sigma) \subseteq \{x_1, \ldots, x_k\}$. Every such σ is a finite expression, therefore can be encoded as a natural number $\ulcorner\sigma\urcorner$. Now consider the set

$$R \overset{\text{def}}{=} \{(\ulcorner\sigma\urcorner, n_1, \ldots, n_k, m_1, \ldots, m_k) \in \mathbb{N}^{2k+1} \mid (\overline{n}, \overline{m}) \in \mathfrak{m}_{\mathbb{N}}(\sigma)\},$$

where $\overline{n}$ is the state that assigns n_i to x_i for $1 \leq i \leq k$ and 0 to the remaining variables. The state $\overline{m}$ is defined similarly. Clearly R is a recursive set and there is first-order formula $\gamma(y, x_1, \ldots, x_k, z_1, \ldots, z_k)$ that defines R in $\mathbb{N}$. We can assume that the variables $y, z_1, \ldots, z_k$ do not occur in ψ_L. Let $\varphi_\alpha(y)$ be a formula defining the set $\{\ulcorner\sigma\urcorner \mid \sigma \in CS(\alpha)\}$. The desired formula φ_L is

$$\forall y \, \forall z_1 \, \ldots \, \forall z_k \, (\varphi_\alpha(y) \wedge \gamma(y, x_1, \ldots, x_k, z_1, \ldots, z_k) \quad \rightarrow \quad \psi_L[x_1/z_1, \ldots, x_k/z_k]).$$

The remaining cases we leave as an exercise (Exercise 12.5).   ∎

The significance of this result is that in principle, one can carry out all reasoning about programs interpreted over $\mathbb{N}$ in the first-order logic $L_{\omega\omega}$ by translating each DL formula into a first-order equivalent. The translation is effective, as this proof shows. Moreover, Theorem 12.6 holds for any arithmetical structure containing the requisite coding power. As mentioned earlier, every structure can be extended to an arithmetical one.

However, the translation of Theorem 12.6 produces unwieldly formulas having little resemblance to the original ones. This mechanism is thus somewhat unnatural and does not correspond closely to the type of arguments one would find in practical program verication. In Section 14.2, a remedy is provided that makes the process more orderly.

We now show that over $\mathbb{N}$, $\mathsf{DL}(\text{rich-test r.e.})$ has considerably more power than the equivalent logics of Theorem 12.6. This too is true for any arithmetical structure.

THEOREM 12.7:   Over $\mathbb{N}$, $\mathsf{DL}(\text{rich-test r.e.})$ defines precisely the Δ_1^1 (hyperarithmetic) sets.

Proof We will show in Theorem 13.6 that the set

$$\{\psi \in \mathsf{DL}(\text{rich-test r.e.}) \mid \mathbb{N} \vDash \psi\} \tag{12.2.2}$$

is hyperarithmetic. Any $\mathsf{DL}(\text{rich-test r.e.})$-definable set

$$\{(a_1,\dots,a_n) \mid \mathbb{N} \vDash \varphi[x_1/a_1,\dots,x_n/a_n]\} \tag{12.2.3}$$

defined by a $\mathsf{DL}(\text{rich-test r.e.})$ formula φ with free variables $x_1,\dots,x_n$ reduces by simple substitution[2] to (12.2.2). The set (12.2.3) is therefore hyperarithmetic.

For the other direction, we use the characterization of Δ_1^1 as the subsets of $\mathbb{N}$ defined by total IND programs; equivalently, by IND programs that always halt within "time" bounded by a recursive ordinal. This generalized notion of time is defined formally by the ordinal mapping $\text{ord} : T \to \mathbf{Ord}$ on recursive well-founded trees as discussed in Section 2.2. The time of a halting IND computation is the ordinal associated with the root of the computation tree.

Given an IND program π over $\mathbb{N}$ with program variables $x_1,\dots,x_n$ and a recursive ordinal represented by a well-founded recursive tree $T \subseteq \omega^*$ as described in Section 2.2, we define a family of $\mathsf{DL}(\text{rich-test r.e.})$ formulas φ_ℓ^w with free variables $x_1,\dots,x_n$, where $w \in T$ and ℓ is a statement label of π. The formula $\varphi_\ell^w[x_1/a_1,\dots,x_n/a_n]$ says that π halts and accepts in at most $\text{ord}(w)$ steps when started at statement ℓ in a state in which x_i has value a_i, $1 \le i \le n$.

The definition of φ_ℓ^w is inductive on the well-founded tree T. In the following definition, $c(\ell)$ refers to the continuation of statement ℓ in π; that is, the first statement of π if ℓ is the last statement, otherwise the statement immediately following ℓ.

The formulas φ_ℓ^w are defined as follows. If ℓ is the statement $x_i := \exists$, define

$$\varphi_\ell^w \stackrel{\text{def}}{=} \ \texttt{<}\{x_i := m \mid m \in \omega\}\texttt{><}\{\varphi_{c(\ell)}^{wn}? \mid n \in \omega, \ wn \in T\}\texttt{>}\mathbf{1}.$$

If ℓ is the statement $x_i := \forall$, define

$$\varphi_\ell^w \stackrel{\text{def}}{=} \ \texttt{[}\{x_i := m \mid m \in \omega\}\texttt{]<}\{\varphi_{c(\ell)}^{wn}? \mid n \in \omega, \ wn \in T\}\texttt{>}\mathbf{1}.$$

If ℓ is either **accept** or **reject**, define φ_ℓ^w to be $\mathbf{1}$ or $\mathbf{0}$, respectively. Finally, if ℓ is the statement **if r then go to ℓ'**, define

$$\varphi_\ell^w \stackrel{\text{def}}{=} \ \texttt{<if } r \text{ then } \{\varphi_{\ell'}^{wn}? \mid n \in \omega, \ wn \in T\} \text{ else } \{\varphi_{c(\ell)}^{wn}? \mid n \in \omega, \ wn \in T\}\texttt{>}\mathbf{1}.$$

The top-level statement asserting that π halts and accepts in ordinal time bounded by $\text{ord}(T)$ is $\varphi_{\ell_0}^\varepsilon$, where ℓ_0 is the first statement of π and ε is the null string. ∎

---

2 We assume the coding scheme for $\mathsf{DL}(\text{rich-test r.e.})$ formulas has been designed to permit effective identification of and substitution for free variables.

Theorem 12.6 says that over $\mathbb{N}$, the languages DL and DL(r.e.) each define precisely the arithmetic (first-order definable) sets, and Theorem 12.7 says that DL(rich-test r.e.) defines precisely the hyperarithmetic or Δ_1^1 sets. Since the inclusion between these classes is strict—for example, first-order number theory is hyperarithmetic but not arithmetic—we have

COROLLARY 12.8:   DL(r.e.) $<_\mathbb{N}$ DL(rich-test r.e.).

12.3   Bibliographical Notes

Uninterpreted reasoning in the form of program schematology has been a common activity ever since the work of Ianov (1960). It was given considerable impetus by the work of Luckham et al. (1970) and Paterson and Hewitt (1970); see also Greibach (1975). The study of the correctness of interpreted programs goes back to the work of Turing and von Neumann, but seems to have become a well-defined area of research following Floyd (1967), Hoare (1969) and Manna (1974).

Embedding logics of programs in $L_{\omega_1\omega}$ is based on observations of Engeler (1967). Theorem 12.3 is from Meyer and Parikh (1981). Theorem 12.6 is from Harel (1979) (see also Harel (1984) and Harel and Kozen (1984)); it is similar to the expressiveness result of Cook (1978). Theorem 12.7 and Corollary 12.8 are from Harel and Kozen (1984).

Arithmetical structures were first defined by Moschovakis (1974) under the name *acceptable structures*. In the context of logics of programs, they were reintroduced and studied in Harel (1979).

Exercises

12.1. Consider DL with deterministic **while** programs over the first-order vocabulary of $\mathbb{N}$. Show that the set of valid DL formulas over this vocabulary is not recursively enumerable. (*Hint.* Using the formula $\Theta_\mathbb{N}$ defined in Section 12.1 that defines the natural numbers up to isomorphism, show that if the set of valid DL formulas were r.e., then so would be the set of formulas true in $\mathbb{N}$, thus contradicting Gödel's incompleteness theorem.)

12.2. Show that nondeterministic **while** programs and regular programs are equivalent over any structure.

12.3. Show that in the uninterpreted sense, allowing only atomic formulas instead of all quantifier-free formulas as tests does not diminish the expressive power of DL.

12.4. Argue by induction on the well-founded recursive tree T that the construction of the DL(rich-test r.e.) formulas φ_ℓ^w in the proof of Theorem 12.7 is correct.

12.5. Fill in the missing cases in the proof of Theorem 12.6.

12.6. Give a precise definition of an arithmetical structure. Let $L_1 \leq_A L_2$ denote relative expressibility in arithmetical structures; that is, $L_1 \leq_A L_2$ holds if for any arithmetical structure $\mathfrak{A}$ and any formula φ in L_1, there is a formula ψ in L_2 such that $\mathfrak{A} \models \varphi \leftrightarrow \psi$. Define $L_1 \equiv_A L_2$ accordingly. Show that Theorem 12.6 holds for arithmetical structures; that is,

$$L_{\omega\omega} \quad \equiv_A \quad \mathsf{DL} \quad \equiv_A \quad \mathsf{DL(r.e.)}.$$

13 Complexity

This chapter addresses the complexity of first-order Dynamic Logic.

Section 13.1 discusses the difficulty of establishing validity in DL. As in Chapter 12, we divide the question into uninterpreted and interpreted versions. On the uninterpreted level, we deal with the complexity of deciding validity of a given formula of an arbitrary signature over all interpretations for that signature. On the interpreted level, we are interested in the truth in $\mathbb{N}$ of a number-theoretic DL formula or validity over arithmetical structures.

In Section 13.2 we turn our attention to some of the programming languages defined in Chapter 11 and analyze their *spectral complexity*, a notion that measures the difficulty of the halting problem over finite structures. Spectral complexity will become useful in comparing the expressive power of variants of DL in Chapter 15.

13.1 The Validity Problem

Since all versions of DL subsume first-order logic, truth can be no easier to establish than in $L_{\omega\omega}$. Also, since DL(r.e.) is subsumed by $L_{\omega_1^{ck}\omega}$, truth will be no harder to establish than in $L_{\omega_1^{ck}\omega}$. These bounds hold for both uninterpreted and interpreted levels of reasoning.

The Uninterpreted Level: Validity

In this section we discuss the complexity of the validity problem for DL. By the remarks above and Theorems 3.60 and 3.67, this problem is between Σ_1^0 and Π_1^1. That is, as a lower bound it is undecidable and can be no better than recursively enumerable, and as an upper bound it is in Π_1^1. This is a rather large gap, so we are still interested in determining more precise complexity bounds for DL and its variants. An interesting related question is whether there is some nontrivial[1] fragment of DL that is in Σ_1^0, since this would allow a complete axiomatization.

In the following, we consider these questions for full DL(reg), but we also consider two important subclasses of formulas for which better upper bounds are derivable:

- partial correctness assertions of the form $\psi \rightarrow [\alpha]\varphi$, and
- termination or total correctness assertions of the form $\psi \rightarrow \langle\alpha\rangle\varphi$,

---

1 *Nontrivial* here means containing $L_{\omega\omega}$ and allowing programs with iteration. The reason for this requirement is that loop-free programs add no expressive power over first-order logic.

where φ and ψ are first-order formulas. The results are stated for regular programs, but they remain true for the more powerful programming languages too. They also hold for deterministic **while** programs (Exercises 13.3 and 13.4).

We state the results without mentioning the underlying first-order vocabulary Σ. For the upper bounds this is irrelevant. For the lower bounds, we assume the Σ contains a unary function symbol and ternary predicate symbols to accommodate the proofs.

THEOREM 13.1:   The validity problem for DL is Π_1^1-hard, even for formulas of the form $\exists x\ [\alpha]\varphi$, where α is a regular program and φ is first-order.

Proof For convenience, we phrase the proof in terms of satisfiablity instead of validity, carrying out a reduction from the Σ_1^1-complete tiling problem of Proposition 2.22: Given a finite set T of tile types, can the infinite $\omega \times \omega$ grid with blue south and west boundaries be tiled so that the color red occurs infinitely often?

We will adapt the encoding of Theorem 3.67 to our needs. Let us recall that the vocabulary contains one constant symbol a, one unary function symbol f, and four ternary relation symbols SOUTH, NORTH, WEST and EAST.

As in the proof of Theorem 3.67, define the formula

$$\text{RED}(x,y) \quad \overset{\text{def}}{\Longleftrightarrow} \quad \text{NORTH}(x,y,f^{\text{red}}(a)) \vee \text{SOUTH}(x,y,f^{\text{red}}(a))$$
$$\vee\ \text{EAST}(x,y,f^{\text{red}}(a)) \vee \text{WEST}(x,y,f^{\text{red}}(a)),$$

which says intuitively that the tile at position x,y has a red side. Let ψ_T be the conjunction of the five formulas (3.4.3)–(3.4.7) used in the proof of Theorem 3.60 and the formula

$$\forall x <y := x; z := x; (y := f(y))^*; (z := f(z))^* > \text{RED}(y,z). \tag{13.1.1}$$

The claim is that ψ_T is satisfiable iff T can tile the $\omega \times \omega$ grid so that the color red occurs infinitely often. The explanations of the encoding in the proof of Theorem 3.60 apply here. Clause (13.1.1) forces the red to appear infinitely often in the tiling. It asserts that no matter how far we go, we always find at least one point with a tile containing red.

As for the required form of the DL formulas, note that the first five clauses can be "pushed under" the diamond and attached as conjuncts to $\text{RED}(x,y)$. Negating the resulting formula in order to accommodate the phrasing of the theorem in terms of validity yields the desired result. ∎

The following is an immediate corollary of Theorem 13.1:

THEOREM 13.2:   The validity problem for DL and DL(rich-test r.e.), as well as all intermediate versions, is Π_1^1-complete.

To soften the negative flavor of these results, we now show that the special cases of unquantified one-program DL(r.e.) formulas have easier validity problems (though, as mentioned, they are still undecidable). We first need a lemma.

LEMMA 13.3:   For every r.e. program α and for every first-order formula φ, there exists an r.e. set $\{\varphi_\sigma \mid \sigma \in CS(\alpha)\}$ of first-order formulas such that

$$\vDash \ [\alpha]\varphi \ \leftrightarrow \ \bigwedge_{\sigma \in CS(\alpha)} \varphi_\sigma.$$

Proof For every seq σ, we define a mapping $(\ )_\sigma$ that transforms first-order formulas into first-order formulas as follows:[2]

$$\varphi_\varepsilon \ \overset{\text{def}}{=} \ \varphi, \quad \text{where } \varepsilon \text{ is the null seq;}$$
$$\varphi_{x:=t \,;\, \sigma} \ \overset{\text{def}}{=} \ \varphi_\sigma[x/t];$$
$$\varphi_{\psi? \,;\, \sigma} \ \overset{\text{def}}{=} \ \psi \to \varphi_\sigma.$$

Verification of the conclusion of the lemma is left to the reader. ∎

THEOREM 13.4:   The validity problem for the sublanguage of DL(r.e.) consisting of formulas of the form $\langle\alpha\rangle\varphi$, where φ is first-order and α is an r.e. program, is Σ_1^0-complete.

Proof It suffices to show that the problem is in Σ_1^0, since the sublanguage $L_{\omega\omega}$ is already Σ_1^0-complete. By Lemma 13.3, $\langle\alpha\rangle\varphi$ is equivalent to $\bigvee_{\sigma \in CS(\alpha)} \varphi_\sigma$, and all the φ_σ are first-order. By the compactness of first-order logic, there is some finite subset $\Gamma \subseteq \{\varphi_\sigma \mid \sigma \in CS(\alpha)\}$ such that $\vDash \langle\alpha\rangle\varphi$ iff $\vDash \bigvee \Gamma$. Each such finite disjunction is a first-order formula, hence the finite subsets Γ can be generated and checked for validity in a recursively enumerable manner. ∎

It is easy to see that the result holds for formulas of the form $\psi \to \langle\alpha\rangle\varphi$, where ψ is also first-order (Exercise 13.1). Thus, termination assertions for nondeterministic programs with first-order tests (or total correctness assertions for deterministic programs), on the uninterpreted level of reasoning, are recursively enumerable and

---

2 The reader may wish to compare this mapping with the mapping defined in the proof of Proposition 12.2.

therefore axiomatizable. We shall give an explicit axiomatization in Chapter 14.
We now turn to partial correctness.

THEOREM 13.5:   The validity problem for the sublanguage of DL(r.e.) consisting
of formulas of the form $[\alpha]\varphi$, where φ is first-order and α is an r.e. program, is
Π_2^0-complete. The Π_2^0-completeness property holds even if we restrict α to range
over deterministic **while** programs.

Proof For the upper bound, we have by Lemma 13.3 that $\vDash [\alpha]\varphi$ iff $\vDash$
$\bigwedge_{\sigma \in CS(\alpha)} \varphi_\sigma$. It follows that the validity of the latter is co-r.e. in the r.e. problem of validity of first-order formulas, hence it is in Π_2^0.
       For the lower bound, we carry out a reduction (to the dual satisfiability problem)
from the Σ_2^0-complete tiling problem of Proposition 2.21. Let us recall that this
problem calls for a finite set T of tile types to tile the positive quadrant of the
integer grid in such a way that the colors on the south boundary form a finite
sequence of colors followed by an infinite sequence of blue.
       For our encoding, we again adapt the proof of Theorem 3.60. We use the notation
from that proof. We take ψ_T' to be the conjunction of the clauses (3.4.3), (3.4.6),
and (3.4.7) used in the proof of Theorem 3.60 together with the clause

$$\forall x \; \text{SOUTH}(x, a, f^{\text{blue}}(a)) \quad \rightarrow \quad \text{SOUTH}(f(x), a, f^{\text{blue}}(a)).$$

This clause expresses the property that the color blue, when occurring on the south
boundary, remains there from the first occurrence on. Now we can combine ψ_T'
with the requirement that blue actually occurs on the south boundary to obtain
the formula

$$\psi_T \;\stackrel{\text{def}}{=}\; \texttt{<}x := a; \textbf{while } \neg\text{SOUTH}(x, a, f^{\text{blue}}(a)) \textbf{ do } x := f(x)\texttt{>}\psi_T'.$$

The claim is that ψ_T is satisfiable iff T can tile the grid with the additional
constraint on the colors of south boundary. We leave the verification of this claim
to the reader.   ∎

       Theorem 13.5 extends easily to partial correctness assertions; that is, to formulas
of the form $\psi \rightarrow [\alpha]\varphi$, where ψ is also first-order (Exercise 13.2). Thus, while Π_2^0
is obviously better than Π_1^1, it is noteworthy that on the uninterpreted level of
reasoning, the truth of even simple correctness assertions for simple programs is not
r.e., so that no finitary complete axiomatization for such validities can be given.

The Interpreted Level: Validity over $\mathbb{N}$

The characterizations of the various versions of DL in terms of classical static logics established in Section 12.2 provide us with the precise complexity of the validity problem over $\mathbb{N}$.

THEOREM 13.6:   The $\mathbb{N}$-validity problem for DL(dreg) and DL(rich-test r.e.), as well as all intermediate versions, when defined over the vocabulary of $\mathbb{N}$, is hyperarithmetic (Δ_1^1) but not arithmetic.

Proof   Let

$$X \overset{\text{def}}{=} \{\varphi \in \mathsf{DL}(\text{rich-test r.e.}) \mid \mathbb{N} \models \varphi\}.$$

Let $\Theta_\mathbb{N}$ be the DL(dreg) formula that defines $\mathbb{N}$ up to isomorphism (see Proposition 12.1). Since for every $\varphi \in$ DL(rich-test r.e.) we have

$$\varphi \in X \iff \models \Theta_\mathbb{N} \to \varphi,$$

by Theorem 13.2 we have that X is in Π_1^1. On the other hand, since for every sentence φ we have $\varphi \notin X$ iff $\neg\varphi \in X$, it follows that X is also in Σ_1^1, hence it is in Δ_1^1.

That $\mathbb{N}$-validity for any of the intermediate versions is not arithmetic follows from the fact that the first-order theory of $\mathbb{N}$ is already not arithmetic.   ∎

13.2   Spectral Complexity

We now introduce the *spectral complexity* of a programming language. As mentioned, this notion provides a measure of the complexity of the halting problem for programs over finite interpretations.

Recall that a *state* is a finite variant of a constant valuation w_a for some $a \in A$ (see Section 11.3), and a state w is *initial* if it differs from w_a for individual variables only. Thus, an initial state can be uniquely defined by specifying its relevant portion of values on individual variables. For $m \in \mathbb{N}$, we call an initial state w an *m-state* if for some $a \in A$ and for all $i \geq m$, $w(x_i) = a$. An m-state can be specified by an $(m+1)$-tuple of values $(a_0, \dots, a_m)$ that represent values of w for the first $m+1$ individual variables $x_0, \dots, x_m$. Call an m-state $w = (a_0, \dots, a_m)$ *Herbrand-like* if the set $\{a_0, \dots, a_m\}$ generates A; that is, if every element of A can be obtained as a value of a term in the state w.

Coding Finite Structures

Let Σ be a finite first-order vocabulary, and assume that the symbols of Σ are linearly ordered as follows. Function symbols are smaller in the order than predicate symbols. Function symbols are ordered according to arity; that is, symbols of smaller arity are smaller than symbols of larger arity. Function symbols of the same arity are ordered in an arbitrary but fixed way. Predicate symbols are ordered similarly.

Let $\mathfrak{A}$ be a structure for Σ. We define a *natural chain* in $\mathfrak{A}$ as a particular way of linearly ordering all elements in the substructure of $\mathfrak{A}$ generated by the empty set. A natural chain is a partial function $C_{\mathfrak{A}} : \mathbb{N} \to A$ defined for $k \in \mathbb{N}$ as follows:

$$
C_{\mathfrak{A}}(k) \stackrel{\text{def}}{=} \begin{cases} f_i^{\mathfrak{A}}(C_{\mathfrak{A}}(i_1),\dots,C_{\mathfrak{A}}(i_n)), & \text{if } (i, i_1, \dots, i_n) \text{ is the first vector in lexicographic order such that } f_i \text{ is an } n\text{-ary function symbol in } \Sigma, i_1, \dots, i_n < k, \text{ and } f_i^{\mathfrak{A}}(C_{\mathfrak{A}}(i_1),\dots,C_{\mathfrak{A}}(i_n)) \notin \{C_{\mathfrak{A}}(j) \mid j < k\}; \\ \text{undefined}, & \text{otherwise.} \end{cases}
$$

Observe that if Σ has no constant symbols, then $C_{\mathfrak{A}} = \varnothing$. From now on, we assume that Σ has at least one constant symbol.

Let Σ be a first-order vocabulary and let $c_0, \dots, c_m$ be symbols not occurring in Σ. An *expanded vocabulary* $\Sigma \cup \{c_0, \dots, c_m\}$ is obtained from Σ by adding $c_0, \dots, c_m$ as constant symbols. If the symbols of Σ were linearly ordered in some way, then assuming a linear order on the new constants, the symbols of $\Sigma \cup \{c_0, \dots, c_m\}$ are ordered as in Σ, except that the new constants come just after the old constants and before the function symbols of Σ.

Let $\Sigma' = \Sigma \cup \{c_0, \dots, c_m\}$. For every Σ-structure $\mathfrak{A}$ and for every m-state $w = (a_0, \dots, a_m)$ in $\mathfrak{A}$, we expand $\mathfrak{A}$ into a Σ'-structure $\mathfrak{A}_w$ by interpreting each c_i by a_i and leaving the interpretation of the old symbols unchanged.

The next result shows that the natural chain in $\mathfrak{A}_w$ can be uniformly computed by a deterministic program with an algebraic stack.

PROPOSITION 13.7: For every $m > 0$, there exists a deterministic program NEXT_m with an algebraic stack such that for every Σ-structure $\mathfrak{A}$, m-state w in $\mathfrak{A}$, and $b \in A$,

$$\mathfrak{A}, w[x_{m+1}/b] \vDash \langle \text{NEXT}_m \rangle \mathbf{1} \iff b \in C_{\mathfrak{A}_w}(\mathbb{N}).$$

Moreover, if $b = C_{\mathfrak{A}_w}(k)$ for some k, then NEXT_m terminates for the input $w[x_{m+1}/b]$ in some state in which x_{m+1} has value $C_{\mathfrak{A}_w}(k+1)$ if $C_{\mathfrak{A}_w}(k+1)$ is defined, b if not.

Proof Following the recursive definition of $C_\mathfrak{A}$, it is easy to write a recursive procedure that computes the successor of $b \in A$ with respect to the natural chain in $\mathfrak{A}_w$. This procedure is further translated into the desired deterministic program with an algebraic stack (see Section 11.2). ∎

It follows that for every structure $\mathfrak{A}$ and input w that is an m-state, there is a canonical way of computing a successor function on the elements generated by the input.

PROPOSITION 13.8: Let $\mathfrak{A}_1$ and $\mathfrak{A}_2$ be Σ-structures on the same carrier generated by the empty set (that is, every element is named by a ground term), and assume that $C_{\mathfrak{A}_1} = C_{\mathfrak{A}_2}$. Then $\mathfrak{A}_1$ and $\mathfrak{A}_2$ are isomorphic iff $\mathfrak{A}_1 = \mathfrak{A}_2$.

Proof Let $f : \mathfrak{A}_1 \to \mathfrak{A}_2$ be an isomorphism. One proves by a straightforward induction on k in the domain of $C_{\mathfrak{A}_1}$ that $f(C_{\mathfrak{A}_1}(k)) = C_{\mathfrak{A}_2}(k)$. Thus f is the identity and $\mathfrak{A}_1 = \mathfrak{A}_2$. ∎

Let Σ be a first-order vocabulary. Recall that we assume that Σ contains at least one function symbol of positive arity. In this section we actually assume that Σ is *rich*; that is, either it contains at least one predicate symbol[3] or the sum of arities of the function symbols is at least two. Examples of rich vocabularies are: two unary function symbols, or one binary function symbol, or one unary function symbol and one unary predicate symbol. A vocabulary that is not rich will be called *poor*. Hence a poor vocabulary has just one unary function symbol and possibly some constants, but no relation symbols other than equality. The main difference between rich and poor vocabularies is that the former admit exponentially many pairwise non-isomorphic structures of a given finite cardinality, whereas the latter admit only polynomially many. In this section we will cover rich vocabularies. The case of poor vocabularies will be covered in the exercises (Exercises 13.9, 13.13, and 13.14).

We say that the vocabulary Σ is *mono-unary* if it contains no function symbols other than a single unary one. It may contain constants and predicate symbols.

Let $\mathfrak{A}$ be a Σ-structure generated by the empty set and let $\#A = n$. Without loss of generality, we can assume that $A = \{0, 1, \ldots, n-1\}$ and that $C_\mathfrak{A}(k) = k$ for all $k < n$. Every structure can be transformed into one satisfying this property by renaming elements if necessary. Let S_n be the set of all such structures over a fixed vocabulary Σ. Clearly, the set S_n depends on the vocabulary Σ. We shall

---

3 The equality symbol is not counted here.

write S_n^L when we want to make the dependence on Σ explicit. It follows from Proposition 13.8 that if $\mathfrak{A}, \mathfrak{B} \in S_n$ are different, then they are not isomorphic. Also every n-element Σ-structure with no proper substructures is isomorphic to precisely one element of S_n.

We encode every element $\mathfrak{A}$ of S_n by a binary string $\ulcorner \mathfrak{A} \urcorner \in \{0,1\}^*$ as follows. All elements of $\{0, \dots, n-1\}$ are encoded in binary using the same length, $\lfloor \log(n-1) \rfloor + 1$. The code of $\mathfrak{A}$ consists of concatenating the values of consecutive symbols of Σ in the order in which they occur in Σ, where the values of any function or predicate[4] in $\mathfrak{A}$ are listed for consecutive arguments in lexicographic order with respect to the natural order in $\{0, \dots, n-1\}$. It is easy to see that for every $\mathfrak{A} \in S_n$, the length of $\ulcorner \mathfrak{A} \urcorner$ is polynomial in n.[5]

Let us illustrate the coding technique with an example.

EXAMPLE 13.9:   Let $\mathfrak{A} = (\{0,1,2\}, c, f, \leq)$, where c is a constant that denotes 1, f is the binary operation of addition modulo 3, and $\leq$ is the linear order $0 \leq 1 \leq 2$. Clearly, $\mathfrak{A}$ is generated by the empty set. The natural chain in $\mathfrak{A}$ is $1, 2, 0$, thus $\mathfrak{A} \notin S_3$. However, $\mathfrak{A}$ is isomorphic to $\mathfrak{A}' = (\{0,1,2\}, c', f', \leq')$, where c' denotes 0, $f'(x,y) = x + y + 1 \pmod 3$, and $\leq'$ is the linear order $2 \leq' 0 \leq' 1$. The natural chain in $\mathfrak{A}'$ is $0, 1, 2$, therefore $\mathfrak{A}' \in S_3$. In order to help read off the code of $\mathfrak{A}'$, we abbreviate 00 by 0, 01 by 1, and 10 by 2. The code of $\mathfrak{A}'$ is given below.

$$0 \underbrace{1\,2\,0\,2\,0\,1\,0\,1\,2}_{\text{code of } f'} \underbrace{1\,1\,0\,0\,1\,0\,1\,1\,1}_{\text{code of } \leq'}$$

Spectra

We are now ready to define the notion of a *spectrum* of a programming language. Let K be a programming language and let $\alpha \in K$ and $m \geq 0$. The mth *spectrum of* α is the set

$SP_m(\alpha)$

$\overset{\text{def}}{=} \{\ulcorner \mathfrak{A}_w \urcorner \mid \mathfrak{A} \text{ is a finite } \Sigma\text{-structure}, w \text{ is an } m\text{-state in } \mathfrak{A}, \text{ and } \mathfrak{A}, w \vDash \texttt{<}\alpha\texttt{>}1\}.$

The *spectrum* of K is the set

$SP(K) \overset{\text{def}}{=} \{SP_m(\alpha) \mid \alpha \in K, \ m \in \mathbb{N}\}.$

---

4 Truth values of a predicate are represented using the correspondence 0 for **0** and 1 for **1**.

5 However, this polynomial depends on Σ.

Given $m \geq 0$, observe that structures in $S_n^{\Sigma \cup \{c_0, \ldots, c_m\}}$ can be viewed as structures of the form $\mathfrak{A}_w$ for a certain Σ-structure $\mathfrak{A}$ and an m-state w in $\mathfrak{A}$. This representation is unique.

In this section we establish the complexity of spectra; that is, the complexity of the halting problem in finite interpretations. Let us fix $m \geq 0$, a rich vocabulary Σ, and new constants $c_0, \ldots, c_m$. Since not every binary string is of the form $\ulcorner \mathfrak{A} \urcorner$ for some Σ-structure $\mathfrak{A}$ and m-state w in $\mathfrak{A}$, we will restrict our attention to strings that are of this form. Let

$$H_m^\Sigma \stackrel{\text{def}}{=} \{\ulcorner \mathfrak{A} \urcorner \mid \mathfrak{A} \in S_n^{\Sigma \cup \{c_0, \ldots, c_m\}} \text{ for some } n \geq 1\}.$$

It is easy to show that the language H_m^Σ is in $LOGSPACE$ for every vocabulary Σ and $m \geq 0$. Later, we shall need the following result.

LEMMA 13.10:   Let $m \geq 0$ and let L be a rich vocabulary. For every language $X \subseteq \{0,1\}^*$, there is a language $Y \subseteq H_m^\Sigma$ such that

$$X \quad \leq_{\log} \quad Y \quad \leq_{\log} \quad X.$$

Proof The proof is structured according to the symbols that belong to Σ. Let us consider the case in which Σ contains a unary relation symbol r and a unary function symbol f. The other cases are dealt with similarly, and we leave them to the reader.

Let $x \in \{0,1\}^*$. We define a Σ-structure $\mathfrak{B}_x$ and an Herbrand-like m-state u. Let $n = |x|$ be the length of x. The carrier of $\mathfrak{B}_x$ is the set $U = \{0, 1, \ldots, n\}$. The interpretation of f in $\mathfrak{B}_x$ is the successor function modulo $n+1$. The interpretation of r is as follows. For $i \in U$, we let $r^{\mathfrak{B}_x}(i)$ hold iff $1 \leq i \leq n$ and the ith bit in x is 1.

All other function symbols, including constants, are interpreted as functions constantly equal to 0. All other relation symbols are interpreted as empty relations. The state u assigns 0 to every variable. We leave it to the reader to show that there is a $LOGSPACE$-computable function $\Theta : \{0,1\}^* \to \{0,1\}^*$ such that $\Theta(x) = \ulcorner \mathfrak{B}_x, u \urcorner$. Since $\mathfrak{B}_x$ and $\mathfrak{B}_y$ are not isomorphic for $x \neq y$, it follows that Θ is one-to-one.

Let us describe a computation of another function $\Psi : \{0,1\}^* \to \{0,1\}^*$. Given an input $y \in \{0,1\}^*$, it checks whether $y \in H_m^\Sigma$. If so, it finds the cardinality (in binary) of a structure $\mathfrak{A}$ whose code is y. It then reads off from the code whether $f^{\mathfrak{A}}$ is the successor, whether all other operations of $\mathfrak{A}$ are constantly equal to 0, and whether all relations besides $r^{\mathfrak{A}}$ are empty. If so, it reads off from the code of $r^{\mathfrak{A}}$ the bits of a string x such that $\ulcorner \mathfrak{B}_x, u \urcorner = y$. If on any of these tests the machine computing Ψ should fail, the computation is aborted and the value of $\Psi(y)$ is the empty string. The reader can easily check that Ψ is indeed computable by a *LOGSPACE* transducer and that

$$\Psi(\Theta(x)) \;=\; x \quad \text{for all } x \in \{0,1\}^*,$$
$$\Theta(\Psi(y)) \;=\; y \quad \text{for all } y \in \Theta(\{0,1\}^*).$$

Given $X \subseteq \{0,1\}^*$, let $Y = \Theta(X)$. It follows that Θ establishes the reduction $X \leq_{\log} Y$, while Ψ establishes the reduction $Y \leq_{\log} X$. ∎

We are now ready to connect complexity classes with spectra. Let K be any programming language and let $C \subseteq 2^{\{0,1\}^*}$ be a family of sets. We say that $SP(K)$ *captures* C, denoted $SP(K) \approx C$, if

- $SP(K) \subseteq C$, and
- for every $X \in C$ and $m \geq 0$, if $X \subseteq H_m^\Sigma$, then there is a program $\alpha \in K$ such that $SP_m(\alpha) = X$.

For example, if C is the class of all sets recognizable in polynomial time, then $SP(K) \approx P$ means that

- the halting problem over finite interpretations for programs from K is decidable in polynomial time, and
- every polynomial-time-recognizable set of codes of finite interpretations is the spectrum of some program from K.

We conclude this section by establishing the spectral complexity of some of the programming languages introduced in Chapter 11.

THEOREM 13.11:   Let Σ be a rich vocabulary. Then

(i) $SP(\text{dreg}) \subseteq LOGSPACE$.
(ii) $SP(\text{reg}) \subseteq NLOGSPACE$.

Moreover, if Σ is mono-unary, then $SP(\text{dreg})$ captures $LOGSPACE$ and $SP(\text{reg})$ captures $NLOGSPACE$.

Proof We first show (i). Let α be a deterministic regular program and let $m \geq 0$. A deterministic off-line $O(\log n)$-space-bounded Turing machine M_α that accepts $SP_m(\alpha)$ can be constructed as follows. For a given input string $z \in \{0,1\}^*$, it checks whether z is the code of an expanded structure $\mathfrak{A}_w \in S_n^{\Sigma \cup \{c_0, \ldots, c_m\}}$ for some $n \geq 1$. This can be done in $O(\log n)$ space. If so, it starts a simulation of a computation of α in $\mathfrak{A}$, taking the values given by w as initial values for the registers of α. At any stage of the simulation, the current values of the registers of α are stored on the work tape of M_α using their binary representations of length $O(\log n)$. The necessary tests and updates of values of the registers of α can be read off from the input string z. The machine M_α halts iff α halts for $(\mathfrak{A}, w)$.

The proof of (ii) is essentially the same, except that M_α will be nondeterministic.

For the second part of the theorem, assume that Σ is mono-unary. We show that $SP(\mathrm{dreg})$ captures $LOGSPACE$. The argument for $SP(\mathrm{reg})$ is similar and is omitted. Let $X \in LOGSPACE$ and $X \subseteq H_m^\Sigma$ for some $m \geq 0$. We describe a deterministic regular program α such that for every $n \geq 1$ and every $\mathfrak{A}_w \in S_n^{\Sigma \cup \{c_0, \ldots, c_m\}}$,

$$\mathfrak{A}, w \vDash \langle \alpha \rangle 1 \iff \ulcorner \mathfrak{A}_w \urcorner \in X.$$

First, let us consider the case in which the carrier of $\mathfrak{A}$ has only one element. There are only finitely many pairwise nonisomorphic structures over a one-element carrier. They differ only by different interpretations of the predicate symbols. Let $\mathfrak{A}_1, \ldots, \mathfrak{A}_k$ all be one-element structures such that $\ulcorner \mathfrak{A}_w^i \urcorner \in X$. Since $\mathfrak{A}^i$ has only one element, it follows that w is uniquely determined.

The program α first checks whether the structure generated by the input has exactly one element. If so, it checks whether this structure is one of the $\mathfrak{A}^i$ listed above, in which case it halts. Otherwise it diverges.

From now on, we assume that $\mathfrak{A}$ has more than one element. Let M be a deterministic off-line $O(\log n)$-space-bounded Turing machine that accepts X. Without loss of generality, we can assume that M's tape alphabet is $\{0, 1\}$. Moreover, since the length of the input $\ulcorner \mathfrak{A}_w \urcorner$ for M is polynomial in $\#\mathfrak{A} = n$, we can assume without loss of generality that the work tape of M has length $k \lfloor \log n \rfloor$, where k is constant. Hence, the contents of this tape can be stored by α in k registers, each holding a value $a \in A$ whose binary expansion represents the relevant portion of the work tape.

In order to store head positions of M, the program α uses counters, which are simulated as follows. Since Σ is mono-unary, one can define a deterministic regular program that plays the role of the program NEXT_m of Proposition 13.7. This is the only place where we crucially use the assumption about Σ. Hence, α can compute the successor function that counts up to $n - 1$ in an n-element structure. Using several registers, α can thus count up to a polynomial number of steps.

The bits of the code $\ulcorner \mathfrak{A}_w \urcorner$ can be read off directly from $\mathfrak{A}$ and the first $m+1$ registers $x_0, \ldots, x_m$, which store the initial values of w. For this it is enough to have polynomial-size arithmetic on counters, as explained above.

Now α can simulate the computation of M step by step, updating the contents of M's work tape and M's head positions. It halts if and only if M eventually reaches an accepting state. ■

THEOREM 13.12:   Over a rich vocabulary Σ, $SP(\text{dstk})$ and $SP(\text{stk})$ capture P.

Proof The proof is very similar to the proof of Theorem 13.11. Instead of mutual simulation with $O(\log n)$-space-bounded Turing machines, we work with Cook's $O(\log n)$ *auxiliary pushdown automata* (APDAs); see Chapter 14 of Hopcroft and Ullman (1979) for the definition. The pushdown store of the APDA directly simulates the algebraic stack of a regular program. It follows from Cook's theorem (see Theorem 14.1 of Hopcroft and Ullman (1979)) that languages accepted by deterministic/nondeterministic $O(\log n)$ APDAs coincide with P. The program NEXT_m of Proposition 13.7 is used to simulate counters as in the proof of Theorem 13.11. ■

THEOREM 13.13:   If Σ is a rich vocabulary, then $SP(\text{darray})$ and $SP(\text{array})$ capture *PSPACE*.

Proof Again, the proof is very similar to that of Theorem 13.11. This time we mutually simulate deterministic/nondeterministic regular programs with arrays and deterministic/nondeterministic polynomial space Turing machines. By Savitch's theorem (Hopcroft and Ullman, 1979, Theorem 12.11) it follows that both models of Turing machines accept the same class of languages, namely *PSPACE*. To simulate counters for the backwards reduction, we need a deterministic regular program with arrays that performs the same function as the program NEXT_m of Proposition 13.7. The easy details are left to the reader. ■

13.3   Bibliographical Notes

The Π_1^1-completeness of DL was first proved by Meyer, and Theorem 13.1 appears in Harel et al. (1977). The proof given here is from Harel (1985). Theorem 13.4 is from Meyer and Halpern (1982). That the fragment of DL considered in Theorem 13.5 is not r.e., was proved by Pratt (1976). Theorem 13.6 follows from Harel and Kozen (1984).

The name "spectral complexity" was proposed by Tiuryn (1986), although the main ideas and many results concerning this notion were already present in Tiuryn and Urzyczyn (1983); the reader may consult Tiuryn and Urzyczyn (1988) for the full version. This notion is an instance of the so-called *second-order spectrum* of a formula. First-order spectra were investigated by Sholz (1952), from which originates the well known *Spectralproblem*. The reader can find more about this problem and related results in the survey paper by Börger (1984). Proposition· 13.7 and the notion of a natural chain is from Urzyczyn (1983a). The results of Section 13.2 are from Tiuryn and Urzyczyn (1983, 1988); see the latter for the complete version. A result similar to Theorem 13.12 in the area of finite model theory was obtained by Sazonov (1980) and independently by Gurevich (1983). Higher-order stacks were introduced in Engelfriet (1983) to study complexity classes. Higher-order arrays and stacks in DL were considered by Tiuryn (1986), where a strict hierarchy within the class of elementary recursive sets was established. The main tool used in the proof of the strictness of this hierarchy is a generalization of Cook's auxiliary pushdown automata theorem for higher-order stacks, which is due to Kowalczyk et al. (1987).

Exercises

13.1. Prove Theorem 13.4 for termination or total correctness formulas of the form $\psi \to \langle \alpha \rangle \varphi$.

13.2. Prove Theorem 13.5 for partial correctness assertions of the form $\psi \to [\alpha] \varphi$.

13.3. Prove Theorem 13.2 for DL(dreg).

13.4. Prove Theorem 13.5 for DL(dreg).

13.5. Show that for every structure $\mathfrak{A}$, the image $C_{\mathfrak{A}}(\mathbb{N})$ is the substructure of $\mathfrak{A}$ generated by the empty set; that is, the least substructure of $\mathfrak{A}$.

13.6. Write a recursive procedure that computes the successor function with respect to the natural chain in $\mathfrak{A}_w$ (see Proposition 13.7).

13.7. Show that if a vocabulary Σ contains no function symbols of positive arity, then DL(r.e.) reduces to first-order logic over all structures.

13.8. Show that for a rich vocabulary Σ and a given $n > 0$, there are exponentially many (in n) pairwise nonisomorphic Σ-structures $\mathfrak{A}$ such that $\#A = n$ and $\mathfrak{A}$ is generated by the empty set.

13.9. Show that for a poor vocabulary Σ and for a given $n > 0$, there are polynomially many (in n) pairwise nonisomorphic Σ-structures $\mathfrak{A}$ such that $\#A = n$ and $\mathfrak{A}$ is generated by the empty set.

13.10. Let Σ be a rich vocabulary. Show that for every $\mathfrak{A} \in S_n$, the length of $\ulcorner\mathfrak{A}\urcorner$ is polynomial in n.

13.11. Show that for every rich vocabulary Σ and $m \geq 0$, the language H_m^Σ is in *LOGSPACE*.

13.12. (Tiuryn (1986)) Show that if the vocabulary Σ is rich, then the spectra of deterministic/nondeterministic regular programs with an algebraic stack and arrays capture *EXPTIME*.

13.13. Let Σ be a poor vocabulary. Give an encoding $\ulcorner\ulcorner\mathfrak{A}\urcorner\urcorner \in \{0,1\}^*$ of finite structures $\mathfrak{A} \in S_n$ such that the length of $\ulcorner\ulcorner\mathfrak{A}\urcorner\urcorner$ is $O(\log n)$.

13.14. Let Σ be a poor vocabulary. Redefine the notion of a spectrum following the encoding of structures for poor vocabularies, and show that the complexity classes thus captured by spectra become exponentially higher. For example:

- spectra of deterministic regular programs capture $DSPACE(n)$;
- spectra of nondeterministic regular programs capture $NSPACE(n)$;
- spectra of regular programs with an algebraic stack capture $DTIME(2^{O(n)})$;
- spectra of regular programs with arrays capture $DSPACE(2^{O(n)})$ (see Tiuryn and Urzyczyn (1988)).

14 Axiomatization

This chapter deals with axiomatizing first-order Dynamic Logic. We divide our treatment along the same lines taken in Chapters 12 and 13, dealing with the uninterpreted and interpreted cases separately. We must remember, though, that in both cases the relevant validity problems are highly undecidable, something we will have to find a way around.

14.1   The Uninterpreted Level

Recall from Section 13.1 that validity in DL is Π_1^1-complete, but only r.e. when restricted to simple termination assertions. This means that termination (or total correctness when the programs are deterministic) can be fully axiomatized in the standard sense. This we do first, and we then turn to the problem of axiomatizing full DL.

Completeness for Termination Assertions

Although the reader may feel happy with Theorem 13.4, it should be stressed that only very simple computations are captured by valid termination assertions:

PROPOSITION 14.1: . Let $\varphi \to <\alpha>\psi$ be a valid formula of DL, where φ and ψ are first-order and α contains first-order tests only. There exists a constant $k \geq 0$ such that for every structure $\mathfrak{A}$ and state u, if $\mathfrak{A}, u \vDash \varphi$, there is a computation sequence $\sigma \in CS(\alpha)$ of length at most k such that $\mathfrak{A}, u \vDash <\sigma>\psi$.

Proof   The proof is left as an exercise (Exercise 14.1). ■

Nevertheless, since the validity problem for such termination assertions is r.e., it is of interest to find a nicely-structured complete axiom system. We propose the following.

AXIOM SYSTEM 14.2:

Axiom Schemes

- all instances of valid first-order formulas;
- all instances of valid formulas of PDL;
- $\varphi[x/t] \to <x := t>\varphi$,   where φ is a first-order formula.

Inference Rules

- modus ponens:

$$\frac{\varphi, \; \varphi \to \psi}{\psi}$$

We denote provability in Axiom System 14.2 by $\vdash_{s_1}$.

LEMMA 14.3:   For every first-order formula ψ and for every sequence σ of atomic assignments and atomic tests, there is a first-order formula ψ_σ such that

$$\vDash \psi_\sigma \; \leftrightarrow \; <\sigma>\psi.$$

Proof   The proof is left as an exercise (Exercise 14.2).   ∎

THEOREM 14.4:   For any **DL** formula of the form $\varphi \to <\alpha>\psi$, for first-order φ and ψ and program α containing first-order tests only,

$$\vDash \varphi \to <\alpha>\psi \; \iff \; \vdash_{s_1} \varphi \to <\alpha>\psi.$$

Proof   Soundness ($\Longleftarrow$) is obvious. The proof of completeness ($\Longrightarrow$) proceeds by induction on the structure of α and makes heavy use of the compactness of first-order logic. We present the case for $\varphi \to <\beta \cup \gamma>\psi$.

By assumption, $\vDash \varphi \to <\beta \cup \gamma>\psi$, therefore $\vDash \varphi \to \bigvee_{\sigma \in CS(\beta \cup \gamma)} \psi_\sigma$, where ψ_σ is the first-order equivalent to $<\sigma>\psi$ from Lemma 14.3. By the compactness of first-order logic, $\vDash \varphi \to \bigvee_{\sigma \in C} \psi_\sigma$ for some finite set of seqs $C \subseteq CS(\beta \cup \gamma) = CS(\beta) \cup CS(\gamma)$. This can be written

$$\vDash \varphi \; \to \; \left(\bigvee_{\sigma \in C_1} \psi_\sigma \vee \bigvee_{\tau \in C_2} \psi_\tau \right)$$

for some finite sets $C_1 \subseteq CS(\beta)$ and $C_2 \subseteq CS(\gamma)$. Since the last formula is first-order and valid, by the completeness of first-order logic we have

$$\vdash_{s_1} \varphi \; \to \; \left(\bigvee_{\sigma \in C_1} \psi_\sigma \vee \bigvee_{\tau \in C_2} \psi_\tau \right). \tag{14.1.1}$$

However, since $C_1 \subseteq CS(\beta)$ and $C_2 \subseteq CS(\gamma)$, we have $\vDash \bigvee_{\sigma \in C_1} \psi_\sigma \to <\beta>\psi$ and $\vDash \bigvee_{\tau \in C_2} \psi_\tau \to <\gamma>\psi$. Applying the inductive hypothesis to each yields $\vdash_{s_1} \bigvee_{\sigma \in C_1} \psi_\sigma \to <\beta>\psi$ and $\vdash_{s_1} \bigvee_{\tau \in C_2} \psi_\tau \to <\gamma>\psi$. By (14.1.1) and propositional reasoning, we obtain

$$\vdash_{S_1} \varphi \;\rightarrow\; (<\beta>\psi \vee <\gamma>\psi),$$

which together with an instance of the PDL tautology $<\beta>\psi \vee <\gamma>\psi \rightarrow <\beta \cup \gamma>\psi$ yields $\vdash_{S_1} \varphi \rightarrow <\beta \cup \gamma>\psi$. ∎

REMARK 14.5: The result also holds if α is allowed to involve tests that are themselves formulas as defined in the theorem.

Infinitary Completeness for the General Case

Given the high undecidability of validity in DL, we cannot hope for a complete axiom system in the usual sense. Nevertheless, we do want to provide an orderly axiomatization of valid DL formulas, even if this means that we have to give up the finitary nature of standard axiom systems.

In this section, we present a complete infinitary axiomatization of DL that includes an inference rule with infinitely many premises. Before doing so, however, we must get a certain technical complication out of the way. We would like to be able to consider valid first-order formulas as axiom schemes, but instantiated by general formulas of DL. In order to make formulas amenable to first-order manipulation, we must be able to make sense of such notions as "a free occurrence of x in φ" and the substitution $\varphi[x/t]$. For example, we would like to be able to use the axiom scheme of the predicate calculus $\forall x \; \varphi \rightarrow \varphi[x/t]$, even if φ contains programs.

The problem arises because the dynamic nature of the semantics of DL may cause a single occurrence of a variable in a DL formula to act as both a free and bound occurrence. For example, in the formula $<\textbf{while } x \leq 99 \textbf{ do } x := x + 1>\textbf{1}$, the occurrence of x in the expression $x + 1$ acts as both a free occurrence (for the first assignment) and as a bound occurrence (for subsequent assignments).

There are several reasonable ways to deal with this, and we present one for definiteness. Without loss of generality, we assume that whenever required, all programs appear in the special form

$$<\bar{z} := \bar{x} \,;\, \alpha \,;\, \bar{x} := \bar{z}>\varphi \tag{14.1.2}$$

where $\bar{x} = (x_1, \ldots, x_n)$ and $\bar{z} = (z_1, \ldots, z_n)$ are tuples of variables, $\bar{z} := \bar{x}$ stands for

$$z_1 := x_1 \,;\, \cdots \,;\, z_n := x_n$$

(and similarly for $\bar{x} := \bar{z}$), the x_i do not appear in α, and the z_i are new variables appearing nowhere in the relevant context outside of the program α. The idea is to make programs act on the "local" variables z_i by first copying the values of the x_i into the z_i, thus freezing the x_i, executing the program with the z_i, and then restoring the x_i. This form can be easily obtained from any DL formula by consistently changing all variables of any program to new ones and adding the appropriate assignments that copy and then restore the values. Clearly, the new formula is equivalent to the old. Given a DL formula in this form, the following are bound occurrences of variables:

- all occurrences of x in a subformula of the form $\exists x \; \varphi$;
- all occurrences of z_i in a subformula of the form (14.1.2) (note, though, that z_i does not occur in φ at all);
- all occurrences of x_i in a subformula of the form (14.1.2) except for its occurrence in the assignment $z_i := x_i$.

Every occurrence of a variable that is not bound is free. Our axiom system will have an axiom that enables free translation into the special form discussed, and in the sequel we assume that the special form is used whenever required (for example, in the assignment axiom scheme below).

As an example, consider the formula:

$$\forall x \; (<y := f(x); \; x := g(y,x)>p(x,y))$$
$$\rightarrow \quad <z_1 := h(z); \; z_2 := y; \; z_2 := f(z_1); \; z_1 := g(z_2,z_1); \; x := z_1; \; y := z_2>p(x,y).$$

Denoting $<y := f(x); x := g(y,x)>p(x,y)$ by φ, the conclusion of the implication is just $\varphi[x/h(z)]$ according to the convention above; that is, the result of replacing all free occurrences of x in φ by $h(z)$ after φ has been transformed into special form. We want the above formula to be considered a legal instance of the assignment axiom scheme below.

Now consider the following axiom system.

Axiom System 14.6:

Axiom Schemes

- all instances of valid first-order formulas;
- all instances of valid formulas of PDL;
- $<x := t>\varphi \leftrightarrow \varphi[x/t]$;
- $\varphi \leftrightarrow \widehat{\varphi}$, where $\widehat{\varphi}$ is φ in which some occurrence of a program α has been replaced

by the program $z := x$; α'; $x := z$ for z not appearing in φ, and where α' is α with all occurrences of x replaced by z.

Inference Rules

- modus ponens:

$$\frac{\varphi,\ \varphi \to \psi}{\psi}$$

- generalization:

$$\frac{\varphi}{[\alpha]\varphi} \quad \text{and} \quad \frac{\varphi}{\forall x \varphi}$$

- infinitary convergence:

$$\frac{\varphi \to [\alpha^n]\psi,\ n \in \omega}{\varphi \to [\alpha^*]\psi}$$

Provability in Axiom System 14.6, denoted by $\vdash_{s_2}$, is the usual concept for systems with infinitary rules of inference; that is, deriving a formula using the infinitary rule requires infinitely many premises to have been previously derived.

Axiom System 14.6 consists of an axiom for assignment, facilities for propositional reasoning about programs and first-order reasoning with no programs (but with programs possibly appearing in instantiated first-order formulas), and an infinitary rule for $[\alpha^*]$. The dual construct, $<\alpha^*>$, is taken care of by the "unfolding" validity of PDL:

$$<\alpha^*>\varphi \ \leftrightarrow \ (\varphi \vee <\alpha; \alpha^*>\varphi).$$

See Example 14.8 below.

The main result here is:

THEOREM 14.7:   For any formula φ of DL,

$$\models \varphi \ \Longleftrightarrow \ \vdash_{s_2} \varphi.$$

Proof sketch.   Soundness is straightforward. Completeness can be proved by adapting any one of the many known completeness proofs for the classical infinitary logic, $L_{\omega_1\omega}$. Algebraic methods are used in Mirkowska (1971), whereas Harel (1984) uses Henkin's method. For definiteness, we sketch an adaptation of the proof given in Keisler (1971).

Take the set At of *atoms* to consist of all consistent finite sets of formulas possibly involving elements from among a countable set G of new constant symbols. By an atom A being consistent, we mean that it is not the case that $\vdash_{S2} \neg \widehat{A}$, where $\widehat{A} = \bigwedge_{\varphi \in A} \varphi$. It is now shown how to construct a model for any $A \in At$. The result will then follow from the fact that for any consistent formula φ, $\{\varphi\} \in At$.

Given an atom A, we define its *closure* $CL(A)$ to be the least set of formulas containing all formulas of A and their subformulas, exactly as is done for the Fischer-Ladner closure $FL(\varphi)$ in Section 6.1, but which is also closed under substitution of constants from G for arbitrary terms, and which contains $c = d$ for each $c, d \in G$. An infinite sequence of atoms $A = A_0 \subseteq A_1 \subseteq A_2 \subseteq \cdots$ is now constructed. Given $A_i \in At$, A_{i+1} is constructed by considering φ_i, the ith closed formula of $CL(A)$ in some fixed ordering, and checking whether $A_i \cup \{\varphi_i\} \in At$. If so, certain formulas are added to A_i to produce A_{i+1}, depending on the form of φ_i.

A typical rule of this kind is the following. If $\varphi_i = \langle \alpha^* \rangle \psi$, then we claim that there must be some n such that $\widehat{A}_i \vee \langle \alpha^n \rangle \psi$ is consistent; then we take A_{i+1} to be $A_i \cup \{\varphi_i, \langle \alpha^n \rangle \psi, \ t_i = c\}$, where t_i is the ith item in some fixed enumeration of the basic terms over the current vocabulary, but with constants from G, and where $c \in G$ does not occur in A_i. To see that such an n exists, assume to the contrary that $\vdash_{S2} \neg(\widehat{A}_i \wedge \langle \alpha^n \rangle \psi)$ for every n. Then $\vdash_{S2} \widehat{A}_i \to [\alpha^n] \neg \psi$ for each n. By the infinitary convergence rule, $\vdash_{S2} \widehat{A}_i \to [\alpha^*] \psi$, which is $\vdash_{S2} \neg(\widehat{A}_i \wedge \langle \alpha^* \rangle \psi)$. But this contradicts the fact that $A_i \cup \{\varphi_i\} \in At$.

Now let $A_\infty = \bigcup_i A_i$ and let $\widehat{c} = \{d \in G \mid (c = d) \in A_\infty\}$. The structure $\mathfrak{A} = (D, \mathfrak{m}_\mathfrak{A})$ is obtained by taking the carrier to be $D = \{\widehat{c} \mid c \in G\}$ and for example setting $\mathfrak{m}_\mathfrak{A}(p)(\widehat{c}_1, \ldots, \widehat{c}_k)$ to be true iff $p(c_1, \ldots, c_k) \in A_\infty$. A straightforward induction on the complexity of formulas shows that all formulas of A_∞ are true in $\mathfrak{A}$. ∎

EXAMPLE 14.8:   We use Axiom System 14.6 to prove the validity of the following formula:

$$x = y \quad \to \quad [(x := f(f(x)))^*] \langle (y := f(y))^* \rangle x = y.$$

To that end, we show that for every n,

$$\vdash_{S2} \quad x = y \quad \to \quad [(x := f(f(x)))^n] \langle (y := f(y))^* \rangle x = y$$

and then apply the infinitary convergence rule to obtain the result. Let n be fixed.

We first prove

$$\vdash_{S2} \; x = y \;\; \rightarrow \;\; [x := f(f(x))] \, [x := f(f(x))] \ldots [x := f(f(x))]$$
$$\langle y := f(y) \rangle \langle y := f(y) \rangle \ldots \langle y := f(y) \rangle \; x = y \qquad (14.1.3)$$

with n occurrences of $[x := f(f(x))]$ and $2n$ occurrences of of $\langle y := f(y) \rangle$. This is done by starting with the first-order validity $\vdash_{S2} x = y \rightarrow f^{2n}(x) = f^{2n}(y)$ (where $f^{2n}(\cdot)$ abbreviates $f(f(\cdots(\cdot)\cdots))$ with $2n$ occurrences of f), and then using the assignment axiom with propositional manipulation n times to obtain

$$\vdash_{S2} \; x = y \;\; \rightarrow \;\; [x := f(f(x))] \ldots [x := f(f(x))] x = f^{2n}(y),$$

and again $2n$ times to obtain (14.1.3). Having proved (14.1.3), we use the PDL validity $\varphi \rightarrow \langle \alpha^* \rangle \varphi$ with φ taken to be $x = y$ and α taken to be $y := f(y)$, then apply the PDL validity $\langle \alpha \rangle \langle \alpha^* \rangle \varphi \rightarrow \langle \alpha^* \rangle \varphi$ $2n$ times with the same instantiation, using the monotonicity rules

$$\frac{\varphi \rightarrow \psi}{\langle \alpha \rangle \varphi \rightarrow \langle \alpha \rangle \psi} \qquad\qquad \frac{\varphi \rightarrow \psi}{[\alpha] \varphi \rightarrow [\alpha] \psi}$$

to obtain

$$\vdash_{S2} \; x = y \;\; \rightarrow \;\; [x := f(f(x))] \ldots [x := f(f(x))] \langle (y := f(y))^* \rangle x = y.$$

Now $n - 1$ applications of the PDL validity $[\alpha] [\beta] \varphi \rightarrow [\alpha; \beta] \varphi$ yield the desired result.

14.2   The Interpreted Level

Proving properties of real programs very often involves reasoning on the interpreted level, where one is interested in $\mathfrak{A}$-validity for a particular structure $\mathfrak{A}$. A typical proof might use induction on the length of the computation to establish an invariant for partial correctness or to exhibit a decreasing value in some well-founded set for termination. In each case, the problem is reduced to the problem of verifying some domain-dependent facts, sometimes called *verification conditions*. Mathematically speaking, this kind of activity is really an effective transformation of assertions about programs into ones about the underlying structure.

In this section, we show how for DL this transformation can be guided by a direct induction on program structure using an axiom system that is complete *relative to* any given arithmetical structure $\mathfrak{A}$. The essential idea is to exploit the existence, for any given DL formula, of a first-order equivalent in $\mathfrak{A}$, as guaranteed by Theorem

12.6. In the axiom systems we construct, instead of dealing with the Π_1^1-hardness of the validity problem by an infinitary rule, we take all $\mathfrak{A}$-valid first-order formulas as additional axioms. Relative to this set of axioms, proofs are finite and effective.

In Section 14.2 we take advantage of the fact that for partial correctness assertions of the form $\varphi \to [\alpha]\psi$ with φ and ψ first-order and α containing first-order tests, it suffices to show that DL reduces to the first-order logic $L_{\omega\omega}$, and there is no need for the natural numbers to be present. Thus, the system we present in Section 14.2 works for finite structures too. In Section 14.2, we present an *arithmetically complete* system for full DL that does make explicit use of natural numbers.

Relative Completeness for Correctness Assertions

It follows from Theorem 13.5 that for partial correctness formulas we cannot hope to obtain a completeness result similar to the one proved in Theorem 14.4 for termination formulas. A way around this difficulty is to consider only *expressive* structures.

A structure $\mathfrak{A}$ for the first-order vocabulary Σ is said to be *expressive* for a programming language K if for every $\alpha \in K$ and for every first-order formula φ, there exists a first-order formula ψ_L such that $\mathfrak{A} \vDash \psi_L \leftrightarrow [\alpha]\varphi$. Examples of structures that are expressive for most programming languages are finite structures and arithmetical structures.

Consider the following axiom system:

AXIOM SYSTEM 14.9:

Axiom Schemes

- all instances of valid formulas of PDL;
- $<x := t>\varphi \leftrightarrow \varphi[x/t]$ for first-order φ.

Inference Rules

- modus ponens:

$$\frac{\varphi,\ \varphi \to \psi}{\psi}$$

- generalization:

$$\frac{\varphi}{[\alpha]\varphi}.$$

Note that Axiom System 14.9 is really the axiom system for PDL from Chapter 7 with the addition of the assignment axiom. Given a DL formula φ and a structure $\mathfrak{A}$, denote by $\mathfrak{A} \vdash_{S3} \varphi$ provability of φ in the system obtained from Axiom System 14.9 by adding the following set of axioms:

- all $\mathfrak{A}$-valid first-order sentences.

THEOREM 14.10:   For every expressive structure $\mathfrak{A}$ and for every formula ξ of DL of the form $\varphi \to [\alpha]\psi$, where φ and ψ are first-order and α involves only first-order tests, we have

$$\mathfrak{A} \vDash \xi \quad \Longleftrightarrow \quad \mathfrak{A} \vdash_{S3} \xi.$$

Proof Soundness is trivial. For completeness, one proceeds by induction on the structure of α. We present the case for $\alpha = \beta^*$.

By the assumption, $\mathfrak{A} \vDash \varphi \to [\beta^*]\psi$. Consider the first-order formula $([\beta^*]\psi)_L$, which exists by the expressiveness of $\mathfrak{A}$, and denote it by χ. Clearly, $\mathfrak{A} \vDash \varphi \to \chi$ and $\mathfrak{A} \vDash \chi \to \psi$. Since both these formulas are first-order and are $\mathfrak{A}$-valid, they are axioms, so we have:

$$\mathfrak{A} \ \vdash_{S3} \ \varphi \to \chi \tag{14.2.1}$$
$$\mathfrak{A} \ \vdash_{S3} \ \chi \to \psi. \tag{14.2.2}$$

However, by the semantics of β^* we also have $\mathfrak{A} \vDash \chi \to [\beta]\chi$, from which the inductive hypothesis yields $\mathfrak{A} \vdash_{S3} \chi \to [\beta]\chi$. Applying the generalization rule with $[\beta^*]$ and using modus ponens with the PDL induction axiom of Chapter 7 yields $\mathfrak{A} \vdash_{S3} \chi \to [\beta^*]\chi$. This together with (14.2.1), (14.2.2), and PDL manipulation yields $\mathfrak{A} \vdash_{S3} \varphi \to [\beta^*]\psi$. ∎

REMARK 14.11:   The theorem holds also if α is allowed to involve tests of the form $\langle\alpha\rangle\chi$, where χ is first-order and α is constructed inductively in the same way.

Arithmetical Completeness for the General Case

In this section we prove the completeness of an axiom system for full DL. It is similar in spirit to the system of the previous section in that it is complete relative to the formulas valid in the structure under consideration. However, this system works for arithmetical structures only. It is not tailored to deal with other expressive structures, notably finite ones, since it requires the use of the natural numbers. The kind of completeness result proved here is thus termed *arithmetical*.

As in Section 12.2, we will prove the results for the special structure $\mathbb{N}$, omitting the technicalities needed to deal with general arithmetical structures, a task we leave to the exercises. The main difference in the proofs is that in $\mathbb{N}$ we can use variables n, m, etc., knowing that their values will be natural numbers. We can thus write $n + 1$, for example, assuming the standard interpretation. When working in an unspecified arithmetical structure, we have to precede such usage with appropriate predicates that guarantee that we are indeed talking about that part of the domain that is isomorphic to the natural numbers. For example, we would often have to use the first-order formula, call it $\text{nat}(n)$, which is true precisely for the elements representing natural numbers, and which exists by the definition of an arithmetical structure.

Consider the following axiom system:

AXIOM SYSTEM 14.12:

Axiom Schemes

- all instances of valid first-order formulas;
- all instances of valid formulas of PDL;
- $<x := t>\varphi \leftrightarrow \varphi[x/t]$ for first-order φ.

Inference Rules

- modus ponens:

$$\frac{\varphi, \; \varphi \to \psi}{\psi}$$

- generalization:

$$\frac{\varphi}{[\alpha]\varphi} \quad \text{and} \quad \frac{\varphi}{\forall x \varphi}$$

- convergence:

$$\frac{\varphi(n+1) \to <\alpha>\varphi(n)}{\varphi(n) \to <\alpha^*>\varphi(0)}$$

for first order φ and variable n not appearing in α.

REMARK 14.13:   For general arithmetical structures, the +1 and 0 in the rule of convergence denote suitable first-order definitions.

As in Axioms System 14.9, denote by $\mathfrak{A} \vdash_{S4} \varphi$ provability of φ in the system obtained from Axiom System 14.12 by adding all $\mathfrak{A}$-valid first-order sentences as axioms.

Interestingly, the infinitary system 14.6 and the arithmetical system 14.12 deal with α^* in dual ways. Here we have the arithmetical convergence rule for $<\alpha^*>$, and $[\alpha^*]$ is dealt with by the **PDL** induction axiom, whereas in 14.6 we have the infinitary rule for $[\alpha^*]$, and $<\alpha^*>$ is dealt with by the **PDL** unfolding axiom.

Before we address arithmetical completeness, we prove a slightly more specific version of the expressiveness result of Theorem 12.6. Again, we state it for $\mathbb{N}$, but an appropriately generalized version of it holds for any arithmetical structure.

LEMMA 14.14:   For any **DL** formula φ and program α, there is a first-order formula $\chi(n)$ with a free variable n such that for any state u in the structure $\mathbb{N}$, we have

$$\mathbb{N}, u \vDash \chi(n) \quad \Longleftrightarrow \quad \mathbb{N}, u \vDash <\alpha^{u(n)}>\varphi.$$

(Recall that $u(n)$ is the value of variable n in state u.)

Proof The result is obtained as in the proof of Theorem 12.6 in the following way: $\chi(n)$ will be constructed just as $(<\alpha>\varphi)_L$ in that proof. Instead of taking $\varphi_\alpha(y)$ which defines the set $\{\ulcorner\sigma\urcorner \mid \sigma \in CS(\alpha)\}$, we take a formula $\varphi_\alpha(n,y)$ defining the r.e. set

$$\{(n, \ulcorner\sigma_1 \cdots \sigma_n\urcorner) \in \mathbb{N}^2 \mid \sigma_1, \ldots, \sigma_n \in CS(\alpha)\}.$$

The rest of the proof is as in Theorem 12.6. ∎

We first show that Axiom System 14.12 is arithmetically complete for first-order termination assertions.

THEOREM 14.15:   For every formula ξ of **DL** of the form $\varphi \to <\alpha>\psi$, for first-order formulas φ and ψ and program α involving only first-order tests,

$$\mathbb{N} \vDash \xi \quad \Longleftrightarrow \quad \mathbb{N} \vdash_{S4} \xi.$$

Proof Soundness is trivial. For completeness, we proceed by induction on the structure of α. As in Theorem 14.10, we present the case for $\alpha = \beta^*$.

By assumption, $\mathbb{N} \vDash \varphi \to <\beta^*>\psi$. Consider the first-order formula $\chi(n)$ of Lemma 14.14 for ψ and α. Clearly $\mathbb{N} \vDash \varphi \to \exists n\ \chi(n)$ for n not appearing in φ, ψ

or α, and $\mathbb{N} \vDash \chi(0) \to \psi$. Hence, these being first-order, we have

$$\mathbb{N} \vdash_{S4} \varphi \to \exists n \, \chi(n),$$
$$\mathbb{N} \vdash_{S4} \chi(0) \to \psi.$$

However, from the meaning of $\chi(n)$, we also have $\mathbb{N} \vDash \chi(n+1) \to {<}\beta{>}\chi(n)$. By the inductive hypothesis, we obtain $\mathbb{N} \vdash_{S4} \chi(n+1) \to {<}\beta{>}\chi(n)$. The convergence rule now yields $\mathbb{N} \vdash_{S4} \chi(n) \to {<}\beta^*{>}\chi(0)$. Applying the generalization rule with $\forall n$ and using first-order manipulation, we obtain $\mathbb{N} \vdash_{S4} \exists n \, \chi(n) \to {<}\beta^*{>}\chi(0)$, which together with the two formulas above gives the result. ∎

The main result here is the following, which holds for any arithmetical structure (see Exercise 14.6):

THEOREM 14.16:   For every formula ξ of DL,

$$\mathbb{N} \vDash \xi \iff \mathbb{N} \vdash_{S4} \xi.$$

Proof Soundness is obvious. For completeness, let $\mathbb{N} \vDash \xi$. Define k_ξ to be the sum of the number of programs in ξ and the number of quantifiers prefixing non-first-order formulas in ξ. (Of course, we also count those quantifiers and programs that appear within tests.) We proceed by induction on k_ξ.

If $k_\xi = 0$, ξ must be first-order, so that $\mathbb{N} \vdash_{S4} \xi$. For $k_\xi > 0$, we can assume that ξ is in conjunctive normal form and then deal with each conjunct separately. Without loss of generality (see Exercise 14.7), it suffices to deal with formulas of the form $\varphi \to op \, \psi$, where $op \in \{\forall x, \exists x, {<}\alpha{>}, [\alpha]\}$ for some x or α, and where $op \, \psi$ is not first-order. This way, we have $k_\varphi, k_\psi < k_\xi$.

Now consider the first-order formulas φ_L and ψ_L, which exist by the expressiveness of $\mathbb{N}$. Clearly, since $\mathbb{N} \vDash \varphi \to op \, \psi$, we also have $\mathbb{N} \vDash \varphi_L \to op \, \psi_L$. We now claim that this implication is in fact provable:

$$\mathbb{N} \vdash_{S4} \varphi_L \to op \, \psi_L. \qquad (14.2.3)$$

For $op \in \{\forall x, \exists x\}$, the claim is trivial, since the formula is first-order. For the cases $[\alpha]$ and ${<}\alpha{>}$, the proof proceeds by induction on α exactly as in the proofs of Theorems 14.10 and 14.15, respectively. The only difference is that the main inductive hypothesis of the present proof is employed in dealing with non-first-order tests.

Now, from $\mathbb{N} \vDash \varphi \to \varphi_L$ and $\mathbb{N} \vDash \psi_L \to \psi$, we deduce $\mathbb{N} \vdash_{S4} \varphi \to \varphi_L$ and $\mathbb{N} \vdash_{S4} \psi_L \to \psi$ by the inductive hypothesis, since $k_\varphi, k_\psi < k_\xi$. These combine with rase and prove Theorems 14.15 and 14.16 for general arithmetical struc-

ustify the special form of formulas that is used in the proof of Theorem

Formulate a more liberal rule of convergence as in the discussion following rem 14.16. Prove that if the convergence rule of Axiom System 14.12 is replaced the new one, the resulting system is arithmetically complete.

. Extend Axiom Systems 14.6 and 14.12 to handle array assignments, and prove infinitary and arithmetical completeness, respectively, of the resulting systems.

(14.2.3) and some PDL and first-order manipulation to yield $\mathbb{N} \vdash_{S4} \varphi \rightarrow op\,\psi$, as desired. ∎

The use of the natural numbers as a device for counting down to 0 in the convergence rule of Axiom System 14.12 can be relaxed. In fact, any well-founded set suitably expressible in any given arithmetical structure suffices. Also, it is not necessary to require that an execution of α causes the truth of the parameterized $\varphi(n)$ in that rule to decrease exactly by 1; it suffices that the decrease is positive at each iteration.

EXAMPLE 14.17:   Consider the following program for computing v^w for natural numbers v and w.

$(z, x, y) := (1, v, w);$
while $y > 0$ **do**
  if $even(y)$
    then $(x, y) := (x^2, y/2)$
    else $(z, y) := (zx, y - 1)$

We shall prove using Axiom System 14.12 that this program terminates and correctly computes v^w in z. Specifically, we show

$$\mathbb{N} \quad \vdash_{S4} \quad (z = 1 \land x = v \land y = w)$$
$$\rightarrow \; \langle(((y > 0 \land even(y))?;\; x := x^2;\; y := y/2)$$
$$\cup \; (odd(y)?;\; z := z \cdot x;\; y := y - 1))^*\rangle \; (y = 0 \land z = v^w).$$

Consider the formula above as $\varphi \rightarrow \langle(\alpha \cup \beta)^*\rangle\psi$. We construct a first-order formula $\chi(n)$, for which we show

(i) $\mathbb{N} \vdash_{S4} \varphi \rightarrow \exists n\, \chi(n)$
(ii) $\mathbb{N} \vdash_{S4} \chi(0) \rightarrow \psi$
(iii) $\mathbb{N} \vdash_{S4} \chi(n+1) \rightarrow \langle\alpha \cup \beta\rangle\chi(n).$

Application of the convergence rule to (iii) and further manipulation yields the result.
  Let

$$\chi(n) \;\overset{\text{def}}{=}\; zx^y = v^w \;\land\; n = \lfloor \log_2 y \rfloor + 1bin(y).$$

Here $1bin(y)$ is the function yielding the number of 1's in the binary representation of y. Clearly, $1bin(y)$, $even(y)$, $odd(y)$ and $\lfloor \log_2 y \rfloor$ are all computable, hence they are first-order definable in $\mathbb{N}$. We consider their appearance in $\chi(n)$ as abbreviations. Also, consider $y := y/2$ as an abbreviation for the obvious equivalent program over $\mathbb{N}$, which need be defined only for even y.

To prove (i) and (iii), all we need to show is that the formulas therein are $\mathbb{N}$-valid, since they are first-order and will thus be axioms. For example, $\chi(0) \rightarrow \psi$ is

$$(zx^y = v^w \ \wedge \ 0 = \lfloor \log_2 y \rfloor + 1bin(y)) \ \rightarrow \ (y = 0 \ \wedge \ z = v^w),$$

which is clearly $\mathbb{N}$-valid, since $1bin(y) = 0$ implies $y = 0$, which in turn implies $zx^y = z$.

To prove (iii), we show

$$\mathbb{N} \ \vdash_{S4} \ (\chi(n+1) \wedge y > 0 \wedge even(y)) \ \rightarrow \ \langle\alpha\rangle\chi(n) \tag{14.2.4}$$

and

$$\mathbb{N} \ \vdash_{S4} \ (\chi(n+1) \wedge odd(y)) \ \rightarrow \ \langle\beta\rangle\chi(n). \tag{14.2.5}$$

PDL and first-order reasoning will then yield the desired (iii). Indeed, (14.2.4) is obtained by applying the assignment axiom and the PDL axiom for tests to the following formula:

$$(zx^y = v^w \ \wedge \ n+1 = \lfloor \log_2 y \rfloor + 1bin(y) \ \wedge \ y > 0 \ \wedge \ even(y))$$
$$\rightarrow \ (y > 0 \ \wedge \ even(y) \ \wedge \ z = (x^2)^{y/2} = v^w \ \wedge \ n = \lfloor \log_2(y/2) \rfloor + 1bin(y/2)).$$

This formula is $\mathbb{N}$-valid (and hence an axiom), since for any even y, $1bin(y) = 1bin(y/2)$ and $\lfloor \log_2(y) \rfloor = 1 + \lfloor \log_2(y/2) \rfloor$.

Similarly, (14.2.5) is obtained from the formula:

$$(zx^y = v^w \ \wedge \ n+1 = \lfloor \log_2 y \rfloor + 1bin(y) \ \wedge \ odd(y))$$
$$\rightarrow (odd(y) \ \wedge \ zxx^{y-1} = v^w \ \wedge \ n = \lfloor \log_2(y-1) \rfloor + 1bin(y-1)).$$

This formula is also $\mathbb{N}$-valid, since for odd y, $1bin(y) = 1 + 1bin(y-1)$ and $\lfloor \log_2 y \rfloor = \lfloor \log_2(y-1) \rfloor$.

Note that the proof would have been easier if the truth of $\chi(n)$ were allowed to "decrease" by more than 1 each time around the loop. In such a case, and with a more liberal rule of convergence (see Exercise 14.8), we would not have had to be so pedantic about finding the exact quantity that decreases by 1. In fact, we could have taken $\chi(n)$ to be simply $zx^y = v^w \wedge n = y$. The example was chosen in its present form to illustrate the fact (which follows from the completeness result) that in principle the strict convergence rule can always be used.

In closing, we note that appropriately restricted this chapter are complete for DL(dreg). In particular the Hoare **while**-rule

$$\frac{\varphi \wedge \xi \rightarrow [\alpha]\varphi}{\varphi \rightarrow [\textbf{while} \ \xi \ \textbf{do} \ \alpha](\varphi \wedge \neg\xi)}$$

results from combining the generalization rule with the of PDL, when $*$ is restricted to appear only in the cont that is, only in the form $(\xi?;p)^*;(\neg\xi)?$.

14.3 Bibliographical Notes

Completeness for termination assertions (Theorem 14.4) is from (1982). Infinitary completeness for DL (Theorem 14.7) is based for Algorithmic Logic (see Section 16.1) by Mirkowska (1971) presented here is an adaptation of Henkin's proof for $L_{\omega_1\omega}$ ap (1971).

The notion of relative completeness and Theorem 14.10 are due The notion of arithmetical completeness and Theorems 14.15 and Harel (1979).

The use of invariants to prove partial correctness and of well-fo prove termination are due to Floyd (1967). An excellent survey of and the corresponding completeness results appears in Apt (1981).

Some contrasting negative results are contained in Clarke (1979), Li and Wand (1978).

Exercises

14.1. Prove Proposition 14.1.

14.2. Prove Lemma 14.3.

14.3. Complete the proof of Theorem 14.4.

14.4. Show that every finite structure is expressive for the regular programs of DL

14.5. Complete the proof of Theorem 14.10.

(14.2.3) and some **PDL** and first-order manipulation to yield $\mathbb{N} \vdash_{S4} \varphi \to op\,\psi$, as desired. ∎

The use of the natural numbers as a device for counting down to 0 in the convergence rule of Axiom System 14.12 can be relaxed. In fact, any well-founded set suitably expressible in any given arithmetical structure suffices. Also, it is not necessary to require that an execution of α causes the truth of the parameterized $\varphi(n)$ in that rule to decrease exactly by 1; it suffices that the decrease is positive at each iteration.

EXAMPLE 14.17: Consider the following program for computing v^w for natural numbers v and w.

$(z, x, y) := (1, v, w);$
while $y > 0$ **do**
   if $even(y)$
      then $(x, y) := (x^2, y/2)$
      else $(z, y) := (zx, y - 1)$

We shall prove using Axiom System 14.12 that this program terminates and correctly computes v^w in z. Specifically, we show

$$\mathbb{N} \vdash_{S4} \quad (z = 1 \wedge x = v \wedge y = w)$$
$$\to \; \texttt{<}(((y > 0 \wedge even(y)))?; \; x := x^2; \; y := y/2)$$
$$\cup \; (odd(y)?; \; z := z \cdot x; \; y := y - 1))^*\texttt{>} \; (y = 0 \wedge z = v^w).$$

Consider the formula above as $\varphi \to \texttt{<}(\alpha \cup \beta)^*\texttt{>}\psi$. We construct a first-order formula $\chi(n)$, for which we show

(i) $\mathbb{N} \vdash_{S4} \varphi \to \exists n \; \chi(n)$
(ii) $\mathbb{N} \vdash_{S4} \chi(0) \to \psi$
(iii) $\mathbb{N} \vdash_{S4} \chi(n + 1) \to \texttt{<}\alpha \cup \beta\texttt{>}\chi(n)$.

Application of the convergence rule to (iii) and further manipulation yields the result.
    Let

$$\chi(n) \;\overset{\text{def}}{=}\; zx^y = v^w \;\wedge\; n = \lfloor \log_2 y \rfloor + 1bin(y).$$

Here $1bin(y)$ is the function yielding the number of 1's in the binary representation of y. Clearly, $1bin(y)$, $even(y)$, $odd(y)$ and $\lfloor \log_2 y \rfloor$ are all computable, hence they are first-order definable in $\mathbb{N}$. We consider their appearance in $\chi(n)$ as abbreviations. Also, consider $y := y/2$ as an abbreviation for the obvious equivalent program over $\mathbb{N}$, which need be defined only for even y.

To prove (i) and (iii), all we need to show is that the formulas therein are $\mathbb{N}$-valid, since they are first-order and will thus be axioms. For example, $\chi(0) \rightarrow \psi$ is

$$(zx^y = v^w \wedge 0 = \lfloor \log_2 y \rfloor + 1bin(y)) \quad \rightarrow \quad (y = 0 \wedge z = v^w),$$

which is clearly $\mathbb{N}$-valid, since $1bin(y) = 0$ implies $y = 0$, which in turn implies $zx^y = z$.

To prove (iii), we show

$$\mathbb{N} \ \vdash_{S4} \ (\chi(n+1) \wedge y > 0 \wedge even(y)) \ \rightarrow \ \langle\alpha\rangle\chi(n) \tag{14.2.4}$$

and

$$\mathbb{N} \ \vdash_{S4} \ (\chi(n+1) \wedge odd(y)) \ \rightarrow \ \langle\beta\rangle\chi(n). \tag{14.2.5}$$

PDL and first-order reasoning will then yield the desired (iii). Indeed, (14.2.4) is obtained by applying the assignment axiom and the PDL axiom for tests to the following formula:

$$(zx^y = v^w \ \wedge \ n + 1 = \lfloor \log_2 y \rfloor + 1bin(y) \ \wedge \ y > 0 \ \wedge \ even(y))$$
$$\rightarrow \ (y > 0 \ \wedge \ even(y) \ \wedge \ z = (x^2)^{y/2} = v^w \ \wedge \ n = \lfloor \log_2(y/2) \rfloor + 1bin(y/2)).$$

This formula is $\mathbb{N}$-valid (and hence an axiom), since for any even y, $1bin(y) = 1bin(y/2)$ and $\lfloor \log_2(y) \rfloor = 1 + \lfloor \log_2(y/2) \rfloor$.

Similarly, (14.2.5) is obtained from the formula:

$$(zx^y = v^w \ \wedge \ n + 1 = \lfloor \log_2 y \rfloor + 1bin(y) \ \wedge \ odd(y))$$
$$\rightarrow (odd(y) \ \wedge \ zxx^{y-1} = v^w \ \wedge \ n = \lfloor \log_2(y-1) \rfloor + 1bin(y-1)).$$

This formula is also $\mathbb{N}$-valid, since for odd y, $1bin(y) = 1 + 1bin(y-1)$ and $\lfloor \log_2 y \rfloor = \lfloor \log_2(y-1) \rfloor$.

Note that the proof would have been easier if the truth of $\chi(n)$ were allowed to "decrease" by more than 1 each time around the loop. In such a case, and with a more liberal rule of convergence (see Exercise 14.8), we would not have had to be so pedantic about finding the exact quantity that decreases by 1. In fact, we could have taken $\chi(n)$ to be simply $zx^y = v^w \wedge n = y$. The example was chosen in its present form to illustrate the fact (which follows from the completeness result) that in principle the strict convergence rule can always be used.

In closing, we note that appropriately restricted versions of all axiom systems of this chapter are complete for DL(dreg). In particular, as pointed out in Section 5.7, the Hoare **while**-rule

$$\frac{\varphi \wedge \xi \rightarrow [\alpha]\varphi}{\varphi \rightarrow [\textbf{while } \xi \textbf{ do } \alpha](\varphi \wedge \neg \xi)}$$

results from combining the generalization rule with the induction and test axioms of PDL, when * is restricted to appear only in the context of a **while** statement; that is, only in the form $(\xi?;p)^*;(\neg\xi)?$.

14.3   Bibliographical Notes

Completeness for termination assertions (Theorem 14.4) is from Meyer and Halpern (1982). Infinitary completeness for DL (Theorem 14.7) is based upon a similar result for Algorithmic Logic (see Section 16.1) by Mirkowska (1971). The proof sketch presented here is an adaptation of Henkin's proof for $L_{\omega_1\omega}$ appearing in Keisler (1971).

The notion of relative completeness and Theorem 14.10 are due to Cook (1978). The notion of arithmetical completeness and Theorems 14.15 and 14.16 are from Harel (1979).

The use of invariants to prove partial correctness and of well-founded sets to prove termination are due to Floyd (1967). An excellent survey of such methods and the corresponding completeness results appears in Apt (1981).

Some contrasting negative results are contained in Clarke (1979), Lipton (1977), and Wand (1978).

Exercises

14.1. Prove Proposition 14.1.

14.2. Prove Lemma 14.3.

14.3. Complete the proof of Theorem 14.4.

14.4. Show that every finite structure is expressive for the regular programs of DL.

14.5. Complete the proof of Theorem 14.10.

14.6. Phrase and prove Theorems 14.15 and 14.16 for general arithmetical structures.

14.7. Justify the special form of formulas that is used in the proof of Theorem 14.16.

14.8. Formulate a more liberal rule of convergence as in the discussion following Theorem 14.16. Prove that if the convergence rule of Axiom System 14.12 is replaced with the new one, the resulting system is arithmetically complete.

14.9. Extend Axiom Systems 14.6 and 14.12 to handle array assignments, and prove the infinitary and arithmetical completeness, respectively, of the resulting systems.

15 Expressive Power

The subject of study in this chapter is the relative expressive power of languages. We will be primarily interested in comparing, on the uninterpreted level, the expressive power of various versions of DL. That is, for programming languages P_1 and P_2 we will study whether $\mathsf{DL}(P_1) \leq \mathsf{DL}(P_2)$ holds. Recall from Chapter 12 (Section 12.1) that the latter relation means that for each formula φ in $\mathsf{DL}(P_1)$, there is a formula ψ in $\mathsf{DL}(P_2)$ such that $\mathfrak{A}, u \vDash \varphi \leftrightarrow \psi$ for all structures $\mathfrak{A}$ and initial states u.

Before describing the contents of this chapter, we pause to make two comments. The first is that by studying the expressive power of logics, rather than the computational power of programs, we are able to compare, for example, deterministic and nondeterministic programming languages. More on this will appear in Section 15.2. The second comment is that the answer to the fundamental question "$\mathsf{DL}(P_1) \leq \mathsf{DL}(P_2)$?" may depend crucially on the vocabulary over which we consider logics and programs. Indeed, as we will see later, the answer may change from "yes" to "no" as we move from one vocabulary to another. For this reason we always make clear in the theorems of this chapter our assumptions on the vocabulary.

Section 15.1 introduces the very useful concept of the unwinding of a program. Some basic properties of this notion are proved there. Section 15.2 establishes the fundamental connection between spectra of formulas (i.e. codes of finite interpretations in which a given formula holds) and the relative expressive power of logics of programs. This section also makes some connections with computational complexity theory.

Section 15.3 studies the important question of the role nondeterminism plays in the expressive power of logic. We discuss separately the case of regular programs (Section 15.3) and regular programs with a Boolean stack (Section 15.3). The more powerful programs are discussed in Section 15.3.

In Section 15.4 we study the question of the impact on the expressive power of bounded vs. unbounded memory. We discuss separately the cases of a polyadic vocabulary (Section 15.4) and a monadic vocabulary (Section 15.4).

The power of a Boolean stack vs. an algebraic stack and vs. pure regular programs is discussed in Section 15.5. Finally, in Section 15.6 we discuss some of the aspects of adding wildcard assignment to other programming constructs.

For now, we adopt a very liberal notion of a program. Let Σ be a finite vocabulary. All we assume about the programming language is that for every program α we have a set $CS(\alpha)$ of seqs that describe the semantics of α in all structures of the same signature. Hence, for every Σ-structure $\mathfrak{A}$ we have a binary input/output relation $m_{\mathfrak{A}}(\alpha) \subseteq S^{\mathfrak{A}} \times S^{\mathfrak{A}}$ defined by the equation

$$m_{\mathfrak{A}}(\alpha) \;=\; \bigcup \{m_{\mathfrak{A}}(\sigma) \mid \sigma \in CS(\alpha)\}.$$

We assume that with each program $\alpha \in K$ there is associated a finite set of individual variables $FV(\alpha) \subseteq V$ that occur in α. The property that we need is that for all $u, v \in S^{\mathfrak{A}}$, if $(u, v) \in m_{\mathfrak{A}}(\alpha)$ then $u(x) = v(x)$ for all $x \in V - FV(\alpha)$; that is, α does not change the values of individual variables that are not in $FV(\alpha)$.

15.1   The Unwind Property

We present a powerful technique that can be sometimes used to establish that one logic is strictly less expressive than another. This technique is based on the notion of the *unwind property*. We say that α *unwinds* in a structure $\mathfrak{A}$ if there exists $m \in \mathbb{N}$ and seqs $\sigma_1, \ldots, \sigma_m \in CS(\alpha)$ such that

$$m_{\mathfrak{A}}(\alpha) \;=\; m_{\mathfrak{A}}(\sigma_1) \cup \cdots \cup m_{\mathfrak{A}}(\sigma_m).$$

The next result says that the unwind property is invariant under elementary equivalence of structures.

PROPOSITION 15.1:   The unwind property is invariant under elementary equivalence of structures. That is, for every program α and for all structures $\mathfrak{A}$ and $\mathfrak{B}$ that are elementarily equivalent,

$$m_{\mathfrak{A}}(\alpha) = m_{\mathfrak{A}}(\sigma_1) \cup \cdots \cup m_{\mathfrak{A}}(\sigma_m) \;\Longrightarrow\; m_{\mathfrak{B}}(\alpha) = m_{\mathfrak{B}}(\sigma_1) \cup \cdots \cup m_{\mathfrak{B}}(\sigma_m),$$

where $\sigma_1, \ldots, \sigma_m \in CS(\alpha)$.

Proof   Assume that α unwinds in $\mathfrak{A}$; that is, there are $m \in \mathbb{N}$ and $\sigma_1, \ldots, \sigma_m \in CS(\alpha)$ such that

$$m_{\mathfrak{A}}(\alpha) \;=\; m_{\mathfrak{A}}(\sigma_1) \cup \cdots \cup m_{\mathfrak{A}}(\sigma_m). \tag{15.1.1}$$

For each $i \in \mathbb{N}$, let φ_i be a first-order formula describing the input-output relation of σ_i; that is, if $x_1, \ldots, x_n$ are all registers of α and $y_1, \ldots, y_n$ are new variables, then

$$\models \varphi_i \;\leftrightarrow\; \langle \sigma_i \rangle (x_1 = y_1 \wedge \cdots \wedge x_n = y_n).$$

By Lemma 14.3, we know that there exists such a formula.

It follows from (15.1.1) that for all $i \in \mathbb{N}$, the formula

$$\forall x_1 \ldots \forall x_n \; \forall y_1 \ldots \forall y_n \; (\varphi_i \to (\varphi_1 \vee \cdots \vee \varphi_n))$$

holds in $\mathfrak{A}$. Thus, it holds in $\mathfrak{B}$ as well, therefore

$$\mathfrak{m}_{\mathfrak{B}}(\alpha) \quad \subseteq \quad \mathfrak{m}_{\mathfrak{B}}(\sigma_1) \cup \cdots \cup \mathfrak{m}_{\mathfrak{B}}(\sigma_m).$$

Since the opposite inclusion always holds, it follows that α unwinds in $\mathfrak{B}$. ∎

LEMMA 15.2:   If φ is a DL formula over a programming language P and $\mathfrak{A}$ is a structure such that all programs that occur in φ unwind in $\mathfrak{A}$, then there is a first-order formula $\overline{\varphi}$ such that

$$\mathbf{Th}\,\mathfrak{A} \;\models\; \varphi \leftrightarrow \overline{\varphi}.$$

Proof The proof is by induction on φ. The only non-trivial step is when φ is $[\alpha]\varphi'$. If the program α unwinds in $\mathfrak{A}$, then for some $m \in \mathbb{N}$ and for some $\sigma_1, \ldots, \sigma_m \in CS(\alpha)$, the programs α and $\sigma_1 \cup \cdots \cup \sigma_m$ are equivalent in $\mathfrak{A}$, and by Proposition 15.1 they are equivalent in all models of $Th(\mathfrak{A})$. By Lemma 14.3, there is a first-order formula ψ_α that in all models describes the input-output relation of $\sigma_1 \cup \cdots \cup \sigma_m$; that is,

$$\models \psi_\alpha \quad \leftrightarrow \quad {<}\sigma_1 \cup \cdots \cup \sigma_m{>}(x_1 = y_1 \wedge \cdots \wedge x_n = y_n),$$

where $x_1, \ldots, x_n$ are all the registers of α and $y_1, \ldots, y_n$ are fresh variables. By the inductive hypothesis, there is a first-order formula $\overline{\varphi}'$ such that

$$\mathbf{Th}\,\mathfrak{A} \;\models\; \varphi' \leftrightarrow \overline{\varphi}'.$$

Assuming that $y_1, \ldots, y_n$ do not occur free in φ', we have

$$\mathbf{Th}\,\mathfrak{A} \;\models\; [\alpha]\varphi' \leftrightarrow \forall y_1 \ldots \forall y_n \; (\psi_\alpha \to \overline{\varphi}'[x_1/y_1, \ldots, x_n/y_n]),$$

which completes the proof. ∎

Lemma 15.2 gives a useful method for showing that some programs do not unwind. We illustrate it with the program $\textsc{Next}_0$ of Proposition 13.7.

PROPOSITION 15.3:   If $\mathfrak{A}$ is an infinite structure without proper substructures, then $\textsc{Next}_0$ does not unwind in $\mathfrak{A}$.

Proof   Observe that the formula

$$\forall x_0 \ \forall x_1 \ \langle \text{NEXT}_0 \rangle \mathbf{1}$$

holds in a structure $\mathfrak{A}$ iff $\mathfrak{A}$ has no proper substructures. Now, take an infinite structure $\mathfrak{A}$ without proper substructures. If NEXT_0 unwinds in $\mathfrak{A}$, then by Lemma 15.2 there is a first-order formula φ such that

$$\mathbf{Th}\,\mathfrak{A} \ \models \ \varphi \ \leftrightarrow \ \forall x_0 \forall x_1 \ \langle \text{NEXT}_0 \rangle \mathbf{1}.$$

This contradicts the upward Löwenheim–Skolem theorem (Theorem 3.59) since $\mathbf{Th}\,\mathfrak{A}$ contains uncountable models. ∎

The following result shows that the unwind property can be used to separate the expressive power of logics of programs.

THEOREM 15.4:   Let P_1 and P_2 be two programming languages over the same first-order vocabulary, and assume that there is a program $\alpha \in P_1$ such that for an arbitrary finite set $\{\beta_1, \dots, \beta_m\} \subseteq P_2$ there exists a structure $\mathfrak{A}$ with the property that all the $\beta_1, \dots, \beta_m$ unwind in $\mathfrak{A}$ but α does not. Then $\mathsf{DL}(P_2)$ is not reducible to $\mathsf{DL}(P_1)$.

Proof   Let $CS(\alpha) = \{\sigma_i \mid i \geq 0\}$. Let $FV(\alpha) = \{x_1, \dots, x_n\}$ be all the input registers of α. Let $y_1, \dots, y_n$ be new variables. We prove that the formula

$$\psi \ = \ \langle \alpha \rangle (x_1 = y_1 \wedge \cdots \wedge x_n = y_n)$$

is equivalent to no formula of $\mathsf{DL}(P_2)$. Indeed, assume that ψ is equivalent to a formula φ of $\mathsf{DL}(P_2)$. Let $\beta_1, \dots, \beta_m$ be all the programs occurring in φ, and take a structure $\mathfrak{A}$ in which each β_i unwinds and α does not. The latter property means that the set

$$\{\psi\} \ \cup \ \{\neg \langle \sigma_0 \cup \cdots \cup \sigma_k \rangle (x_1 = y_1 \wedge \cdots \wedge x_n = y_n) \mid k \geq 0\}$$

is finitely satisfiable in $\mathfrak{A}$.

For $k \geq 0$, let ψ_k be a first-order formula that is equivalent to

$$\neg \langle \sigma_0 \cup \cdots \cup \sigma_k \rangle (x_1 = y_1 \wedge \cdots \wedge x_n = y_n)$$

in all models (see Lemma 14.3).

By Lemma 15.2, there is a first-order formula $\overline{\varphi}$ that is equivalent to φ over all structures elementarily equivalent to $\mathfrak{A}$; that is,

Th $\mathfrak{A}$ $\models$ $\varphi \leftrightarrow \overline{\varphi}$.

Since φ is equivalent to ψ, it follows that the set

Th $\mathfrak{A}$ $\cup$ $\{\overline{\varphi}\}$ $\cup$ $\{\psi_k \mid k \geq 0\}$

is finitely satisfiable. By the compactness property for predicate logic (Theorem 3.57), it has a model $\mathfrak{B}$. This model is such that φ holds but ψ does not. This contradiction completes the proof. ∎

15.2 Spectra and Expressive Power

The goal of the present section is to relate the question of comparing the expressive power of Dynamic Logic over various programming languages to the complexity of spectra of the corresponding programming languages. As we will see later, for sufficiently powerful programming languages, the only way to distinguish between the corresponding logics is by investigating the behavior of the programs over finite interpretations.

An important notion often studied in the area of comparative schematology is that of translatability of one programming language into another. Let K_1 and K_2 be programming languages. We say that a program $\beta \in K_2$ *simulates* a program $\alpha \in K_1$ if for every Σ-structure $\mathfrak{A}$ the following holds:

$\{(u, v \restriction FV(\alpha)) \mid (u,v) \in \mathfrak{m}_{\mathfrak{A}}(\alpha), \ u \text{ is initial}\}$
$= \{(u, v \restriction FV(\alpha)) \mid (u,v) \in \mathfrak{m}_{\mathfrak{A}}(\beta), \ u \text{ is initial}\}.$

The reason for restricting v in the above formula to $FV(\alpha)$ is to allow β to use auxiliary variables and perhaps some other data types. We say that a program $\alpha \in K_1$ is *translatable into* K_2, if there exists $\beta \in K_2$ that simulates α. Finally, K_1 is translatable into K_2, denoted $K_1 \leq K_2$, if every program of K_1 is translatable into K_2.

A programming language K is said to be *admissible* if:

(i) it is translatable into the class of r.e. programs;

(ii) all atomic regular programs and all tests are translatable into K;

(iii) K is semantically closed under composition, **if-then-else** and **while-do**; e.g., closure under composition means that if $\alpha, \beta \in K$, then there is $\gamma \in K$ such that for every $\mathfrak{A}$, $\mathfrak{m}_{\mathfrak{A}}(\gamma) = \mathfrak{m}_{\mathfrak{A}}(\alpha) \circ \mathfrak{m}_{\mathfrak{A}}(\beta)$, and similarly for the other constructs.

Thus, if K is admissible, we will treat it as being syntactically closed under the above constructs. This will allow us to write expressions like **if** φ **then** α **else** β, where φ is a quantifier free formula and $\alpha, \beta \in K$. Such expressions, even though they do not necessarily belong to K, are semantically equivalent to programs in K. This convention will simplify notation and should never lead to confusion.

The relation of translatability can be further weakened if all we care about is the expressive power of the logic. For example, as we will see later, there are programming languages K_1 and K_2 such that $\mathsf{DL}(K_1) \leq \mathsf{DL}(K_2)$ holds, even though K_1 contains nondeterministic programs and K_2 contains only deterministic programs, so that $K_1 \leq K_2$ is impossible. It follows from the next result that all that really matters for the expressive power of the relevant logic are the termination properties of programs in the programming language.

PROPOSITION 15.5:   Let K be admissible. For every formula φ of $\mathsf{DL}(K)$ there is a formula φ' of $\mathsf{DL}(K)$ that is equivalent in all interpretations to φ and such that for every program α that occurs in φ', if α occurs in the context $[\alpha]\psi$, then $\psi = \mathbf{0}$.

Proof If α occurs in φ in the context $[\alpha]\psi$ with $\psi \neq \mathbf{0}$, then we replace $[\alpha]\psi$ with

$$\forall y_1 \ldots \forall y_m \ (\neg[\alpha; (x_1 = y_1 \wedge \cdots \wedge x_m = y_m)?]\mathbf{0} \ \rightarrow \ \psi[x_1/y_1, \ldots, x_m/y_m]),$$

where $x_1, \ldots, x_m$ are all variables that occur freely in α and $y_1, \ldots, y_m$ are fresh variables that occur neither in α nor in ψ. Since K is admissible, it follows that $\alpha; (x_1 = y_1 \wedge \cdots \wedge x_m = y_m)?$ belongs to K. After a finite number of steps we transform φ into the desired formula φ'. ∎

The above comments motivate the following definition. K_2 is said to *termination-subsume* K_1, denoted $K_1 \preceq_T K_2$, if for every $\alpha \in K_1$ there is $\beta \in K_2$ such that for every Σ-structure $\mathfrak{A}$ and for every state $u \in S^{\mathfrak{A}}$, we have

$$\mathfrak{A}, u \vDash \langle\alpha\rangle\mathbf{1} \ \Longleftrightarrow \ \mathfrak{A}, u \vDash \langle\beta\rangle\mathbf{1}.$$

Notice that the above is equivalent to

$$\mathfrak{A}, u \vDash [\alpha]\mathbf{0} \ \Longleftrightarrow \ \mathfrak{A}, u \vDash [\beta]\mathbf{0}.$$

PROPOSITION 15.6:   Let K_1 and K_2 be admissible programming languages.

(i) If $K_1 \leq K_2$, then $K_1 \preceq_T K_2$.

(ii) If $K_1 \preceq_T K_2$, then $\mathsf{DL}(K_1) \leq \mathsf{DL}(K_2)$.

Proof The first part is immediate. The second follows immediately from Proposition 15.5. ∎

An admissible programming language K is said to be *semi-universal* if for every $m > 0$, the program NEXT_m of Proposition 13.7 is translatable into K.

Examples of semi-universal programming languages include r.e. programs, regular programs with an algebraic stack, and regular programs with arrays. A corollary of the following result is that the expressive power of DL over a semi-universal programming language can be determined by investigating finite interpretations only.

Recall that a state u is Herbrand-like (see the beginning of Section 13.2) if the values assigned by u to the individual variables (there are finitely many of them) generate the structure.

PROPOSITION 15.7:   If K is semi-universal, then for every r.e. program α there is $\beta \in K$ such that α and β have the same termination properties over all infinite interpretations; that is, for every infinite Σ-structure $\mathfrak{A}$ and for every Herbrand-like state u in $\mathfrak{A}$,

$$\mathfrak{A}, u \vDash \text{<}\alpha\text{>}\mathbf{1} \iff \mathfrak{A}, u \vDash \text{<}\beta\text{>}\mathbf{1}.$$

Proof sketch.   We sketch the proof, leaving the details to the reader. Let α be an arbitrary r.e. program and let $FV(\alpha) \subseteq \{x_0, \ldots, x_m\}$. Clearly, the termination of α in any interpretation depends only on the values of variables in $FV(\alpha)$ and on the substructure generated by these values. Thus, we can assume that the state u in the conclusion of the proposition is an Herbrand-like m-state. Let us start by observing that using NEXT_m and working in an infinite interpretation gives us *counters*, with a successor function that corresponds to the particular order in which all elements of the substructure generated by the input occur in the natural chain. Zero is represented here as the first element of the natural chain; testing for zero and testing the equality of counters can be done easily. The control structure of a deterministic regular program with these counters is strong enough to compute every partial recursive function.

Now, we can use counters to simulate the Turing machine that computes $CS(\alpha) = \{\sigma_n \mid n \in \mathbb{N}\}$. The regular program β that will simulate α searches through all seqs σ_n starting with σ_0, trying to find the first one that terminates. It halts as soon as it finds one such σ_n.

In order to simulate the computation of σ_n, β has to be able to compute the value of any term t with variables in $\{x_0, \ldots, x_m\}$. This can be done as follows. Given t, the program β computes the value of t with respect to the actual values stored in $x_0, \ldots, x_m$ by first computing the values for subterms of t of depth 1, then of depth 2, etc. Of course, in order to do this, β has to store the intermediate values. For this we use the power of counters and the program NEXT_m. Using counters, β can encode arbitrary finite sequences of natural numbers. Using NEXT_m gives β a natural encoding of all the elements of the substructure generated by the input.

Now, it should be clear that being able to compute the value of any term with variables in $\{x_0, \ldots, x_m\}$, the program β can perform the computation of every σ_n. Since K is admissible, it follows that the program described above is equivalent to a program in K. ∎

An admissible programming language K is *divergence-closed* if for every $\alpha \in K$ there exists $\beta \in K$ and two variables $x, y \in V$ such that for every finite Herbrand-like interpretation $(\mathfrak{A}, u)$ with A having at least two elements,

$$\mathfrak{A}, u \vDash \texttt{<}\alpha\texttt{>}\mathbf{1} \iff \mathfrak{A}, u \vDash \texttt{<}\beta\texttt{>}(x = y),$$
$$\mathfrak{A}, u \vDash [\alpha]\mathbf{0} \iff \mathfrak{A}, u \vDash \texttt{<}\beta\texttt{>}(x \neq y).$$

Informally, β decides without diverging whether α possibly terminates.

LEMMA 15.8:   If K is divergence-closed, then for every $\alpha \in K$ there exists $\gamma \in K$ such that for every finite Herbrand-like interpretation $(\mathfrak{A}, u)$ with A having at least two elements, we have both

$$\mathfrak{A}, u \vDash \texttt{<}\alpha\texttt{>}\mathbf{1} \iff \mathfrak{A}, u \vDash [\gamma]\mathbf{0}$$
$$\mathfrak{A}, u \vDash [\alpha]\mathbf{0} \iff \mathfrak{A}, u \vDash \texttt{<}\gamma\texttt{>}\mathbf{1}.$$

Proof Take as γ the program $\beta; (x \neq y)?$, where β is a program that corresponds to α by the definition of K being divergence-closed. Since K is admissible, it follows that γ (semantically) belongs to K. ∎

We now list some languages that are semi-universal and divergence-closed. In some cases this depends on the vocabulary Σ.

PROPOSITION 15.9:   The following programming languages are semi-universal and divergence-closed:

(i) For every Σ containing at least one function symbol of arity at least two, or at least two unary function symbols:

  • (deterministic/nondeterministic) regular programs with algebraic stack;

- (deterministic/nondeterministic) regular programs with arrays.

(ii) For every mono-unary Σ:

- deterministic regular programs;
- deterministic regular programs with a Boolean stack.

Proof sketch.   First, we sketch the proof of (i). In the proof of Theorem 13.12 there is a sketch of a mutual simulation between Cook's $\log n$-APDA's and deterministic regular programs with an algebraic stack. It follows from the proof of Cook's theorem (see Chapter 14 of Hopcroft and Ullman (1979)) that we can assume without loss of generality that deterministic $\log n$-APDA's halt for every input. Since the simulation of a deterministic $\log n$-APDA by a deterministic regular program α with algebraic stack is step by step, it follows that α can find out in a finite number of steps whether the $\log n$-APDA accepts or rejects the input. Then α halts, assigning the same value to the special variables x and y if the input is accepted, and assigning two different values to x and y otherwise. The same remarks hold for nondeterministic regular programs with an algebraic stack.

The same argument applies to regular programs with arrays. Here the mutual simulation is with polynomial-space bounded Turing machines, and without loss of generality we may assume that these Turing machines halt for every input. This proves (i).

For part (ii), we use an argument similar to the one used above, except that now we work with log-space bounded Turing machines (see Theorem 13.11). This proves the result for deterministic regular programs. The second part of (ii) follows immediately from (i) and from the fact that over a mono-unary vocabulary regular programs with a Boolean stack are computationally equivalent to regular programs with an algebraic stack (Exercise 15.10). ■

It is not known whether the class of all regular programs is divergence-closed for vocabularies richer than mono-unary.

It turns out that for semi-universal and divergence-closed programming languages, the DL theory of finite interpretations reduces to termination properties.

PROPOSITION 15.10:   If K is semi-universal and divergence-closed, then for every formula φ of $\mathsf{DL}(K)$ there exists a program $\alpha_\varphi \in K$ such that for every finite Σ-structure $\mathfrak{A}$, for every $m \geq 0$, and for every Herbrand-like m-state w in $\mathfrak{A}$, we have

$$\mathfrak{A}, w \ \vDash \ \varphi \ \leftrightarrow \ \langle\alpha_\varphi\rangle\mathbf{1}.$$

Proof Let us fix $m \geq 0$. We first prove the conclusion of the proposition by induction on φ, assuming that A has at least two elements. For the case when φ is of the form $\varphi_1 \rightarrow \varphi_2$, we use the divergence tests for the programs obtained by the induction hypothesis. For the case when φ is of the form $\forall z \; \varphi_1$, in addition to using the divergence test for the program corresponding to φ_1, we have to use NEXT_m to search A; that is, the structure generated by the input. Finally, for the case when φ is of the form $[\alpha]\psi$, we find by the inductive hypothesis β_ψ such $<\beta_\psi>\mathbf{1}$ and ψ are equivalent over all finite Herbrand-like interpretations. For β_ψ, we find γ_ψ such that $<\beta_\psi>\mathbf{1}$ and $[\gamma]_\psi\mathbf{0}$ are equivalent over all finite Herbrand-like interpretations with at least two elements (we apply Lemma 15.8 here). Thus, it follows that φ and $[\alpha;\gamma_\psi]\mathbf{0}$ are equivalent over all finite Herbrand-like interpretations with at least two elements. Applying Lemma 15.8 again to the program $\alpha;\gamma_\psi$ yields the desired α_φ.

In order to extend the result to one element structures, we have to perform a test to see whether the structure is indeed of one element only. For this, denote by ψ the conjunction of the following formulas:

- $x_i = x_j$,   for $0 \leq i, j \leq m$,
- $f(x_0, \dots, x_0) = x_0$,   where f ranges over all function symbols of Σ.

The next observation we need for the case of one element structures is that there are at most 2^k different isomorphism types of such structures, where k is the number of relation symbols in the vocabulary. Each such structure is uniquely determined by a conjunction of formulas of the form $r(x_0, \dots, x_0)$ or $\neg r(x_0, \dots, x_0)$, where r ranges over all relation symbols of Σ.

Now, given φ, let $\gamma_1, \dots, \gamma_n$ be all the formulas that describe the one element structures in which φ holds. Let α' be the program found for φ in the first part of the proof; that is, the one that works correctly in structures containing at least two different elements. The program α we are looking for is:

if ψ
   then if $\gamma_1 \vee \cdots \vee \gamma_n$
     then skip
     else fail
   else α'

This completes the proof.   ∎

Observe that the above proof does not give an effective construction of the program α from φ. The reason is that in general there is no effective procedure to determine whether a given formula of $\mathsf{DL}(K)$ holds in a one-element structure. For example, for an r.e. program α, it is undecidable whether α terminates in a given one-element interpretation.

We are now ready to present the main result of this section. It relates complexity classes and spectra to the expressive power of Dynamic Logic. This result proves to be a strong tool for establishing relative expressive power of several logics of programs. We will use it in a number of places in the present chapter.

THEOREM 15.11 (SPECTRAL THEOREM): Let Σ be a rich vocabulary. Let K_1 and K_2 be programming languages over Σ such that K_1 is acceptable and K_2 is semi-universal and divergence-closed. Let $C_1, C_2 \subseteq 2^{\{0,1\}^*}$ denote families of sets that are downward closed under logarithmic space reductions. Let $SP(K_i) \approx C_i$ for $i = 1, 2$. The following statements are equivalent:

(i) $\mathsf{DL}(K_1) \leq \mathsf{DL}(K_2)$;
(ii) $SP_m(K_1) \subseteq SP_m(K_2)$ for all $m \geq 0$;
(iii) $C_1 \subseteq C_2$;
(iv) $K_1 \preceq_T K_2$.

Proof For the implication (i) $\Longrightarrow$ (ii), consider any $m \geq 0$ and any $\alpha \in K_1$. It follows from (i) that there exists a formula φ of $\mathsf{DL}(K_2)$ such that $<\alpha>1$ and φ are equivalent in all interpretations. By Proposition 15.10, there is a $\beta \in K_2$ such that

$$\mathfrak{A}, w \quad \vDash \quad <\beta>1 \leftrightarrow \varphi$$

holds for every finite Σ-stucture $\mathfrak{A}$ and every Herbrand-like m-state w. Thus $SP(\alpha) = SP(\beta)$, which proves (ii).

Now for (ii) $\Longrightarrow$ (iii). Consider any $X \in C_1$. By Lemma 13.10, there is a language $Y \subseteq H_0^L$ such that

$$X \leq_{\log} Y \leq_{\log} X. \tag{15.2.1}$$

Hence $Y \in C_1$, and since $SP(K_1)$ captures C_1, it follows that there exists $\alpha \in K_1$ such that $Y = SP_0(\alpha)$. By (ii), there is $\beta \in K_2$ such that $SP_0(\alpha) = SP_0(\beta)$, therefore $Y \in C_2$. Since C_2 is downward closed under log-space reductions, it follows from (15.2.1) that $X \in C_2$. This proves (iii).

For the proof of (iii) $\Longrightarrow$ (iv), consider any $\alpha \in K_1$. We describe a program $\beta \in K_2$ such that for all Σ-structures $\mathfrak{A}$ and states w, we have

$$\mathfrak{A}, w \vDash <\alpha>1 \quad \Longleftrightarrow \quad \mathfrak{A}, w \vDash <\beta>1.$$

Let $FV(\alpha) \subseteq \{x_0, \ldots, x_m\}$ and let $\gamma \in K_2$ be such that $SP_m(\alpha) = SP_m(\gamma)$. Since K_1 is admissible, it follows that there is an r.e. program α' that is equivalent to α in all interpretations. Let $\beta' \in K_2$ be the program of Proposition 15.7, which has the same termination properties as α' in all infinite interpretations.

In the first phase of the simulation of α by β, the latter runs β' to find out whether α', and therefore α, has terminated. The simulation is performed under the assumption that the substructure $\mathfrak{A}'$ of $\mathfrak{A}$ generated by $\{w(x_0), \ldots, w(x_m)\}$ is infinite. Either the simulation succeeds with α terminating, in which case β terminates too, or else β' discovers that $\mathfrak{A}'$ is finite. The finiteness of $\mathfrak{A}'$ is discovered by finding out that the value of x_{m+1} returned by NEXT_m equals the previous value of x_{m+1}. Having discovered this, β aborts the simulation and runs the program γ on the restored initial valuation of $x_0, \ldots, x_m$. If γ uses any variable x_n with $n > m$, then prior to running γ, β resets its value by the assignment $x_n := x_m$. Since $\mathfrak{A}'$ is finite, γ terminates iff α terminates. This proves $K_1 \preceq_T K_2$.

The implication (iv) $\implies$ (i) is just Proposition 15.6. ∎

We conclude this section with an example of how the Spectral Theorem can be applied. We will see more applications of this theorem later in the book.

THEOREM 15.12:   Let Σ be a rich vocabulary. Then

(i) DL(stk) $\leq$ DL(array).

(ii) DL(stk) $\equiv$ DL(array) iff $P = PSPACE$.

Moreover, the same holds for deterministic regular programs with an algebraic stack and deterministic regular programs with arrays.

Proof The result follows immediately from Theorem 15.11, Proposition 15.9, Theorem 13.12, and Theorem 13.13. ∎

A similar result can be proved for poor vocabularies. The complexity classes change, though. This is treated in the exercises (Exercise 15.12).

We remark that part (i) of Theorem 15.12 can be proved directly by showing that (deterministic) regular programs with an algebraic stack are translatable into (deterministic) regular programs with arrays.

15.3   Bounded Nondeterminism

In this section we investigate the role that nondeterminism plays in the expressive power of logics of programs. As we shall see, the general conclusion is that for a programming language of sufficient computational power, nondeterminism does not increase the expressive power of the logic.

Regular Programs

We start our discussion of the role of nondeterminism with the basic case of regular programs. Recall that DL and DDL denote the logics of nondeterministic and deterministic regular programs, respectively.

For the purpose of this subsection, fix the vocabulary to consist of two unary function symbols f and g. Any given nonempty prefix-closed subset $A \subseteq \{0,1\}^*$ determines a structure $\mathfrak{A} = (A, f^{\mathfrak{A}}, g^{\mathfrak{A}})$, where

$$f^{\mathfrak{A}}(w) \;=\; \begin{cases} w \cdot 0, & \text{if } w \cdot 0 \in A \\ w, & \text{otherwise.} \end{cases}$$

In the above definition, $w \cdot 0$ denotes the result of concatenating 0 at the right end of word w. The definition of $g^{\mathfrak{A}}$ is similar with 1 replacing 0. Such structures are called *treelike structures*.

Throughout this subsection, we will be referring to the algebra $\mathfrak{A}$ by indicating its carrier A. This will not lead to confusion. In particular, we will be interested in the algebras $T_n = \{w \in \{0,1\}^* \mid |w| \le n\}$ for $n \in \mathbb{N}$. The main combinatorial part of our proof demonstrates that the number of elements of T_n that a deterministic regular program can visit is at most polynomial in n. Thus, for sufficiently large n, there will be elements in T_n that are not visited during a computation starting from the root of T_n. This bound depends on the program—the larger the program, the larger n will be.

On the other hand, the following simple nondeterministic regular program visits all the elements of any T_n:

while $x \neq y$? **do** $(x := f(x) \cup x := g(x))$.

Thus, the formula

$$\varphi \;=\; \exists x \, \forall y \; \text{<\textbf{while} } x \neq y? \textbf{ do } (x := f(x) \cup x := g(x))\text{>}\mathbf{1} \qquad (15.3.1)$$

states that there is an element from which every element of the domain is reachable by a finite number of applications of the operations f and g. It can be shown that this formula is equivalent to no formula of DDL.

For technical reasons, we represent **while** programs here as consisting of *labeled* statements. Thus, deterministic **while** programs contain the following three kinds of statements:

- $\ell: \ x_i := \xi(x_j)$,   where $\xi(x_j)$ is either x_j, $f(x_j)$, or $g(x_j)$;
- $\ell: \ $**halt**;
- $\ell: \ $**if** $x_i = x_j$ **then** ℓ' **else** ℓ''.

The computational behavior of a program α in a structure $A \subseteq \{0,1\}^*$ is represented by a sequence of states $\pi = (\ell_1, a^1), \ldots, (\ell_i, a^i), \ldots$, where ℓ_i is a label of the statement to be executed at the ith step and a^i is the vector of current values stored in the registers of α. To represent a computation of α, π must satisfy the following properties:

- (ℓ_1, a^1) is the initial state; that is, ℓ_1 is the label of the first statement to be executed by α, and a^1 represents the input.
- To move from (ℓ_i, a^i) to (ℓ_{i+1}, a^{i+1}), the statement labeled ℓ_i is executed, which determines the next statement ℓ_{i+1}, and a^{i+1} is the vector of the new values after executing ℓ_i. If ℓ_i is a label of **halt**, then there is no next state.

By an *L-trace* of a computation π we mean the sequence $Ltr(\pi) = \ell_1, \ldots, \ell_n, \ldots$ of labels of the consecutive statements of π.

Let $Cmp(\alpha, A)$ denote the set of all computations of α in A. Call a computation π *terminating* if it is finite and the last pair of π contains the **halt** statement. Since we are dealing with deterministic programs, every nonterminating finite computation can be uniquely extended to a longer computation. The *length* of a computation is the number of pairs in it. Let $LtrCmp(\alpha, A, n)$ denote the set of all L-traces of computations of α in A whose length is at most n.

Let $L = \ell_1, \ell_2, \ldots$ be a sequence of labels. We define a *formal computation of α along L* as a sequence $t^0, t^1, \ldots$ of k-tuples of terms, where k is the number of registers of α. This sequence represents a history of values that are stored in registers, assuming that the computation followed the sequence L of labels. The values are terms. They depend on the input, which is represented by variables[1]

---

[1] We do not make a clear distinction between registers of a program and variables. We usually think of registers as part of the computer on which the program is being executed, while variables are part of a formal language (usually they appear in terms) that is used to describe properties of a computation.

$x_1, \ldots, x_k$. Let $1 \leq i \leq k$ and $0 \leq m < |L|$. We define t_i^m by induction on m:

$$t_i^0 \stackrel{\text{def}}{=} x_i$$

$$t_i^{m+1} \stackrel{\text{def}}{=} \begin{cases} \xi(t_j^m), & \text{if } \ell_m \text{ is a label of } x_i := \xi(x_j) \\ t_i^m, & \text{otherwise.} \end{cases}$$

In the above formula, we use the abbreviation $\xi(x)$ to denote one of x, $f(x)$ or $g(x)$.

Take any sequence $L = \ell_1, \ell_2, \ldots$ of labels and a formal computation $t^0, t^1, \ldots$ of α along L. For registers x_i and x_j of α, we say that x_i and x_j *witness a left turn* at the mth step of L and write $W_L(i,j) = m$ if $m > 0$ is the smallest number such that ℓ_{m-1} is a label of a statement **if** $x_p = x_q$ **then** ℓ_m **else** ℓ', the element t_p^m contains the variable x_i, and t_q^m contains the variable x_j (or conversely). If there is no such m, then we say that x_i and x_j do not witness a left turn, and in that case we let $W_L(i,j) = 0$.

The general form of a term is $\xi_1 \cdots \xi_m(x)$, where each ξ_i is either f or g. Taking into account the interpretation of function symbols in $\mathfrak{A}$, we can represent such a term by the word $x w_m \cdots w_1$, where $w_i \in \{0,1\}^*$ is 0 if ξ_i is f and to 1 if ξ_i is g. This representation of a term supports the intuition that, given a value for x as a word $u \in A$, the result of evaluating this term is obtained from u by traveling along the path $w = w_m \cdots w_1$. Of course, we apply here our convention that we follow the path w as long as we stay within the elements of A, i.e. the "true" result is $u w_n \cdots w_1$, where $w_n \cdots w_1$ is the longest prefix of w such that $u w_n \cdots w_1 \in A$.

LEMMA 15.13: Let α be a deterministic **while** program, and let $\pi, \pi' \in Cmp(\alpha, T_n)$ be computations with input values a and a', respectively. Let $L = Ltr(\pi)$ and $L' = Ltr(\pi')$ be the L-traces of the corresponding computations. Assume that

(i) $|L| = |L'|$,
(ii) For all $1 \leq i, j \leq k$, $W_L(i,j) = W_{L'}(i,j)$,
(iii) For all $1 \leq i \leq k$, $|a_i| = |a_i'|$.

Then $L = L'$.

Proof Let $L = \ell_1, \ell_2, \ldots$ and $L' = \ell_1', \ell_2', \ldots$. We prove by induction on $0 < m < |L|$ that $\ell_m = \ell_m'$ for all m.

For $m = 1$, this is obvious, since $\ell_1 = \ell_1'$ is the label of the start statement of α. Let $1 < m < |L|$ and assume that $\ell_r = \ell_r'$ for all $r < m$. Consider the statement labeled $\ell_{m-1} = \ell_{m-1}'$. If this is an assignment statement, then the next statement is uniquely determined by α, hence $\ell_m = \ell'_m$.

Assume now that ℓ_{m-1} labels **if** $x_p = x_q$ **then** ℓ **else** ℓ' and $\ell_m = \ell$, $\ell'_m = \ell'$, $\ell \neq \ell'$. If there exist $1 \leq i, j \leq k$ such that $W_L(i, j) = m$, then $W_{L'}(i, j) = m$ and $\ell_m = \ell'_m$. So assume now that

$$W_L(i, j) \neq m, \quad 1 \leq i, j \leq k. \tag{15.3.2}$$

Consider a formal computation $t^0, t^1, \ldots, t^{m-1}$ of α along $\ell_1, \ldots, \ell_{m-1}$. Let $t_p^{m-1} = x_i w$ and $t_q^{m-1} = x_j w'$, for some $1 \leq i, j \leq k$, and let $w, w' \in T_n$. Thus, we have

$$T_n \ \models \ a_i w = a_j w' \tag{15.3.3}$$

$$T_n \ \models \ a'_i w \neq a'_j w'. \tag{15.3.4}$$

Let $m_0 = W_L(i, j)$. It follows from (15.3.3) that $m_0 > 0$, and by (15.3.2) we conclude that $m_0 < m$. It also follows from (15.3.3) that a_i is a prefix of a_j, or conversely, a_j is a prefix of a_i. Without loss of generality we may assume the former. Hence, for some $\xi \in \{0, 1\}^*$, we have

$$T_n \ \models \ a_j = a_i \xi. \tag{15.3.5}$$

By (15.3.4) and (iii), we have

$$T_n \ \models \ a'_j \neq a'_i \xi. \tag{15.3.6}$$

Since at step m_0 both computations run through the "yes"-branch of some **if-then-else** statement, it follows that for some $u, u' \in \{0, 1\}^*$ we have

$$T_n \models a_i = a_j u' \quad \text{and} \quad T_n \models a'_i u = a'_j u'. \tag{15.3.7}$$

Again, by (iii) and (15.3.7) it follows that there is a common $\xi' \in \{0, 1\}^*$ such that

$$T_n \models a_j = a_i \xi' \quad \text{and} \quad a'_j = a'_i \xi'.$$

Thus, by (15.3.5) we have $\xi = \xi'$, which yields a contradiction with (15.3.6). This completes the proof. ∎

LEMMA 15.14:   Let α be a deterministic **while** program with k registers. Then for all $n, p \in \mathbb{N}$ we have

$$\#LtrCmp(\alpha, T_n, p) \ \leq \ n^k p^{k^2}.$$

Proof It follows from Lemma 15.13 that an L-trace L of a given length $r \leq p$ is uniquely determined by the left-turn-witness function W_L and the length of the input data. The number of possible functions W_L is $r^{k^2} \leq p^{k^2}$, and the number of possible lengths of values for k input variables in T_n is n^k. Thus the total number of all L-traces of length at most p is no greater than $n^k \cdot p^{k^2}$. ∎

Lemma 15.14 fails for nondeterministic programs. It holds for programs that are more powerful than **while** programs, though they still have to be deterministic.

For every $1 \leq i \leq k$, we define a function $G_i : \mathbb{N} \to \mathbb{N}$ as follows. For $n \in \mathbb{N}$, $G_i(n)$ is the maximum number $m \in \mathbb{N}$ such that there is a computation $\pi \in Cmp(\alpha, T_n)$ and an i-element set $B \subseteq T_n$ such that for m consecutive steps of π (not necessarily starting at the beginning of the computation), some registers of α store all the elements of B. Moreover, we require that no state in π repeats.

Observe now that the number of states of the program α is at most $2^{c \cdot n^k}$, where $c > 0$ depends on $|\alpha|$. Thus

$$G_i(n) \quad \leq \quad 2^{cn^k}$$

holds for all $1 \leq i \leq k$. We show that the G_i can in fact be bounded by a polynomial in n. Clearly, $G_k(n) \leq |\alpha|$ for all $n \in \mathbb{N}$.

LEMMA 15.15:   For every $1 \leq i < k$ and $n \geq 1$,

$$G_i(n) \quad \leq \quad (n+1)G_{i+1}(n) + |\alpha|^{k+1} n^{k^3 + k^2}.$$

Proof Take any $1 \leq i < k$ and $n \geq 1$. Let $B \subseteq T_n$ be an i-element set. Let $\pi \in Cmp(\alpha, T_n)$ be a computation without repeating states. Moreover, assume that starting from step $p \geq 1$, the values from B occur in every state after the pth state.

For any $q \geq 0$, let $V(B, q)$ be the set of values obtainable from B within q steps of π. The precise definition is by induction on q:

- $V(B, 0) = B$,

- $w \in V(B, q+1)$ iff either $w \in V(B, q)$ or there exist $r > p$, registers x_{j_1}, x_{j_2} of α, and a value $u \in V(B, q)$ such that $w = u \cdot 0$ or $w = u \cdot 1$, u occurs in the rth step of π in register x_{j_1}, and the rth statement of π is $x_{j_2} := f(x_{j_1})$ or $x_{j_2} := g(x_{j_1})$, depending on whether $w = u \cdot 0$ or $w = u \cdot 1$.

Take any state (ℓ, a) that occurs in π at position $q > p$. Let $m \leq n$, and assume that $q + (m+1)G_{i+1}(n) < |\pi|$. Let (ℓ', b) be a state that occurs in π at position

$q + (m + 1)G_{i+1}(n)$. We prove the following property:

For all $1 \leq j \leq k$, $(|b_j| = m \implies b_j \in V(B, m))$.   (15.3.8)

The proof is by induction on $0 \leq m \leq n$. Let $m = 0$, and assume that $|b_j| = 0$. Since there is no way to set a register to value ε other than by assigning to it the contents of another register containing ε, it follows that ε must have been stored in registers throughout π. If $\varepsilon \notin B$, then $B \cup \{\varepsilon\}$ has been stored in states of π from the pth step on. There are more than $G_{i+1}(n)$ steps in π after the pth (since $p + G_{i+1}(n) < q + G_{i+1}(n) < |\pi|$), and we obtain a contradiction. Hence, $\varepsilon \in B$ and $b_j \in V(B, 0)$.

For the induction step, let $0 < r \leq n$, and assume that (15.3.8) holds for all $m < r$. Assume that $q + (r + 1)G_{i+1}(n) < |\pi|$ and let (ℓ', b) be a state that occurs in π in position $q + (r + 1)G_{i+1}(n)$. Let $1 \leq j \leq k$ be such that $|b_j| = r$. If $b_j \notin B$, then b_j must have been created sometime after step $q + rG_{i+1}(n)$. Thus, there is a state (ℓ'', b') at a position later than $q + rG_{i+1}(n)$ such that the value b_j was obtained in a certain register x from a certain b'_{j_1} via an assignment of the form $x := f(x_{j_1})$ or $x := g(x_{j_1})$. Thus $|b'_{j_1}| = r - 1$. By the inductive hypothesis, we have $b'_{j_1} \in V(B, r - 1)$, therefore $b_j \in V(B, r)$ as required. This proves (15.3.8).

It follows from (15.3.8) that all values occurring in π after step $p + (n+1)G_{i+1}(n)$ belong to $V(B, n)$. Thus, after $p + (n + 1)G_{i+1}(n) + |\alpha| \cdot \#V(B, n)^k$ steps of π, at least one state must repeat. Therefore,

$$G_i(n) \leq (n + 1)G_{i+1}(n) + |\alpha| \cdot \#V(B, n)^k.$$

By Lemma 15.14, we have that the number of possible L-traces of fragments of computations of α of length at most n is no greater than $|\alpha|n^k n^{k^2}$. Thus

$$\#V(B, n) \leq |\alpha|n^{k^2 + k}.$$

From this we obtain

$$G_i(n) \leq (n + 1)G_{i+1}(n) + |\alpha|^{k+1}n^{k^3 + k^2},$$

which completes the proof. ∎

Let $\mathbf{Moves}(\alpha, T_n)$ be the set of all words $w \in \{0, 1\}^*$ such that there is a terminating computation $\pi \in Cmp(\alpha, T_n)$ and a variable x such that xw occurs in the formal computation along $Ltr(\pi)$. Thus, $\mathbf{Moves}(\alpha, T_n)$ is the set of all possible moves that α can perform on one of its inputs in a terminating computation. It turns out that this set is polynomially bounded.

PROPOSITION 15.16:   For every deterministic **while**-program α there is a constant $c > 0$ such that

$$\#\mathbf{Moves}(\alpha, T_n) \;\leq\; (|\alpha|n)^{ck^5}.$$

Proof It follows from Lemma 15.15 that $G_0(n)$, the maximum number of steps α makes in T_n before terminating or repeating a state, is at most

$$k \cdot |\alpha|^{k+1}(n+1)^k n^{k^3+k^2} \;\leq\; (|\alpha|n)^{c'k^3}$$

for some $c' > 0$, which depends on α. Thus, by Lemma 15.14, the number of different L-traces of terminating computations in T_n is at most $(|\alpha|n)^{c''k^5}$ for some $c'' > 0$. Since an L-trace L of length p brings at most kp terms in the formal computation along L, it follows that

$$\#\mathbf{Moves}(\alpha, T_n) \;\leq\; k(|\alpha|n)^{c'k^3}(|\alpha|n)^{c''k^5} \;\leq\; (|\alpha|n)^{ck^5}$$

for a suitable $c > 0$. This completes the proof. ∎

For a word $w \in \{0,1\}^*$, let

$$T^*(w) \;\overset{\text{def}}{=}\; \{w^n u \mid n \in \mathbb{N},\; u \in \{0,1\}^*,\; \text{and}\; |u| \leq |w|\}.$$

This set can be viewed as an infinite sequence of the trees $T_{|w|}$ connected along the path w.

PROPOSITION 15.17:   Let α be a deterministic **while** program with k registers, and let $w \in \{0,1\}^*$ be a word of length $n \geq 2k$. If $w \notin \mathbf{Moves}(\alpha, T_n)$, then α unwinds in $T^*(w)$.

Proof Let α have registers $x_1, \ldots, x_k$, and choose n with $n \geq 2k$. We shall describe a deterministic **while** program β whose computation in T_n for a specially chosen input will simulate the computation of α in $T^*(w)$ for every w with $|w| = n$. In fact, β will not depend on w; the correctness of the simulation will follow from the choice of a suitable input for β. If we view $T^*(w)$ as consisting of an infinite number of copies of T_n, each connected along w to the next copy, then β will be doing the same in one block of T_n as α does in $T^*(w)$. Obviously, β has to remember when values stored in the registers of α enter the same block. The assumption that $w \notin \mathbf{Moves}(\alpha, T_n)$ implies that no value of α can be moved all the way along w.

The program β has k registers $x_1, \ldots, x_k$ that will hold the values of the registers of α truncated to a single T_n. It has two registers b and e, which will be initialized to the root of T_n and the node w, respectively.[2] In addition, the program β has k registers $z_1, \ldots, z_k$, where z_i stores the name of the block in which α has the value stored in x_i. These names are represented by words of the form 0^m, where $1 \leq m \leq 2k$. The essential information, sufficient to carry out the simulation, is whether two variables store a value from the same block or from adjacent blocks. Two values that are at least one block apart are not accessible from each other.

For each statement in α of the form

$$\ell : \; x_i := \xi x_j, \quad \xi \in \{0, 1, \varepsilon\},$$

the program β will have the corresponding statement

$$\ell : \; x_i := \xi x_j; \; \textbf{if } x_i = e \textbf{ then } z_i := 0 \cdot z_i; x_i := b \textbf{ else } z_i := z_j.$$

Each statement of α of the form

$$\ell : \; \textbf{if } x_i = x_j \textbf{ then } \ell' \textbf{ else } \ell''$$

is replaced in β by

$$\ell : \; \textbf{if } x_i = x_j \wedge z_i = z_j \textbf{ then } \ell' \textbf{ else } \ell''.$$

Let us now take any $w \in \{0, 1\}^*$ with $|w| = n$. Every value $a \in T^*(w)$ can be uniquely represented as $a = w^m u$, where $m \geq 0$, $|u| \leq n$, and $u \neq w$. Given an initial valuation v for α in $T^*(w)$, where $v(x_i) = w^{m_i} u_i$ (with $|u_i| \leq n$ and $u_i \neq w$), we define an initial valuation $\overline{v}$ for β in T_n as follows:

$$
\begin{aligned}
\overline{v}(x_i) &= u_i \\
\overline{v}(b) &= \varepsilon \\
\overline{v}(e) &= w \\
\overline{v}(z_i) &= 0^p,
\end{aligned}
$$

where p in the above definition is the position of m_i in the set

$$\{m_j \mid j = 1, \cdots, k\} \; \cup \; \{m_j + 1 \mid j = 1, \cdots, k\},$$

counting from the smallest to the largest element starting from 1. The above enumeration of blocks takes into account whether two values are in the same block or in adjacent blocks or whether they are at least one full block apart. Now, if $w \notin \textbf{Moves}(\alpha, T_n)$, then α terminates in $T^*(w)$ for the initial evaluation v iff β terminates in T_n for the corresponding evaluation $\overline{v}$. (An easy proof of this is left

---

2 We do not fix the word w at this stage—it will be introduced via a suitable valuation.

to the reader.) Morever, the simulation of α by β is faithful, in the sense that for every step of α there are at most 4 steps of β after which the above described correspondence $[v \mapsto \overline{v}]$ between valuations is maintained. Thus, α terminates in $T^*(w)$ for an input v iff it terminates in at most $|\beta| \cdot n^{2 \cdot k + 2}$ steps. Hence α unwinds in $T^*(w)$. $\blacksquare$

PROPOSITION 15.18:   For every finite set $\{\alpha_1, \ldots, \alpha_p\}$ of deterministic **while** programs over the vocabulary containing two unary function symbols, there is a word $w \in \{0, 1\}$ such that each α_i unwinds in $T^*(w)$.

Proof   Take n sufficiently large that

$$\{0,1\}^n - \bigcup_{i=1}^{p} \mathbf{Moves}(\alpha_i, T_n) \ \neq \ \varnothing.$$

By Proposition 15.16, there is such an n. Then by Proposition 15.17, each α_i unwinds in $T^*(w)$, where $w \in \{0,1\}^n - \bigcup_{i=1}^{p} \mathbf{Moves}(\alpha_i, T_n)$. $\blacksquare$

Observe that the infinite structure $T^*(w)$ is constructed separately for each finite set $\{\alpha_1, \ldots, \alpha_p\}$ of deterministic **while** programs. That is, we do not construct one structure in which all deterministic **while** programs unwind. Still, it is enough for our purposes in this section. In fact, a stronger result can be shown.

THEOREM 15.19:   There exists an infinite treelike structure $\mathfrak{A}$ in which all deterministic **while** programs unwind.

We do not prove this result here, since the proof is quite complicated and technical. The main idea is to build an infinite treelike structure $\mathfrak{A}$ as a limit of a sequence of finite treelike structures. This sequence is constructed inductively in such a way that if a deterministic **while** program tries to follow one of the very few infinite paths in $\mathfrak{A}$, then it must exhibit a periodic behavior. The interested reader is referred to Urzyczyn (1983b) for details.

We can now state the main result that separates the expressive power of deterministic and nondeterministic **while** programs.

THEOREM 15.20:   For every vocabulary containing at least two unary function symbols or at least one function symbol of arity greater than one, DDL is strictly less expressive than DL; that is, DDL < DL.

Proof For the vocabulary containing two unary function symbols, the theorem is an immediate corollary of Proposition 15.18 and Theorem 15.4. The case of a vocabulary containing a function symbol of arity greater than one is easily reducible to the former case. We leave the details as an exercise (Exercise 15.3). ∎

It turns out that Theorem 15.20 cannot be extended to vocabularies containing just one unary function symbol without solving a well known open problem in complexity theory.

THEOREM 15.21:   For every rich mono-unary vocabulary, the statement "DDL is strictly less expressive than DL" is equivalent to $LOGSPACE \neq NLOGSPACE$.

Proof This follows immediately from the Spectral Theorem (Theorem 15.11), Proposition 15.9 (ii), and Theorem 13.11. ∎

Boolean Stacks

We now turn our attention to the discussion of the role non-determinism plays in the expressive power of regular programs with a Boolean stack. We will show that for a vocabulary containing at least two unary function symbols, nondeterminism increases the expressive power of DL over regular programs with a Boolean stack.
There are two known approaches to proving this result. These are similar in terms of the methods they use—they both construct an infinite treelike algebra in which deterministic regular programs with a Boolean stack unwind. This property is achieved by exhibiting a periodic behavior of deterministic regular programs with a Boolean stack. We sketch the main steps of both approaches, leaving out the technical details that prove the periodicity.
For the rest of this section, we let the vocabulary contain two unary function symbols. The main result of the section is the following.

THEOREM 15.22:   For a vocabulary containing at least two unary function symbols or a function symbol of arity greater than two, DL(dbstk) < DL(bstk).

For the purpose of this section, we augment the deterministic **while** programs of Section 15.3 with instructions to manipulate the Boolean stack. Thus, a computation of a program α with a Boolean stack is a sequence of the form

$$(\ell_1, a^1, \sigma_1), \ldots, (\ell_i, a^i, \sigma_i), \ldots$$

where ℓ_i is a label of the statement to be executed at the ith step, a^i is a vector of current values stored in the registers of α prior to the ith step and $\sigma_i \in \{0,1\}^*$ is the contents of the Boolean stack prior to the ith step. We do not assume here that ℓ_1 is the label of the first instruction of α, nor that σ_1 is empty.

If for every $n \geq 0$ the number of **push** statements is greater than or equal to the number of **pop** statements during the first n steps

$$(\ell_1, a^1, \sigma_1), \ldots, (\ell_n, a^n, \sigma_n),$$

then such a computation will be called *legal*.

Let $\mathfrak{A}$ be a Σ-structure, let $r > 0$, and let α be a deterministic **while** program with a Boolean stack. A computation

$$(\ell_1, a^1, \sigma_1), \ldots, (\ell_i, a^i, \sigma_i), \ldots$$

of α in $\mathfrak{A}$ is said to be *strongly r-periodic* if there is $n < r$ such that for all $i \in \mathbb{N}$,

$$\ell_{n+i} = \ell_{n+r+i} \quad \text{and} \quad a^{n+i} = a^{n+r+i}.$$

A program α is said to be *uniformly periodic* in $\mathfrak{A}$ if for every $\sigma \in \{0,1\}^*$ there exists $r > 0$ such that for every label ℓ and every vector a of values, the computation that starts from (ℓ, a, σ) is strongly r-periodic.

Let $m \geq 2$. A computation

$$(\ell_1, a^1, \sigma_1), \ldots, (\ell_i, a^i, \sigma_i), \ldots$$

is said to be *upward periodic for m-periods* if there exist $r > 0$ and $n < r$ such that for all $0 \leq i < (m-1)r$,

$$\ell_{n+i} \quad = \quad \ell_{n+r+i},$$

and moreover, the computation

$$(\ell_n, a^n, \sigma_n), \ldots, (\ell_{n+r-1}, a^{n+r-1}, \sigma_{n+r-1})$$

is legal. Hence, the sequence of labels repeats for m times, and each of the m cycles is legal, i.e. it never inspects the contents of the Boolean stack with which the cycle started.

Adian Structures

Adian structures arise from the well known solution to the Burnside problem in group theory. In 1979, S. I. Adian proved that for every odd $n \geq 665$ there exists an infinite group G_n generated by two elements satisfying the identity $x^n = 1$, where 1 is the unit of the group (Adian (1979)).

Every such group G_n induces in a natural way a Σ-algebra $\mathfrak{G}_n = <G_n, f, g>$, where f and g are unary functions defined by

$$f(x) = ax, \qquad g(x) = bx,$$

where a and b are the generators of G_n.

Since in G_n we have $a^{-1} = a^{n-1}$ and $b^{-1} = b^{n-1}$, it follows that every term over G_n can be represented by a string in $\{a, b\}^*$, assuming that the unit 1 is represented by the empty string ε. Thus G_n induces an equivalence relation on $\{0, 1\}^*$: for $u, w \in \{0, 1\}^*$, $u \equiv w$ iff the terms obtained from u and w by replacing 0 with a and 1 with b are equal in G_n. The quotient $\{0, 1\}^*/\equiv$ can be viewed as an infinite directed graph in which every node is of out-degree 2. This graph is not a treelike structure, since it contains loops of length greater than 1. It might also be possible that for paths $u, w \in \{0, 1\}^*$ we have $0u \equiv 1w$.

Cyclicity of G_n implies periodic behavior of deterministic **while** programs with a Boolean stack. The reader interested in the details of the proof of the following result is referred to Stolboushkin (1983).

THEOREM 15.23:   For every odd $n \geq 665$, any deterministic **while** program with a Boolean stack is uniformly periodic in $\mathfrak{G}_n$.

It follows immediately from Theorem 15.23 that every deterministic **while** program with a Boolean stack unwinds in $\mathfrak{G}_n$. On the other hand, the ordinary non-deterministic regular program

$$x := \varepsilon \,;\, x := g(x)^*$$

does not unwind in $\mathfrak{G}_n$. Hence, Theorem 15.22 follows immediately from Theorem 15.4.

Traps

The method of trapping programs from a given class $\mathcal{K}$ of programs consists of building a treelike structure $\mathfrak{A}$ satisfying the following two properties:

- Programs from $\mathcal{K}$, when computing in $\mathfrak{A}$, exhibit some form of limited periodic behavior.

- The structure $\mathfrak{A}$ contains only one infinite path, and this path has the property that there are very few repetitions of subwords on that path.

As a result of these two properties, no computation in $\mathfrak{A}$ can stay for a sufficiently long time on that infinite path. This yields the unwind property in $\mathfrak{A}$ of programs from $\mathcal{K}$. Of course, in this section we are only interested in deterministic regular programs with a Boolean stack.

Let $m \geq 2$, and let $\mathcal{T}$ be a class of treelike structures. We say that a program α *exhibits m repetitions* in $\mathcal{T}$ if there exists $n \in \mathbb{N}$ such that for every $\mathfrak{A} \in \mathcal{T}$, each legal fragment of length n of any computation of α in $\mathfrak{A}$ is upward periodic for m periods. We stress that the bound n is uniform for all structures in $\mathcal{T}$.

Let $\mathfrak{A}$ be a treelike structure and let $n \geq 0$. We say that level n is *incomplete* in $\mathfrak{A}$ if there is $w \in A$ such that $|w| = n$ and either $w0 \notin A$ or $w1 \notin A$. Otherwise, level n in $\mathfrak{A}$ is said to be *complete*.

The treelike structure $\mathfrak{A}$ is called *p-sparse* if every two incomplete levels in $\mathfrak{A}$ are separated by at least p complete levels.

The following theorem is the main tool used in establishing limited periodic behavior of deterministic **while** programs with a Boolean stack when the programs are run over certain treelike structures.

THEOREM 15.24:   For every deterministic **while** program α with a Boolean stack and for every $m \geq 2$, there exists $p \in \mathbb{N}$ such that α exhibits m repetitions over the class of all p-sparse structures.

We are now ready to build a trap.

THEOREM 15.25:   For every finite set $\{\alpha_1, \ldots, \alpha_n\}$ of deterministic **while** programs with a Boolean stack, there is an infinite treelike structure $\mathfrak{A}$ such that every α_i unwinds in $\mathfrak{A}$.

Proof Let W be an infinite cube-free string; that is, no finite non-empty string of the form uuu is a substring of W. It is known that such strings exist (see Salomaa (1981)). Let k be an upper bound on the number of registers used by each α_i. It is not hard to prove that there exists a number $r \in \mathbb{N}$ such that for every function $f : \{1, \ldots, k\} \to \{1, \ldots, k\}$, the rth power f^r of f is idempotent; that is, $f^r f^r = f^r$. We fix such an r and let $m = 4r$. We now apply Theorem 15.24 to m and to each α_i. Let $p_i \in \mathbb{N}$ be such that α_i exhibits m repetitions over the class of p_i-sparse structures. Clearly, we can choose a common p by taking the largest p_i.

We now cut W into pieces, each of length p; that is, $W = w_1 w_2 \cdots$, where

$|w_i| = p$ for all $i \geq 1$. Our trap structure is defined as follows.

$$A \overset{\text{def}}{=} \{u \in \{0,1\}^* \mid \exists j \geq 0 \; \exists u' \in \{0,1\}^* \; u = w_1 w_2 \cdots w_j u' \text{ and } |u'| < p\}.$$

The set A can be viewed as sequence of blocks of full binary trees of depth p connected along the infinite path W. Since $\mathfrak{A}$ is p-sparse, it follows that every α_i exhibits m repetitions in $\mathfrak{A}$. Let $q \geq 0$ be such that every legal fragment of length q of any computation of α_i in $\mathfrak{A}$ is upward periodic for m-periods. Take any computation of α_i that starts with an empty stack and any initial valuation in $\mathfrak{A}$. Assume that the computation is of length at least q, and consider the first q steps in this computation. Thus, this fragment is upward periodic for m periods.

Consider the first period. After it has been completed, the value of any register, say x_j, depends on the value of a certain register $x_{j'}$ at the entering point of this period. That is, upon completing the first period, x_j is equal to $\xi x_{j'}$ for a certain $\xi \in \{0,1\}^*$. This gives rise to a function $f : \{1, \ldots, k\} \to \{1, \ldots, k\}$ whose value at j is $f(j) = j'$. Thus, after r periods, the contents of register x_j depends on the value stored in register $x_{f^r(j)}$ at the beginning of the first period. By the same argument, it follows that after $2r$ periods, the contents of x_j depends on the value stored in register $x_{f^r(j)}$ at the beginning of the $(r+1)^{\text{st}}$ period. The latter value depends on the contents stored in register $x_{f^r f^r(j)} = x_{f^r(j)}$ at the beginning of the first period. It follows that after $4r$ periods, the value stored in x_j is obtained from the value stored in $x_{f^r(j)}$ at the beginning of the first period by applying a term of the form $\xi_1 \xi_2 \xi_2 \xi_2$.

We have shown that after $4r$ periods, all values stored in registers of every α_i are outside the path W. Therefore, the computation cannot proceed to the next block, which implies that every program α_i unwinds in $\mathfrak{A}$. ∎

We now derive Theorem 15.22 from Theorem 15.25 in exactly the same way as in the case of Adian structures and Theorem 15.23.

Algebraic Stacks and Beyond

It turns out that for programming languages that use sufficiently strong data types, nondeterminism does not increase the expressive power of Dynamic Logic.

THEOREM 15.26:   For every vocabulary,

(i) DL(dstk) $\equiv$ DL(stk).

(ii) DL(darray) $\equiv$ DL(array).

Proof Both parts follow immediately from the Spectral Theorem (Theorem 15.11), Proposition 15.9, and either Theorem 13.12 for case (i) or Theorem 13.13 for case (ii). ∎

It can be shown that even though r.e. programs are not divergence closed, nondeterminism does not increase the expressive power. We leave this as an exercise (see Exercise 15.2).

15.4 Unbounded Memory

In this section we show that allowing unbounded memory increases the expressive power of the corresponding logic. However, this result depends on assumptions about the vocabulary Σ.

Recall from Section 11.2 that an r.e. program α has *bounded memory* if the set $CS(\alpha)$ contains only finitely many distinct variables from V, and if in addition the nesting of function symbols in terms that occur in seqs of $CS(\alpha)$ is bounded. This restriction implies that such a program can be simulated in all interpretations by a device that uses a fixed finite number of registers, say $x_1, \dots, x_n$, and all its elementary steps consist of either performing a test of the form

$$r(x_{i_1}, \dots, x_{i_m})?,$$

where r is an m-ary relation symbol of Σ, or executing a simple assignment of either of the following two forms:

$$x_i := f(x_{i_1}, \dots, x_{i_k}) \qquad x_i := x_j.$$

In general, however, such a device may need a very powerful control (that of a Turing machine) to decide which elementary step to take next.

An example of a programming language with bounded memory is the class of regular programs with a Boolean stack. Indeed, the Boolean stack strengthens the control structure of a regular program without introducing extra registers for storing algebraic elements. We leave it as an exercise (Exercise 15.5) to prove that regular programs with a Boolean stack have bounded memory. On the other hand, regular programs with an algebraic stack or with arrays are programming languages with unbounded memory.

It turns out that the results on expressive power depend on assumptions on the vocabulary. Recall that a vocabulary Σ is *polyadic* if it contains a function symbol of arity greater than one. Vocabularies whose function symbols are all unary are called *monadic*. We begin our discussion with polyadic vocabularies and then move to the more difficult case of monadic ones.

Polyadic Vocabulary

We need some technical machinery for the proof of the main result of this section. We first discuss *pebble games* on dags, then exhibit a dag that is hard to pebble. The technical results will be used in the proof of Proposition 15.29.

A Pebble Game on Dags

Let $\mathcal{D} = (D, \to_{\mathcal{D}})$ be a dag, and let $n \geq 1$. We describe a game on $\mathcal{D}$ involving n pebbles. The game starts with some of the pebbles, perhaps all of them, placed on vertices of $\mathcal{D}$, at most one pebble on each vertex. A *move* consists of either removing pebbles from the graph or placing a free pebble on some vertex d. The latter move is allowed only if all direct predecessors of d (vertices c such that $c \to_{\mathcal{D}} d$) are pebbled, i.e., are occupied by pebbles. We also allow a pebble to be moved from a predecessor of d directly to d, provided all predecessors of d are pebbled.

The rules of the n-pebble game can be expressed more precisely by introducing the notion of an *n-configuration* and the relation of *succession* on the set of n-configurations. An *n-configuration* C is any subset of D of cardinality at most n. For n-configurations C and C', we say that C' *n-succeeds* C if either of the following two conditions hold:

(i) $C' \subseteq C$; or
(ii) for some d, $C' - C = \{d\}$ and $\{c \in D \mid c \to_{\mathcal{D}} d\} \subseteq C$.

A sequence of n-configurations $C_0, C_1, \ldots, C_m$ is called an *n-pebble game* if C_{i+1} n-succeeds C_i for $0 \leq i \leq m - 1$.

The following lemma is useful for transforming an n-pebble game into an $(n-1)$-pebble game. It will be applied to a special dag constructed in the next section.

LEMMA 15.27:   Let $\mathcal{D} = (D, \to_{\mathcal{D}})$ be a dag, and let $a \in D$. Define

$$A \stackrel{\text{def}}{=} \{d \mid a \to_{\mathcal{D}}^* d\},$$

where $\to_{\mathcal{D}}^*$ is the reflexive transitive closure of $\to_{\mathcal{D}}$. Let $C_0, \ldots, C_m$ be an n-pebble game in $\mathcal{D}$, $n \geq 2$. Suppose that for every $0 \leq i \leq m$, $A \cap C_i \neq \varnothing$. Then there is an $(n-1)$-pebble game $B_0, \ldots, B_m$ such that

$$\bigcup_{i=0}^{m} C_i \quad \subseteq \quad A \cup \bigcup_{i=0}^{m} B_i. \tag{15.4.1}$$

Proof For each $0 \leq i \leq m$, let $B_i = C_i - A$. Surely, (15.4.1) holds. Since A and

C_i intersect, B_i is an $(n-1)$-configuration. It remains to show that B_{i+1} $(n-1)$-succeeds B_i for $0 \le i \le m-1$. In case (i), we have $C_{i+1} \subseteq C_i$, so that $B_{i+1} \subseteq B_i$ as well. In case (ii), we have $C_{i+1} - C_i = \{d\}$. Either $d \in A$, in which case $B_{i+1} \subseteq B_i$; or $d \notin A$, in which case $B_{i+1} - B_i = \{d\}$. However, if $d \notin A$, then no predecessor of d is in A, and since $\{c \mid c \to_{\mathcal{D}} d\} \subseteq C_i$, we must have $\{c \mid c \to_{\mathcal{D}} d\} \subseteq B_i$ too.   ∎

A Hard Dag

In this section we describe a dag that cannot be pebbled with finitely many pebbles. Let

$$\mathcal{A} \stackrel{\text{def}}{=} (\mathbb{N}, \to_{\mathcal{A}})$$

be a dag defined as follows.

$$\to_{\mathcal{A}} \stackrel{\text{def}}{=} \{(n, n+1) \mid n \in \mathbb{N}\} \cup \{(n, 2n+1) \mid n \in \mathbb{N}\} \cup \{(n, 2n+2) \mid n \in \mathbb{N}\}.$$

The dag $\mathcal{A}$ can be viewed as a union of the chain of successive natural numbers and the infinite binary tree that has 0 as its root and for each n has $2n+1$ as the left child and $2n+2$ as the right child. A parent of the node n is $\lfloor (n-1)/2 \rfloor$ (we will call it a *tree-parent* of n).

Observe that

$$n \to_{\mathcal{A}}^* m \iff n \le m.$$

Let $C \subseteq \mathbb{N}$ and $k \in \mathbb{N}$. We define the *k-neighborhood* of C, denoted $N(C, k)$, by

$$N(C, k) \stackrel{\text{def}}{=} \{j \in \mathbb{N} \mid (\exists i \in C \cup \{0\})\ i \le j \le i + k\}.$$

Finally, define a function $f : N \to N$ inductively, by

$$f(0) \stackrel{\text{def}}{=} 0,$$

$$f(n+1) \stackrel{\text{def}}{=} 4(n+1)(f(n) + 1).$$

The following lemma shows that $\mathcal{A}$ cannot be pebbled with finitely many pebbles.

LEMMA 15.28:   For every $n \ge 1$ and for every n-configuration C of $\mathcal{A}$, if $C, C_1, \ldots, C_r$ is an n-pebble game in $\mathcal{A}$, then $C_r \subseteq N(C, f(n))$.

Proof We prove the result by induction on n. For $n = 1$, the result is obvious.

For $n > 1$, assume that there is an n-configuration C of $\mathcal{A}$ and an n-pebble game $C, C_1, \ldots, C_r$ in $\mathcal{A}$ such that for some $k \in C_r$, $k \notin N(C, f(n))$. We will find an $(n-1)$-configuration and an $(n-1)$-pebble game that contradict the conclusion of the lemma.

Let $j \in C \cup \{0\}$ be the largest element such that $j < k$. It follows that $f(n) < k - j$. Let $m = \lceil (k - j + 1)/2 \rceil + j + 1$, which is roughly the middle of the interval between j and k. Observe that this interval does not contain any node from C. In order to move a pebble from j to k, the n-game $C, C_1, \ldots, C_r$ must have moved at least one pebble through all the intermediate nodes. Let i_0 be the smallest number such that $m \in C_{i_0}$ and each configuration after C_{i_0} contains a node between m and k. In order to move a pebble through all these nodes, we must also move a pebble through the tree-parents of these nodes. Call these tree-parent nodes *red*.

Since the tree-parent of a node $i > 0$ is $\lfloor (i-1)/2 \rfloor$, it follows that all red nodes are smaller than or equal to $\lfloor (k-1)/2 \rfloor$. On the other hand we have

$$\lceil (k - j + 1)/2 \rceil + j + 1 \;\; \geq \;\; \frac{k + j + 3}{2} \;\; > \;\; \lfloor k/2 \rfloor,$$

thus $m > \lfloor k/2 \rfloor$, so every red node is smaller than m. We can now apply Lemma 15.27 to $\mathcal{A}$, the node m, and the n-pebble game $C_{i_0}, \ldots, C_r$. We obtain an $(n-1)$-pebble game $B_1, \ldots, B_p$ such that every red node is in $\bigcup_{i=1}^{p} B_i$. By the inductive hypothesis, we have

$$\# \textstyle\bigcup_{i=1}^{p} B_i \;\; \leq \;\; \# N(B_1, f(n-1)) \;\; \leq \;\; n(f(n-1) + 1). \tag{15.4.2}$$

On the other hand, the number of red nodes is half the number of nodes in the interval m through k; that is, it is at least $(k-j)/2$. We thus have

$$\frac{k - j}{2} \;\; > \;\; \frac{f(n)}{2} \;\; = \;\; 2n(f(n-1) + 1).$$

Thus, the number of red nodes is larger than $n(f(n-1) + 1)$, which contradicts (15.4.2). This completes the induction step. ∎

The Unwind Property

We first define a structure

$$\mathfrak{A} \;\; \overset{\text{def}}{=} \;\; (\mathbb{N}, g, 0)$$

over the vocabulary that consists of one constant symbol 0 and one binary function symbol $g : \mathbb{N}^2 \to \mathbb{N}$ defined as follows:

$$g(m, n) \quad \overset{\text{def}}{=} \quad \begin{cases} n + 1, & \text{if } n > 0 \text{ and } m = \lfloor (n - 1)/2 \rfloor \\ 0, & \text{otherwise.} \end{cases}$$

We can now prove the main technical result of this section.

PROPOSITION 15.29:   Every r.e. program with bounded memory unwinds in $\mathfrak{A}$.

Proof Let α be an r.e. program with bounded memory, and let $CS(\alpha) = \{\sigma_i \mid i \in \mathbb{N}\}$. Let $x_1, \dots, x_n$ be all the variables that occur in seqs of $CS(\alpha)$. We claim that each seq $\sigma_i \in CS(\alpha)$ can be viewed as a simultaneous assignment

$$(x_1, \dots, x_n) := (t_{1,i}, \dots, t_{n,i}),$$

which is performed subject to the satisfiability of a quantifier-free condition (guard) φ_i. In other words, σ_i is equivalent to

$$\varphi_i? \, ; \, (x_1, \dots, x_n) := (t_{1,i}, \dots, t_{n,i}).$$

This claim can be proved by a routine induction on the number of steps in σ_i, and we leave it to the reader.

From now on, we assume that the seqs in $CS(\alpha)$ are of the above form. Let $T(\alpha)$ be the least set of terms that contains all terms occurring in $CS(\alpha)$ and that is closed under subterms. For every $a_1, \dots, a_n \in \mathbb{N}$, let

$$T^{\mathfrak{A}}(a_1, \dots, a_n) \quad \overset{\text{def}}{=} \quad \{t^{\mathfrak{A}}(a_1, \dots, a_n) \mid t \in T(\alpha)\}.$$

Observe that every element in $b \in T^{\mathfrak{A}}(a_1, \dots, a_n)$ can be computed by simple assignments using only n variables. Hence b can be viewed as being reachable by an n-pebble game from the initial configuration $\{a_1, \dots, a_n\}$. It follows from Lemma 15.28 that

$$T^{\mathfrak{A}}(a_1, \dots, a_n) \quad \subseteq \quad N(\{a_1, \dots, a_n\}, f(n)),$$

thus

$$\#T^{\mathfrak{A}}(a_1, \dots, a_n) \quad \leq \quad (n + 1) \cdot (f(n) + 1). \tag{15.4.3}$$

We can conclude that the computation starting from any given input lies in the partial subalgebra of $\mathfrak{A}$ of cardinality $(n + 1) \cdot (f(n) + 1)$.

Since the number of pairwise non-isomorphic partial subalgebras of $\mathfrak{A}$ of bounded cardinality is finite, it follows that there exists $m \geq 0$ such that α and $\sigma_1 \cup \cdots \cup \sigma_m$ represent the same input-output relation in $\mathfrak{A}$. To see this, suppose that we have two isomorphic partial subalgebras of $\mathfrak{A}$, say $(\mathfrak{B}_1, a_1, \ldots, a_n)$ and $(\mathfrak{B}_2, b_1, \ldots, b_n)$. Moreover, assume that the computation of α for input $a_1, \ldots, a_n$ lies in $\mathfrak{B}_1$, and similarly that the computation of α for input $b_1, \ldots, b_n$ lies in $\mathfrak{B}_2$. Then

$$\{i \in \mathbb{N} \mid \mathfrak{B}_1 \models \varphi_i(a_1, \ldots, a_n)\} \;=\; \{i \in \mathbb{N} \mid \mathfrak{B}_2 \models \varphi_i(b_1, \ldots, b_n)\}.$$

Let I denote this set. It follows from (15.4.3) that the set

$$\{(t_{1,i}^{\mathfrak{A}}(a_1, \ldots, a_n), \ldots, t_{n,i}^{\mathfrak{A}}(a_1, \ldots, a_n)) \mid i \in I\}$$

is finite. Let $m \in \mathbb{N}$ be such that

$$\{(t_{1,i}^{\mathfrak{A}}(a_1, \ldots, a_n), \ldots, t_{n,i}^{\mathfrak{A}}(a_1, \ldots, a_n)) \mid i \in I\}$$
$$= \{(t_{1,i}^{\mathfrak{A}}(a_1, \ldots, a_n), \ldots, t_{n,i}^{\mathfrak{A}}(a_1, \ldots, a_n)) \mid i \in I,\ i \leq m\}.$$

It follows that the number m depends only on the isomorphism class of $(\mathfrak{B}_1, a_1, \ldots, a_n)$, not on the particular choice of this subalgebra. Since there are only finitely many isomorphism classes of bounded cardinality, it suffices to take the largest such m. Then

$$\alpha^{\mathfrak{A}} \;=\; \sigma_1^{\mathfrak{A}} \cup \cdots \cup \sigma_m^{\mathfrak{A}},$$

which completes the proof. ∎

THEOREM 15.30: For every vocabulary containing at least one function symbol of arity greater than one, no **DL** over a programming language with bounded memory is reducible to any **DL** over a programming language that contains a program equivalent to NEXT_0.

Proof For a vocabulary containing a binary function symbol, the result follows immediately from Proposition 15.29, Theorem 15.4, and Proposition 15.3. The case of a vocabulary containing only function symbols of arity greater than two we leave as an exercise (Exercise 15.8). ∎

THEOREM 15.31: For every vocabulary containing a function symbol of arity greater than one, **DL**(dbstk) < **DL**(dstk) and **DL**(bstk) < **DL**(stk).

Proof This is an immediate corollary of Theorem 15.30 and the fact that regular programs with a Boolean stack have bounded memory (see Exercise 15.5). ■

Monadic Vocabulary

For monadic vocabularies the situation is much less clear. The method of pebbling, which is applicable to polyadic vocabularies, does not work for monadic vocabularies, since every term (viewed as a dag) can be pebbled with a single pebble. For this reason, formally speaking, the issue of unbounded memory in programs over a monadic vocabulary disappears. Nevertheless, it makes sense to compare the expressive power of regular programs with or without a Boolean stack and programs equipped with an algebraic stack.

It is not known whether $DL(reg) < DL(stk)$ holds for monadic vocabularies. For deterministic regular programs, however, we have the following result.

THEOREM 15.32:   Let the vocabulary be rich and mono-unary. Then

$$DL(dreg) \equiv DL(dstk) \iff LOGSPACE = P.$$

Proof Since deterministic regular programs over mono-unary vocabularies are semi-universal and divergence closed (see Proposition 15.9), the result follows immediately from Theorem 15.11, Theorem 13.12 and Theorem 13.11. ■

The case of poor vocabularies is treated in Exercise 15.12.

For monadic vocabularies, the class of nondeterministic regular programs with a Boolean stack is computationally equivalent to the class of nondeterministic regular programs with an algebraic stack (see Exercise 15.11). Hence, we have:

THEOREM 15.33:   For all monadic vocabularies, $DL(bstk) \equiv DL(stk)$.

For deterministic programs, the situation is slightly different.

THEOREM 15.34:

(i) For all mono-unary vocabularies, $DL(dbstk) \equiv DL(dstk)$.

(ii) For all monadic vocabularies containing at least two function symbols, $DL(dbstk) < DL(dstk)$.

Proof Part (i) follows from Exercise 15.10. For part (ii), we observe that $DL(bstk) \leq DL(stk)$; hence, the result follows immediately from Theorem 15.22 and Theorem 15.26. ■

It is not known whether $\mathsf{DL}(\text{bstk}) < \mathsf{DL}(\text{stk})$ holds for monadic vocabularies. The case of poor vocabularies is treated in the exercises (Exercise 15.12).

15.5   The Power of a Boolean Stack

Regular programs with a Boolean stack are situated between pure regular programs and regular programs with an algebraic stack. We start our discussion by comparing the expressive power of regular programs with and without a Boolean stack. The only known definite answer to this problem is given in the following result, which covers the case of deterministic programs only.

THEOREM 15.35:   If the vocabulary contains at least one function symbol of arity greater than one or at least two unary function symbols, then $\mathsf{DL}(\text{dreg}) < \mathsf{DL}(\text{dbstk})$.

Proof sketch.   The main idea of the proof is as follows. We start with an infinite treelike structure $\mathfrak{A}$ in which all deterministic **while** programs unwind. Theorem 15.19 provides such structures. Next, we pick up an infinite path in $\mathfrak{A}$, cut it into finite pieces, and separate each two consecutive pieces u and w by inserting w^R in between them (the string w in reversed order). The hard part is to prove that all deterministic **while** programs still unwind in the transformed structure. However, it should be much clearer that there is a deterministic **while** program with a Boolean stack that can follow the entire infinite path; it simply stores on its stack the inserted strings and uses the stored string in order to find a way through the next piece of the infinite path. The technical details are rather complicated. The reader can consult Urzyczyn (1987) for the details.   ∎

It is not known whether Theorem 15.35 holds for nondeterministic programs, and neither is its statement known to be equivalent to any of the well known open problems in complexity theory. In contrast, it follows from Exercise 15.10 and from Theorem 15.32 that for rich mono-unary vocabularies the statement "$\mathsf{DL}(\text{dreg}) \equiv \mathsf{DL}(\text{dbstk})$" is equivalent to $LOGSPACE = P$. Hence, this problem cannot be solved without solving one of the major open problems in complexity theory.

The comparison of the expressive power of a Boolean stack and an algebraic stack is discussed in Theorem 15.31 for polyadic vocabularies and in Theorem 15.33 and Theorem 15.34 for monadic vocabularies.

15.6   Unbounded Nondeterminism

The wildcard assignment statement $x := ?$ discussed in Section 11.2 chooses an element of the domain of computation nondeterministically and assigns it to x. It is a device that represents *unbounded nondeterminism* as opposed to the binary nondeterminism of the nondeterministic choice construct $\cup$. The programming language of regular programs augmented with wildcard assignment is not an acceptable programming language, since a wildcard assignment can produce values that are outside the substructure generated by the input.

Our first result shows that wildcard assignment increases the expressive power in quite a substantial way; it cannot be simulated even by r.e. programs.

THEOREM 15.36:   Let the vocabulary Σ contain two constants c_1, c_2, a binary predicate symbol p, the symbol $=$ for equality, and no other function or predicate symbols. There is a formula of DL(wild) that is equivalent to no formula of DL(r.e.), thus DL(wild) $\not\leq$ DL(r.e.).

Proof   Consider the DL(wild) formula

$$\varphi \overset{\text{def}}{=} \ \text{<}(x := c_1; z := ?; p(x, z)?; x := z)^*\text{>} \ x = c_2,$$

which is true in a structure $\mathfrak{A}$ iff (c_1, c_2) belongs to the transitive closure of p. Since the vocabulary contains no function symbols, it follows that every DL(r.e.) formula is equivalent to a first-order formula. It is well known (and in fact can be proved quite easily by the compactness of predicate logic) that there is no first-order formula capable of expressing the transitive closure of a binary relation.   ∎

It is not known whether any of the logics with unbounded memory are reducible to DL(wild). An interesting thing happens when both wildcard and array assignments are allowed. We show that in the resulting logic, it is possible to define the finiteness of (the domain of) a structure, but not in the logics with either of the additions removed. Thus, having both memory and nondeterminism unbounded provides more power than having either of them bounded.

THEOREM 15.37:   Let vocabulary Σ contain only the symbol of equality. There is a formula of DL(array+wild) equivalent to no formula of either DL(array) or DL(wild).

Proof Let F be a unary function variable and consider the formula

$$\varphi \stackrel{\text{def}}{=} \text{<}\alpha\text{>} \forall y \, \exists x \, \text{<}z := F(x)\text{>} \, z = y,$$

where $\alpha = (x := ?; y := ?; F(x) := y)^*$. This program stores some elements in some locations of F. In a model $\mathfrak{A}$, the formula φ expresses the fact that we can store all elements of the domain in the variable F in a finite number of steps, thus the domain is finite. That finiteness cannot be expressed in DL(array) should be clear: since DL(array) is reducible over this vocabulary to first-order logic, another routine application of the compactness of predicate logic suffices.

We show that over our vocabulary, DL(wild) is also reducible to first-order logic. For this it is enough to observe that for our simple vocabulary, every regular program with wildcard assignments unwinds in every structure. Given a regular program α with wildcard assignments, let $x_1, \ldots, x_k$ be all the variables occurring in α. Seqs in $CS(\alpha)$ are sequences of the following three kinds of atomic programs:

$$x_i := x_j \qquad x_i := ? \qquad \varphi?,$$

where $i, j \in \{1, \ldots, k\}$ and φ is a Boolean combination of atomic formulas of the form $x_i = x_j$. It is easy to show that for each seq $\sigma \in CS(\alpha)$, there is a program γ and a first-order formula ψ such that for every structure $\mathfrak{A}$,

$$\mathfrak{m}_{\mathfrak{A}}(\sigma) \quad = \quad \{(u, v) \in \mathfrak{m}_{\mathfrak{A}}(\gamma) \mid u \in \mathfrak{m}_{\mathfrak{A}}(\psi)\}.$$

The program γ uses only variables from $\{x_1, \ldots, x_k\}$, and it is a sequence of assignments (ordinary or wildcard) such that no variable on the left side of an assignment appears twice in γ. Moreover, ψ is a conjunction of formulas of the form $\exists x_{i_1} \ldots \exists x_{i_m} \, \varphi$, where each $x_{i_j} \in \{x_1, \ldots, x_k\}$ and φ is a Boolean combination of atomic formulas of the form $x_i = x_j$. Since there are only finitely many different γ and ψ satisfying the above conditions, it follows that that there are only finitely many semantically different seqs in $CS(\alpha)$, therefore α unwinds in all structures. ∎

15.7 Bibliographical Notes

Many of the results on relative expressiveness presented herein answer questions posed in Harel (1979). Similar uninterpreted research, comparing the expressive power of classes of programs (but detached from any surrounding logic) has taken place under the name *comparative schematology* quite extensively ever since Ianov (1960); see Greibach (1975) and Manna (1974).

The results of Section 15.1 are folklore. However, Kfoury (1985) contained the first proposal to use the notion of the unwind property as a tool for separating the expressive power of logics of programs (Theorem 15.4). Kreczmar (1977) studied the unwind property over the fields of real and complex numbers as well as over Archimedian fields (the unwind property for deterministic **while** programs holds for each of these structures). A systematic study of the unwind property, mainly for regular programs, was carried out in the PhD thesis of Urzyczyn (1983c).

The material of Section 15.2, relating spectra of logics of programs to their relative expressive power, is due to Tiuryn and Urzyczyn. It started with Tiuryn and Urzyczyn (1983) (see Tiuryn and Urzyczyn (1988) for the full version). The general Spectral Theorem (Theorem 15.11) is from Tiuryn and Urzyczyn (1984). However, some of the definitions presented in our exposition are simpler than in the papers cited above. In particular, the notion of *admissibility* of a programming language has been simplified here, and an auxiliary notion of *termination subsumption* has been introduced. As a result, some of the proofs have become simpler too. In particular, our proof of the Spectral Theorem is simpler than that in Tiuryn and Urzyczyn (1984).

The main result of Section 15.3, Theorem 15.20, appears in Berman et al. (1982) and was proved independently in Stolboushkin and Taitslin (1983). These results extend in a substantial way an earlier and much simpler result for the case of regular programs without equality in the vocabulary, which appears in Halpern (1981). A simpler proof of the special case of the quantifier-free fragment of the logic of regular programs appears in Meyer and Winklmann (1982). The proof of Theorem 15.20 presented here is from Tiuryn (1989). Theorem 15.19 is due to Urzyczyn (1983b), and as a corollary it yields Theorem 15.20. Theorem 15.21 is from Tiuryn and Urzyczyn (1984).

Theorem 15.22 is from Stolboushkin (1983). The proof, as in the case of regular programs (see Stolboushkin and Taitslin (1983)), uses Adian's result from group theory (Adian (1979)). Theorem 15.23 is also from Stolboushkin (1983). The method of trapping programs is from Kfoury (1985). Theorems 15.24 and 15.25 are from Kfoury (1985). Observe that Theorem 15.25 is strong enough to yield Theorem 15.20. Theorem 15.26 is from Tiuryn and Urzyczyn (1983, 1988).

The main result of Section 15.4, Theorem 15.30, is from Erimbetov (1981) and was proved independently by Tiuryn (1981b) (see Tiuryn (1984) for the full version). Erimbetov (1981) contains a somewhat special case of this result, namely that $DL(dreg) < DL(dstk)$. Both proofs applied similar methods: pebble games on finite trees. The proof given here is based on the idea presented in Kfoury (1983). In particular, Proposition 15.29 is from Kfoury (1983). However, the proof of this Proposition was further simplified by Kfoury and Stolboushkin (1997). We follow the latter proof in our exposition.

Chapter 15

Theorem 15.35 is from Urzyczyn (1987). There is a different proof of this result, using Adian structures, which appears in Stolboushkin (1989). Exercise 15.11 is from Urzyczyn (1988), which also studies programs with Boolean arrays.

Wildcard assignments were considered in Harel et al. (1977) under the name *nondeterministic assignments*. Theorem 15.36 is from Meyer and Winklmann (1982). Theorem 15.37 is from Meyer and Parikh (1981).

In our exposition of the comparison of the expressive power of logics, we have made the assumption that programs use only quantifier-free first-order tests. It follows from the results of Urzyczyn (1986) that allowing full first-order tests in many cases results in increased expressive power. Urzyczyn (1986) also proves that adding array assignments to nondeterministic r.e. programs increases the expressive power of the logic. This should be contrasted with the result of Meyer and Tiuryn (1981, 1984) to the effect that for deterministic r.e. programs, array assignments do not increase expressive power.

Makowski (1980) considers a weaker notion of equivalence between logics common in investigations in abstract model theory, whereby models are extended with interpretations for additional predicate symbols. With this notion it is shown in Makowski (1980) that most of the versions of logics of programs treated here become equivalent.

Exercises

15.1. Show that program equivalence is not invariant under elementary equivalence of structures.

15.2. (Meyer and Tiuryn (1981, 1984)) Define the class of *deterministic r.e. programs* over a given vocabulary. Show that DL(r.e.) has the same expressive power as DL over deterministic r.e. programs. Notice that r.e. programs are not divergence-closed.

15.3. In Theorem 15.20, reduce the case of a vocabulary containing a function symbol of arity greater than one to the case of a vocabulary containing two unary function symbols.

15.4. Define super-atomic seqs as those that use only simple assignments in which the terms have depth at most one. Show that a term t has pebble complexity at most n iff there is a super-atomic seq with at most n variables that computes it.

15.5. Show that every nondeterministic **while** program with a Boolean stack has bounded memory.

15.6. Show that regular programs with an algebraic stack are translatable into regular programs with arrays. (*Hint.* Prove that for every regular program α with an algebraic stack, there is a polynomial $p(n)$ such that in every terminating computation of α over an n-element interpretation, the maximal depth of the stack is at most $p(n)$.)

15.7. Prove that regular programs with two algebraic stacks have the same computational power as arbitrary r.e. programs.

15.8. Prove Theorem 15.30 for vocabularies containing only symbols of arity greater than two.

15.9. Show that over a vocabulary containing no function symbols of arity greater than one all terms have pebble complexity one.

15.10. Show that over a mono-unary vocabulary, regular programs with a Boolean stack have the same computational power as regular programs with an algebraic stack. Show that the same result holds for deterministic programs. Conclude that the two version of **DL** over these programming languages are of equal expressive power.

15.11. Prove that over a monadic vocabulary, nondeterministic regular programs with a Boolean stack have the same computational power as nondeterministic regular programs with an algebraic stack.

15.12. Prove that for any poor vocabulary,

(a) $\mathsf{DL}(\text{stk}) \equiv \mathsf{DL}(\text{array})$ iff $DTIME(2^{O(n)}) = DSPACE(2^{O(n)})$;
(b) $\mathsf{DL}(\text{dreg}) \equiv \mathsf{DL}(\text{reg})$ iff $DSPACE(n) = NSPACE(n)$;
(c) $\mathsf{DL}(\text{dreg}) \equiv \mathsf{DL}(\text{dstk})$ iff $DSPACE(n) = DTIME(2^{O(n)})$.

In this section we consider some restrictions and extensions of **DL**. We are interested mainly in questions of comparative expressive power on the uninterpreted level. In arithmetical structures these questions usually become trivial, since it is difficult to go beyond the power of first-order arithmetic without allowing infinitely many distinct tests in programs (see Theorems 12.6 and 12.7). In regular **DL** this luxury is not present.

16.1 Algorithmic Logic

Algorithmic Logic (**AL**) is the predecessor of Dynamic Logic. The basic system was defined by Salwicki (1970) and generated an extensive amount of subsequent research carried out by a group of mathematicians working in Warsaw. Two surveys of the first few years of their work can be found in Banachowski et al. (1977) and Salwicki (1977).

The original version of **AL** allowed deterministic **while** programs and formulas built from the constructs

$$\alpha\varphi \qquad \cup\,\alpha\varphi \qquad \cap\,\alpha\varphi$$

corresponding in our terminology to

$$<\!\alpha\!>\!\varphi \qquad <\!\alpha^*\!>\!\varphi \qquad \bigwedge_{n\in\omega} <\!\alpha^n\!>\!\varphi,$$

respectively, where α is a deterministic **while** program and φ is a quantifier-free first-order formula.

In Mirkowska (1980, 1981a,b), **AL** was extended to allow nondeterministic **while** programs and the constructs

$$\nabla\alpha\varphi \qquad \Delta\alpha\varphi$$

corresponding in our terminology to

$$<\!\alpha\!>\!\varphi \qquad \mathbf{halt}(\alpha) \wedge [\alpha]\varphi \wedge <\!\alpha\!>\!\varphi,$$

respectively. The latter asserts that all traces of α are finite and terminate in a state satisfying φ.

A feature present in **AL** but not in **DL** is the set of "dynamic terms" in addition to dynamic formulas. For a first-order term t and a deterministic **while** program

α, the meaning of the expression αt is the value of t after executing program α. If α does not halt, the meaning is undefined. Such terms can be systematically eliminated; for example, $P(x, \alpha t)$ is replaced by $\exists z\ (\langle\alpha\rangle(z = t) \land P(x, z))$.

The emphasis in the early research on AL was in obtaining infinitary completeness results (as in Section 14.1), developing normal forms for programs, investigating recursive procedures with parameters, and axiomatizing certain aspects of programming using formulas of AL. As an example of the latter, the algorithmic formula

$$(\textbf{while } s \neq \varepsilon \textbf{ do } s := \textbf{pop}(s))\textbf{1}$$

can be viewed as an axiom connected with the data structure *stack*. One can then investigate the consequences of such axioms within AL, regarding them as properties of the corresponding data structures.

Complete infinitary deductive systems for first-order and propositional versions are given in Mirkowska (1980, 1981a,b). The infinitary completeness results for AL are usually proved by the algebraic methods of Rasiowa and Sikorski (1963).

Constable (1977), Constable and O'Donnell (1978) and Goldblatt (1982) present logics similar to AL and DL for reasoning about deterministic **while** programs.

16.2   Nonstandard Dynamic Logic

Nonstandard Dynamic Logic (NDL) was introduced by Andréka, Németi, and Sain in 1979. The reader is referred to Németi (1981) and Andréka et al. (1982a,b) for a full exposition and further references. The main idea behind NDL is to allow nonstandard models of time by referring only to first-order properties of time when measuring the length of a computation. The approach described in Andréka et al. (1982a,b) and further research in NDL is concentrated on proving properties of flowcharts, i.e., programs built up of assignments, conditionals and **go to** statements.

Nonstandard Dynamic Logic is well suited to comparing the reasoning power of various program verification methods. This is usually done by providing a model-theoretic characterization of a given method for program verification. To illustrate this approach, we briefly discuss a characterization of Hoare Logic for partial correctness formulas. For the present exposition, we choose a somewhat simpler formalism which still conveys the basic idea of nonstandard time.

Let Σ be a first-order vocabulary. For the remainder of this section we fix a deterministic **while** program α over Σ in which the **while-do** construct does not occur (such a program is called *loop-free*). Let $\overline{z} = (z_1, \ldots, z_n)$ contain all variables occurring in α, and let $\overline{y} = (y_1, \ldots, y_n)$ be a vector of n distinct individual variables disjoint from $\overline{z}$.

Since α is loop-free, it has only finitely many computation sequences. One can easily define a quantifier-free first-order formula θ_α with all free variable among $\overline{y}, \overline{z}$ that defines the input/output relation of α in all Σ-structures $\mathfrak{A}$ in the sense that the pair of states (u, v) is in $\mathfrak{m}_{\mathfrak{A}}(\alpha)$ if and only if

$$\mathfrak{A}, v[y_1/u(z_1), \ldots, y_n/u(z_n)] \models \theta_\alpha$$

and $u(x) = v(x)$ for all $x \in V - \{z_1, \ldots, z_n\}$.

Let α^+ be the following deterministic **while** program:

$\overline{y} := \overline{z};$

$\alpha;$

while $\overline{z} \neq \overline{y}$ **do** $\overline{y} := \overline{z};\ \alpha$

where $\overline{z} \neq \overline{y}$ stands for $z_1 \neq y_1 \vee \cdots \vee z_n \neq y_n$ and $\overline{y} := \overline{z}$ stands for $y_1 := z_1;\ \cdots;\ y_n := z_n$. Thus program α^+ executes α iteratively until α does not change the state.

The remainder of this section is devoted to giving a model-theoretic characterization, using NDL, of Hoare's system for proving partial correctness assertions involving α^+ relative to a given first-order theory T over Σ. We denote provability in Hoare Logic by $\vdash_{\mathsf{HL}}$.

Due to the very specific form of α^+, the Hoare system reduces to the following rule:

$$\frac{\varphi \to \chi, \ \chi[\overline{z}/\overline{y}] \wedge \theta_\alpha \to \chi, \ \chi[\overline{z}/\overline{y}] \wedge \theta_\alpha \wedge \overline{z} = \overline{y} \to \psi}{\varphi \to [\alpha^+]\psi}$$

where φ, χ, ψ are first-order formulas and no variable of $\overline{y}$ occurs free in χ.

The next series of definitions introduces a variant of NDL. A structure $\mathfrak{I}$ for the language consisting of a unary function symbol $+1$ (*successor*), a constant symbol 0, and equality is called a *time model* if the following axioms are valid in $\mathfrak{I}$:

- $x + 1 = y + 1 \to x = y$
- $x + 1 \neq 0$
- $x \neq 0 \to \exists y\ y + 1 = x$
- $x \neq x \underbrace{+1 + 1 + \cdots + 1}_{n}$, for any $n = 1, 2, \ldots$

Let $\mathfrak{A}$ be a Σ-structure and $\mathfrak{I}$ a time model. A function $\rho : \mathfrak{I} \to \mathfrak{A}^n$ is called a *run* of α in $\mathfrak{A}$ if the following infinitary formulas are valid in $\mathfrak{A}$:

- $\bigwedge_{i \in \mathfrak{I}} \theta_\alpha [\overline{y}/\rho(i), \overline{z}/\rho(i+1)]$;
- for every first-order formula $\varphi(\overline{z})$ over Σ,

$$\varphi(\rho(0)) \wedge \bigwedge_{i \in \mathfrak{I}} (\varphi(\rho(i)) \to \varphi(\rho(i+1))) \quad \to \quad \bigwedge_{i \in \mathfrak{I}} \varphi(\rho(i)).$$

The first formula says that for $i \in \mathfrak{I}$, $\rho(i)$ is the valuation obtained from $\rho(0)$ after i iterations of the program α. The second formula is the induction scheme along the run ρ.

Finally, we say that a partial correctness formula $\varphi \to [\alpha^+]\psi$ *follows from T in nonstandard time semantics* and write $T \vDash_{\text{NT}} \varphi \to [\alpha^+]\psi$ if for every model $\mathfrak{A}$ of T, time model $\mathfrak{I}$, and run ρ of α in $\mathfrak{A}$,

$$\mathfrak{A} \vDash \varphi[\overline{z}/\rho(0)] \quad \to \quad \bigwedge_{i \in \mathfrak{I}} (\rho(i) = \rho(i+1) \to \psi[\overline{z}/\rho(i)]).$$

The following theorem characterizes the power of Hoare Logic for programs of the form α^+ over nonstandard time models.

THEOREM 16.1:   For every first-order theory T over Σ and first-order formulas φ, ψ over Σ, the following conditions are equivalent:

(i) $T \vdash_{\text{HL}} \varphi \to [\alpha^+]\psi$;

(ii) $T \vDash_{\text{NT}} \varphi \to [\alpha^+]\psi$.

Other proof methods have been characterized in the same spirit. The reader is referred to Makowski and Sain (1986) for more information on this issue and further references.

16.3   Well-Foundedness

As in Section 10.6 for PDL, we consider adding to DL assertions to the effect that programs can enter infinite computations. Here too, we shall be interested both in LDL and in RDL versions; i.e., those in which **halt** α and **wf** α, respectively, have been added inductively as new formulas for any program α. As mentioned there, the connection with the more common notation **repeat** α and **loop** α (from which the L and R in the names LDL and RDL derive) is by:

$$\mathbf{loop}\,\alpha \;\overset{\text{def}}{\iff}\; \neg\mathbf{halt}\,\alpha$$
$$\mathbf{repeat}\,\alpha \;\overset{\text{def}}{\iff}\; \neg\mathbf{wf}\,\alpha.$$

We now state some of the relevant results. The first concerns the addition of $\mathbf{halt}\,\alpha$:

THEOREM 16.2:

LDL $\equiv$ DL.

Proof sketch. In view of the equivalences (10.6.2)–(10.6.5) of Section 10.6, it suffices, for each regular program α, to find a DL formula φ_α such that

$$\vDash [\alpha^*]\mathbf{halt}\,\alpha \;\to\; (\varphi_\alpha \leftrightarrow \mathbf{wf}\,\alpha).$$

Given such φ_α, $\mathbf{halt}\,(\alpha^*)$ is equivalent to $[\alpha^*]\mathbf{halt}\,\alpha \wedge \varphi_\alpha$.

Consider the computation tree $T_\alpha(s)$ corresponding to the possible computations of α in state s. The tree is derived from α by identifying common prefixes of seqs. A node of $T_\alpha(s)$ is labeled with the state reached at that point. The tree $T_\alpha(s)$, it should be noted, is obtained from the syntactic tree T_α by truncating subtrees that are rooted below false tests. Then $s \vDash \mathbf{halt}\,\alpha$ holds iff $T_\alpha(s)$ contains no infinite path.

For any program of the form α^*, consider the tree $S_\alpha(s)$ derived from $T_{\alpha^*}(s)$ by eliminating all states internal to executions of α. Thus t is an immediate descendant of t' in $S_\alpha(s)$ iff t' is reached from s by some execution of α^* and t is reached from t' by an additional execution of α.

If $s \vDash [\alpha^*]\mathbf{halt}\,\alpha$, then by König's lemma $S_\alpha(s)$ is of finite outdegree. It can be shown that in this case $S_\alpha(s)$ has an infinite path iff either some state repeats along a path or there are infinitely many states t, each of which appears only within bounded depth in $S_\alpha(s)$ but for which there is a state appearing for the first time at depth greater than that of the last appearance of t.

This equivalent to "$S_\alpha(s)$ contains an infinite path" is then written in DL using the fact that a state is characterized by a finite tuple of values corresponding to the finitely many variables in α.

As an example of a typical portion of this definition, the following is a DL equivalent of the statement: "There is a state in $S_\alpha(s)$ appearing for the first time at depth greater than the greatest depth at which a given state $\bar{y}$ appears."

$$\exists \bar{z}\,(<\alpha^*>\bar{x} = \bar{z} \wedge [\bar{z}' := \bar{x}; (\alpha; \alpha[\bar{z}'/\bar{x}])^*; \bar{z}' = \bar{z}?; \alpha^*]\neg\bar{x} = \bar{y}).$$

Here $\overline{y}, \overline{z}$ and $\overline{z}'$ are n-tuples of new variables denoting states matching the n-tuple $\overline{x}$ of variables appearing in α. Assignments and tests are executed pointwise, as is the substitution $\alpha[\overline{z}'/\overline{x}]$, which replaces all occurrences of the variables in α with their $\overline{z}'$ counterparts. The inner program runs α simultaneously on $\overline{x}$ and $\overline{z}'$, reaches $\overline{z}$ and then continues running α on $\overline{x}$. The assertion is that $\overline{y}$ cannot be obtained in this manner. ∎

In contrast to this, we have:

THEOREM 16.3:

LDL   <   RDL.

Proof sketch. The result is proved by showing how to state in RDL that a binary function g is a well-order, where one first constrains the domain to be countable, with the unary f acting as a successor function starting at some "zero" constant c. The result then follows from the fact that well-order is not definable in $L_{\omega_1\omega}$ (see Keisler (1971)). ∎

Turning to the validity problem for these extensions, clearly they cannot be any harder to decide than that of DL, which is Π_1^1-complete. However, the following result shows that detecting the absence of infinite computations of even simple uninterpreted programs is extremely hard.

THEOREM 16.4:   The validity problems for formulas of the form $\varphi \to \mathbf{wf}\,\alpha$ and formulas of the form $\varphi \to \mathbf{halt}\,\alpha$, for first-order φ and regular α, are both Π_1^1-complete. If α is constrained to have only first-order tests then the $\varphi \to \mathbf{wf}\,\alpha$ case remains Π_1^1-complete but the $\varphi \to \mathbf{halt}\,\alpha$ case is r.e.; that is, it is Σ_1^0-complete.

Proof sketch. That the problems are in Π_1^1 is easy. The Π_1^1-hardness results can be established by reductions from the recurring tiling problem of Proposition 2.22 similarly to the proof of Theorem 13.1. As for $\mathbf{halt}\,\alpha$ formulas with first-order tests in Σ_1^0, compactness and König's lemma are used. Details appear in Harel and Peleg (1985). ∎

Axiomatizations of LDL and RDL are discussed in Harel (1984). We just mention here that the additions to Axiom System 14.12 of Chapter 14 that are used to obtain an arithmetically complete system for RDL are the axiom

$$[\alpha^*](\varphi \to {<}\alpha{>}\varphi) \quad \to \quad (\varphi \to \neg\mathbf{wf}\,\alpha)$$

and the inference rule

$$\frac{\varphi(n+1) \to [\alpha]\varphi(n), \; \neg\varphi(0)}{\varphi(n) \to \mathbf{wf}\,\alpha}$$

for first-order φ and n not occurring in α.

16.4 Dynamic Algebra

Dynamic algebra provides an abstract algebraic framework that relates to PDL as Boolean algebra relates to propositional logic. Dynamic algebra was introduced in Kozen (1980b) and Pratt (1979b) and studied by numerous authors; see Kozen (1979c,b, 1980a, 1981b); Pratt (1979a, 1980a, 1988); Németi (1980); Trnkova and Reiterman (1980). A survey of the main results appears in Kozen (1979a). A *dynamic algebra* is defined to be any two-sorted algebraic structure $(K, B, \cdot)$, where $B = (B, \to, 0)$ is a Boolean algebra, $K = (K, +, \cdot, {}^*, 0, 1)$ is a Kleene algebra (see Section 17.5), and $\cdot : K \times B \to B$ is a scalar multiplication satisfying algebraic constraints corresponding to the dual forms of the PDL axioms (Axioms 5.5). For example, all dynamic algebras satisfy the equations

$$
\begin{aligned}
(\alpha\beta) \cdot \varphi &= \alpha \cdot (\beta \cdot \varphi) \\
\alpha \cdot 0 &= 0 \\
0 \cdot \varphi &= 0 \\
\alpha \cdot (\varphi \vee \psi) &= \alpha \cdot \varphi \vee \alpha \cdot \psi,
\end{aligned}
$$

which correspond to the PDL validities

$$
\begin{aligned}
<\alpha\,;\,\beta>\varphi &\leftrightarrow <\alpha><\beta>\varphi \\
<\alpha>0 &\leftrightarrow \mathbf{0} \\
<0?>\varphi &\leftrightarrow \mathbf{0} \\
<\alpha>(\varphi \vee \psi) &\leftrightarrow <\alpha>\varphi \vee <\alpha>\psi,
\end{aligned}
$$

respectively. The Boolean algebra B is an abstraction of the formulas of PDL and the Kleene algebra K is an abstraction of the programs.

Kleene algebra is of interest in its own right, and we defer a more detailed treatment until Section 17.5. In short, a Kleene algebra is an idempotent semiring under $+, \cdot, 0, 1$ satisfying certain axioms for * that say essentially that * behaves like the asterate operator on sets of strings or reflexive transitive closure on binary relations. There are finitary and infinitary axiomatizations of the essential properties of * that are of quite different deductive strength. A Kleene algebra satisfying the stronger infinitary axiomatization is called *-*continuous* (see Section 17.5).

The interaction of scalar multiplication with iteration can be axiomatized in a finitary or infinitary way. One can postulate

$$\alpha^* \cdot \varphi \;\; \le \;\; \varphi \vee (\alpha^* \cdot (\neg\varphi \wedge (\alpha \cdot \varphi))) \tag{16.4.1}$$

corresponding to the diamond form of the PDL induction axiom (Axiom 5.5(viii)). Here $\varphi \le \psi$ in B iff $\varphi \vee \psi = \psi$. Alternatively, one can postulate the stronger axiom of *-*continuity*:

$$\alpha^* \cdot \varphi \;\; = \;\; \sup_n (\alpha^n \cdot \varphi). \tag{16.4.2}$$

We can think of (16.4.2) as a conjunction of infinitely many axioms $\alpha^n \cdot \varphi \le \alpha^* \cdot \varphi$, $n \ge 0$, and the infinitary Horn formula

$$(\bigwedge_{n \ge 0} \alpha^n \cdot \varphi \le \psi) \;\; \rightarrow \;\; \alpha^* \cdot \varphi \le \psi.$$

In the presence of the other axioms, (16.4.2) implies (16.4.1) (Kozen (1980b)), and is strictly stronger in the sense that there are dynamic algebras that are not *-continuous (Pratt (1979a)).

A standard Kripke frame $\mathfrak{K} = (U, \mathfrak{m}_\mathfrak{K})$ of PDL gives rise to a *-continuous dynamic algebra consisting of a Boolean algebra of subsets of U and a Kleene algebra of binary relations on U. Operators are interpreted as in PDL, including 0 as $\mathbf{0}$? (the empty program), 1 as $\mathbf{1}$? (the identity program), and $\alpha \cdot \varphi$ as $<\alpha>\varphi$. Nonstandard Kripke frames (see Section 6.3) also give rise to dynamic algebras, but not necessarily *-continuous ones. A dynamic algebra is *separable* if any pair of distinct Kleene elements can be distinguished by some Boolean element; that is, if $\alpha \ne \beta$, then there exists $\varphi \in B$ with $\alpha \cdot \varphi \ne \beta \cdot \varphi$.

Research directions in this area include the following.

- *Representation theory.* It is known that any separable dynamic algebra is isomorphic to some possibly nonstandard Kripke frame. Under certain conditions, "possibly nonstandard" can be replaced by "standard," but not in general, even for *-continuous algebras (Kozen (1980b, 1979c, 1980a)).

- *Algebraic methods in* PDL. The small model property (Theorem 6.5) and completeness (Theorem 7.6) for PDL can be established by purely algebraic considerations (Pratt (1980a)).

- *Comparative study of alternative axiomatizations of* *. For example, it is known that separable dynamic algebras can be distinguished from standard Kripke frames by a first-order formula, but even $L_{\omega_1\omega}$ cannot distinguish the latter from *-continuous separable dynamic algebras (Kozen (1981b)).

- *Equational theory of dynamic algebras.* Many seemingly unrelated models of computation share the same equational theory, namely that of dynamic algebras (Pratt (1979b,a)).

In addition, many interesting questions arise from the algebraic viewpoint, and interesting connections with topology, classical algebra, and model theory have been made (Kozen (1979b); Németi (1980)).

16.5   Probabilistic Programs

There is wide interest recently in programs that employ probabilistic moves such as coin tossing or random number draws and whose behavior is described probabilistically (for example, α is "correct" if it does what it is meant to do with probability 1). To give one well known example taken from Miller (1976) and Rabin (1980), there are fast probabilistic algorithms for checking primality of numbers but no known fast nonprobabilistic ones. Many synchronization problems including digital contract signing, guaranteeing mutual exclusion, etc. are often solved by probabilistic means.

This interest has prompted research into formal and informal methods for reasoning about probabilistic programs. It should be noted that such methods are also applicable for reasoning probabilistically about ordinary programs, for example, in average-case complexity analysis of a program, where inputs are regarded as coming from some set with a probability distribution.

Kozen (1981d) provided a formal semantics for probabilistic first-order **while** programs with a random assignment statement $x := ?$. Here the term "random" is quite appropriate (contrast with Section 11.2) as the statement essentially picks an element out of some fixed distribution over the domain D. This domain is assumed to be given with an appropriate set of measurable subsets. Programs are then interpreted as measurable functions on a certain measurable product space of copies of D.

In Feldman and Harel (1984) a probabilistic version of first-order Dynamic Logic, $Pr(\mathsf{DL})$, was investigated on the interpreted level. Kozen's semantics is extended as described below to a semantics for formulas that are closed under Boolean connectives and quantification over reals and integers and that employ terms of the form $Fr(\varphi)$ for first-order φ. In addition, if α is a **while** program with nondeterministic assignments and φ is a formula, then $\{\alpha\}\varphi$ is a new formula.

The semantics assumes a domain D, say the reals, with a measure space consisting of an appropriate family of *measurable subsets* of D. The states $\mu, \nu, \ldots$ are then taken to be the positive measures on this measure space. Terms are interpreted as functions from states to real numbers, with $Fr(\varphi)$ in μ being the *frequency* (or simply, the *measure*) of φ in μ. Frequency is to positive measures as probability is to probability measures. The formula $\{\alpha\}\varphi$ is true in μ if φ is true in ν, the state (i.e., measure) that is the result of applying α to μ in Kozen's semantics. Thus $\{\alpha\}\varphi$ means "after α, φ" and is the construct analogous to $<\alpha>\varphi$ of DL.

For example, in $Pr(\mathsf{DL})$ one can write

$$Fr(1) = 1 \quad \rightarrow \quad \{\alpha\}Fr(1) \geq p$$

to mean, "α halts with probability at least p." The formula

$$Fr(1) = 1 \quad \rightarrow \quad [i := 1; x := ?; \textbf{while } x > 1/2 \textbf{ do } (x := ?; i := i + 1)]$$
$$\forall n \, ((n \geq 1 \rightarrow Fr(i = n) = 2^{-n}) \wedge (n < 1 \rightarrow Fr(i = n) = 0))$$

is valid in all structures in which the distribution of the random variable used in $x := ?$ is a uniform distribution on the real interval $[0, 1]$.

An axiom system for $Pr(\mathsf{DL})$ was proved in Feldman and Harel (1984) to be complete relative to an extension of first-order analysis with integer variables, and for discrete probabilities first-order analysis with integer variables was shown to suffice.

Various propositional versions of probabilistic DL have also been proposed; see Reif (1980); Makowsky and Tiomkin (1980); Ramshaw (1981); Feldman (1984); Parikh and Mahoney (1983); Kozen (1985). In Ramshaw (1981), Ramshaw gave a Hoare-like logic, but observed that even the if-then-else rule was incomplete. Reif (1980) gave a logic that was not expressive enough to define if-then-else; moreover, the soundness of one of its proof rules was later called into question (Feldman and Harel (1984)). Makowsky and Tiomkin (1980) gave an infinitary system and proved completeness. Parikh and Mahoney (1983) studied the equational properties of probabilistic programs. Feldman (1984) gave a less expressive version of $Pr(\mathsf{DL})$, though still with quantifiers, and proved decidability by reduction to the first-order theory of $\mathbb{R}$ (Renegar (1991)). Kozen (1985) replaced the truth-functional propositional operators with analogous arithmetic ones, giving an arithmetical calculus closer in spirit to the semantics of Kozen (1981d). Three equivalent semantics were given: a Markov transition semantics, a generalized operational semantics involving measure transformers, and a generalized predicate transformer semantics involving measurable function transformers. A small model property and *PSPACE* decision procedure over well-structured programs were given. A deductive calculus was proposed and its use demonstrated by calculating the expected running time of a random walk.

In a different direction, Lehmann and Shelah (1982) extend propositional temporal logic (Section 17.2) with an operator C for "certainly" where $C\varphi$ means essentially, "φ is true with probability 1." Actual numerical probabilities, like p or 2^{-n} in the examples above, are not expressible in this language. Nevertheless, the system can express many properties of interest, especially for finite state protocols that employ probabilistic choice, such as probabilistic solutions to such synchronization problems as mutual exclusion. In many such cases the probabilistic behavior of the program can be described without resorting to numerical values and is independent of the particular distribution used for the random choices.

For example, one can write

$$\textbf{at } L_1 \quad \rightarrow \quad (\neg C \neg \bigcirc \textbf{at } L_2 \wedge \neg C \neg \bigcirc \textbf{at } L_3)$$

meaning "if execution is at label L_1, then it is possible (i.e., true with nonzero probability) to be at L_2 in the next step, and similarly for L_3." Three variants of the system, depending upon whether positive probabilities are bounded from below or not, and whether or not the number of possibilities is finite, are shown in Lehmann and Shelah (1982) to be decidable and complete with respect to finite effective axiomatizations that extend those of classical modal or temporal logic.

Probabilistic processes and model checking have recently become a popular topic of research; see Morgan et al. (1999); Segala and Lynch (1994); Hansson and Jonsson (1994); Jou and Smolka (1990); Pnueli and Zuck (1986, 1993); Baier and Kwiatkowska (1998); Huth and Kwiatkowska (1997); Blute et al. (1997). The relationship between all these formal approaches remains an interesting topic for further work.

16.6   Concurrency and Communication

As in Section 10.7 for PDL, we can add to DL the concurrency operator for programs, so that $\alpha \wedge \beta$ is a program, inductively, for any α and β. As in concurrent PDL, the meaning of a program is then a relation between states and sets of states.

It is not known whether the resulting logic, *concurrent* DL, is strictly more expressive than DL, but this is known to be true if both logics are restricted to allow only quantifier-free first-order tests in the programs.

Also, the four axiom systems of Chapter 14 can be proved complete with the appropriate addition of the valid formulas of the concurrent versions of PDL.

16.7   Bibliographical Notes

Algorithmic logic was introduced by Salwicki (1970). Mirkowska (1980, 1981a,b) extended AL to allow nondeterministic **while** programs and studied the operators ∇ and Δ. Complete infinitary deductive systems for propositional and first-order versions were given by Mirkowska (1980, 1981a,b) using the algebraic methods of Rasiowa and Sikorski (1963). Surveys of early work in AL can be found in Banachowski et al. (1977); Salwicki (1977). Constable (1977), Constable and O'Donnell (1978) and Goldblatt (1982) presented logics similar to AL and DL for reasoning about deterministic **while** programs.

Nonstandard Dynamic Logic was introduced by Németi (1981) and Andréka et al. (1982a,b). Theorem 16.1 is due to Csirmaz (1985). See Makowski and Sain (1986) for more information and further references on NDL. Nonstandard semantics has also been studied at the propositional level; see Section 6.4.

The **halt** construct (actually its complement, **loop**) was introduced in Harel and Pratt (1978), and the **wf** construct (actually its complement, **repeat**) was investigated for PDL in Streett (1981, 1982). Theorem 16.2 is from Meyer and Winklmann (1982), Theorem 16.3 is from Harel and Peleg (1985), Theorem 16.4 is from Harel (1984), and the axiomatizations of LDL and PDL are discussed in Harel (1979, 1984).

Dynamic algebra was introduced in Kozen (1980b) and Pratt (1979b) and studied by numerous authors; see Kozen (1979c,b, 1980a, 1981b); Pratt (1979a, 1980a, 1988); Németi (1980); Trnkova and Reiterman (1980). A survey of the main results appears in Kozen (1979a).

The PhD thesis of Ramshaw (1981) contains an engaging introduction to the subject of probabilistic semantics and verification. Kozen (1981d) provided a formal semantics for probabilistic programs. The logic $Pr(DL)$ was presented in Feldman and Harel (1984), along with a deductive system that is complete for Kozen's semantics relative to an extension of first-order analysis. Various propositional versions of probabilistic DL have been proposed in Reif (1980); Makowsky and Tiomkin (1980); Feldman (1984); Parikh and Mahoney (1983); Kozen (1985). The temporal approach to probabilistic verification has been studied in Lehmann and Shelah (1982); Hart et al. (1982); Courcoubetis and Yannakakis (1988); Vardi (1985a). Interest in the subject of probabilistic verification has undergone a recent revival; see Morgan et al. (1999); Segala and Lynch (1994); Hansson and Jonsson (1994); Jou and Smolka (1990); Baier and Kwiatkowska (1998); Huth and Kwiatkowska (1997); Blute et al. (1997).

Concurrent DL is defined in Peleg (1987b), in which the results mentioned in Section 16.6 are proved. Additional versions of this logic, which employ various mechanisms for communication among the concurrent parts of a program, are also considered in Peleg (1987c,a).

17 Other Approaches

In this chapter we describe some topics that are the subject of extensive past and present research and which are all closely related to Dynamic Logic. Our descriptions here are very brief and sketchy and are designed to provide the reader with only a most superficial idea of the essence of the topic, together with one or two central or expository references where details and further references can be found.

17.1 Logic of Effective Definitions

The Logic of Effective Definitions (**LED**), introduced by Tiuryn (1981a), was intended to study notions of computability over abtract models and to provide a universal framework for the study of logics of programs over such models. It consists of first-order logic augmented with new atomic formulas of the form $\alpha = \beta$, where α and β are *effective definitional schemes* (the latter notion is due to Friedman (1971)):

if φ_1 **then** t_1
    else if φ_2 **then** t_2
        else if φ_3 **then** t_3
            else if ...

where the φ_i are quantifier-free formulas and t_i are terms over a bounded set of variables, and the function $i \mapsto (\varphi_i, t_i)$ is recursive. The formula $\alpha = \beta$ is defined to be true in a state if both α and β terminate and yield the same value, or neither terminates.

Model theory and infinitary completeness of **LED** are treated in Tiuryn (1981a).

Effective definitional schemes in the definition of **LED** can be replaced by any programming language K, giving rise to various logical formalisms. The following result, which relates **LED** to other logics discussed here, is proved in Meyer and Tiuryn (1981, 1984).

THEOREM 17.1: For every signature L,

$$\text{LED} \quad \equiv \quad \text{DL(r.e.)}.$$

17.2   Temporal Logic

Temporal Logic (TL) is an alternative application of modal logic to program specification and verification. It was first proposed as a useful tool in program verification by Pnueli (1977) and has since been developed by many authors in various forms. This topic is surveyed in depth in Emerson (1990) and Gabbay et al. (1994).

TL differs from DL chiefly in that it is *endogenous*; that is, programs are not explicit in the language. Every application has a single program associated with it, and the language may contain program-specific statements such as **at** L, meaning "execution is currently at location L in the program." There are two competing semantics, giving rise to two different theories called *linear-time* and *branching-time* TL. In the former, a model is a linear sequence of program states representing an execution sequence of a deterministic program or a possible execution sequence of a nondeterministic or concurrent program. In the latter, a model is a tree of program states representing the space of all possible traces of a nondeterministic or concurrent program. Depending on the application and the semantics, different syntactic constructs can be chosen. The relative advantages of linear and branching time semantics are discussed in Lamport (1980); Emerson and Halpern (1986); Emerson and Lei (1987); Vardi (1998a).

Modal constructs used in TL include

$\Box\varphi$ "φ holds in all future states"
$\Diamond\varphi$ "φ holds in some future state"
$\bigcirc\varphi$ "φ holds in the next state"

for linear-time logic, as well as constructs for expressing

"for all traces starting from the present state ... "
"for some trace starting from the present state ... "

for branching-time logic.

Temporal logic is useful in situations where programs are not normally supposed to halt, such as operating systems, and is particularly well suited to the study of concurrency. Many classical program verification methods such as the *intermittent assertions method* are treated quite elegantly in this framework; we give an example of this below.

Temporal logic has been most successful in providing tools for proving properties of concurrent *finite state* protocols, such as solutions to the *dining philosophers* and *mutual exclusion* problems, which are popular abstract versions of synchronization and resource management problems in distributed systems.

The Inductive Assertions Method

In this section we give an example to illustrate the inductive assertions method. We will later give a more modern treatment using TL. For purposes of illustration, we use a programming language in which programs consist of a sequence of labeled statements. Statements may include simple assignments, conditional and unconditional **go to** statements, and **print** statements. For example, the following program computes $n!$.

EXAMPLE 17.2:

$$L_0 \quad : \quad x := 1$$
$$L_1 \quad : \quad y := 1$$
$$L_2 \quad : \quad y := y + 1$$
$$L_3 \quad : \quad x := x \cdot y$$
$$L_4 \quad : \quad \textbf{if } y \neq n \textbf{ then go to } L_2$$
$$L_5 \quad : \quad \textbf{print } x$$

In this program, the variable n can be considered free; it is part of the input. Note that the program does not halt if $n = 1$. Suppose we wish to show that whenever the program halts, x will contain the value $n!$. Traditionally one establishes an *invariant*, which is a statement φ with the properties

(i) φ is true at the beginning,

(ii) φ is preserved throughout execution, and

(iii) φ implies the output condition.

In our case, the output condition is $x = n!$, and the appropriate invariant φ is

$$\begin{aligned}
&\quad \textbf{at } L_1 \rightarrow x = 1 \\
\wedge &\quad \textbf{at } L_2 \rightarrow x = y! \\
\wedge &\quad \textbf{at } L_3 \rightarrow x = (y-1)! \\
\wedge &\quad \textbf{at } L_4 \rightarrow x = y! \\
\wedge &\quad \textbf{at } L_5 \rightarrow x = y! \wedge y = n
\end{aligned} \qquad (17.2.1)$$

where **at** L_i means the processor is about to execute statement L_i. Then (i) holds, because at the beginning of the program, **at** L_0 is true, therefore all five conjuncts are vacuously true. To show that (ii) holds, suppose we are at any point in the program, say L_3, and φ holds. Then $x = (y-1)!$, since **at** $L_3 \to x = (y-1)!$ is a conjunct of φ. In the next step, we will be at L_4, and $x = y!$ will hold, since we will have just executed the statement $L_3 : x := x \cdot y$. Therefore **at** $L_4 \to x = y!$ will hold, and since **at** L_4 holds, all the other conjuncts will be vacuously true, so φ will hold. In this way we verify, for each possible location in the program, that φ is preserved after execution of one instruction. Finally, when we are about to execute L_5, φ ensures that x contains the desired result $n!$.

The Temporal Approach

To recast this development in the framework of Temporal Logic, note that we are arguing that a certain formula φ is preserved throughout time. If we define a *state* of the computation to be a pair (L_i, u) where L_i is the label of a statement and u is a valuation of the program variables, then we can consider the trace

$$\sigma = s_0 s_1 s_2 \cdots$$

of states that the program goes through during execution. Each state s_i contains all the information needed to determine whether φ is true at s_i. We write $s_i \vDash \varphi$ if the statement φ holds in the state s_i.

There is also a binary relation NEXT that tells which states can immediately follow a state. The relation NEXT depends on the program. For example, in the program of Example 17.2,

$$((L_2, x = 6, y = 14), (L_3, x = 6, y = 15)) \in \text{NEXT}.$$

In the sequence σ above, s_0 is the start state $(L_0, x = 0, y = 0)$ and s_{i+1} is the unique state such that $(s_i, s_{i+1}) \in \text{NEXT}$. In ordinary deterministic programs, each state has at most one NEXT-successor, but in concurrent or nondeterministic programs, there may be many possible NEXT-successors.

Define

$s \vDash \bigcirc\varphi \overset{\text{def}}{\Longleftrightarrow}$ for all states t such that $(s, t) \in \text{NEXT}$, $t \vDash \varphi$

$s \vDash \Box\varphi \overset{\text{def}}{\Longleftrightarrow}$ starting with s, all future states satisfy φ

$\Longleftrightarrow$ for all t such that $(s, t) \in \text{NEXT}^*$, $t \vDash \varphi$

where NEXT^* is the reflexive transitive closure of NEXT

$s \vDash \Diamond\varphi \overset{\text{def}}{\Longleftrightarrow} s \vDash \neg\Box\neg\varphi.$

In other words, $s \vDash \bigcirc\varphi$ if all NEXT-successors of s satisfy φ. In the trace σ, if s_{i+1} exists, then $s_i \vDash \bigcirc\varphi$ iff $s_{i+1} \vDash \varphi$. The formula $\bigcirc\varphi$ does not imply that a

NEXT-successor exists; however, the dual operator $\neg \bigcirc \neg$ can be used where this is desired:

$$s \vDash \neg \bigcirc \neg \varphi \quad \Longleftrightarrow \quad \text{there exists } t \text{ such that } (s,t) \in \text{NEXT and } t \vDash \varphi.$$

In the trace σ, $s_i \vDash \Box \varphi$ iff $\forall j \geq i$, $s_j \vDash \varphi$.

To say that the statement φ of (17.2.1) is an *invariant* means that every s_i satisfies $\varphi \to \bigcirc \varphi$; that is, if $s_i \vDash \varphi$ then $s_{i+1} \vDash \varphi$. This is the same as saying

$$s_0 \quad \vDash \quad \Box(\varphi \to \bigcirc \varphi).$$

To say that φ holds at the beginning of execution is just

$$s_0 \quad \vDash \quad \varphi.$$

The principle of induction on $\mathbb{N}$ allows us to conclude that φ will be true in all reachable states; that is,

$$s_0 \quad \vDash \quad \Box \varphi.$$

We can immediately derive the correctness of the program, since (17.2.1) implies our desired output condition.

The induction principle of **TL** takes the form:

$$\varphi \wedge \Box(\varphi \to \bigcirc \varphi) \quad \to \quad \Box \varphi. \tag{17.2.2}$$

Note the similarity to the **PDL** induction axiom (Axiom 5.5(viii)):

$$\varphi \wedge [\alpha^*](\varphi \to [\alpha]\varphi) \quad \to \quad [\alpha^*]\varphi.$$

This is a classical program verification method known as *inductive* or *invariant assertions*.

The operators $\Box$, $\bigcirc$, and $\Diamond$ are called *temporal operators* because they describe how the truth of the formula φ depends on time. The inductive or invariant assertions method is really an application of the temporal principle (17.2.2). The part $\Box(\varphi \to \bigcirc \varphi)$ of the formula φ of (17.2.2) says that φ is an *invariant*; that is, at all future points, if φ is true, then φ will be true after one more step of the program.

This method is useful for proving *invariant* or *safety properties*. These are properties that can be expressed as $\Box \varphi$; that is, properties that we wish to remain true throughout the computation. Examples of such properties are:

- *partial correctness*—see Example 17.2;
- *mutual exclusion*—no two processes are in their critical sections simultaneously;

- *clean execution*—for example, a stack never overflows, or we never divide by 0 at a particular division instruction;

- *freedom from deadlock*—it is never the case that all processes are simultaneously requesting resources held by another process.

Another very important class of properties that one would like to reason about are *eventuality* or *liveness properties*, which say that something will eventually become true. These are expressed using the $\Diamond$ operator of TL. Examples are:

- *total correctness*—a program eventually halts and produces an output that is correct;

- *fairness* or *freedom from starvation*—if a process is waiting for a resource, it will eventually obtain access to it;

- *liveness of variables*—if a variable x is assigned a value through the execution of an assignment statement $x := t$, then that variable is used at some future point.

There are two historical methods of reasoning about eventualities. The first is called the *method of well-founded sets*; the second is called *intermittent assertions*.

Recall from Section 1.3 that a strict partial order $(A, <)$ is *well-founded* if every subset has a minimal element. This implies that there can be no infinite descending chains

$$a_0 \; > \; a_1 \; > \; a_2 \; > \; \cdots$$

in A. One way to prove that a program terminates is to find such a well-founded set $(A, <)$ and associate with each state s of the computation an element $a_s \in A$ such that if $(s, t) \in \text{NEXT}$ then $a_s > a_t$. Thus the program could not run forever through states $s_0, s_1, s_2, \ldots$, because then there would be an infinite descending chain

$$a_{s_0} \; > \; a_{s_1} \; > \; a_{s_2} \; > \; \cdots,$$

contradicting the assumption of well-foundedness. For example, in the program (17.2), if we start out with $n > 1$, then every time through the loop, y is incremented by 1, so progress is made toward $y = n$ which will cause the loop to exit at L_4. One can construct a well-founded order $<$ on states that models this forward progress. However, the expression describing it would be a rather lengthy and unnatural arithmetic combination of the values of n and y and label indices L_i, even for this very simple program.

A more natural method is the *intermittent assertions method*. This establishes eventualities of the form $\psi \to \Diamond\varphi$ by applications of rules such as

$$\frac{\psi \to \Diamond\theta, \quad \theta \to \Diamond\varphi}{\psi \to \Diamond\varphi} \tag{17.2.3}$$

among others. This method may also use well-founded relations, although the well-founded relations one needs to construct are often simpler. For example, in the program of Example 17.2, total correctness is expressed by

$$\text{at } L_0 \wedge n > 1 \quad \to \quad \Diamond(\text{at } L_5 \wedge x = n!). \tag{17.2.4}$$

Using (17.2.3), we can prove

$$\text{at } L_0 \wedge n > 1 \quad \to \quad \Diamond(\text{at } L_4 \wedge y \le n \wedge x = y!) \tag{17.2.5}$$

from the four statements

$$
\begin{aligned}
\text{at } L_0 \wedge n > 1 \quad &\to \quad \bigcirc(\text{at } L_1 \wedge n > 1 \wedge x = 1) \\
\text{at } L_1 \wedge n > 1 \wedge x = 1 \quad &\to \quad \bigcirc(\text{at } L_2 \wedge n > 1 \wedge x = 1 \wedge y = 1) \\
\text{at } L_2 \wedge n > 1 \wedge y = 1 \quad &\to \quad \bigcirc(\text{at } L_3 \wedge n > 1 \wedge x = 1 \wedge y = 2) \\
\text{at } L_3 \wedge n > 1 \wedge x = 1 \wedge y = 2 \quad &\to \quad \bigcirc(\text{at } L_4 \wedge n > 1 \wedge x = 2 \wedge y = 2) \\
&\to \quad \bigcirc(\text{at } L_4 \wedge y \le n \wedge x = y!).
\end{aligned}
$$

Similarly, one can prove using (17.2.3) that for all values a,

$$\text{at } L_4 \wedge y = a \wedge y < n \wedge x = y! \to \Diamond(\text{at } L_4 \wedge y = a + 1 \wedge y \le n \wedge x = y!) \tag{17.2.6}$$

by going through the loop once. This implies that every time through the loop, the value of $n - y$ decreases by 1. Thus we can use the well-founded relation $<$ on the natural numbers to get

$$\text{at } L_4 \wedge y \le n \wedge x = y! \quad \to \quad \Diamond(\text{at } L_4 \wedge y = n \wedge x = y!) \tag{17.2.7}$$

from (17.2.6), using the principle

$$\exists m \; \psi(m) \wedge \forall m \; \Box(\psi(m + 1) \to \Diamond\psi(m)) \quad \to \quad \Diamond\psi(0).$$

Finally, we observe that

$$\text{at } L_4 \wedge y = n \wedge x = y! \to \bigcirc(\text{at } L_5 \wedge x = n!),$$

so we achieve our proof of the total correctness assertion (17.2.4) by combining (17.2.5), (17.2.6), and (17.2.7) using (17.2.3).

Expressiveness

Recall

$$s \vDash \bigcirc\varphi \quad \overset{\text{def}}{\Longleftrightarrow} \quad \forall t \; (s,t) \in \text{Next} \to t \vDash \varphi$$

$$s \vDash \square\varphi \quad \overset{\text{def}}{\Longleftrightarrow} \quad \forall t \; (s,t) \in \text{Next}^* \to t \vDash \varphi$$

$$s \vDash \Diamond\varphi \quad \overset{\text{def}}{\Longleftrightarrow} \quad s \vDash \neg\square\neg\varphi$$

$$\quad\quad\quad \Longleftrightarrow \quad \exists t \; (s,t) \in \text{Next}^* \wedge t \vDash \varphi.$$

Here are some interesting properties that can be expressed with $\bigcirc$, $\Diamond$, and $\square$ over linear-time interpretations.

EXAMPLE 17.3:

(i) The trace consists of exactly one state:

halt $\overset{\text{def}}{\Longleftrightarrow}$ $\bigcirc\mathbf{0}$

(ii) The trace is finite, that is, the computation eventually halts:

fin $\overset{\text{def}}{\Longleftrightarrow}$ $\Diamond$**halt**

(iii) The trace is infinite:

inf $\overset{\text{def}}{\Longleftrightarrow}$ $\neg$**fin**

(iv) The formula φ is true at infinitely many points along the trace (a formula is true at a state on a trace if the formula is satisfied by the suffix of the trace beginning at that state):

inf $\wedge\, \square\Diamond\varphi$

(v) The formula φ becomes true for the first time at some point, then remains true thereafter:

$\Diamond\varphi \wedge \square(\varphi \to \square\varphi)$

(vi) The trace has exactly one nonnull interval on which φ is true, and it is false elsewhere:

$\Diamond\varphi \wedge \square((\varphi \wedge \bigcirc\neg\varphi) \to \bigcirc\square\neg\varphi)$

(vii) The formula φ is true at each multiple of 4 but false elsewhere:

$$\varphi \wedge \Box(\varphi \to \bigcirc(\neg\varphi \wedge \bigcirc(\neg\varphi \wedge \bigcirc(\neg\varphi \wedge \bigcirc\varphi))))$$

The Until Operator

One useful operator that cannot be expressed is **until**. This is a binary operator written in infix (e.g., $\varphi\,\textbf{until}\,\psi$). It says that there exists some future point t such that $t \vDash \psi$ and that all points strictly between the current state and t satisfy φ.

The operators $\bigcirc$, $\Diamond$, and $\Box$ can all be defined in terms of **until**:

$$\bigcirc\varphi \iff \neg(\textbf{0 until}\,\neg\varphi)$$
$$\Diamond\varphi \iff \varphi \vee (\textbf{1 until}\,\varphi)$$
$$\Box\varphi \iff \varphi \wedge \neg(\textbf{1 until}\,\neg\varphi)$$

In the definition of $\bigcirc$, the subexpression $\textbf{0 until}\,\neg\varphi$ says that some future point t satisfies $\neg\varphi$, but all points strictly between the current state and t satisfy $\textbf{0}$ (*false*); but this can happen only if there are no intermediate states, that is, t is the next state. Thus $\textbf{0 until}\,\neg\varphi$ says that there exists a NEXT-successor satisfying $\neg\varphi$. The definition of $\Diamond$ says that φ is true now or sometime in the future, and all intermediate points satisfy $\textbf{1}$ (*true*).

It has been shown in Kamp (1968) and Gabbay et al. (1980) that the **until** operator is powerful enough to express anything that can be expressed in the first-order theory of $(\omega, <)$. It has also been shown in Wolper (1981, 1983) that there are very simple predicates that cannot be expressed by **until**; for example, "φ is true at every multiple of 4." Compare Example 17.3(vii) above; here, we do not say anything about whether φ is true at points that are not multiples of 4.

The **until** operator has been shown to be very useful in expressing non-input/output properties of programs such as: "If process p requests a resource before q does, then it will receive it before q does." Indeed, much of the research in TL has concentrated on providing useful methods for proving these and other kinds of properties (see Manna and Pnueli (1981); Gabbay et al. (1980)).

Concurrency and Nondeterminism

Unlike DL, TL can be applied to programs that are not normally supposed to halt, such as operating systems, because programs are interpreted as *traces* instead of pairs of states. Up to now we have only considered deterministic, single-process programs, so that for each state s, if $(s, t) \in$ NEXT then t is unique. There is no reason however not to apply TL to *nondeterministic* and *concurrent (multiproces-sor)* systems, although there is a slight problem with this, which we discuss below.

In the single-processor environment, a *state* is a pair (L_i, u), where L_i is the instruction the program is about to execute, and u is a valuation of the program variables. In a multiprocessor environment, say with n processors, a *state* is a tuple $(L_1, \ldots, L_n, u)$ where the ith process is just about to execute L_i. If s and t are states, then $(s, t) \in$ NEXT if t can be obtained from s by letting just one process p_i execute L_i while the other processes wait. Thus each s can have up to n possible next states. In a nondeterministic program, a statement

L_i : **go to** L_j **or** L_k

can occur; to execute this statement, a process chooses nondeterministically to go to either L_j or L_k. Thus we can have two next states. In either of these situations, multiprocessing or nondeterminism, the computation is no longer a single trace, but many different traces are possible. We can assemble them all together to get a *computation tree* in which each node represents a state accessible from the start state.

As above, an *invariance property* is a property of the form $\Box\varphi$, which says that the property φ is preserved throughout time. Thus we should define

$$s \vDash \Box\varphi \overset{\text{def}}{\iff} t \vDash \varphi \text{ for every node } t \text{ in the tree below } s.$$

The problem is that the dual $\Diamond$ of the operator $\Box$ defined in this way does not really capture what we mean by *eventuality* or *liveness* properties. We would like to be able to say that *every* possible trace in the computation tree has a state satisfying φ. For instance, a nondeterministic program is *total* if there is no chance of an infinite trace out of the start state s; that is, every trace out of s satisfies $\Diamond$**halt**. The dual $\Diamond$ of $\Box$ as defined by $\Diamond\varphi = \neg\Box\neg\varphi$ does not really express this. It says instead

$$s \vDash \Diamond\varphi \iff \text{there is } some \text{ node } t \text{ in the tree below } s \text{ such that } t \vDash \varphi.$$

This is not a very useful statement.

There have been several proposals to fix this. One way is to introduce a new modal operator A that says, "For all traces in the tree ... ," and then use $\Box$, $\Diamond$ in the sense of linear TL applied to the trace quantified by A. The dual of A is E, which says, "There exists a trace in the tree ... ." Thus, in order to say that the computation tree starting from the current state satisfies a safety or invariance property, we would write

$A\Box\varphi,$

which says, "For all traces π out of the current state, π satisfies $\Box\varphi$," and to say that the tree satisfies an eventuality property, we would write

$A\Diamond\varphi,$

which says, "For all traces π out of the current state, π satisfies $\Diamond\varphi$; that is, φ occurs somewhere along the trace π." The logic with the linear temporal operators augmented with the trace quantifiers A and E is known as CTL; see Emerson (1990); Emerson and Halpern (1986, 1985); Emerson and Lei (1987); Emerson and Sistla (1984).

An alternative approach that fits in well with PDL is to bring the programs α back into the language explicitly, only this time interpret programs as sets of traces instead of pairs of states. We could then write

$[\alpha]\Diamond\varphi$

$[\alpha]\Box\varphi$

which would mean, respectively, "For all traces π of program α, $\pi \vDash \Diamond\varphi$" and "For all traces π of α, $\pi \vDash \Box\varphi$," and these two statements would capture precisely our intuitive notion of *eventuality* and *invariance*. We discuss such a system, called *Process Logic*, below in Section 17.3.

Complexity and Deductive Completeness

A useful axiomatization of linear-time TL is given by the axioms

$$
\begin{aligned}
\Box(\varphi \to \psi) \;&\to\; (\Box\varphi \to \Box\psi) \\
\Box(\varphi \wedge \psi) \;&\leftrightarrow\; \Box\varphi \wedge \Box\psi \\
\Diamond\varphi \;&\leftrightarrow\; \varphi \vee \bigcirc\Diamond\varphi \\
\bigcirc(\varphi \vee \psi) \;&\leftrightarrow\; \bigcirc\varphi \vee \bigcirc\psi \\
\bigcirc(\varphi \wedge \psi) \;&\leftrightarrow\; \bigcirc\varphi \wedge \bigcirc\psi \\
\varphi \wedge \Box(\varphi \to \bigcirc\varphi) \;&\to\; \Box\varphi \\
\forall x\, \varphi(x) \;&\to\; \varphi(t) \quad (t \text{ is free for } x \text{ in } \varphi) \\
\forall x\, \Box\varphi \;&\to\; \Box\forall x\, \varphi
\end{aligned}
$$

and rules

$$\frac{\varphi, \quad \varphi \to \psi}{\psi} \qquad \frac{\varphi}{\Box \varphi} \qquad \frac{\varphi}{\forall x \; \varphi}.$$

Compare the axioms of PDL (Axioms 5.5). The propositional fragment of this deductive system is complete for linear-time propositional TL, as shown in Gabbay et al. (1980).

Sistla and Clarke (1982) and Emerson and Halpern (1985) have shown that the validity problem for most versions of propositional TL is *PSPACE*-complete for linear structures and *EXPTIME*-complete for branching structures.

Embedding TL in DL

TL is subsumed by DL. To embed propositional TL into PDL, take an atomic program a to mean "one step of program p." In the linear model, the TL constructs $\bigcirc\varphi$, $\Box\varphi$, $\Diamond\varphi$, and $\varphi\, \mathbf{until}\, \psi$ are then expressed by $[a]\varphi$, $[a^*]\varphi$, $<a^*>\varphi$, and $<(a;\varphi?)^*; a>\psi$, respectively.

17.3 Process Logic

Dynamic Logic and Temporal Logic embody markedly different approaches to reasoning about programs. This dichotomy has prompted researchers to search for an appropriate process logic that combines the best features of both. An appropriate candidate should combine the ability to reason about programs compositionally with the ability to reason directly about the intermediate states encountered during the course of a computation.

Pratt (1979c), Parikh (1978b), Nishimura (1980), and Harel et al. (1982) all suggested increasingly more powerful propositional-level formalisms in which the basic idea is to interpret formulas in *traces* rather than in states. In particular, Harel et al. (1982) present a system called *Process Logic* (PL), which is essentially a union of TL and test-free regular PDL. That paper proves that the satisfiability problem is decidable and gives a complete finitary axiomatization.

We present here an extended version that includes tests. In order to interpret the **while** loop correctly, we also include an operator ω for infinite iteration. We allow only poor tests (see Section 10.2).

Syntactically, we have programs $\alpha, \beta, \dots$ and propositions $\varphi, \psi, \dots$ as in PDL. We have atomic symbols of each type and compound expressions built up from the operators $\to$, $\mathbf{0}$, ;, $\cup$, *, ? (applied to Boolean combinations of atomic formulas only), ω, and [ ]. In addition we have the temporal operators **first** and **until**. The temporal operators are available for expressing and reasoning about trace properties, but programs are constructed compositionally as in PDL. Other operators are defined as in PDL (see Section 5.1) except for **skip**, which we handle specially below.

Semantically, both programs and propositions are interpreted as sets of traces. We start with a Kripke frame $\mathfrak{K} = (K, \mathfrak{m}_{\mathfrak{K}})$ as in Section 5.2, where K is a set of *states* $s, t, \ldots$ and the function $\mathfrak{m}_{\mathfrak{K}}$ interprets atomic formulas p as subsets of K and atomic programs a as binary relations on K.

A *trace* σ is a finite or infinite sequence of states

$$\sigma \;\; = \;\; s_0 s_1 s_2 \cdots$$

(repetitions allowed). A trace is of length n if it contains $n + 1$ states; thus a single state constitutes a trace of length 0. The first state of a trace σ is denoted $\mathrm{first}(\sigma)$, and the last state (if it exists) is denoted $\mathrm{last}(\sigma)$. The state $\mathrm{last}(\sigma)$ exists iff σ is finite.

If $\sigma = s_0 s_1 \cdots s_k$ and $\tau = s_k s_{k+1} \cdots$ are traces, then the *fusion* of σ and τ is the trace

$$\sigma\tau \;\; = \;\; s_0 s_1 \cdots s_{k-1} s_k s_{k+1} \cdots$$

Note that s_k is written only once. The traces σ and τ cannot be fused unless σ is finite and $\mathrm{last}(\sigma) = \mathrm{first}(\tau)$. If σ is infinite, or if σ is finite but $\mathrm{last}(\sigma) \neq \mathrm{first}(\tau)$, then $\sigma\tau$ does not exist. A trace τ is a *suffix* of a trace ρ if there exists a finite trace σ such that $\rho = \sigma\tau$. It is a *proper suffix* if there exists such a σ of nonzero length. If A and B are sets of traces, we define

$$A \cdot B \;\; \overset{\mathrm{def}}{=} \;\; \{ \sigma\tau \mid \sigma \in A, \; \tau \in B \}$$
$$A \circ B \;\; \overset{\mathrm{def}}{=} \;\; A \cdot B \; \cup \; \{\text{infinite traces in } A\}.$$

It is not hard to verify that $\cdot$ and $\circ$ are associative.

We define the interpretation of the temporal operators first. The definition is slightly different from that of Section 17.2, but the concept is similar.

For p an atomic proposition and σ a finite trace, define

$$\sigma \vDash p \;\; \overset{\mathrm{def}}{\iff} \;\; \mathrm{last}(\sigma) \in \mathfrak{m}_{\mathfrak{K}}(p).$$

The right-hand side is given by the specification of the Kripke frame $\mathfrak{K}$. If σ is infinite, or if σ is finite and $\text{last}(\sigma) \notin \mathfrak{m}_{\mathfrak{K}}(p)$, then $\sigma \nvDash p$. We also define

$$\sigma \vDash \textbf{first}\, \varphi \quad \overset{\text{def}}{\Longleftrightarrow} \quad \text{first}(\sigma) \vDash \varphi$$

$\sigma \vDash \varphi\, \textbf{until}\, \psi \quad \overset{\text{def}}{\Longleftrightarrow} \quad$ there exists a proper suffix τ of σ such that $\tau \vDash \psi$, and for all proper suffixes ρ of σ such that τ is a proper suffix of ρ, $\rho \vDash \varphi$.

The following trace satisfies $(\textbf{first}\, (q \wedge \neg p))\, \textbf{until}\, \textbf{first}\, \neg q$:

q	q	q	q	q	$\neg q$	q	q
p	$\neg p$	$\neg p$	$\neg p$	$\neg p$	p	p	$\neg p$

As in Section 17.2, if we define

$$\bigcirc \varphi \quad \overset{\text{def}}{\Longleftrightarrow} \quad \neg(\textbf{0}\, \textbf{until}\, \neg \varphi)$$

$$\Box \varphi \quad \overset{\text{def}}{\Longleftrightarrow} \quad \varphi \wedge \neg(\textbf{1}\, \textbf{until}\, \neg \varphi)$$

$$\Diamond \varphi \quad \overset{\text{def}}{\Longleftrightarrow} \quad \neg \Box \neg \varphi$$

$$\Longleftrightarrow \quad \varphi \vee (\textbf{1}\, \textbf{until}\, \varphi),$$

then we get

$\sigma \vDash \bigcirc \varphi \quad \Longleftrightarrow \quad$ the maximal proper suffix of σ, if it exists, satisfies φ,

$\sigma \vDash \Box \varphi \quad \Longleftrightarrow \quad$ all suffixes of σ, proper or not, satisfy φ,

$\sigma \vDash \Diamond \varphi \quad \Longleftrightarrow \quad$ there exists a suffix of σ, proper or not, satisfying φ.

Now we wish to extend the definition of $\mathfrak{m}_{\mathfrak{K}}$ to give meanings to programs. The extended meaning function $\mathfrak{m}_{\mathfrak{K}}$ will assign a set of traces to each program.

The meaning of an atomic program a is the binary relation $\mathfrak{m}_{\mathfrak{K}}(a)$ as determined by the frame $\mathfrak{K}$, considered as a set of traces of length one. We define

$$\mathfrak{m}_{\mathfrak{K}}(\alpha \cup \beta) \quad \overset{\text{def}}{=} \quad \mathfrak{m}_{\mathfrak{K}}(\alpha) \cup \mathfrak{m}_{\mathfrak{K}}(\beta)$$

$$\mathfrak{m}_{\mathfrak{K}}(\alpha\, ;\, \beta) \quad \overset{\text{def}}{=} \quad \mathfrak{m}_{\mathfrak{K}}(\alpha) \circ \mathfrak{m}_{\mathfrak{K}}(\beta)$$

$$= \quad \mathfrak{m}_{\mathfrak{K}}(\alpha) \cdot \mathfrak{m}_{\mathfrak{K}}(\beta) \cup \{\text{infinite traces in } \mathfrak{m}_{\mathfrak{K}}(\alpha)\}$$

$$\mathfrak{m}_{\mathfrak{K}}(\alpha^*) \quad \overset{\text{def}}{=} \quad \bigcup_{n \geq 0} \mathfrak{m}_{\mathfrak{K}}(\alpha^n), \text{ where } \mathfrak{m}_{\mathfrak{K}}(\alpha^0) \overset{\text{def}}{=} K \text{ and } \mathfrak{m}_{\mathfrak{K}}(\alpha^{n+1}) \overset{\text{def}}{=} \mathfrak{m}_{\mathfrak{K}}(\alpha \alpha^n)$$

$$\mathfrak{m}_{\mathfrak{K}}(\alpha^\omega) \quad \overset{\text{def}}{=} \quad \{\sigma_0 \sigma_1 \cdots \mid \sigma_n \in \mathfrak{m}_{\mathfrak{K}}(\alpha),\ n \geq 0\} \cup \{\text{infinite traces in } \mathfrak{m}_{\mathfrak{K}}(\alpha^*)\}$$

$$\mathfrak{m}_{\mathfrak{K}}(\varphi?) \quad \overset{\text{def}}{=} \quad \mathfrak{m}_{\mathfrak{K}}(\varphi) \cap \{\text{traces of length } 0\}.$$

We do not define **skip** as **1**? as in PDL, but rather as the relation

$$\mathbf{skip} \ \stackrel{\text{def}}{=} \ \{(s, s) \mid s \in K\}.$$

The reason for including the ω operator is to model the **while** loop correctly. In PDL, we had

$$\textbf{while } \varphi \textbf{ do } \alpha \ = \ (\varphi? \,;\, \alpha)^* \,;\, \neg\varphi?$$

which was all right for binary relation semantics, since if the test φ never becomes false, there will be no output state. However, with trace semantics, such a computation would result in an infinite trace obtained by concatenating infinitely many finite α traces. This is given by α^ω and should be included in the semantics of the **while** loop. Thus for PL, we define

$$\textbf{while } \varphi \textbf{ do } \alpha \ \stackrel{\text{def}}{=} \ (\varphi? \,;\, \alpha)^* \,;\, \neg\varphi? \ \cup \ (\varphi? \,;\, \alpha)^\omega.$$

We would also like infinite traces in $\mathfrak{m}_{\mathfrak{K}}(\alpha)$ included in $\mathfrak{m}_{\mathfrak{K}}(\alpha \,;\, \beta)$. Intuitively, such traces would result if α ran forever without terminating, thus they would also result from running $\alpha \,;\, \beta$.

For the semantics of the modal operator [ ], we define $\sigma \in \mathfrak{m}_{\mathfrak{K}}([\alpha]\varphi)$ iff either of the following two conditions holds:

(i) σ is finite, and for all traces $\tau \in \mathfrak{m}_{\mathfrak{K}}(\alpha)$ such that $\sigma\tau$ exists, $\sigma\tau \in \mathfrak{m}_{\mathfrak{K}}(\varphi)$; or

(ii) σ is infinite and $\sigma \in \mathfrak{m}_{\mathfrak{K}}(\varphi)$.

Intuitively, either σ represents a finite computation and all extensions τ of σ obtained by running the program α satisfy φ; or σ is an infinite computation satisfying φ already.

The addition of clause (ii) takes care of the possibility that α does not halt. It causes the PDL axiom $[\alpha \,;\, \beta]\varphi \leftrightarrow [\alpha][\beta]\varphi$ to be satisfied.

Axiomatization

Trace models satisfy (most of) the PDL axioms. As in Section 17.2, define

$$\begin{aligned}
\textbf{halt} \ &\stackrel{\text{def}}{\Longleftrightarrow} \ \circ\mathbf{0} \\
\textbf{fin} \ &\stackrel{\text{def}}{\Longleftrightarrow} \ \Diamond\textbf{halt} \\
\textbf{inf} \ &\stackrel{\text{def}}{\Longleftrightarrow} \ \neg\textbf{fin},
\end{aligned}$$

which say that the trace is of length 0, of finite length, or of infinite length, respectively. Define two new operators $⟦\ ⟧$ and $≪\ ≫$:

$$⟦α⟧φ \quad \overset{\text{def}}{\iff} \quad \textbf{fin} \to [α]φ$$

$$≪α≫φ \quad \overset{\text{def}}{\iff} \quad ¬⟦α⟧¬φ \quad \iff \quad \textbf{fin} \land <α>φ.$$

Then

$$\mathfrak{m}_{\mathfrak{K}}(⟦α⟧φ) \;=\; \{σ \mid \text{for all } τ \in \mathfrak{m}_{\mathfrak{K}}(α), \text{ if } στ \text{ exists, then } στ \in \mathfrak{m}_{\mathfrak{K}}(φ)\}$$

$$\mathfrak{m}_{\mathfrak{K}}(≪α≫φ) \;=\; \{σ \mid \text{there exists } τ \in \mathfrak{m}_{\mathfrak{K}}(α) \text{ such that } στ \text{ exists and } στ \in \mathfrak{m}_{\mathfrak{K}}(φ)\}.$$

The operator $≪\ ≫$ is just $<\ >$ restricted to finite traces.

By definition of $[\ ]$ and $<\ >$, the following are valid formulas of PL:

$$\begin{aligned}
[α]φ \quad &\leftrightarrow \quad (\textbf{fin} \to ⟦α⟧φ) \land (\textbf{inf} \to φ) \\
&\leftrightarrow \quad (\textbf{fin} \land ⟦α⟧φ) \lor (\textbf{inf} \land φ) \\
<α>φ \quad &\leftrightarrow \quad (\textbf{fin} \to ≪α≫φ) \land (\textbf{inf} \to φ) \\
&\leftrightarrow \quad (\textbf{fin} \land ≪α≫φ) \lor (\textbf{inf} \land φ).
\end{aligned}$$

First we show that the modal axioms

$$[α](φ \land ψ) \quad \leftrightarrow \quad ([α]φ \land [α]ψ) \tag{17.3.1}$$

$$[α](φ \to ψ) \quad \to \quad ([α]φ \to [α]ψ) \tag{17.3.2}$$

are satisfied. To show (17.3.1), first observe that

$$⟦α⟧(φ \land ψ) \quad \leftrightarrow \quad ⟦α⟧φ \land ⟦α⟧ψ$$

is valid. Then

$$\begin{aligned}
[α](φ \land ψ) \quad &\leftrightarrow \quad (\textbf{fin} \to ⟦α⟧(φ \land ψ)) \land (\textbf{inf} \to (φ \land ψ)) \\
&\leftrightarrow \quad (\textbf{fin} \to (⟦α⟧φ \land ⟦α⟧ψ)) \land (\textbf{inf} \to (φ \land ψ)) \\
&\leftrightarrow \quad (\textbf{fin} \to ⟦α⟧φ) \land (\textbf{fin} \to ⟦α⟧ψ) \land (\textbf{inf} \to φ) \land (\textbf{inf} \to ψ) \\
&\leftrightarrow \quad [α]φ \land [α]ψ.
\end{aligned}$$

To show (17.3.2), by propositional reasoning, it suffices to show

$$[α](φ \to ψ) \land [α]φ \quad \to \quad [α]ψ.$$

First observe that

$$⟦α⟧(φ \to ψ) \land ⟦α⟧φ \quad \to \quad ⟦α⟧ψ$$

is valid. Then

$$[\alpha]\,(\varphi \to \psi) \land [\alpha]\,\varphi$$

$$\leftrightarrow \quad (\mathbf{fin} \to [\![\alpha]\!]\,(\varphi \to \psi)) \land (\mathbf{inf} \to (\varphi \to \psi)) \land (\mathbf{fin} \to [\![\alpha]\!]\,\varphi) \land (\mathbf{inf} \to \varphi)$$

$$\to \quad (\mathbf{fin} \to ([\![\alpha]\!]\,\varphi \to [\![\alpha]\!]\,\psi)) \land (\mathbf{inf} \to (\varphi \to \psi)) \land (\mathbf{fin} \to [\![\alpha]\!]\,\varphi) \land (\mathbf{inf} \to \varphi)$$

$$\leftrightarrow \quad (\mathbf{fin} \to ([\![\alpha]\!]\,\varphi \land ([\![\alpha]\!]\,\varphi \to [\![\alpha]\!]\,\psi))) \land (\mathbf{inf} \to (\varphi \land (\varphi \to \psi)))$$

$$\to \quad (\mathbf{fin} \to [\![\alpha]\!]\,\psi) \land (\mathbf{inf} \to \psi)$$

$$\leftrightarrow \quad [\alpha]\,\psi.$$

The argument for the axiom

$$[\alpha \cup \beta]\varphi \quad \leftrightarrow \quad [\alpha]\varphi \land [\beta]\varphi$$

is similar and uses the property

$$[\![\alpha \cup \beta]\!]\varphi \quad \leftrightarrow \quad [\![\alpha]\!]\varphi \land [\![\beta]\!]\varphi.$$

The axiom $[\alpha \,;\, \beta]\varphi \leftrightarrow [\alpha]\,[\beta]\varphi$ is obtained as follows. Suppose σ is finite. Arguing semantically, $\sigma \in \mathfrak{m}_\mathfrak{K}([\![\alpha \,;\, \beta]\!]\varphi)$ iff

- for all infinite α-traces τ such that $\sigma\tau$ exists, $\sigma\tau \vDash \varphi$; and
- for all finite α-traces τ such that $\sigma\tau$ exists, for all β-traces ρ such that $\sigma\tau\rho$ exists, $\sigma\tau\rho \vDash \varphi$.

Thus

$$[\![\alpha \,;\, \beta]\!]\varphi \quad \leftrightarrow \quad [\![\alpha]\!]\,(\mathbf{inf} \to \varphi) \land [\![\alpha]\!]\,(\mathbf{fin} \to [\![\beta]\!]\varphi)$$

$$\leftrightarrow \quad [\![\alpha]\!]\,((\mathbf{inf} \to \varphi) \land (\mathbf{fin} \to [\![\beta]\!]\varphi))$$

$$\leftrightarrow \quad [\![\alpha]\!]\,[\beta]\varphi$$

and

$$[\alpha \,;\, \beta]\varphi \quad \leftrightarrow \quad (\mathbf{fin} \to [\![\alpha \,;\, \beta]\!]\varphi) \land (\mathbf{inf} \to \varphi)$$

$$\leftrightarrow \quad (\mathbf{fin} \to [\![\alpha]\!]\,[\beta]\varphi) \land (\mathbf{inf} \to \varphi)$$

$$\leftrightarrow \quad (\mathbf{fin} \to [\![\alpha]\!]\,[\beta]\varphi) \land (\mathbf{inf} \to [\beta]\varphi)$$

$$\leftrightarrow \quad [\alpha]\,[\beta]\varphi.$$

The penultimate step uses the fact that φ and $[\beta]\varphi$ are equivalent for infinite traces.

The * operator is the same as in PDL. It can be shown that the two PDL axioms

$$\varphi \wedge [\alpha][\alpha^*]\varphi \;\leftrightarrow\; [\alpha^*]\varphi$$
$$\varphi \wedge [\alpha^*](\varphi \rightarrow [\alpha]\varphi) \;\rightarrow\; [\alpha^*]\varphi$$

hold by establishing that

$$\bigcup_{n \geq 0} \mathfrak{m}_{\mathfrak{K}}(\alpha^n) \;=\; \mathfrak{m}_{\mathfrak{K}}(\alpha^0) \cup (\mathfrak{m}_{\mathfrak{K}}(\alpha) \circ \bigcup_{n \geq 0} \mathfrak{m}_{\mathfrak{K}}(\alpha^n))$$
$$=\; \mathfrak{m}_{\mathfrak{K}}(\alpha^0) \cup ((\bigcup_{n \geq 0} \mathfrak{m}_{\mathfrak{K}}(\alpha^n)) \circ \mathfrak{m}_{\mathfrak{K}}(\alpha)).$$

The axiom for the test operator ? is not quite the same as in PDL. The PDL axiom $[\psi?]\varphi \leftrightarrow (\psi \rightarrow \varphi)$ is valid only for weak tests and finite traces. If either one of these restrictions is lifted, then the formula is no longer valid. Instead we postulate

$$(\mathbf{fin} \rightarrow ([\psi?]\varphi \leftrightarrow (\psi \rightarrow \varphi))) \quad \wedge \quad (\mathbf{inf} \rightarrow ([\psi?]\varphi \leftrightarrow \varphi)) \tag{17.3.3}$$

for weak tests only.

In our formulation, tests are instantaneous. One may argue that this interferes with the semantics of programs such as **while 1 do** φ?, which rightfully should generate an infinite trace but does not. This suggests an alternative approach in which tests would be interpreted as binary relations (traces of length one). However, the latter approach is even more problematic. For one thing, it is not clear how to axiomatize $[\psi?]\varphi$; certainly (17.3.3) is no longer valid. Since we can assert the length of a trace, our axiomatization would be encumbered by such irrelevancies as **length** 17 $\rightarrow$ **[1?]length** 18. Worse, Boolean algebra would no longer be readily available, at least in any simple form. For example, $\varphi?\,;\,\varphi?$ and $\varphi?$ would no longer be equivalent. We thus prefer the formulation we have given. Note, however, that if we restrict programs to ordinary **while** programs in which $\varphi?$ must occur in the test of a conditional or while statement, then pathological programs such as **while 1 do** φ? are disallowed, and all is well. The program **while 1 do skip** generates an infinite trace because of the redefinition of **skip**.

Finally, what can we say about ω? One property that is certain is

$$\mathfrak{m}_{\mathfrak{K}}(\alpha^\omega) \;=\; \mathfrak{m}_{\mathfrak{K}}(\alpha) \circ \mathfrak{m}_{\mathfrak{K}}(\alpha^\omega)$$
$$=\; \mathfrak{m}_{\mathfrak{K}}(\alpha^\omega) \circ \mathfrak{m}_{\mathfrak{K}}(\alpha),$$

which leads to the axioms

$$[\alpha^{\omega}]\varphi \quad \leftrightarrow \quad [\alpha\alpha^{\omega}]\varphi$$
$$\leftrightarrow \quad [\alpha^{\omega}\alpha]\varphi.$$

One might expect the formula $[\alpha^{\omega}]\mathbf{inf}$ to be valid, but this is not the case. For example, $m_{\hat{\mathfrak{R}}}(\mathbf{1}?^{\omega})$ contains all and only traces of length 0. However, if any trace $\sigma \in m_{\hat{\mathfrak{R}}}(\alpha^{\omega})$ has a *state* satisfying φ—that is, if σ has a suffix satisfying **first** φ—then some prefix of σ in $m_{\hat{\mathfrak{R}}}(\alpha^{*})$ also has this property. Thus

$$[\alpha^{*}]\Diamond\mathbf{first}\,\varphi \quad \rightarrow \quad [\alpha^{\omega}]\Diamond\mathbf{first}\,\varphi \qquad\qquad\qquad (17.3.4)$$

is valid. We cannot replace **first** φ by an arbitrary property ψ; for instance, (17.3.4) does not necessarily hold for $\psi = \mathbf{inf}$.

As mentioned, the version of PL of Harel et al. (1982) is decidable (but, it seems, in nonelementary time only) and complete. It has also been shown that if we restrict the semantics to include only finite traces (not a necessary restriction for obtaining the results above), then PL is no more expressive than PDL. Translations of PL structures into PDL structures have also been investigated, making possible an elementary time decision procedure for deterministic PL; see Halpern (1982, 1983). An extension of PL in which **first** and **until** are replaced by regular operators on formulas has been shown to be decidable but nonelementary in Harel et al. (1982). This logic perhaps comes closer to the desired objective of a powerful decidable logic of traces with natural syntactic operators that is closed under attachment of regular programs to formulas.

First-order PL has not been properly investigated yet, perhaps because the "right" logic has not yet been agreed upon. It is also not quite clear yet whether the PL approach has pragmatic advantages over TL in reasoning about concurrent programs. The exact relationship of PL with the second order theory of n successors (see Rabin (1969)), to which the validity problem is reduced for obtaining decidability, seems also worthy of further study.

17.4   The μ-Calculus

The μ-calculus was suggested as a formalism for reasoning about programs in Scott and de Bakker (1969) and was further developed in Hitchcock and Park (1972), Park (1976), and de Bakker (1980).

The heart of the approach is μ, the *least fixpoint* operator, which captures the notions of iteration and recursion. The calculus was originally defined as a first-order-level formalism, but propositional versions have become popular.

The μ operator binds relation variables. If $\varphi(X)$ is a logical expression with a free relation variable X, then the expression $\mu X.\varphi(X)$ represents the least X such that $\varphi(X) = X$, if such an X exists. For example, the reflexive transitive closure R^* of a binary relation R is the least binary relation containing R and closed under reflexivity and transitivity; this would be expressed in the first-order μ-calculus as

$$R^* \stackrel{\text{def}}{=} \mu X(x,y).(x = y \vee \exists z \; (R(x,z) \wedge X(z,y))). \tag{17.4.1}$$

This should be read as, "the least binary relation $X(x,y)$ such that either $x = y$ or x is related by R to some z such that z and y are already related by X." This captures the usual fixpoint formulation of reflexive transitive closure (Section 1.7). The formula (17.4.1) can be regarded either as a recursive program computing R^* or as an inductively defined assertion that is true of a pair (x,y) iff that pair is in the reflexive transitive closure of R.

The existence of a least fixpoint is not guaranteed except under certain restrictions. Indeed, the formula $\neg X$ has no fixpoint, therefore $\mu X.\neg X$ does not exist. Typically, one restricts the application of the binding operator μX to formulas that are *positive* or *syntactically monotone* in X; that is, those formulas in which every free occurrence of X occurs in the scope of an even number of negations. This implies that the relation operator $X \mapsto \varphi(X)$ is (semantically) monotone in the sense of Section 1.7, which by the Knaster–Tarski theorem (Theorem 1.12) ensures the existence of a least fixpoint.

The first-order μ-calculus can define all sets definable by first-order induction and more. In particular, it can capture the input/output relation of any program built from any of the DL programming constructs we have discussed. Since the first-order μ-calculus also admits first-order quantification, it is easily seen to be as powerful as DL.

It was shown by Park (1976) that finiteness is not definable in the first-order μ-calculus with the monotonicity restriction, but well-foundedness is. Thus this version of the μ-calculus is independent of $L_{\omega_1^{ck}\omega}$ (and hence of DL(r.e.)) in expressive power. Well-foundedness of a binary relation R can be written

$$\forall x \; (\mu X(x).\forall y \; (R(y,x) \to X(y))).$$

A more severe syntactic restriction on the binding operator μX is to allow its application only to formulas that are *syntactically continuous* in X; that is, those formulas in which X does not occur free in the scope of any negation or any universal quantifier. It can be shown that this syntactic restriction implies semantic continuity (Section 1.7), so the least fixpoint is the union of $\varnothing$, $\varphi(\varnothing)$, $\varphi(\varphi(\varnothing))$, ... As shown in Park (1976), this version is strictly weaker than $L_{\omega_1^{ck}\omega}$.

In Pratt (1981a) and Kozen (1982, 1983), propositional versions of the μ-calculus were introduced. The latter version consists of propositional modal logic with a least fixpoint operator. It is the most powerful logic of its type, subsuming all known variants of PDL, game logic of Parikh (1983), various forms of temporal logic (see Section 17.2), and other seemingly stronger forms of the μ-calculus (Vardi and Wolper (1986c)). In the following presentation we focus on this version, since it has gained fairly widespread acceptance; see Kozen (1984); Kozen and Parikh (1983); Streett (1985a); Streett and Emerson (1984); Vardi and Wolper (1986c); Walukiewicz (1993, 1995, 2000); Stirling (1992); Mader (1997); Kaivola (1997).

The language of the propositional μ-calculus, also called the *modal μ-calculus*, is syntactically simpler than PDL. It consists of the usual propositional constructs $\rightarrow$ and $\mathbf{0}$, atomic modalities $[a]$, and the least fixpoint operator μ. A greatest fixpoint operator dual to μ can be defined:

$$\nu X.\varphi(X) \quad \overset{\text{def}}{\Longleftrightarrow} \quad \neg\mu X.\neg\varphi(\neg X).$$

Variables are monadic, and the μ operator may be applied only to syntactically monotone formulas. As discussed above, this ensures monotonicity of the corresponding set operator. The language is interpreted over Kripke frames in which atomic propositions are interpreted as sets of states and atomic programs are interpreted as binary relations on states.

The propositional μ-calculus subsumes PDL. For example, the PDL formula $<a^*>\varphi$ for atomic a can be written $\mu X.(\varphi \vee <a>X)$. The formula $\mu X.<a>[a]X$, which expresses the existence of a forced win for the first player in a two-player game, and the formula $\mu X.[a]X$, which expresses well-foundedness and is equivalent to **wf** a (see Section 10.6), are both inexpressible in PDL, as shown in Streett (1981); Kozen (1981c). Niwinski (1984) has shown that even with the addition of the **halt** construct, PDL is strictly less expressive than the μ-calculus.

The propositional μ-calculus satisfies a finite model theorem, as first shown in Kozen (1988). Decidability results were obtained in Kozen and Parikh (1983); Vardi and Stockmeyer (1985); Vardi (1985b), culminating in a deterministic exponential-time algorithm of Emerson and Jutla (1988) based on an automata-theoretic lemma of Safra (1988). Since the μ-calculus subsumes PDL, it is *EXPTIME*-complete.

In Kozen (1982, 1983), an axiomatization of the propositional μ-calculus was proposed and conjectured to be complete. The axiomatization consists of the axioms and rules of propositional modal logic, plus the axiom

$$\varphi[X/\mu X.\varphi] \quad \rightarrow \quad \mu X.\varphi$$

and rule

$$\frac{\varphi[X/\psi] \rightarrow \psi}{\mu X.\varphi \rightarrow \psi}$$

for μ. Completeness of this deductive system for a syntactically restricted subset of formulas was shown in Kozen (1982, 1983). Completeness for the full language was proved by Walukiewicz (1995, 2000). This was quickly followed by simpler alternative proofs by Ambler et al. (1995); Bonsangue and Kwiatkowska (1995); Hartonas (1998). Bradfield (1996) showed that the alternating μ/ν hierarchy (least/greatest fixpoints) is strict. An interesting open question is the complexity of *model checking*: does a given formula of the propositional μ-calculus hold in a given state of a given Kripke frame? Although some progress has been made (see Bhat and Cleaveland (1996); Cleaveland (1996); Emerson and Lei (1986); Sokolsky and Smolka (1994); Stirling and Walker (1989)), it is still unknown whether this problem has a polynomial-time algorithm.

The propositional μ-calculus has become a popular system for the specification and verification of properties of transition systems, where it has had some practical impact (Steffen et al. (1996)). Several recent papers on model checking work in this context; see Bhat and Cleaveland (1996); Cleaveland (1996); Emerson and Lei (1986); Sokolsky and Smolka (1994); Stirling and Walker (1989). A comprehensive introduction can be found in Stirling (1992).

17.5   Kleene Algebra

Kleene algebra (KA) is the algebra of regular expressions. It is named for S. C. Kleene (1909–1994), who among his many other achievements invented regular expressions and proved their equivalence to finite automata in Kleene (1956).

Kleene algebra has appeared in various guises and under many names in relational algebra (Ng (1984); Ng and Tarski (1977)), semantics and logics of programs (Kozen (1981b); Pratt (1988)), automata and formal language theory (Kuich (1987); Kuich and Salomaa (1986)), and the design and analysis of algorithms (Aho et al. (1975); Tarjan (1981); Mehlhorn (1984); Iwano and Steiglitz (1990); Kozen (1991b)). As discussed in Section 16.4, Kleene algebra plays a prominent role in dynamic algebra as an algebraic model of program behavior.

Beginning with the monograph of Conway (1971), many authors have con-

tributed over the years to the development of the algebraic theory; see Backhouse
(1975); Krob (1991); Kleene (1956); Kuich and Salomaa (1986); Sakarovitch (1987);
Kozen (1990); Bloom and Ésik (1992); Hopkins and Kozen (1999). See also Kozen
(1996) for further references.

A *Kleene algebra* is an algebraic structure $(K, +, \cdot, {}^*, 0, 1)$ satisfying the axioms

$$\alpha + (\beta + \gamma) = (\alpha + \beta) + \gamma$$
$$\alpha + \beta = \beta + \alpha$$
$$\alpha + 0 = \alpha + \alpha = \alpha$$
$$\alpha(\beta\gamma) = (\alpha\beta)\gamma$$
$$1\alpha = \alpha 1 = \alpha$$
$$\alpha(\beta + \gamma) = \alpha\beta + \alpha\gamma$$
$$(\alpha + \beta)\gamma = \alpha\gamma + \beta\gamma$$
$$0\alpha = \alpha 0 = 0$$
$$1 + \alpha\alpha^* = 1 + \alpha^*\alpha = \alpha^* \tag{17.5.1}$$
$$\beta + \alpha\gamma \le \gamma \;\rightarrow\; \alpha^*\beta \le \gamma \tag{17.5.2}$$
$$\beta + \gamma\alpha \le \gamma \;\rightarrow\; \beta\alpha^* \le \gamma \tag{17.5.3}$$

where $\le$ refers to the natural partial order on K:

$$\alpha \le \beta \;\overset{\text{def}}{\Longleftrightarrow}\; \alpha + \beta = \beta.$$

In short, a KA is an idempotent semiring under $+$, $\cdot$, 0, 1 satisfying (17.5.1)–
(17.5.3) for *. The axioms (17.5.1)–(17.5.3) say essentially that * behaves like the
asterate operator on sets of strings or reflexive transitive closure on binary relations.
This particular axiomatization is from Kozen (1991a, 1994a), but there are other
competing ones.

The axioms (17.5.2) and (17.5.3) correspond to the reflexive transitive closure
rule (RTC) of PDL (Section 5.6). Instead, we might postulate the equivalent axioms

$$\alpha\gamma \le \gamma \;\rightarrow\; \alpha^*\gamma \le \gamma \tag{17.5.4}$$
$$\gamma\alpha \le \gamma \;\rightarrow\; \gamma\alpha^* \le \gamma, \tag{17.5.5}$$

which correspond to the loop invariance rule (LI). The induction axiom (IND) is
inexpressible in KA, since there is no negation.

A Kleene algebra is *-*continuous* if it satisfies the infinitary condition

$$\alpha\beta^*\gamma = \sup_{n\ge 0} \alpha\beta^n\gamma \tag{17.5.6}$$

where

$$\beta^0 \stackrel{\text{def}}{=} 1 \qquad \beta^{n+1} \stackrel{\text{def}}{=} \beta\beta^n$$

and where the supremum is with respect to the natural order $\leq$. We can think of (17.5.6) as a conjunction of the infinitely many axioms $\alpha\beta^n\gamma \leq \alpha\beta^*\gamma$, $n \geq 0$, and the infinitary Horn formula

$$(\bigwedge_{n\geq 0} \alpha\beta^n\gamma \leq \delta) \quad \rightarrow \quad \alpha\beta^*\gamma \leq \delta.$$

In the presence of the other axioms, the *-continuity condition (17.5.6) implies (17.5.2)–(17.5.5) and is strictly stronger in the sense that there exist Kleene algebras that are not *-continuous (Kozen (1990)).

The fundamental motivating example of a Kleene algebra is the family of regular sets of strings over a finite alphabet, but other classes of structures share the same equational theory, notably the binary relations on a set. In fact it is the latter interpretation that makes Kleene algebra a suitable choice for modeling programs in dynamic algebras. Other more unusual interpretations are the min, + algebra used in shortest path algorithms (see Aho et al. (1975); Tarjan (1981); Mehlhorn (1984); Kozen (1991b)) and KAs of convex polyhedra used in computational geometry as described in Iwano and Steiglitz (1990).

Axiomatization of the equational theory of the regular sets is a central question going back to the original paper of Kleene (1956). A completeness theorem for relational algebras was given in an extended language by Ng (1984); Ng and Tarski (1977). Axiomatization is a central focus of the monograph of Conway (1971), but the bulk of his treatment is infinitary. Redko (1964) proved that there is no finite equational axiomatization. Schematic equational axiomatizations for the algebra of regular sets, necessarily representing infinitely many equations, have been given by Krob (1991) and Bloom and Ésik (1993). Salomaa (1966) gave two finitary complete axiomatizations that are sound for the regular sets but not sound in general over other standard interpretations, including relational interpretations. The axiomatization given above is a finitary universal Horn axiomatization that is sound and complete for the equational theory of standard relational and language-theoretic models, including the regular sets (Kozen (1991a, 1994a)). Other work on completeness appears in Krob (1991); Boffa (1990, 1995); Archangelsky (1992).

The literature contains a bewildering array of inequivalent definitions of Kleene algebras and related algebraic structures; see Conway (1971); Pratt (1988, 1990); Kozen (1981b, 1991a); Aho et al. (1975); Mehlhorn (1984); Kuich (1987); Kozen (1994b). As demonstrated in Kozen (1990), many of these are strongly related.

One important property shared by most of them is closure under the formation of $n \times n$ matrices. This was proved for the axiomatization of Section 16.4 in Kozen (1991a, 1994a), but the idea essentially goes back to Kleene (1956); Conway (1971); Backhouse (1975). This result gives rise to an algebraic treatment of finite automata in which the automata are represented by their transition matrices.

The equational theory of Kleene algebra is *PSPACE*-complete (Stockmeyer and Meyer (1973)); thus it is apparently less complex than **PDL**, which is *EXPTIME*-complete (Theorem 8.5), although the strict separation of the two complexity classes is still open.

Kleene Algebra with Tests

From a practical standpoint, many simple program manipulations such as loop unwinding and basic safety analysis do not require the full power of **PDL**, but can be carried out in a purely equational subsystem using the axioms of Kleene algebra. However, *tests* are an essential ingredient, since they are needed to model conventional programming constructs such as conditionals and **while** loops and to handle assertions. This motivates the definition of the following variant of **KA** introduced in Kozen (1996, 1997b).

A *Kleene algebra with tests* (**KAT**) is a Kleene algebra with an embedded Boolean subalgebra. Formally, it is a two-sorted algebra

$$(K,\ B,\ +,\ \cdot,\ {}^{*},\ {}^{-},\ 0,\ 1)$$

such that

- $(K,\ +,\ \cdot,\ {}^{*},\ 0,\ 1)$ is a Kleene algebra
- $(B,\ +,\ \cdot,\ {}^{-},\ 0,\ 1)$ is a Boolean algebra
- $B \subseteq K$.

The unary negation operator $^{-}$ is defined only on B. Elements of B are called *tests* and are written $\varphi, \psi, \dots$. Elements of K (including elements of B) are written $\alpha, \beta, \dots$. In **PDL**, a test would be written $\varphi?$, but in **KAT** we dispense with the symbol ?.

This deceptively concise definition actually carries a lot of information. The operators $+, \cdot, 0, 1$ each play two roles: applied to arbitrary elements of K, they refer to nondeterministic choice, composition, fail, and skip, respectively; and applied to tests, they take on the additional meaning of Boolean disjunction, conjunction, falsity, and truth, respectively. These two usages do not conflict—for example, sequential testing of two tests is the same as testing their conjunction—and their coexistence admits considerable economy of expression.

For applications in program verification, the standard interpretation would be a Kleene algebra of binary relations on a set and the Boolean algebra of subsets of the identity relation. One could also consider trace models, in which the Kleene elements are sets of traces (sequences of states) and the Boolean elements are sets of states (traces of length 0). As with **KA**, one can form the algebra $n \times n$ matrices over a **KAT** (K, B); the Boolean elements of this structure are the diagonal matrices over B.

KAT can express conventional imperative programming constructs such as conditionals and while loops as in **PDL**. It can perform elementary program manipulation such as loop unwinding, constant propagation, and basic safety analysis in a purely equational manner. The applicability of **KAT** and related equational systems in practical program verification has been explored in Cohen (1994a,b,c); Kozen (1996); Kozen and Patron (2000).

There is a language-theoretic model that plays the same role in **KAT** that the regular sets play in **KA**, namely the algebra of regular sets of *guarded strings*, and a corresponding completeness result was obtained by Kozen and Smith (1996). Moreover, **KAT** is complete for the equational theory of relational models, as shown in Kozen and Smith (1996). Although less expressive than **PDL**, **KAT** is also apparently less difficult to decide: it is *PSPACE*-complete, the same as **KA**, as shown in Cohen et al. (1996).

In Kozen (1999a), it is shown that **KAT** subsumes propositional Hoare Logic in the following sense. The partial correctness assertion $\{\varphi\}\, \alpha\, \{\psi\}$ is encoded in **KAT** as the equation $\varphi\alpha\overline{\psi} = 0$, or equivalently $\varphi\alpha = \varphi\alpha\psi$. If a rule

$$\frac{\{\varphi_1\}\, \alpha_1\, \{\psi_1\}, \ \ldots, \ \{\varphi_n\}\, \alpha_n\, \{\psi_n\}}{\{\varphi\}\, \alpha\, \{\psi\}}$$

is derivable in propositional Hoare Logic, then its translation, the universal Horn formula

$$\varphi_1\alpha_1\overline{\psi_1} = 0 \wedge \cdots \wedge \varphi_n\alpha_n\overline{\psi_n} = 0 \ \to \ \varphi\alpha\overline{\psi} = 0,$$

is a theorem of **KAT**. For example, the **while** rule of Section 4.4 becomes

$$\sigma\varphi\alpha\overline{\varphi} = 0 \ \to \ \varphi(\sigma\alpha)^*\overline{\sigma}\,\overline{\overline{\sigma}\varphi} = 0.$$

More generally, all relationally valid Horn formulas of the form

$$\gamma_1 = 0 \wedge \cdots \wedge \gamma_n = 0 \ \to \ \alpha = \beta$$

are theorems of **KAT** (Kozen (1999a)).

Horn formulas are important from a practical standpoint. For example, commutativity conditions are used to model the idea that the execution of certain instructions does not affect the result of certain tests. In light of this, the complexity of the universal Horn theory of KA and KAT are of interest. There are both positive and negative results. It is shown in Kozen (1997c) that for a Horn formula $\Phi \rightarrow \varphi$ over *-continuous Kleene algebras,

- if Φ contains only commutativity conditions $\alpha\beta = \beta\alpha$, the universal Horn theory is Π_1^0-complete;
- if Φ contains only monoid equations, the problem is Π_2^0-complete;
- for arbitrary finite sets of equations Φ, the problem is Π_1^1-complete.

On the other hand, commutativity assumptions of the form $\alpha\varphi = \varphi\alpha$, where φ is a test, and assumptions of the form $\gamma = 0$ can be eliminated without loss of efficiency, as shown in Cohen (1994a); Kozen and Smith (1996). Note that assumptions of this form are all we need to encode Hoare Logic as described above.

In typed Kleene algebra introduced in Kozen (1998, 1999b), elements have types $s \rightarrow t$. This allows Kleene algebras of nonsquare matrices, among other applications. It is shown in Kozen (1999b) that Hoare Logic is subsumed by the type calculus of typed KA augmented with a typecast or coercion rule for tests. Thus Hoare-style reasoning with partial correctness assertions reduces to typechecking in a relatively simple type system.

References

Abrahamson, K. (1980). *Decidability and expressiveness of logics of processes.* Ph. D. thesis, Univ. of Washington.

Adian, S. I. (1979). *The Burnside Problem and Identities in Groups.* Springer-Verlag.

Aho, A. V., J. E. Hopcroft, and J. D. Ullman (1975). *The Design and Analysis of Computer Algorithms.* Reading, Mass.: Addison-Wesley.

Ambler, S., M. Kwiatkowska, and N. Measor (1995, November). Duality and the completeness of the modal μ-calculus. *Theor. Comput. Sci. 151*(1), 3–27.

Andréka, H., I. Németi, and I. Sain (1982a). A complete logic for reasoning about programs via nonstandard model theory, part I. *Theor. Comput. Sci. 17*, 193–212.

Andréka, H., I. Németi, and I. Sain (1982b). A complete logic for reasoning about programs via nonstandard model theory, part II. *Theor. Comput. Sci. 17*, 259–278.

Apt, K. R. (1981). Ten years of Hoare's logic: a survey—part I. *ACM Trans. Programming Languages and Systems 3*, 431–483.

Apt, K. R. and E.-R. Olderog (1991). *Verification of Sequential and Concurrent Programs.* Springer-Verlag.

Apt, K. R. and G. Plotkin (1986). Countable nondeterminism and random assignment. *J. Assoc. Comput. Mach. 33*, 724–767.

Archangelsky, K. V. (1992). A new finite complete solvable quasiequational calculus for algebra of regular languages. Manuscript, Kiev State University.

Arnold, A. (1997a). An initial semantics for the μ-calculus on trees and Rabin's complementation lemma. Technical report, University of Bordeaux.

Arnold, A. (1997b). The μ-calculus on trees and Rabin's complementation theorem. Technical report, University of Bordeaux.

Backhouse, R. C. (1975). *Closure Algorithms and the Star-Height Problem of Regular Languages.* Ph. D. thesis, Imperial College, London, U.K.

Backhouse, R. C. (1986). *Program Construction and Verification.* Prentice-Hall.

Baier, C. and M. Kwiatkowska (1998, April). On the verification of qualitative properties of probabilistic processes under fairness constraints. *Information Processing Letters 66*(2), 71–79.

Banachowski, L., A. Kreczmar, G. Mirkowska, H. Rasiowa, and A. Salwicki (1977). An introduction to algorithmic logic: metamathematical investigations in the theory of programs. In Mazurkiewitz and Pawlak (Eds.), *Math. Found. Comput. Sci.*, pp. 7–99. Banach Center, Warsaw.

Barwise, J. (1975). *Admissible Sets and Structures.* North-Holland.

Bell, J. S. and A. B. Slomson (1971). *Models and Ultraproducts.* North Holland.

Ben-Ari, M., J. Y. Halpern, and A. Pnueli (1982). Deterministic propositional dynamic logic: finite models, complexity and completeness. *J. Comput. Syst. Sci. 25*, 402–417.

Berman, F. (1978). Expressiveness hierarchy for PDL with rich tests. Technical Report 78-11-01, Comput. Sci. Dept., Univ. of Washington.

Berman, F. (1979). A completeness technique for D-axiomatizable semantics. In *Proc. 11th Symp. Theory of Comput.*, pp. 160–166. ACM.

Berman, F. (1982). Semantics of looping programs in propositional dynamic logic. *Math. Syst. Theory 15*, 285–294.

Berman, F. and M. Paterson (1981). Propositional dynamic logic is weaker without tests. *Theor. Comput. Sci. 16*, 321–328.

Berman, P., J. Y. Halpern, and J. Tiuryn (1982). On the power of nondeterminism in dynamic logic. In Nielsen and Schmidt (Eds.), *Proc 9th Colloq. Automata Lang. Prog.*, Volume 140 of *Lect. Notes in Comput. Sci.*, pp. 48–60. Springer-Verlag.

Bhat, G. and R. Cleaveland (1996, March). Efficient local model checking for fragments of the modal μ-calculus. In T. Margaria and B. Steffen (Eds.), *Proc. Second Int. Workshop Tools and*

Algorithms for the Construction and Analysis of Systems (TACAS'96), Volume 1055 of *Lect. Notes in Comput. Sci.*, pp. 107–112. Springer-Verlag.

Birkhoff, G. (1935). On the structure of abstract algebras. *Proc. Cambridge Phil. Soc. 31*, 433–454.

Birkhoff, G. (1973). *Lattice Theory* (third ed.). American Mathematical Society.

Bloom, S. L. and Z. Ésik (1992). Program correctness and matricial iteration theories. In *Proc. Mathematical Foundations of Programming Semantics, 7th Int. Conf.*, Volume 598 of *Lecture Notes in Computer Science*, pp. 457–476. Springer-Verlag.

Bloom, S. L. and Z. Ésik (1993). Equational axioms for regular sets. *Math. Struct. Comput. Sci. 3*, 1–24.

Blute, R., J. Desharnais, A. Edelat, and P. Panangaden (1997). Bisimulation for labeled Markov processes. In *Proc. 12th Symp. Logic in Comput. Sci.*, pp. 149–158. IEEE.

Boffa, M. (1990). Une remarque sur les systèmes complets d'identités rationnelles. *Informatique Théoretique et Applications/Theoretical Informatics and Applications 24*(4), 419–423.

Boffa, M. (1995). Une condition impliquant toutes les identités rationnelles. *Informatique Théoretique et Applications/Theoretical Informatics and Applications 29*(6), 515–518.

Bonsangue, M. and M. Kwiatkowska (1995, August). Re-interpreting the modal μ-calculus. In A. Ponse, M. van Rijke, and Y. Venema (Eds.), *Modal Logic and Process Algebra*, pp. 65–83. CSLI Lecture Notes.

Boole, G. (1847). *The Mathematical Analysis of Logic*. MacMillan, Barclay and MacMillan, Cambridge.

Börger, E. (1984). Spectralproblem and completeness of logical decision problems. In G. H. E. Börger and D. Rödding (Eds.), *Logic and Machines: Decision Problems and Complexity, Proccedings*, Volume 171 of *Lect. Notes in Comput. Sci.*, pp. 333–356. Springer-Verlag.

Bradfield, J. C. (1996). The modal μ-calculus alternation hierarchy is strict. In U. Montanari and V. Sassone (Eds.), *Proc. CONCUR'96*, Volume 1119 of *Lect. Notes in Comput. Sci.*, pp. 233–246. Springer.

Burstall, R. M. (1974). Program proving as hand simulation with a little induction. *Information Processing*, 308–312.

Chandra, A., D. Kozen, and L. Stockmeyer (1981). Alternation. *J. Assoc. Comput. Mach. 28*(1), 114–133.

Chang, C. C. and H. J. Keisler (1973). *Model Theory*. North-Holland.

Chellas, B. F. (1980). *Modal Logic: An Introduction*. Cambridge University Press.

Clarke, E. M. (1979). Programming language constructs for which it is impossible to obtain good Hoare axiom systems. *J. Assoc. Comput. Mach. 26*, 129–147.

Cleaveland, R. (1996, July). Efficient model checking via the equational μ-calculus. In *Proc. 11th Symp. Logic in Comput. Sci.*, pp. 304–312. IEEE.

Cohen, E. (1994a, April). Hypotheses in Kleene algebra. Available as ftp://ftp.bellcore.com/pub/ernie/research/homepage.html.

Cohen, E. (1994b). Lazy caching. Available as ftp://ftp.bellcore.com/pub/ernie/research/homepage.html.

Cohen, E. (1994c). Using Kleene algebra to reason about concurrency control. Available as ftp://ftp.bellcore.com/pub/ernie/research/homepage.html.

Cohen, E., D. Kozen, and F. Smith (1996, July). The complexity of Kleene algebra with tests. Technical Report 96-1598, Computer Science Department, Cornell University.

Constable, R. L. (1977, May). On the theory of programming logics. In *Proc. 9th Symp. Theory of Comput.*, pp. 269–285. ACM.

Constable, R. L. and M. O'Donnell (1978). *A Programming Logic*. Winthrop.

Conway, J. H. (1971). *Regular Algebra and Finite Machines*. London: Chapman and Hall.

Cook, S. A. (1971). The complexity of theorem proving procedures. In *Proc. Third Symp. Theory of Computing*, New York, pp. 151–158. Assoc. Comput. Mach.

Cook, S. A. (1978). Soundness and completeness of an axiom system for program verification. *SIAM J. Comput. 7*, 70–80.

Courcoubetis, C. and M. Yannakakis (1988, October). Verifying temporal properties of finite-state probabilistic programs. In *Proc. 29th Symp. Foundations of Comput. Sci.*, pp. 338–345. IEEE.

Cousot, P. (1990). Methods and logics for proving programs. In J. van Leeuwen (Ed.), *Handbood of Theoretical Computer Science*, Volume B, pp. 841–993. Amsterdam: Elsevier.

Csirmaz, L. (1985). A completeness theorem for dynamic logic. *Notre Dame J. Formal Logic 26*, 51–60.

Davis, M. D., R. Sigal, and E. J. Weyuker (1994). *Computability, Complexity, and Languages: Fundamentals of Theoretical Computer Science*. Academic Press.

de Bakker, J. (1980). *Mathematical Theory of Program Correctness*. Prentice-Hall.

Ehrenfeucht, A. (1961). An application of games in the completeness problem for formalized theories. *Fund. Math. 49*, 129–141.

Emerson, E. A. (1985). Automata, tableax, and temporal logics. In R. Parikh (Ed.), *Proc. Workshop on Logics of Programs*, Volume 193 of *Lect. Notes in Comput. Sci.*, pp. 79–88. Springer-Verlag.

Emerson, E. A. (1990). Temporal and modal logic. In J. van Leeuwen (Ed.), *Handbook of theoretical computer science*, Volume B: formal models and semantics, pp. 995–1072. Elsevier.

Emerson, E. A. and J. Y. Halpern (1985). Decision procedures and expressiveness in the temporal logic of branching time. *J. Comput. Syst. Sci. 30*(1), 1–24.

Emerson, E. A. and J. Y. Halpern (1986). "Sometimes" and "not never" revisited: on branching vs. linear time temporal logic. *J. ACM 33*(1), 151–178.

Emerson, E. A. and C. Jutla (1988, October). The complexity of tree automata and logics of programs. In *Proc. 29th Symp. Foundations of Comput. Sci.*, pp. 328–337. IEEE.

Emerson, E. A. and C. Jutla (1989, June). On simultaneously determinizing and complementing ω-automata. In *Proc. 4th Symp. Logic in Comput. Sci.* IEEE.

Emerson, E. A. and C.-L. Lei (1986, June). Efficient model checking in fragments of the propositional μ-calculus. In *Proc. 1st Symp. Logic in Comput. Sci.*, pp. 267–278. IEEE.

Emerson, E. A. and C. L. Lei (1987). Modalities for model checking: branching time strikes back. *Sci. Comput. Programming 8*, 275–306.

Emerson, E. A. and P. A. Sistla (1984). Deciding full branching-time logic. *Infor. and Control 61*, 175–201.

Engeler, E. (1967). Algorithmic properties of structures. *Math. Syst. Theory 1*, 183–195.

Engelfriet, J. (1983). Iterated pushdown automata and complexity classes. In *Proceedings of the Fifteenth Annual ACM Symposium on Theory of Computing*, Boston, Massachusetts, pp. 365–373.

Erimbetov, M. M. (1981). On the expressive power of programming logics. In *Proc. Alma-Ata Conf. Research in Theoretical Programming*, pp. 49–68. In Russian.

Feldman, Y. A. (1984). A decidable propositional dynamic logic with explicit probabilities. *Infor. and Control 63*, 11–38.

Feldman, Y. A. and D. Harel (1984). A probabilistic dynamic logic. *J. Comput. Syst. Sci. 28*, 193–215.

Ferman, A. and D. Harel (2000). In preparation.

Fischer, M. J. and R. E. Ladner (1977). Propositional modal logic of programs. In *Proc. 9th Symp. Theory of Comput.*, pp. 286–294. ACM.

Fischer, M. J. and R. E. Ladner (1979). Propositional dynamic logic of regular programs. *J. Comput. Syst. Sci. 18*(2), 194–211.

Fischer, P. C. (1966). Turing machines with restricted memory access. *Information and Control 9*(4), 364–379.

Fischer, P. C., A. R. Meyer, and A. L. Rosenberg (1968). Counter machines and counter languages. *Math. Systems Theory 2*(3), 265–283.

Floyd, R. W. (1967). Assigning meanings to programs. In *Proc. Symp. Appl. Math.*, Volume 19, pp. 19–31. AMS.

Friedman, H. (1971). Algorithmic procedures, generalized Turing algorithms, and elementary recursion theory. In Gandy and Yates (Eds.), *Logic Colloq. 1969*, pp. 361–390. North-Holland.

Gabbay, D. (1977). Axiomatizations of logics of programs. Unpublished.

Gabbay, D., I. Hodkinson, and M. Reynolds (1994). *Temporal Logic: Mathematical Foundations and Computational Aspects.* Oxford University Press.

Gabbay, D., A. Pnueli, S. Shelah, and J. Stavi (1980). On the temporal analysis of fairness. In *Proc. 7th Symp. Princip. Prog. Lang.*, pp. 163–173. ACM.

Garey, M. R. and D. S. Johnson (1979). *Computers and Intractibility: A Guide to the Theory of NP-Completeness.* W.H. Freeman.

Gödel, K. (1930). Die Vollständigkeit der Axiome des logischen Funktionenkalküls. *Monatsh. Math. Phys. 37*, 349–360.

Goldblatt, R. (1982). *Axiomatising the Logic of Computer Programming*, Volume 130 of *Lect. Notes in Comput. Sci.* Springer-Verlag.

Goldblatt, R. (1987). Logics of time and computation. Technical Report Lect. Notes 7, Center for the Study of Language and Information, Stanford Univ.

Graham, R., D. Knuth, and O. Patashnik (1989). *Concrete Mathematics: A Foundation for Computer Science.* Addison-Wesley.

Grätzer, G. (1978). *Universal Algebra.* Springer-Verlag.

Greibach, S. (1975). *Theory of Program Structures: Schemes, Semantics, Verification*, Volume 36 of *Lecture Notes in Computer Science.* Springer Verlag.

Gries, D. (1981). *The Science of Programming.* Springer-Verlag.

Gries, D. and F. B. Schneider (1994). *A Logical Approach to Discrete Math.* Springer-Verlag. Third printing.

Gurevich, Y. (1983). Algebras of feasible functions. In *24-th IEEE Annual Symposium on Foundations of Computer Science*, pp. 210–214.

Halmos, P. R. (1960). *Naive Set Theory.* Van Nostrand.

Halpern, J. Y. (1981). On the expressive power of dynamic logic II. Technical Report TM-204, MIT/LCS.

Halpern, J. Y. (1982). Deterministic process logic is elementary. In *Proc. 23rd Symp. Found. Comput. Sci.*, pp. 204–216. IEEE.

Halpern, J. Y. (1983). Deterministic process logic is elementary. *Infor. and Control 57*(1), 56–89.

Halpern, J. Y. and J. H. Reif (1981). The propositional dynamic logic of deterministic, well-structured programs. In *Proc. 22nd Symp. Found. Comput. Sci.*, pp. 322–334. IEEE.

Halpern, J. Y. and J. H. Reif (1983). The propositional dynamic logic of deterministic, well-structured programs. *Theor. Comput. Sci. 27*, 127–165.

Hansson, H. and B. Jonsson (1994). A logic for reasoning about time and probability. *Formal Aspects of Computing 6*, 512–535.

Harel, D. (1979). *First-Order Dynamic Logic*, Volume 68 of *Lect. Notes in Comput. Sci.* Springer-Verlag.

Harel, D. (1984). Dynamic logic. In Gabbay and Guenthner (Eds.), *Handbook of Philosophical Logic*, Volume II: Extensions of Classical Logic, pp. 497–604. Reidel.

Harel, D. (1985). Recurring dominoes: Making the highly undecidable highly understandable. *Annals of Discrete Mathematics 24*, 51–72.

Harel, D. (1992). *Algorithmics: The Spirit of Computing* (second ed.). Addison-Wesley.

Harel, D. and D. Kozen (1984). A programming language for the inductive sets, and applications. *Information and Control 63*(1–2), 118–139.

Harel, D., D. Kozen, and R. Parikh (1982). Process logic: Expressiveness, decidability, completeness. *J. Comput. Syst. Sci. 25*(2), 144–170.

Harel, D., A. R. Meyer, and V. R. Pratt (1977). Computability and completeness in logics of programs. In *Proc. 9th Symp. Theory of Comput.*, pp. 261–268. ACM.

Harel, D. and M. S. Paterson (1984). Undecidability of **PDL** with $L = \{a^{2^i} \mid i \geq 0\}$. *J. Comput. Syst. Sci. 29*, 359–365.

Harel, D. and D. Peleg (1985). More on looping vs. repeating in dynamic logic. *Information Processing Letters 20*, 87–90.

Harel, D., A. Pnueli, and J. Stavi (1983). Propositional dynamic logic of nonregular programs. *J. Comput. Syst. Sci. 26*, 222–243.

Harel, D., A. Pnueli, and M. Vardi (1982). Two dimensional temporal logic and **PDL** with intersection. Unpublished.

Harel, D. and V. R. Pratt (1978). Nondeterminism in logics of programs. In *Proc. 5th Symp. Princip. Prog. Lang.*, pp. 203–213. ACM.

Harel, D. and D. Raz (1993). Deciding properties of nonregular programs. *SIAM J. Comput. 22*, 857–874.

Harel, D. and D. Raz (1994). Deciding emptiness for stack automata on infinite trees. *Information and Computation 113*, 278–299.

Harel, D. and R. Sherman (1982). Looping vs. repeating in dynamic logic. *Infor. and Control 55*, 175–192.

Harel, D. and R. Sherman (1985). Propositional dynamic logic of flowcharts. *Infor. and Control 64*, 119–135.

Harel, D. and E. Singerman (1996). More on nonregular PDL: Finite models and Fibonacci-like programs. *Information and Computation 128*, 109–118.

Hart, S., M. Sharir, and A. Pnueli (1982). Termination of probabilistic concurrent programs. In *Proc. 9th Symp. Princip. Prog. Lang.*, pp. 1–6. ACM.

Hartmanis, J. and R. E. Stearns (1965). On the complexity of algorithms. *Trans. Amer. Math. Soc. 117*, 285–306.

Hartonas, C. (1998). Duality for modal μ-logics. *Theor. Comput. Sci. 202*(1–2), 193–222.

Henkin, L. (1949). The completeness of the first order functional calculus. *J. Symb. Logic 14*, 159–166.

Hennessy, M. C. B. and G. D. Plotkin (1979). Full abstraction for a simple programming language. In *Proc. Symp. Semantics of Algorithmic Languages*, Volume 74 of *Lecture Notes in Computer Science*, pp. 108–120. Springer-Verlag.

Hitchcock, P. and D. Park (1972). Induction rules and termination proofs. In M. Nivat (Ed.), *Int. Colloq. Automata Lang. Prog.*, pp. 225–251. North-Holland.

Hoare, C. A. R. (1969). An axiomatic basis for computer programming. *Comm. Assoc. Comput. Mach. 12*, 576–580, 583.

Hopcroft, J. E. and J. D. Ullman (1979). *Introduction to Automata Theory, Languages and Computation*. Addison-Wesley.

Hopkins, M. and D. Kozen (1999, July). Parikh's theorem in commutative Kleene algebra. In *Proc. Conf. Logic in Computer Science (LICS'99)*, pp. 394–401. IEEE.

Hughes, G. E. and M. J. Cresswell (1968). *An Introduction to Modal Logic*. Methuen.

Huth, M. and M. Kwiatkowska (1997). Quantitative analysis and model checking. In *Proc. 12th Symp. Logic in Comput. Sci.*, pp. 111–122. IEEE.

Ianov, Y. I. (1960). The logical schemes of algorithms. In *Problems of Cybernetics*, Volume 1, pp. 82–140. Pergamon Press.

Iwano, K. and K. Steiglitz (1990). A semiring on convex polygons and zero-sum cycle problems. *SIAM J. Comput. 19*(5), 883–901.

Jou, C. and S. Smolka (1990). Equivalences, congruences and complete axiomatizations for probabilistic processes. In *Proc. CONCUR'90*, Volume 458 of *Lecture Notes in Comput. Sci.*, pp. 367–383. Springer-Verlag.

Kaivola, R. (1997, April). *Using Automata to Characterise Fixed Point Temporal Logics*. Ph. D. thesis, University of Edinburgh. Report CST-135-97.

Kamp, H. W. (1968). *Tense logics and the theory of linear order*. Ph. D. thesis, UCLA.

Karp, R. M. (1972). Reducibility among combinatorial problems. In R. E. Miller and J. W. Thatcher (Eds.), *Complexity of Computer Computations*, pp. 85–103. Plenum Press.

Keisler, J. (1971). *Model Theory for Infinitary Logic*. North Holland.

Kfoury, A. (1983). Definability by programs in first-order structures. *Theoretical Computer Science 25*, 1–66.

Kfoury, A. and A. Stolboushkin (1997). An infinite pebble game and applications. *Information and Computation 136*, 53–66.

Kfoury, A. J. (1985). Definability by deterministic and nondeterministic programs with applications to first-order dynamic logic. *Infor. and Control 65*(2–3), 98–121.

Kleene, S. C. (1943). Recursive predicates and quantifiers. *Trans. Amer. Math. Soc. 53*, 41–74.

Kleene, S. C. (1952). *Introduction to Metamathematics*. D. van Nostrand.

Kleene, S. C. (1955). On the forms of the predicates in the theory of constructive ordinals (second paper). *Amer. J. Math. 77*, 405–428.

Kleene, S. C. (1956). Representation of events in nerve nets and finite automata. In C. E. Shannon and J. McCarthy (Eds.), *Automata Studies*, pp. 3–41. Princeton, N.J.: Princeton University Press.

Knijnenburg, P. M. W. (1988, November). On axiomatizations for propositional logics of programs. Technical Report RUU-CS-88-34, Rijksuniversiteit Utrecht.

Koren, T. and A. Pnueli (1983). There exist decidable context-free propositional dynamic logics. In *Proc. Symp. on Logics of Programs*, Volume 164 of *Lecture Notes in Computer Science*, pp. 290–312. Springer-Verlag.

Kowalczyk, W., D. Niwiński, and J. Tiuryn (1987). A generalization of Cook's auxiliary–pushdown–automata theorem. *Fundamenta Informaticae XII*, 497–506.

Kozen, D. (1979a). Dynamic algebra. In E. Engeler (Ed.), *Proc. Workshop on Logic of Programs*, Volume 125 of *Lecture Notes in Computer Science*, pp. 102–144. Springer-Verlag. chapter of *Propositional dynamic logics of programs: A survey* by Rohit Parikh.

Kozen, D. (1979b). On the duality of dynamic algebras and Kripke models. In E. Engeler (Ed.), *Proc. Workshop on Logic of Programs*, Volume 125 of *Lecture Notes in Computer Science*, pp. 1–11. Springer-Verlag.

Kozen, D. (1979c, October). On the representation of dynamic algebras. Technical Report RC7898, IBM Thomas J. Watson Research Center.

Kozen, D. (1980a, May). On the representation of dynamic algebras II. Technical Report RC8290, IBM Thomas J. Watson Research Center.

Kozen, D. (1980b, July). A representation theorem for models of *-free *PDL*. In *Proc. 7th Colloq. Automata, Languages, and Programming*, pp. 351–362. EATCS.

Kozen, D. (1981a). Logics of programs. Lecture notes, Aarhus University, Denmark.

Kozen, D. (1981b). On induction vs. *-continuity. In Kozen (Ed.), *Proc. Workshop on Logic of Programs*, Volume 131 of *Lecture Notes in Computer Science*, New York, pp. 167–176. Springer-Verlag.

Kozen, D. (1981c). On the expressiveness of μ. Manuscript.

Kozen, D. (1981d). Semantics of probabilistic programs. *J. Comput. Syst. Sci. 22*, 328–350.

Kozen, D. (1982, July). Results on the propositional μ-calculus. In *Proc. 9th Int. Colloq. Automata, Languages, and Programming*, Aarhus, Denmark, pp. 348–359. EATCS.

Kozen, D. (1983). Results on the propositional μ-calculus. *Theor. Comput. Sci. 27*, 333–354.

Kozen, D. (1984, May). A Ramsey theorem with infinitely many colors. In Lenstra, Lenstra, and van Emde Boas (Eds.), *Dopo Le Parole*, pp. 71–72. Amsterdam: University of Amsterdam.

Kozen, D. (1985, April). A probabilistic *PDL*. *J. Comput. Syst. Sci. 30*(2), 162–178.

Kozen, D. (1988). A finite model theorem for the propositional μ-calculus. *Studia Logica 47*(3), 233–241.

Kozen, D. (1990). On Kleene algebras and closed semirings. In Rovan (Ed.), *Proc. Math. Found. Comput. Sci.*, Volume 452 of *Lecture Notes in Computer Science*, Banska-Bystrica, Slovakia, pp. 26–47. Springer-Verlag.

Kozen, D. (1991a, July). A completeness theorem for Kleene algebras and the algebra of regular events. In *Proc. 6th Symp. Logic in Comput. Sci.*, Amsterdam, pp. 214–225. IEEE.

Kozen, D. (1991b). *The Design and Analysis of Algorithms*. New York: Springer-Verlag.

Kozen, D. (1994a, May). A completeness theorem for Kleene algebras and the algebra of regular events. *Infor. and Comput. 110*(2), 366–390.

Kozen, D. (1994b). On action algebras. In J. van Eijck and A. Visser (Eds.), *Logic and Information Flow*, pp. 78–88. MIT Press.

Kozen, D. (1996, March). Kleene algebra with tests and commutativity conditions. In T. Margaria and B. Steffen (Eds.), *Proc. Second Int. Workshop Tools and Algorithms for the Construction and Analysis of Systems (TACAS'96)*, Volume 1055 of *Lecture Notes in Computer Science*, Passau, Germany, pp. 14–33. Springer-Verlag.

Kozen, D. (1997a). *Automata and Computability*. New York: Springer-Verlag.

Kozen, D. (1997b, May). Kleene algebra with tests. *Transactions on Programming Languages and Systems 19*(3), 427–443.

Kozen, D. (1997c, June). On the complexity of reasoning in Kleene algebra. In *Proc. 12th Symp. Logic in Comput. Sci.*, Los Alamitos, Ca., pp. 195–202. IEEE.

Kozen, D. (1998, March). Typed Kleene algebra. Technical Report 98-1669, Computer Science Department, Cornell University.

Kozen, D. (1999a, July). On Hoare logic and Kleene algebra with tests. In *Proc. Conf. Logic in Computer Science (LICS'99)*, pp. 167–172. IEEE.

Kozen, D. (1999b, July). On Hoare logic, Kleene algebra, and types. Technical Report 99-1760, Computer Science Department, Cornell University. Abstract in: Abstracts of 11th Int. Congress Logic, Methodology and Philosophy of Science, Ed. J. Cachro and K. Kijania-Placek, Krakow, Poland, August 1999, p. 15. To appear in: Proc. 11th Int. Congress Logic, Methodology and Philosophy of Science, ed. P. Gardenfors, K. Kijania-Placek and J. Wolenski, Kluwer.

Kozen, D. and R. Parikh (1981). An elementary proof of the completeness of *PDL*. *Theor. Comput. Sci. 14*(1), 113–118.

Kozen, D. and R. Parikh (1983). A decision procedure for the propositional μ-calculus. In Clarke and Kozen (Eds.), *Proc. Workshop on Logics of Programs*, Volume 164 of *Lecture Notes in Computer Science*, pp. 313–325. Springer-Verlag.

Kozen, D. and M.-C. Patron (2000, July). Certification of compiler optimizations using Kleene algebra with tests. In U. Furbach and M. Kerber (Eds.), *Proc. 1st Int. Conf. Computational Logic*, London. To appear.

Kozen, D. and F. Smith (1996, September). Kleene algebra with tests: Completeness and decidability. In D. van Dalen and M. Bezem (Eds.), *Proc. 10th Int. Workshop Computer Science Logic (CSL'96)*, Volume 1258 of *Lecture Notes in Computer Science*, Utrecht, The Netherlands, pp. 244–259. Springer-Verlag.

Kozen, D. and J. Tiuryn (1990). Logics of programs. In van Leeuwen (Ed.), *Handbook of Theoretical Computer Science*, Volume B, pp. 789–840. Amsterdam: North Holland.

Kreczmar, A. (1977). Programmability in fields. *Fundamenta Informaticae I*, 195–230.

Kripke, S. (1963). Semantic analysis of modal logic. *Zeitschr. f. math. Logik und Grundlagen d. Math. 9*, 67–96.

Krob, D. (1991, October). A complete system of B-rational identities. *Theoretical Computer Science 89*(2), 207–343.

Kuich, W. (1987). The Kleene and Parikh theorem in complete semirings. In T. Ottmann (Ed.), *Proc. 14th Colloq. Automata, Languages, and Programming*, Volume 267 of *Lecture Notes in Computer Science*, New York, pp. 212–225. EATCS: Springer-Verlag.

Kuich, W. and A. Salomaa (1986). *Semirings, Automata, and Languages*. Berlin: Springer-Verlag.

Ladner, R. E. (1977). Unpublished.

Lamport, L. (1980). "Sometime" is sometimes "not never". *Proc. 7th Symp. Princip. Prog. Lang.*, 174–185.

Lehmann, D. and S. Shelah (1982). Reasoning with time and chance. *Infor. and Control 53*(3), 165–198.

Lewis, H. R. and C. H. Papadimitriou (1981). *Elements of the Theory of Computation*. Prentice Hall.

Lipton, R. J. (1977). A necessary and sufficient condition for the existence of Hoare logics. In *Proc. 18th Symp. Found. Comput. Sci.*, pp. 1–6. IEEE.

Luckham, D. C., D. Park, and M. Paterson (1970). On formalized computer programs. *J. Comput. Syst. Sci. 4*, 220–249.

Mader, A. (1997, September). *Verification of Modal Properties Using Boolean Equation Systems*. Ph. D. thesis, Fakultt fr Informatik, Technische Universitt Mnchen.

Makowski, J. A. (1980). Measuring the expressive power of dynamic logics: an application of abstract model theory. In *Proc. 7th Int. Colloq. Automata Lang. Prog.*, Volume 80 of *Lect. Notes in Comput. Sci.*, pp. 409–421. Springer-Verlag.

Makowski, J. A. and I. Sain (1986). On the equivalence of weak second-order and nonstandard time semantics for various program verification systems. In *Proc. 1st Symp. Logic in Comput. Sci.*, pp. 293–300. IEEE.

Makowsky, J. A. and M. L. Tiomkin (1980). Probabilistic propositional dynamic logic. Manuscript.

Manna, Z. (1974). *Mathematical Theory of Computation*. McGraw-Hill.

Manna, Z. and A. Pnueli (1981). Verification of concurrent programs: temporal proof principles. In D. Kozen (Ed.), *Proc. Workshop on Logics of Programs*, Volume 131 of *Lect. Notes in Comput. Sci.*, pp. 200–252. Springer-Verlag.

Manna, Z. and A. Pnueli (1987, January). Specification and verification of concurrent programs by ∀-automata. In *Proc. 14th Symp. Principles of Programming Languages*, pp. 1–12. ACM.

McCulloch, W. S. and W. Pitts (1943). A logical calculus of the ideas immanent in nervous activity. *Bull. Math. Biophysics 5*, 115–143.

Mehlhorn, K. (1984). *Graph Algorithms and NP-Completeness*, Volume II of *Data Structures and Algorithms*. Springer-Verlag.

Meyer, A. R. and J. Y. Halpern (1982). Axiomatic definitions of programming languages: a theoretical assessment. *J. Assoc. Comput. Mach. 29*, 555–576.

Meyer, A. R. and R. Parikh (1981). Definability in dynamic logic. *J. Comput. Syst. Sci. 23*, 279–298.

Meyer, A. R., R. S. Streett, and G. Mirkowska (1981). The deducibility problem in propositional dynamic logic. In E. Engeler (Ed.), *Proc. Workshop Logic of Programs*, Volume 125 of *Lect. Notes in Comput. Sci.*, pp. 12–22. Springer-Verlag.

Meyer, A. R. and J. Tiuryn (1981). A note on equivalences among logics of programs. In D. Kozen (Ed.), *Proc. Workshop on Logics of Programs*, Volume 131 of *Lect. Notes in Comput. Sci.*, pp. 282–299. Springer-Verlag.

Meyer, A. R. and J. Tiuryn (1984). Equivalences among logics of programs. *Journal of Computer and Systems Science 29*, 160–170.

Meyer, A. R. and K. Winklmann (1982). Expressing program looping in regular dynamic logic. *Theor. Comput. Sci. 18*, 301–323.

Miller, G. L. (1976). Riemann's hypothesis and tests for primality. *J. Comput. Syst. Sci. 13*, 300–317.

Minsky, M. L. (1961). Recursive unsolvability of Post's problem of 'tag' and other topics in the theory of Turing machines. *Ann. Math. 74*(3), 437–455.

Mirkowska, G. (1971). On formalized systems of algorithmic logic. *Bull. Acad. Polon. Sci. Ser. Sci. Math. Astron. Phys. 19*, 421–428.

Mirkowska, G. (1980). Algorithmic logic with nondeterministic programs. *Fund. Informaticae III*, 45–64.

Mirkowska, G. (1981a). PAL—propositional algorithmic logic. In E. Engeler (Ed.), *Proc. Workshop Logic of Programs*, Volume 125 of *Lect. Notes in Comput. Sci.*, pp. 23–101. Springer-Verlag.

Mirkowska, G. (1981b). PAL—propositional algorithmic logic. *Fund. Informaticae IV*, 675–760.

Morgan, C., A. McIver, and K. Seidel (1999). Probabilistic predicate transformers. *ACM Trans. Programming Languages and Systems 8*(1), 1–30.

Moschovakis, Y. N. (1974). *Elementary Induction on Abstract Structures*. North-Holland.

Moschovakis, Y. N. (1980). *Descriptive Set Theory*. North-Holland.

Muller, D. E., A. Saoudi, and P. E. Schupp (1988, July). Weak alternating automata give a simple explanation of why most temporal and dynamic logics are decidable in exponential time. In *Proc. 3rd Symp. Logic in Computer Science*, pp. 422–427. IEEE.

Németi, I. (1980). Every free algebra in the variety generated by the representable dynamic algebras is separable and representable. Manuscript.

Németi, I. (1981). Nonstandard dynamic logic. In D. Kozen (Ed.), *Proc. Workshop on Logics of Programs*, Volume 131 of *Lect. Notes in Comput. Sci.*, pp. 311–348. Springer-Verlag.

Ng, K. C. (1984). *Relation Algebras with Transitive Closure*. Ph. D. thesis, University of California, Berkeley.

Ng, K. C. and A. Tarski (1977). Relation algebras with transitive closure, abstract 742-02-09. *Notices Amer. Math. Soc. 24*, A29–A30.

Nishimura, H. (1979). Sequential method in propositional dynamic logic. *Acta Informatica 12*, 377–400.

Nishimura, H. (1980). Descriptively complete process logic. *Acta Informatica 14*, 359–369.

Niwinski, D. (1984). The propositional μ-calculus is more expressive than the propositional dynamic logic of looping. University of Warsaw.

Parikh, R. (1978a). The completeness of propositional dynamic logic. In *Proc. 7th Symp. on Math. Found. of Comput. Sci.*, Volume 64 of *Lect. Notes in Comput. Sci.*, pp. 403–415. Springer-Verlag.

Parikh, R. (1978b). A decidability result for second order process logic. In *Proc. 19th Symp. Found. Comput. Sci.*, pp. 177–183. IEEE.

Parikh, R. (1981). Propositional dynamic logics of programs: a survey. In E. Engeler (Ed.), *Proc. Workshop on Logics of Programs*, Volume 125 of *Lect. Notes in Comput. Sci.*, pp. 102–144. Springer-Verlag.

Parikh, R. (1983). Propositional game logic. In *Proc. 23rd IEEE Symp. Foundations of Computer Science*.

Parikh, R. and A. Mahoney (1983). A theory of probabilistic programs. In E. Clarke and D. Kozen (Eds.), *Proc. Workshop on Logics of Programs*, Volume 164 of *Lect. Notes in Comput. Sci.*, pp. 396–402. Springer-Verlag.

Park, D. (1976). Finiteness is μ-ineffable. *Theor. Comput. Sci. 3*, 173–181.

Paterson, M. S. and C. E. Hewitt (1970). Comparative schematology. In *Record Project MAC Conf. on Concurrent Systems and Parallel Computation*, pp. 119–128. ACM.

Pecuchet, J. P. (1986). On the complementation of Büchi automata. *Theor. Comput. Sci. 47*, 95–98.

Peleg, D. (1987a). Communication in concurrent dynamic logic. *J. Comput. Sys. Sci. 35*, 23–58.

Peleg, D. (1987b). Concurrent dynamic logic. *J. Assoc. Comput. Mach. 34*(2), 450–479.

Peleg, D. (1987c). Concurrent program schemes and their logics. *Theor. Comput. Sci. 55*, 1–45.

Peng, W. and S. P. Iyer (1995). A new type of pushdown-tree automata on infinite trees. *Int. J. of Found. of Comput. Sci. 6*(2), 169–186.

Peterson, G. L. (1978). The power of tests in propositional dynamic logic. Technical Report 47, Comput. Sci. Dept., Univ. of Rochester.

Pnueli, A. (1977). The temporal logic of programs. In *Proc. 18th Symp. Found. Comput. Sci.*, pp. 46–57. IEEE.

Pnueli, A. and L. D. Zuck (1986). Verification of multiprocess probabilistic protocols. *Distributed Computing 1*(1), 53–72.

Pnueli, A. and L. D. Zuck (1993, March). Probabilistic verification. *Information and Computation 103*(1), 1–29.

Post, E. (1943). Formal reductions of the general combinatorial decision problem. *Amer. J. Math. 65*, 197–215.

Post, E. (1944). Recursively enumerable sets of positive natural numbers and their decision problems. *Bull. Amer. Math. Soc. 50*, 284–316.

Pratt, V. (1988, June). Dynamic algebras as a well-behaved fragment of relation algebras. In D. Pigozzi (Ed.), *Proc. Conf. on Algebra and Computer Science*, Volume 425 of *Lecture Notes in Computer Science*, Ames, Iowa, pp. 77–110. Springer-Verlag.

Pratt, V. (1990, September). Action logic and pure induction. In J. van Eijck (Ed.), *Proc. Logics in AI: European Workshop JELIA '90*, Volume 478 of *Lecture Notes in Computer Science*, New York, pp. 97–120. Springer-Verlag.

Pratt, V. R. (1976). Semantical considerations on Floyd-Hoare logic. In *Proc. 17th Symp. Found. Comput. Sci.*, pp. 109–121. IEEE.

Pratt, V. R. (1978). A practical decision method for propositional dynamic logic. In *Proc. 10th Symp. Theory of Comput.*, pp. 326–337. ACM.

Pratt, V. R. (1979a, July). Dynamic algebras: examples, constructions, applications. Technical Report TM-138, MIT/LCS.

Pratt, V. R. (1979b). Models of program logics. In *Proc. 20th Symp. Found. Comput. Sci.*, pp. 115–122. IEEE.

Pratt, V. R. (1979c). Process logic. In *Proc. 6th Symp. Princip. Prog. Lang.*, pp. 93–100. ACM.

Pratt, V. R. (1980a). Dynamic algebras and the nature of induction. In *Proc. 12th Symp. Theory of Comput.*, pp. 22–28. ACM.

Pratt, V. R. (1980b). A near-optimal method for reasoning about actions. *J. Comput. Syst. Sci. 20*(2), 231–254.

Pratt, V. R. (1981a). A decidable μ-calculus: preliminary report. In *Proc. 22nd Symp. Found. Comput. Sci.*, pp. 421–427. IEEE.

Pratt, V. R. (1981b). Using graphs to understand **PDL**. In D. Kozen (Ed.), *Proc. Workshop on Logics of Programs*, Volume 131 of *Lect. Notes in Comput. Sci.*, pp. 387–396. Springer-Verlag.

Rabin, M. O. (1969). Decidability of second order theories and automata on infinite trees. *Trans. Amer. Math. Soc. 141*, 1–35.

Rabin, M. O. (1980). Probabilistic algorithms for testing primality. *J. Number Theory 12*, 128–138.

Rabin, M. O. and D. S. Scott (1959). Finite automata and their decision problems. *IBM J. Res. Develop. 3*(2), 115–125.

Ramshaw, L. H. (1981). *Formalizing the analysis of algorithms*. Ph. D. thesis, Stanford Univ.

Rasiowa, H. and R. Sikorski (1963). *Mathematics of Metamathematics*. Polish Scientific Publishers, PWN.

Redko, V. N. (1964). On defining relations for the algebra of regular events. *Ukrain. Mat. Z. 16*, 120–126. In Russian.

Reif, J. (1980). Logics for probabilistic programming. In *Proc. 12th Symp. Theory of Comput.*, pp. 8–13. ACM.

Renegar, J. (1991). Computational complexity of solving real algebraic formulae. In *Proc. Int. Congress of Mathematicians*, pp. 1595–1606. Springer-Verlag.

Rice, H. G. (1953). Classes of recursively enumerable sets and their decision problems. *Trans. Amer. Math. Soc. 89*, 25–59.

Rice, H. G. (1956). On completely recursively enumerable classes and their key arrays. *J. Symbolic Logic 21*, 304–341.

Rogers, H. (1967). *Theory of Recursive Functions and Effective Computability*. McGraw-Hill.

Rogers, Jr., H. (1967). *Theory of Recursive Functions and Effective Computability*. McGraw-Hill.

Rosen, K. H. (1995). *Discrete Mathematics and Its Applications* (3rd ed.). McGraw-Hill.

Safra, S. (1988, October). On the complexity of ω-automata. In *Proc. 29th Symp. Foundations of Comput. Sci.*, pp. 319–327. IEEE.

Sakarovitch, J. (1987). Kleene's theorem revisited: A formal path from Kleene to Chomsky. In A. Kelemenova and J. Keleman (Eds.), *Trends, Techniques, and Problems in Theoretical Computer Science*, Volume 281 of *Lecture Notes in Computer Science*, New York, pp. 39–50. Springer-Verlag.

Salomaa, A. (1966, January). Two complete axiom systems for the algebra of regular events. *J. Assoc. Comput. Mach. 13*(1), 158–169.

Salomaa, A. (1981). *Jewels of Formal Language Theory*. Pitman Books Limited.

Salwicki, A. (1970). Formalized algorithmic languages. *Bull. Acad. Polon. Sci. Ser. Sci. Math. Astron. Phys. 18*, 227–232.

Salwicki, A. (1977). Algorithmic logic: a tool for investigations of programs. In Butts and Hintikka (Eds.), *Logic Foundations of Mathematics and Computability Theory*, pp. 281–295. Reidel.

Saudi, A. (1989). Pushdown automata on infinite trees and omega-Kleene closure of context-free tree sets. In *Proc. Math. Found. of Comput. Sci.*, Volume 379 of *Lecture Notes in Computer Science*, pp. 445–457. Springer-Verlag.

Sazonov, V. (1980). Polynomial computability and recursivity in finite domains. *Elektronische Informationsverarbeitung und Kibernetik 16*, 319–323.

Scott, D. S. and J. W. de Bakker (1969). A theory of programs. IBM Vienna.

Segala, R. and N. Lynch (1994). Probabilistic simulations for probabilistic processes. In *Proc. CONCUR'94*, Volume 836 of *Lecture Notes in Comput. Sci.*, pp. 481–496. Springer-Verlag.

Segerberg, K. (1977). A completeness theorem in the modal logic of programs (preliminary report). *Not. Amer. Math. Soc. 24* (6), A–552.

Shoenfield, J. R. (1967). *Mathematical Logic*. Addison-Wesley.

Sholz, H. (1952). Ein ungelöstes Problem in der symbolischen Logik. *The Journal of Symbolic Logic 17*, 160.

Sistla, A. P. and E. M. Clarke (1982). The complexity of propositional linear temporal logics. In *Proc. 14th Symp. Theory of Comput.*, pp. 159–168. ACM.

Sistla, A. P., M. Y. Vardi, and P. Wolper (1987). The complementation problem for Büchi automata with application to temporal logic. *Theor. Comput. Sci. 49*, 217–237.

Soare, R. I. (1987). *Recursively Enumerable Sets and Degrees*. Springer-Verlag.

Sokolsky, O. and S. Smolka (1994, June). Incremental model checking in the modal μ-calculus. In D. Dill (Ed.), *Proc. Conf. Computer Aided Verification*, Volume 818 of *Lect. Notes in Comput. Sci.*, pp. 352–363. Springer.

Steffen, B., T. Margaria, A. Classen, V. Braun, R. Nisius, and M. Reitenspiess (1996, March). A constraint oriented service environment. In T. Margaria and B. Steffen (Eds.), *Proc. Second Int. Workshop Tools and Algorithms for the Construction and Analysis of Systems (TACAS'96)*, Volume 1055 of *Lect. Notes in Comput. Sci.*, pp. 418–421. Springer.

Stirling, C. (1992). Modal and temporal logics. In S. Abramsky, D. Gabbay, and T. Maibaum (Eds.), *Handbook of Logic in Computer Science*, pp. 477–563. Clarendon Press.

Stirling, C. and D. Walker (1989, March). Local model checking in the modal μ-calculus. In *Proc. Int. Joint Conf. Theory and Practice of Software Develop. (TAPSOFT89)*, Volume 352 of *Lect. Notes in Comput. Sci.*, pp. 369–383. Springer.

Stockmeyer, L. J. and A. R. Meyer (1973). Word problems requiring exponential time. In *Proc. 5th Symp. Theory of Computing*, New York, pp. 1–9. ACM: ACM.

Stolboushkin, A. (1983). Regular dynamic logic is not interpretable in deterministic context-free dynamic logic. *Information and Computation 59*, 94–107.

Stolboushkin, A. (1989, June). Some complexity bounds for dynamic logic. In *Proc. 4th Symp. Logic in Comput. Sci.*, pp. 324–332. IEEE.

Stolboushkin, A. P. and M. A. Taitslin (1983). Deterministic dynamic logic is strictly weaker than dynamic logic. *Infor. and Control 57*, 48–55.

Stone, M. H. (1936). The representation theorem for Boolean algebra. *Trans. Amer. Math. Soc. 40*, 37–111.

Streett, R. (1985a). Fixpoints and program looping: reductions from the propositional μ-calculus into propositional dynamic logics of looping. In Parikh (Ed.), *Proc. Workshop on Logics of Programs 1985*, pp. 359–372. Springer. Lect. Notes in Comput. Sci. 193.

Streett, R. and E. A. Emerson (1984). The propositional μ-calculus is elementary. In *Proc. 11th Int. Colloq. on Automata Languages and Programming*, pp. 465–472. Springer. Lect. Notes in Comput. Sci. 172.

Streett, R. S. (1981). Propositional dynamic logic of looping and converse. In *Proc. 13th Symp. Theory of Comput.*, pp. 375–381. ACM.

Streett, R. S. (1982). Propositional dynamic logic of looping and converse is elementarily decidable. *Infor. and Control 54*, 121–141.

Streett, R. S. (1985b). Fixpoints and program looping: reductions from the propositional μ-calculus into propositional dynamic logics of looping. In R. Parikh (Ed.), *Proc. Workshop on Logics of Programs*, Volume 193 of *Lect. Notes in Comput. Sci.*, pp. 359–372. Springer-Verlag.

Tarjan, R. E. (1981). A unified approach to path problems. *J. Assoc. Comput. Mach.*, 577–593.

Tarski, A. (1935). Die Wahrheitsbegriff in den formalisierten Sprachen. *Studia Philosophica 1*, 261–405.

Thiele, H. (1966). Wissenschaftstheoretische untersuchungen in algorithmischen sprachen. In

Theorie der Graphschemata-Kalkale Veb Deutscher Verlag der Wissenschaften. Berlin.

Thomas, W. (1997, May). Languages, automata, and logic. Technical Report 9607, Christian-Albrechts-Universität Kiel.

Tiuryn, J. (1981a). A survey of the logic of effective definitions. In E. Engeler (Ed.), *Proc. Workshop on Logics of Programs*, Volume 125 of *Lect. Notes in Comput. Sci.*, pp. 198–245. Springer-Verlag.

Tiuryn, J. (1981b). Unbounded program memory adds to the expressive power of first-order programming logics. In *Proc. 22nd Symp. Found. Comput. Sci.*, pp. 335–339. IEEE.

Tiuryn, J. (1984). Unbounded program memory adds to the expressive power of first-order programming logics. *Infor. and Control 60*, 12–35.

Tiuryn, J. (1986). Higher-order arrays and stacks in programming: an application of complexity theory to logics of programs. In Gruska and Rovan (Eds.), *Proc. Math. Found. Comput. Sci.*, Volume 233 of *Lect. Notes in Comput. Sci.*, pp. 177–198. Springer-Verlag.

Tiuryn, J. (1989). A simplified proof of DDL < DL. *Information and Computation 81*, 1–12.

Tiuryn, J. and P. Urzyczyn (1983). Some relationships between logics of programs and complexity theory. In *Proc. 24th Symp. Found. Comput. Sci.*, pp. 180–184. IEEE.

Tiuryn, J. and P. Urzyczyn (1984). Remarks on comparing expressive power of logics of programs. In Chytil and Koubek (Eds.), *Proc. Math. Found. Comput. Sci.*, Volume 176 of *Lect. Notes in Comput. Sci.*, pp. 535–543. Springer-Verlag.

Tiuryn, J. and P. Urzyczyn (1988). Some relationships between logics of programs and complexity theory. *Theor. Comput. Sci. 60*, 83–108.

Trnkova, V. and J. Reiterman (1980). Dynamic algebras which are not Kripke structures. In *Proc. 9th Symp. on Math. Found. Comput. Sci.*, pp. 528–538.

Turing, A. M. (1936). On computable numbers with an application to the Entscheidungsproblem. *Proc. London Math. Soc. 42*, 230–265. Erratum: Ibid., 43 (1937), pp. 544–546.

Urzyczyn, P. (1983a). A necessary and sufficient condition in order that a Herbrand interpretation be expressive relative to recursive programs. *Information and Control 56*, 212–219.

Urzyczyn, P. (1983b). Nontrivial definability by flowchart programs. *Infor. and Control 58*, 59–87.

Urzyczyn, P. (1983c). *The Unwind Property.* Ph. D. thesis, Warsaw University. In Polish.

Urzyczyn, P. (1986). "During" cannot be expressed by "after". *Journal of Computer and System Sciences 32*, 97–104.

Urzyczyn, P. (1987). Deterministic context-free dynamic logic is more expressive than deterministic dynamic logic of regular programs. *Fundamenta Informaticae 10*, 123–142.

Urzyczyn, P. (1988). Logics of programs with Boolean memory. *Fundamenta Informaticae XI*, 21–40.

Valiev, M. K. (1980). Decision complexity of variants of propositional dynamic logic. In *Proc. 9th Symp. Math. Found. Comput. Sci.*, Volume 88 of *Lect. Notes in Comput. Sci.*, pp. 656–664. Springer-Verlag.

van Dalen, D. (1994). *Logic and Structure* (Third ed.). Springer-Verlag.

van Emde Boas, P. (1978). The connection between modal logic and algorithmic logics. In *Symp. on Math. Found. of Comp. Sci.*, pp. 1–15.

Vardi, M. (1998a). Linear vs. branching time: a complexity-theoretic perspective. In *Proc. 13th Symp. Logic in Comput. Sci.*, pp. 394–405. IEEE.

Vardi, M. and P. Wolper (1986a). Automata-theoretic techniques for modal logics of programs. *J. Comput. Sys. Sci. 32*, 183–221.

Vardi, M. Y. (1985a, October). Automatic verification of probabilistic concurrent finite-state programs. In *Proc. 26th Symp. Found. Comput. Sci.*, pp. 327–338. IEEE.

Vardi, M. Y. (1985b). The taming of the converse: reasoning about two-way computations. In R. Parikh (Ed.), *Proc. Workshop on Logics of Programs*, Volume 193 of *Lect. Notes in Comput. Sci.*, pp. 413–424. Springer-Verlag.

Vardi, M. Y. (1987, June). Verification of concurrent programs: the automata theoretic framework. In *Proc. 2nd Symp. Logic in Comput. Sci.*, pp. 167–176. IEEE.

Vardi, M. Y. (1998b, July). Reasoning about the past with two-way automata. In *Proc. 25th Int. Colloq. Automata Lang. Prog.*, Volume 1443 of *Lect. Notes in Comput. Sci.*, pp. 628–641. Springer-Verlag.

Vardi, M. Y. and L. Stockmeyer (1985, May). Improved upper and lower bounds for modal logics of programs: preliminary report. In *Proc. 17th Symp. Theory of Comput.*, pp. 240–251. ACM.

Vardi, M. Y. and P. Wolper (1986b, June). An automata-theoretic approach to automatic program verification. In *Proc. 1st Symp. Logic in Computer Science*, pp. 332–344. IEEE.

Vardi, M. Y. and P. Wolper (1986c). Automata-theoretic techniques for modal logics of programs. *J. Comput. Syst. Sci. 32*, 183–221.

Walukiewicz, I. (1993, June). Completeness result for the propositional μ-calculus. In *Proc. 8th IEEE Symp. Logic in Comput. Sci.*

Walukiewicz, I. (1995, June). Completeness of Kozen's axiomatisation of the propositional μ-calculus. In *Proc. 10th Symp. Logic in Comput. Sci.*, pp. 14–24. IEEE.

Walukiewicz, I. (2000, February–March). Completeness of Kozen's axiomatisation of the propositional μ-calculus. *Infor. and Comput. 157*(1–2), 142–182.

Wand, M. (1978). A new incompleteness result for Hoare's system. *J. Assoc. Comput. Mach. 25*, 168–175.

Whitehead, A. N. and B. Russell (1910–1913). *Principia Mathematica.* Cambridge University Press. Three volumes.

Wolper, P. (1981). Temporal logic can be more expressive. In *Proc. 22nd Symp. Foundations of Computer Science*, pp. 340–348. IEEE.

Wolper, P. (1983). Temporal logic can be more expressive. *Infor. and Control 56*, 72–99.

Notation and Abbreviations

$\mathbb{Z}$	integers	3
$\mathbb{Q}$	rational numbers	3
$\mathbb{R}$	real numbers	3
$\mathbb{N}$	natural numbers	3
ω	finite ordinals	3
$\Longrightarrow$	meta-implication	3
$\rightarrow$	implication	3
$\Longleftrightarrow$	meta-equivalence	3
$\leftrightarrow$	equivalence	3
iff	if and only if	3
$\overset{\text{def}}{=}$	definition	3
$\overset{\text{def}}{\Longleftrightarrow}$	definition	3
$|\sigma|$	length of a sequence	3
A^*	set of all finite strings over A	3
ε	empty string	3
w^R	reverse of a string	3
$A, B, C, \ldots$	sets	3
$\in$	set containment	3
$\subseteq$	set inclusion, subset	3
$\subset$	strict inclusion	4
$\#A$	cardinality of a set	4
2^A	powerset	4
$\varnothing$	empty set	4
$A \cup B$	union	4
$A \cap B$	intersection	4
$\bigcup \mathcal{A}$	union	4
$\bigcap \mathcal{A}$	intersection	4
$B - A$	complement of A in B	4
$\sim A$	complement	4
$A \times B$	Cartesian product	4
$\prod_{\alpha \in I} A_\alpha$	Cartesian product	4
A^n	Cartesian power	4
π_β	projection function	4

ZFC	Zermelo–Fraenkel set theory with choice	4
$P, Q, R, \ldots$	relations	5
$\varnothing$	empty relation	6
$R(a_1, \ldots, a_n)$	$(a_1, \ldots, a_n) \in R$	6
$a\,R\,b$	$(a, b) \in R$	6
$\circ$	relational composition	7
ι	identity relation	7
R^n	n-fold composition of a binary relation	7
$^-$	converse	7
R^+	transitive closure	8
R^*	reflexive transitive closure	8
$[a]$	equivalence class	9
$f, g, h, \ldots$	functions	9
$f : A \to B$	function with domain A and range B	9
$A \to B$	function space	9
B^A	function space	9
$\mapsto$	anonymous function specifier	9
$\upharpoonright$	function restriction	10
$\circ$	function composition	10
f^{-1}	inverse	10
$f[a/b]$	function patching	10
$\sup B$	supremum	11
WFI	well-founded induction	12
$\alpha, \beta, \gamma, \ldots$	ordinals	14
Ord	class of all ordinals	14
ZF	Zermelo–Fraenkel set theory	16
$\tau^\dagger$	least prefixpoint operator	18
curry	currying operator	25
$\vdash, \dashv$	endmarkers	27
$\sqcup$	blank symbol	28
δ	transition function	28
$\alpha, \beta, \gamma, \ldots$	Turing machine configurations	29

$\xrightarrow[M,x]{1}$	next configuration relation	29
$z[i/b]$	string replacement operator	29
$\xrightarrow[M,x]{*}$	reflexive transitive closure of $\xrightarrow[M,x]{1}$	30
$L(M)$	strings accepted by a Turing machine	30
δ	transition relation	33
HP	halting problem	37
MP	membership problem	37
$DTIME(f(n))$	deterministic time complexity class	39
$NTIME(f(n))$	nondeterministic time complexity class	39
$ATIME(f(n))$	alternating time complexity class	39
$DSPACE(f(n))$	deterministic space complexity class	39
$NSPACE(f(n))$	nondeterministic space complexity class	39
$ASPACE(f(n))$	alternating space complexity class	39
$EXPTIME$	deterministic exponential time	40
$NEXPTIME$	nondeterministic exponential time	40
P	deterministic polynomial time	40
NP	nondeterministic polynomial time	40
$M[B]$	oracle Turing machine	41
Σ_1^0	r.e. sets	43
Π_1^0	co-r.e. sets	43
Δ_1^0	recursive sets	43
$\Sigma_n^0, \Pi_n^0, \Delta_n^0$	arithmetic hierarchy	43
Π_1^1	second-order universal relations	45
Δ_1^1	hyperarithmetic relations	45
IND	programming language for inductive sets	45
ω_1	least uncountable ordinal	50
ω_1^{ck}	least nonrecursive ordinal	50
ord	labeling of well-founded tree	50
$\leq_m$	many-one reducibility	54
$\leq_m^{log}$	logspace reducibility	54
$\leq_m^p$	polynomial-time reducibility	54
$\vDash$	satisfiability relation	69

Th Φ	logical consequences of a set of formulas	69
$\vdash$	provability relation	70
$\neg$	negation	70
$p, q, r, \ldots$	atomic propositions	71
$\wedge$	conjunction	71
$\vee$	disjunction	71
1	truth	71
0	falsity	71
$\varphi, \psi, \rho, \ldots$	propositional formulas	72
S, K	axioms of propositional logic	77
DN	double negation	77
MP	modus ponens	77
EFQ	e falso quodlibet	78
Σ	vocabulary	87
$a, b, c, \ldots$	constants	87
$=$	equality symbol	87
$x, y, \ldots$	individual variables	87
$s, t, \ldots$	terms	87
$T_\Sigma(X)$	set of terms	87
T_Σ	ground terms	87
$\mathfrak{A} = (A, \mathfrak{m}_\mathfrak{A})$	Σ-algebra	88
$\mathfrak{m}_\mathfrak{A}$	meaning function	88
$f^\mathfrak{A}$	meaning of a function in a structure	88
$|\mathfrak{A}|$	carrier of a structure	88
$T_\Sigma(X)$	term algebra	89
$u, v, w, \ldots$	valuations	90
$t^\mathfrak{A}$	meaning of a ground term in a structure	90
Mod Φ	models of a set of formulas	91
Th $\mathfrak{A}$	theory of a structure	91
Th $\mathcal{D}$	theory of a class of structures	91
$[a]$	congruence class	94
$a \equiv b \pmod{n}$	number theoretic congruence	95
$a \equiv b \ (I)$	congruence modulo an ideal	95

$\triangleleft$	normal subgroup	95
$\mathfrak{A}/\equiv$	quotient algebra	96
REF	reflexivity rule	99
SYM	symmetry rule	99
TRANS	transitivity rule	99
CONG	congruence rule	99
$\prod_{i \in I} \mathfrak{A}_i$	product algebra	100
H	closure operator for homomorphic images	101
S	closure operator for subalgebras	101
P	closure operator for products	101
$\forall$	universal quantifier	102
$\exists$	existential quantifier	102
$p, q, r, \ldots$	predicate symbols	102
$\varphi, \psi, \rho, \ldots$	first-order formulas	103
$p(t_1, \ldots, t_n)$	atomic formula	103
$L_{\omega\omega}$	first-order predicate logic	103
$\varphi[x_1/t_1, \ldots, x_n/t_n]$	simultaneous substitution	105
$\varphi[x_i/t_i \mid 1 \le i \le n]$	simultaneous substitution	105
$\mathfrak{A} = (A, \mathfrak{m}_{\mathfrak{A}})$	relational structure	105
GEN	generalization rule	111
$\bigwedge_{\alpha \in A} \varphi_\alpha$	infinitary conjunction	120
$\bigvee_{\alpha \in A} \varphi_\alpha$	infinitary disjunction	120
$\square$	modal necessity operator	127
$\diamond$	modal possibility operator	127
$\mathfrak{K} = (K, R_{\mathfrak{K}}, \mathfrak{m}_{\mathfrak{K}})$	Kripke frame for modal logic	127
GEN	modal generalization	130
$a, b, c, \ldots$	modalities	130
$[a]$	multimodal necessity operator	131
$<a>$	multimodal possibility operator	131
$\mathfrak{K} = (K, \mathfrak{m}_{\mathfrak{K}})$	Kripke frame for multimodal logic	131
$\mathrm{first}(\sigma)$	first state of a path	132
$\mathrm{last}(\sigma)$	last state of a path	132
$x := t$	assignment	145

$\alpha \,;\, \beta$	sequential composition	148
$\varphi?$	test	148
$\alpha \cup \beta$	nondeterministic choice	148
α^*	iteration	148
$\sigma, \tau, \ldots$	seqs	150
$CS(\alpha)$	computation sequences of a program	150
$\{\varphi\}\,\alpha\,\{\psi\}$	partial correctness assertion	156
$\varphi, \psi, \ldots$	propositions	164
$\alpha, \beta, \gamma, \ldots$	programs	164
$a, b, c, \ldots$	atomic programs	164
Π_0	set of atomic programs	164
$p, q, r, \ldots$	atomic propositions	164
Φ_0	set of atomic propositions	164
Π	set of programs	164
Φ	set of propositions	164
$[\alpha]$	DL box operator	165
$\langle\alpha\rangle$	DL diamond operator	166
skip	null program	167
fail	failing program	167
$\mathfrak{K} = (K, \mathfrak{m}_{\mathfrak{K}})$	Kripke frame for PDL	167
$\mathfrak{m}_{\mathfrak{K}}$	meaning function	167
$u, v, w, \ldots$	states	167
RTC	reflexive transitive closure rule	182
LI	loop invariance rule	182
IND	induction axiom	182
$FL(\varphi)$	Fischer–Ladner closure	191
$FL^{\square}(\varphi)$	Fischer–Ladner closure auxiliary function	191
$\mathfrak{K}/FL(\varphi)$	filtration of a Kripke frame	195
PDA	pushdown automaton	227
$a^{\Delta} b a^{\Delta}$	a nonregular program	228
PDL + L	extension of PDL with a nonregular program	229
SkS	monadic second-order theory of k successors	229
CFL	context-free language	238

UDH	unique diamond path Hintikka tree	241
PTA	pushdown tree automaton	242
A_ℓ	local automaton	244
$A_\square$	box automaton	245
$A_\diamond$	diamond automaton	247
DWP	deterministic **while** programs	259
WP	nondeterministic **while** programs	260
DPDL	deterministic PDL	260
SPDL	strict PDL	260
SDPDL	strict deterministic PDL	260
$\Phi^{(i)}$	programs with nesting of tests at most i	264
PDL$^{(i)}$	PDL with programs in $\Phi^{(i)}$	264
PDL$^{(0)}$	test-free PDL	264
APDL	automata PDL	267
$-\alpha$	complement of a program	268
$\alpha \cap \beta$	intersection of programs	268
IPDL	PDL with intersection	269
$\bar{}$	converse operator	270
$TC(\varphi, \alpha, \psi)$	total correctness assertion	271
μ	least fixed point operator	271
wf	well-foundedness predicate	272
halt	halt predicate	272
loop	loop operator	272
repeat, Δ	repeat operator	272
RPDL	PDL with well-foundedness predicate	272
LPDL	PDL with halt predicate	272
CRPDL	RPDL with converse	274
CLPDL	LPDL with converse	274
$\wedge$	concurrency operator	277
$F(t_1, \ldots, t_n) := t$	array assignment	288
push(t)	push instruction	289
pop(y)	pop instruction	289
$x := ?$	wildcard assignment	290

w_a	constant valuation	293
DL(r.e.)	DL with r.e. programs	297
DL(array)	DL with array assignments	297
DL(stk)	DL with algebraic stack	297
DL(bstk)	DL with Boolean stack	297
DL(wild)	DL with wildcard assignment	297
DL(dreg)	DL with **while** programs	297
$\mathsf{DL}_1 \leq \mathsf{DL}_2$	no more expressive than	304
$\mathsf{DL}_1 < \mathsf{DL}_2$	strictly less expressive than	304
$\mathsf{DL}_1 \equiv \mathsf{DL}_2$	equivalent in expressive power	304
DL(rich-test r.e.)	rich test DL of r.e. programs	304
$L_{\omega_1^{ck}\omega}$	constructive infinitary logic	305
$\mathsf{DL}_1 \leq_{\mathbb{N}} \mathsf{DL}_2$	relative expressiveness over $\mathbb{N}$	308
$C_{\mathfrak{A}}$	natural chain in a structure	318
$\mathfrak{A}_w$	expansion of a structure by constants	318
NEXT_m	program computing a natural chain	318
S_n	collection of n-element structures	319
$\ulcorner\mathfrak{A}\urcorner$	code of a structure	320
$SP_m(\alpha)$	m^{th} spectrum of a program	320
$SP(K)$	spectrum of a class of programs	320
H_m^{Σ}	language of codes of structures	321
$SP(K) \approx C$	spectrum $SP(K)$ captures complexity class C	322
APDA	auxiliary pushdown automaton	324
$\vdash_{S1}$	provability in DL Axiom System 14.2	328
$\varphi[x/t]$	substitution into DL formulas	329
$\vdash_{S2}$	provability in DL Axiom System 14.6	331
$\vdash_{S3}$	provability in DL Axiom System 14.9	335
$\vdash_{S4}$	provability in DL Axiom System 14.12	337
$FV(\alpha)$	free variables of an abstract program	344
$K_1 \leq K_2$	translatability	347
$K_1 \preceq_T K_2$	termination subsumption	348
T_n	full binary tree of depth n	355
$Ltr(\pi)$	L-trace of a computation	356

$Cmp(\alpha, A)$	computations of a program in a set	356
$LtrCmp(\alpha, A, n)$	L-traces of length at most n	356
$\mathfrak{G}_n$	structure arising from an Adian group	366
$N(C, k)$	k-neighborhood of a subset of $\mathbb{N}$	371
AL	Algorithmic Logic	383
NDL	Nonstandard Dynamic Logic	384
$\vdash_{\text{HL}}$	provability in Hoare Logic	385
$\mathfrak{J}$	time model	385
$\models_{\text{NT}}$	satisfiability in nonstandard time semantics	386
LDL	DL with halt predicate	386
RDL	DL with well-foundedness predicate	386
$Pr(\text{DL})$	probabilistic DL	391
LED	Logic of Effective Definitions	397
TL	Temporal Logic	398
$\Box\varphi$	box operator of temporal logic	398
$\Diamond\varphi$	diamond operator of temporal logic	398
$\bigcirc\varphi$	nexttime operator of temporal logic	398
at L_i	at statement	399
NEXT	next relation of TL	400
fin	finiteness predicate of TL	404
inf	infiniteness predicate of TL	404
until	until operator of TL	405
A	temporal operator "for all traces"	406
E	temporal operator "there exists a trace"	406
PL	Process Logic	408
first	temporal operator of PL	408
until	temporal operator of PL	408
$\text{first}(\sigma)$	first state in σ	409
$\text{last}(\sigma)$	last state in σ	409
$[\![\ ]\!]$	trace operator of PL	412
$\ll\ \gg$	trace operator of PL	412
$\mu X.\varphi(X)$	least fixpoint of $\varphi(X)$	416
KA	Kleene algebra	418

KAT   Kleene algebra with tests.................................421
$\bar{b}$ negation of a Boolean element in KAT.....................421

Index

* operator,
   See iteration operator
*-continuity, 419
*-continuous Kleene algebra,
   See Kleene algebra
*-continuous dynamic algebra,
   See dynamic algebra

$\mathfrak{A}$-validity, 297
Abelian group, 92
accept configuration, 35
acceptable structure, 311
acceptance, 28, 30, 35, 36
accepting subtree, 35
accessibility relation, 127
acyclic, 13
Adian structure, 365, 380
admissibility, 347, 379
AEXPSPACE, 40
AEXPTIME, 40
AL,
   See Algorithmic Logic
algebra
   dynamic,
     See dynamic algebra
   Kleene,
     See Kleene algebra
   Σ-, 88
   term, 89
algebraic stack, 290
Algorithmic Logic, 383–384, 394
ALOGSPACE, 39
α-recursion theory, 64
alternating Turing machine,
   See Turing machine
analytic hierarchy, 45
and-configuration, 35
annihilator, 22
anti-monotone, 26
antichain, 11
antisymmetric, 6
APSPACE, 40
APTIME, 39
argument of a function, 9
arithmetic hierarchy, 42–45
arithmetical
   completeness, 334, 335, 338, 341
   structure, 308, 311, 334
arity, 5, 283, 288
array, 288
   assignment, 288
   variable, 288
     nullary, 292
as expressive as, 229, 304
assignment

array, 288
   nondeterministic,
     See wildcard
   random, 290
   rule, 156
   simple, 147, 283, 284
   wildcard, xiii, 288, 290, 377, 380
associativity, 83, 166
asterate, 3, 98
ATIME, 39
atom, 82
atomic
   formula, 284
   program, 147, 283, 284
   symbol, 164
   test, 147
automata PDL, 267
automaton
   auxiliary pushdown, 324, 351
   box, 245
   counter, 63
   diamond, 247
   finite, 131, 266
   local, 244
   ω-, 266
   pushdown, 227
   pushdown k-ary ω-tree, 242
auxiliary pushdown automaton,
   See automaton
axiom, 69
   of choice, 16
   of regularity, 16
   scheme, 71
axiomatization
   DL, 327–341
   equational logic, 99
   equational theory of regular sets, 420
   infinitary logic, 122
   μ-calculus, 417
   PDL, 173–174, 203
   PL, 411
   predicate logic, 111
     with equality, 115
   propositional logic, 77, 82

bijective, 10
binary, 6
   function symbol, 86
   nondeterminism, 377
   relation, 6–8, 420
Birkhoff's theorem, 140
Boolean algebra, 82, 86, 93, 136, 138
   of sets, 137, 138
Boolean satisfiability,
   See satisfiability, propositional

bound occurrence of a variable, 104
bounded memory, 287, 369
box
    automaton, 245
    operator, 165, 398
branching-time TL, 398
Büchi acceptance, 243

canonical homomorphism, 96
Cantor's set theory, 5
capture
    of a complexity class by a spectrum, 322
    of a variable by a quantifier, 104
cardinality, 4
    of $FL(\varphi)$, 194
carrier, 88, 105, 291
Cartesian
    power, 4
    product, 4
chain, 16
    of sets, 17
change of bound variable, 109
choice
    axiom of, 16
    operator, xiv, 164
class, 5
closed, 18
    formula, 105
closure
    congruence, 95, 99
    Fischer–Ladner, 191–195, 267
    of a variety under homomorphic images, 93
    operator, 19
    ordinal, 21, 51
    universal, 105
CLPDL, 274
co-r.e., 42
    in B, 41
coarsest common refinement, 9
coding of finite structures, 318, 320
coinductive, 50
commutativity, 83
compactness, 122, 142, 181, 210, 220, 303
    first-order, 115–116
    propositional, 81–82
comparative schematology, 347, 378
complete disjunctive normal form, 83
complete lattice, 13
completeness, 303
    DL, 341
    equational logic, 99–100
    first-order, 112–115
        with equality, 115
    for a complexity class, 57

    for termination assertions, 341
    infinitary logic, 124–126
    LED, 397
    μ-calculus, 418
    of a deductive system, 70
    of a set of connectives, 75, 135
    PDL, 203–209
    propositional logic, 79–81
    relative, 341
    TL, 407
complexity, 38–40
    class, 57
    of DL, 313
    of DL, 313–324
    of infinitary logic, 126–127
    of PDL, 211–224
    of spectra, 321
composition, 148, 175
    functional, 10, 54
    operator, 164
    relational, 7, 168
    rule, 156, 186
    sequential, xiv
compositionality, 157
comprehension, 5
computability, 27
    relative, 40–41
computation, 356, 364
    formal, 356
    history, 44
    legal, 365
    on an infinite tree, 243
    sequence, 150, 170
    strongly r-periodic, 365
    terminating, 356
    upward periodic, 365
computational complexity, 64
conclusion, 70
concurrent DL, 393
concurrent PDL, 277
concurrent systems, 406
conditional, 148, 167
    rule, 156, 186
configuration, 29, 243
    n-, 370
congruence, 94
    class, 94
    closure,
        See closure
connective, 71
coNP, 57
    -completeness, 57
    -hardness, 57
consequence

deductive, 70
  logical, 69, 91
consistency, 70, 138, 174, 203
constant, 86, 284
  test, 148
constructive $L_{\omega_1\omega}$, 305
context-free
  DL, 298
  language
    simple-minded, 238
  PDL, 230
  program, 227, 230
  set of seqs, 151
continuity, 11, 17, 417
  *- (star-),
    See *-continuity
  of <> in presence of converse, 179
contraposition, 136
converse, 7, 10, 177, 203, 270
Cook's theorem, 57
correctness
  partial,
    See partial correctness
  specification, 152
  total,
    See total correctness
countable, 16
  ordinal,
    See ordinal
countably infinite, 16
counter automaton,
    See automaton
counter machine,
    See Turing machine
CRPDL, 274
currying, 25, 142

dag, 13
De Morgan law, 83, 137
  infinitary, 123, 143
decidability, 37, 42
  of PDL, 191, 199
  of propositional logic, 75
deduction theorem, 79, 209
  first-order, 111–112
  infinitary, 124
deductive consequence, 70
deductive system, 67
Δ_1^0, 43
Δ_n^0, 43
Δ_1^1, 45, 51
ΔPDL, 272
dense, 6, 120
descriptive set theory, 64

deterministic
  Kripke frame, 259
  semantically, 188, 259
  while program, 147
diagonalization, 38, 63
diamond
  automaton, 247
  operator, 166, 398
difference sequence, 250
directed graph, 13
disjunctive normal form, 83
distributivity, 83
  infinitary, 123, 143
divergence-closed, 350
DL,
    See Dynamic Logic
  concurrent, 393
DN, 77
domain, 88, 105
  of a function, 9
  of computation, 145, 283, 291
double negation, 77, 83, 136
double-exponential time, 39
DPDL, 260
$DSPACE$, 39
$DTIME$, 39
duality, 135–136, 166, 172
duplicator, 119
DWP, 259
dyadic, 6
dynamic
  formula, 383
  term, 383
dynamic algebra, 389–391
  *-continuous, 390
  separable, 390
Dynamic Logic, 133
  axiomatization, 329
  basic, 284
  context-free, 298
  poor test, 148, 284
  probabilistic, 391
  rich test, 148, 285, 286
    of r.e. programs, 304

edge, 13
effective definitional scheme, 397
EFQ, 78
Ehrenfeucht–Fraïssé games, 119–120
emptiness problem
  for PTA, 243
empty
  relation, 6
  sequence, 3

set, 4
  string, 3
endogenous, 157, 398
enumeration machine, 63
epimorphism, 90
equal expressive power, 304
equality symbol, 284
equation, 88
equational logic, 86–102
  axiomatization, 99
equational theory, 91
equationally defined class,
  See variety
equivalence
  class, 9
  of Kripke frames, 132
  of logics, 304, 380
  relation, 6, 8–9
eventuality, 402
excluded middle, 136
exogenous, 157
expanded vocabulary, 318
exponential time, 39
expressive structure, 334
expressiveness
  of DL, 353
  relative, 343, 378
  over $\mathbb{N}$, 308
EXPSPACE, 40
EXPTIME, 40

fairness, 290
filter, 138
filtration, 191, 195–201, 273
  for nonstandard models, 199–201, 204
finitary, 17
finite
  automaton, 131, 266
  branching, 65
  intersection property, 81
  model property,
    See small model property
  model theorem,
    See small model theorem
  satisfiability, 81, 115
  variant, 293
first-order
  logic,
    See predicate logic
  spectrum, 325
  test, 380
  vocabulary, 283
Fischer–Ladner closure, 191–195, 267
fixpoint, 18

forced win, 119
formal computation, 356
formula, 283
  atomic, 284
  DL, 286, 297
  dynamic, 383
  first-order, 103
  Horn, 88
  positive in a variable, 416
free, 97
  algebra, 97–99
  Boolean algebra, 137
  commutative ring, 98
  for a variable in a formula, 104
  monoid, 98
  occurrence of a variable, 104
    in DL, 329
  variable, 105
  vector space, 99
function, 9–10
  patching, 10, 105, 106, 292
  projection, 4
  Skolem, 142
  symbol, 283
functional composition,
  See composition
fusion of traces, 409

Galois connection, 25
game, 48
generalization rule, 111, 173, 203
generate, 89
generating set, 89
graph, 13
  directed, 13
greatest lower bound,
  See infimum
ground term, 87, 103
guarded command, 167, 187
guess and verify, 34, 40

halt, 30
halt, 272, 386
halting problem, 37, 55
  for IND programs, 65
  over finite interpretations, 322
  undecidability of, 63
hard dag, 371
hardness, 57
Herbrand-like state, 317, 349
Hilbert system, 69
Hoare Logic, 133, 156, 186
homomorphic image, 90
homomorphism, 76, 89

canonical, 96
Horn formula, 88, 140
    infinitary, 140
HSP theorem, 100–102
hyperarithmetic relation, 50
hyperelementary relation, 50, 51

ideal
    of a Boolean algebra, 138
    of a commutative ring, 95
idempotence, 83
    infinitary, 143
identity relation, 7, 88
image of a function, 10
IND, 45–51, 64
independence, 16
individual, 88
    variable, 284, 286
induction
    axiom
        PDL, 173, 182, 183, 201
        Peano arithmetic, 174, 183
    principle, 12, 13
        for temporal logic, 401
        transfinite, 14
    structural, 12, 157
    transfinite, 12, 15–16, 117
    well-founded, 12–13
inductive
    assertions method, 399, 401
    definability, 45–53, 64
    relation, 49, 51
infimum, 13
infinitary completeness
    for DL, 341
infinitary logic, 120–127
infinite descending chain, 24
infix, 87
initial state, 293, 304, 317
injective, 10
input variable, 147
input/output
    pair, 168, 291
    relation, 147, 169, 287, 293
    specification, 153, 154
intermittent assertions method, 398, 402
interpretation of temporal operators in PL, 409
interpreted reasoning, 307, 333
intuïtionistic propositional logic, 79, 136
invariant, 399, 401
invariant assertions method, 157, 401
inverse, 10
IPDL,
    See PDL with intersection

irreflexive, 6
isomorphism, 90
    local, 119
iteration operator, xiv, 164, 181, 390

join, 11

K, 77
k-counter machine,
    See Turing machine
k-fold exponential time, 39
k-neighborhood, 371
KA,
    See Kleene algebra
KAT,
    See Kleene algebra with tests
kernel, 90
Kleene algebra, 389, 418
    *-continuous, 390, 419
    typed, 423
    with tests, 421
Kleene's theorem, 51, 63, 64
Knaster–Tarski theorem, 20–22, 37, 416
König's lemma, 61, 65, 387, 388
Kripke frame, 127, 167, 291, 292
    nonstandard, 199, 204, 205, 210, 211

$LOGSPACE$, 39
L-trace, 356
language, 67–68
    first-order DL, 283
lattice, 13, 92
    complete, 13
LDL, 386
leaf, 50
least fixpoint, 49, 415, 416
least upper bound, 11
LED, 397
legal computation, 365
lexicographic order, 23
limit ordinal,
    See ordinal
linear
    order,
        See total order
    recurrence, 255, 257
linear-time TL, 398
literal, 82
liveness property, 402
local
    automaton, 244
    isomorphism, 119
logarithmic space, 39

logic, 67
Logic of Effective Definitions, 397
logical consequence, 69, 91, 106, 172
  in PDL, 209, 216, 220–224
logical equivalence, 106, 163
$L_{\omega_1\omega}$, 120, 142, 305
  constructive, 305
$L_{\omega_1^{ck}\omega}$, 120, 142, 304, 305
$L_{\omega\omega}$,
  See predicate logic
loop, 30
  -free program, 385
  invariance rule, 182, 184, 201
loop, 272, 386
Löwenheim–Skolem theorem, 116–117, 302
  downward, 116, 122, 126
  upward, 116, 122, 142, 346
lower bound
  for PDL, 216–220
LPDL, 272

m-state, 317
many-one reduction, 53
maximal consistent set, 204
meaning,
  See semantics
  function, 167, 291
meet, 13
membership problem, 37, 55
meta-equivalence, 3
meta-implication, 3, 73
method of well-founded sets, 402
min,+ algebra, 420
modal logic, xiv, 127–134, 164, 167, 191
modal μ-calculus,
  See μ-calculus
modality, 130
model, 68, 106
  nonstandard, 384
model checking, 199, 202, 211
  for the μ-calculus, 418
model theory, 68
modus ponens, 77, 111, 173, 203
monadic, 6
mono-unary vocabulary, 319
monoid, 92
  free, 98
monomorphism, 90
monotone, 11, 17
  Boolean formula, 135
monotonicity, 416
MP, 77
m^{th} spectrum, 320
μ operator, 415

μ-calculus, 271, 415, 417
multimodal logic, 130–132
multiprocessor systems, 406

n-ary
  function symbol, 86
  relation, 6
n-configuration, 370
n-pebble game, 120, 370
natural chain, 318, 325
natural deduction, 69
NDL, 384, 394
necessity, 127
neighborhood, 371
NEXPSPACE, 40
NEXPTIME, 40
next configuration relation, 29
nexttime operator, 398
NLOGSPACE, 39
nondeterminism, 63, 151, 158
  binary, 377
  unbounded, 377
nondeterministic
  assignment,
    See wildcard assignment
  choice, xiv, 175
  program, 133
  Turing machine,
    See Turing machine
  while program, 285
nonstandard
  Kripke frame, 199, 204, 205, 210, 211
  model, 384
Nonstandard DL, 384–386, 394
normal subgroup, 95
not-configuration, 36
not-state, 36
NP, 40, 57
  -completeness, 57, 220
  -hardness, 57
NPSPACE, 39
NPTIME, 39
NTIME, 39
nullary, 6
  array variable, 292
  function symbol, 86
number theory, 103, 140
  second-order, 45

occurrence, 104
ω-automaton, 266
ω_1^{ck}, 50
one-to-one, 10
  correspondence, 10

onto, 10
or-configuration, 35
oracle, 41
 Turing machine,
  See Turing machine
ord, 50, 124
ordinal, 14
 countable, 50
 limit, 14, 15
 recursive, 45
 successor, 14, 15
 transfinite, 13–15
output variable, 147

P, 40
p-sparse, 367
$P=NP$ problem, 40, 76
pairing function, 142
parameterless recursion, 227, 290
parentheses, 72, 166
partial
 correctness, 154
  assertion, 133, 167, 187, 313, 316, 325, 385
 order, 6, 10–12
  strict, 6, 11
partition, 9
path, 50, 132
PDL, 163–277
 automata, 267
 concurrent, 277
 poor test, 263
 regular, 164
 rich test, 165, 263
 test-free, 264
 with intersection, 269
$PDL^{(0)}$, 224
Peano arithmetic
 induction axiom of, 174
pebble game, 120, 370
Peirce's law, 136
Π_1^0, 43
Π_n^0, 43
Π_1^1, 45, 51, 126
 -completeness, 222
PL,
 See Process Logic
polyadic, 369
polynomial, 98
 space, 39
 time, 39
poor
 test, 148, 263, 284
 vocabulary, 319
positive, 49

possibility, 127
postcondition, 154
postfix, 87
precedence, 72, 103, 166
precondition, 154
predicate logic, 102–119
predicate symbol, 283
prefix, 87
prefixpoint, 18
premise, 70
prenex form, 45, 109
preorder, 6, 10
probabilistic program, 391–393
Process Logic, 408
product, 100
program, 145, 283, 287
 atomic, 147, 283, 284
 DL, 284
 loop-free, 385
 operator, 147
 probabilistic, 391–393
 r.e., 287, 296
 regular, 148, 169, 285
 schematology, 311
 scheme, 302
 simulation, 347
 uniformly periodic, 365
 variable, 286
 while, 149
 with Boolean arrays, 380
programming language
 semi-universal, 349
projection function, 4
proof, 70
proper class,
 See class
proposition, 72
propositional
 formula, 72
 logic, 71–86
  intuitionistic, 136
 operators, 71
 satisfiability,
  See satisfiability
Propositional Dynamic Logic,
 See PDL
$PSPACE$, 39
$PTIME$, 39
pushdown
 k-ary ω-tree automaton, 242
 automaton, 227
 store,
  See stack

quantifier, 102
  depth, 119
quasiorder,
  See preorder
quasivariety, 140
quotient
  algebra, 96
  construction, 96–97

Ramsey's theorem, 24
random assignment,
  See assignment
range of a function, 9
RDL, 386
r.e., 30, 42, 63
  in *B*, 41
  program, 287, 296
reasoning
  interpreted, 307, 333
  uninterpreted, 301, 327
recursion, 149, 289
  parameterless, 227, 290
recursive, 30, 42
  call, 149
  function theory, 63
  in *B*, 41
  ordinal, 45, 50–51
  tree, 50–51
recursively enumerable,
  See r.e.
reducibility, 54
  relation, 53–56, 63
reductio ad absurdum, 136
reduction
  many-one, 53
refinement, 6, 9
reflexive, 6
reflexive transitive closure, 8, 20, 47, 182, 183,
  200
refutable, 70
regular
  expression, 164, 169, 190
  program, 148, 169, 285
    with arrays, 288
    with Boolean stack, 364
    with stack, 289
  set, 170, 420
reject configuration, 35
rejection, 28, 30
relation, 5
  binary, 6–8
  empty, 6
  hyperarithmetic, 50
  hyperelementary, 50, 51

next configuration, 29
  reducibility, 53–56, 63
  symbol, 283
  universal, 45
  well-founded,
    See well-founded
relational
  composition,
    See composition
  structure, 105
relative
  completeness, 341
  computability, 40–41
  expressiveness, 343, 378
    over ℕ, 308
repeat, 272, 386
representation by sets, 76–77
resolution, 69
rich
  test, 148, 165, 263, 285, 286
  vocabulary, 319
ring, 92
  commutative, 92
RPDL, 272
rule of inference, 69
run, 386
Russell's paradox, 5

S, 77
safety property, 401
satisfaction
  equational logic, 90
  first-order, 106
  PDL, 168
  propositional, 74
  relation, 106
  TL, 400
satisfiability
  algorithm for **PDL**, 191, 213
  Boolean,
    See satisfiability, propositional
  DL, 297, 298
  finite, 81
  modal logic, 128
  PDL, 171, 191, 211
  propositional, 57, 74, 76, 129, 220
scalar multiplication, 390
schematology, 302, 347, 378
scope, 104
SDPDL, 224, 260
second-order number theory, 45
Segerberg axioms,
  See axiomatization, **PDL**
semantic determinacy, 188, 259

semantics, 67, 68
  abstract programs, 344
  DL, 291–298
  equational logic, 88
  infinitary logic, 120
  modal logic, 127
  multimodal logic, 131
  PDL, 167–170
  predicate logic, 105–109
    with equality, 115
  propositional logic, 73–74
semi-universal, 349, 350
semigroup, 92
semilattice, 13, 92
sentence, 69, 105
separable dynamic algebra,
  See dynamic algebra
seq, 150, 170, 287
sequent, 69
sequential composition,
  See composition
set operator, 16–22
Σ-algebra, 88
Σ_1^0, 43
Σ_n^0, 43
signature,
  See vocabulary
simple assignment,
  See assignment
simple-minded
  context-free language, 238, 256
  pushdown automaton, 238
simulation, 37, 347
Skolem function, 142
Skolemization, 142
SkS, 229
small model
  property, 191, 198, 227
  theorem, 198, 211
soundness, 70
  equational logic, 99–100
  modal logic, 128
  PDL, 172, 174
SPDL, 260
specification
  correctness, 152
  input/output, 153, 154
spectral
  complexity, 317, 321, 322
  theorem, 353, 379
spectrum, 379
  first-order, 325
  m^{th}, 320
  of a formula, 320

second-order, 325
spoiler, 119
stack, 149, 288, 289
  algebraic, 290
  automaton, 249
  Boolean, 290
  configuration, 243
  higher-order, 325
  operation, 289
standard Kripke frame, 390
* operator,
  See iteration operator
*-continuity, 419
*-continuous dynamic algebra,
  See dynamic algebra
*-continuous Kleene algebra,
  See Kleene algebra
start configuration, 29
state, 127, 146, 167, 291, 293, 400
  Herbrand-like, 317, 349
  initial, 293, 304, 317
  m-, 317
static logic, 304
stored-program computer, 37
strict partial order, 6, 11
strictly more expressive than, 229, 304
strongly r-periodic, 365
structural induction,
  See induction
structure, 68
  acceptable, 311
  Adian, 365
  arithmetical, 308
  expressive, 334
  p-sparse, 367
  relational, 105
  treelike, 261, 262, 355, 367
subalgebra, 89
  generated by, 89
subexpression relation, 191
substitution, 90
  in DL formulas, 329
  instance, 90, 222
  operator, 105, 106
  rule, 84, 138
succession, 370
successor ordinal,
  See ordinal
supremum, 11
surjective, 10
symbol
  atomic, 164
  constant, 284
  equality, 284

function, 283
predicate, 283
relation, 102, 283
symmetric, 6
syntactic
    continuity, 416
    interpretation, 89
    monotonicity, 416
syntax, 67

tableau, 69
tail recursion, 150
tautology, 74, 129
    infinitary, 142
Temporal Logic, 133, 157, 398
    branching-time, 133
    linear-time, 133
temporal operators, 401
    interpretation in PL, 409
term, 87, 103
    algebra, 89
    dynamic, 383
    ground, 87, 103
termination, 166, 356
    assertion, 327
    properties of finite interpretations, 351
    subsumption, 348, 379
ternary, 6
    function symbol, 86
test, 147, 175
    -free, 264
    atomic, 147
    first-order, 380
    operator, xiv, 165, 284
    poor,
        See poor test
    rich,
        See rich test
theorem, 70
theory, 69
tile, 58
tiling problem, 58–63, 117, 126, 222
time model, 385
time-sharing, 42, 53
TL,
    See temporal logic
topology, 81
total, 30
    correctness, 155, 271, 327
        assertion, 313
    order, 6, 11
trace, 146
    in PL, 409
    L-, 356

quantifier, 406
transfinite
    induction,
        See induction
    ordinal,
        See ordinal
transition function, 28
transitive, 6
    closure, 8, 19
    set, 14
transitivity, 192
    of implication, 78
    of reductions, 54
translatability, 347
trap, 366
tree, 50
    model, 143, 239
    model property, 239
    structure, 239
    well-founded, 50
tree-parent, 371
treelike structure, 132, 261, 262, 355, 367
truth, 106
    assignment, 74
    table, 134
    value, 73, 74
Turing machine, 27–37, 63
    alternating, 34–37, 46, 216, 225
        with negation, 36–37
    deterministic, 28
    nondeterministic, 33–34
    oracle, 40–42
    universal, 37, 63
    with k counters, 32–33
    with two stacks, 31–32
typed Kleene algebra,
    See Kleene algebra

UDH tree, 241
ultrafilter, 138
unary, 6
    function symbol, 86
unbounded nondeterminism, 377
undecidability, 37, 42
    of predicate logic, 117–119
    of the halting problem, 63
uniform
    periodicity, 365
    simulation, 37
uninterpreted reasoning, 301, 327
unique diamond path Hintikka tree,
    See UDH tree
universal
    closure,

See closure
formula, 141
model, 208, 211
relation, 7, 45
Turing machine,
    See Turing machine
universality problem, 62
universe, 127
until operator, 405
unwind property, 344, 379
unwinding, 132
upper bound, 11
    least, 11
upper semilattice, 13
upward periodic, 365
use vs. mention, 73

validity, 69
    𝔄-, 297
    DL, 297, 298, 313
    equational logic, 91
    first-order, 106
    modal logic, 128
    PDL, 171
    propositional, 74
valuation, 90, 105, 146, 283, 291, 292
value of a function, 9
variable, 145
    array, 288
    individual, 87, 284, 286
    program, 286
    work, 147
variety, 92
vector space, 93
verification conditions, 333
vertex, 13
vocabulary, 86
    expanded, 318
    first-order, 102, 283
    monadic, 369
    mono-unary, 319
    polyadic, 369
    poor, 319
    rich, 319

weakening rule, 156, 186
well order, 6
well ordering principle, 16
well partial order, 12
well quasiorder, 12
well-founded, 6, 11, 121, 271, 402
    induction,
    See induction
    relation, 12, 48

tree, 50
well-foundedness, 386–389
wf, 272, 386
while
    loop, 167, 260
    operator, 148
    program, 149, 259
        deterministic, 285
        nondeterministic, 285
        with arrays, 288
        with stack, 289
    rule, 156, 186
wildcard assignment,
    See assignment
work variable, 147
world, 127
WP, 260

Zermelo's theorem, 16
Zermelo–Fraenkel set theory, 4, 16
ZF, 16
ZFC, 4, 16
Zorn's lemma, 16, 138